IRISH   FAMILIES

IRISH FAMILIES

Their Names, Arms and Origins

By

EDWARD MacLYSAGHT,

D.Litt., M.R.I.A.

Chairman of the Irish Manuscripts Commission
(formerly Chief Herald of Ireland)

Illustrated by

MYRA MAGUIRE,

Heraldic Artist to the Genealogical Office
Dublin Castle

DUBLIN

HODGES FIGGIS & CO. LTD.

1957

By the same author :
   IRISH LIFE IN THE SEVENTEENTH CENTURY
   SHORT STUDY OF A TRANSPLANTED FAMILY
   EAST CLARE 1916–1921
   AN AIFRIC THEAS
   CÚRSAÍ THOMÁIS
   TOIL DÉ
   etc.

Edited for the Irish Manuscripts Commission :
   THE KENMARE MANUSCRIPTS
   THE ORRERY PAPERS
   ANALECTA HIBERNICA NOS. 14 AND 15

MADE AND PRINTED IN THE REPUBLIC OF IRELAND
BY ALEXANDER THOM AND CO. LTD., DUBLIN

CONTENTS

CONTENTS

APPENDICES

PREFACE

The *raison d'être* of this book is fully explained in Chapter I. Briefly it is to correct errors long current and to present in easily accessible form essential facts about Irish nomenclature and families.

In the course of the twelve years during which I have been collecting material with this object I have received information from many people—especially my colleagues in the National Library. It would not, I hope, be invidious to mention four of these by name : Mr. T. P. O'Neill, who is a walking dictionary of national biography ; Mr. Alfred MacLochlainn, whose controversial mind I have always found stimulating ; Mr. Basil O'Connell, who probably knows more about the ramifications of Munster families since 1700 than anyone living ; and Mr. Gerard Slevin, the present Chief Herald of Ireland. Mr. Slevin most kindly undertook the laborious task of reading the book before it went to the printer and Mr. O'Connell read it in proof. I am indebted to them for the correction of some errors of fact and for many helpful suggestions, nearly all of which I was glad to adopt. I should add that Mr. Slevin does not agree with me in one or two matters of opinion relating to heraldic practice. It has been suggested that, as I have been Chief Herald and Keeper of Manuscripts in the National Library and the author of historical works of an academic nature, I should not write a book which is intended to have a popular appeal. However, the need for such a book is generally admitted and it seems to me that only a man who writes with authority can hope to succeed in correcting popular misconceptions.

E. McL.

PART ONE

Chapter I

INTRODUCTORY

The subject of Irish families is one in which much interest is evinced, but the popular books usually consulted and regarded as authoritative, particularly in America, are in fact unreliable. The inaccurate and misleading information thus imparted with cumulative effect is, however, much more deplorable in the armorial sphere than in the genealogical.

It is an indisputable fact that the publication presenting colour plates of Irish arms which is probably most widely consulted is no less than seventy per cent inaccurate, not only in mere detail, but often in points of primary importance and of an elementary kind. Apart from their many grotesque heraldic blunders the compilers of this work seem to have had a sort of rule of thumb; if they could not find arms for one Irish sept they looked for the name of another somewhat resembling it in sound: thus, for example, they coolly assigned the arms of Boylan to Boland. This frequently resulted in the arms of some purely English family being inserted in their book of "Irish Arms", the Saxon Huggins being equated with O'Higgins, and so on. When this arbitrary method failed them they fell back on the arms of some great Irish sept. To quote one instance of this: Gleeson, Downey, Noonan and MacFadden are all given the arms of O'Brien, though none of these septs had any connexion whatever with the O'Briens or with each other. Consequently many Americans of Irish descent are in good faith using erroneous and often English arms derived from the spurious source in question.

A certain cachet has been given to this because, in the more recent editions of O'Hart's *Irish Pedigrees*, these same coloured plates, have been inserted as if they were an integral part of O'Hart's book. The serious genealogist uses O'Hart with caution, if at all, for he is a far from reliable authority except for the quite modern period. John O'Hart, however, undoubtedly did a vast amount of research, no matter how he used the information he acquired: I know that some of these errors of ascription can actually be traced to him, but it is surely an injustice to him that his well-known name should be used as a cover for the propagation of false and often ludicrous heraldic statements.

It is a common popular error to speak of coats of arms as "crests".* This is another heraldic *faux pas* of which this extraordinary production is guilty. It can now be dismissed from further consideration.

* Many of the oldest armorial bearings have no crests. In some cases different crests were in use by the several branches of a family or sept, while the arms were common to all. A crest on the other hand cannot exist except as an apanage of a coat of arms.

Turning to another aspect of our subject, it is a pleasure to be able to say that there exists a book which deserves high praise : the Reverend Patrick Woulfe's *Sloinnte Gaedheal is Gall* (*Irish Names and Surnames*). It is unfortunately little used abroad. I take this early opportunity of acknowledging my indebtedness to Father Woulfe's work. The errors in it are very few and it is open to adverse criticism in only two respects, neither of primary importance : first his guesswork in the matter of the derivation of Irish names—for this a knowledge of Middle Irish is essential, for Middle Irish differs from Modern Irish more widely than does modern English speech from that of Chaucer ; and secondly his tendency to turn the blind eye to the extent of English immigration. For example, while he tells his readers that Ford, Hearn, Matthews and Moore can be either of English or Gaelic origin, Boyle, Collins and even Ellison and Freeman are treated as if they were exclusively Gaelic. There are a great many instances of this inconsistency. Notwithstanding these minor defects his book is most valuable.

His primary objective was to provide in dictionary form the Gaelic and English equivalent of every extant Gaelic-Irish surname and of the commoner foreign names now found in Ireland, with some account of their origin and history. To accomplish the latter adequately for some 3,500 names within the compass of a single volume was obviously an impossibility. In parts II and IV of the present work this is done more fully for some 500 surnames. The names thus dealt with are those which are most numerous in Ireland to-day, or most famous, together with some rarer ones which are included in the illustrated armorial section.

The selection of the 243 armorial bearings illustrated in Part III needs some explanation. Why, for example, are such well-known and numerous names as MacCormack and Healy missing there, while Troy, Mulvihil and O'Davoren, comparatively rare names, are included ? The answer to this is that not all ancient Irish families have traditional arms recorded in authoritative heraldic sources. The Genealogical Office in Dublin Castle, formerly known as the Office of Arms, is of course, the principal source for such information.

Grants and even Confirmations of Arms to individual members of a sept do not give to other persons of the same name, not included in the terms of the grant or confirmation, any right to use such arms. There are, however, a number of coats of arms on record which by custom are regarded as appertaining to all members of a sept. The majority of these are illustrated in Part III.

At this point it would be well to consider what we mean by the term " sept "— the word " clan " has been avoided because its use might imply the existence in Ireland of a clan system like that so highly developed in Scotland, which in fact we never had in this country.*

The term " sept " has never, as far as I know, been given an authoritative

---

* *Vide* p. 14 *infra.*

technical definition. It can perhaps best be explained by saying that it is a collective term describing a group of persons who, or whose immediate and known ancestors, bore a common surname and inhabited the same locality.

Some danger exists of persons not of the true ancestry of a sept being inextricably identified with it. There is no doubt that up to the middle of the seventeenth century many of the labouring class had no hereditary surnames. As this interesting point is discussed in Chapter II it is referred to here only to indicate a possible objection to a wide interpretation of sept arms, namely that " serfs " (as they have been called in this connexion) may, when the practice of using transitory surnames died out, have assumed as their permanent surnames those of their masters, rather in the same way as the negroes of the plantations in the West Indies sometimes assumed planter surnames. While this contention is not without substance, the consensus of opinion is that such assumption was not at all widespread.

The elasticity inherent in the concept of sept arms is repugnant to British heraldic practice. In England armorial bearings are held to emanate from the Sovereign and are hereditary, though devoid of sanctions to protect what may be regarded as a family heirloom and personal property ; in Scotland the right to bear arms is strictly regulated by law ; on the Continent, again, heraldic usage differs considerably from British.

Ulster King of Arms (as the head of the Irish Office of Arms in Dublin was called) who derived his authority, like Garter and Lyon, from the King of Great Britain and Ireland, continued to exercise his functions in Ireland until March 31, 1943, when his office was transferred to the Government of Ireland and has since been known as the Genealogical Office, its head being entitled Chief Herald of Ireland. This transfer took place more than twenty years after the establishment of the Irish Free State.

On taking over we were at first inclined to adopt the British attitude in heraldic matters ; but after a few years the particular conditions existing in Ireland, politically and historically, induced a modification of outlook, especially in regard to sept arms. In England and Scotland all arms to be found in the records of the heraldic authorities, if not extinct, can be claimed by certain specific individuals. Sept arms, as recorded in the Office of Arms in Dublin Castle, as I have said, have come somewhat loosely to be regarded as appertaining to all members of the sept.

The peculiar circumstances of Ireland, it may be added, were recognized two centuries before the transfer to an Irish authority took place, since Confirmations of Arms, based on use, were issued in Ireland, but not in Great Britain where settled conditions existed.

It must be emphasized that the acceptance of the principle of sept arms in no way implies that arms appertain to a surname as such. It does not mean, for example, that every man called Kelly or O'Kelly may legitimately use the well-known arms of O'Kelly of Ui Máine. There were several distinct septs of O'Kelly ; and O'Kellys of the Meath or Kilkenny septs have no better title to the said arms than a Murphy or an O'Brien. No one, however, can reasonably object to an O'Kelly taking a proprietary interest in those arms, provided that he is unquestionably of a family originating in the O'Kelly country in Connacht.

Briefly, then, the position is that the arms illustrated in Part III of this book may be displayed without impropriety by any person of the sept indicated if he really does belong to that sept. Nevertheless anyone wishing to bear arms in the true heraldic sense, e.g. to have them inscribed on silver or seal or in stone carving, would be well advised to apply for a Confirmation of such arms from the Chief Herald at Dublin Castle, which can be obtained at a moderate fee on production of evidence of descent. Corroborative evidence of " user " is also required in all cases where the proof afforded by descent is inadequate. Searches to obtain such evidence are undertaken by the Genealogical Office.

All the arms in this book have been taken from the archives of the Irish Office of Arms (Genealogical Office) and the depiction has been done by the heraldic artist employed by that authority. They may, therefore, be regarded as authentic and accurate. The genealogical data to be found in the body of the work has been derived from a variety of sources. Here again the records of the Genealogical Office, which date back to its establishment in 1552, are the main primary source. There is also much genealogical and nomenclatural material in the (as yet) uncatalogued collection of family archives in the National Library with which, as Keeper of Manuscripts in that institution, I have most fortunately had exceptional opportunities of familiarizing myself.

The printed works which I have used are for the most part listed in the bibliography at the end of this book. The most helpful of these are undoubtedly " The Four Masters " and the other Annals (Loch Cé, Innisfallen, etc.), " The Topographical Poems " and the many publications of the Irish Archaeological Society, and particularly John O'Donovan's notes thereon ; among works issued by the Irish Manuscripts Commission, many of which have been frequently consulted, the so-called Census of 1659 was especially valuable ; the diocesan and county histories were helpful in varying degrees ; while papers printed in the archaeological and historical journals, particularly the *Journal of the Royal Society of Antiquaries, Ireland*, have proved a mine of information. These, I fear, are too numerous to specify separately. I have consulted numerous family histories, some of which indeed are scholarly works, but as many of these were written by enthusiastic and uncritical amateurs the statements they contain can as a rule only be accepted where independent evidence is forthcoming : in short they are useful chiefly as pointers to more authentic sources.

Finally, a word should be said about a Government publication of an unusual kind. It is entitled *Special Report on Surnames in Ireland*, but it is ordinarily cited as " Matheson " from the name of the Registrar-General of Births Deaths and Marriages under whom it was produced. It was published in 1894 with a re-issue in 1909. In addition to a general dissertation on the subject and some very interesting examples of the vagaries of spelling and even recent translation of Irish surnames, it lists every name for which five or more births were registered in 1890 and it usually gives the county or counties in which each name is most prevalent. It is possible to say " is " rather than " was " in this connexion, because various tests (which will be indicated at the appropriate places in the book) show that the distribution of surnames in Ireland has not altered materially in the sixty years which have since elapsed : the revolution in transport, emigration and all the other disturbing elements of modern life, which might be expected to change the pattern, have not in fact done so. Matheson, therefore, has been found very useful, especially in the preparation of Part II of this book. A further bluebook sponsored by Matheson was issued in 1901 : this is entitled *Synonymes of Irish Surnames* and is of considerable interest.

The unsettled conditions produced by successive invasions, rebellions, agrarian revolution and emigration have resulted in the wholesale loss of family papers so that, though every effort is now being made to save what remains, we have in Ireland nothing comparable to the family and local archives in which Britain is so rich. The destruction of the Public Record Office in 1922 was also a major disaster to Irish genealogists, particularly to searchers concerned with the seventeenth and eighteenth centuries. Nevertheless there are compensating factors. The Gaelic order was essentially aristocratic in character, and the Norman invaders who were assimilated into it were no less so. Thus was created a unique corpus of mediaeval genealogical material, the greater part of which has been preserved. In this we may include not only the actual genealogies and genealogical tracts and poems but also the Annals, the " Book of Rights " and such like works. These sources are of the greatest value in the preparation of a book on Irish families.

Finally, reference should be made to a vast and, until quite recently, almost unexplored manuscript source, namely the papers relating to the Wild Geese and their descendants now for the most part stored in Continental archives, particularly in France, Austria and Spain. These, together with much ecclesiastical material, are becoming available for consultation in Dublin, thanks to the initiative and energy of Dr. R. J. Hayes, Director of the National Library of Ireland, whose comprehensive scheme for the microfilming of Continental records relating to Ireland is already well advanced.

Having indicated in this preliminary chapter the nature of the problems inherent in Irish genealogy and heraldry we may now proceed to consider our subject in its various aspects. This I hope to do in a way calculated to interest the general reader as well as the student.

CHAPTER II

MAC AND O

The successive invasions of Ireland from Strongbow to Cromwell, culminating in the final destruction of the Gaelic order and the long drawn out subjection of the Irish people under the eighteenth century penal code, together with the plantations of foreign settlers and the more peaceful infiltration of Englishmen in the commercial life of the country, have made Irish surnames more mixed than those of a nation with a less disturbed history. The situation can no doubt be paralleled in several mid-European states, but there is nothing comparable to it in any of our nearer neighbours such as England, France, Germany, Holland or Spain, where foreign names are exceptional and native ones are seldom hidden under alien guise. This latter is a phenomenon which is extremely common in Ireland.

It has often been stated that surnames were introduced into Ireland by King Brian Boru. Though this cannot be accepted as historically accurate it is a fact that Ireland was one of the first countries to adopt a system of hereditary surnames ; or perhaps it would be truer to say that such a system developed spontaneously. At any rate the Macs and O's were well established as such more than a century before the coming of the Cambro-Normans or, as they are more usually called, the Anglo-Normans.

It is hardly necessary to state that these prefixes denote descent, *mac* (son) indicating that the surname was formed from the personal name, or sometimes calling, of the father of the first man to bear that surname, while O names are derived from a grandfather or even earlier ancestor, *ó* or *ua* being the Irish word for grandson, or more loosely male descendant.

Many instances occur of Mac names and some of O names in the Annals, lists of bishops and other records relating to the centuries between the time of St. Patrick and that of Brian Boru. These, however, were not hereditary surnames, but merely indicated the father (or grandfather) of the man in question. Thus to take, by way of example, two successors of St. Patrick in the see of Armagh, Torbac MacGormain (d. 812) and Diarmuid Ó Tighearnaigh (d. 852), these were not members of families called MacGorman and O'Tierney, but were respectively son of a man whose baptismal name was Gorman and grandson of one who was christened Tierney.

Prior to the introduction of surnames there was in Ireland a system of clan-names, which the use of surnames gradually rendered obsolete except as territorial designations. Groups of families, many of them descended from a common ancestor, were known by collective clan-names such as Dál Cais (whence the adjective Dalcassian), Ui Máine (or Hy Many), Cinel Eoghain, Clann Cholgain, Corca Laidhe. The expression " tribe-names ", used by John O'Donovan in this connexion, is perhaps more expressive, though a more modern authority, Professor Eoin MacNeill, objected to this term as misleading. In some cases the tribe-name did subsequently become the surname of a leading family of the clan or tribe, but as a rule this did not happen ; and, as the tribe name was usually identical with the surname acquired by some quite unrelated sept in another part of the country, confusion is apt to arise. Thus the Clann Daly embraced the O'Donnells and other northern septs, Clann Cahill became O'Flanagans etc., Munter Gilligan was chiefly composed of the O'Quins of Annaly and Hy Regan was the tribe name of the O'Dunns. It would be outside the scope of this book to pursue this aspect of Gaelic nomenclature. A brief account of it will be found in Woulfe's *Sloinnte* and it is more fully dealt with in MacNeill's *Celtic Ireland*.

The location of the clans or tribes to which allusion is made in Part II, as well as ancient territories such as Thomond, Breffny and Ossory, is indicated on the Barony Map (*facing* p. 284).

A study of this map shows that many of the tribe names have been perpetuated in the names of baronies, some like Keenaght, Pubblebrien and Iraghticonnor easy to identify, but more hardly recognizable in their English guise as, for example, Iverk (Ui Eirc), Tirerrill (Tir Oilella) and Tullyhaw (Teallach Eachdhach).

The first of the major invasions of Ireland in historical times (1169–1172) resulted in the formation of a new set of surnames belonging to the Norman families which in due course became *Hiberniores Hibernicis ipsis*. The old Latin cliché is applicable to the names as well as to the people who bore them, for no one to-day would regard Fitzgerald or Burke as any less Irish than O'Connor or MacCarthy.

Names in this category* are numerous and widespread in Ireland, and most of them have in the course of time become exclusively Irish, as for example Burke, Costello, Cusack, Cogan, Dalton, Dillon, Fitzgerald, Keating, Nagle, Nugent, Power, Roche, Sarsfield and Walsh. Some of them, of course, like Barry and Purcell, though generally regarded as Irish, are found in England also since the twelfth century. To-day, no doubt, almost all the Norman-Irish surnames which are increasingly common in England became established there as a result of nineteenth century and particularly of recent emigration from Ireland.

The second great upheaval, five hundred years later, was of a more devastating character. In the seventeenth century the dire effects of conquest were intensified by religious persecution and the three main events of that century resulting from military aggression—the Plantation of Ulster, the Cromwellian Settlement and the Williamite forfeitures—followed by the Penal Code which was at its severest in the first half of the eighteenth century, inevitably led to a lack of accord between the new settlers and the old inhabitants of the country. The natural process of assimilation was thus retarded, indeed it is not too much to say that it was deliberately prevented. Thus the Elizabethan immigrants and those that followed them in the next century did not become hibernicized as the Normans had. Part IV of this book

* These are included in Appendix E.

is devoted to a consideration of the place of their descendants in the Irish nation of modern times.

A feature of the degradation of the Gael and the inferiority complex it produced was the wholesale discarding of the distinctive prefixes O and Mac. Nor was this confined to the down-trodden peasantry. The few Catholic gentry who managed to maintain to some extent their social position, while keeping their O's and Macs within the ambit of their own entourage (usually in the remoter parts of the country) were so deeply conscious of belonging to a conquered nation that they frequently omitted the prefixes when dealing with Protestants, not only in legal matters but also in ordinary social intercourse. Thus we find Daniel O'Connell's uncle, that picturesque figure universally known as " Hunting Cap ", signing himself Maurice Connell as late as 1803 when approaching the Knight of Kerry to enlist his influence in a court case ; while MacDermot, Chief of the Name, though ranking as a prince among his own people and himself a prominent banker in the middle of the eighteenth century, invariably signed himself simply Anthony Dermott.

It has been stated that one of the causes of the disuse of the prefixes Mac and O in the eighteenth century was the inclusion in the Penal Code of a provision to that effect. I can find no such clause in any of the relevant Acts. No legislation dealing with this question was ever passed except in so far as the Statute of Kilkenny (1367) affected the Irish of the Pale. This indeed had no bearing on the use of Mac and O ; but it did, no doubt, mark the beginning of the practice of translating Irish names into English, which in the eighteenth and nineteenth centuries became widespread and, I may add, proved more often to be mistranslation than translation. Nevertheless pressure was exerted in other ways to bring about the degaelicization of surnames. For example, even two generations before the Penal Code was in full force we find O'Conor Roe entering into a composition in which he binds the Irish chiefs under his influence to " forego the customs and usages of their Brehon law . . . and to give up prefixes to their surnames ".* We may be sure that this undertaking was made by O'Conor with his tongue in his cheek and that it was ignored, but it serves to indicate the official outlook in this respect.

I may refer here to the widespread belief outside Ireland that Mac is essentially a Scottish prefix. To us this idea is absurd, for many of our foremost Irish families bear Mac names such as MacCarthy, MacDermot, MacGuinness, MacGrath, MacGillycuddy, MacKenna, MacMahon, MacNamara and so on. Nevertheless, it is a fallacy widely held. It is true, of course, that many Mac names in Ulster are Scottish in origin, having come in with the seventeenth century planters ; and these tended to retain their Gaelic prefix when those of Catholic Ireland fell into disuse. In any case the Scottish Gaels are originally of Irish stock and Scotland herself took her name from the word *Scotia* which in Latin was at first used to denote the land inhabited by the Irish race.

* 5 Jan. 1637. This quotation, taken from Genealogical Office MS. 178, p. 293, is by no means an isolated case.

16

At the beginning of the present century under the growing influence of the Gaelic League a general reversal of the process began to be perceptible. Yet even to-day there are scores of Gaelic names with which the prefix is seldom, if ever, seen, e.g. Boland, Brophy, Connolly, Corrigan, Crowe, Garvey, Hennessy, Kirby, Larkin, to mention a few of the commonest.

The extent of this resumption can best be illustrated by the mere fact that while in 1890, according to Matheson's calculations, there were twice as many Connells as O'Connells, to-day, (judging by such tests as directories) we have nine O'Connells for every Connell. I do not know the present proportion of O'Kellys to Kellys, but I am sure it is very much higher than it was in 1890 when the official estimate for all Ireland was 55,900 Kellys and only a mere 400 O'Kellys.

As I will devote some detailed attention to this matter in Chapter IV, I will pass now to another class of Mac surnames which is of considerable interest. This is the assumption by Norman families of surnames of a Gaelic type and the formation under those designations of what practically amount to septs or sub-septs on the Gaelic model. The majority of these, such as MacSherone *ex* Prendergast and MacRuddery *ex* Fitzsimon, are nearly extinct to-day, as are the various offshoots of the Burkes, though no doubt some of their descendants did revert to their original surnames. Berminghams, however, survive under the name of MacCorish or Corish, Stauntons as MacEvilly, Archdeacons as MacOda or Coady and Nangles as Costello (formerly MacCostello). Woulfe says that the latter was the first Norman Mac name. Not all such Norman name assumptions retained a Gaelic form, for d'Exeter, first gaelicized as MacSiurtain, eventually became Jordan (now a common name in the West) and the Jenningses, formerly MacSeoinin, were originally Burkes.

This practice of forming sub-septs was not confined to Norman families. Among the offshoots of O'Brien were MacConsidine and MacLysaght. MacShane stemmed from O'Neill: in due course this was turned by translation into Johnson and as such is found in that numerous class of concealed Gaelic surnames referred to in Appendix A. So the name MacShera, now rare, was adopted by some of the Fitz-patricks. MacSherry (whence the place name Courtmacsherry) on the other hand was a Gaelic patronymic assumed by the English family Hodnett. MacSherry, it should be noted, is also an indigenous Gaelic surname in Breffny.

Fitzpatrick, which up to the seventeenth century was MacGilpatrick, is in a class by itself, being the only Fitz name which is Gaelic: otherwise Fitz (from French *fils*) always denotes a Norman origin. It is possible, however, that some of the Fitzhenrys may originally have been MacEnery.

Unless we adopt an exclusive and doctrinaire attitude we must admit Fitzgerald, Fitzgibbon and Fitzmaurice as Irish. As I have already remarked many other Norman surnames are among our best-known surnames to-day. It would be ridicul-ously pedantic to regard these as anything but Irish. Not only have they been

17

continuously in Ireland for seven or eight centuries, but they are also not found in England except, of course, when introduced by Irish settlers there. The Norman name Power, indeed, holds first place for County Waterford.

One of the most striking and interesting of the phenomena to be observed in a study of our subject is the tenacity with which families have continued to dwell for centuries, down to the present day, in the very districts where their names originated. This obtains in almost every county in Ireland. Thus, according to Matheson's returns, the births registered for the distinctive Kerry names of Brick, Brosnan, Culloty, Kissane, MacElligott and MacGillycuddy, to take more or less random examples, are entirely confined to that county. I will revert to this point later on in Chapter IV.*

In many cases local association has been perpetuated in place names. Indeed it is a characteristic of Irish place names, particularly those beginning with Bally, Dun, Clon etc., that a large proportion of them are formed from personal names. Bally-mahon, Lettermacaward, Drumconor, Toomevara are a few examples to illustrate this point. Many such will be noticed in Part II of this book. It is dangerous to jump to conclusions and easy to make mistakes in this field : thus Kilodonnell in Co. Donegal is the church of O'Toner, not of O'Donnell as would appear at first sight. Similarly Doonamurray has nothing to do with the surname Murray, being a corruption of *Dún na móna* ; nor has Drumreilly any etymological connexion with the sept of O'Reilly. Of course the association, especially in the case of the *Kil* words, is often ecclesiastical rather than genealogical, for many are formed from the names of pre-surname saints and hermits, and so have no interest for the student of surnames. Those place names beginning with Bally and other Irish words were almost all formed before the seventeenth century and too often when a family was thus distinguished it has ceased to exist or has almost died out in the immediate neighbourhood of the particular townland so designated, but in many cases they are still numerous there. Nearly all such are Gaelic or Hiberno-Norman family names. There are, however, some exceptions such as Ballybunion and Ballyviniter, which are formed from the English surnames Bunyan and Viniter.

After the 1602 débâcle, as we must regard the battle of Kinsale, place names with the prefix Castle and Mount or the suffix Town and Bridge like Castlepollard and Crookstown, and occasionally a combination of both like Castletownconyers, began to be used. For the most part these names honoured planter families, with whom must be classed renegade Gaels who forsook their own people and religion and backed the winning side—or at least the then winning side, for the tables are turned now ; though where they represent translations from older Irish place names, as in the case of O'Brien's Bridge and Castledermot, this of course does not apply. This aspect of our subject can be dismissed without further examination : it can be studied by anyone interested in it by a perusal of a map or gazeteer, or better still the Index

* See also Appendix F.

of Townlands, Parishes etc. officially published in connexion with the decennial censuses of the nineteenth century.

Of more interest to us here is the converse, i.e. those surnames which were actually formed from places. In England they constitute one of the most numerous classes ; in Ireland they are comparatively rare : so much so indeed that all of them that I know can be enumerated here, being too few to make one of our Appendix lists. Apart from Anglo-Irish names taken from places in England like Sutton, Preston etc., the only Irish place names so used I have met are Ardagh, Athy, Bray, Corbally, Finglas, Galbally, Kilcash, Rath, Santry, Slane and Trim, some of which are very rare. Dease (and Deasy), Desmond, Lynagh, Meade and Minnagh, formed from extensive territories, may also perhaps be included. Not all place names found as surnames can be accepted in this category. Cavan for example is not taken from the town but is a synonym of Keevane or occasionally an abbreviation of Kavanagh ; Navan is Mac Cnaimhin, Limerick is Ó Luimbric, Kilkenny is Mac Giolla Choinnigh and Ormonde is found in County Waterford oddly enough as a corruption of Ó Ruaidh. The most numerous of these in Ireland to-day is Galway or Galwey. It does, it is true, derive from a place, but the place is Galloway in Scotland.

Deasy, mentioned above, might be placed in the class which we may call descriptive. It indicates " a native of the Decies ", as Lynagh means " a Leinster-man ", Moynagh " a Munsterman " and Meade (with its earlier form Miagh) " a Meathman ". These have a topographical significance, as have Spain, Switzer, Wallace, Brett, London. Quite a number of descriptive surnames, which at some period must have superseded a normal family surname, are formed from adjectives such as Bane (white), Begg (small), Crone (brown), Creagh (branchy), Duff (black), Gall (foreign), Glass (green), Lawder (strong), Reagh (brindled).

Phair or Fair is also one of these, but it has been subjected to translation, being the Irish adjective *fionn*.

Akin to adjectives are names in the genitive case, of which a few are found among genuine Irish surnames, e.g. Glenny (sometimes Glenn) for *a' ghleanna* and Maghery for *an mhachaire*. Here also the process has in some cases been carried a stage further, *an chnuic* becoming Hill and *an mhuilinn* Mills ; but when met to-day Hill and Mills are more likely to be of English origin.

Everyone knows the old rhyme which ends with the lines " And if he lack both O and Mac no Irishman is he ". Like most general statements this is not wholly true for, disregarding the undoubted claims of the Burkes, Fitzgeralds etc., we must admit Creagh, Deasy, Crone, Maghery and the other descriptive surnames as genuinely Gaelic. Indeed two of the best known and essentially Irish names, Kavanagh and Kinsella, have neither O nor Mac, for they are of the descriptive type.

Both of these, however, sometimes have an O tacked on to them erroneously. There are some curious instances of this error. A' Preith (meaning " of the cattle spoil ") is well known in County Down for generations under the anglicized form of

O'Prey. Gorham was formerly credited with an O in Co. Galway. De Horseys became O'Horseys before ever the influence of the Gaelic League revival brought bogus O's and Macs into being. Two of the most remarkable, not to say ridiculous, of these mistakes are to be found in Limerick city and county where Mackessy (in Irish Ó Macasa and *recte* O'Mackessy in English) appears as McKessy; and Odell, a purely English name, as O'Dell.

In this connexion, I should refer to those Mac names which through long usage in the spoken language have become O's. The best known of these are O'Growney and O'Gorman. Other examples of this appear here and there in Part II.

We have already noticed instances of the sub-division of the great septs and the consequent formation in the middle ages of new surnames like MacConsidine. This arose for various reasons, not the least of which was the desirability of readily distinguishing between a number of people of the same name. For a similar reason a system of nomenclature exists to-day, particularly in the western counties, whereby the father's christian name is added to a man's legal name. Thus in Clare, where there may well be several Patrick O'Briens in a single townland, they are known as Patrick O'Brien John, Patrick O'Brien Michael and so on. This is not merely a colloquial convenience, for these designations are used in ordinary business transactions such as completing an order form or supplying milk to a creamery, and they appear very frequently in the official voters' lists.

A similar practice, very much in vogue in Limerick in the seventeenth century, has misled some writers unfamiliar with Irish conditions. The normal method was to add the father's name, as in the example given above, but with the prefix Fitz. Thus, to take a well known Limerick surname, John Arthur son of Stephen Arthur was almost invariably described as John Arthur FitzStephen, so that to the un-initiated the man's surname appears to be FitzStephen.

There are many examples in the sixteenth and seventeenth century records of persons whose names as set down therein are a veritable genealogy. John MacMahon MacWilliam MacOwen MacShane was, of course, John MacMahon whose father's christian name was William and his great grandfather's was Shane. Ignorance of this practice on the part of the enumerators probably accounts for the extraordinary number of MacShanes and MacTeiges returned as surnames in such records as the 1659 census all over the country. According to this there were large numbers of MacWilliams, MacEdmunds, MacDavids, MacRichards etc., and in the same way Fitzjames (sometimes alias MacJames) appears as a common surname. The prevalence, according to these returning officers, of Oge as a surname bears out this assumption. Similarly Bane is given as a common surname, though there is little doubt that it was in fact, like Oge, merely an epithet. Bane does exist as a modern surname; Oge, however, does not, though it may have occasionally survived by translation, as Young. The Ormond Deeds, especially those of the sixteenth century, contain a great many names formed by prefixing Mac to a christian name. Besides those mentioned above, MacNicholas, MacPhelim, MacRory, MacThomas and MacWalter are of most frequent occurrence. Of all these names the only two to be found in any considerable numbers as surnames to-day are MacShane and MacTigue, as it is now spelt. The latter has in some places been shorn of its Mac and is written Tighe.

In this connexion it must not be forgotten that a not inconsiderable number of people in the lower stratum of society did not use hereditary surnames even as late as 1650. In examining family documents I have met with cases of this: a witness signs himself James MacThomas, whom we know to be the son of Thomas MacTeige— or more probably being illiterate he makes his mark beside the name. Nevertheless it can safely be stated that the great majority even of the labouring class did have hereditary Mac and O surnames at least from the middle of the sixteenth century. By the eighteenth, of course, the cottier and small farmer class had come to include a considerable proportion of the old Gaelic aristocracy.

CHAPTER III

THE DISTORTION OF OUR SURNAMES

Even in Ireland, where there is a genealogical tradition, it is quite common for people to be uncertain of their ancestry for more than three generations. Consequently a man in those circumstances whose name is, say, Collins or Rogers, to take two common in Ireland, cannot assert with certainty that he bears a native Irish surname. However, if he is a Collins, born and living in Dublin perhaps, whose people came from West Cork the odds are very strongly in favour of the true name being the Gaelic Ó Coileain. Smith, the commonest surname in England, comes high up in the Irish list—fifth in that given by Matheson. There can be no doubt that many of our Irish Smiths are the descendants of English settlers and traders, but it is equally probable that at least eighty per cent of the Smiths of County Cavan are of native stock, being MacGowans or O'Gowans who, under pressure of alien legislation or social influence, accepted the translated form and have used it ever since.

It is in this class of surname that Woulfe must be used with caution. In the case of some fifty per cent of the names which I have listed in Appendix A there is nothing in his *Sloinnte* to indicate that there is an English surname exactly identical with the form used in Ireland as the anglicized version of a Gaelic surname. Some examples of this, taken almost at random, were given in Chapter I.

Many of these dual-origin surnames are translations, like Smith and Oaks, or more often pseudo-translations such as Kidney and Bird. Some indeed of the latter are very far-fetched, even ridiculous, as for example the grotesque transformation of Mac Giolla Eoin into Monday from a fancied resemblance of the last part of that name to the Irish word *Luain*.

So far we have been considering English names which in Ireland may conceal those of genuine Gaelic families. The list given in Appendix A includes the commoner surnames in that category. In a smaller number (see Appendix B) the converse obtains.

Such names as Moore, Hart, Hayes and Boyle, which are, of course, genuinely Irish and are often regarded as exclusively so, are also found as indigenous surnames in England. So here again there is no certainty in the absence of an authentic pedigree, or at least of a well-founded tradition, as a guide. It has been pointed out for example that Guinness, which stout has made world-famous as an Irish name, and is in that case probably rightly derived from Magennis or MacGuinness of County Down, occurs in English records of some centuries ago in the rural county of Devonshire.

Probably the most reliable and scholarly work on English surnames is that of Professor Weekley. Yet he includes in his lists, without any mention of Ireland, several like Geary, Garvin, Grennan and Quigley: typical Gaelic-Irish surnames which, while they are no doubt occasionally found with the French or Anglo-Saxon background he indicates, when met in England at the present time are much more likely to have been brought there by Irish immigrants.

Apart from these surnames of possible English origin there are many indisputably Irish surnames not indigenous in England which assumed in their anglicized form a completely English appearance. What, for example, could be more English in appearance than Gleeson, Buggy, Cashman, Halfpenny and Doolady, to cite only a few examples. All of these are genuine Gaelic surnames. The list given in Appendix C shows them to be surprisingly numerous.

Once again the converse of this is also true. No one unacquainted with the subject would doubt that such very Irish sounding names as Gernon, Laffan, Gogan, Henebry and Tallon, and even O'Dell, all quite common in Ireland, are Irish, yet none of them is of Gaelic origin. This list, however, is not so long—see Appendix D.

Some Gaelic surnames in their modern anglicized form have acquired an equally un-Irish guise but have a foreign rather than an English look. Coen, a variant of Coyne, and Levy, a common abbreviation of Dunlevy, suggest the Jew; I know a Lomasney who is always refuting the erroneous belief that he is of French origin, and I expect Lavelles and even Delargys and Delahuntys may have the same difficulty; Hederman and Hessian have rather a German sound, while Nihil, well known in County Clare, and Melia, synonym of O'Malley, might be Latin words. Most of this class, however, are occasional variants, such as Gna and Gina for (Mac) Kenna or Manasses for Mannix, or rare surnames like Schaill, Thulis and Gaussen.

In some cases the anglicization process has had very unfortunate results. The beautiful name Mac Giolla Iosa, for example, usually rendered as MacAleese, takes the form MacLice in some places. The picturesque and heroic Ó Dathlaoich in County Galway ridiculously becomes Dolly and the equally distinguished Ó Sealbhaigh which is anglicized Shelly in its homeland (Co. Cork) is Shallow in Co. Tipperary. Schoolboys of these families, unless they use the Irish form, need no nicknames; Grimes, too, is a miserable substitute for its Gaelic counterpart Ó Greachain, which has also Grehan as a more euphonious anglicized form.

These corruptions, of course, are due to the influence of the English language, the spread of which in Ireland was contemporary with the subjection and eclipse of the old Catholic Irish nation: names of tenants were inscribed in rentals by strangers brought in to act as clerks, who attempted to write down phonetically what they regarded as outlandish names; in the same way Gaelic-speaking litigants, deponents and witnesses in law cases were arbitrarily dubbed this and that at the whim of the recording official.* It was not until the nineteenth century that uniformity in the spelling of names began to be observed, but the seventeenth century was the period during which our surnames assumed approximately the forms ordinarily in use in Ireland to-day.

The corruptions we have noticed above have been cited as examples of the

* See O'Broder, p. 64 *infra*.

tendency to give Irish names an English appearance. Most of them have at least some phonetic resemblance to their originals or else were frankly translations or supposed translations. There is, too, a large class of Irish surnames anglicized in a way which makes them quite unrecognizable. Often these distortions are aesthetically most unpleasing, as Mucklebreed for Mac Giolla Bríde and Gerty for Mag Oireachtaigh.

Citing only official registrations with the Registrar-General, Matheson notes a particularly flagrant example, viz. a family of O'Hagans in County Dublin who have actually become Hog, which in the absence of his testimony one would naturally assume to be simply the well-known English surname of Hogg*. Rather less cacophonous is Ratty for Hanratty. Forker for Farquhar (in County Down) may perhaps be regarded as comparable to the contraction in England of Cholmondeley to Chumley and Featherstonehaugh to Fanshawe in less aristocratic circles, these of course being phonetic spellings. The most curious instance of phonetic abbreviation recorded by Matheson is the birth registration of a Dalzell child at Dundalk *tout court* as " D.L.", that being the peculiar pronunciation of Dalzell in its native Scotland.

The commonest of all Irish surnames, though not aesthetically objectionable, is a good illustration of decadence, for Murphy is a far cry from MacMurrough and O'Morchoe, as is Dunphy from its synonym O'Donoghue. My own name, which I am glad to say is a true Dalcassian (Co. Clare) one, is an excellent example of the distortion we are considering, for no one would readily connect MacLysaght, especially when shorn of its Mac, with Mac Giolla Iasachta. The seventeenth century officials did at first render it as McGillysaghta, etc. in documents in English, but this proved too much of a mouthful to last long.

This name is also an example of that fairly numerous class in which the initial letter (excluding the prefix) is misleading. The L of Lysaght and of Leland derives from the gioLLa. The initial L of Lally on the other hand is to be found in the MaoL of the original. In the same way the C of Clancy, the K of Keogh and the Q of Quaid are from MaC ; the G of Gaynor and Gorevan from the MaG† prefix, while the Il of Ilhenny can again be traced to the gIOLla of the Gaelic form.

Another tendency in the anglicization of Irish surnames is the absorption of uncommon names in common ones. Blowick, for example, tends to become Blake, Kindellan is merged in Connellan, Cormican in McCormick, Sullahan in Sullivan, Kehilly and Killkelly in Kelly, and so on. Certain well-known family names such as Courtney, Conway and Leonard have gobbled up in the course of time, not one, but half a dozen or more minor ones. We must presume that this was a result of the general Gaelic depression, part of the same indifference and hopelessness which acquiesced in the lopping off of the Mac and O from so many old Irish surnames.

---

* O'Hagan is unlucky in this respect. According to Woulfe the very English and plebeian-sounding Huggins is one of its synonyms in Ireland.

† Mag is a form of Mac frequently used with names beginning with a vowel.

THE DISTORTION OF OUR SURNAMES

I have said that the mutilation and corruption of Irish surnames took place in the seventeenth and to a lesser extent in the eighteenth centuries. It must be admitted, however, that even to-day, fifty years after the foundation of the Gaelic League, the gradual re-gaelicization of names resulting from its influence is to some extent counterbalanced by the opposing forces of de-nationalization. This is found more in pronunciation than in spelling : though even in this official registration age pronunciation does tend to affect spelling. A notable example of what I have in mind is the internal H. The English seem unable to cope with this sound which presents no difficulty to an Irishman : for Mahony they say Mah-ney (or, as they would write it, Marney, since the internal R is also dead in England). Now Dublin and suburbs with over 650,000 people contains more than one fifth of the population of the Republic and one seventh of the whole country ; and Dublin for all its genuine political nationalism is in most ways becoming more English, or perhaps it would be more accurate to say, more cosmopolitan, in character. The contrast between Connacht and Dublin is as marked as that between Dublin and England. Of course the good old Dublin accent has lost none of its distinctive raciness, but it is only to be heard in the mouths of one section of the citizens. The gradual disappearance of regional Irish accents is much to be deplored : it is due to a number of causes including the B.B.C., the cinema, the much increased intercourse with England resulting from the recent mass emigration to that country, and perhaps I may add the " refinement " aimed at in convent education. However, I must not allow myself to go off at a tangent on this interesting topic, which is irrelevant except in so far as it is concerned with the pronunciation of surnames.

In America the distortion of the name Mahony takes a different form, for it is often mispronounced Ma-hōney, just as the wrong vowel is stressed in Carmody and Connell. In Ireland one does not yet hear Ma(r)ney for Mahony or Clossey for Cloghessy, but boggling at the internal H has come to Dublin now. I know a family in Dublin named Fihilly : the parents insist quite rightly that there are three syllables in the word, but the younger generation are content to answer to " Feeley " and so pronounce the name themselves ; Gallaghers in Sydney, after a long losing battle with Australian philistinism, have had to accept " Gallagger " with the best grace they could. This, however, may be partly due to the ocular influence of the middle G. There is another difference in these two cases, besides the fact that the Fihilly deterioration took place in Ireland itself : Feeley has actually become a recognized way of spelling that name. Similarly there are Dawneys who were originally Doheny.

The surnames Hehir and Cahir in Thomond are still dissyllables, but the latter when denoting the town of that name in Co. Tipperary has become immutably " Care ". This again prompts a long digression on place names : but that subject, so full of pitfalls for all but the most learned, would be out of place in this book.

The internal H is not the only stumbling-block for English people and anglicized Dubliners. They pronounce Linnane as Linnayne and Kissane Kissayne. Our *ane* sound, which is intermediate between the English " Anne " and " aunt ", is not heard in English speech. Similarly O'Dea is called O'Dee. These emasculated pronunciations sound like affectation to people who come from the places where those names originated and still abound. This is not to deny that there is actually a name O'Dee, but that is not a Clare name, as O'Dea emphatically is.

Some English inspired innovations fortunately do not last. During the first World War a neighbour of mine in Co. Clare named Minogue joined the British army ; in due course he returned as Capt. Minogue—Captain " Minnow-gew ", if you please, not " Minnóg " ! He may have first got the idea from the mistake of a fellow soldier but he adopted the monstrosity and even insisted on it.

One of the most irritating of the examples of capitulation to English influence is the adoption of the essentially Saxon termination *ham* for the Irish *ahan*, *ann*, etc. This is not confined to surnames : the Gaelic word *banbh*, called bonnive in English in the less anglicized counties, is bonham in most places. Rathfarnham, *recte* Rathfarnnan, is the best known place so anglicized ; while on our own ground we have the very English-looking Markham, a Clare surname of which the normal version should be, and indeed formerly was, Markahan (cf. the place name Bally-markahan in Co. Clare).

In the same way, but less noticeably, the final S so dear to English tongues de-gaelicizes Higgin(s), while the addition of an unnecessary D has somewhat the same effect on Boland. This D seems to have been a matter of chance for Noland is almost as rare as Bolan.

Quite often the anglicization of a Gaelic surname resulted in the adoption in English, whether consciously or not, of one which carried a certain social cachet like D'Evelyn for the usual Devlin, Molyneux for Mulligan or Delacour for Dilloughery. Montague for MacTadhg or Mactague probably arose in the same way, the sound Montag at some period giving way to Montagew through the ocular influence of the spelling. The cognate Minnogew for Minogue was just " swank ". We may assume that the good captain's descendants have gone back to plain Minnóg, as it is only a matter of pronunciation in their case.

There are other examples of this tendency which cannot be shed so easily. When Mulvihil has thus become Melville and Loughnane Loftus, resumption of the true patronymic necessitates (in practice, though not in strict law)* certain legal formalities. I am told that there are people whose name was originally Mullins (Ó Maolain) using the form de Moleyns. I have not met a case myself. According to Burke's *Peerage* the best known family of the name, the head of which is Lord Ventry, are not true Irish Mullinses at all, and they presumably had justification for assuming the form de Moleyns in place of Mullins, a step which they took in 1841.

Some people with Mac names insist on the Mac being written in full, others prefer Mc, and formerly M' was quite usual. It is hard to understand why any objection

* See Chapter VI.

should be taken to Mc or even M', since these are simply abbreviations of Mac.*
The practice of some indexers, notably in the recently published *Century Cyclopaedia
of Names*, of differentiating between Mac and Mc is to be deplored, since the reader
must seek the name he wants in two places—in the Macs, which are interspersed
among such words as Maccabees and Macedonia, and in the Mcs many pages further
on. It is impossible to differentiate satisfactorily. Take MacGillycuddy for example :
it appears in the work in question as MacGillycuddy's Reeks, yet the Chief of the
Name always subscribes himself McGillycuddy of the Reeks. The idea that Mac is
Irish and Mc Scottish is just another popular error. Mcc, however, may fairly be
called an affectation, being merely the perpetuation of a seventeenth century scribe's
slip of the pen.

The most prevalent of peculiarities in the spelling of names—the use of two
small f's for a capital F—would seem to have arisen not through snobbery but from
ignorance : the originators of this now carefully treasured blunder were probably
unaware of the fact that in seventeenth century documents the normal way of
writing F was ff, a symbol almost indistinguishable from f f.

* Throughout this book I use Mac in full merely for the sake of consistency. I have also put an apostrophe after
the prefix O because, though there is no logical reason for this (unless it be a relic of the accent in Irish), it has become
so universally accepted that to omit it might seem to be an affectation.

Chapter IV

DISTRIBUTION AND CONTINUITY

From the time of the early missionaries, whose names—St. Columban, St. Finan, St. Gall and a hundred others—are famous in the history of Europe, the Irish have been a roving race. Descendants of Irishmen who, some voluntarily, more perforce, became emigrants are to be found abroad to-day not only in the United States, Great Britain, Australia and other English-speaking countries, but throughout Europe where the posterity of the Wild Geese are still numerous, though their Irish names are often disguised under forms more consonant with the language of the country of their adoption. Just as the French D'Aubyn and Joie became Tobin and Joyce when naturalized in Ireland so did our O'Dwyer and Shea become Audoyer and Chaix in France. In Spain the alteration has been less marked : O'Donoghue, for example, is O Donoju there.

At home, however, the extent to which the present-day descendants of the old Gaelic families still inhabit the territories occupied by the mediaeval septs from which they stem is most remarkable. Examples of this phenomenon occur repeatedly in the articles on the septs which form Part II of this book : in fact, exceptions to the rule are rare.

In this chapter three areas have been taken for consideration in this connexion. I have chosen Counties Limerick and Clare, taken together, for particular attention for two reasons : first because, being myself of Co. Clare by ancestry and lifelong residence, I have made a closer study of the families and surnames of Thomond than of other places, and secondly because an analysis on the lines about to be presented to the reader was made for the county of Limerick by Father Woulfe some years before his *Sloinnte* was published. The other two areas, Donegal and Leix, were chosen almost at random as typical counties suitable for such a survey in Ulster and Leinster. I have also dealt briefly with Antrim and Down, which differ remarkably from all the other counties of Ireland.

Father Woulfe's articles* dealt only with the County Limerick. He based his findings on the current (1914) voters' lists which showed that of the 19,000 persons then registered approximately 14,500 had surnames of native Irish, 2,100 of Norman and 1,700 of English origin (the remainder being doubtful or miscellaneous). As I am dealing here with the two counties of Limerick and Clare, and as the number of voters is now much greater than it was in 1914, I found it impossible in the time at my disposal to make an exhaustive count of the current registers for both Clare and Limerick. However, a complete count was made for over 50 names in the County

* *Journal of the North Munster Archaeological Society* IV. 1. 16–27 ; IV. 2. 75–111 ; IV. 3. 197–206.

Clare lists, and I made considerable use of those of Limerick County and City in other ways as will appear later in this chapter.

Taking the number of births in the year as indicative of the numerical strength of various names, Matheson found that the following twelve names were the commonest in the country as a whole: Murphy, Kelly, Sullivan, Walsh, Smith, O'Brien, Byrne, Ryan, Connor, O'Neill, Reilly, Doyle. There is no precise way, short of a detailed examination of the last census or the voters' lists for the thirty-two counties to check the accuracy of this list for the present time. A rough and ready test, however, is to be found in the Telephone Directory or in Thom's Directory of Dublin. Any capital city is, as far as names are concerned, more or less a reflection or microcosm of the whole country. By these tests the position is seen to be almost unchanged, the only noticeable difference being that Kennedy comes up into the first dozen and Byrne, as might be expected where Dublin is concerned, rises from seventh to second place.

If we now take the figures given by Father Woulfe for County Limerick and compare them in the subjoined table with the returns in the 1659 census we find that the same surnames predominate at both periods.

	Position in List	20th Century (No. of Voters)	17th Century (No. of Families)	Position in List
Ryan . .	1	644	145	5 (mostly Mulrian then)
O'Brien . .	2	375	201	2
O'Connor . .	3	364	172	3 (including MacConnor)*
Fitzgerald .	4	309	62	12
Sullivan . .	5	244	39	17
Murphy . .	6	235	51	14
Hayes . .	7	233	153	4 (O'Hea then)
O'Connell . .	8	220	57	13
Walsh . .	9	218	66	11
O'Donnell .	10	215	205	1 (including MacDonnell)*

Matheson's Report substantially corroborates the modern figures. It is true that he found that Moloney occupies the tenth place—it is only twenty-first in Woulfe's list—but the influence of County Clare in the composition of Limerick city (which is not in Father Woulfe's count) probably accounts for the inclusion of this well known Clare name.

* In the 1659 "census" much confusion exists as between Mac and O. In the case of MacConnor the prefix Mac appears to have been used carelessly by the enumerator instead of O; on the other hand MacDonnell and O'Donnell should be kept separate and distinct, but the presentation of the figures in the census makes this impossible.

In computing the order of the 1659 count the names McShane (242), McTeige (227), McDonagh (126) and McDermot (74) were disregarded, as in the majority of cases these were not hereditary surnames.*

A similar comparison for County Clare is expressed in the following table. In this case the figures for the twentieth century are taken from a recent voters' register —hence the great increase in the number of voters, women's suffrage and indeed adult suffrage having been introduced subsequent to the date of Father Woulfe's survey.

	Position in List	20th century (No. of Voters)	17th century (No. of Families)	Position in List
MacMahon . .	1	1,594	124	2
MacNamara . .	2	1,358	90	5
O'Brien . . .	3	945	88	6
Molony . . .	4	922	141	1
Kelly . . .	5	832	28†	
Keane . . .	6	713	14†	
MacInerney . .	7	690	29†	
Ryan . . .	8	685	10†	
Murphy . . .	9	592	31†	
Lynch . . .	10	574	12†	
O'Connor . . .	11	549	107	3
Hogan . . .	12	488	62	10
O'Loughlin . .	13	460	34	19
O'Halloran . .	14	447	73	8
Griffin . . .	15	426	26†	
Considine . . .	16	400	21†	

In this case the interval between the date of the modern figures given above and that of Matheson's is some sixty years, but once again the remarkable constancy of the statistics is demonstrated ; and the next four names, which would be in both lists, are the typical Clare names Hickey, Clancy, MacDonnell and Moroney. Of these all but Moroney come in the first twenty of the 1659 list.

We are also able to compare Matheson's birth registration figures for 1890 with the census returns of 1921, thanks to the statistical information collected by Jeremiah

* See Chapter II, pp. 20, 19 *supra*.

† There were undoubtedly a greater number of families of these names than is indicated in the tables. The published returns do not give all the information collected in the census. They state for each barony the number of families only in the case of the more numerous names in that barony. Thus, if there were, say, four families of a given name in each of the eleven baronies, that name would not appear in the returns though there would be actually forty-four families so called. They would, however, be included in the population total.

DISTRIBUTION AND CONTINUITY

King in his *Kerry Past and Present.* The result here is striking, for the eighteen most numerous Kerry surnames specified by Matheson are the same as the eighteen most numerous names in the census with the single exception of O'Donoghue, which is tenth in the census though surprisingly not included in Matheson's list. They are : Sullivan, Connor, Shea, Murphy, MacCarthy, Moriarty, Fitzgerald, Griffin, Connell, Brosnan, Foley, Leary, Clifford, Walsh, Cronin, Lynch, Mahony and Daly, in that order. The positional variation in the 1921 census is slight. The latter indicates that Casey, O'Brien, Kelly, Moynihan, Keane, Stack, Kelleher and Sugrue come next in numerical strength. The Petty census of 1659 tells us that most of the names mentioned above were numerous in Kerry in the seventeenth century.

Having satisfied myself by these and other tests that the birth registrations as given by Matheson can be confidently used as the basis of modern population distribution, at least as far as the more numerous names are concerned, I have taken his figures for my comparison in the case of County Donegal.

	Position in List	Modern (No. of births in a year)	17th century (No. of Families)	Position in List
Gallagher . .	1	196	160	2
Doherty . .	2	160	267	1
Boyle . }	3	102	82	5
O'Donnell . }		102	88	4
MacLoughlin .	5	81	153	3
(Mac)Sweeney .	6	50	46	9
Ward . .	7	40	17	28 (MacAward)
Kelly . }	8	37	61	6 (including O'Cally)
MacGinley . }		37	21	22
MacFadden . .	10	33	20	23 (including MacPaden)

In the first fifteen in 1659 are O'Cunigan (alias Cunningham), MacDevitt, MacMurray, O'Brolloghan and MacColgan, all names intimately associated with north-west Ulster.

Leix, like most of the midland counties, is less satisfactory for our purpose, so far as the modern figures are concerned, because there no names preponderate like Gallagher, Doherty etc. in Donegal or MacMahon and MacNamara in Clare. Dunne, the leading name in Leix (or Queen's County as it then was) had only 34 births registered in the test year taken by Matheson in contrast to the 196 registered for Gallagher in Donegal. The figures for Leix, set out as for the other counties are :

	Position in List	Modern (No. of Births in a year)	17th century (No. of Families)	Position in List
Dunne . .	1	34	105	6
Delany . .	2	30	217	2 (spelt Dullany then)
Phelan (and Whelan)	3	30	263	1 (includes 10 Heelan)
Conry or Conroy .	4	19	39	18 (returned as Conrahy)
Lalor . .	5	18	141	3
Fitzpatrick . .	6	17	134	4
Ryan . .	7	13	—	—
Carroll . .	8	12	45	15
Byrne . .	9	11	72	9
Kavanagh .	10	11	—	—
Kennedy .		11	—	—

The ubiquitous Kelly and Murphy, and the local Ossory Brennan follow with ten births. The 1659 return includes in the first dozen Kelly (121), Bergin (80), MacEvoy (77), Brophy (65) with Moore (53) thirteenth, all traditional Leix names still found there. The absence of Ryan from the "census" is notable.*

It will be seen that the commonest surnames in County Leix in our own day are all of Gaelic origin, as is also the case in County Donegal where Campbell, which comes far down the list, is the only one of planter stock, though Donegal was one of the counties included in the Plantation of Ulster. In County Limerick, on the other hand, as we have already seen, Father Woulfe found that about eleven per cent of the people bear Norman surnames.

As might be expected, Norman names are much less in evidence in County Clare than in County Limerick, and those which are at all numerous such as Burke and the ubiquitous Walsh are immigrant families from other counties and not, like Herbert, Fitzgerald and de Lacy in County Limerick, original Norman settlers. In fact, the only Norman name which appears to belong in that sense to County Clare is Miniter ; Studdert, though it might now, perhaps, be classed as a Clare name, is of much later introduction.

It will be observed that the prefix Mac is much less common in Limerick than in Clare, where the two most numerous surnames are Macs with a third, MacInerney, not far behind. I estimate that in County Clare some twenty-seven per cent of the indigenous Gaelic surnames are Mac names, whereas in County Limerick the proportion is less than twelve per cent.

Oddly enough in County Clare though MacMahon considerably outnumbers Macnamara it is invariably the latter which is indicated by the use in ordinary

* See footnote on p. 30.

parlance of the plain Mac as an abbreviation : indeed so usual is this that it is often written in the abbreviated form, generally with the addition of a K—Mack. This is also done in County Limerick where a similar practice obtains with Fitzgerald, which is commonly abbreviated to Fitz. In other counties, particularly in County Down, the abbreviation is Fitch, which does duty for Fitzpatrick and Fitzsimons and, according to Matheson, is often actually used in registering births.

We have already observed that families still tend to be found in considerable numbers in the county or district of their origin. A glance at the tables given on p. 30 above will show that this is true of the commoner names in County Clare, for 13 out of the 20 cited are of Thomond origin and the remainder (apart from the ubiquitous Murphy, Walsh and Sullivan) belong to an adjacent county. In this connexion it is interesting to observe that the following less common surnames, also of Clare origin, are all given by Matheson as still far more numerous in their original habitat than anywhere else. For this purpose Limerick must be included with Clare, owing to the position of the city on the county border and for the reasons put forward by Dr. John Ryan, S.J., in an informative article on the Dalcassians.*

Cloghessy	Hehir	Minogue
Clune	Hickey	Mulqueen
Crowe	Killeen	Nestor
O'Dea	Lahiff	Neylon
Enright	Liddy	Normoyle
Grady	Looney	Quinlivan
McGuane	Loughlin	Sheedy
Halpin	Lysaght	Talty
Haran		

In the foregoing list I have omitted the Mac and O except in the case of O'Dea and MacGuane, which in County Clare are seldom if ever found without the prefix. Of course, many Loughlins and Gradys, and some Hehirs and Hickeys use the O, while Lysaght, like Clancy in the earlier list, though usually truncated, is often met with its Mac attached ; but none of the other seventeen, nor Moloney, Griffin, Moroney and Considine in the list of commoner names, are ever, I think, to be seen to-day with the Gaelic hallmark to which they are really entitled.

On the other hand certain names for some reason never lost the prefix. O'Brien and O'Neill seldom shed the O, except in colloquial speech, and in County Clare at any rate O'Donnell always retained it ; while among the Macs MacMahon is seldom Mahon and, for philological or phonetic reasons MacNamara and MacInerney escaped.

We have noted in Chapter II how general has been the resumption of Mac and O

* *Journal of the North Munster Archaeological Society*, Vol. II, No. 4, p. 202 *et. seq.*

throughout Ireland. Though as I have just remarked there are many names in Thomond which have not responded to this tendency it has occurred there to a marked extent in others.

The following table shows the position in this respect regarding the name O'Sullivan for Limerick. It is based on the voters' lists :—

		No. of O'Sullivans	No. of Sullivans	Percentage using the prefix O
1914	. .	51	193	21%
1944	. .	191	90	60%

If we take the well-known Clare name Halloran, which Matheson returns as Halloran (67) O'Halloran (25), we find that in the current voters' lists for County Clare quite fifty per cent are now called O'Halloran. In this connexion it may be remarked that the use of these voters' lists for this purpose probably results in a considerable underestimate of the extent of the resumption, as in going through them I noticed several examples of people who appear in the register without the prefix, notwithstanding the fact that to my own knowledge they do ordinarily use the Mac or O, as the case may be.

The most remarkable case of " resumption " is probably O'Gorman. This name, so far as Clare is concerned, is really MacGorman, but so completely was the Mac dropped in the eighteenth century that it appears to have been forgotten, and when the Gormans began to re-gaelicize their patronymic they put an O before it instead of a Mac. The first offender was probably the famous Chevalier, though it is hard to understand why he, with his antiquarian knowledge, can have been guilty of such an error, unless he had some evidence that he himself was actually an O'Gorman ; for there is undoubtedly such a name, though it is very rare and apparently un-connected with Thomond.

Another example of confusion between Mac and O is to be found in the Limerick Mackessy. This, as mentioned in Chapter II, is an O name (Ó Macasa), but I find some of them calling themselves McKissy : they are so described in the recent voters' lists for Limerick city on which I worked.

There are also examples not of resumption but of erroneous assumption. The use of the form MacArthur, for example, is quite without authority so far as Ireland, and especially Limerick, is concerned. There are, of course, the Scottish MacArthurs ; but our Arthurs are of Norse origin and they did not at any period prefix a Mac to their name : to do so now is therefore not a resumption but a solecism.

Reverting to the matter of the prevalence of surnames from which I digressed to discuss the use and disuse of Mac and O, it is worthy of remark that some essentially Clare names which are quite numerous in the voters' lists do not appear

34

in Matheson's table, though he states that it includes every name of which five or more births were registered in the selected year, e.g. Rynne (95 voters), Nihil (55). A few others, like Durack and Gallery, appear to be dwindling, since in each case there were less than five births registered in 1890 and there are less than thirty Clare voters at the present time.

By the same test it might be thought that the good old Clare name of O'Honeen, or O'Huonyn as it was formerly spelled, was likewise almost extinct. There is good reason to believe, however, that this is one of those names which, having undergone a process of translation or pseudo-translation, are no longer found in anything like their original form and, just as Ó Fiachnach is Hunt in County Clare and Ó Mocheirghe of Leitrim is always Early, so the English name Greene was substituted for O'Honeen.

Names in that category are not common in Thomond but we have a number which suffered severely in the process of anglicization and would seem to those unfamiliar with them to be typically English. Some of these have already been noticed in Chapter II. Essentially Thomond names of this class are Arkins (Ó hOrcháin), Crowe (Mac Conchradha), Kett (Ó Ceit), Long (Ó Longaigh), Sexton (Ó Seasnáin), Shine (Ó Seighin) and Thynne (Ó Teimhin).

Of the names mentioned above one or two, e.g. Long and Greene, may in certain cases be not only English in appearance but English in origin. They belong to that numerous class of Irish surname whose anglicized form is the same as a common English name, with which we have already dealt in Chapter II.

As this chapter deals largely with County Limerick it may not be out of place here to mention an element of the population scarcely found outside that county: I refer to those families which we know as the Palatines. They were planted in County Limerick in 1709 and for many generations remained a distinct and un-assimilated race. Their descendants are still there, but none in sufficient numbers to be included in Matheson's birth registration statistics. Ruttle and Switzer, Palatine names, do appear, but in both cases the figures relate to migrants to Dublin. The voters' lists, however, show that Ruttles are still quite numerous in West Limerick.

To some extent the same observations apply to Huguenot names, though of course the Huguenot settlers were not, like the Palatines, confined to one area. Irish families of Huguenot ancestry have produced a number of prominent men—the names La Touche, Lefanu, Cannon and Maturin, for example, attest this, but numerically they form an insignificant proportion of the population.

Before leaving this aspect of our subject reference may be made to another useful source of evidence, namely estate rentals. I examined many of these during the period I was inspector for the Irish Manuscripts Commission, and a large number also passed through my hands in the manuscripts department of the National Library. A few of the great estates, such as Ormond, Inchiquin, Kenmare and Lismore, have rentals for the seventeenth century. The majority, however, are of the nineteenth century. While these corroborate the statement that surnames are found at all periods in the area of their origin, it is also abundantly clear from a perusal of them that many surnames which were numerous even as late as a hundred years ago are now extremely rare if not extinct. To take one or two typical examples : Larminee and Varrily both appear very frequently in the O'Donnell (Co. Mayo) rentals of 1826–1830, but have almost disappeared from the same estate in 1862. Other names in the former, now rare, are Dordan, Dyra, MacEvea, Gettins and Toorish. Similarly in the Westby (Co. Clare) estate rental of 1850 we find many Fennells, a name now scarce in Co. Clare. The Inchiquin rental for 1699, however, which comprises parts of Co. Limerick and Co. Tipperary as well as Clare, has surprisingly few rare names, though older forms such as MacEncroe (mod. Crowe) and Dawley (mod. Daly) occur frequently. The recurrence of names now rare or extinct is particularly notice-able in the Elphin diocesan census of 1749, an extremely interesting document now in the Public Record Office, Dublin.

It can be accepted that the two main conclusions to be drawn from the data given for the counties dealt with in this chapter are to a great extent applicable to the whole country, namely that the commoner names in each area to-day are in fact the names of septs belonging to that county, and the uncommon names originat-ing in a county or district are still chiefly found there. It would be impracticable and tedious to examine every county in detail ; but the following list, compiled from Matheson's report showing the commonest names in each county, is added here both as additional evidence and because it will probably be found of general interest.

It will be noticed that in seven of the nine Ulster counties the most numerous name is a Gaelic-Irish one. The other two—Antrim and Down—include the city of Belfast where there was, and is, a large British element in the population. The surnames of these two counties are the subject of a detailed analysis made just a century ago and published in the *Ulster Journal of Archaeology* (1857 and 1858). These most informative articles are accompanied by maps and statistical tables which show the location and numerical strength of some 250 family names for Down and nearly 200 for Antrim. From these it appears that, even disregarding the Belfast area, the majority of the people in Antrim and Down were of British origin ; and Matheson's figures for more than a generation later corroborate this. The Gaelic element, however, was numerous. The principal Gaelic names were : (for Antrim) MacMullan, MacNeill, MacAlister, MacAwley, Kennedy, Kilpatrick, MacBride, O'Neill, Hamill, MacDowell, MacCormick, McKeown, MacDonnell, in that order ; and (for Down) MacKee, Magee, MacCullogh, Murphy, MacDowell, MacConnell, O'Hare, Lowry, Kelly, Quin. Some of these, of course, have a Scottish background. O'Neill and Neill were listed separately : if taken together they would stand higher. Many interesting facts emerge from a study of these maps and tables. For example, the concentration of O'Haras in the barony of Glenarm and of O'Hares in the barony

36

of Iveagh, or the prevalence of families called MacKeating, chiefly in the barony of Lecale, Co. Down.

CONNACHT

Galway : Kelly
Leitrim : Kelly
Mayo : Walsh
Roscommon : Kelly
Sligo : Brennan

LEINSTER

Carlow : Murphy
Dublin : Byrne
Kildare : Kelly
Kilkenny : Brennan
Leix : Dunne
Longford : Reilly
Louth : Byrne
Meath : Reilly
Offaly : Kelly
Westmeath : Lynch
Wexford : Murphy
Wicklow : Byrne

MUNSTER

Clare : MacMahon
Cork : Sullivan
Kerry : Sullivan
Limerick : Ryan
Tipperary : Ryan
Waterford : Power

ULSTER

Antrim : Smith
Armagh : Murphy
Cavan : Reilly
Derry : Doherty
Donegal : Gallagher
Down : Thompson
Fermanagh : Maguire
Monaghan : Duffy
Tyrone : Quinn

CHAPTER V

CHRISTIAN NAMES

Though of minor importance in comparison with surnames the question of the prevalence of christian names is of sufficient interest to merit a brief examination.

In America and in England the use of surnames as christian names has become very widespread since the end of the nineteenth century. In Great Britain famous surnames like Cecil, Douglas, Gordon, Leslie and Stanley are now regarded there as recognized christian names and are common as such; while in the United States you are more likely to meet, say, a Calvin D. Smith than a plain Tom Smith. The almost universal initial representing a second forename is, of course, characteristically American. Mr. Harry S. Truman, twice President of the United States, (who, by the way, was given a genuine christian name at baptism) is reported to have often said that he did not know what his S. stands for and rather thought it was just an ornamental initial and no more.

In Ireland fancy forenames—we can hardly call Berkeley, Melville, Spencer and the like christian names—are almost unknown, except in Protestant families of " West British " outlook, with whom in Victorian times the " Castle Catholics " could be coupled. Nor do we find the Old Testament biblical names, once so popular in England, adopted to any appreciable extent in Irish families at any period; and we never had in Ireland anything comparable to the extravagance of the Cromwellian Puritans who condemned their children to bear such extraordinary forenames as " Praise-God ", " Christ-died-to-save-us ", and the like.

In modern times in Ireland, particularly in Catholic Ireland, christian names are generally chosen from those of saints: but we still have a fair number of old Gaelic personal names in use, such as Brian, Connor, Dermot and Manus, which are not to be found in Irish hagiology. However, most of the old Gaelic names were actually borne by some early Irish saint: the commonest of them to-day are Aidan, Brendan, Colman, Donough, Fergus, Finbar, Fintan, Kevin, Kieran, Lorcan and Phelim among men, and Brigid, Dympna and Ita among women.

Gaelic names such as those just referred to have become more popular of late years, but the great majority of our people bear christian names which are not of Irish origin; and this has been the case since the destruction of the old Gaelic order. In a number of cases, however, Gaelic names are disguised under the foreign synonyms arbitrarily chosen to represent them. Thus Connor was equated with Cornelius, Cormac and Callagh with Charles, Donough with Denis, Lorcan with Laurence, Rory with Roger, Teig with Timothy, and, most far-fetched of all, Dermot with Jeremiah. An examination of the Fiants and other late sixteenth century sources shows that Gaelic christian names were still usual up to that time; but from the seventeenth century onwards the conditions now obtaining prevailed, and the only changes to be observed are the waning and waxing of the popularity of certain individual names, while the common use in one part of the country of some which are scarce in another is also an interesting point to which reference will be made further on in this chapter.

The numerical strength of our various christian names can best be shown by means of a statistical table. That which follows has been compiled from the voters' lists of four counties. For simplicity of comparison the extensive counts made for this purpose have been reduced to a common ratio, and the figures given below represent the number of persons per thousand of that county's population who bear a particular christian name. It should be mentioned that the modern tendency to substitute Gaelic forms for English, e.g. Sean for John or Liam for William, hardly noticeable yet in the registers, is likely to be more apparent in future; and also that the figures given for the less common names must be regarded as only approximate.

	Limerick	Clare	Donegal	Offaly
John .	175	204	168	159
Patrick	149	170	158	135
Michael	114	171	52	129
William	94	26	64	69
Thomas	72	95	39	60
James	71	75	124	82
Denis	40	8	18	16
Daniel	35	25	38	27
Edmund	24	3	—	—
Timothy	23	15	2	25
Maurice	19	2	—	—
Cornelius	19	8	—	10
Joseph	18	32	44	59
Christopher .	17	4	2	10
Laurence	15	1	2	10
Edward	14	10	40	32
David	12	2	4	2
Martin	10	27	3	28
Jeremiah	9	6	1	—
Peter	8	17	29	29
Stephen	6	13	1	1
Francis	5	18	24	17
Robert	1	—	24	7
Hugh	—	—	46	8
Charles	—	—	38	12
Bernard	—	—	20	15

Other names :

Limerick	*Clare*	*Donegal*	*Offaly*
Bartholomew	Austin	Anthony	Andrew
Brian	Andrew	Owen	Bartholomew
Gerald	Henry	Roger (Rory)	George
George	Brian		Kieran
Nicholas	Matthew		Philip

A similar count was undertaken for the mid-seventeenth century, a number of sources being chosen for this purpose such as the Civil Survey, the Books of Survey and Distribution, the Cromwellian Certificates, etc. This field is too extensive to allow of the production of exact figures, but the result is quite accurate enough to enable us to assess the comparative popularity of christian names in 1650 and in 1950. Then as now John headed the list though its proportion of the whole—approximately nine per cent—was much less than that of the present day. Thomas, William, James and Edmund come next with about five per cent each. The old Gaelic names Connor, Dermot, Donough, Rory and Teig (with of course many varieties of spelling) each accounted for nearly three per cent of the Catholic population, and with these names may be included the equally popular Hugh or Ee (Aodh) and Daniell (or Donell). Patrick, Richard and Nicholas were little less numerous. Then come Maurice, Edward and Robert approximately equal with the Gaelic Brian and Murrough. The list of those names which each exceeded one per cent is completed by Andrew, Christopher, Francis, Garrett, Henry, Loughlin, Mahon, Peter, Piers and Terlagh. It will be observed that Michael and Joseph, which are among the most numerous christian names in Ireland to-day, have not been mentioned : of these, Joseph is very rarely met with in seventeenth century records, but Michael does occur occasionally.

The main conclusions to be drawn from the foregoing are that while John is, and has been consistently since 1650, the most popular christian name throughout the country, the great popularity of its present day rivals Patrick and Michael is of comparatively recent date. Growing devotion to the Archangel may account for the latter. As regards Patrick it has frequently been stated that it was almost unknown as a christian name before the time of Patrick Sarsfield and that its widespread adoption can be attributed to the honour in which that celebrated Irish soldier was held. It is, I think, true that the name Patrick was thus first popularized ; but it is quite erroneous to say that the name was uncommon before his time, as we have already seen in considering the 1650 figures. It has been suggested that the mediaeval Gaels had so great a veneration for the patron saint of Ireland that they refrained from giving his name to their sons, just as they did not call their daughters Muire, the Irish name for the Blessed Virgin, Máire being used for Mary ; and it is true that the form Giolla Pádraig (Gilpatrick) is found in mediaeval records.

Nevertheless the Annals, the ecclesiastical registers etc. contain many Patricks from Patrick O'Scannell, Bishop of Raphoe (1261–1265), onwards.

Even within the past half century certain tendencies can be perceived. For County Limerick we have a ready means of comparison without having recourse to the labour of making a count of the voters' lists of fifty years ago : for Father Woulfe published many years before the appearance of his *magnum opus* an analysis of the names of County Limerick, including the christian names. For the most part their comparative popularity remains much the same, but it is of interest to note that there has been a very marked fall in the number of Jeremiahs, and Bartholomew and Philip share this decline ; while a very considerable increase is noticeable in the name Joseph and also, though in a less degree, in Christopher and Martin.

All over the country, and particularly in County Limerick, William is and was a favourite name. The association of William of Orange with a disastrous period of Irish history has surprisingly had no effect on its popularity. On the other hand the odium attaching to Cromwell has made Oliver a hated name in Ireland, but this is offset by the reverence felt for the martyred Oliver Plunkett, especially since his beatification.

As we have seen, the old Irish forenames fell into disuse with the submergence of the Gael. The persecution of the Catholic Church and its adherents, which was an integral part of the policy of conquest, had the effect of making the Irish people more conscious of their religion and stiffened their determination not to relinquish it : it is from this period we may date the practice of calling children by the names of saints.

Every diocese has its patron saint. In some his name is to be found in frequent use as a christian name in that diocese : thus Kierans are quite numerous in the counties embraced by the dioceses of Clonmacnois and Ossory, but not elsewhere ; similarly Brendan is not uncommon in Kerry and Clonfert, Finbar in Cork, Colman in Cloyne, Malachy in Down and Armagh, Eugene in Derry, Kevin and Laurence in Dublin, Phelim in Kilmore and Nicholas in Galway. On the other hand many of them have never been adopted : it is indeed very seldom one hears of a boy called Mel (Ardagh), Jarlath (Tuam), Nathy (Achonry), Munchin (Limerick), Fachanan (Kilfenora and Ross) or Otteran (Waterford). The name of another saint associated with County Waterford, however—St. Declan—is often used in that county, but seldom elsewhere.

Certain christian names are also closely associated with particular surnames. Thus Florence (a curious anglicization of Finghin or Fineen) suggests MacCarthy and Tiernan O'Rourke. Other familiar combinations are Garrett Fitzgerald, Niall O'Boyle, Myles O'Reilly, Quentin O'Kane, Heber MacMahon, Randal MacDonnell ; Aeneas and Manus are associated with O'Donnell, and Donough, Kennedy and Lucius with O'Brien, while Boetius was a favourite name with the MacEgans and the MacClancys.

Little has been said in this chapter about women's christian names. Historically the sources for statistical information are meagre since the records available, dealing as they do with agrarian, ecclesiastical and military affairs, relate almost entirely to men. The modern voters' lists, of course, contain as many women as men, but there are much fewer women's christian names than men's and much less variation geographically. Mary is by far the commonest of these, exceeding even John in numbers. In the seventeenth century it was rare. Brigid, until comparatively recent almost as popular as Mary, has of late years been sadly neglected. Another present-day tendency to be noted is the marked increase in the use of old Gaelic names such as Nuala, Sive, Sheila and Una.

Chapter VI

CHANGES OF NAME

The Adaptation of Enactments Acts of 1922 embraced not only laws applicable to Ireland enacted by Statute but also the common law as it existed at the time of the establishment of the Irish Free State. The law of the land relating to personal names, which was and is for the most part determined by usage, not statute, is therefore substantially the same as that in Great Britain. It is so lax that it surprises, even shocks, continental observers of Irish life and customs.

That it should be possible for Moses Solomon to become Maurice Salmon without any official act involving registration or fee seems odd enough to them; but that Jacob Isaacs can become first Jack Ivers, and that Jack Ivers may later merge into John McIntyre or even Pat Murphy, entirely *motu proprio*, seems incredible. Indeed the metamorphosis can be accomplished without any intermediate onomatopoeic stage.

As the law stands a person's name is determined by "common repute". So well established is that principle that there have been cases in the British courts in which marriages have been declared void on account of the use by one of the parties in the publication of the banns of the name appearing in his or her baptismal record rather than that acquired by common repute; and this would seem to be in accordance with common sense if the publication of banns is to be regarded as more than a formality.

The general idea is that a deed-poll is required to effect a change of name. This is a popular error.

According to Linell and other authorities on the law governing changes of name, and the various judicial judgements given both in Great Britain and Ireland during the past ninety years, there are (apart from a special Act of Parliament or Oireachtas) two methods of changing a name, viz. by Royal Licence, and by prescription. As the law stands, therefore, a name cannot legally be changed by deed-poll, a deed-poll being merely evidence of the intention to acquire (or occasionally of the fact of having already acquired) a new name by prescription. The growing practice of resorting to a deed-poll with the object of effecting a change of name *motu proprio* is a contrivance of comparatively modern introduction, the first isolated instance of its use in England being in 1851 and in Ireland much later. It has, however, obtained a sort of quasi-legal sanction, especially since the further step of registering such deed-poll at the Central Office of the High Court became part of the usual procedure in these cases. This indeterminate state of affairs is far from satisfactory, for not only does it enable undesireable foreigners to acquire Irish names with a minimum of difficulty and expense, it also gives a colour of legality to the assumption by an impostor of such a designation as, say, " The O'Carroll ", to which he has no shadow of claim.

43

If we except the rectification by parents of an error in registration, a point to which I will revert later, there is, therefore, apart from prescription by common repute (and its corollary deed-poll), only one way in which a name can be changed by legal process, viz. by Government Licence. This is simply a republican adaptation of the Royal Licence which obtains in England and was available here also up to 1922. By that means a man's name can be changed, as it were overnight, with no possibility of legal doubt. This method, however, costs a considerable sum (£60) and is seldom employed except in the case of landed estates long in the possession of one family whose last male representative wishes to perpetuate their surname and so leaves the property on condition that the heir assumes that of his predecessors.

I have referred already to another type of name change—a minor one—viz. the correction of registration errors. These, which usually occur when the registration is done by someone other than a parent, are quite frequent and are seldom detected until the person in question is in his or her teens, when a birth certificate is required for school or employment purposes. The Registrar-General accepts corrections when vouched for by the parents ; but on the certificate both the original error and the correction appear. Thus if John Mackessy is entered as John McKessy, the latter can never be expunged, though it is a blunder, since MacKessy, as we saw in Chapter II, is an O name. However, there is no immediate necessity for codification in this respect.

We now come to a category which includes a great many of the older generation of Irishmen : those who have resumed the prefix O or Mac, dropped by their ancestors during the period of Gaelic submergence. " Common repute " has of course covered their case as the law now stands ; but new legislation on the subject, since it must necessarily abolish the validity of prescription by common repute, would have to provide for the acceptance of such resumptions and their registration at a nominal fee by the competent authority. A difficulty arises here, for that authority (who it would be, will be considered later) should be competent in more than the legal sense of the word. It would be ridiculous to allow people with obviously non-Gaelic names to " resume " imaginary prefixes, to become, for example, O'Hodge or MacParker. These would be easy enough to detect, but how would an untrained official know when to allow Moore to become O'Moore and Johnson MacShane, or when a Smith was genuinely a MacGowan ? Indeed even an expert would be confronted with many difficulties, so great has been the destruction of Irish records.

The latter really belong to the next class of name change I have in mind : re-translation. We have already seen in Chapter III how numerous are those names of English appearance which were formed by the translation or pseudo-translation of old Gaelic patronymics—Banks, Hand, Woods and so on. Should these be allowed to resume their original form on the same easy terms as the Mac and O people ? Is anyone called Smith, even if he is the son of a recent English immigrant, to have an equal right with a genuine County Cavan MacGowan to that form of the name ?

Clearly the " competent authority " would need a very knowledgeable advisory council to help him decide such knotty problems.

I may mention, *en passant*, that there is at present, at any rate for the simple resumers of Mac and O, a very easy expedient for the parent who is chiefly interested in his children and posterity. All Mr. Sullivan has to do is to enter his own name as O'Sullivan when registering his children's births and they become O'Sullivans automatically thereby.

I have cited already some examples to show that the allowance of indiscriminate and uncontrolled name-changes can be, and is in fact, an abuse : discretion forbids me to quote any of the more flagrant actual cases which have come under my notice officially. In the same way our easy-going system of birth registration can be, and occasionally is, abused. A person registering the birth of his child can make any statement he chooses as to his own name, rank, profession etc. Thus John Smith, bookmaker, of Clontarf (I trust there is no such person in existence—if there is I apologize for the accidental use of his name) can, when registering his son's birth, describe himself as the Prince of the Blasket Islands, adding K.M., D.Litt., V.C. and any other bogus degrees or distinctions he likes. It is not the function of officials accepting civil registration entries to question the accuracy of statements made, and, unless they contain something obviously blasphemous or obscene, they do not in fact do so. No doubt if confronted with an entry giving the child's name as Dirty Pig and the father's as, say, Mahomet or Buddha some query would be raised as to the sanity of the parent, but in practice anything not definitely offensive passes. In Britain some control is exercised under the Criminal Justice Act of 1925 and the Registration Regulations of 1927 but these of course do not apply to this country.

In this connexion I may mention that there are other ways of procuring quasi-official recognition of a fake title, as for example by registering a bogus deed at the Registry of Deeds and obtaining there a copy in the form of an imposing looking legal document : this in fact does not purport to be in any way a guarantee of the factual accuracy of the original, but can easily be used to impress the uninitiated, and particularly foreigners who are accustomed to a more rigid code in such matters. I have in the past few years met actual instances both of birth registration and of registration of deeds of the most outrageous character, but regret that for obvious reasons I cannot cite them here.

I think enough has already been said to indicate that legislation is needed to create a more rational state of affairs in the matter of the use and control of personal names ; unless, as sometimes seems incredibly enough to be the case, we wish, like the Government of Northern Ireland, to adopt a legislative policy of step-by-step with Britain. Perhaps the first move in this direction might be the setting up of a commission to consider the whole question, though, having regard to the fate of the findings of so many commissions in the past, both under the Union and since we became independent, I hesitate to advocate this.

It may be assumed that the main principles of the Bill would not give rise to controversy. It must provide that a person's only legal name is that which appears on the birth certificate and further that this can be changed if only the change be carried out in proper legal form.

As intentionally misleading statements in birth registration are very rare and would be difficult to prevent, we may take it that little or no amendment need be contemplated in this respect.

Turning to the question of name-changing we can probably also take it as axiomatic that changes should not be allowed unless good cause for such action be forthcoming. This postulates, as I have already remarked, a really Competent Authority and a properly qualified Advisory Council, and possibly also an Appeal Board. If the Competent Authority must be an existing higher civil servant the choice would lie between the Registrar-General, who is now responsible for birth certificates, and the Chief Herald, who is the official through whom at the Genealogical Office changes of name by Government Licence are carried out under existing arrangements. That office keeps an official register for this purpose. There has also been established at the Genealogical Office a register of persons who have submitted adequate evidence of change of name by prescription (without the execution of a deed-poll)—cases frequently occur particularly in connexion with illegitimacy and adoption—and the Chief Herald's certificate to that effect is in fact more conclusive as evidence of such change of name than a deed-poll, since it testifies to an established and fully proved fact and is not given where any doubt exists as to the propriety of such changes ; whereas, as I have said, a deed-poll is usually no more than the expression of an intention. This register at the Genealogical Office has no legal sanction beyond being excellent evidence of change by prescription.

The Competent Authority, whoever he might be, and his advisors or the Appeal Board, would no doubt have many difficult border-line cases to decide on. No opposition could, of course, be offered to testamentary or marriage settlement changes, to resumptions of Mac and O, to genuine re-translations and to other equally simple cases. Less obvious would be those applications prompted by aesthetic considerations. For example, many people would greatly dislike bearing surnames like Bugg, Bastard, Coward, Death or Grubb.

These are all well-known English surnames occasionally found in Ireland : we have nothing in the anglicized versions of our Irish names to vie with these, and those like Buggy, Levy and Looney which are suggestive or lacking in harmony have only to be changed back to their original form to become unobjectionable.

If I were the official to make the decision I would have no hesitation in granting a Mr. Bugg's application to make a change ; I would, however, have something to say about the name he took in place of it. If, for example, he proposed to call himself O'Connor or MacMahon I would agree if his mother belonged to those families ; otherwise I would not permit the assumption by outsiders of ancient Gaelic patronymics. There is much food for thought and study in this aspect of the question but it would be tedious to pursue it in further detail here.

A scale of fees would have to be prescribed to cover the various types of name-change. If Government Licences were retained in the schedule they would head the list even if the present rate were reduced. The lowest would enable a person registered in one of the official languages of this country to use for legal purposes its form in the other. Hitherto the need for revision in this respect has been felt chiefly by students of the National University who wish to use the Gaelic form of a name registered in its anglicized version, and find that they are obliged to follow exactly the form and spelling shown on their birth certificates. (Oddly enough, Trinity College is less strict in this way).

But for the necessity of guarding against freak gaelicization this fee could be fixed at something quite nominal, just to cover the cost of registration. No case, however, even the most obvious, should be passed without the approval of some responsible and trained official. Many clerical officers are as well-informed and well-educated as their superiors ; but if one of the ignorant or indeed of the casual easy-going type happened to be in charge of the machinery of such registration it is by no means improbable that some invention such as Ó hEidhin (Hynes) for Heinz or even a concoction like Mac a' Rosa for Rosenbaum might slip through unnoticed. Once again it would be tedious to pursue this by-path further.

There is one other class of name variant to which I have made no reference in this chapter : stage names and *noms de plume*. Difficulties do exist at present, but our suggested Act would automatically remove them, for they arise from the doctrine of " common repute ". I am able here to quote an actual case to illustrate the interesting complications which can arise, as the gentleman in question has told me he has no objection to being cited. Some thirty-five years ago a young man from County Westmeath called John Weldon wrote a very striking first novel under the nom-de-plume of Brinsley MacNamara, and he followed this up with Abbey plays and other works which established him as one of the leading figures in the Irish literary movement, always under the name of Brinsley MacNamara. Indeed, very few people were aware that that was not his original name : so much so that when at the age of fifty or so he became Registrar at the National Gallery his letter of appointment was made out to Brinsley MacNamara, not to John Weldon, and in spite of the fact that the error was pointed out to the authorities the name MacNamara was and is still used in all official documents. It is therefore the indisputable fact that under the present law we find here a man who has two entirely different and equally valid legal names ; for though by common repute and prescription he has irrevocably become MacNamara he has never relinquished his original name which he retains for domestic and family purposes : thus when he attended the wedding of his son (who is called Weldon) he was described in the reports as Weldon, not MacNamara.

No better example of the lack of precision in the law now governing nomenclature in Ireland could be found. In itself it is merely interesting and does not illustrate an abuse. That abuses under the present system can and do exist has I think been demonstrated earlier in this chapter. It is to be hoped that some event such as a *cause célèbre* turning on the misuse of a name will occur to make headlines in the newspapers and so focus attention on the necessity for codification.

PART TWO

IRISH FAMILIES

O'AHERNE, Hearne, (O'Heffron).

This Irish surname was first anglicized O'Hagherin, which is a fair phonetic approximation of the original Gaelic Ó hEachtighearna, derived from the Irish words *each* a horse and *tighearna* a lord. Later this was corrupted to O'Aherne and finally the prefix O was dropped. The O'Ahernes were originally a Dalcassian sept and up to the middle of the fourteenth century they were dynasts of Ui Cearnaigh, their territory being in the neighbourhood of Sixmilebridge, Co. Clare, not far from the city of Limerick. In the course of time they migrated southwards and in 1659, when Petty's census was taken, the name was numerous throughout Counties Cork and Waterford. At the present time it is almost confined to Counties Cork and Limerick; but in the form Hearn and Hearne it is also well-established in Co. Waterford. In this connexion it should be observed that Hearn is a fairly common indigenous name in England, so that persons so called in Ireland may be immigrants from that country.

The Bishop of Kerry from 1336 to 1347 is described in the records as Alan O'Hathern alias O'Hachierane. The most noteworthy of the name in modern history were John Aherne (c. 1769–1806), United Irishman and intimate friend of Wolfe Tone, who, after the latter's death, became an officer in Napoleon's Irish Legion; and John Aheron author of the first book on architecture printed in Ireland (1754).

The Gaelic name Ó hUidhrín, that of an Offaly sept, has also been anglicized Hearne, Heron etc., though Heffron and Haveran are more usual forms in English. Giollananaomh Ó hUidhrín (d. 1420), who completed O'Dugan's celebrated " Topographical Poem," is usually called O'Heerin in English.

Arms illustrated on Plate I.

ATHY.

No records exist for Galway prior to the date of the Anglo-Norman invasion : among the earliest preserved the name Athy appears as a leading family in that city. It subsequently became one of the " Tribes of Galway ",* which appellation, according to Hardiman, was invented as a term of opprobrium by the Cromwellian forces who regarded unfavourably the close bond of friendship and relationship between the chief families of the city, and it was afterwards adopted by them as a mark of distinction. Nevertheless the first time the name Athy comes into prominence

*The "Tribes" were fourteen in number, viz. Athy, Blake, Bodkin, Browne, Deane, Darcy, Fant, French, Joyce, Kirwan, Lynch, Martin, Morris and Skerrett. Some authorities reckon the number as thirteen, omitting Deane ; but as this name appears as early as 1448 in a responsible position in Galway, whereas the Morris family did not go there until 1485, it seems proper to include Deane among the Tribes.

in the history of the city is (c. 1320) as a party to a series of deadly disputes between the Blakes and the Athys in which the Athys were worsted. They were never comparable in influence with the more powerful of the Tribes, but several of them held important posts, e.g., William de Athy, Treasurer of Connacht 1388.

The surname Athy, now scarce, is of a type which is common in most countries but very rare in Ireland, being formed from a place name. The Athys were of Norman stock, settled at Athy, Co. Kildare, whence they soon migrated to Galway.

MacAULIFFE.

The name MacAuliffe is almost peculiar to Co. Cork and is scarcely found outside Munster. The MacAuliffes are a branch of the MacCarthys and their chief resided at Castle MacAuliffe near Newmarket, Co. Cork. Their territory in that part of the country is described in a grant of land to a stranger in 1612 as " Clan Auliffe ". It should be noted however that the term Clan Auliffe normally refers to a branch of the O'Farrells of Co. Longford and has no connexion with the sept of MacAuliffe. The last recognized Chief of the name, Michael MacAuliffe, was according to Dalton a colonel in the Spanish army and died in Spain in 1720 ; O'Donovan however ascribes that position to a minor official at Kenmare in 1840. In Irish the name is Mac Amhlaoibh, i.e., son of Auliffe (*anglice* Humphrey). The same Gaelic name is also anglicized MacAuley, which is an entirely different sept (q.v. *infra*). The famous French physician Joseph Oliffe (1808–1869) was actually born in Cork, his ancestral name being MacAuliffe.

Arms illustrated on Plate I.

MacAWLEY, Cauley, Magawley.

This name is spelt in many different ways, the most usual being MacAuley, MacCauley, Cawley, Macaulay, MacGawley and Magawley. There are two main Irish septs of MacAuley etc. entirely different in origin and location. One is Mac Amhalghaidh, i.e. son of Auley, an old Irish personal name now obsolete. This sept was at one time of considerable importance, being lords of a wide territory in the west of Co. Westmeath and north of Offaly : in the Elizabethan Fiants this is called " McGawley's Country," the centre of which was Ballyloughnoe in Co. Westmeath. The Four Masters describe them as Chiefs of Calry. They are descended from Niall of the Nine Hostages, their surname being taken from his descendant Auley, who flourished in the thirteenth century. Their pedigree is recorded in the Office of Arms, Dublin

50

Castle, in great detail ; the Chief of the Name a century ago was Count Magawley Cerati, son of the Prime Minister of the Empress Maria Louisa. Up till that time they preserved a close connexion with their homeland in Co. Westmeath.

The other sept was called in Irish Mac Amhlaoibh. They are a branch of the MacGuires and belong to Co. Fermanagh, where they have given their name to the barony of Clanawley.

It should be noted that Mac Amhlaoibh is also the name of a quite distinct Munster sept, the anglicized form there being MacAuliffe (q.v. p. 50 *supra*). The same Gaelic form is used by the Scottish clan of Macaulay. Many of the Irish born Macauleys and MacAuleys, particularly those living in the counties adjacent to Belfast, are descendants of Scottish settlers in Ulster.

The outstanding figure of the name in Irish history is Catherine MacAuley (1787–1841), foundress of the Order of Mercy.

Arms illustrated on Plate I.

BARRETT, MacPadine, (MacEvilly, Staunton).

The surname Barrett came to Ireland with the Anglo-Norman invaders at the end of the twelfth century, and, in due course, became hibernicized, though not to the extent that some others such as Fitzgerald and Burke did, inasmuch as Barrett is still a common name in England.

Though they came to Ireland at the same period, the ancestors of the Irish Barretts were of two quite distinct families whose names were at first different and who settled in widely separated parts of the country. The surname Barrett to-day is most numerous in Co. Cork and in the Mayo-Galway area, in fact approximately where their forefathers established themselves more than seven centuries ago. The former were Barratt (in Irish Baróid) ; the latter Barrett (in Irish Bairéid). O'Donovan states that both lines were Welsh ; Woulfe, who writing sixty years later usually accepts O'Donovan's opinions, disagrees and regards Baróid as of Norman origin (from the Norman French name Baraud), and Bairéid as Anglo-Saxon.

The Munster Barretts, though numerically stronger than those of Connacht, were of less importance in the mediaeval or Gaelic period ; nevertheless they were influential enough to give their name to an extensive territory, viz. Barrett's Country, i.e. approximately the present barony of Barretts in Co. Cork. They did not, however, become entirely gaelicized like their Connacht namesakes. Those Barretts who early acquired a large part of north Mayo were lords of Tirawley and founded there a sept on the Irish model. The chief of this sept was known as Mac-Wattin—it is spelt MacVaittin by O'Donovan in his translation of the Four Masters, and it so appears in the Annals at various dates in the fourteenth and fifteenth centuries. In the sixteenth, however, the " Composition Book of Connacht " (1585) which includes the names of many Mayo Barretts, as do the Fiants of approximately the same date, describes the then Chief of the Name as Richard Barrett, alias Mac-Padine ; and it is interesting to note that the surname MacPadden is found in Mayo to-day, while MacWattin is unknown. It must also be remembered that the name MacPadine was adopted by certain families of the Stauntons, another of the Anglo-Norman invaders. Some of these again adopted as their Gaelic surname Mac an Mhileadha (*anglice* MacEvilly), so that confusion may easily arise, especially as there is an Ulster name MacPhaidín (MacFadden, MacFadyen, etc.), and this is also found in Gaelic Scotland.

The Munster Barretts, in spite of their somewhat dishonourable treatment by Sir John Perrott and later by John St. Leger, managed to retain the bulk of their property until 1691 when the Williamite confiscation deprived Col. John Barrett, the head of the family at that time, of 12,000 acres. This Col. Barrett had raised a regiment of infantry for King James's army in Ireland, and subsequently was killed in the French service at the battle of Landen in 1693.

In the eighteenth century Richard Barrett (c. 1740–1810), " the Poet of Erris ", was also a prominent United Irishman, and George Barrett (d. 1784) was a celebrated landscape painter. Rev. John Barrett (1753–1821), of Dublin University, was a noted Hebrew scholar. In the nineteenth century Michael Barrett, the Fenian, condemned for the attempt to blow up Clerkenwell prison, was executed in 1868—the last public execution in England. Laurence Barrett (1838–1891), a leading American actor, was the son of an Irish emigrant, but the other Barrett family of American actors were of English extraction.

Arms illustrated on Plate I.

BARRY.

Though not peculiar to Ireland, Barry is one of the names introduced into the country following the Anglo-Norman invasion—like Burke, Roche, Fitzgerald, etc.—which can now be regarded as essentially Irish. As early as 1179 Philip de Barri obtained extensive grants of land in Co. Cork (in the baronies of Barrymore, Orrery and Kinelea). Philip's posterity prospered and multiplied, and the several branches of the family formed septs somewhat in the Irish fashion, the chief of which were the important Barry Mór, Barry Óg, Barry Roe, while minor branches became Barry Maol (bald) and Barry Láidir (strong). The Barrys of Rathcormac, Co. Cork, adopted the surname MacAdam, taken from one Adam Barry—Adam being a common Christian name in Anglo-Norman families. The baronies of Barrymore and Barryroe were so named from the two most important of these septs. The former is very large and the latter very small, due to the fact that by Elizabethan times when the boundaries of the baronies became stabilized, the area of the Barryroe lordship had been very much reduced.

The name, since the twelfth century, has always been principally associated with Co. Cork, and modern statistics indicate that quite fifty per cent of the Barrys in Ireland belong to that county, the majority of the remainder being also from the province of Munster. In this connexion it should be stated that there is a Gaelic surname Ó Beargha belonging to a sept which, at one time, were lords of a territory in the barony of Kenry, Co. Limerick. Except in cases where a pedigree is preserved, or a family tradition exists, it is not possible to be certain of the origin of the Barrys in Co. Limerick and north Cork, but it is probable that even there many, if not most of them, are of Norman stock—though, of course, continued intermarriage with their Gaelic neighbours has made them indistinguishable from the older race.

One of the leading descendants of Philip de Barry became Baron Barry in 1490, and his family was advanced in the peerage as Viscount Buttevant in 1535 and Earl of Barrymore in 1627. The Four Masters record that in 1507, Barry Roe, accompanied by the chief men of his people, went from Cork on a pilgrimage to Spain and that all were lost at sea on the return journey.

Among the many distinguished Irishmen of the name are two soldiers of the 1641 war—David Barry, Earl of Barrymore (1605–1642), and Gerald Barry who was also an author of note—the former was killed in that war and the latter outlawed and exiled to Spain. There was a Capt. Barry in the Irish Brigade in France who would have been arrested for his anti-revolutionary sympathies at the time of the French Revolution but for the fact that the letter he had written, expressing these views, was in the Irish language and there was no one among his captors who could translate it. Kevin Barry (1902–1920), may also be included in that category for he was an active member of the I.R.A. in the Irish War of Independence and was hanged for his part in it.

In the field of literature " Lo " (probably James) Barry (b. c. 1591) is regarded as the first Irish dramatist; while John Milner Barry (1768–1822), Sir Samuel Barry (1696–1776) and Sir David Barry (1780–1835), all physicians, wrote widely on medical subjects; while James Greene Barry (1841–1931), did valuable work as a historian in his native Co. Limerick. In art James Barry (1741–1806), was a celebrated painter, and Sir Charles Barry (1795–1860), was the architect of the London Houses of Parliament. Spranger Barry (1719–1777), himself a fine actor, built theatres in Dublin and Cork. The most renowned of all Irish Barrys did not, like most of the foregoing, come from Co. Cork: he was John Barry (1745–1803), who was born in Co. Wexford and is known as the " father of the American navy ". He is one of the very few individuals who have been commemorated by the issue of an Irish postage stamp. Another who made a name in America was also born far from Co. Cork— Belfast-born Patrick Barry (1816–1890), leading horticultural authority in the U.S.A.

Gerald de Barri, or Barry (c. 1145–c. 1220), better known as Giraldus Cambrensis, though famous for his commentary on twelfth century Ireland, was, of course, himself Welsh not Irish.

Arms illustrated on Plate I.

O'BEIRNE.

Though the pronunciation of this name is very similar to O'Byrne there is no connexion between the two septs. O'Beirne belongs almost exclusively to Connacht. One branch, allied to the MacDermots and the other leading Roscommon families, in the thirteenth century displaced the O'Monahans as chiefs of a territory called Tir Briuin na Sinna between Elphin and Jamestown on the Co. Roscommon side of the Shannon, and they appear as such in the " Composition Book of Connacht " (1585) ; and in 1850 there was still an O'Beirne of Dangan-I-Beirn in that territory. The other branch possessed territory in the adjoining county of Mayo, north of Ballinrobe. At the present time O'Beirnes are chiefly found in Counties Roscommon and Leitrim.

While no O'Beirne has left a lasting mark on the history of Ireland several distinguished themselves in the service of France in the eighteenth century. The sept has produced one or two interesting characters who may be mentioned here. Thomas Lewis O'Beirne (1748–1823), though reared a Catholic (his brother was a Parish Priest in Co. Meath) became Protestant Bishop of Meath in 1789 ; and Henry O' Beirne (b. 1851), an Irish emigrant, was well known in America on account of his writings about the Texas Indians, among whom he settled permanently.

Arms illustrated on Plate I.

BLAKE, Caddell, (Blowick).

The Blakes are one of the " Tribes of Galway ". They descend from Richard Caddell, also called Blake, who was Sheriff of Connacht in 1303. It was not until the seventeenth century that the name Blake finally supplanted Caddell : for three hundred years they appear in the records of the city as " Caddell alias Blake " or " Blake alias Caddell ", Blake being originally an epithet—*le blac*, i.e. black. The name, of course, is also well-known in England : for a note on the poet William Blake, see O'Neill (p. 242). Apart from their activities in the city government and in the ecclesiastical wardenship of Galway, the most distinguished member of this family was Sir Richard Blake who was chairman or speaker of the Assembly of

Confederate Catholics at Kilkenny in 1647, Francis Blake, being also on the Supreme Council. William Rufus Blake (1805–1863), the popular American actor, was of Galway parentage. The man who killed Red Hugh O'Donnell by poison is said to have been one James Blake. William Hume Blake (1809–1870), an emigrant from Ireland, became the head of the Canadian judiciary and his son, Edward Blake (1833–1912), was a leading statesman in Canada. Martin Joseph Blake (1853–1931), should also be mentioned on account of his extensive genealogical researches, partly published in *Blake Family Records*.

The Blakes were among the most extensive landowners in Connacht in the sixteenth century and this was equally true in the nineteenth: their principal estates were at Ardfry, Balglunin, Kiltullagh, Menlo and Renvyle, all in Co. Galway.

A branch of the Galway Blakes settled in Co. Kildare where they gave their name to Blakestown in that county.

It should be added that there are some scattered families of Blake in the west of Ireland who are of Gaelic origin, for Ó Blathmhaic, *anglice* Blowick, is known to have become Blake in certain places in Co. Mayo, being an example of the unfortunate tendency of rare Irish surnames to become merged in common ones of a somewhat similar sound.

Arms illustrated on Plate I.

BODKIN.

This un-Irish sounding name is intimately connected with Galway, the Bodkins being one of the fourteen " tribes " of that city. They are, in fact, an offshoot of the Fitzgeralds, being descended from Maurice Fitzgerald the ancestor of the Earls of Desmond and Kildare. Richard, Maurice's grandson, acquired extensive lands in east Galway in 1242. The name Bodkin is said to have originated from an incident in the career of Richard's son, Thomas Fitzgerald—the tradition being that in the course of a famous single combat he gained the victory by means of using a short spear called a baudekin, whence the expression *buaidh baudekin*, from which the surname was formed. Be that as it may there is no doubt as to the authenticity of their descent from the Fitzgeralds.

It was in the fourteenth century that the Bodkins, then called Boudakyn and later Bodekin, established themselves in the city of Galway, and from that time until the Cromwellian upheaval and the submergence of prominent Catholic families, they were one of the more important of the " tribes ". There were several mediaeval bishops of the name and a number of officers in King James II's army in Ireland. Walter and Dominick Bodkin were members of the Supreme Council of the Confederation of Kilkenny in 1647. One of them, at the siege of Galway in 1652 refused to sign the articles of surrender. Forty years later Col. John Bodkin, was a prominent

Jacobite leader. Francis Bodkin was a notorious pirate captain : in 1673 his crew were captured but he escaped.

O'BOLAND, Bolan.

The older form of this name—O'Bolan—is almost obsolete, though it is occasionally found without the prefix O. The usual modern form—Boland—never has the O, though entitled to it, the Gaelic original being Ó Beolláin. The addition of the D at the end of the name is an anglicized affectation comparable to changing -ahan into -ham, as in the case of Markham for Markahan. This final D does not once appear in the Elizabethan Fiants though the name in four different forms occurs nine times in those records, principally in Co. Sligo.

There are at least two distinct septs of the name, one of the Ui Fiachrach line, seated at Doonaltan, (barony of Tireragh, Co. Sligo) ; the other being Dalcassian, of Thomond. The former may be distinct from that of Drumcliff, also in Co. Sligo, where O'Bolans were erenaghs of the church of St. Columban. The Thomond sept is descended from Mahon, brother of Brian Boru : for this we have the authority of " An Leabhar Muimhneach," but MacFirbis traces them to another Mahon, less closely related to the great Brian. Present day representatives of these septs are chiefly found in north Connacht and in east Clare where the picturesque fishing village of Mountshannon on Lough Derg perpetuates the homeland of the sept in its Gaelic name Baile ui Beoláin (or Ballybolan). In the seventeenth century it was also numerous in Offaly. References to the name Ó Beolláin occur occasionally in the Annals in early mediaeval times, but since the Anglo-Norman invasion they have not been prominent in the political or cultural history of the country. To-day Boland is a household word in the milling industry of Dublin, and is also prominent in the person of Frederick Boland, formerly Ambassador to Great Britain and later Ireland's permanent representative in the United Nations Organization.

Arms illustrated on Plate I.

O'BOYLAN, Boyland.

The O'Boylan sept of Oriel, which sprang originally from the same stock as the O'Flanagans of Fermanagh, were in early mediaeval times located in a widespread territory stretching from Fermanagh to Louth. Later they were reduced by the MacMahons, but still retained the greater part of the barony of Dartry in Co. Monaghan. O'Dugan in his fourteenth century " Topographical Poem " praises them for their horsemanship and comments on their blue eyes, calling them " the bold Kings of Dartry ". They are still more numerous in the Monaghan-Cavan-Meath area than elsewhere. In Irish the name is Ó Baoigheálláin which is etymologically akin to Ó Baoighill, *anglice* Boyle (q.v. *infra*). The prefix O is seldom if ever used with Boylan in modern times, but the alternative form Boyland is sometimes found. The name does not appear prominently in Irish political or military history. Teresa Boylan (b. 1868) was a poetess of some note. At the present day Monsignor Patrick Boylan, the distinguished Hebrew scholar and orientalist, was recently President of the Royal Irish Academy.

Arms illustrated on Plate I.

O'BOYLE.

Boyle is Ó Baoighill in modern Irish, the derivation of which is possibly from the old Irish word *baigell*, i.e. having profitable pledges : modern scholars reject the derivation *baoith-geall*. It is thus of course a true native Irish surname and the O'Boyles were a strong sept in Co. Donegal with a regularly initiated chieftain seated at Cloghineely : they shared with the O'Donnells and the O'Doughertys the leadership of the north-west. Ballyweel, near Donegal town, is a phonetic rendering of Baile ui Bhaoighill (i.e. the home of the O'Boyles). These O'Boyles were noted for their ruddy complexion. Nevertheless the best-known Boyles connected with Ireland were men of English race. When Richard Boyle landed in Ireland in 1588 as a young man without influence few could have anticipated that he would become what has been termed the " first colonial millionaire ". He acquired the extensive property of the executed Sir Walter Raleigh in Co. Waterford. This formed the nucleus of the vast estates he was to bequeath to his numerous family on his death in 1643, by which time he was Earl of Cork and had held high government office. The best known of his sons (born in Ireland) were Roger Boyle (1621–1679) Earl of Orrery, and Robert Boyle (1627–1691), chemist and experimental physicist. It is worthy of note that of 15 Boyles in the *Dictionary of National Biography* 14 belong to this Anglo-Irish family. Some Gaelic-Irish Boyles or O'Boyles have also distinguished themselves, notably William Boyle (1853–1922) Abbey Theatre dramatist, John Boyle (d. 1832) the well-known wit, and Richard Boyle (1822–1908) the railway engineer whose heroism during the Indian Mutiny won renown. The name is common (being included in the fifty most numerous in Ireland), particularly in the Ulster counties of Donegal, Tyrone and Armagh (it takes third place in the first named). It is only in comparatively recent times that the discarded prefix O has been at all widely restored.

Arms illustrated on Plate II.

MacBRADY.

In Irish the name Brady is Mac Bradaigh so that it should correctly be MacBrady in the anglicized form ; the prefix Mac, however, has seldom if ever been used in modern times. The MacBradys were a powerful sept belonging to Breffny, their chief holding sway over a territory lying a few miles east of Cavan town. The Four Masters record many illustrious chiefs of the name there. The historian Abbé Mac-Geoghegan says that the MacBradys are a branch of the O'Carrolls of Calry, Co. Leitrim, a statement which has been often repeated, but modern authorities refute this. In any case they have always been pre-eminently associated with Co. Cavan ; and it is in Co. Cavan and adjacent areas the Bradys are mostly found to-day. They are indeed very numerous in Ireland with an estimated population of nearly 10,000 persons so called.

A number of families of Brady are also to be found in the district around the village of Tuamgraney, Co. Clare. These are in fact not truly Bradys at all but O'Gradys, of the same family as O'Grady of Kilballyowen, Co. Limerick*: from the time of Henry VIII onwards these O'Gradys identified themselves with the English cause : for that reason, perhaps, they adopted the form Brady instead of Grady. The first Protestant Bishop of Meath, for example, was Hugh Brady, a Clareman, son of Donough O'Grady. The Limerick branch, on the other hand, having been Brady for a generation or two, reverted to the correct form O'Grady.

All the Bradys who have distinguished themselves in the cultural and political history of Ireland were from Co. Cavan. The most notable of these are Fiachra MacBrady (fl. 1710), and Rev. Philip MacBrady (d. 1719), both Gaelic poets, the latter of whom became a Protestant clergyman and was very popular with the people of Co. Cavan, perhaps because he satirized his colleagues. In this category we may also place Phelim Brady (fl. 1710), usually referred to as " bold Phelim Brady the bard of Armagh ". Thomas Brady (1752–1827), a farmer's son from Cootehill, Co. Cavan, became a Field Marshal in the Austrian service ; another who was prominent in military service outside Ireland was Michael Brady : he was executed for his part in the service of the " Young Pretender " in 1745. In the ecclesiastical sphere Gilbert MacBrady was Bishop of Ardagh from 1396 to 1400 ; and three MacBradys were bishops of Kilmore in the fifteenth and sixteenth centuries : in 1580 John MacBrady was succeeded in the same see by Richard Brady a distinguished Franciscan. Andrew MacBrady in 1454 was the first bishop of Kilmore to provide a cathedral church for the diocese. Hugh Brady, Protestant Bishop of Meath, has already been mentioned. Apart from the Gaelic poets the most important literary man of the name was William Maziere Brady (1825–1894), author of *Episcopal Succession in England, Scotland and Ireland*.

Arms illustrated on Plate II.

* Vide O'Grady p. 165, *infra*.

58

O'BRALLAGHAN, Bradley.

Few Irish surnames have been more barbarously maltreated as a result of the introduction of the English language into Ireland than Ó Brollacháin, which for some extraordinary reason was generally given as its anglicized form the common English name of Bradley, though in a few places, notably in Co. Derry, it is quite rationally called in English O'Brallaghan. No doubt a proportion of the Bradleys in Ireland are descendants of English settlers, but those who bear the name in the counties adjacent to Co. Derry and also in Co. Cork have justification for believing that they are really O'Brallaghans, because it was in those areas that the sept originated, the Cork line being a branch which in early times migrated southwards. Actually they are first heard of in Co. Tyrone, the county adjacent to Co. Derry on its southern border. It is interesting to note that modern statistics show that Counties Derry, Tyrone and Donegal are still the homeland of most Irish Bradleys, with Cork their main stronghold in the south.

A remarkable number of O'Brallaghans (or rather O'Brollachain for the English language was then unknown in Ireland) distinguished themselves in the eleventh and twelfth centuries : Maelbrighde O'Brollacháin (d. 1029) builder ; his sons Aedh (d. 1095), professor, and Maelbrighde, bishop of Kildare (1097–1100) ; another, Donal O'Brollachain (d. 1202), was Abbot of Derry ; while Flaibhertach O'Brollachain (d. 1175) rebuilt the Cathedral at Derry in 1164. The only Irishman of special note called Bradley was Most Rev. Denis Mary Bradley (1846–1903), a Kerryman popular with all denominations in his diocese of Manchester (New England).

O'BREEN, MacBREEN.

At the present time the Breens are distributed widely throughout Ireland. They are always called simply Breen though originally there were both MacBreens and O'Breens. The former, Mac Braoin in Irish, were an Ossory sept seated near Knocktopher in Co. Kilkenny ; but after the Anglo-Norman invasion they were dispersed by the Walshes and sank in importance. Though in 1659 they were noted as still numerous in Ossory—the prefix Mac had even then been dropped—Co. Wexford, adjacent to Co. Kilkenny, is the area in which the name Breen is now chiefly found, and it is reasonable to assume that these are MacBreens. The most important O'Breen (Ó Braoin) sept in mediaeval times was that possessed of territory in Counties Westmeath and Offaly near Athlone. Their chief was Lord of Brawney. As late as 1421 O'Breen of Brawney is mentioned in a contemporary document with O'Conor and MacMorogh as a great chieftain of the Irish nation. The name Breen is seldom met with in that area to-day, but it is said to be now disguised there under the alias

O'Brien. The infamous Jemmy O'Brien, of 1798 notoriety, was an O'Breen, not an O'Brien of Thomond. It is also a fact that a comparable corruption occurred in the case of the O'Breens of north Connacht who in course of time became Bruen in Co. Roscommon, a name fairly common there now (which Breen is not), and Browne in Mayo. William Browne (1777–1857), of Foxford, famous Argentine admiral, was possibly of the Connacht O'Breens.* Finally the name has been common in Co. Kerry, at least since the seventeenth century. Henry H. Breen (1805–1882), the poet, was a Kerryman. Francis Breen, the 1798 rebel, was from Co. Wexford. The Brawney sept is represented in history by Tighearnach Ó Braoin, the annalist, who died at Clonmacnois, where he was abbot, in 1088, and by Donal O'Breen, Bishop of Clonmacnois from 1303 to 1324. Elizabeth Breen was one of the Irish nuns arrested in France in 1793 during the Terror. Patrick Breen (d. 1808), whose diary of the Donner exploration party is remarkable for its stark realism, was born in Ireland. In our own day the best known bearer of the name is Dan Breen, T.D. one of the most prominent fighters on the Irish side during the War of Independence 1916–1921.

O'BRENNAN, MacBRENNAN.

In modern Ireland there are many Brennans: the name comes twenty-eighth in the statistical list of Irish surnames. Here and there one is met with the prefix O, but to-day the form MacBrennan is seldom if ever found.

The simple form Brennan is used in the anglicized form of two quite distinct Gaelic Irish surnames, viz. O Braonáin and Mac Branáin. The former is the appellation of four different unrelated septs; the latter of one only. Judging by the present day distribution of the name, two of these five have survived in large numbers in the districts around their original habitats. It is sufficient, therefore, just to mention *en passant* the three others which were located respectively in counties Galway, Westmeath and Kerry.

Mac Branáin was chief of Corcachlann, the old name of a territory in the eastern part of Co. Roscommon: a succession of these chiefs appear in the Annals between 1159 and 1488. While the leading members of the sept retained the Mac until the submergence of the Gaelic order in the seventeenth century, the substitution of O for Mac, in some cases, is noted as early as 1360. The present day Brennans of Counties Roscommon, Sligo and Mayo, however, are nearly all MacBrennans, or more correctly MacBrannans.

The principal O'Brennan sept was that of Ossory: they were chiefs of Ui Duach (mod. Idough) in the northern part of Co. Kilkenny. Their influence naturally waned

* See p. 65 *infra*.

as English power became paramount in Leinster, and though several O'Brennans retained some portion of their former estates, the seventeenth century reduced many of them to the status of rapparee—indeed several famous or notorious bands of tories in Leinster were led by Brennans, and in the next century, one of the most intrepid and chivalrous of all Irish highwaymen, James Freney, was, he asserted, instructed in his calling by the last of these tory Brennans.

The most distinguished of the sept was Most Rev. John Brennan (1625–1693), Bishop of Waterford and Archbishop of Cashel, friend of Geoffrey Keating and Blessed Oliver Plunkett : though constantly the object of special attention from priest-hunters, he was elusive enough to remain continuously in his dioceses which he administered with marked wisdom, and his periodical reports to Rome are of the greatest value to the historian of the seventeenth century. Another John Brennan (1768–1830), popularly called the " wrestling doctor " and well known in his day for his satires on Dublin doctors, was also of the Ossory sept of O'Brennan and considered to be chief of the name. Among exiles of the name we may mention the Abbé Peter O'Brennan who was executed in 1794 for his resistance to the French Revolution.

An interesting account of the O'Brennans of Ossory will be found in the *Journal of the Royal Society of Antiquaries*, vol. I, pp. 230–254.

Arms illustrated on Plate II.

MacBRIDE, Kilbride.

MacBride is Mac Giolla Brighde in Irish i.e. son of the follower or devotee of St. Brigid. The name is numerous in Ulster, particularly in Counties Donegal and Down. They are first heard of as erenaghs of Raymunterdoney, Co. Donegal, a parish which includes Tory Island. In the seventeenth century they settled at Gweedore in the same county. Several of the sept were bishops of Raphoe, the most distinguished of whom was John MacGilbride (d. 1440). A branch of the sept was established in Co. Down and in the 1659 census MacBride appears as a principal Irish name in three different baronies of that county.

MacBride is also a well known name in Scotland.

Though the majority of Irish MacBrides are Catholics four prominent Ulster Protestants of the name are noteworthy, all being of the same family : David Mac-Bride (1726–1778), physician and inventor ; John MacBride (1730–1800), admiral in the British navy ; Rev. John MacBride (1650–1718), Presbyterian author ; and John David MacBride (1778–1868), scholar and head of Magdalen College, Oxford. The minaturist Alexander MacBride (1798–1852), was born in Co. Monaghan. The Minister for External Affairs in a recent Irish government, Seán MacBride (b. 1904), is the son of the late Major John MacBride (1865–1916), executed after the 1916 Rising, and Maud Gonne MacBride (1865–1953), who was one of the most picturesque figures in the modern Irish political scene.

In Connacht the name MacBride sometimes takes the form Kilbride.

O'BRIEN.

In these brief accounts of Irish septs and families in which only a page or two is devoted to each subject, it is impossible to do justice to the greatest of them, such as the O'Briens, the O'Connors and the O'Neills, about whom whole volumes have been written and more has yet to be added. From the tenth century, when the sept rose to the High Kingship of Ireland in the person of Brian Boru, down to the present day, the O'Briens have always been prominent in the history of the country.

Before Brian Boru's time, the Dalcassian clan, known as the Ui Toirdealbhaigh, to which they belonged, was not of outstanding importance in Thomond : the greatness of Brian gave them pre-eminence there and in due course the sept, which took the surname O'Brien from him, divided into several branches and possessed a great part of Munster, of which they were frequently kings. The O'Briens of Ara (north Tipperary), a territory they acquired from the O'Donegans about the year 1300, had as chief Mac Ui Bhriain Ara ; those of Co. Limerick gave their name to the barony of Pubblebrien ; another branch was located around Aherlow by the Galtees ; and another south of the Comeragh Mountains on the rich lands near Dungarvan. In all those areas, and especially in Co. Clare they are numerous to-day : the name, in fact, is so common that it comes sixth in the statistical list relating to Irish surnames, with an estimated population of more than thirty thousand persons. In this connexion it may be observed, that though fifty years ago one third of the people of the name were registered as plain Brien, nowadays it is rarely to be found without the prefix O.

The outstanding figure is, of course, Brian Boru (925–1014), whose remarkable career as High King of Ireland ended with his death on the field of the battle of Clontarf when the Norsemen were finally subdued. Brian, in fact, used no surname ; it was, however, in regular use forty years after his death. From 1055 up to 1616, the last year recorded by the Four Masters, O'Briens figure in the annals of every generation, over 300 individuals of the name finding a place in that great work. In this respect they are outnumbered only by the O'Connors, the O'Neills and the O'Donnells. In the " Annals of Innisfallen," which deal principally with the southern half of Ireland, the O'Briens appear more often than any other sept, though in this the MacCarthys run them close.

Coming to modern times, the difficulty is to select a few names from the many O'Briens who have been prominent in the political and cultural history of the country. The descendants of Brian Boru, in the main line, have been peers of the realm under three titles, Earls and Marquises of Thomond, Barons and Earls of Inchiquin and Viscounts Clare. The two former have more often than not been on the side of England, notably Murrough O'Brien, sixth Earl of Thomond (d. 1551), who was one of the first great Gaelic chiefs to acknowledge Henry VIII, and the other notorious Murrough O'Brien, sixth Earl of Inchiquin (1614–1674), whose exploits during the war of 1641–1650 earned him the sobriquet "Murrough of the Burnings". The Viscounts Clare, on the other hand, present a different picture ; the first of these, Daniel O'Brien (1577–1663), was a member of the Supreme Council of the Catholic Confederates ; it was the third Viscount, also Daniel O'Brien (d. 1690), who raised the famous Irish Brigade regiment known as Clare's Dragoons, which was later commanded in many famous battles on the continent by the fifth Viscount, Charles O'Brien, whose distinguished military career ended when he was killed at the battle of Ramillies in 1706, while his son, Charles O'Brien, sixth Viscount (1699–1771), upheld the family tradition at Dettingen and Fontenoy, and became a Marshal of France. Younger branches of these noble families produced William Smith O'Brien (1803–1864), who broke away from the "landlord" tradition of his relatives and became one of the best known of the Young Irelanders. His daughter, Charlotte Grace O'Brien (1845–1909), was a philanthropist, author and zealous Gaelic Leaguer, and his brother, Edward O'Brien (1808–1840), devoted his short life to similar causes.

Other O'Briens whose names are honoured for their part in the struggle for the restoration of Irish independence are Most Rev. Terence Albert O'Brien (1600–1651), Dominican Bishop of Emly, who was hanged by Ireton after the Siege of Limerick ; James Francis Xavier O'Brien (1828–1905), the Fenian, and William O'Brien (1852–1928), who devised the "Plan of Campaign" and founded the United Irish League. Another William O'Brien (b. 1881), nationalist, labour leader and friend of James Connolly, is still active in Irish affairs. Add to all these Fitzjames O'Brien (1828–1862), the Irish author who was killed fighting in the American Civil War ; Jeremiah O'Brien (1740–1818), with his brothers John and William, heroes of naval exploits against the British in the American War of Independence ; Most Rev. John O'Brien (d. 1767) and Rev. Paul O'Brien (1763–1820), two noted Gaelic scholars ; and there are still many names which may justly be considered worthy of a place in this brief account of a great and famous Irish sept.

Arms illustrated on Plate II.

O'BRODER, Broderick, Brothers.

Broderick is a fairly common indigenous surname in England. Nevertheless very few Irish Brodericks are of English extraction. The name affords a good example of the practice, which grew up during the two centuries of English and Protestant domination in Ireland after the Williamite Wars, of assimilating old Gaelic surnames to well-known English names somewhat resembling them. Thus for Lehane Lane was widely adopted, MacFirbis became generally Forbes and Cunnigan Cunningham ; and in the same way Ó Bruadair and Mac Bruadair, which were at first anglicized as Broder and Brouder, acquired the forms Broderick and Brothers. Father McErlean, in his introduction to the poems of David Ó Bruadair, referring to a recent generation remarks " those who to their neighbours are Broders become Brodericks when they go marketing in the county town or when they enter a rent office or a court of law." It has been held that this sept is of Norse origin but there is no basis for this beyond the fact that Bruadar was a common name in the Scandinavian countries. Even had it been taken from this source that is no proof of Norse blood, but the fact is that many Bruadars are on record in Ireland before the " Danish " invasions began and before surnames came into existence. Several distinct septs of Ó Bruadair existed in early mediaeval times of which two may be mentioned here since their descendants are still found in or near their original territory. One was located in Co. Cork—in the barony of Barrymore—to which David or Daithi Ó Bruadair the poet belonged. It was presumably a branch of this which settled as a Munster family in Iverk (Ossory), where they were well established in the seventeenth century. In Co. Limerick, where the name is now quite numerous, they are registered as Brouder and Broderick in about equal numbers. The other belonged to Co. Galway, the most famous of whom was Fr. Anthony O'Bruadair, O.S.F., the martyr. The best known of all Broderick families in Ireland is that of which Lord Midleton is the head. The first of these to come to Ireland was an Englishman, Sir Alan Broderick who was appointed Surveyor General of Ireland in 1660.

Arms illustrated on Plate II.

BROWNE.

Though this is one of the commonest of all surnames in England (more often without the E there), it is included here because the Brownes were one of the " Tribes " of Galway. The arms illustrated on Plate II are those of the Galway Brownes. There are many other distinguished families of Browne in Ireland, notably in Connacht—that of Lord Oranmore and Browne and the Brownes of Breaghwy, Co. Mayo—and in Kerry the Brownes of Killarney, whose historic Kenmare peerage has recently become extinct. No less important were the Brownes of Camus, Co. Limerick, of whom General Ulysses Browne (1705–1757), was the best known.

The Galway Brownes are descended from a Norman, le Brun, who came to Ireland at the time of the Anglo-Norman invasion. The Brownes, or Brunachs, are mentioned by MacFirbis in his Hy Fiachrach as one of the four Norman tribes who wrested the territory of Tirawley from the Fiachrach following the invasion. They established themselves in Galway by intermarriage with its leading family, the Lynches. By similiar alliance with the O'Flahertys and the O'Malleys they secured their position as an Irish family in the West. The Brownes of Killarney, on the other hand, stem from an Elizabethan Englishman, but there again intermarriage with influential Gaelic families in Kerry consolidated their position. A very full account of this family is given in *The Kenmare Manuscripts*, published by the Irish Manuscripts Commission.

Admiral William Browne (1777–1857), celebrated as the creator of the Argentine navy, was born at Foxford, Co. Mayo. It is thought that his family was a branch of the Connacht O'Breens whose name appears in the sixteenth century Fiants, inter alia, as O'Browne. No conclusive proof, however, of this descent is as yet forthcoming.

Two of the most important men in Galway city to-day are Brownes: Most Rev. Michael Browne, Bishop of Galway, and Monsignor Patrick Browne, President of University College, Galway, and a Gaelic poet of distinction.
Arms illustrated on Plate II.

O'BUHILLY, Buckley.

The Irish surname Ó Buachalla (derived from the Gaelic word *buachal* a boy) is usually anglicized Buckley. Buckley is of course a common English name, but it is safe to say that few Irish-born Buckleys are of English extraction. The more Irish-looking forms Boughla and Buhilly are used in one area of Co. Offaly. It is not, however, numerous in that part of Ireland now, though it was in mediaeval times; and in 1659 it appears there in Petty's census as an Irish principal name in the barony of Ballycowan as Bohelly. A family of Buckley or Buhilly resident at Lemanaghan, Co. Offaly, claimed to be descendants of the cowherd of St. Manahan and hereditary bearers of his shrine, the custodians of which were the O'Mooneys (q.v. p. 227 *infra*). As Bouhilly it was numerous at the same date in Iffa and Offa, i.e. the south western corner of Co. Tipperary.

William Bulkely (1768–1793), who was guillotined for his prominent part in the royalist counter-revolution, was born at Clonmel and apparently his real name was Buckley. The famous family of Bulkely in France was, however, according to O'Callaghan, of English origin.

To-day the name Buckley is chiefly found in Counties Cork and Kerry: eighty per cent of the large number of births recorded for the name (it has a place in the hundred commonest Irish surnames) are in Munster.

The American botanist, Samuel Buckley (1809–1883), was possibly of Irish origin, though he was a Wesleyan. The last Governor-General of the Irish Free State was Donal Ó Buachalla.

BURKE, Bourke, de Burgh.

Burke is much the most numerous of the Hiberno-Norman surnames. It is estimated that there are some 19,000 people of the name in Ireland to-day: with its variant Bourke it comes fourteenth in the list of commonest names. It came to Ireland at the time of the Anglo-Norman invasion in the person of William Fitzadelm de Burgo (called William the Conqueror by Irish annalists), who succeeded Strongbow as Chief Governor. In 1179 vast estates in Connacht were granted to the de Burgos, or Burkes, but beyond sporadic ravaging, they did not, properly speaking, possess the territory until the next generation when it was regranted to Sir Richard de Burgo, or Burke, by Henry III. Having regard to the large number of Burkes, or Bourkes, now living—the figure 19,000, given above, must be multiplied several times to include emigrants of Irish stock to America and elsewhere—it is hardly possible that they all stem from the one ancestor (the name, it may be remarked, is not found in England except in families of Irish background); nevertheless, even if several different Burkes came to Ireland in the wake of Strongbow, it is the one great family, mentioned above, which has been so prominent in Irish history.

The Burkes became more completely hibernicized than any other Norman family. They adopted Brehon Law and proclaimed themselves chiefs after the Irish fashion, forming, indeed, several septs of which the two most important were known as MacWilliam Uachtar (Galway) and MacWilliam Iochtar (Mayo). Minor branches became MacDavie, MacGibbon, MacHugo, MacRedmond and MacSeoinin. Of these the name Mac Seoinin is extant in Counties Mayo and Galway as Jennings, and MacGibbon as Gibbons. As late as 1518, when the City of the Tribes was still hostile to its Gaelic neighbours and the order was made that " neither O nor Mac should strut or swagger through the streets of Galway ", a more specific instruction was issued forbidding the citizens to admit into their houses " Burkes, MacWilliams, Kellys or any other sept ". The original form of the name was often used even as late as the sixteenth century: two de Burgos were bishops of Clonfert between 1508 and 1580.

After the battle of Kinsale at which Lord Burke of Castleconnell distinguished himself (on the English side), the leading Burkes displayed more loyalty to their king than to their country, though when the two loyalties coincided during the reign of James II, they were to be found among the leading men of the Confederate Catholics and many of the name were attainted and deprived of their estates, much of which, however, was recovered by them after the Restoration. The Earl of Clanrickarde, whose peerage dated from 1543, commanded one of the infantry regiments in James II's army. Of the many Burkes who took service with continental powers after the defeat of that King, none was more distinguished than Toby Bourke (c. 1674–c. 1734), whose connexion was with Spain. Raymond Bourke (1773–1847), a peer of France descended from the Mayo Burkes, accompanied Wolfe Tone to Ireland in the 1798 expedition and later became a famous Napoleonic commander. Several other Bourkes or Burkes distinguished themselves in the army of France.

Later in the eighteenth century the outstanding Burkes were the famous states-man Edmund Burke (1729–1797), whose only son, Richard Burke (1758–1794), was agent of the Catholic Committee, and Dr. Thomas Burke (1705–1776), Dominican Bishop of Ossory, author of *Hibernia Dominicana*. Another Dominican of note was Rev. Thomas Nicholas Burke (1830–1883), whose fame as a preacher, especially during his visit to America, was phenomenal—Pope Pius IX called him " the prince of preachers ". His contemporary, also Galway born, Canon Ulick Bourke, P.P. (1829–1887), was a pioneer of the Irish language revival. The death of Richard Southwell Burke, sixth Earl of Mayo (1822–1872), caused a sensation as he was assassinated during his term of office as Governor General of India. Another sensation relating to a Burke of humbler origin was the trial and execution of the notorious William Burke (1792–1829) ; his activities in smothering the victims whose bodies he sold for dissection have added a verb—to burke—to the English language. Galway born Robert O'Hara Burke (1820–1861), also made headlines in his day when under conditions of almost incredible hardship he succeeded in crossing the Australian desert on foot : he died of starvation on the return journey. Many other Burkes, Bourkes, and de Burghs might also be mentioned. No account of the name, however brief, would be adequate which omitted Sir Bernard Burke (1814–1892), Ulster King of Arms, and his father, John Burke (1787–1848), a Co. Tipperary man, celebrated for their work on genealogy, peerages and family history.

Arms illustrated on Plate II.

BUTLER.

Butler is a name now to be found in every walk of life in Ireland. The same is true of England. In the absence of a reliable pedigree, or at least a well established tradition, the origin of individual Butlers in Ireland to-day cannot be suggested with confidence. The history of the Ormond Butlers, however, is very well authenticated—indeed for more than seven centuries their history is the history of Anglo-Irish relations—from 1171 when Theobald Fitzwalter accompanied Henry II to Ireland, till our own time when the ancestral castle of Kilkenny was abandoned as the seat of the family and the voluminous Ormond manuscript collection was taken over by the National Library of Ireland, where it forms an invaluable source for Irish as well as for Butler family history.

The surname Butler, as far as Ireland is concerned, dates from about the year 1220 : it arose from the fact that in 1177 the Theobald Fitzwalter, mentioned above, was created Chief Butler of Ireland. The seventh in descent from him was created Earl of Ormond in 1328. In 1391 the head-quarters of the Ormonds was removed from Gowran to Kilkenny Castle.

For centuries a rivalry existed between the Butlers and the Geraldines (see Fitzgerald *infra*), and it may be said that up to the death of the Great Duke of Ormond in 1688, the effective government of the country (or, at least, as much of it as for the time being acknowledged allegiance to the King of England) was in the hands of one or the other of these great Norman houses. The Butlers have generally been regarded as more consistently loyal to the sovereign than their rivals, but as Standish O'Grady in his edition of *Pacata Hibernia* points out, being weaker than the Geraldines they were forced to lean on the State, and on the only occasion in which they were wronged they were just as ready to rebel as any other sept. In this connexion it may be mentioned that a branch of the Butlers, for a while in the fifteenth century, took MacRichard as their surname and had an important chief somewhat in the Gaelic fashion : eventually, however, they reverted to the name Butler. Among the numerous Catholic Butlers who were loyal Jacobites perhaps the most noteworthy were the Abbé James Butler of Nantes, who was chaplain to Prince Charles Edward (the " Young Pretender ") in the 1745 expedition ; and Pierce Butler (1652–1740), third Viscount Galmoy, who fought with Sarsfield in all his Irish and French campaigns.

A branch of the Butler family has long been established in Co. Clare : a very full account of them is to be found in *The Butlers of Co. Clare* by Sir Henry Butler Blackall.

Arms illustrated on Plate II.

O'BYRNE.

O'Byrne is in Irish Ó Broin i.e. descendant of Bran (earlier form Broen), King of Leinster, who died in 1052. With the O'Tooles the O'Byrnes were driven from their original territory in the modern Co. Kildare at the time of the Anglo-Norman invasion and settled in the wilder country of south Wicklow about the year 1200. There were two main branches of the O'Byrnes of which the senior soon sank into obscurity, but the junior line, which occupied the country between Rathdrum and

Shillelagh, became a sept of great importance and, like their neighbours the O'Tooles in north Wicklow, were particularly noteworthy for their persistent and largely successful resistance to English aggression. They continued regularly to inaugurate chiefs of the sept up to the end of the sixteenth century. The seat of their chiefs was at Ballinacor and their territory was called Crioch Branach, the sept itself being known as Ui Broin or Branaigh. Many of these were renowned in the military history of Ireland, the most famous being Feagh or Fiacha MacHugh (or son of Aodh) O'Byrne (1544–1597) who, though he was prominent in rebellion and was killed in battle, is perhaps best remembered for his part in the escape of Hugh Roe O'Donnell from his prison in Dublin Castle in 1591. His son Phelim O'Byrne was the victim of one of the many unscrupulously trumped-up charges which disgraced English seventeenth century administration in Ireland : the Viceroy Falkland was in turn disgraced, but notwithstanding that the O'Byrnes lost the greater part of their estates in consequence of his action.

The celebrated " Leabhar Branach " or " Book of the O'Byrnes " is a collection of Gaelic poetry by some thirty-five different authors, dealing for the most part with the exploits and personalities of the O'Byrnes in the sixteenth century : it was made about 1662. In the next century O'Byrnes were prominent in the 1798 insurrection, notably the brothers Garret Byrne (1774–1830) and William Byrne (1775–1799), the latter of whom was hanged ; and Miles Byrne (1780–1862), who subsequently distinguished himself in France and was awarded the Legion of Honour. Other O'Byrnes have been notable in France : one branch, which was admitted to the ranks of the French nobility in 1770, was a leading family in Bordeaux before the Revolution and Garret Byrne, mentioned above, was among the distinguished exiles to that country ; while in America, Irish-born Most Rev. Dr. Andrew Byrne (1802–1862), first bishop of Little Rock, is remembered as a pioneer Catholic in Indian territory. In our own time one of the best known and most popular figures in the life of the Irish capital was Alderman Alfred Byrne (1882–1956), who was ten times Lord Mayor of Dublin.

The Byrnes, who in recent generations have increasingly resumed the discarded prefix O, are very numerous in Ireland to-day, the name being in the seventh place in the list of Commonest Names. The great majority of these were born in Dublin, in Co. Wicklow and adjacent counties.

Arms illustrated on Plate III.

MacCABE.

The MacCabes came from the western isles of Scotland about the year 1350 as gallowglasses to the O'Reillys and the O'Rourkes, the principal septs of Breffny. They became themselves a recognized Breffny sept, their chief being " Constable

69

of the two Breffnys ". Modern statistics show that they are still much more numerous in the Breffny area than anywhere else. As landed proprietors they were as much associated with Co. Monaghan as with Co. Cavan; however the principal families of MacCabe lost their estates in the Catholic débâcle after the battle of Aughrim in 1691.

William Putnam McCabe (1776–1821) was one of the most romantic figures among the United Irishmen. Earlier in the eighteenth century Cathaoir MacCabe (d. 1740), himself a Cavan bard, is best remembered as the life long friend of Turlogh O'Carolan (1670–1738), whose death he commemorated in a fine elegy in Irish (Carolan had previously written an elegy on MacCabe having been hoaxed by him into believing he was dead). In more recent times Edward Cardinal McCabe (1816–1885) and Bernard MacCabe (1801–1891), the author, may be mentioned. Outside Ireland the best known man of the name was Charles Caldwell MacCabe (1836–1906), grandson of a Co. Tyrone man, an American Protestant bishop, known as " chaplain MacCabe " of the Civil War.

Arms illustrated on Plate III.

MacCAFFREY, (MacCafferky).

The MacCaffreys are a branch of the MacGuires of Fermanagh. The townland of Ballymacaffrey near Fivemiletown on the Tyrone border marks their homeland. The great majority of persons of the name to-day belong to families located in Fermanagh and Tyrone: a little further south in Cavan and north Meath there are a considerable number of Caffreys, i.e. the same surname but with the prefix Mac dropped. In Irish it is Mac Gafraidh (son of Godfrey). At one time this was anglicized MacGoffrey by some families which migrated from Fermanagh to Roscommon; and that of course is phonetically more correct than MacCaffrey. The best known of the name was Rev. James MacCaffrey (d. 1875), the ecclesiastical historian, who was born in Co. Tyrone.

The Mayo name MacCafferky, sometimes called MacCafferty, has occasionally been corrupted to MacCaffrey. This is MacEachmharcaigh in Irish, formed from the words *each* a steed and *marcach* a rider.

O'CAHILL.

In early mediaeval times the most important sept of O'Cahill was that located in Co. Galway near the Clare border, the head of which was Chief of Kinelea (Aughty), but by the middle of the thirteenth century their former position as the leading family in Kilmacduagh had been taken by the O'Shaughnessys. The name is uncommon there now, but is found in Co. Clare where a branch of the sept was also established. There were several quite distinct septs of O'Cahill: one of these was located near Lough Leane in Kerry and another in Co. Tipperary between Thurles and Templemore. There are no less than three townlands called Ballycahill in Co. Tipperary which perpetuate the original habitat of that sept. Two other Ballycahills, one in Co. Galway, between Portumna and Killimor, the other in Co. Clare near Ballyvaughan, also indicate the location of those septs. To-day the great majority of Cahills are to be found in the three Munster counties of Tipperary, Cork and Kerry.

In Irish the name is Ó Cathail, i.e. descendant of Cathal, a Christian name which, Dr. M. A. O'Brien informs me, is derived from the Old Irish *catu-ualos* meaning powerful in battle. Cahill is one of those surnames seldom if ever found in modern times with its proper prefix O. O'Cahill is one of the earliest surnames on record: Flann O'Cahill was martyred in 938.

The most notable man of the name was that versatile priest Father Daniel William Cahill (1796–1864), schoolmaster, newspaper editor and prolific lecturer in the U.S.A. and elsewhere on behalf of Catholic institutions.

Arms illustrated on Plate III.

O'CALLAGHAN, (Kelaghan).

The name O'Callaghan, in Irish Ó Ceallacháin, was taken from Ceallachán (Callaghan), King of Munster (d. 952), the eponymous ancestor of the sept. Dispossessed of their original territory in the barony of Kinelea, Co. Cork, after the Anglo-Norman invasion, they acquired a large area of north Co. Cork near Mallow and retained it until again dispossessed under the Cromwellian régime. The leading family of the sept was transplanted then to Co. Clare, where the village of O'Callaghan's Mills bears their name and where they are represented by the family of O'Callaghan (now O'Callaghan-Westropp) of Lismehane. The humbler members of the sept, as was usually the case, were not transplanted; and to-day Co. Cork is the area in which O'Callaghans are chiefly to be found. Although they are mainly concentrated in that area the total number of O'Callaghans and Callaghans in Ireland to-day is about 13,000, which places the name among the forty most numerous in the country. It may here be observed that Callaghan is one of those names in which the resumption of the prefix O, dropped during the period of Gaelic submergence, has been most widely resumed: fifty years ago Callaghans without the O outnumbered those who used the prefix by five to one, while to-day O'Callaghans are much more numerous than Callaghans.

In addition to King Callaghan mentioned above there have been a number of distinguished Irishmen of the name, among them Father Richard Callaghan (1738–1807), the Jesuit educationist, two historians in the persons of Edmund O'Callaghan (1797–1883), and John Cornelius O'Callaghan (1805–1883), and Sir Francis O'Callaghan (1839–1909), the engineer. The name is also one of distinction in the records of the Irish Brigades in France. It is a curious fact that the Abbé John O'Callaghan (1605–1654), who was a very prominent Jansenist in France, gives the name of his father, a gentleman of Macroom, Co. Cork, as MacCallaghan. The records of the O'Callaghans in Spain are very extensive in the archives of that country. O'Callaghan is one of the few families of which a modern Chief of the Name is certified by the Genealogical Office. The present holder of that designation is a citizen of Spain.

The name O'Callaghan is sometimes found in Oriel (Armagh, Louth and Monaghan). This is an entirely different sept, O Ceileacháin in Irish, properly anglicized O'Kelaghan or Kealahan ; this name has become O'Callaghan in some families through a not uncommon process of attraction, but the form Kelaghan is still in use in Co. Westmeath.

Arms illustrated on Plate III.

MacCANN, (Canny).

In Irish Mac Anna (son of Annadh) it has become, by the attraction of the C of Mac, Mac Canna in Irish and MacCann in English. The MacCanns were lords of Clanbrassil, a district of Co. Armagh on the southern shore of Lough Neagh—a territory originally occupied by the O'Garveys. One of these, Amhlaibh Mac Canna, who died in 1155, is described by the Four Masters as " pillar of chivalry and vigour of Cinel Eoghain " ; the last to be mentioned in their Annals was killed in 1260, after which they do not appear prominently in the history of the country. Donnell MacCanna was, however, still styled Chief of Clanbrassil as late as 1598 and the name is still numerous in the vicinity of Lough Neagh, though uncommon elsewhere. The most noteworthy of the name, in modern times, is Michael Joseph MacCann (1824–1883), author of the poem " O'Donnell Abu ". Patrick MacCanna, a native of Armagh, was the hero of an unusual incident at the height of the Terror in the French Revolution—he not only defended the Irish College from the mob but won them from hostility to friendship toward Irishmen by his well chosen words : this MacCanna was a member of Wolfe Tone's expedition to Ireland, and finally became a leading merchant in Boulogne.

The cognate name Mac Annaidh is called Canny in English and as such is well known in Co. Clare and Limerick.

Arms illustrated on Plate III.

O'CANNON, (MacCannon).

Cannon is a common English surname derived from the ecclesiastical word canon. It is also the anglicized form of the name of two quite distinct Irish septs. Though identical in English these two are different in Irish. One is Ó Canáin: this is a Hy Many (Ui Máine) sept of the same stock as the O'Maddens and belongs to southern Co. Galway though nearly extinct there now. The other is Ó Canannáin abbreviated to Ó Canann, an old Tirconnell sept, whose chiefs the annalists call Kings of Cinel Connaill: it was subjugated by the powerful O'Donnells in the thirteenth century and sank into obscurity. Descendants of minor families of the sept, however, remained in their ancestral territory: in the seventeenth century they were numerous in Co. Donegal; priests called Cannon appear from time to time in the records of the diocese of Raphoe; and to-day they are still more numerous in Co. Donegal than anywhere else in Ireland.

The name MacCannon is found in Dublin at the present time and in the records of the city at least as far back as 1744; in the 1659 census it is recorded as numerous in Meath and in 1687 one of the name was Sheriff of Co. Monaghan.

A further point in connexion with the name in Ireland is that several families called Cannon are the descendants of French Protestant refugees. Joseph Gurney Cannon (1836–1926), Speaker of Congress (U.S.A.), for example, was the grandson of an Irishman of Huguenot stock, as also was Charles James Cannon (1800–1860), well-known in New York in his day as an author. Another writer of some distinction was the Franciscan friar Rev. Francis Cannon (d. 1850), a native of Co. Donegal.

The site of the ancient castle of the O'Cannons was near Letterkenny which is said on good authority to denote the hillside of the O'Cannons, Kenny being used in that district as a synonym of Cannon.

It should be added that Cannon is not used as an abbreviated form of the well-known Connacht name Concannon.

CAREY, O'Keary, (Carr).

The O'Kearys, in Irish Ó Ciardha, who in later times always used the anglicized form Carey, belonged to the southern Ui Neill and were lords of Carbury (Co. Kildare) until dispersed by the invasion of the Anglo-Normans. Carey, however, has also been used as the anglicized form of several other Gaelic patronymics. Besides the now almost extinct surname MacFhiachra formerly both of Tyrone and Galway, Carey is found as a synonym of Kerin i.e. Ó Céirín in Mayo and Ó Ciaráin in Co. Cork. It is also used as the English form of Mac Giolla Céire which is sometimes further corrupted to Carr in Co. Galway. Carr, however, when not of English origin, more often represents Ó Carra (Co. Galway) and Mac Giolla Chathair (Co. Donegal). The name Carey, arising from these different origins, is now numerous and widespread: it is found more in the Munster counties of Cork, Kerry and Tipperary than elsewhere. The three brothers John Carey (1756–1826), classical scholar and inventor of the shipwreck rocket, William Carey (1759–1839), and Mathew Carey (1760–1839), authors of note, were all born in Dublin, as was James Carey (1845–1883), the " Invincible " who informed on his comrades after the Phoenix Park murders and was subsequently shot in reprisal.

O'CAROLAN, Carleton.

Two distinct septs whose surname is not identical in Irish are called O'Carolan in English. As recognized septs these both disappear from history by the end of the thirteenth century, though individuals of the names continued to dwell in their ancient territory long after that. Ó Cairealláin was chief of Clan Diarmada, whence comes the name of the parish of Clondermot in Co. Derry. Ó Cairealláin assumed the anglicized form of Carleton as well as Carolan. The family of William Carleton (1794–1869), the novelist, is an example of this. The sept of Ó Cearbhalláin was also of Ulster, being located chiefly in Cavan and Monaghan, whence they crossed into the north Leinster county of Meath. There was born Turlough O'Carolan (1670–1738), the celebrated bard. The mediaeval ecclesiastical records of the dioceses of Raphoe and Derry contain the names of many priests called O'Carolan, three of whom were bishops of Derry in the thirteenth century. Hugh O'Carolan, Bishop of Clogher from 1535 to 1568, was one of the most distinguished Catholic prelates in that stormy period.

O'CARROLL, MacCARROLL, MacCarvill.

Prior to the Gaelic resurgence, at the end of the last century, under the influence of the Gaelic League, and later of the Rising of 1916, a minor result of which was the resumption of the prefixes O and Mac so widely discarded two or three centuries earlier, the simple form Carroll was almost universally used. As MacCarroll, an entirely distinct surname (a note on which appears at the end of this section), is also often shorn of its prefix Mac, confusion may well arise in the case of the name Carroll. However, undoubtedly, the great majority of people called Carroll are, in fact, O'Carrolls.

Before the Anglo-Norman invasion, there were six distinct septs of O'Carroll, the two most important of which were O'Carroll of Ely O'Carroll (Tipperary and Offaly) and O'Carroll of Oriel (Monaghan and Louth). The others disappeared, except as individuals, before the end of the thirteenth century and need not be considered here—O'Carroll of Oriel lost his status of chief and his sept disintegrated as a result of the Anglo-Norman invasion (they cease to appear in the Annals after 1193), but the clansmen themselves were not dispersed, and a fair number have remained in their territory to this day. The very large and well-known tobacco firm, Carrolls of Dundalk, have their factory in this area, though it may be mentioned that, curiously enough, the head of it has substantiated a claim to be descended from the O'Carrolls of Ely O'Carroll. That sept retained its Gaelic way of life and its distinct independence until the end of the sixteenth century, and its activities are frequently recorded throughout the Annals. They derive their name Ó Cearbhaill from Cearbhal, lord of Ely, who was one of the leaders of the victorious army at Clontarf (1014), and thus descend from King Oilioll Olum. Before the advent of the powerful Norman Butlers they possessed a very extensive territory in Co. Tipperary, but they were later restricted to the district around Birr, Co. Offaly.

Carroll has a high position in the list of most numerous surnames in Ireland, taking twenty-second place with an estimated population at the present time of approximately 16,000, the majority of whom belong to the four counties stretching from Cork to Kilkenny.

Many noteworthy O'Carrolls figure in the " Annals of the Four Masters." Maol-suthain O'Carroll (d. 1031), confessor of Brian Boru and contributor to the " Book of Armagh," was of the Kerry sept; Margaret O'Carroll (d. 1451), famous for hospitality, encouragement of learning, and as builder of churches, roads and bridges, belonged to the Ely O'Carroll sept, as did Charles Carroll (1737–1832), who is remembered as an Irish signatory of the American Declaration of Independence. It is with America rather than with the home country, that notable Carrolls have been associated during the past two centuries : the *Dictionary of American Biography* includes four others closely related to the Carrollton family, for so their place in Maryland was called (not to be confused with Carrollton, a town in Georgia, U.S.A.), the most distinguished of them being Most Rev. John Carroll (1735–1815), the first Catholic bishop in U.S.A., and the first Archbishop of Baltimore. Rev. Anthony Carroll, S.J. (1722–1794), who was robbed and murdered in a London street, was a brother of the Archbishop. Three members of the Ely O'Carroll sept distinguished themselves in the armies of James II and of France. The best known of these was Brigadier Daniel O'Carroll (d. 1712).

As we have seen there is a distinct sept of MacCarroll : the Irish Mac Cearbhaill is now more usually anglicized as MacCarvill in Ulster where its mediaeval territory is indicated by the place name Ballymaccarroll. One of these, Donslevy MacCarroll

(d. 1357), is described by the Four Masters as " a noble master of music and melody, the best of his time " ; and another, Mulrory MacCarroll (d. 1328), was called Chief Minstrel of Ireland and Scotland : indeed the family was noted for its musicians. James MacCarroll (1814–1892), who emigrated to U.S.A. at the age of 17, was a well-known American poet, dramatist and inventor. A Bishop of Cork and three Arch-bishops of Cashel, in the thirteenth and fourteenth centuries, were MacCarrolls, but these were probably of the Ely O'Carroll sept : it appears that its members sometimes used the prefix Mac instead of O during that period.

The name Lewis Carroll, famous as the author of *Alice in Wonderland*, is a *nom de plume* and has no connexion with O'Carroll or MacCarroll.

Arms illustrated on Plate III.

MacCARTAN, (Carton).

The Irish surname MacArtain became, in English, MacCartan, or sometimes Carton : this is an example of an error often found with Mac names beginning with a vowel where the letter C of Mac was carried forward to form the initial of the name proper (cf., MacCann, MacCoy etc.).   The name is derived from the common christian name Art, of which Artan is a dimunitive. The earlier anglicized form was more correctly MacArtan. The MacArtans, or MacCartans, were a northern sept, tributary to the O'Neills and they were chiefs of Kinelarty, a territory in Co. Down, generally known as MacArtan's Country. They appear frequently in the Annals as such up to the end of the fifteenth century : for a short time, about 1350, the chief of Kinel-arty was also lord of Iveagh, otherwise known as MacGennis's country—normally they were subordinate to the MacGennises.   Carew mentions the MacArtans as still powerful in 1599.

Counties Down and Armagh are the main places where MacCartans are found to-day. Cartons, however, belong chiefly to Dublin and Wexford ; but most of these are not, in fact, MacCartans whose families dropped the Mac—the well known Carton family of Dublin for instance, is of Huguenot origin. A branch of the sept migrated from Co. Down to Co. Cork in the sixteenth century, but there the name became absorbed in MacCurtin : Father Conor Curtin, an eighteenth century Gaelic poet of Co. Cork, is believed to have been in fact a MacCartan not a MacCurtin.

Arms illustrated on Plate III.

MacCARTHY.

No other Irish Mac name approaches MacCarthy in numerical strength.   The abbreviated form Carthy is fairly common, but MacCarthy is a name which has very generally retained the prefix. It is among the dozen commonest names in Ireland as a whole, due to the very large number of MacCarthys in Co. Cork which accounts for some sixty per cent of them. Charles O'Conor describes the sept as "the most eminent by far of the noble families of the south".

The name from the earliest times has been associated with south Munster or Desmond. The third century King of Munster, Oilioll Olum, had two sons Eoghan and Cormac Cas. At his death North Munster (Thomond) was inherited by the latter (whence the Dalcassians), and south Munster (Desmond) by Eoghan. The families which descended from this Eoghan were known, before the introduction of surnames, as the Eoghanacht, and the surname MacCarthy (in Irish Mac Cárthaigh) is derived from Cárthach, lord of the Eoghannacht, who, the Four Masters tell us, met his death in a house deliberately set on fire by one of the Lonergans in 1045. The number of references to the MacCarthys in the Annals, especially the "Annals of Innisfallen," is very great. This Cárthach was the son of Saorbreathach, a Gaelic name which is anglicized as Justin, and in the latter form has been in continuous use among various branches of MacCarthys for centuries. Another christian name similarly associated with them is Finghin, *anglice* Fineen, but for some centuries past, for some obscure reason, Florence (colloquially Flurry) has been used as the English form.

From the thirteenth century, when Fineen MacCarthy decisively defeated the Geraldines in 1261, down to the present day, Fineen or Florence MacCarthys and Justin MacCarthys have been very prominent among the many distinguished men of the name in Irish military, political and cultural history. Fineen (Florence) MacCarthy (1562–1640), Chief of the MacCarthy Reagh branch of the sept, after a term of service in the army of Queen Elizabeth, spent much of his time a prisoner in the Tower of London where, being a man of great erudition, he wrote a history of ancient Ireland. Rev. Dr. Florence MacCarthy (1761–1810), V.G. of Cork, and Denis Florence MacCarthy (1817–1882), poet, were others of note. Justin MacCarthy (d. 1694), created Earl of Mountcashell by James II, commander of a regiment in that King's army in Ireland and, subsequently, of the Irish Brigade in France ; Justin Count MacCarthy (1744–1812), famous book-collector in France where he was enobled by Louis XVI ; Justin MacCarthy (1830–1912), novelist, historian and politician, and his son, Justin Huntley MacCarthy (1861–1936), also a writer of note, are a few of the many noted men christened Justin. Cormac (or Charles) is another christian name common among MacCarthys, especially in the Muskerry branch. One, who died in 1640, was created Viscount Muskerry ; his father, also Cormac MacCarthy (d. 1616), served under Carew at Kinsale ; another Cormac MacCarthy (d. 1536), known as lord of Muskerry, grandfather of the last named, a soldier of note, was in his day favourable to the English interest. In modern times a Charles Mac-Carthy (1873–1921), was noteworthy as an American political scientist : he was the son of a Fenian emigrant. When we remember, moreover, that in 1172 the MacCarthy Mor of the day did homage to Henry II, and another MacCarthy Mor accepted the earldom of Glencar from Queen Elizabeth, it would appear that the leading men of the various branches of the sept have little claim to be regarded as Irish heroes, though in this connexion it must not be forgotten that the modern conception of nationality and nationalism was non-existent until the end of the seventeenth century. On the other hand Viscount Muskerry was a member of the Supreme Council of Confederate Catholics in 1646, and MacCarthy Reagh with two others of the name were also in the Commons of that body; Muskerry, indeed, was expressly exempted from pardon by the Cromwellian authority in 1652. Lady Eleanor MacCarthy, too, has an honoured place in Irish history for her protection of Garrett Fitzgerald after the murder of his five uncles by Henry VIII in 1537.

Passing reference has been made above to different branches of the MacCarthy sept. MacCarthy Mór was located in Kerry and the direct line was thought to be extinct*. MacCarthy Reagh was of Carbery in West Cork; while the Muskerry branch were in the barony of Muskerry in that county: the famous Blarney Castle was the chief's principal residence. There were also minor branches known as Glas etc.

The name Carty is not as a rule an abbreviation of MacCarthy, but is more often the appellation of the small and scattered sept of O'Carty.

Arms illustrated on Plate III.

O'CASEY, (MacCasey).

There were originally at least six distinct and unrelated septs of Ó Cathasaigh: the most important of these in early times were respectively lords of the Suaithni (whose territory comprised the modern barony of Balrothery West, Co. Dublin) and erenaghs of Devenish, Co. Fermanagh; both these, however, have long been dispersed though the name is not uncommon in the former of these places. It is chiefly found now in the south-west of Munster, and also, in smaller numbers, in north Connacht. These two areas correspond with the locations of four of the septs mentioned above: one of these was Dalcassian and was seated at Liscannon near Bruff in Co. Limerick, and another near Mitchelstown, Co. Cork, while the third and fourth were in Tirawley, Co. Mayo, where they were erenaghs of Kilarduff, and in Co. Roscommon where they were erenaghs of Clondara in the barony of Athlone.

The interesting archaeological remains called " Casey's Lios " at Ballygunnermore indicate the residence of Caseys near Waterford. The so-called census of 1659 indicates that the name was then quite numerous in that county, but mainly in the south-western corner of it; from the same source we learn that the O'Caseys or, as they were

*On the death of the last of the senior line in 1773 the MacCarthy Mór estates passed to the family of his maternal grandfather, Herbert of Kilcow. Their beautiful Muckross estate, near Killarney, is now the property of the nation, through the Bourne-Vincent Trust. The style MacCarthy Mór, used in France by a cousin, has long disappeared. Search for nearly 120 years for the descendants of an earlier MacCarthy Mór has in 1957, at last been successful and one junior branch has been traced to Montreal.

then usually called, the O'Cahassys were, at that time, principally found in Co. Limerick and adjacent areas. The best known people of the name are Admiral Joseph Gregory O'Casey (1787–1862), of a Co. Limerick family, Minister of Marine in the Government of France, John Keegan Casey (1846–1870), poet and Fenian, and Seán O'Casey (b. 1884), Dublin labourer and famous playwright. Five minor poets of the nineteenth century, as well as John Keegan Casey, are included in O'Donoghue's *Poets of Ireland*.

In addition to the O'Caseys dealt with above there was also a sept of MacCasey, located in Oriel : few survivors of this are to be found to-day, but in the mediaeval period it was numerous in Co. Monaghan and three bishops named MacCasey occupied the see of Clogher in the fourteenth century.

Arms illustrated on Plate III.

O'CASSIDY.

The O'Cassidys belong to Fermanagh ; this, and the borders of adjacent counties, is their principal homeland to-day and it is there their sept originated. It provided hereditary physicians to the great Maguire sept and numerous O'Cassidys are recorded as ollavs and physicians to the Maguires between 1300 and 1600 A.D. The name first appears in the field of literature in the person of Giolla Moduda O'Cassidy (d. 1143), whose Gaelic poetry is still preserved. One of the O'Cassidys, Rory, Archdeacon of Clogher, is said to have assisted Cathal Maguire in the compilation of the fifteenth century " Annals of Ulster ". Equally deserving of literary renown is Thomas Cassidy (fl. 1740), expelled Augustinian friar and subsequently soldier of fortune and itinerant, whose racy autobiography has been likened to the work of Rabelais. He and others of the sept were sometimes called MacCassidy as well as O'Cassidy.

After the plantation of Ulster in the early seventeenth century the O'Cassidys, like nearly all the leading Gaelic septs of that province, sank into obscurity. We find them only in such records as the presentments relating to priests under the Penal Code, chiefly in counties Fermanagh and Monaghan. Many, of course, emigrated: the grandson of one of these was William Cassidy (1815–1873), Catholic politician in the United States and lifelong enemy of Great Britain.

Arms illustrated on Plate IV.

MacCLANCY, Glanchy.

Clancy is a Mac name : the initial C of Clancy is in fact the last letter of the prefix Mac. In Irish it is Mac Fhlannchaidh, (son of Flannchadh, *flann* meaning reddish). The aspirated F is silent. In recent years some Clancys have resumed the prefix and become once more MacClancy. The alternative form Glanchy was often used in the seventeenth century and is still occasionally found.

There are two septs of the name. The more important is that of Thomond: they are a branch of the Macnamaras of Co. Clare and were hereditary brehons to the O'Briens. They became established in north Clare, some distance from the main Macnamara country. The place name Cahermacclancy locates the area. They are still more numerous in Co. Clare and in the adjoining counties of Galway and Tipperary than elsewhere. The only other county in which they are found in considerable numbers to-day is Leitrim; and this is as might be expected, since the second MacClancy sept belongs to that locality, the head of the family having been Chief of Dartry or Rosclogher. Up to the time of the final collapse of the Gaelic order the MacClancys were very influential in Co. Clare. Boetius Clancy (Boetius was a common christian name in that family) represented Clare in the Parliament of 1585. One of the last of the hereditary brehons is said to have saved Murrough O'Brien (the then O'Brien chief) from the fury of his formerly devoted clansmen when he returned to Clare after accepting a peerage from Henry VIII in 1543. Boetius Glancy (sic) was one of the " nobility of the diocese of Killaloe " who sent a memorial to Cardinal Veralto, the Protector of Ireland, in 1624. After the second siege of Limerick, in the defence of which city several Clancys took part, many of them took service abroad as Wild Geese and distinguished themselves in the Irish Brigades. One settled at Nantes in France where he founded bursarships for the education of priests. One who did not leave Limerick, though he married a Protestant lady of an influential family, remained a staunch Catholic and his wife became one—a rare event for a Protestant in the height of the Penal Laws period.

Peadar Clancy was one of the three prisoners (Dick McKee and Conor Clune were the others) who were murdered by British Auxiliaries in Dublin Castle, after " Bloody Sunday " in November, 1920.

Arms illustrated on Plate IV.

O'CLERY, Clarke, (MacCleary, Clerkin).

Clery, often spelt Cleary, is one of the Gaelic Irish surnames which has kept the prefix O to some extent in modern times. O'Clery is Ó Cleirigh in Irish probably derived from the word *cléireach* meaning a clerk or cleric. The name itself means descendant of Cleireach, who was of the line of the famous Guaire the Hospitable, King of Connacht. Cleireach was born about the year 820 A.D. some two centuries before hereditary surnames began to be generally used. That of O'Clery, however, was one of the earliest recorded surnames: it dates from the middle of the tenth century. The O'Clerys were the chief family in that part of the present Co. Galway which is covered by the diocese of Kilmacduagh, but their influence gradually declined and by the middle of the thirteenth century they had been driven out of their original territory and settled elsewhere. By far the most important of these branches was that which became domiciled in Counties Donegal and Derry : many of its members distinguished themselves as poets and antiquarians there. Since the Plantation of Ulster in the seventeenth century, and the consequent anglicization of what was formerly the most Irish of the four Provinces, the common English surname Clarke has been very widely substituted for O'Clery there, and also indeed elsewhere in Ireland. Without a reliable pedigree or at least a strong family tradition it is therefore impossible to say whether an Irish Clarke is an O'Clery in disguise or the descendant of an English settler ; but it is probable that most of our Clarkes are in fact O'Clerys. The branch which settled in Co. Cavan has almost disappeared (at least as Clery, though Clarke is fairly common to-day in Co. Cavan), but the third, which went to Co. Kilkenny, is still to be found in considerable numbers if not actually in Co. Kilkenny, in the adjacent counties of Tipperary and Waterford. Clery and Cleary are also found as variants of Clerkin (Ó Cleirchín) a sept located in the barony of Coshma, Co. Limerick.

Clarke, with an estimated population of over 14,000 persons comes as high as thirty-second in the list of the hundred commonest surnames in Ireland (this of course includes all persons of the name whether their origin be Irish or English). Clery (including Cleary, O'Clery and O'Cleary) musters some 5,000 persons.

The O'Clerys of the seventeenth century who left their mark on the literary history of Ireland are too numerous to mention individually. The most famous were Michael, his brother Conary and their cousin Cucoigchriche (sons of Lughaigh O'Clery the chieftain and historian), who with Fearfasa O'Mulconry compiled the " Annals of the Four Masters " which was finished in 1636. A modern historian of the name was Arthur Patrick O'Clery (1841-1915), a Limerick man. Of the many distinguished Irish Clarkes we may mention Rev. John Clarke, S.J. (1662-1723), born at Kilkenny, the missionary to Irish and Scots soldiers in the Low Countries ; Dr. Joseph Clarke (1758-1834), the Derryman who did so much for the Rotunda Hospital, Dublin ; and in our own time Thomas Clarke (1857-1916), first signatory to the republican proclamation in 1916 who was executed after the Easter Week Rising. Two sisters, Julie Cleary and Desirée Cleary (1781-1860), daughters of an Irish merchant in Marseilles, became respectively Queens of Spain and Sweden under Napoleon.

There is another Gaelic surname which has become Clery in English in some places, though more usually MacCleary or MacAlary. This is Mac Giolla Arraith, a branch of the O'Haras, who went with them to Co. Antrim and became established there.

Arms illustrated on Plate IV.

81

O'COFFEY, Cowhig.

In Irish this name is Ó Cobhthaigh, pronounced O'Coffey as in English : it is probably derived from the word *cobhthach,* meaning victorious.   Coffey is one of those surnames which have not resumed the prefix O, dropped during the period of Gaelic submergence.   Several distinct septs were prominent in mediaeval times, of which two are still well represented in their original homeland.   These are O'Coffey of Corcalaoidhe in south-west Co. Cork, where local pronounciation often makes the name Cowhig or Cowhey, as in the place name Dunocowhey, called after them.   This sept is of the same stock as the O'Driscolls.   A second minor sept was a branch of the O'Maddens of Ui Máine, whose descendants are found to-day in Co. Roscommon. A third, once of considerable importance but now scattered, belonged to Co. West-meath where they were famous as a bardic family.   The most distinguished of these was Dermot O'Coffey (fl. 1580), the Gaelic poet.   Six other poets of this family are represented in Gaelic literature.   In more recent times the Leinster Coffeys are re-presented by Charles Coffey (1700–1745), dramatist and actor, the first to introduce Irish airs in a play.   George Coffey (1857–1916), the archaeologist, though his family has long associations with Dublin, was descended from the Munster sept.   The place-name Rathcoffey occurs both in Co. Kildare and Co. Leix.

Arms illustrated on Plate IV.

MacCOGHLAN, O'COUGHLAN, (Cohalan).

There are two quite distinct septs of Coughlan, one being MacCoughlan (Mac-Cochláin) of Offaly and the other O'Coughlan (Ó Cochláin) of Co. Cork—who were not the same, it should be observed, as Ó Cathaláin (*anglice* Cohalan and Culhane) also of that county.   Down to the eighteenth century the former were far the more important of the two, but since then they have dwindled and become dispersed. The MacCoughlan country comprised the modern barony of Garrycastle, Co. Offaly, where they had many strong castles in the Banagher-Clonmacnois area : no less than ten of these are mentioned in the sixteenth century by the Four Masters.   The head of the sept, which was by origin Dalcassian, was known as Chief of Delvin MacCoughlan (to be distinguished from Delvin or Delvin Mor in Co. Westmeath): Sir John MacCoughlan, so styled, died in 1590.   They are prominent in the Annals from the twelfth century ;   and even after the destruction of the Gaelic order the family remained influential in their native territory for nearly two centuries.   A MacCoughlan represented Banagher in the Irish Parliament of 1689 and another held the same seat in 1790.   In 1665 two McCoughlans possessed 3,400 acres in Co. Offaly.   In 1828 they were still found as landlords at Cloghan, near Banagher ; but fifty years later they were no longer there.

The Coughlans of Co. Cork belonged to the baronies of Carbery and Ballymore where, as they are to-day, they were numerous at the time of Petty's census. Even then the prefix O had in their case already been almost entirely lost.

Arms illustrated on Plate IV.

MacCOLGAN.

In early mediaeval times the prefix O was found with Colgan as well as Mac. O'Dugan, who died in 1372, mentions O'Colgan as lord of a territory in the modern barony of Tirkeeran, Co. Derry. This was the homeland of one of the two distinct septs of Colgan. Later, when somewhat reduced in influence, they were erenaghs of Donaghmore in Inishowen. In the course of time these O'Colgans became Mac-Colgans, influenced no doubt by the fact that the more important sept, located in Offaly, was MacColgan. There is a reference to these in the Four Masters as early as 1212. Rev. John Colgan (d. 1658), Franciscan friar, professor of theology at Louvain and author of *Acta Sanctorum Hiberniae* etc., was of the Tirkeeran (Derry) O'Colgan sept, but his relative a hundred years later, who was Bishop of Derry and suffered severely in the penal times, was known as John MacColgan (d. 1765). Mac-Colgan, as we know from tombstones and other records, was the usual form of the name in Counties Derry and Donegal up to the beginning of the nineteenth century. Another notable missionary prelate was Most Rev. Joseph Colgan (1824–1911), Archbishop of Madras. He came from Westmeath, not far from the ancient seat of the chiefs of his sept, which was Kilcolgan in Offaly. This sept was of the same stock as the O'Dempseys and the O'Dunnes of Leix and Offaly.

The name is not common in Ireland to-day : it is found chiefly in Offaly and also to some extent in northern Ulster.

Arms illustrated on Plate IV.

O'COLMAN, Coleman, (Clifford).

Though families called Coleman are known to have settled in Ireland as early as the thirteenth century, having come from England, where the name is numerous, Coleman in Ireland almost always denotes a Gaelic origin. The sept of Ó Colmáin, a branch of the Ui Fiachrach, was located in the barony of Tireragh, Co. Sligo, and representatives of it are still living in north Connacht. Colemans, however, are more numerous in Co. Cork. These are of a sept called Ó Clúmháin in Irish which, like the foregoing, originated in Co. Sligo. The branch of it which migrated to Munster became numerically strong. Indeed they are even more numerous than would appear from statistics at first sight, because Ó Clúmháin has also been anglicized Clifford and there are many Cliffords in Kerry and Cork. Clifford, like Coleman, is a well known indigenous surname in England, but only a small proportion of Irish Cliffords are of English origin.

O'CONCANNON.

The name Concannon is rarely found outside the territory in which it originated. All the 21 births registered for the name in the last available statistical return took place in Co. Galway or in contiguous areas of adjacent counties. O'Concannon, in Irish Ó Concheanainn, is a sept of the Hy Many (Ui Máine), descended from Cuceannan who was killed in 991. From the eleventh to the fifteenth centuries their chiefs are described in the Annals as lords of Ui Diarmada (i.e. Kilkerrin, Co. Galway), and a century later the " Composition Book of Connacht " (1585) records the Chief of the Name as still resident in their old seat at Kultullagh in the parish of Kilkerrin or Corcamoe. An interesting fourteenth century monumental slab to one Maurice O'Concannon can be seen in Knockmoy Abbey, Co. Galway. It will be observed from the number of births registered in one year, indicated above, that the sept has dwindled to comparatively small proportions in modern times. The head of the family in 1848 still retained some of the ancestral property in the parish of Kilkerrin, Co. Galway, but this estate does not appear in the list of landowners of 500 acres and over in 1878.

Arms illustrated on Plate IV.

CONDON.

The north-eastern division of Co. Cork, close to the adjoining counties of Limerick and Tipperary, is called the barony of Condons. This was named after the family of Condon which was in possession of much of that area, their principal stronghold being the Castle of Cloghleagh near Kilworth, which however actually lies outside the boundary of the said barony. They may indeed be described as a sept rather than as a family. They are not, it is true, of native Gaelic stock, having come to Ireland at the time of the Anglo-Norman invasion, but they always counted themselves as a sept, and as late as 1605, we find David Condon, in a letter to the Secretary of State, describing himself as " Chief of his Sept ". Nevertheless, though often fighting side by side with the McCarthys and other native septs, they did not become thoroughly gaelicized like many of the Norman families, but were proud of their English descent, and this claim stood them in good stead at least up to the beginning of the seventeenth century. In 1641, however, they were as Irish as any. No less than

21 Condons were attainted at that time and several more suffered for their adhesion to James II in 1690. It was during this period that the Gaelic poet David Condon lived. Historical and religious causes and intermarriage with Gaelic Irish families have, of course, now made the Condons completely Irish. One of them was a well-known Fenian, Edward O'Meagher Condon (1835–1915), an emigrant who had become an American citizen—a fact which saved him from the gallows, as he was condemned to death in 1867 for his part in the Manchester raid. He was from Co. Cork. That county and south Tipperary are, as might be expected, the homeland of the great majority of Condons to-day.

There was formerly an Ulster family called Ó Condubháin whose name was anglicized Condon, but this is now very rare if not extinct.

Arms illustrated on Plate IV.

O'CONNELL, (Gunning).

Though in early mediaeval times there were undoubtedly several distinct and unrelated septs of O'Connell, those of Ulster and Connacht are seldom heard of even as late as the fourteenth century. O'Dugan (d. 1372) in the " Topographical Poems " mentions Ó Conaill as a family of Oirghiall and another, again, as of Ui Máine. The name does not appear in the Four Masters after 1117 when the death of Cathasach Ó Conaill, "noble Bishop of Connacht ", is recorded. Another of the name, Bishop of Thomond (Killaloe) is mentioned in the " Annals of Innisfallen " under date 927 A.D. ; but if this be a true surname it is one of the earlier examples. The "Annals of Connacht" have no reference to the name.

These septs can, in fact, be regarded as extinct and we may confine our attention to the one sept of O'Connell which has not only become numerous but has also, during the past two centuries, produced many outstanding Irishmen.

As regards numerical strength O'Connell and Connell, taken together, are listed by Matheson as among the 25 commonest surnames in Ireland : sixty years ago Connells outnumbered O'Connells by two to one ; since then the resumption of the prefix has been so widespread in this case that Connell without the O to-day accounts for less than 20 per cent. of the total. The great majority of the O'Connells came from south-west Munster. This is as might be expected for the O'Connells are by origin a Kerry sept.

Traditionally the genealogy is traced back to the Eremonian Aengus Tuirmeach who was said to have been the High King of Ireland about 280 B.C.. Coming to historical times we find an O'Connell chief of Magunihy in East Kerry. The name is spelt Ó Conghail in O'Heerin's continuation of the " Topographical Poem ". In the eleventh century pressure by the powerful O'Donoghues pushed them towards the

Atlantic coast, and they became hereditary castellans of Ballycarbery under the MacCarthy Mor chiefs. Nearby is the romantically situated Derrynane, home of Daniel O'Connell, now preserved for the nation by private subscription, though not officially a national monument. The disasters of the seventeenth century submerged them for a time—it was under the Cromwellian settlement that the head of the sept was transplanted to Co. Clare, where a branch has remained since as a Catholic landed family. The barony of Magunihy, in which Killarney is situated, is still the homeland of the leading family of O'Connell to-day, the present representative of which is Sir Morgan O'Connell, Bart.

Unless we cite the Capuchin Father Robert O'Connell (c. 1621–1678), the first O'Connell to become a figure of national importance was Daniel Count O'Connell (1743–1833), "the last colonel of the Irish Brigade," as his biographer, Mrs. M. J. O'Connell, calls him. His kinsman and contemporary, Baron Moritz (or Murty) O'Connell (1738–1830), was another Kerry exile who, as well as being chamberlain to three emperors, served with military distinction on the continent. The famous Daniel O'Connell (1775–1847), "the Liberator", needs no description. His uncle, Maurice O'Connell (1727–1825), squire, patriarch, autocrat and smuggler, was a celebrated character known as "Hunting Cap", but Daniel's three sons, though also public men, were not of the same calibre as their father. An earlier member of this family, who should not be forgotten, was the Friar John O'Connell who about the year 1700 composed the historical poem "Tuireadh na hÉireann". One O'Connell from Co. Clare merits a place in the national roll of honour, Peter O'Connell (1775–1826)—described by Prof. T. F. O'Rahilly as "the best Irish scholar in the Ireland of a century ago."

The remarkably thorough genealogical researches of Mr. Basil O'Connell, much of which has been printed, will be found of great value to anyone desiring detailed information about the O'Connells of Kerry and allied families during the past three centuries.

It should be observed that Castle Connell, the town near Limerick, is a misnomer since it takes its name not from the O'Connells but from the Dalcassian family of Ó Connaing (now anglicized Gunning).

Arms illustrated on Plate IV.

O'CONNELLAN, Conlan, Conlon.

Conlon, Conlan and Connellan are all synonyms (readers outside Ireland who might tend to stress the second syllable—ell—of Connellan may need to be told that in fact it is barely audible, Connellan and Conlan being pronounced almost alike). Several different Irish surnames have been so anglicized. The principal septs so called in English are Ó Conalláin of Roscommon and Galway and Ó Coinghiolláin of Co. Sligo : their present day representatives are chiefly found in north Connacht—in Counties Mayo and Sligo. The name is also fairly numerous in Co. Meath and the midlands, where however they are also called Quinlan—Ó Coindealbháin in Irish : they descend from an important sept seated near Trim which traces back to Laoghaire, King of Ireland in the time of St. Patrick, but was dispossessed at the Anglo-Irish invasion. In Munster Ó Caoindealbháin, usually anglicized Quinlevan, is sometimes made Conlon. (For Quinlan and Quinlevan see p. 251 *infra*).

In the seventeenth century the name was very numerous and widespread. In Petty's census (1659) it appears, under seven different spellings, as one of the commoner names in Counties Roscommon, Clare, Sligo, Longford, Westmeath, Offaly, Kildare and Louth.

The spelling Connellan is infrequent in modern times, compared with Conlan and Conlon, only about ten per cent. using that form ; but so far as distinguished men of the name are concerned Connellans are outstanding. " The Book of the O'Connellans," a mediaeval work in Irish, deals with Tirconnell genealogies. Abraham O'Connellan was Archbishop of Armagh from 1247 to 1260 and Thomas O'Connellan, Bishop of Achonry from 1492 to 1508. Thomas O'Connellan (c. 1620–1695), was a composer of Irish airs and noted harper, as was his brother Laurence, who was well known in Scotland as a wandering harper after 1700. Owen Connellan (1800–1869), another north Connacht man, was an eminent Gaelic scholar ; and Joseph Connellan, Nationalist Six-County M.P. was one of the active pioneers of Sinn Fein and the Gaelic Athletic Association in Ulster.

The well known war-cry " Conlan abu " was not connected with any of these septs : it was used by the O'Mores of Leix.

O'CONNOLLY.

Owing to the lack of precision frequently found in the anglicization of Gaelic surnames due to the fact that their English forms were often determined by the phonetic attempts of lawyers and others in the seventeenth century who were unfamiliar with the Irish language, the name Connolly has been much confused with Conneely and Kinnealy (q.v.p. 202 *infra*). The people now called Connolly mostly derive their descent from three Gaelic septs. These were Ó Conghalaigh or Ó Conghaile of Connacht and of Monaghan, and Ó Coingheallaigh of Munster, for which Mac Coingheallaigh was previously an alias ; the other Connacht sept was of the Ui Máine and the same stock as the O'Maddens. That associated with Co. Monaghan was in early times the most important, being one of the " four tribes of Tara " and a branch of the southern Ui Néill, but it was forced out of its original territory by the Anglo-Norman invasion and driven northwards to Co. Monaghan. As late as 1591 Tirlogh Ó Connola is recorded in the Fiants relating to Co. Monaghan as Chief of his Name and late vice-marshal to MacMahon. The Munster Connollys were established in West Cork where they were subject to the paramount O'Donovans of that area. At the present time the name is most numerous in each of the aforesaid places, viz. Counties Galway, Monaghan and Cork, while it is still found in and around County Meath.

The best known representative of the last was William Connolly (c. 1660–1729), " squire," Speaker of the House of Commons and reputedly the richest man in Ireland, whose seat was Castletown, Co. Kildare ; his relative Thomas Connolly (1738–1803), was another politician of note. Most Rev. John Connolly (1750–1825), notable Dominican Archbishop of New York, was also of a Meath family. James Connolly (1868–1916), labour leader, signatory of the Irish Declaration of Independence, wounded in the Rising and executed while still unable to stand, is usually stated to have been born at Clones, Co. Monaghan in 1870. It has however recently been discovered that he was born in Edinburgh of Irish parents on June 5, 1868. Another who left his mark on the course of Irish history, though in a very different sense, was Owen O'Connelly, a Monaghan man, whose betrayal of the plans for the 1641 Rising did irreparable harm. A number of exiles have kept the name in the forefront both in America and France : William Connolly was of the noblesse of Bordeaux at the time of the French Revolution while in the United States, besides the archbishop referred to above, Henry Connolly (1800–1866), was a famous pioneer ; Pierce Francis Connolly (b. 1841) was a sculptor of note ; his mother, Mrs. Cornelia Connelly (1809–1879), was foundress of the Society of the Holy Child Jesus (she and her husband, Pierce Connolly, were converts, the latter becoming a priest but later apostasizing : his subsequent conduct shed no lustre on the name).

The arms illustrated in Plate V belong to the family of Co. Kildare and must not be regarded as traditional sept arms.

Arms illustrated on Plate V

O'CONNOR.

O'Connor, or O'Conor, is perhaps the most illustrious of all Irish surnames, though this view would, no doubt, be disputed by the O'Neills, the O'Briens, the O'Donnells and one or two other great and famous septs. It is borne by six distinct septs located in different parts of the country of whom four survive in considerable numbers. The most important are the O'Connors of Connacht—the main branches of this sept being O'Conor Don, O'Conor Roe and O'Conor Sligo. These are descended from Conchobhar, King of Connacht (d. 971), and the last two High-Kings of Ireland

88

were of this line, viz., Turlough O'Connor (1088–1156) and Roderick O'Connor (1116–1198), both of whom were progressive monarchs. Their direct descendant, as certified by the Genealogical Office, Dublin Castle, is the present O'Conor Don : he is a Jesuit priest, and it is interesting to note that this important and aristocratic family consistently maintained its position notwithstanding the fact that they remained inflexibly Catholic. Evidence of this is abundant in all the sixteenth, seventeenth and eighteenth century manuscripts.

In dealing with the landed proprietors of Connacht, among the distinguished members of the O'Conor Don stock four O'Conors of Belnagare are outstanding in the field of culture : Charles O'Conor (1710–1791), antiquary and collector of Irish manuscripts ; his two grandsons, Rev. Charles O'Conor, D.D., P.P. (1764–1828), librarian at Stowe and author, *inter alia*, of *Rerum Hibernicarum Scriptores Veteres*, and Mathew O'Conor (1773–1844), author of *History of the Irish Catholics* etc. ; and Charles Owen O'Conor, O'Conor Don (1838–1906), President of the Royal Irish Academy and of the Society for Preserving the Irish Language and author of *The O'Conors of Connacht*. In the military sphere Cabrach O'Conor (1584–1655) and Hugh O'Conor (d. 1669), respectively son and grandson of O'Conor Don, took a prominent part in the 1641–1652 wars. Three of this sept were outstanding in the Irish Brigade. More recently, one of the Sligo branch, General Sir Luke O'Connor (1832–1915), who had enlisted as a private soldier in the British army, won the V.C. and a commission for his remarkably bravery at the battle of Alma.

O'Connor Kerry, as the chief of the Munster O'Connors was called, derives his name from a different Conchobhar. He was lord of an extensive area in north Kerry, but after the invasion of 1170 Anglo-Norman pressure pushed the O'Connors northwards towards the Shannon estuary. However, they still retained a considerable territory, in fact the greater part of the modern barony of Iraghticonor, which is an attempt at a phonetic spelling of Oireacht ui Chonchobhair, i.e. O'Connor's district or government : their chief stronghold in Iraghticonor was Carrigafoyle Castle. From this sept came a number of distinguished officers of the Irish Brigade in France, the best known of whom was Arthur O'Connor (1763–1852), United Irishman and later a general in Napoleon's army ; his brother Roger O'Connor (1761–1834), an erratic character who was also a member of the United Irishmen, and the latter's son, Fergus O'Connor (1794–1855), the chartist. Some of this family changed their name to Conner. The three most notable Irish-American O'Connors were of this sept : the brothers Michael O'Connor (1810–1872), and James O'Connor (1823–1890), both Catholic bishops in U.S.A., and Patrick Edward Connor (1820–1871), pioneer, Indian fighter and soldier in the Civil War on the Confederate side. The O'Connor sept of Kerry is at the present day much the most numerous of them all. It is estimated that there are almost 30,000 persons of the name in Ireland to-day—it comes ninth in the list of commonest surnames and the vast majority of these are from Kerry or from the adjoining counties of Cork and Limerick.

The O'Connors of Corcomroe, a barony in north Clare on the shores of the Atlantic, are still extant. The eponymous ancestor in this case was Conchobhar, lord of Corcomroe (d. 1002).

The fourth of the surviving septs was O'Connor of Offaly. O'Connor Faly, as the chief was called, was of royal descent, his ancestor being Cathaoir Mor, King of Ireland in the second century. The eponymous Conchobhar in this case was much later than Cathaoir and belongs to historical times as he died in 979. This sept was constantly engaged in war with the invader until the middle of the sixteenth century when they were vanquished and dispossessed of most of their estates. They were still in Offaly in 1689, as Col. John O'Connor was member for Philipstown in King James II's Parliament and they were represented by the family of O'Connor-Morris of the same county until quite recently.

It should be added that there was also a powerful sept of O'Connor in Keenaght (Derry), which in the twelfth century was overpowered by the O'Kanes. They are mentioned here because, though as a sept they were eliminated, families of O'Connor are still found in that part of Ulster and it may be assumed that they are descended from the once famous O'Connors of Glengiven who were of royal blood, their ancestor being Cian, son of Oilioll Olum, King of Munster in the third century.

The history of the O'Connors, particularly those of Connacht, forms the subject of a number of books which can be consulted for detailed information concerning these important septs.

Arms illustrated on Plate V.

O'CONRY, CONROY, O'Mulconry, (King).

Though the surnames Conry and Conroy are, properly speaking, quite distinct, they are dealt with together here because in modern times they have become almost interchangeable. To illustrate this we may refer to the list of synonyms issued by the Registrar-General of Births, Deaths and Marriages in the year 1901. At that comparatively recent date births in families usually called Conroy were also registered as Conary, Conrahy, Conree, Cunree, Cory, King and also Mulconry and Conry; the synonyms for Conry were Connery, Mulconry and Conroy. All that can be done to elucidate the resultant confusion is to give a brief account of the background of the several Gaelic surnames which have assumed the various anglicized forms given above.

The most important of these is Ó Maolconaire, i.e. descendant of the follower of Conaire, from which O'Mulconry and its abbreviation, Conry, naturally derive, though, as we have seen, Conroy is also used by modern descendants of this sept. However, it should be stated that in the homeland of the Ó Maolconaire sept, whose patrimony was the parish of Clooncraff in the neighbourhood of Strokestown, Co. Roscommon, they are usually called Conry not Conroy. The O'Mulconrys were hereditary poets and chroniclers to the Kings of Connacht, and many such are recorded in the "Annals of Connacht," the "Annals of the Four Masters" etc., the most notable of whom were Fearfasa O'Mulconry, who was himself one of the Four Masters (whose work was completed 1636), and Maurice O'Mulconry whose copy of the "Book of Fenagh," made in 1517, is an exceptionally beautiful manuscript. Most Rev. Florence Conry (1561–1629), Archbishop of Tuam, was also of this sept. His name is so spelt in the Franciscan records, but in some other contemporary documents he appears as Conroy, and also as O'Maolconaire. This most distinguished Franciscan was associated with the foundation of the Irish College at Louvain, and wrote many important works including a theological treatise in Irish. He was chaplain in the Spanish Armada and to Hugh O'Donnell at his death. Charles O'Mulconry (son of John O'Mulconry, who fought in the Cromwellian war and lost his estate in Co. Roscommon) was an ardent Jacobite and was killed at the Battle of the Boyne in 1690. Another John O'Mulconry, the famous Gaelic poet and chronicler, whose family had settled at Ardkyle in Co. Clare, was of this sept. He presided over a school of poets at Ardkyle from about 1440 to 1470. Hardiman's inclusion of the Mulconrys among the Dalcassian septs is an error.

Other Gaelic surnames which are anglicized Conry and Conroy in Connacht are Ó Conraoi of Ui Máine or Hy Many, i.e. the territory otherwise known as O'Kelly's Country in east Galway and south Roscommon, and Mac Conraoi of Moycullen, called by the Four Masters Lord of Delvin of the Two Lakes (viz. Lough Corrib and Lough Lurgan—an old name for the Bay of Galway). The "Books of Survey and Distribution," and other seventeenth century records, show that MacConrys or MacConroys were there at that period. Pádraic O'Conaire (1883–1928), one of the best known of all the modern writers in Irish, was a Galway man—his statue is to be seen in Eyre Square in Galway City. He spelt his name Ó Conaire, though this form is usually found in Munster and anglicized Connery, and is quite distinct from the Galway sept just mentioned. O'Connery is included in Smith's *History of County Waterford* among the principal inhabitants of the county at the end of the sixteenth century.

A further complication is the use of the surname King as a synonym for MacConraoi, and even for Ó Conraoi and also for Mac Fhearadhaigh. This arose from the similarity in sound of these Mac names and Mac an Righ : the latter means son of the king, and so became King in English by a process of mistranslation very common in the late seventeenth and eighteenth centuries. In fact nearly all the MacConroys of Moycullen use the name King, and in the nineteenth century they called their ancestral seat of Ballymaconry Kingstown. King, of course, is a common English name, and it is also the anglicized form of the Gaelic surname Ó Cionga or Ó Cingeadh (first anglicized O'Kinga), a family which in mediaeval times were seated on the Island of Inismor in Lough Ree, and were influential in Co. Westmeath up to the end of the sixteenth century.

Statistics of the modern distribution of population indicate that Conrys are found in considerable numbers in Leix and Offaly, as well as in Connacht. This might well be expected because, in addition to the septs referred to above, there was also a not unimportant sept called Ó Conratha, alias Mac Conratha, of the same stock as the MacCoughlans of Offaly. Their arms are quite different from those of O'Mulconry as can be seen by reference to Plate V.

Arms illustrated on Plate V.

MacCONSIDINE.

The prefix Mac is never used with this name nowadays, but MacConsidine is found in old documents in English. In Irish it is Mac Consaidín, an example of a Gaelic surname formed from a foreign christian name : it denotes son of Constantine. As a surname Considine is of comparatively late introduction. The Considines, like their kinsmen the MacLysaghts, were a branch of the O'Briens, being descended from Domhnall Mór O'Brien, King of Munster, who died in 1194. They are thus of illustrious Dalcassian origin but they are seldom heard of in Irish history or literature, though they appear frequently in local histories of Co. Clare as people of substance. In 1627 we find one Cornelius MacConsidine among the distinguished Irish exiles in Brussels.

Arms illustrated on Plate V.

MacCONWAY, O'CONWAY, (Conboy, Convey).

Conway, in spite of its English or Welsh appearance, is a true Gaelic Irish surname. It looks more Irish as MacConaway, the form used in some parts of Donegal and north Connacht. Conway is the anglicized form of several different Irish surnames and the resultant confusion is very difficult to elucidate, particularly as the prefixes O and Mac have been used in some places indifferently with this name.

MacConway was the usual form in Co. Donegal in the seventeenth century and is extant there to-day. However, I have discovered no sept of MacConway belonging to Donegal. There was one in the adjacent county of Sligo, where the name Conway is still found : they were located in the parish of Easky ; but these are O'Conway not MacConway being Ó Conbhuidhe in Irish which is alternatively anglicized Conboy. Nearby in Co. Mayo we have the sept of Ó Connmhacháin, of the same stock as the

O'Haras, whose name, first anglicized as O'Conoughan etc. and later Kanavaghan, has now been corrupted to Conway and sometimes Convey. Mayo accounts for about twenty-five per cent of all the Conway births registered in Ireland.

MacConway, in Irish Mac Conmheadha or Mac Connmhaigh, belongs properly to Thomond, where the MacConways were a sept of importance up to the end of the fourteenth century : they were among the septs which rallied to O'Brien's standard in 1317. In 1360 the death of Gillananaev Ó Connmhaigh (The Four Masters use the prefix O not Mac), described as chief professor of music in Thomond is recorded.

As regards the derivations of these surnames it has been suggested to me by Dr. M. A. O'Brien, Director of the School of Celtic, Dublin Institute for Advanced Studies, that Connmhaigh comes from old Irish *condmach* meaning head-smashing. Conbhuidhe is probably from *cú buidhe*, yellow hound.

The Conways in King James's Irish Army were of Welsh extraction : their family is credited with the prefix Mac in error.

Two O'Conways were Bishops of Kilmacduagh in the early fifteenth century ; and Father Richard Conway (1586–1623), was one of the intrepid Jesuits who did so much to promote the counter-reformation in Ireland.

One of the Conways of Connacht, Roderick William Conway (1782–1853), was a prominent advocate of Catholic Emancipation but fell out with Daniel O'Connell. Thomas Conway (1735–1800), second Count Conway, was one of the many distinguished Irish exiles who rose to high military rank—he became a Major-General, Governor of all the French possessions in India and also a general in the American War of Independence. This family, of which several were distinguished soldiers, was of Cloghane and Glenbehy, Co. Kerry. It should not be confused with the Anglo-Irish family of Conway (Barons Conway), who unlike so many of the " ascendancy," were notable for the fact that they were landlords who were of the improving type and not absentees, particularly in the latter half of the seventeenth and early eighteenth centuries.

O'COONEY.

The sept of O'Cooney—Ó Cuana in Irish—was formerly of considerable importance. Originating in Ulster (Tyrone), they migrated westwards to north Connacht at an early date. In 1248, the most distinguished member of the sept died, viz. Diarmid Ó Cuana : he is described as " the great priest of Elphin " both by the Four Masters and in the " Annals of Loch Cé." The diocese of Elphin lies in the counties of Roscommon, Sligo and Galway. Three centuries later they were still in that area, as evidenced by the Elizabethan Fiants. They gradually spread southwards, for in the census of 1659 they were numerous in Co. Clare. The place Ballycooney is in the southern part of Co. Galway. To-day, as in the sixteenth century, they are chiefly found in north Connacht.

In modern times the Cooneys have not been prominent. The most noteworthy person of the name was Mary Cooney, an Irish poetess who had a reputation in America as well as in Ireland in the 1880's.

Cooney is used in Co. Cork as a variant of the north Munster name Ó Cuanacháin, normally anglicized Counihan.

O'CORCORAN, MacCORCORAN.

The Irish forename Corcoran is derived from the Gaelic word *corcair*, now used to denote purple but formerly meaning ruddy. The sept called MacCorcoran was of some importance in the Ely O'Carroll country : they were still people of substance in Offaly and Tipperary at the end of the sixteenth century and the name is fairly numerous in Counties Tipperary and Cork to-day. The O'Corcorans belonged to Fermanagh and produced a number of ecclesiastics from the eleventh to the fifteenth century whose field of activity was around Lough Erne. One of these was Bishop of Clogher in 1373. The name is rare there now : probably there was a westward migration as it is found in Counties Mayo and Sligo. From the latter came Brigadier General Michael Corcoran (1827–1863), who recruited an Irish Legion in the United States in 1861. Edmund O'Corcoran, " the hero of Limerick " (i.e. the siege of 1691), was the subject of one of O'Carolan's well-known poems.

MacCORMACK, (O'Cormacan).

MacCormack or MacCormick is a very common name in Ireland and is distributed widely throughout the four provinces. There was a minor sept of the name in Co. Longford, but for the most part the name appears to have come into existence independently in many places at a comparatively late date, individuals whose fathers' christian name happened to be Cormac describing themselves as MacCormaic which thereafter was continued as a surname by subsequent generations. MacTeige and MacShane are other examples of this tendency. In the sixteenth century—in 1576, 1598 and again in 1600—MacCormacks are recorded as leading gentry in Co. Cork and one, of Muskerry, was influential enough to raise a large force to assist Desmond in the Elizabethan wars. The Four Masters record the deaths of several prominent MacCormacks of Fermanagh ; the last of these died in 1431. Possibly the MacCormacs of Co. Armagh were descendants of these : two of them were very prominent in the medical profession : Henry MacCormac (1800–1886), and his son Sir William Mac-Cormac (1836–1901) ; while a third medical man, Robert MacCormack (1800–1890), best known as an Arctic navigator, was of Tyrone parentage. The name is universally recognized as Irish on account of the fame of John Count MacCormack (1885–1945), the tenor.

MacCormack has also been adopted in place of the surnames O'Cormack and O'Cormacan, borne by small septs located in Counties Roscommon, Galway, Clare, Cork, Down and Derry. Thus even when MacCormack is a substitute for those names it is very widely scattered. Three of the name O'Cormacan were Bishops of Killaloe in the thirteenth and fourteenth centuries.

O'CORRIGAN, Carrigan.

This name is Ó Corragáin in Irish. The sept belongs primarily to Fermanagh being of the same stock as the Maguires. Corrigans—the prefix O is seldom used—are still in that part of Ulster, but the name to-day is very scattered, being found in most counties, except in Munster. This was already the case in the sixteenth century when it appears in localities as far apart as Offaly, Roscommon, Meath and Monaghan. In the 1659 census Corrigan and O'Corrigan are among the more numerous Irish names in Offaly, Longford and Fermanagh. The majority of the references to it in the Four Masters are to abbots and other ecclesiastics in Co. Fermanagh. The place called Ballycorrigan is near Nenagh in Co. Tipperary, indicating that a leading family of Corrigan was seated there not later than the middle of the seventeenth century. The Most Rev. Michael Augustine Corrigan (1839–1902), Archbishop of New York, came from a Meath family, while Sir Dominic John Corrigan (1802–1880), the eminent physician, was a Dublin man. Carrigan is a variant of Corrigan.
Arms illustrated on Plate VI.

MacCOSTELLO, Nangle.

The Costelloes were originally Nangles, or de Angulos, as that great Norman family was called when, soon after the invasion, the Anglo-Normans occupied Conn-acht. The first reference to them in the Four Masters is in the year 1193 when they were called the sons of Oistealb, who was a son of the famous Gilbert de Nangle,

95

whence was formed the surname Mac Oisdealbh, later Mac Oisdealbhaigh, *anglice* MacCostello. Curtis calls their eponymous ancestor Gocelin (or Jocelin) and gives the Irish form as Mac Goisdelbh. It is the first recorded instance of a Norman family assuming a Mac name. Thenceforward they became thoroughly Irish. There are many traditional tales of the feuds between the MacCostelloes and MacDermots : none more poignant than the tragic love story of Una, daughter of Charles MacDermot (the last inaugurated chieftain of that name), and the son of the head of the Mac-Costello family, who lie in adjoining graves beside the ruins of the church on Trinity Island. Their lands were in Co. Mayo and the barony of Costello, in the east of that county, was named from the MacCostelloes who possessed it up to the end of the sixteenth century. In 1565 their chief seat was near Ballaghadereen, which is now included in Co. Roscommon. The name Costello (the Mac has been entirely dropped) is found to-day chiefly in Counties Mayo and Galway—in south Galway and Clare it is usually spelt Costelloe. The erroneous form O'Costello instead of MacCostello probably arose through the practice in the spoken Irish language of shortening the Mac with names beginning with C : thus 'ac Costello was turned into O'Costello.

The Costelloes were one of the many great Irish families which, in the ruin of the seventeenth century destruction of the Gaelic order, produced famous rapparees. Dudley (or Dubhaltach) Costello was an officer in the army of the Confederate Catholics in 1642, and later became a colonel in the Spanish service. Returning to Ireland after the Restoration and disappointed by his failure to recover the family estates, he devoted the rest of his life to wreaking vengeance on the new Cromwellian proprietors. His chief lieutenant in this private war was, appropriately enough, named Nangle : both of them were killed in action in fights with the British soldiery. Arthur Dudley Costello (1803–1865) and his sister, Louise Stuart Costello (1799–1870), English born of Irish stock, were both novelists and travel writers of note ; while William Costello (1800–1867), a surveyor, wrote much on medical subjects. The Taoiseach (Prime Minister) of the Republic of Ireland from 1948 to 1951, and again 1954–1957 was John A. Costello (b. 1891).

Arms illustrated on Plate VI.

MacCOTTER.

MacCotter is one of the quite numerous class of surnames with the initial C which should properly begin with a vowel, the C being transferred by attraction from the prefix Mac. In Irish this is Mac Oitir which in the same way is found also as Mac Coitir. The latter is unquestionably a corruption ; the surname is formed from the popular Norse personal name Oitir. It does not follow that the Cotters (who in modern times do not use the prefic Mac) are of Norse descent since several families of un-disputed Gaelic Irish origin have surnames derived from Norse personal names as, for example, McAuliffe, McManus, McRannall. Probably the first mention of it in Irish records is in the Four Masters under date 1142 when the son of Mac Ottir assumed " the chieftainship and government of Dublin." The Mac Ottir referred to was one of the Gaels of the Hebrides. Whether there is any connexion between him and the Mac Oitir (Cotter) family, which was well established in Co. Cork at least as early as 1300, is still an open question. The sixteenth century Fiants have many references to MacCotters, all these being in Co. Cork. By the seventeenth century they had become Cotter. William and Thomas Cotter were Gaelic poets of that century whose songs have survived till our own day. Sir James Cotter was in command of King James II's troops in Co. Clare. His son, James Cotter (1689–1720), ended his life somewhat unjustly on the gallows. His son, another Sir James Cotter (1714–1770), having forsaken the religion and politics of his forebears, was created a baronet and among his posterity were a number of Protestant clergymen in Co. Cork, including Rev. George Sackville Cotter (1754–1831), who was translator of classical works of some merit. The name is still almost peculiar to Co. Cork. There are no less than eight place names in that county which incorporate the surname, e.g. Ballymacotters and ScartMcCotters near Cloyne.

Arms illustrated on Plate VI.

MacCOY, (MacCooey).

MacCoy is a fairly common name in Ireland : it is chiefly to be found in Ulster on both sides of the border (Armagh-Monaghan area) with a sprinkling in Cork and Limerick. It is a variant of MacKay, in Irish MacAodha (i.e. son of Hugh). The MacKays and MacCoys are not by origin Irish in the usual sense of the word, since they came to Ireland as gallowglasses in the wake of the MacDonnells, their home territory being the southern isles of Scotland (Islay etc.)—though the Gaelic settlers in Alba came, no doubt, originally from Ireland. Like the MacDonnells some of the MacCoys went south, hence the families in Munster mentioned above. The name has not been very noteworthy in the political and cultural history of Ireland, but in this connexion Rev. Edward MacCoy (1839–1872), Gaelic writer, may be cited. Sir Frederick MacCoy (1823–1899), the Dublin-born naturalist, is best known for his work in that field in Australia. Several MacCoys have been prominent in America, but these do not appear to have had any connexion with Ireland. Less distinguished, if equally prominent, were the MacCoys of the gang so called. The origin of the expression " the rale MacCoy " is in dispute : some authorities state that it is a corruption of the Portugese word Macao (i.e. heroin from Macao) ; others connect it with an individual viz. the boxer " Kid " MacCoy, who was somewhat of a dandy. The Ulster Gaelic poet Art MacCoy (c. 1715–1774), was also known as MacCooey in English, his name in Irish being Mac Cobhthaigh.

COYNE, Kilcoyne, Kyne, Coen.

The remarkable extent to which this name and its synonyms appertain to the province of Connacht, and particularly to the counties of Galway and Mayo, is illustrated by the following birth statistics :

Form of Name	Total births registered in one year	In Connacht	In Leinster	In Munster	In Ulster
Coyne	54	39	13	1	1
Kyne	27	27	0	0	0
Coen	27	21	1	2	3
Kilcoyne	15	15	0	0	0

The majority of the 14 born in Leinster were probably of Connacht families settled in the metropolitan area of Dublin. The first three names given above are variant anglicized forms of the Irish Ó Cadhain, a minor sept originating near Partry, Co. Mayo. Coen (and especially the form Cohen) appears Jewish, but when met in Ireland it is almost always a true Irish name ; it may, however, often be an anglicized form of Ó Comhdháin (also of north Connacht) and not of Ó Cadhain. There is another synonym of Coyne which is found around Castlebar, viz. Barnacle, a surname which was adopted because the Irish word *cadhan* means wild goose. Kilcoyne is definitely found in the birth registrations as an alias of Coyne, or perhaps it would be more accurate to say that Coyne is an alias of Kilcoyne. Kilcoyne, however, as a rule is not the same name in Irish as Coyne and Kyne, but comes from Mac Giolla Chaoine, i.e. son of a follower of St. Caoin. Hardiman states that the Quins, one of the assimilated families of Galway City, are in fact Coynes whose name was altered to Quin. The 15 births recorded for Kilcoyne as above were all in Counties Mayo and Sligo. The Coens were nearly all in Galway and Roscommon. The name is more closely associated with literary than with political or other activities ; apart from the distinguished Jesuit, Father Coyne of our own day, Joseph Sterling Coyne (1803–1868), was a very well known playwright and satirist and was one of the founders of the English *Punch* ; Rev. Joseph Coyne, P.P. (1839–1891), was also an author of repute and contributor to the *Nation*, as was John Coen (b. circa 1820).

CREAGH.

This name presents one of the few examples of a cognomen superseding an original surname. The Creaghs are a branch of the O'Neills of Co. Clare, the tradition being that in a battle with the Norsemen at Limerick they carried green branches with them. The Irish word *craobhach* is the adjective formed from the noun *craobh*, a branch : Craobhach is the Irish form of the surname. This tradition is, of course, the *raison d'être* of the laurel branches in the Creagh coat of arms and crest.

The Creaghs were reckoned among the leading gentry of Co. Clare. The main branch for generations gave its sons to the British Army. General Sir O'Moore Creagh (1848–1923), was the most celebrated of this line of soldiers. A number of Clare Creaghs were officers in the Irish Brigades on the continent including his ancestor who, unlike most Wild Geese, returned to Ireland and retained the family estate by conforming to the established church. Very few, however, became Protestants and some of the most distinguished of Irish Catholic bishops and archbishops have been Creaghs. Those who remained steadfast Catholics were to be found chiefly in the nearby city of Limerick and figure prominently in its records. Several Creaghs were transplanted from Co. Limerick as papists by Cromwell. Thence came at least six of the distinguished bishops and archbishops called Creagh in the roll of the Irish hierarchy. General James Creagh (1701–c. 1790), many times severely wounded when serving in the Irish Brigade, was born in Co. Cork.

At the trial of Dr. Pierce Creagh, Archbishop of Dublin, under the penal code in 1705, the floor of the courthouse collapsed, the only two participants not buried in the ruins being the prisoner and the judge, who " cried out that Heaven itself acquitted him." Other prelates, even before the notorious Penal Code came fully into force, were not so fortunate. Most Rev. Richard Creagh (1525–1585), Archbishop of Armagh, died in the Tower of London after 18 years imprisonment there, having twice escaped and twice been recaptured.

In addition to the Creaghs of Counties Clare and Limerick, there is a branch of the same name in Co. Cork which was established there before the sixteenth century. Christopher Creagh was Mayor of Cork in 1541. All these branches use the same arms. Unlike the majority of old Gaelic surnames that of Creagh is not widely dispersed among all classes of the population.

Arms illustrated on Plate VI.

O'CREAN, Crehan, (Cregan).

According to MacFirbis, O'Crean and O'Cregan are synonymous, Crehan again being a variant of Crean. In Irish Crean and Crehan are Ó Croidheáin (spelt Ó Craidhen by the Four Masters) and Creegan or Cregan is Ó Croidheagáin. These families formed a minor sept of the Cineal Eoghan belonging to Donegal, with a branch in the neighbouring county of Sligo. They are twice mentioned by the Four Masters as wealthy merchants, which is somewhat unusual in the Annals : in 1506 as of Co. Donegal ; in 1572 as of Sligo. The Clongowes manuscript " The State of Ireland in 1598 " gives them a higher status : the then head of the family was John O'Crean of Ballynegare, and in another place in the manuscript O'Crean of Annagh is stated to have been one of the leading families of Co. Sligo in the sixteenth century. According to the " Annals of Loch Cé " the Bishop of Elphin in 1582 was an O'Crean, but he was " removed " in 1584. Father Daniel O'Crean (d. c. 1616) of Holy Cross, Sligo, was Provincial of the Dominican order in a period of intensive persecution.

The form Crehan is usual in Co. Galway ; in Co. Mayo these are called Crean, Grehan and even Graham. Creegan alone of these variants can be said to belong now to Co. Sligo. Crean is mostly found to-day in south-west Munster, but families of the name in Kerry and Cork are in most cases Creen, *recte* Curreen, i.e. Ó Corraidhín. A further complication in regard to the name Crean arises from the fact that Ó Corráin, normally Curran in English, has become Crean in some places. The arms illustrated in Plate VI are those of O'Crean of Donegal and Sligo and do not belong to the Creans of Munster.

Arms illustrated on Plate VI.

O'CROWLEY.

The history of this sept presents an example of a junior branch which emigrated to a distant province prospering and multiplying in its new territory while the main stem dwindled and almost disappeared from its original homeland. The sept of O'Crowley began as an off-shoot of the MacDermots of Moylurg (Co. Roscommon). Their eponymous ancestor was one Cruadhlaoch (*cruadh*—hard, *laoch*—hero) : hence the Irish form of the surname Ó Cruadhlaoich. The branch referred to above settled in the territory near Dunmanway (Co. Cork) and in due course became a distinct sept with a recognized chief residing at Kilshallow. Many of the sept were employed as professional soldiers, like the MacSheehys and MacSweenys. The O'Crowleys usually fought for the MacCarthys. By the middle of the seventeenth century the extensive estates of the O'Crowleys had nearly all been forfeited. A large proportion of them fell into the hands of Richard Boyle, first Earl of Cork. So much are they now identified with Co. Cork that seventy-five per cent of Crowley and O'Crowley births are registered in Co. Cork and most of the remaining twenty-five per cent in other Munster counties : only three per cent are Connacht registrations. The claim that the Munster O'Crowleys are really Mac Roghallaigh seems to have little foundation ; and in this connexion it is interesting to note that arms, long officially recorded, are the same for O'Crowley of Connacht and O'Crowley of Munster.

Two persons of the name may be mentioned as distinguished Irishmen : Nicholas Joseph Crowley (1819–1857), portrait-painter ; and Peter O'Neill Crowley (1832–1867), mortally wounded in the Fenian outbreak.

Arms illustrated on Plate VI.

O'CULLANE, COLLINS.

Collins is of course a common English surname : of 29 Collins biographies in the *Dictionary of National Biography* 27 are of Englishmen. Nevertheless in Ireland Collins may be regarded as a genuinely indigenous Irish name : in fact it is one of our most numerous surnames, being number 30 in the relevant statistical list with an estimated Collins population of 14,000 persons. The great majority of these come from Counties Cork and Limerick. This is as might be expected because the sept of O'Coileáin (possibly derived from the word *coileán*, a whelp or young dog) originated in North Desmond which extended into the modern Co. Limerick, where they were lords of the baronies of Connello, until in the thirteenth century they were driven southwards by the Geraldines and settled in West Cork near the country possessed by their kinsmen the O'Donovans. The well known Gaelic poem, translated as " Lament over Timoleague Abbey " has immortalized Seán Ó Coileáin, or John Collins (1754–1817), one of this sept. It should be observed that in the very territory to which they migrated was a sept called O'Cuilleáin also subsequently anglicized Collins : these were of the Corca Laoidhe.

The most famous of all Irish Collinses was from West Cork—Michael Collins (1890–1922), who combined in the highest degree the qualities of soldier and administrator, till the promise of a brilliant career was tragically cut short by his death in the Civil War which followed the establishment of the Irish Free State. Another who lost his life for Ireland was Father Dominic Collins, S.J. (1553–1602), who was hanged in Dublin Castle. Father Collins, O.P., led the Confederate Catholic army to a successful attack on Bunratty Castle in 1647. Jerome Collins (d. 1850), the arctic explorer, was a Co. Cork man. David Collins (1756–1810), who was born in Offaly, was one of the founders of the city of Sydney. A Co. Wicklow family of Collins produced three distinguished men : William Collins (1740–1812), author, his son, William Collins (1788–1847), painter and Royal Academician, and grandson William Wilkie Collins (1824–1889), the well known novelist. In America Edward Knight Collins (1802–1878) was a pioneer ship-owner who early adopted steam in place of sail ; his ancestor emigrated from Ireland in 1635.

Arms illustrated on Plate VI.

O'CULLEN.

Several quite distinct septs or families of Cullen existed formerly but only one has survived to any extent and this one is very numerous to-day : Cullen in fact has eighty-fourth place in the list of the hundred commonest surnames in Ireland, with an estimated population of nearly 8,000 persons. The great majority of these are found in the south-eastern counties—Dublin, Wicklow and Wexford. It is there the sept originated. They possessed Glencullen, Co. Wicklow, a place name which is said to be derived from the Irish word *cuileann* a holly tree not from the possession of it by Cullens, as does the barony of Kilcullen on the Wicklow border of Co. Kildare. As a power in that land they were overshadowed by the O'Byrnes and the O'Tooles about the year 1300, but they continued to dwell there uninterruptedly up to the present day. That they retained a position of some importance is evidenced by the fact that Cullen of Cullenstown is listed among the leading gentry of Co. Wexford in the Clongowes manuscript (1598). Cullen is the normal anglicized form of this name but there are many variants in the spelling of it, such as Quillen and Cullion, recorded here and there, though seldom in its original habitat. The usual modern form of the name in Irish is Ó Cuilinn. Several other minor Gaelic sept names have become Cullen by attraction, notably Ó Cuileamhain, *recte* Culloon or Culhoun, of south Leinster, to which, according to O'Curry, Cardinal Cullen belonged; and Mac Cuilin (MacCullen) of Leitrim whose name is sometimes confused with MacQuillan. In the 1659 census the name in various spellings was then numerous in Donegal and south-east Leinster.

Two famous Catholic bishops of the name should be mentioned. Patrick O'Cullen, Bishop of Clogher from 1517–1542, composer of the famous " Hymn to St. Maccartin "; and Paul Cullen (1803–1878), Cardinal and Archbishop of Dublin. The Gaelic poet John O'Cullane belonged to a different sept, whose name is usually Collins in modern speech though occasionally anglicized Cullen.* Descendants of Irish exiles named O'Cullen now fill important positions in the Argentine Republic and in Tenerife.

Arms illustrated on Plate VI.

O'CULLINAN, Quillinane.

Cullinan is the usual anglicized spelling of the name Ó Cuileannáin in Co. Clare and Cullinane in Co. Cork and east Munster. The prefix O is seldom found with Cullinan or Cullinane nowadays. One important sept so called originated in Tirconaill (Donegal), but there the name has been changed to Cullen. Up to the end of the seventeenth century they were still using the form O'Cullinan. They were closely associated with the O'Donnells and their seat was at Mullinashee. One of their sixteenth century chiefs was remarkable on account of the careers of his sons, of whom one was a bishop and six were abbots. Dr. John Cullinan (1585–1653), was Bishop of Raphoe and suffered much persecution as such: he was a prominent supporter of Rinuccini at the Confederation of Kilkenny. His brother Glaisne O'Cullinan (1558–1584), Cistercian Abbot of Boyle, was martyred. The

* See O'Collins *supra* and O'Cullinan *infra*.

O'Cullinanes of Co. Cork are a branch of the Corca Laidhe and their territory was in the barony of Barryroe. The Civil Survey and the 1659 census indicate that the name was very numerous in Co. Cork in the seventeenth century not only in Barryroe but also in the surrounding baronies : two from Kinalea were among the Irish who sailed for Spain after the battle of Kinsale. At that time, as to-day, branches of the sept were well established in Co. Clare and in Co. Waterford ; in the latter the spelling of the name was then Quillinane, a form still occasionally met with in Munster.

Cormac Mac Cuileannáin, King and Bishop of Cashel, who was slain in battle 908 A.D., is famous as the compiler of the genealogical tract called the " Psalter of Cashel " and as the first Irish language lexicographer. He cannot, however, properly be called a Cullinane because he lived before the era of surnames : his father's christian name was Cuileannán.

Arms illustrated on Plate VI.

CUMMINS, Comyn, Commons.

Notwithstanding its very English appearance Cummins is a Gaelic Irish surname quite distinct from the English Cummings and Cumming, though sometimes the original Ó Coimín takes those forms as its anglicized synonyms. Indeed the number of variants in English is considerable—Commons, Comyns, Kimmons, Commane and even MacSkimmins are recorded by the Registrar-General as being used as interchangeable with Cummins. Ó Coimín is first found in Connacht : the family were erenaghs of the church of St. Cuimín Fada, and the parish of Kilcummin on the western side of the Bay of Killala is named after them. The form Commons is now the most usual in Co. Mayo. It is a name about which much confusion is inevitable. It appears as Ó Comáin in Munster, whence come the majority of present day Cumminses (also called Commane) now found in Counties Tipperary and Cork. There they are sometimes called Hurley, through a mistranslation, *camán* being the Gaelic word for a hurley-stick. In some parts of Ulster the form in Irish is Mac Coimín, which is of long standing, for a deed relating to land in Co. Armagh, dated 1264, contains the name of Patrick MacCumyn. To add to the complexity the name Comyn is that of a prominent Norman-Irish family long established in this country : John Comyn, an Anglo-Norman, was Archbishop of Dublin from 1182–1213.

In one form or another the name appears in the roll of distingusihed Irishmen from a very early date. In the sixth century, long before the introduction of surnames, St. Common, pupil of St. Finian, went from Ulster as missionary to Connacht and founded Roscommon and other monasteries in that province. Cormac Ó Cuimín, or Comon (1703–1786), was one of the many blind bards and shanachies of the eighteenth century. Another famous Gaelic poet of that era was Michael Comyn (1688–1760), of Kilcorcoran, Co. Clare. His son Michael Comyn (b. 1704), emigrated to France where he was accepted as one of the nobility of France* and his grandson, John Francis Comyn (1742–1793), was guillotined as an aristocrat during the French Revolution, while David Comyn (1853–1907), another Clareman, was particularly active in the movements which led up to the formation of the Gaelic League. Some families of Comyn came to north Clare as papists transplanted under the Cromwellian régime from east of the Shannon, but the Inquisitions of earlier in the seventeenth century prove that families of the name were already well established in the county before that period. William Cumming (1769–1852), famous as a portrait-painter, was an Irishman who lived and worked in Ireland.

O'CUNIGAN, MacCunigan, Cunningham, (Dongan, Counihan).

The surname Cunningham or Conyngham is among the 75 most numerous in Ireland, the estimated number of persons so called in 1954 being 8,550. They are distributed over all four provinces, the majority being found in the Ulster counties of Down and Antrim and in the Connacht counties of Galway and Roscommon. In the former the families in question are for the most part of Scottish origin ; in the latter they are native Irish. The original Irish-Gaelic forms Ó Connagáin and Mac Cuinneagáin were first written in English as O'Cunnigan and MacCunnigan. Under the anglicizing influence of three centuries of British occupation many old Gaelic families, having dropped the O or Mac, gradually assumed an English or Scottish name approximating to theirs in sound. Thus Cunnigan became Cunningham.

There is hardly another name in Ireland which appears in the Registrar-General's records, voters' lists and so forth in so many different guises. Side by side with the standard form Cunningham, we find Coonaghan, Counihan, Cunnighan, Kinningham, Kinighan, Kinagam, Kinnegan and MacCunnigan in Ulster, while Conaghan and Kinaghan are two of the many variants elsewhere. Counihan and Coonaghan, however, are properly the anglicized forms of the north Munster name Ó Cuanacháin.

The true Irish Cunninghams trace their descent from two sources in Connacht, the Gaelic forms given above denoting son (mac) or descendant (ó) of Connagan, which is a diminutive of the personal name Conn. One branch stems from Fiachra, brother of the famous Niall of the Nine Hostages and father of the last pagan King of Ireland, and was located in Co. Sligo ; the other is a sept of the Ui Máine (often called Hy Many), a widespread group of septs centred in Counties Galway and Roscommon of which O'Kelly was the most important.

*Descendants of Wild Geese of the name were also enrolled among the nobility of Spain.

As is not unusual in the case of smaller families which, notwithstanding the destruction of the Gaelic order after 1603, refused to accept English rule, no arms are on record at the Office of Arms in Dublin Castle for O'Cunnigan or MacCunnigan. The well-known Cunningham arms are those of a Scottish family, several branches of which settled in Ireland in the seventeenth century and became influential in the north. There is a tradition that these Cunninghams were originally Irish settlers in Scotland : be that as it may they were in Scotland as early as the eleventh century, since their arms and their motto " over fork over " are based on an incident which occurred about the year 1050 when the Cunninghams' ancestor saved the life of Malcolm Canmore, afterwards King of Scotland, by covering him with hay and thus concealing him from MacBeth's pursuing forces.

The most distinguished Irishman of the name was probably Timothy Cunningham (d. 1761), the antiquarian, member and benefactor of the Royal Irish Academy. Mention may also be made of Henry first Marquess Conyngham (1766–1832), who was an Irish representative peer and a man of influence in England in the reign of George IV, and also of John Cunningham (1729–1773), the Irish actor and poet.

Some of the Cunninghams in Ulster acquired their surname in quite a different way from those dealt with above. There was a minor sept of MacDonegan in Co. Down, one of whom, John Dongan or MacDonnegan, was Bishop of Down from 1395 to 1412, while earlier in the fourteenth century Florence MacDonnagan was Bishop of Dromore. In this area the name was first corrupted to MacConegan and later some of these MacConegans changed this to Cunningham in imitation of the Scottish settlers. Others, however, retained the more correct modernized form Dunnigan, and Dunnigans are still to be found in Co. Down. This name is not to be confused with Donegan or Dongan—Ó Donnagáin in Irish—an important sept of Muskerry, Co. Cork, whose territory was around Rathluirc. Thomas Donegan (1634–1715), last Earl of Limerick (of the first creation), Governor of New York from 1683 to 1691, was the most distinguished man of this name.

MacCUNNEEN, O'Cunneen, Kenyon, (Kinnane).

The fact that Cunneen is never found nowadays with a prefix hides the fact that it represents actually two quite distinct surnames. MacCoinín is that of a literary family of Erris, Co. Mayo. It is anglicized Kenning and Kenyon, as well as Cunneen, and also by pseudo-translation as Rabbitt. Cunneen, and Rabbitt too, are the forms used in English for the Offaly family of Ó Coinín. A variant of this is Ó Cuinín which in turn is used as a variant of Ó Cuineáin, quite a different name in Irish : this is now indistinguishable from Ó Cuinneáin, a surname well-known in north Tipperary in its anglicized form Kinnane or Kinane. Here again there is also a Mac form viz. Mac Cuineáin *anglice* Cunnane. As this is almost exclusively found in north Connacht it is probably basically the same name as MacCunneen of Co. Mayo referred to at the beginning of this note. Father John Kenyon (1812–1869) of Templederry, Co. Tipperary, was a leading figure in the Young Ireland movement of 1848.

MacCURLEY, Kerley, Turley, Terry.

Curley is the usual modern form of this surname. Disregarding the Dublin metropolitan area, in which names from all the provinces are of course found, it is almost entirely confined to Connacht and particularly the counties of Galway and Roscommon. Though it has an English sound Curley is a genuine Gaelic Irish name, the initial C being the last letter of its prefix Mac : in Irish it is Mac Thoirdealbhaigh and so a variant of Turley—the meaning is simply son of Turlough, hence the use in some places of Terence and Terry as alternative anglicized forms. Terry is a surname found in Munster to-day. In the census of 1659 MacTerlagh and MacTurlogh both appear among the principal Irish names in Co. Limerick, but possibly these were not true surnames (see p. 14 *supra*). The connexion of Curley with Roscommon is emphasized by the place names Ballymacurley and Curley's Island both in that county. The sept was not particularly prominent in early or mediaeval times nor do people of the name find a place in the roll of distinguished Irish writers or politicians. The best known to-day is Archbishop Curley.

O'CURRAN.

The surname Curran is numerous and widespread in Ireland, equally in all the four provinces to-day. The census of 1659 reveals that it was then chiefly found in Co. Waterford and thence northwards towards Kildare, and also in Kerry and in Leitrim. Curran is the usual form, but Currane is more usual in Kerry. Kirrane and Curreen are other modern synonyms. There was a sept of the Ui Máine called Ó Curráin of the same stock as the O'Maddens, one of whom Simon O'Currin, O.P. (d. 1302), was Bishop of Kilfenora. James O'Corren was Bishop of Killaloe from 1526 to 1546. Of the south Leinster sept was Andrew O'Curran, O.S.B., who, after an interesting case of dispensation by the Pope, was appointed Prior of Glascarrig in 1411. The Leitrim Currans were a bardic family. There are few names as numerous as Curran about the background of which so little is recorded. Reference is made to this name in the article on Crean (p. 99 *supra*).

The outstanding historical personage of the name, John Philpot Curran (1750–1817), orator and patriot, needs no description. He was born in Co. Cork. His daughter Sarah Curran (1781–1808), a romantic and tragic figure, was engaged to be married to Robert Emmet.

O'CURRY, (Corry).

The Irish name Curry or O'Curry has no connexion with the Scottish Currie. In Irish Ó Comhraidhe, it sometimes takes the form Corry or Corra, especially in the northern counties, where in the few early records in which the name is found the prefix Mac is usually substituted for O. There was a little known sept of O'Curry in Co. Cork, now often Corry. The most important of the several distinct septs of O'Curry was that of Thomond from which sprang Eugene O'Curry (1796–1862), one of Ireland's greatest pioneer Gaelic scholars. The O'Currys were a leading sept in Co. Clare in the fourteenth century.

MacCURTIN.

Curtin, more usually nowadays without the prefix Mac, is probably popularly regarded as a Co. Cork surname, and it is undoubtedly more common there than in any other county, though found also in Limerick and Clare. The MacCurtins are, in fact, an ancient Thomond sept, whose territory was near Ennistymon in the barony of Corcomroe, Co. Clare. There they and the MacBrodys were hereditary ollaves to the O'Briens of Thomond. Nor was this in any sense a nominal position, for from generation to generation the Clare MacCurtins distinguished themselves as poets and Gaelic scholars. Four of them were recorded as such in the fourteenth and fifteenth centuries by the Four Masters. The best known in more modern times were Hugh Buidhe MacCurtin (1680–1755), styled " Chief of the Sept," who was a lexicographer as well as a poet, his cousin, Andrew MacCurtin (c. 1690–1749), and Hugh Og MacCurtin (c. 1680–1755). In the present century the name is honoured in the person of Thomas MacCurtin (1885–1920) the patriotic Lord Mayor of Cork who was a victim of the " Black and Tan " terror in that city.

Abroad these Clare MacCurtins have also made the name illustrious. In America

Andrew Gregg Curtin (1815–1894), notable Governor of Pennsylvania, was a son of a Clare emigrant ; and Jeremiah Curtin (c. 1840–1906), an outstanding linguist, was also of Irish ancestry. In France, in the Revolution period, a Jeremiah Curtin was an Irish signatory of the address to the National Convention, and Major General Benjamin MacCurtin was a leader of the Vendean insurgents on the Royalist and Catholic side in 1793.

Arms illustrated on Plate VII.

CUSACK.

Cusack is one of those Norman names introduced into Ireland following the invasion of 1172 which have become completely Irish. The name itself is derived from a place in Guienne, in France, and was first anglicized as de Cussac etc. and rendered de Cíomhsóg in Irish. In the fourteenth century Thomond deeds in the Irish language, printed by Hardiman in the R.I.A. Transactions for 1826, the name is given as MacIosog and Mac Isog : which suggests that, in Clare at any rate, the Cusacks became hibernicized in fact as well as in name.

The first Cusacks, Geoffrey and André de Cusack, who came with King John in 1211, obtained lands in Meath and other counties of the Pale where they held a prominent position down to the seventeenth century, when their continued and uncompromising support of the Catholic cause brought about their ruin as a leading landed family. They were then in possession of extensive estates not only in Meath and Kildare but also in Clare and Roscommon, practically all of which were lost in the 1691 attainders and the forfeitures of 1701. During the period of Catholic resurgence under James II the name appears frequently not only, as might be expected, in King James's Army list, but also in the parliamentary and municipal rolls. In preceding centuries Cusacks are prominent in all spheres of activity : for example, Nicholas Cusack was Bishop of Kildare from 1280 to 1300 ; Thomas Cusack was Mayor of Dublin in 1409 ; and Sir Thomas Cusack (1490–1571) was Lord Chancellor. The last named, though in no sense an Englishman, was prominent in his efforts on behalf of the English interest both in the legal and military spheres. On the other hand Nicholas Cusack was beheaded for his part in the resistence to Elizabethan aggression, and Patrick Cusack was a leader of the Confederate Catholics in the Cromwellian war. After the disasters of the seventeenth century Cusacks continued abroad to distinguish themselves as soldiers : the most famous of these was General Chevalier Richard Edmond de Cusack (1687–1770), who had a brilliant military career under Louis XIV and Louis XV. These and other prominent individuals were Meath or Kildare men, as was Dr. James William Cusack (1788–1861) the famous Dublin surgeon.

108

Although the Cusacks are not closely associated with Connacht in modern times, a branch of the Killeen (Co. Meath) family established itself in Co. Mayo at an early date. Mac Firbis, spelling the name simply Ciosóg, mentions them as one of the four Norman tribes which wrested the territory of Tirawley from the Ui Fiachrach chiefs, and the Four Masters record a sanguinary battle there between the Cusacks and the Barrets in 1281 ; three centuries later the " Composition Book of Connacht " mentions them as landowners in the barony of Tirawley (Co. Mayo). It is somewhat strange, therefore, to find the name now more numerous in Munster than elsewhere—though it is nowhere very common. The best known connected with that province was Margaret Anne Cusack (1832–1899), or Sister Mary Francis Clare, a convert who after being famous for her good works—she was popularly known as " the Nun of Kenmare "—reverted to her former faith and spent the rest of her life attacking Catholicism. One of the best known actors on stage and screen of the present day is Cyril Cusack (b. 1910), formerly of the Abbey Theatre.

Arms illustrated on Plate VII.

DALTON.

Though this name is not Irish in origin it is on record in Dublin and Co. Meath as early as the beginning of the thirteenth century, the family having been established in Ireland following the Anglo-Norman invasion. Its Norman origin is more apparent in the alternative spelling, still sometimes used, viz. D'Alton i.e. of Alton, a place in England. According to family tradition the first Dalton to come to Ireland was one Walter, who had fled to England from France, having incurred the wrath of the French king by secretly marrying his daughter. The early settlers became powerful, having acquired lands in Teffia, Co. Meath, under Henry II. There and in Co. Westmeath (part of which subsequently became known as Dalton's Country) they erected castles and founded religious houses. In the fourteenth century they spread into Counties Tipperary and Cork, but it was not until the middle of the seventeenth century that a branch of the family went to Clare, with which county they were afterwards closely identified. The head of the family was known as Lord of Rathconrath (Co. Westmeath) ; but as territorial magnates they were broken by the Cromwellian and Williamite devastations, having in the course of time completely identified themselves with the native Irish. The humbler families of the name, however, remained in Westmeath and their descendants are there to-day. A number of Irish Daltons distinguished themselves as Wild Geese in foreign service, particularly in that of Austria. Another Irish Dalton to become famous (or notorious) outside Ireland was Robert Dalton, whose short life terminated in 1892 when the band of desperate outlaws he led in Oklahoma and California was finally rounded up. At home the best known of the name in modern times have been John Dalton (1792–1867), the historian, and the present Archbishop of Armagh, Cardinal D'Alton.

Arms illustrated on Plate VII.

O'DALY.

O'Daly may be said to be the greatest name in our Gaelic literature. Other septs may have produced one or two more famous individuals, but the O'Dalys have a continuous record of literary achievement from the twelfth to the seventeenth century and, indeed, even to the nineteenth. Hardiman speaks of no less than thirty O'Dalys distinguished as writers between 1139 and 1680. The first of these famous poets was Cuconnacht Ó Dálaigh (such is the Irish form of O'Daly), who flourished in the early twelfth century. He presided over a bardic school in Co. Meath, not far from the territory traditionally belonging to the parent sept of O'Daly, who were located in the barony of Magheradernon, Co. Westmeath. They were of the southern Ui Neill. Thence they spread to other parts of the country, always continuing the literary tradition and forming sub-septs in each of the places they settled in pursuit of their calling. One was the first of a line of poets in north Clare on the shore of Galway Bay. The most famous of these was Donogh Mór O'Daly (d. 1244), who was born at Finvarra, Co. Clare : he has been called " the Irish Ovid." In the same way the O'Dalys became associated with Co. Cork and Co. Cavan. Diarmuid Og O'Daly was made the official poet of the MacCarthys of West Cork, thus acquiring for his family lands and privileges in the barony of Carbery. One of these, Angus O'Daly (d. 1617), was somewhat of a renegade, being the author of the anti-Irish propagandist satire *The Tribes of Ireland*. The Cavan O'Dalys were similarly attached to the O'Reillys of Breffny. The Dalys, who became Barons Dunsandle in Co. Galway— achieved great wealth and power in the eighteenth and nineteenth centuries.

Not only did the name thus become widespread, but the descendants of these scattered sub-septs increased and multiplied so that the name is now one of the commonest in Ireland, holding as it does twenty-fourth place in the statistical list, with an estimated population of nearly 16,000 persons in Ireland at the present day.

In addition to the mediaeval poets already referred to, two modern O'Dalys have upheld the family tradition, viz., Robert Daly (1783–1872), Protestant Bishop of Cashel, and John O'Daly (1800–1878), both of whom were early contributors to the Gaelic revival. The Catholic Church, besides several mediaeval bishops of western dioceses, has Rev. Dominic O'Daly (1595–1665), a Kerryman who had a most distinguished career in Portugal, both as ecclesiastic and statesman. Many of the name were attainted under the Cromwellian and Williamite régimes for their support of the Irish and Stuart cause. One Richard Daly (1750–1813) was a leading figure in the eighteenth century Dublin theatre as actor and manager. Daly's, opened in Dublin in 1791, was the most celebrated of the club-houses which were a feature of eighteenth century social life. The building is now the office of an insurance company.

Arms illustrated on Plate VII.

DARCY, O'Dorcey, MacDarcy.

This name is often spelt D'Arcy. This is historically correct in the case of those families of the name which descend from Sir John D'Arcy who was Chief Justice of Ireland in the fourteenth century, e.g., the Darcys of Hyde Park, Co. Westmeath, whose chief seat for centuries was Platten, Co. Meath ; and it is reasonable to assume that the Darcys of the east midlands of Ireland are of that stock. It may be mentioned here that though Norman in origin, the name being originally D'Arci, from Arci a place in Normandy, these Darcys did not come to Ireland as early as the Anglo-Norman invasion. There is no justification for the Darcys of Munster and Connacht (with very few exceptions) using the form D'Arcy, because they were of native Irish stock and their name is a corruption of the Gaelic Ó Dorchaidhe, which was first anglicized as O'Dorcey. There were two minor septs so called : one in Co. Mayo was located around Partry near Lough Mask ; the other in east Galway was a branch of the Ui Máine. In the " Annals of Loch Cé " the name MacDarcy appears as that of a Co. Leitrim chieftain in the years 1384 and 1403. O'Donovan in his notes to the Four Masters under the date 1310 places the MacDarcy sept in the parish of Oughteragh, Co. Leitrim.

The most distinguished of the name were the lawyer, Patrick Darcy (1598–1668), a prominent member of the Supreme Council of the Confederation of Kilkenny, and Patrick Count Darcy (1725–1779), Chevalier and Maréchal-de-camp in the service of France, who was a mathematician of note as well as a famous soldier. Oliver Darcy was Bishop of Dromore from 1670 to 1674, having previously held the see of Ardagh.

It has been proved by O'Donovan that the Darcys who became one of the Tribes of Galway were of true Gaelic stock, being descended from the O'Dorceys of Partry, Co. Mayo.

Arms illustrated on Plate VII.

O'DARGAN, Dorgan.

The Gaelic name Ó Deargáin, the root of which is the adjective *dearg* (red), has taken the anglicized form Dargan in Leinster, and Dorgan in Munster. The latter is almost confined to Co. Cork while respectable families of Dargan have long been resident in the midland counties. As a Gaelic sept they were of little importance so that they do not figure in the Annals, the "Book of Rights," the Fiants, the "Topographical Poems", "An Leabhar Muimhneach" or any of the usual sources of genealogical information.

There were two prominent nineteenth century men of the name : William Dargan (1799–1867), the chief builder of Irish railways and promoter of the Dublin International Industrial Exhibition of 1853 ; and Edmund Strother Dargan (1809–1879), the Irish-American judge, a remarkable character of whom many amusing anecdotes are told.

O'DAVOREN.

Formerly a flourishing Thomond sept, the O'Davorens have now dwindled to small numbers but are still found in Clare and the adjoining county of Tipperary. They are described as formerly a learned brehon family seated at Lisdoonvarna, where they had a literary and legal school, among the pupils of which was Duald MacFirbis, the most distinguished of that celebrated family of Irish antiquaries. The Four Masters record the death in 1364 of Gillananaev Ó Duibhdabhoireann— so the name was originally spelt—chief brehon of Corcomroe : it was first anlgicized phonetically as O'Duvdavoren and later shortened to O'Davoren. The "Wars of Torlough" mention Coradh mic Dabhoirenn, i.e. Davoren's weir near Corofin, in 1317. The O'Davorens had a mortuary chapel in the now vanished church of Noughaval in north Co. Clare. *Dubh* (black) *an dá Bhoireann* (of the two Burrens) is the suggested derivation of the name.

Arms illustrated on Plate VII.

O'DEA.

O'Dea is a name associated alike in the past and at present almost exclusively with the County Clare and the areas such as Limerick City and North Tipperary which immediately adjoin it. It is not a common name elsewhere and even in County Clare is not numerous outside the part of the county where it originated. This is indicated by the place names Tully O'Dea and Dysart O'Dea, the site of a famous battle in 1318. The head of the sept was chief of a considerable territory comprising much of the barony of Inchiquin. In Irish the name is Ó Deághaidh. This is pronounced O D(y)aw, hence the occasional variant Daw in English. The normal pronunciation of the name in English is approximately O'Day and in some places it is anglicized as Day, but persons so called are not numerous in Ireland and some may be of English extraction since Day is a common name in England. A variant in Irish, found in Counties Tipperary and Waterford, is O Diaghaidh anglicized as Dee or O'Dee. Some O'Deas call themselves O'Dee—no doubt this pronunciation arose during the period when things Irish were unfashionable, O'Dee sounding more refined.

No outstanding O'Dea appears in the political, military or literary history of Ireland but several are mentioned by the Four Masters and one Cornelius O'Dea (d. 1434), was Archdeacon of Killaloe and later Bishop of Limerick. Another notable bishop of the name was Most Rev. Thomas O'Dea (d. 1923) who as Bishop of Galway administered also the Clare see of Kilfenora. Father Joseph Peter O'Dea (1743–1812), son of an Irish exile, was a noteworthy priest in the diocese of Nantes, where many Irish families settled in the eighteenth century. The well-known comedian of our own day, Jimmy O'Dea, is a Dubliner of Clare ancestry.

Arms illustrated on Plate VII.

O'DELANY, Delane, (Dillane).

Delany is a surname never seen to-day with the prefix O which properly belongs to it. It is Ó Dubhshláine in Irish, Delany being a phonetic rendering of this—the A of Delany was formerly pronounced broad. An earlier anglicized form was O'Dulany e.g. Felix O'Dulany, Bishop of Ossory from 1178 to 1202, who built St. Canice's Cathedral in Kilkenny. *Dubh* means black and *Sláine* is topographical—Slaney in English. If it refers to the river Slaney it suggests that this sept originally possessed a wider territory than that usually assigned to it, namely Coilluachtarach (now Upperwoods) at the foot of Slieve Bloom near the source of the rivers Nore and Barrow in Co. Leix. At the present time the name is chiefly associated with Counties Leix and Kilkenny and in 1659, when Petty's census was made, it appears as a principal Irish name in four baronies of Queen's County (now Leix) and in five of Co. Kilkenny. It is sometimes abbreviated to Delane in Co. Mayo, and this was the form used by Dennis Delane (d. 1750), the celebrated Dublin and London actor. Dillane, however, is not a synonym of Delany, but the anglicized form of O'Duilleáin, a Co. Limerick surname, sometimes disguised as Dillon. Dean Patrick Delany (1684–1768), the friend of Dean Swift, was a Leix man. His wife, the famous Mary Delany (1700–1788), was also prominent in the Swift circle. Michael Ronald (" Ronny ") Delany, champion athlete who brought honours to Ireland in the 1956 Olympic Games, is a Dubliner.

O'DEMPSEY.

The O'Dempseys are of the same stock as the O'Connors of Offaly and were a powerful sept in the territory lying on the borders of Leix and Offaly known as Clanmalier. Hence the title Viscount Clanmalier bestowed by James I of England on Terence O'Dempsey, the family being then and in the reign of Elizabeth I consistently pro-English. An example of their activity in this respect will be found in the section on O'Lalor (v.p. 206 *infra*). However, they took the Irish side later on in the seventeenth century : Edmund O'Dempsey, Bishop of Leighlin, Lewis O'Dempsey, Viscount Clanmalier, and Barnabas O'Dempsey were prominent members of the Confederation of Kilkenny and, with Lysagh O'Dempsey, were exempted from pardon by the Cromwellian victors in 1652 : their loyalty to the Catholic King James II resulted in the loss of their estates. In earlier times, too, they were distinguished in the defence of their country and O'Dempsey, Chief of Offaly, was one of the few Irish leaders who could boast of having defeated Strongbow in a military engagement, which he did in 1172, Strongbow's son-in-law, de Quenci being killed in the battle. Dermot O'Dempsey (d. 1193), Chief of the Name, founded the Cistercian Abbey at Monasterevan. St. Evin, it may be mentioned, who established the church at Monasterevan, a place which bears his name, was the patron saint of the O'Dempseys. The Dempseys, too, were notable among the priests of the penal times, one of them John Dempsey, a relative of Viscount Clanmalier, being Bishop of Kildare.

Arms illustrated on Plate VII.

MacDERMOT, Kermode.

The MacDermots are one of the few septs whose head is recognized by the Irish Genealogical Office as an authentic chieftain, that is to say he is entitled in popular parlance to be called The MacDermot ; and in his case this is enhanced by the further title of Prince of Coolavin, though of course as titles are not recognized under the Irish Constitution the designation is only used by courtesy. The family descends from Tadhg O'Connor, who was King of Connacht before the Norman invasion. The MacDermots divided into three distinct septs, or, if we disregard the branch which early accepted English domination, into two septs. The more important, having precedence, is that of Coolavin, Co. Sligo, formerly of Moylurg, whose territory embraced much of Co. Roscommon ; the other, further south in Co. Galway, owned Kilronan and was called MacDermot Roe (i.e. Red). Madam MacDermot (1659–1739), of Alderford, wife of MacDermot Roe, was noted for her patronage of O'Carolan the harper at a time when aristocratic patronage of the bards was almost a thing of the past. O'Carolan was buried in the MacDermot family vault at Kilronan. The name is numerous—it is included in the hundred commonest in Ireland. It is the second most common in its home county (Roscommon) and is also found frequently in Counties Donegal and Tyrone. It is seldom used without the prefix Mac, except in Co. Leitrim where the simple form Dermott is not uncommon. Its derivation is simple—Mac Diarmada (son of Diarmuid or Dermot). Three men of the name may be mentioned as outstanding : two of these were of the chiefly family of Moylurg—Brian MacDermot (d. 1592), learned owner of the famous manuscript " The Annals of Loch Cé " and Hugh MacDermot (1834–1904), leading barrister and politician ; and a third, Martin MacDermott (1823–1905), Young Irelander and poet of *The Nation*. The name MacDermot is also to be found among the prominent members of exiled Irish families on the continent, both as ecclesiastics and as soldiers.

In some parts of Connacht the name has been corrupted to Kermode, due to the aspiration of the initial D of Mac Diarmada in spoken Irish.

Arms illustrated on Plate VII.

O'DEVINE, Davin, (Devane).

The name Devine is chiefly found to-day in the counties of Tyrone and Fermanagh. Up to the fifteenth century the chief of this sept was Lord of Tirkennedy in Co. Fermanagh. Though the etymology of the name has been questioned we may accept the view of so eminent a scholar as O'Donovan that it is in Irish Ó Daimhín. This is also anglicized as Davin, which is not a common name but it is to be found in and around Co. Tipperary. The Davins of the midlands are probably a branch of the O'Devines of Fermanagh and so ultimately an offshoot of the Maguires. The Four Masters mention one O'Devine as co-arb of Derry in 1066 as well as several who were chiefs of Tirkennedy at various dates up to 1427.

In modern times the best known man of the name was Professor Edward Thomas Devine (1867–1948), of Columbia University, famous as an organizer of American charities.

Another Irish surname which is anglicized Devine in some places is Ó Dubháin, normally anglicized Dwane or Devane in Munster and Duane in Connacht.

O'DEVLIN.

There was once a not unimportant sept of Ó Doibhilin, *anglice* O'Devlin, in what is now the barony of Corran, Co. Sligo. As late as 1316 one of these, Gillananaev O'Devlin, who was standard bearer to O'Connor, was slain in battle. Their descendants, however, have either died out or been dispersed. The principal sept of the name belongs to Co. Tyrone. Their chiefs were lords of the territory known as Munterdevlin on the Tyrone shore of Lough Neagh. Eighty per cent of present day Devlins (the prefix O is seldom if ever used in modern times) are from Ulster, most of whom hail from Tyrone or an adjacent county. In the Elizabethan Fiants they are called Doibilin, but the name is scarcely found in any form in the census of 1659, since the Co. Tyrone is missing from that document. An O'Devlin who died in 1211 was Bishop of Kells. A prominent rebel in the Portadown area in 1641 was Patrick O'Develin; Francis O'Devlin (d. 1735), a Franciscan friar of Prague, born in Co. Tyrone, was a writer of some note; and James Devlin (d. 1825), was a veteran of the American War of Independence. The best known of the name in Irish history, however, was associated with Wicklow not Tyrone—Anne Devlin (1778–1851), the faithful servant of Robert Emmet, who though imprisoned and tortured would not give information against him. Joe Devlin (1872–1934), the Belfast Nationalist M.P., one of the best known figures in Ireland during the first twenty years of the present century, and another Joseph Devlin (b. 1869), who wrote voluminously over the *nom de plume* of "Northern Gael," were both unmistakable Ulstermen.

DILLON.

Although not native Gaelic in origin the name Dillon may now be regarded as hundred per cent Irish: when met outside Ireland it will almost always be found to belong to a person of Irish origin or with Irish connexions. The Dillons came to Ireland at the time of the Anglo-Norman invasion and during the well nigh eight centuries which have elapsed since that event Dillon has been an important name in Irish history and in modern politics. The family never lost the power and influence it acquired at the end of the twelfth century. The large tract of country covering most of the modern county of Westmeath, which was their main territory, became known as Dillon's Country. A branch settled in Co. Mayo. Many Dillons held high government office up to the fall of the Stuarts. Their chief renown thereafter was won as Colonel-Proprietors of Dillon's Regiment, famous in French military annals. The Dillons were created Counts in 1711 and their descendants still live in France. Several holders of the sixteenth century earldom of Roscommon have been noteworthy, the best known being Wentworth Dillon (1633–1685) the fourth earl, a voluminous and at one time much esteemed poet. The present Lord Dillon is nineteenth Viscount of Costello-Gallen in Co. Sligo. Prominent Dillons of later times are too numerous to mention individually, but reference should be made to three generations of a Co. Roscommon Dillon family who have played an important part in Irish politics: John Blake Dillon (1816–1866), Young Irelander; his son John

Dillon (1851–1927), M.P.; and the grandson James Dillon, twice Minister for Agriculture in the Government of the Republic of Ireland. The last named has two brothers in important positions in the educational sphere.

Arms illustrated on Plate VIII.

O'DINNEEN, (Downing).

In our own day the great majority of Dinneens, who rarely if ever have the prefix O in English, belong to Co. Cork families, especially to the south-western part anciently known as Corca Laoidhe. It was there the sept originated. It provided a succession of hereditary poets and historians to the MacCarthys and occasionally, also, to the O'Sullivans. Even after the destruction of the Gaelic order the literary tradition of the O'Dinneens was continued, Tadhg O'Dinneen, poet to the Earl of Clancarty, being a prominent member of the seventeenth century school of poetry at Blarney. The best known man of the name, Father Patrick Dinneen (1860–1934), compiler of the standard Irish-English dictionary, followed the literary tradition of his forbears.

In Irish the name is Ó Duinnín, which in Co. Kerry has a variant O Dúinín, anglicized Downing (v. p. 128 *infra, sub* O'Downey).

Arms illustrated on Plate VIII.

O'DOHERTY, (MacDevitt).

Doherty is an example of a surname in which the resumption of its prefix O during the present century has been very marked. Comparing the statistics of 1890 with 1955 we find that in the former year in Ireland out of 465 births registered only eight i.e. less than two per cent were O'Doherty: at the present time the proportion is approximately fifty per cent. i.e. those calling themselves Doherty and O'Doherty are about equal. Alternative spellings such as Dogherty and Dougherty are rarely met with nowadays. Many Irish surnames in their anglicized forms present problems in regard to their origin. Doherty, however, is simple and straightforward. In Irish Ó Dochartaigh, which is said to be derived from the word *dochartach* meaning obstructive, this large and powerful sept is of the same stock as the O'Donnells. Originating in the barony of Raphoe, Co. Donegal, the O'Doherty chiefs extended their territory till they became Lords of Inishowen in the fourteenth century, but they were greatly reduced as a result of the ill-timed rebellion of Sir Cahir O'Dougherty in 1608. The great majority of the present day bearers of the name live, or at least were born, in Donegal or the areas adjacent to that country. Their numbers give them the fifteenth place in the list of the commonest names in Ireland.

From David O'Doherty, a chief of Cinel Conaill, who was killed in 1208, descend the MacDevitts (in Irish Mac Daibhid, son of David), who are numerous in Inishowen.

Notable people of the name have been very numerous in the past in every walk of Irish life. Sir Cahir O'Dougherty (1587–1608), has already been mentioned ; we may also cite in politics John Doherty (1783–1850), M.P., notorious as the Crown prosecutor in the Doneraile Conspiracy case and subsequently Lord Chief Justice, and Kevin Izod O'Doherty (1823–1905), Young Irelander ; in art William James O'Doherty (1835–1868), the sculptor ; and in literature Thomas Dogherty (d. 1805), legal writer, and Mary Anne O'Doherty (1826–1910), the wife of Kevin Izod O'Doherty.

Arms illustrated on Plate VIII.

O'DOLAN, Doolan.

The name Dolan is fairly common to-day in Ulster—in the Catholic areas of Counties Cavan and Fermanagh—and in the Counties of Roscommon and Galway in Connacht. The latter is the place of origin of this sept which is a branch of the Ui Máine (Hy Many). In the census of 1659 the name appears principally in Counties Roscommon and Fermanagh (the portion dealing with Co. Galway is missing). In Irish it is Ó Dubhláin, Ó Dubhlainn being a variant in Connacht. These are also anglicized as Doolan and sometimes as Dowling. A very well known Irish-American was Thomas Dolan (1834–1914), the capitalist ; in Ireland the best known man of the name was Michael J. Dolan (d. 1953), an outstanding actor in the Abbey Theatre.

MacDONLEVY, Dunleavy, Leavy.

Dunleavy, to give the name its most usual modern form, may be regarded as a Mac surname—Mac Duinnshléibhe in Irish—though in some early manuscripts, e.g., the " Topographical Poems " of O'Dugan and O'Heerin, the prefix O is used. In the " Annals of Loch Cé " the O prefix appears in the sixteenth century, but all those mentioned before that are Mac. In modern times it has many synonyms : besides spelling variants such as Donlevy, there is McAleevy (due to the aspiration of the D), Leevy (by abbreviation) and MacNulty, or in Irish, Mac an Ultaigh, i.e., son of the Ulidian (Ultach). Under date 1395 the Four Masters call the then Chief

Physician of Tir Conaill Paul Ultach; and again for 1586 they record the death of Owen Ultach (i.e. MacDonlevy) who excelled as a medical doctor. The MacDonlevys were originally a royal family of Ulidia (Down and South Antrim) but never recovered from their disastrous defeat by John de Courcy in 1177, though their chief was still officially styled Rex Hibernicorum Ultoniae in 1273. After that they migrated to Tirconnell (Donegal) where they became hereditary physicians to the O'Donnells; and one branch went to Scotland where their descendants are now known as Dunlop and Dunlief. Cormac McDonlevy, one of these hereditary physicians, was a man of note in the fifteenth century on account of his translations of Gaulterus and other medical works into Irish. In the eighteenth century Rev. Andrew Donlevy, D.D., LL.D. (1694–c. 1761), who was Superior of the Irish College in Paris from 1728 to 1746, compiled a catechism in Irish and English and also collaborated with Walter Harris, the historian, who is best known for his work on the Ware manuscripts. Dr. Donlevy was born in Co. Sligo, in which county, not far from Tirconnell, the name Dunleavy is principally found at the present time. Father Christopher Dunlevy, O.F.M. was martyred in 1644.

Arms illustrated on Plate VIII.

MacDONNELL.

McDonnells are to be found widely distributed at the present day all over Ireland and, without including the cognate surname McDonald in the count, the McDonnells in Ireland number nearly ten thousand persons. These have three distinct origins. The most numerous are descendants of a Scottish clan from Argyle whose chief was known as Lord of the Isles. They came to Ireland in the thirteenth century as a military body and having established themselves as gallowglasses to the most power-ful chiefs in the north of Ireland, they gradually acquired territory of their own both as grants for military service and by marriage, and by the middle of the fifteenth century were firmly established in the Glens of Antrim, having largely displaced the MacQuillans. Randal MacSorley MacDonnell, the head of this family, was created Earl of Antrim in 1620. The christian name Randal is of frequent occurrence in their pedigree. Some MacDonnells of Ulster are, however, a distinct Gaelic Irish sept, belonging to Co. Fermanagh, but these would appear to be almost extinct now. Another quite distinct sept of MacDonnells are those of Thomond, who were, before the Gaelic way of life was disrupted by English invasion, bards to the O'Briens. MacDonnells are still found there in Co. Clare. These descend from Domhnall, son of King Murtagh Mór O'Brien. The name in Irish is Mac Domhnaill meaning son of Domhnall (*anglice* Donal). In the seventeenth century the anglicized form Mac-Daniell was more usual than MacDonnell.

There have been many distinguished bearers of the name. In war the most famous were Sorley Boy MacDonnell (1505–1590), a lifelong foe of the English and often successful in his engagements with them, Alastar " Colkitto " MacDonnell, intrepid foe of the Cromwellians killed in action in 1647, and Francis MacDonnell (1656–1702), of the Wild Geese in Austria ; in politics Eneas MacDonnell (1783–1858), of the Catholic Association and Sir Anthony (later Lord) MacDonnell (1844–1915), the devolutionist ; in literature Eneas (q.v. *supra*), Seán Clárach MacDonnell (1691–1754), who was acknowledged by his contemporaries as the supreme poet of Munster, and John de Courcy MacDonnell (1859–1915), notable in Celtic Studies. Alexander MacDonnell (1798–1835), was world chess champion in 1833.

Arms illustrated on Plate VIII.

O'DONNELL.

The O'Donnells have always been both numerous and eminent in Irish life. They are of course chiefly associated with Tirconaill (Donegal) the habitat of the largest and best known O'Donnell sept ; but, as the present distribution of persons of the name implies, there were quite distinct O'Donnell septs in other parts of the country, two of which require special mention, viz. that of Corcabaskin in West Clare, and another, a branch of the Ui Máine (Hy Many) in Co. Galway. All of these descend from some ancestor named Domhnall (*anglice* Donal) and are Ó Domhnaill in Irish. The Donal particularized in the case of the great Tirconaill sept, who died in 901, was himself descended from the famous Niall of the Nine Hostages. Their predominance only dates from the thirteenth century : prior to that they were located in a comparatively restricted area around Kilmacrenan, Co. Donegal. With a total of nearly 13,000 the O'Donnells are among the fifty most common names in Ireland. They have produced many illustrious figures in Irish history, as soldiers, churchmen, authors and politicians. The most famous was Hugh Roe O'Donnell (Red Hugh) (1571–1602), Chief of the Name, whose escape from captivity in Dublin Castle makes an adventure story beloved of young and old. After several brilliant victories over the English army he participated in the disaster at Kinsale and, retiring to Spain, was poisoned, it is said, by one Blake an English agent. Hugh Balderg O'Donnell (d. 1704), Daniel O'Donnell (1666–1735), Calvagh O'Donnell (d. 1566) and Manus O'Donnell (d. 1654), were other soldiers of note in Ireland and on the continent. Rory O'Donnell, first Earl of Tyrconnell, (1575–1608), of the " Flight of the Earls " and Sir Niall Garv O'Donnell (1569–1626), whose activities in Ireland caused him to spend 27 years incarcerated in the Tower of London, were close relatives of Red Hugh, as was the adventurous Mary Stuart O'Donnell (1608–1649).

The Annals are full of the exploits of O'Donnell chiefs and military leaders in the north-west of Ireland, while in more recent times notable O'Donnells have been Frank Hugh O'Donnell, M.P. (1848–1916), John Francis O'Donnell (1837–1874), of the *Nation* and at least three remarkable ecclesiastics, viz. Dr. James Louis O'Donnell, bishop, " the apostle of Newfoundland," Father Hugh O'Donnell (1739–1814), first P.P. of Belfast, and Cardinal Patrick O'Donnell (1856–1927), at one time the youngest bishop in the world. The O'Donnells, Dukes of Tetuan in Spain, are descended from our Tirconaill O'Donnells.

Arms illustrated on Plate VIII.

O'DONNELLAN, Donlon.

The O'Donnellans were a sept of the Ui Máine. They belong, therefore, by origin to the south-eastern part of Co. Galway where the place name Ballydonnellan perpetuates their connexion with the district between Ballinasloe and Loughrea. They claim descent from Domhnallán, lord of Clan Breasail. The original castle of Ballydonnellan is reputed to have been built by them in 936 A.D. ; it was certainly rebuilt by them in 1412 after being destroyed by fire. They are chiefly known as ollavs or poets, many of whom are mentioned in the " Annals of the Four Masters," the " Annals of Connacht" etc. The best known of them was Brian Mac Owen O'Donnellan (fl. c. 1610), poet to MacWilliam of Clanricard, whom Hyde describes as one of the last of the classic poets. His contemporary, Rt. Rev. Nehemiah Donellan (d. 1609), Protestant Archbishop of Tuam, also a Co. Galway man, translated a great part of the New Testament into Irish. He was the direct descendant of Chiefs of the Name, of Ballydonnellan, and ancestor of the Donelans of Sylanmore, Tuam. The majority of the Donelans of this line reverted to the Catholic faith. The name is quite common to-day in Co. Galway and also in the adjacent counties of Clare and Mayo.

It is also spelt Donlan and Donlon. In Irish it is Ó Domhnalláin, indicating descent from the Domhnallán mentioned above.

Arms illustrated on Plate VIII.

O'DONNELLY.

According to the latest available statistics there are not far short of ten thousand persons of the name of Donnelly in Ireland to-day, which places this name among the sixty-five most numerous in the country. Practically all these may be regarded as belonging to the Ulster Donnelly sept—Ó Donnghaile of Cinel Eoghan. This is of the same stock as the O'Neills, the eponymous ancestor of the sept being Donnghaile O'Neill, seventeenth in descent from Niall the Great, ancestor of the royal house of O'Neill. Their territory lay first in Co. Donegal and later further eastwards, centered around the place called Ballydonnelly, Co. Tyrone, which was named from them. The place name Ballydonnelly also occurs twice in that part of Co. Antrim which adjoins Co. Tyrone. This area is still the part of Ireland in which they are most numerous. Their chief was hereditary marshal of O'Neill's military forces and they were noted soldiers in early times, one of the most famous of them, Donnell O'Donnelly, being killed at the battle of Kinsale (1603). Another, Patrick Modardha O'Donnelly, out in 1641, captured the castle of Ballydonnelly from Lord Caulfield. It was subsequently renamed Castle Caulfield. Another sept called in English O'Donnelly, but in Irish Ó Donnghalaigh, belonged to Lower Ormond in Co. Tipperary, but as there appear to be few survivors of it to-day it can be dismissed with a bare mention.

In modern times prominent Donnellys are connected with the U.S.A. rather than Ireland the country of their origin, e.g. Charles Francis Donnelly (1836–1909), the Catholic lawyer ; Ignatius Donnelly (1831–1901), politician and reformer ; and the last named's sister Eleanor Cecilia Donnelly (1838–1917), author of many Catholic devotional works.

Arms illustrated on Plate VIII.

MacDONOGH, (Donaghy).

Like so many well known Irish surnames, especially where like MacDonagh (Irish Mac Donnchadha, i.e. son of Donnchadh, or Donagh) they are formed from a common christian or personal name, MacDonagh is one which came into being independently in two widely separated parts of the country. We usually find the modern descendants of these original ancestors in considerable numbers in the territory of their origin (or, where dispossessed by invasion, in the territory of their subsequent settlement). MacDonagh, however, would appear at first sight to be an exception to that general rule. That MacDonagh sept whose chiefs in Co. Cork held the strong castle of Kanturk and were known as Lords of Duhallow, was a branch of the MacCarthys. The name MacDonagh is now rare there but there is reason to believe that these MacDonaghs in many cases assumed the surname MacCarthy. Taking the last year for which statistics are available we find that of 174 MacDonagh births registered in the period only eleven were in Munster and nine in Ulster, while as many as 141 were in Connacht. As Leinster includes Dublin the 13 recorded for that province may well be the children of Connacht residents in the capital. It is clear from this that the other MacDonagh sept has survived vigorously in the province of its origin.

These MacDonaghs were a branch of the great MacDermot clan, whose chiefs long held sway in Counties Sligo and Roscommon : the MacDonagh chiefs were lords of Corran or Tireril in Co. Sligo. In this note the name has been spelled MacDonagh throughout, but in fact only 100 of the 174 births referred to above were so entered, the other 74 being given as MacDonogh, MacDonough etc. Though lack of uniformity in the spelling of names has little significance prior to the introduction of compulsory registration in 1864, it is noticeable that three individuals who may be cited as noteworthy Irishmen of the name each used a different spelling. John MacDonogh (1779–1850), the Irish-born American philanthropist, is best remembered for his efforts on behalf of slaves ; Thomas MacDonough (1783–1825), another Irish-American, was a naval officer who greatly distinguished himself at the battle of Plattsburg ; while in our own times Thomas MacDonagh (1878–1916), was not only a poet of distinction but also a leader of the Rising of Easter 1916 and a signatory of the Declaration of Independence, being one of those who was a victim of the long-drawn out executions which followed that event. In the military sphere Andrew MacDonagh (b. 1738), who accompanied Wolfe Tone in the Bantry Bay expedition in 1796, was of a Sligo family which was able to boast that forty of its members served France in the Irish Brigade.

The Ulster surname Donaghy, common in Tyrone and Derry, is a variant of MacDonagh.

Arms illustrated on Plate IX.

O'DONOGHUE, Donohoe, Dunphy.

Donoghue or Donohoe, more properly O'Donoghue, is one of the most important as well as the most numerous names in Ireland. In Irish Ó Donnchadha, it denotes descendant of Donnchadh, *anglice* Donogh, a personal name. Several distinct septs of the name existed in early times. Of these the principal are O'Donoghue of Desmond, O'Donoghue of Ui Máine (Hy Many) and O'Donoghue of Co. Cavan. The modern representatives of the two latter usually spell the name Donohoe, and are still found plentifully in Counties Galway and Cavan, while the first-named are mostly in Counties Kerry and Cork, i.e. in the Desmond country. These are of the same stock as the O'Mahonys, descended from Domhnall son of the King of Munster who took part in the battle of Clontarf in 1014. They were originally in West Cork, but having been driven into Kerry by the MacCarthys, they became very powerful in that county, and a district called Onaght O'Donoghue perpetuates their occupation. The sept split into two branches, the head of one being styled O'Donoghue Mór, with his seat on Lough Leine at Ross Castle (still one of the tourist attractions near Killarney) ; the other was O'Donoghue of the Glen.

O'Donoghue Mór's estates were confiscated during the Elizabethan wars, but O'Donoghue of the Glen held on at Glenflesk and the present head of the family is one of the few Chiefs of the Name recognized officially in Ireland as eligible to use that designation, i.e. to be called in popular parlance " The O'Donoghue ". Geoffrey O'Donoghue of the Glen, one of the leading Gaelic poets and scholars of the seventeenth century, if not himself Chief of the Name was most probably son of the chieftain Geoffrey O'Donoghue (d. 1678). Another minor O'Donoghue sept belonged to Ossory but these are now called Dunphy. A hundred years ago the peasantry there were still O'Donoghue, and Dunphy was " genteel ". Dunphy, however, is recorded in the census of 1659 as one of the principal Irish names in the barony of Iverk, Co. Kilkenny.

Like all the great Irish families O'Donoghues distinguished themselves in the armies of continental powers in the eighteenth century. In Spain the name became O'Donoju—Juan O'Donoju (1751–1821) was the last Spanish ruler of Mexico. Donnchadh Ó Donnchadha founded Jerpoint Abbey at the end of the twelfth century. Several O'Donoghues distinguished themselves in the nineteenth century in politics and literature. John O'Donoghue (1812–1893) was the author of *A Historical Memoir of the O'Briens* and other works ; Patrick Donahoe (1811–1901) was founder and first editor of the *Boston Pilot*, while David James O'Donoghue (1866–1917), author of *The Poets of Ireland* etc., was a well-known librarian and research worker.

Arms illustrated on Plate IX.

O'DONOVAN.

There are few families about which we have more authentic information than the O'Donovans, for not only have the Genealogical Office a verified pedigree of the eldest branch from Gaelic times, when they held a semi-royal position, to the present day, but also the notes of Dr. John O'Donovan, one of Ireland's most distinguished antiquarians and a member of a junior branch of the same sept, are available to us. Their place of origin is Co. Limerick, but shortly after the Norman invasion they were forced to migrate to south-west Co. Cork and it is with that area that they have since been chiefly associated. There lives the present officially recognized " Chief of the Name " and there are found the greatest number of persons of the name. In fact, according to the latest available returns of the Registrar General of Births, of 211 births registered in that year, 194 were in Munster and of these 175 were in Co. Cork. From this we may estimate that there are nearly 9,000 persons of the name in Ireland at the present day. An increasing number of these prefix the O to the name : sixty years ago less than two per cent did so. Dr. John O'Donovan, mentioned above, came from Co. Kilkenny where a branch of the sept was also established and spread into Co. Wexford. As a power in the land the O'Donovans were ruined by their adhesion to the Catholic cause in the time of James II. Following his defeat many of them took service in the Irish Brigades in the continental armies. O'Donovan's Infantry was one of the foremost regiments of King James's army in Ireland.

In modern Irish the name is Ó Donnabháin and is formed from two Gaelic words *donn* (brown) and *dubhan* (a derivative of *dubh*—black).

In addition to Dr. John O'Donovan (1809–1861), referred to above, his son Edmund (1844–1883), whose adventures as journalist and soldier in foreign armies were noteworthy, may be mentioned. The most famous of the name in Irish history was Jeremiah O'Donovan (1831–1915), called Rossa, the Fenian who went to America after being released from prison. His funeral to Glasnevin cemetery, Dublin, was one of the largest ever witnessed and was the occasion of a famous and inspiring address by Padraig Pearse.

Arms illustrated on Plate IX.

O'DOOLEY.

The modern form of this name in Irish is Ó Dubhlaoich. The Four Masters write it Ó Dubhlaich, describing their chiefs in the eleventh and twelfth centuries as Lords of Fertullagh, which is in the south-eastern end of Co. Westmeath. They were driven thence by the O'Melaghlins and the Tyrrells and migrated to the Ely O'Carroll country where they acquired a footing on the western slopes of Slieve Bloom. They soon firmly established themselves there, so much so that the head of the family became the inaugurator of O'Carroll, King of Ely. The census of 1659 shows them to be very numerous in Leix and Offaly in the seventeenth century. Offaly, too is the main homeland of present day O'Dooleys, or rather Dooleys, for they seldom if ever use the prefix O in English.

The sept has produced no outstanding personality in Ireland. The name is familiar to many people outside Ireland on account of the humorous character Mr. Dooley (Irish-American saloon-keeper in Chicago), created by Finlay Peter Dunn, whose Mr. Dooley books were published between 1898 and 1919.

In "Linea Antiqua" Ó Dubhalla appears as one of the minor septs of Muskerry, Co. Cork, but this seems to be non-existent now.

O'DORAN, Dorrian.

The O'Dorans have been justly described as "the great brehon family of Leinster," but they are probably better known as traditional antiquarians who kept in their possession from generation to generation one of the three manuscript copies of the " Tripartite Life of St. Patrick ". Originally one of the Seven Septs of Leix, whose leading members were transplanted to Kerry in 1609, they are still found in considerable numbers in Leinster, but rather in Co. Wexford than in their original territory. In 1540 they were seated at Chappell, Co. Wexford, now a well farmed area but then almost a wilderness, with the Blackstairs Mountain in the background. At that time the English accused them of " succouring rebellious plunderers in their judicial [brehon] capacity." A generation later, however, they were actually consulted by the Lord Deputy on a question of government administration ; and in 1608 they are listed as among the principal gentlemen of Co. Wexford. The place-name Doransland emphasizes their association with that county.

They were formerly called O'Deoran in English, the Irish form of the name being Ó Deoráin, itself a contraction of the earlier Ó Deoradháin, which is possibly derived from *deoradh*, an exile.

Dorans are also fairly numerous to-day in counties Armagh and Down, in which counties a sept of the name was early established. A variant of the name found in that area is Dorrian, e.g. Most Rev. Patrick Dorrian (1814–1885), for many years Bishop of Down and Connor. A century earlier the see was held by Edward O'Doran. From Oriel, too, came Dr. John Doran (1807–1878), the poet and historian ; while from the main sept in Leix came Maurice Doran, the Bishop of Leighlin who in 1523 was murdered by his archdeacon, one of the Kavanaghs. Also of the main sept was Charles Guilfoyle Doran (1835–1909), Fenian and book collector, whose voluminous writings, as well as long residence, closely identified him with Cork.

Arms illustrated on Plate IX.

O'DOWD, Dowda, Doody, (Duddy).

This is one of the O names with which the prefix has been widely retained, O'Dowd being more usual than Dowd. Other modern variants are O'Dowda and Dowds, with Doody, another synonym, found around Killarney. All are Ó Dubhda (pronounced O'Dooda) in Irish, the root word being *dubh* black. The sept traces its descent from Fiachra, brother of Niall of the Nine Hostages, through Daithi, the last pagan King of Ireland. For centuries they were the leading sept of the northern Ui Fiachrach. Their territory at its widest embraced the baronies of Erris and Tirawley in Mayo and Tireragh in Sligo. They were considerably reduced by the Anglo-Norman incursion into Connacht in the thirteenth century but were still powerful and in 1354 Sen-Bhrian O'Dowd succeeded in driving all the Anglo-Norman settlers out of Tireragh for a time. The name has been well represented in its original homeland throughout the centuries up to the present day.

A quite distinct minor sept of Ó Dubhda was located in Co. Derry. Survivors of this in Ulster to-day are usually called Duddy.

Several O'Dowds were bishops of the see of Killala. Father John O'Duada, who was tortured and hanged in 1579 was one of the many Irish Franciscan martyrs. Many of the name appear in the ranks of the Confederate Catholics and, later in the seventeenth century, in King James's army. The head of the sept at that time, who was killed at the battle of the Boyne, is said to have been seven feet tall, and it is noteworthy that great height is a feature of this family. In more recent times the best known is Rev. Patrick Dowd (1813–1891), the Irish priest who did so much for the Catholic community of Montreal.

Arms illustrated on Plate IX.

O'DOWLING.

The Dowlings are one of the " Seven Septs of Leix", the leading members of which were transplanted to Tarbert on the border of north Kerry and west Limerick in 1609. This transplantation did not affect the rank and file of the sept who multiplied in their original territory : this lay along the western bank of the River Barrow, anciently called Fearann ua n-Dunlaing i.e. O'Dowling's country. Thence they spread eastwards through Counties Carlow and Kilkenny (where they are most numerous to-day) and even as far as Co. Wicklow—there are no less than four town-lands called Ballydowling in the Rathdrum area of Co. Wicklow. The transplantation to Kerry had little permanent effect as regards numbers ; nevertheless, two or three of the many Dowlings of distinction, nearly all of whom were connected with literary activities in some form, were Kerrymen : viz. Bartholomew Dowling (1823–1863), author of *The Brigade of Fontenoy* and his brother William Dowling, a poet identified with America rather than with his own country ; Most Rev. Austin Dowling (1868–1930), Archbishop of St. Paul's, U.S.A., was of a family which emigrated from Co. Kerry or Co. Limerick. All the others were natives of Leix or one of the adjoining counties. Among these we may mention Vincent Dowling (1787–1844), colonial judge and author of legal treatises, and Vincent George Dowling (1785–1852), founder, and editor for nearly thirty years, of *Bell's Life* and also of *Fistiana*, publications which were carried on in turn by his son Frank Lewis Dowling (1821–1867) ; Richard Dowling (1846–1898), novelist and editor of the Dublin humorous journals *Zozimus* and *Ireland's Eye*, was also a Leix man, as was Dr. Jeremiah Dowling (1830–1906), author of *The Claddagh Boatman ;* and, to go back some three centuries, there was Thady Dowling (1544–1628), annalist and Irish language grammarian.

Arms illustrated on Plate IX.

O'DOWNEY, (MacEldowney).

The O'Downeys were of some importance in early mediaeval times, when there were two distinct septs of Ó Dúnadhaigh. That of Sil Anmchadha, of the same stock as the O'Maddens, several of whom are described in the " Annals of Innisfallen," " Four Masters" etc., as lords of Sil Anmchadha, became submerged as early as the twelfth century : their descendants, however, are still found in quite considerable numbers in that country (i.e. Co. Galway). Though the prefix O is now quite obsolete in English in the case of Downey, in the Irish language Ó Dúnadhaigh is sometimes Mác Dunadhagh in Co. Galway. This, of course, would be anglicized as MacDowney. MacDowney, however, which is actually to be found in Ulster, though a rare name even there, is the anglicized form of quite a different surname, viz. Mac Giolla Domhnaigh, usually rendered MacEldowney in English and sometimes simply Downey. Families named Downey in Ulster are presumably of this origin. MacEldowney is essentially a Co. Derry name, seldom found elsewhere.

As well as the Galway sept there was a more important sept of Ó Dúnadhaigh which was located in Luachair of which their chiefs were lords : they are mentioned as such by O'Heerin who died in 1420. Luachair is the old name of a district lying on the borders of three modern counties, viz. Cork, Kerry, and Limerick ; and, appropriately enough, it is in these counties that families of Downey are mostly found to-day. Some of this sept have anglicized their name as Downing, a well-known name in Co. Kerry.

In modern times few Downeys have been noteworthy. The best known was Most Rev. Richard Downey (1881–1953), Archbishop of Liverpool.

DOYLE, (MacDowell).

Doyle, never found as O'Doyle in modern times, stands high in the list of Irish surnames arranged in order of numerical strength, holding twelfth place with approximately 21,000 souls out of a population of something less than 4½ millions. Though now widely distributed it was always most closely associated with the counties of south-east Leinster (Wicklow, Wexford and Carlow) in which it is chiefly found to-day, as it is in the records of the fifteenth, sixteenth and seventeenth centuries.

The statement that the name is derived from the Irish word *doilbh* (meaning dark, gloomy, melancholy) may be discounted ; it is generally accepted that the correct derivation is *dubh-ghall*, i.e. dark foreigner, and the name in Irish is always written Ó Dubhghaill. As Dubhghall it appears in the " Annals of the Four Masters " at various dates between 978 and 1013. The family is not included in the great Gaelic genealogies, which supports the traditional belief that the eponymous ancestor is in this case a descendant of one of the Norsemen who settled in Ireland in pre-Norman times ; and the fact that Doyles are and were always more numerous in areas adjacent to the sea coast, where Norse settlements existed, tends to confirm this view. Dubh-ghall, it may be mentioned, is the word used in early times to denote a Norseman or Scandinavian. One authority, however, Rev. John Francis Shearman, asserts that the eponymous ancestor of the east Leinster Doyles was Dubhgilla, son of Bruadar, King of Idrone (Co. Carlow) in 851.

There is reason to believe that at the time surnames came into being in Ireland, that is to say for the most part the eleventh and twelfth centuries, more than one quite distinct family acquired that of Ó Dubhghaill or Doyle. It should be added that there is no reliable evidence for the claim which is sometimes made that some Doyles are an offshoot of the great Decies sept of O'Phelan.

Doyle in Ulster is sometimes found as a synonym of MacDowell—Mac Dubhghaill in Irish—a family which came to Ireland as gallowglasses from the Hebrides : the name there is MacDugall. The principal settlement of this family was in Co. Roscommon.

The first bridge built over the Liffey in Dublin was constructed by an O'Doyle. It was, however, in the nineteenth century that men of the name were particularly prominent, none more so than the famous " J.K.L."—James Doyle (1786–1834), Bishop of Kildare and Leighlin, that champion of the Catholic cause. Another outstanding churchman was Father William Doyle, S.J. (1873–1917) ; while the best known outside Ireland was undoubtedly Arthur Conan Doyle (1859–1930), the creator of Sherlock Holmes. His grandfather was Dublin born John Doyle (1797–1868), the famous " H.B." of *Punch*, who resigned his lucrative position on the staff of that well known weekly because of its anti-Catholic bias and it is worthy of note that five closely related Doyles of this branch are included in the *Dictionary of National Biography*, a distinction equalled by very few other families.

Arms illustrated on Plate IX.

O'DRISCOLL.

Few if any families have been so continuously and exclusively associated with the territory of their origin as the Driscolls or O'Driscolls. They belong to Co. Cork. At first they were concentrated in south Kerry but pressure by the O'Sullivans drove them eastwards and they settled then around Baltimore in south-west Cork. There they remained, though pressure by the O'Mahonys and O'Donovans further reduced the extent of their territory. In 1460 the chief of the sept founded the Franciscan monastery there. Their eponymous ancestor was Eidersceoil, the surname being Ó hEidersceoil, later corrupted to Ó Drisceoil. Eidersceoil, who was born about

910 A.D., was descended from Lughaidh Laidhe the principal progenitor of the Corca Laoidhe clan. This clan or group name was applied to that part of Co. Cork embraced by the diocese of Ross. The many septs comprised in it can be seen by reference to the folded map, which shows the locations of the families. The territorial importance of the O'Driscolls waned in the seventeenth century, but many of their leading men were prominent in the army of James II in Ireland. Cornelius O'Driscoll, the son of one of these, when a colonel in the Irish Brigade, greatly distinguished himself at the battle of Ondara in 1707. Notwithstanding successive confiscations members of the sept continued to live in their homeland and it is remarkable that, according to the most recent statistics available, 120 out of 121 Driscoll births recorded for the year were in Munster and nearly all of these in Co. Cork.

O'Driscoll is a notable example of the resumption of the prefixes O and Mac to surnames from which they had been dropped during the two centuries of Gaelic depression. Current directories etc. reveal the fact that the O'Driscolls recorded outnumber the Driscolls by 10 to 1 and in the *Irish Catholic Directory* there are no priests without the prefix while eleven O'Driscolls are inserted. A similar comparison for sixty years ago shows ten times as many Driscolls as O'Driscolls.

Arms illustrated on Plate IX.

O'DUFFY, Duhig, Dowey.

The name Duffy or O'Duffy is widespread in Ireland : it is among the fifty commonest surnames ; standing first in the list for Co. Monaghan, it is also very numerous in north Connacht. It is found in Munster to some extent but there it often takes the form Duhig, while in parts of Donegal it has become Doohey and Dowey. These variants arose from local pronunciations of the Irish Ó Dubhthaigh, a surname in which the root word is *dubh* (black).

There were several distinct septs of O'Duffy. One belongs to the parish of Lower Templecrone in the diocese of Raphoe, Co. Donegal, the patron saint of which is the seventh century Saint Dubhthach, or Duffy. His kinsmen the O'Duffys were erenaghs and coarbs there for eight hundred years. The Connacht sept, the centre of whose territory was Lissonuffy or Lissyduffy near Strokestown, named after them, was remarkable for the number of distinguished ecclesiastics it produced, particularly in the twelfth and thirteenth centuries. Among the many abbots and bishops whose names are recorded in the Annals and in the Rental of Cong Abbey, compiled by Tadhg O'Duffy in 1501, the most noteworthy were Cele (also called Cadhla and Catholicus) O'Duffy, Archbishop of Tuam, who was King Roderick O'Connor's ambassador to Henry II in 1175, and Muiredagh O'Duffy (1075–1150), also Archbishop of Tuam. This family was much occupied with ecclesiastical art and was

130

responsible for making the famous Cross of Cong. They are traditionally believed to have originally been located in east Leinster, of the same stock as the O'Byrnes and O'Tooles. The same origin is claimed for the O'Duffys of Monaghan. There, too, they were remarkable for their contribution to the Church; but in this case not for mediaeval dignitaries, but for the extraordinary number of parish clergy of the name: for example, in the lists of priests and sureties compiled for Co. Monaghan in accordance with the Penal Laws in the eighteenth century Duffy is by far the most numerous name. One other priest must be mentioned, though he has no apparent connexion with these, since he was vicar of Tubrid in the diocese of Waterford, viz. Father Eugene (or Owen) O'Duffy (c. 1527–1615), a famous preacher who always used the Irish language in his sermons: he was the author of the well-known satire on the apostate bishop Miler Magrath.

In other spheres O'Duffys have distinguished themselves in the nineteenth and twentieth centuries. Among these we may mention Edward Duffy (1840–1868), the leading Fenian in Connacht, who died in an English prison; Monaghan born James Duffy (1809–1871), the founder of the well-known Dublin publishing firm; and three members of the Gavan Duffy family (which, by the way, is not a hyphenated name)—Sir Charles Gavan Duffy (1816–1903), also of a Co. Monaghan family, founder of the Young Ireland party and *The Nation* newspaper, subsequently Prime Minister of Victoria, Australia; his son John Gavan Duffy (1844–1917), also an member of the Victoria government, though born in Dublin; and of the third generation a very prominent figure in modern Irish politics, George Gavan Duffy (1882–1951), one of the signatories of the Anglo-Irish Treaty of 1922 and later President of the High Court of Justice of Ireland.

The Mayo surname Ó Doithe, formerly anglicized O'Diff, presents an example of the absorption of uncommon names by common ones: the O'Diffs have now become generally Duffys and so are hardly distinguishable from the O'Duffys of the adjoining county of Roscommon.

O'DUGGAN, O'Dugan.

Duggan, in Irish Ó Dubhagáin, is in some places given in English speech approximately the Irish pronunciation viz. Doogan. The prefix O, dropped in the seventeenth century, has not been resumed. Apart from Dublin the name is now almost entirely confined to Munster, especially the Counties Cork, Tipperary and Waterford; in the seventeenth century it was very numerous in Co. Tipperary. This is as might be expected, because the principal sept of O'Dugan originated in the area around the modern town of Fermoy, where in pre-Norman times its chief was lord of the territory later known as Roche's Country : this borders on the Co. Tipperary. One other sept of O'Dugan was notable : that belonging to the Ui Máine, though not of the same stock as the O'Kellys, which has left its mark not only in some distinguished descendants, but also in the place name Ballyduggan near Loughrea. To that sept belonged John O'Dugan (d. 1372), co-author of the celebrated " Topographical Poems " and author of the valuable work known in English as " The Tribes and Customs of Hy Many." He was one of the hereditary historians and poets to the O'Kellys. A later Gaelic poet Maurice O'Dugan is remembered for the words he put to the air "An Chúil Fhionn." Of the Hy Many sept, too, was Most Rev. Patrick Duggan (1813–1896), Bishop of Clonfert, who was tried for his part in the Galway election of 1872, and acquitted. Peter Paul Duggan (d. 1861), was a historian who attained some fame in America as an artist and it is probable that Augustine Joseph Hickey Duganne (1823–1884), American poet and story writer, was of Irish origin.

Arms illustrated on Plate IX.

O'DUNN, Dunn.

In Irish Ó Duinn or Ó Doinn (*doinn* is the genitive case of the adjective *donn*—brown) it is more often written Dunne than Dunn in English. The form O'Doyne, common in the seventeenth century, is now almost obsolete. In fact of 364 births registered for them in a given year, 313 had the final E and only 51 were Dunn. From this it can be estimated that the total number of people so called in Ireland to-day is approximately 15,000, giving them twenty-seventh place in the list of commonest surnames in Ireland. This sept originated in Co. Leix (Queen's County) and formed one of the principal families of Leinster, their chiefs being lords of Iregan in that county. The sept is one of those specially mentioned in the mid-sixteenth century official orders as hostile and dangerous to the English interest. It is in that part of the country that Dunnes are, appropriately, now to be found in greatest numbers, though they have spread far and wide. Nearly all those who spell the name Dunn come from Ulster. This is a name to which the practice during the present century of resuming the discarded prefixes Mac and O does not apply—the form O'Dunn or O'Dunne is seldom if ever seen to-day. At least one of the name is to be found in the gallery of famous Irishmen, viz., Gillananaomh Ó Duinn (1102–1160), the historian and poet. One was killed at the battle of Aughrim in 1691. Another very active Jacobite was James O'Dunne (c. 1700–1758), Bishop of Ossory, most of whose life was spent in France, in the service of which country several of his relatives distinguished themselves as diplomatists and soldiers. In modern times Charles Dunn

(1799–1872), was a notable judge in the U.S.A. ; and Col. Humphrey O'Dunne was famous for his bravery in the attack on Savannah in 1774. The Irish-American author, Finlay Peter Dunn, has been noticed in the article on Dooley (q.v. p. 125 *supra*). Sir Patrick Dun (1642–1713), five times President of the Royal College of Physicians, Ireland, and Irish M.P., whose memory is perpetuated in Sir Patrick Dun's Hospital, Dublin, was of a Scottish family.

Arms illustrated on Plate X.

O'DWYER.

The O'Dwyers (in Irish Ó Duibhir, descendant of Duibhir) were an important sept in Co. Tipperary, though not comparable in power or extent of territory with the neighbouring great septs. Their lands were in Kilnamanagh, the mountainous area lying between the town of Thurles and the county Limerick. The O'Dwyers were always noted for their staunch resistance to English aggression and many are recorded in this connexion in mediaeval and early modern times. Coming down to 1798, Michael Dwyer (1771–1816) defied the English Government forces for five years : his end, after being sentenced to transportation following his voluntary surrender in 1803, was to become a policeman in Australia. In our own day, Most Rev. Edward O'Dwyer (1842–1917), the Bishop of Limerick, endeared himself to the people of Ireland by his manly stand on behalf of Sinn Féin and the men of 1916. In America Joseph O'Dwyer (1841–1898) was noted as a pioneer physician, particularly in regard to the treatment of diphtheria. William O'Dwyer (b. 1890) also had a remarkable career : starting as an emigrant labourer from Co. Mayo he became Mayor of New York and one of the most notable of United States ambassadors. A very full account of this sept is given in *The O'Dwyers of Kilnamanagh* by Sir Michael O'Dwyer.

Arms illustrated on Plate X.

MacEGAN, Keegan.

In Irish Egan is MacAodhagáin (from the christian name Aodh, *anglice* Hugh), and the surname is really MacEgan, though the prefix Mac is rarely used in modern times except by the family which claims to be head of the sept. The MacEgans were hereditary lawyers : beginning as a brehon family among the Ui Máine (Hy Many) septs, they eventually became dispersed. They settled chiefly in Ormond, i.e. the wide territory comprising all or part of the counties of Tipperary, Kilkenny and Offaly, where they continued to follow their traditional calling and acted as brehons to the chiefs. The most important of these was MacEgan, chief brehon to O'Connor Faly.

Owen Mac Egan (1570–1603), bishop-designate of Ross, was a prominent supporter of Tyrone in the Elizabethan wars and was killed in battle ; other illustrious churchmen were Most Rev. Boetius Egan (1734–1798), Archbishop of Tuam, who, however, was opposed to the Rising of '98 : Most Rev. Cornelius Egan (1780–1856), Bishop of Kerry, and Most Rev. Michael Egan (1761–1814), Bishop of Philadelphia. Two Pierce Egans (1772–1849 and 1814–1880), were popular novelists in their day. John Egan (1750–1810), patriot member of Parliament, was notorious also for his propensity to duelling. In our own day " the MacEgan ", as he styled himself, was an artist noted for his striking portraits of contemporary Irish national leaders.

When the prefixes Mac and O fell into disuse during the period of Gaelic submergence, in some places the C was retained and became K, resulting in Keegan, and this, in turn, gave rise to the corrupt Gaelic form Ó Caogáin now often used in Connacht as the Gaelic equivalent of Keegan. The Keegans are found to-day chiefly in two areas : in Leinster—in Counties Dublin and Wicklow—and in Connacht—in Counties Roscommon and Leitrim, i.e. in places fairly remote from the homeland of the MacEgan sept where the form Egan is always used. The poet John Keegan (1809–1849), was born in Co. Leix.

Arms illustrated on Plate X.

MacELROY, MacGilroy, Kilroy.

This name is Mac Giolla Rua in Irish, i.e. son of the red (haired) youth. The sept originated in Co. Fermanagh where the place name Ballymackilroy is found : their territory was on the east side of Lough Erne. There is another Ballymackilroy in Tyrone and a Ballymacilroy in Co. Antrim. In the seventeenth century census (1659) the name is recorded as very numerous in Co. Fermanagh and also in Co. Leitrim—the latter as MacGilleroy. It is still numerous in the same areas, but in Connacht the modern spelling is often Kilroy or Gilroy without the Mac. The form Kilroy is occasionally used as an anglicized form of the name Mac Giolla Riabhaigh, which has many synonyms in English—MacAreavy, Gallery, Gray etc.

The MacElroys were of some importance in Gaelic Ireland, particularly in the fifteenth century, as their frequent mention in the " Annals of the Four Masters ", " Loch Cé " etc., testifies. For notable persons of the name in modern times we must turn to America. Rev. John MacElroy, S.J. (1782–1877), a native of Co. Fermanagh, where he was educated at a hedge school and was associated with the United Irishmen in 1798, was famous in the U.S.A. as a missionary priest and church builder. Dr. Robert MacElroy (b. 1872), was a distinguished professor of history at Princeton and also at Oxford University.

134

MacENCHROE, Crowe.

The very English-looking name Crowe disguises the genuinely Irish surname McEnchroe, which in its original form is Mac Conchradha. Woulfe states that the form McEnchroe is still in use; but all the members of this sept who live in its original territory, viz. Thomond, are certainly called simply Crowe. The sept was subordinate to that of O'Dea and was located in the western part of the present barony of Inchiquin. The great majority of Crowes either hail from Clare and Tipperary or are of families which migrated to Dublin and other large urban centres from that area. The name is fairly numerous in Belfast but most of these are presumably of British planted stock, Crowe being quite a common name in England. The old form Mac-Enchroe was that almost always used in the transplantation certificates of the 1650's. In one or two cases the form MacCrowe was used. It is preserved in the motto " Skeagh mac en chroe " attached to the coat of arms of the Clare Crowes (see Plate X). It is interesting to note that there is a place-name near Mount Callan in Co. Clare called Skaghvicencrowe which means the thorn bush of MacEncroe. Some branches of the Crowe sept used a thorn bush as the main charge in their arms. The old form was still used in Co. Tipperary in the last century, e.g. by the family of Rev. John McEncroe (1795–1868), who, as well as being the founder of the *Freeman's Journal* of Sydney, is noteworthy for his edition of Donlevy's Catechism. Dermot MacEncroe (fl. 1730), author of many beautiful poems in Latin, was of a French family which had emigrated from Co. Clare and used de la Croix as a French form of MacEncroe. The best known Irish Crowe was O'Beirne Crowe of Cong, Co. Galway, who, though according to tradition he was stupid and ill-educated as a boy, became one of the first professors in the Queen's College (now University College) Galway, and was in the first rank of Gaelic scholars. Eyre Evans Crowe (1799–1868), the historian and novelist, was an Irishman, and his son, Sir Joseph Archer Crowe (1825–1896)— who was, however, reared in England—was also a man of note as a diplomat, art critic and war correspondent.

Arms illustrated on Plate X.

MacENIRY, HENRY, O'Henry, Fitzhenry.

There are some five thousand persons in Ireland to-day bearing the surname Henry—without O or Mac. The majority of these are Ulstermen formerly called O'Henery, the Irish form being Ó hInneirghe. The head of this sept was chief of Cullentra in Co. Tyrone whose territory at one time extended to the valley of Glenconkeine in Co. Derry.

Fitzhenry, sometimes abbreviated to Henry, is the name of a Norman family chiefly associated with Co. Wexford but having a branch in Connacht. The latter, becoming hibernicized like so many Norman families in Connacht, were in the sixteenth century records regarded as an Irish sept : they were tributary to the O' Flahertys of Moycullen and Ballynahinch and were called Mac Einri in Irish, which in due course was made MacHenry in English.

MacHenry is also occasionally to be found as a synonym of MacEnery, in Irish Mac Inneirghe : one of the anglicized variants of this is Kiniry which, pronounced to rhyme with the English word enquiry, is phonetically nearer to the principal form than MacEnery. The sept in question was one of the Ui Cairbre group, of the same stock as the O'Donovans : they were located in the barony of Upper Connelloe, Co. Limerick, at Corcomohid, now Castletown MacEnery. This name is still quite well known in Co. Limerick.

Three James MacHenrys are noteworthy : one (1753–1816) became an American citizen and was private secretary to George Washington ; another (1785–1845) was a poet and novelist ; the third (1816–1891), son of the foregoing, was a leading American financier. James Henry (1798–1876), a product of Trinity College, Dublin, was famous for his Virgilian researches. Mrs. Fitzhenry was a celebrated Irish actress towards the end of the eighteenth century. Augustine Henry (1857–1930), the Irish botanist, will be remembered by the names of the many species of trees and shrubs he discovered, chiefly in Asia, which bear the epithet Henryana.

Arms illustrated on Plate X.

MacEVOY, (MacElwee, MacGilloway, MacVeagh).

The MacEvoys were one of the "Seven Septs of Leix," the leading members of which were transplanted to Co. Kerry in 1609. The lesser clansmen remained in their own territory and Leix is one of the areas in which the name is found fairly commonly to-day. This sept was called Mac Fhiodhbhuidhe which is pronounced Mac-ee-vwee, whence the approximately phonetic anglicization MacEvoy. (*Buidhe*—yellow—was always written " boy " in early attempts to put Irish names into English form). Formerly chiefs of the present barony of Moygish in Co. Westmeath, this sept in early times settled in Leix and became lords of the territory now comprising the parishes of Mountrath and Raheen in that county. The MacEvoys, called Muintir Fhiodhbhuidhe, appear there in a map of Leix dated 1563. Another quite distinct Irish sept, in Gaelic Mac Giolla Buidhe, normally anglicized MacElwee and MacGilloway (names now well known in Counties Donegal and Derry), is shortened in the spoken language to Mac a'bhuidhe, hence the form MacAvoy or MacEvoy in English. Conn Mac Giolla Bhuidhe, Abbot of Mungret in 1100, was one of these. The name MacEvoy is rare in Connacht now but fairly common in Armagh and Louth. There it is a synonym of MacVeagh, i.e. Mac an bheatha, an Oriel sept. Considering their importance in the past it is remarkable that so few MacEvoys appear as distinguished individuals in any sphere of Irish history. Longford born Francis MacEvoy (1751–1804), was a distinguished President of the Royal College of Surgeons of Ireland.

Arms illustrated on Plate X.

FAGAN.

In spite of its very Irish appearance (*gan* is one of the most common terminations of Irish surnames) Fagan must be regarded (subject to a reservation to be mentioned later) as a family name of Norman origin. At the same time it must be pointed out that it is not an English name. It is derived from the Latin word *paganus*. For many centuries it has been associated with Counties Dublin and Meath. As early as the year 1200 one William Fagan was the owner of extensive house property in the city of Dublin and fifty years later we find the family firmly established in the neighbouring counties with a seat, acquired a little later, at Feltrim, Co. Dublin. A branch of this family was also found in Kerry and another in Cork City where Christopher Fagan took refuge in 1497—he had been a supporter of Perkin Warbeck's claim to the throne and Cork was solidly behind that pretender. From the Kerry branch were descended the Fagans who distinguished themselves in the service of France in the eighteenth century and were ennobled in that country. The name is not really numerous in Ireland—it is estimated that about two thousand of the population are so called : almost all of these are natives of Leinster, fifty per cent of whom are Dubliners. There is also, it is true, a Gaelic Irish family of Ó Faodhagáin, anglicized Fagan, which belongs to Co. Louth : it is a corrupt form of the well known name O'Hagan. One of these, Edmund O'Fagan, was an officer in the Ultonia regiment of the Spanish army in 1778.

The two best known Fagans in the past were Robert Fagan (1745–1816), born in Cork, who was a diplomat and portrait painter ; and James Fleming Fagan (1828–1893), American planter, soldier and public official, of Irish descent.

Arms illustrated on Plate X.

O'FAHY.

Apart from modern migrants to the larger cities it can be said that Fahy (also spelt Fahey) is almost exclusively a Co. Galway name, though of course it is also to be found in the areas bordering that county, such as north Tipperary. A sept of the Ui Máine (or Hy Many), the centre of their patrimony, which they held as proprietors up to the time of the Cromwellian upheaval and where most of them still

dwell, is Loughrea : their territory was known as Pobal Mhuintir ui Fhathaigh, which means the country inhabited by and belonging to the Fahys. In this Fahy homeland there is a place the modern name of which is Fahysvillage. Fahy is Ó Fathaigh in Irish. In some places this is anglicized Vahey instead of Fahey, and occasionally Fay which, however, is a distinct surname except in some rare instances in Co. Galway. (*Vide* p. 291 *infra*). The name Green has been used as a synonym for Fahy, a good example of the not uncommon absurd mistranslation of Irish names into English—the Irish word *faithche*, pronounced Fahy, means a green or a lawn. The obvious derivation from *fathach*, a giant, genitive *fathaigh*, is not acceptable, the name being, it is stated, derived from *fothadh*, a foundation. No person of the name is famous in Irish history : Francis Fahy, prominent in the Young Ireland movement of 1848 may, however, be mentioned. Another Francis Fahy (b. 1854) is noteworthy as the author of " The Ould Plaid Shawl " and other popular songs. The universally respected late ceann-comhairle (speaker) of Dáil Éireann, was yet another Francis Fahy (1880–1954), a veteran of the 1916–1921 War of Independence.
Arms illustrated on Plate X.

O'FALLON, Falloon.

The name Fallon or, as it is sometimes written O'Fallon, has from the beginning of history till to-day been closely associated with the counties of Galway and Roscommon, and particularly the area where these two counties adjoin. The head of this sept of the Ui Máine was chief of a territory comprising the present parishes of Camma and Dysart in the barony of Athlone, Co. Roscommon. As late as 1585 the chief was resident in Dysart parish, where the ruins of his castle are still to be seen and there are people of the name dwelling near. Not far away another branch of the family until quite recently owned estates in the Ballinasloe area and lived on them. These claim to be the direct descendants of the " Chiefs of O'Fallon's Country". The name of their place affords an example of the extent to which slavish anglicization of place names as well as surnames went during the period of Gaelic submergence : they changed the old name Runnavota into Rummimead. In pre-Norman times there was a sept of O'Fallon in Meath, but this was dispersed at the invasion. The name in the Annals and early records appears in Irish always as Ó Fallamhain, and I can find no justification for Dalton's statement that O'Fallon is a corruption of Ó Faoláin and that they came from the Decies, i.e. the O'Phelan country. Many references to O'Fallons, chiefs of Clann Udach (the territory referred to above) appear in the Annals (" Four Masters," " Loch Cé " etc.). The sept produced at least two mediaeval bishops (of Elphin and Derry). There was a remarkable family of the name in America : the father James O'Fallon (1749–1794), was born in Ireland, took part as an officer in the American War of Independence and continued his antagonism to the end as an active member, if not the founder, of the Anti-British Society. He anticipated by a century and a half the modern practice of resuming the prefixes O and Mac to Gaelic surnames from which they had been dropped through English influence. His elder son, Col. John O'Fallon (1791–1865), was well known as a philanthropist ; the other, Benjamin O'Fallon (1793–1842), was a more romantic figure, best known for his success in establishing friendly relations with the Indians ; he was called the " Father of the Tribes." Another form of the same surname, written Falloon, is found in Co. Armagh.

Arms illustrated on Plate X.

O'FARRELL, O'Ferrall.

Farrell, with and without the prefix O, is a well known name in many parts of the country and it stands thirty-fifth in the statistical returns showing the hundred commonest names in Ireland. It is estimated that there are over thirteen thousand of the name in Ireland ; the great majority of these were born in Leinster, mainly in Co. Longford and surrounding areas. This is as might be expected for the great Ó Fearghaill (O'Farrell or O'Ferrall) sept was of Annaly in Co. Longford. The chief of the sept, known as Lord of Annaly, resided at Longphuirt Ui Fhearghaill (i.e. O'Farrell's fortress), hence the name of the town and county. So important were they that references to them in the " Annals of the Four Masters " occupy more than seven columns of the index to that monumental work. There were two branches of the sept, the chiefs of which were distinguished as O'Farrell Boy (*buidhe*, i.e. yellow) and O'Farrell Bane (*bán*, i.e. white or fair).

There were a number of distinguished churchmen of the name, of whom the Capuchin Father Richard O'Farrell (c. 1615–1663), of Annaly, was perhaps the most notable. Notwithstanding the misfortunes which befell the great Gaelic families through the conquests and confiscations of the sixteenth and seventeenth centuries the O'Farrells of Annaly were not entirely submerged and many of them took a worthy part in Irish resistance to English aggression. Three sons of Ceadagh O'Ferrall of Annaly, who was killed at the Battle of the Boyne in 1690, greatly distinguished themselves as officers of the Irish Brigade in the service of France. The family settled in Picardy. Later on in the political field Richard More O'Ferrall (1797–1850) was a prominent supporter of Daniel O'Connell. Sir Thomas Farrell (1827–1900) was a noted sculptor, many of whose statues adorn the city of Dublin. The compiler of one of the best known Irish genealogical manuscripts, " Linea Antiqua " (1709) now in the Genealogical Office, Dublin, was Roger O'Ferrall.

Arms illustrated on Plate XI.

O'FARRELLY, Farley.

O'Farrelly—Ó Faircheallaigh in Irish—is the name of a Breffny sept associated in both early and modern times principally with Counties Cavan and Meath. Their leading family were erenaghs of Drumlane, Co. Cavan, and were also co-arbs of St. Mogue until the suppression of the monasteries in the sixteenth century. The Gaelic poet Feardorcha O'Farrelly (d. 1746) was born in Co. Cavan.

The O'Farrelly sept seated at Knockainy, Co. Limerick, mentioned as such by O'Heerin in his fourteenth century "Topographical Poem" and still numerous in Co. Limerick when the 1659 census was compiled, are no longer to be found there : even a century ago O'Donovan commented on the fact that they had disappeared.

In parts of Ulster Farley is used as a synonym of Farrelly, which leads to confusion since Farley is a common English name. Cardinal Farley (1842–1918), Archbishop of New York, who was born in Co. Armagh, is an example of the use of this synonym.

O'FEENEY.

Apart from the quite definite fact that it is essentially a Connacht name it is difficult to be precise in dealing with the surname Feeney. The reason for this is that in Connacht there are two different septs—Ó Fiannaidhe in Sligo and Mayo and Ó Fidhne in Galway and Roscommon ; both of these anglicized their name as Feeney so that, as all these counties are close together, it is hardly possible to determine to which sept present day Feeneys belong—the great majority of these hail from the four counties mentioned above. There are two places named Ballyfeeney, both in Co. Roscommon. The name was more numerous formerly than at present and it appears very frequently in the Elizabethan Fiants and in the census of 1659. Then as now the name was not unknown in Co. Derry—the poet Patrick Feeney (d. 1900) was born there.

O'FINN, Maginn.

The name Finn—it seldom has the prefix O in modern times—is chiefly found in Co. Cork to-day; and this was equally true in the seventeenth century, as Petty's census shows. This is curious because it is almost always a fact that names are still most numerous in the part of Ireland in which they originated. The mediaeval sources on which we chiefly depend for our information on this subject make no mention of a Munster sept of O'Finn, though the Annals record the deaths of several Munster bishops called O'Finn between 1020 and 1331. There were three authenticated O'Finn septs. One of these was of Co. Sligo, where O'Finns were chiefs of Calry on the shore of Lough Gill. The Co. Sligo place name Coolavin, now inseparably associated with the MacDermots, is in Irish Cúil Ó bhFinn, i.e. the refuge place of the O'Finns. The leading family of another sept of O'Finn were erenaghs of Kilcolgan, Co. Galway. The descendants of these are still to be found in Connacht. The third sept, that of Feara Rois in South Oriel, fades out of the records about the time of the Anglo-Norman invasion, though the name survives—probably Rev. John O'Finn, who was vicar of Granard in 1369, was one of them. The form MacFinn is used by the Four Masters for an erenagh of Clonmacnois in 1020 and it appears several times in the mediaeval diocesan registers of Meath. This name has survived, usually in the form MacFhinn or Mag Fhinn, *anglice* Maginn in Ulster, where it is quite common to-day. O'Finn is spelt the same way in both Irish and English. It is presumably derived from the word *fionn* (fair).

In modern history the best known man of the name is Edmund Finn (1767–1810), outlawed member of the United Irishmen, who served with distinction in the French army and was killed in action at Azava. Most. Rev. Edward Maginn (1802–1849), Co-adjutor Bishop of Derry, was notable for his vigorous support of the Young Ireland Movement. The Rev. Francis James Finn, S.J. (1859–1928), was the author of many popular books for boys.

O'FINNEGAN.

There are two distinct septs of Finnegan or Finegan whose name is Ó Fionnagáin in Irish, which means the descendants of Fionnagán, an old Irish personal name derived from the word *fionn*, i.e. fairheaded. One of these septs was located on the border of Counties Galway and Roscommon where are two places called Ballyfinnegan—one in the barony of Ballymoe and the second nearby in the barony of Castlereagh. The other is a Breffny sept. The present day bearers of the name—it is seldom found with its proper prefix O—hail chiefly from the localities of their origin; the majority belong to Cavan and adjacent counties, with a fair proportion to south Connacht. An entry in the "Annals of Loch Cé" telling of the destruction by the O'Byrnes in 1405 of a place called Newcastle O'Finnegan, as well as a reference in one of the Elizabethan Fiants, suggests that in mediaeval times Finnegans were also located in Co. Wicklow. Finnegans have not been prominent in the cultural or political history of Ireland. The name is, of course, familiar on account of the novel *Finnegan's Wake* by James Joyce : the title of his novel is that of an old Dublin ballad from which Joyce took it.

Arms illustrated on Plate XI.

FITZGERALD, (Barron).

The Fitzgeralds of Ireland, who are now very numerous, are said to be all descended from the famous Maurice, son of Gerald, who accompanied Strongbow in the Anglo-Norman invasion. Gerald was constable of Pembroke in Wales and was married to Nesta, Princess of Wales. Fitzgerald simply means son of Gerald—Fitz (French *fils*) becoming Mac in Irish, hence the use of Mac Gearailt as the Gaelic form of the name. There are some thirteen thousand Fitzgeralds in Ireland, principally in Munster, in all classes of life. Two of the most influential noble families in Ireland are Fitzgeralds. The Dukes of Leinster of Maynooth, Co. Kildare, known in history by their earlier titles of Earls of Kildare, are still extant. The Munster branch, headed by the Earls of Desmond, were destroyed as a great family by the devastating wars of the sixteenth century in which they played a conspicuous and leading part. Nevertheless, two branches of it have remained without intermission members of the Irish aristocracy, and are known respectively as the Knights of Glin and the Knights of Kerry. These titles are unique. Three brothers, sons of John Fitzgerald, were in the year 1333 created hereditary Knights by Desmond, by virtue of his royal seigniory as a Count Palatine, and their direct descendants still bear these designations; those of the third brother became Fitzgibbons and the head of that family was the White Knight.

So many Fizgeralds have filled the pages of Irish history that it is impossible here to do more than refer briefly to the most distinguished of them. Every one of the sixteen Earls of Desmond who held that title between 1329 and 1601 finds a place in Webb's *Compendium of Irish Biography*, and similarly all the twenty Earls of Kildare from 1316 to 1766 (when they became Dukes of Leinster) are mentioned in that work. They and their families were known historically as the Geraldines. It is believed that they are of the same stock as the noble Italian family called the Gherardini. While there are few of these thirty-six men of whom it cannot be said that they made history, two are especially memorable: Garrett Fitzgerald, the eighth Earl of Kildare (d. 1513), called the Great Earl, had a remarkable life in Ireland as soldier, Lord Deputy, supporter of Lambert Simnel, political prisoner etc. His adroitness in dealing with successive English sovereigns, with whom he was often in conflict, is typified by one incident. When called upon by Henry VII to account for his action in burning the Cathedral at Cashel he frankly replied that he would not have done so had he not been told that the Archbishop was inside. It was on this occasion that Henry, on being told that all Ireland could not govern this man, replied " then let this man govern all Ireland." Garrett's grandson, Thomas Fitzgerald (1513–1537), tenth Earl, known as " Silken Thomas " on account of the uniform of his gallowglasses, renounced his allegiance to the King of England but, after the resultant campaign, was captured and, to the amazement and consternation of the people of Ireland, was, together with his five uncles, executed at Tyburn, London. The wife of the twelfth Earl, herself a Fitzgerald by birth, called " the Old Countess," is the subject of much popular tradition : the romantic stories about her and the belief that she lived to the age of 139 years have been discounted by historical research —she was 100 years old when she died in 1604. Lord Edward Fitzgerald (1763–1798), the famous rebel, was son of the first Duke of Leinster (i.e. twentieth Earl of Kildare). Another Edward Fitzgerald was prominent in Wexford in the '98 Rising.

Since 1411, when the fifth Earl of Desmond settled at Rouen, having abandoned his Irish territory on account of the unpopularity occasioned by his marriage to a beautiful peasant girl, the Fitzgeralds of Ireland have had connexions with France. In the eighteenth century they were particularly prominent in the Irish Brigade and the Regiment of Fitzgerald won special renown in the War of Spanish Succession. The well-known French family of Giraldin is descended from an Irish emigrant called Fitzgerald.

In literature the best known of the name is Edward Fitzgerald (1809–1883), author of the *Rubaiyat of Omar Khayyam*, but his connexion with Ireland is somewhat remote. Pierce Fitzgerald (1700–1791), the Gaelic poet, however, never forsook his ancient home at Ballymacoda which he retained for his family, as his poems poignantly tell us, by forsaking the religion of his forefathers.

In addition to the spheres of politics and war, Fitzgeralds have distinguished themselves as scientists, surgeons, lawyers, colonial statesmen and even as duellists.

The ape in the crest and supporters of the Kildare arms is commemorative of an incident which occurred in the thirteenth century. Thomas, infant son of Maurice Fitzgerald, is said to have been snatched from his cradle by a tame ape which, having carried the child to the verge of the battlements at the top of the castle and terrified the family by the danger involved, safely returned him to his cradle. This traditional story is also related in a slightly different form of the first Earl of Kildare, but as the said Thomas was nicknamed Tomás an Ápa, or Thomas Simiacus, it may be ascribed to the Desmonds, if not also to their kinsmen the Kildares. The war cry of the Kildares was " Crom abu ", and of the Desmonds " Shanid abu ".

Finally two other branches of the Fitzgeralds should be briefly mentioned. Those settled in the present parish of Mayo (Co. Mayo) were called collectively the Clanmorris and so described in the Annals as late as 1446. In 1450 their chief is called MacMorris of the Bryes. Some of the Fitzgeralds in Co. Waterford, whose ancestor was baron of Burnchurch, Co. Kilkenny, assumed the surname Barron. That name is well known to-day in that part of Ireland.

Arms illustrated on Plate XI.

FITZGIBBON, Gibbons.

In treating of the surname Gibbons in Ireland it must first be mentioned that this is a very common indigenous name in England and in the course of the several plantations of English settlers in this country from 1600 onwards, as well as a result of business infiltration, it is inevitable that at least a small proportion of our Gibbonses must be of English stock. Having said that we may dismiss this element in the population and consider native Irish families bearing the name. Strictly speaking, there are no native Irish families of Gibbons, if by Irish we mean Gaelic Irish. Our Gibbonses are Norman in origin but are now as completely Irish as any of Gaelic stock. Their origin is twofold, each quite distinct, having nothing in common beyond the fact that their descent was Norman Irish not Gaelic Irish. The Gibbons families of the present day are to be found concentrated in the very parts of the country in which they originated. The most numerous are those of Co. Mayo : the ancestors of these were first known as MacGibbon Burke, being a branch of the great Norman Irish sept (for sept it was to all intents and purposes) of Burke in Co. Mayo. They are called Mac Giobúin in Irish just as if they were of Gaelic origin. Ballymacgibbon in Co. Mayo takes its name from them. The others are equally associated with a particular county, in this case Co. Limerick. There, however, though also Mac Giobúin in Irish, they are usually Fitzgibbon in English, the Fitz being frequently dropped and a final S substituted for it in speech but seldom in writing. The head of this family in Co. Limerick was known as The White Knight being one of the three hereditary knights in Desmond, unique among British and Irish titles—the other two being the Knight of Kerry and the Knight of Glin who are Fitzgeralds. Their territory prior to the upheaval of the seventeenth century was the south-eastern corner of Co. Limerick near Co. Cork. One of the Fitzgibbons (MacGibbon) was chief of Clangibbon in Co. Cork.

John Gibbons (d. 1808), a Mayo landowner, took part in the 1798 Rising, was captured, outlawed and escaped to France. His son John was hanged at Westport in 1798, and another son, Edmund (d. 1809), of the Irish Legion, died of wounds. In 1691 Thomas Gibbons, of Mayo, was also a notable outlaw. From the same stock came Cardinal James Gibbons (1834–1921), Archbishop of Baltimore, whose life work was in America. The best known of the Fitzgibbons was John Fitzgibbon (1749–1802), Lord Chancellor of Ireland, whose pro-English activity at the time of the Union made him hated in his own day and his memory reviled since. Two Gerald Fitzgibbons, father and son (1793–1882 and 1837–1909), were outstanding members of the Irish Bar, while Edward Fitzgibbon (1803–1857) wrote several standard works on subjects connected with fishing.

Arms illustrated on Plate XI.

FITZPATRICK, Kilpatrick.

This is the only surname with the prefix Fitz which is of native Irish origin, the others being Norman. The Fitzpatricks are Macgilpatricks—Mac Giolla Phádraig in Irish, meaning son of the servant or devotee of St. Patrick. In sixteenth and even seventeenth century records they are usually called MacGilpatrick or MacKilpatrick ; and in some places they are still so called, other variants being McIlpatrick, Kilpatrick, etc. : the latter is common in Ulster, where, however, it is usually of Scottish origin. Their eponymous ancestor was Giolla Pádraig, a warlike chief in Ossory who lived in the second half of the tenth century. Branches of the sept are now found in many parts of the country : nearly ten thousand persons of the name are estimated to be in Ireland to-day, widely distributed, Leix (alias Queen's Co.) having the greatest number. By far the most important was, and still is, the family whose head was for centuries during the Gaelic period known as Lord of Upper Ossory, at one time almost a royal ruler over counties Leix and Kilkenny. Their power was much reduced by the rise of the Ormond Butlers, but they were by no means dispossessed of all their patrimony. They were one of the first of the great Irish septs to submit to Henry VIII and one Sir Barnaby Fitzpatrick was knighted in 1558. They lost considerably through their loyalty to James II. Nevertheless the head of the family received a peerage in 1714 and in 1878 his descendants are recorded as possessing no less than twenty-two thousand acres of the best land in Ossory.

One branch of the Fitzpatricks of Ossory assumed the surname Mac Séartha, or Shera in English, taken from an ancestor whose christian name that was. Many variants of the name, in addition to those given above, are recorded in the modern birth registers, not only more or less obvious abbreviations like Fitz, Fitch and Patrick, but even Parrican, Parogan and Patchy!

Brian Fitzpatrick (1585–1652), Vicar Apostolic of Ossory, who was murdered by Cromwellian soldiers, was instrumental in saving the " Book of the O'Byrnes ", which he transcribed, from destruction. In modern times, apart from the Earls of Upper Ossory, several Fitzpatricks were prominent in politics, two in the English interest and another Patrick Vincent Fitzpatrick (1792–1865) was one of Daniel O'Connell's most trusted colleagues. Also worthy of mention are William John Fitzpatrick (1830–1895), the biographer, and Thomas Fitzpatrick (1832–1900), an eminent physician.

Arms illustrated on Plate XI.

O'FLAHERTY, (Laverty).

The O'Flahertys possessed the territory on the east side of Lough Corrib until the thirteenth century when, under pressure from the Anglo-Norman penetration into Connacht, they moved westwards to the other side of the lake and became established there. The head of the sept was known as Lord of Moycullen and as Lord of Iar-Connacht, which, at its largest, extended from Killary Harbour to the Bay of Galway and included the Aran Islands. The chieftaincy was continued until the beginning of the eighteenth century. The celebrated historian, Roderick or Rory O'Flaherty (1629–1718), author of *Ogygia*, was the last recognized Chief of the Name. The christian name Rory is associated with the family throughout the centuries. Other christian names much in favour with them were Brian, Donnell, Hugh and Murrough. Birth statistics show that the Flahertys and O'Flahertys are still much more numerous in their original habitat (Co. Galway) than elsewhere. The name in Irish is Ó Flaithbheartaigh. The same surname is found in Ulster, but there the initial F is aspirated thus altering the pronunciation and producing the form O'Laverty, which approximates phonetically to the aspirated Irish form. The chief of this sept was Lord of Aileach (modern Elagh, Co. Donegal). He is also described by the Four Masters as Tanist of Tyrone. The sept may be regarded as distinct from that of Iar-Connacht. The latter is now, and always was, the more important and more numerous of the two. Both have produced eminent writers—Roderick O'Flaherty has already been mentioned. Monsignor James O'Laverty (1828–1906) was another historian of note. At the present time there is Liam O'Flaherty whose works, both in English and Irish are considered to be of great merit.

Arms illustrated on Plate XI.

O'FLANAGAN.

This surname is practically the same in both its Irish and anglicized forms, being in the former Ó Flannagáin, which is probably derived from the adjective *flann* meaning reddish or ruddy. It belongs to Connacht both by origin and location (i.e. present distribution of population). Flanagan, with of course O'Flanagan, for this is one of those names with which the prefix is frequently retained, is numbered among the hundred commonest surnames in Ireland and has the sixty-ninth place on that list. The greatest number of these are found in Co. Roscommon and in the counties of the western seaboard—Mayo, Galway and Clare. They spring from one Flanagan, who was of the same stock as the royal O'Connors and his line held the hereditary post of steward to the Kings of Connacht. These, who were seated between Mantua and Elphin, represent the main O'Flanagan sept. There were also minor septs of the same name in other parts of the country which were still represented in the seventeenth century; of Toorah in north-west Fermanagh and again of the barony of Ballybrit in Offaly. Some descendants of these are still to be found in both those areas.

Donough O'Flanagan (d. 1308), Bishop of Elphin, was famous abroad as well as at home for his hospitality and devotion. Other notable Irishmen of the name were Roderick Flanagan (1828–1861), founder of the *Sydney Chronicle ;* Thomas Flanagan (1814–1865), author of the *History of the Church in England ;* and James Roderick Flanagan (1814–1900), voluminous author on Irish subjects. Theophilus O'Flanagan (1760–1818), was a leading figure in the early Gaelic revival movement.

Arms illustrated on Plate XI.

O'FLANNERY.

The name O'Flannery—or rather Flannery for the prefix O has been almost entirely discarded—is identified with two different areas. One sept of Ó Flannabhra was of the Ui Fiachrach, located at Killala, Co. Mayo ; the other, of the Ui Fidhgheinte, was one of the principal families of the barony of Connelloe, Co. Limerick. It is approximately in these districts that the Flannerys of the present day are to be found, though they may be said now to belong to North Tipperary rather than to Co. Limerick.

John O'Flannery was Bishop of Derry from 1401–1415 ; Thomas Flannery (1840–1916), also of the north Connacht sept, was a pioneer in the Gaelic revival movement. The Rev. (Dean) William Flannery (1830–1902), known as a Canadian poet and author, was born in Co. Tipperary and also died there.

FLEMING.

Fleming, as the word implies, denotes an inhabitant of Flanders, and this surname originated about the year 1200 when many Flemings emigrated to Britain, settling chiefly on the Scottish border and in Wales. Since then it has been chiefly associated with Scotland. Nevertheless it is fairly numerous in Ireland. The ancestors of our Irish Flemings did not, however, come to Ireland from Scotland at the time of the Plantation of Ulster : they were in Ireland some four centuries before that, as they came in the wake of the Normans and then acquired considerable estates in Co. Meath and elsewhere. Christopher Fleming, Lord Slane, still held the Castle of Slane in the seventeenth century, but the adhesion of the family to the cause of James II caused their ruin. Now they are scattered throughout each of the four provinces. Several of the name have been distinguished Churchmen, including Nicholas Fleming, Archbishop of Armagh from 1404 to 1416, the compiler of the

147

valuable document known as " Fleming's Register " ; Meath-born Rev. Richard Fleming, S.J. (1542–1590), professor of philosophy in Paris and other French universities, who has been described as by far the most prominent Irish theologian in the Europe of his time ; Rev. Patrick Fleming (1599–1631), Franciscan friar, author of the *Life of St. Columban*, and most Rev. Thomas Fleming (1593–1666), the Archbishop of Dublin who excommunicated Ormond. Rev. James Fleming (1830–1903), the popular preacher and writer, was, however, a Protestant. Christopher Fleming (1800—1880) was a surgeon of note. John Fleming (1815–1895), was one of the most prominent scholars in the early days of the Gaelic revival. In the Irish language Fleming is written Pléamonn.

Arms illustrated on Plate XI.

O'FLYNN, O'Lynn.

The surname O'Flynn is derived from the Gaelic personal name Flann ; the adjective *flann* denotes a dull red colour and means ruddy when applied to persons. Ó Floinn is the form of the surname in Irish. It is one of those which arose independently in several parts of the country and, as might be expected, is widely distributed. It ranks forty-first in the list of most numerous surnames in Ireland with an estimated total of thirteen thousand persons. These are found chiefly in two main areas—Cork and Waterford in the south, and on the borders of Connacht and Ulster in the adjacent counties of Roscommon, Leitrim and Cavan. Two of the O'Flynn septs originated in Co. Cork. Of these O'Flynn of Ardagh Castle (between Skibbereen and Baltimore) was a branch of the Corca Laoidhe ; and the O'Flynns of Muskerry were lords of Muskerrylinn (Muscraidhe Ui Fhloinn), i.e. the country between Ballyvourney and Blarney. They were pushed thence by the MacCarthys and moved to a more easterly location. The most important of the Connacht septs of the name was O'Flynn of Kiltullagh and Kilkeevin, in Co. Roscommon. In the same county O'Flynns were erenaghs of the Church of St. Dachonna near Boyle. The head of this family had the peculiar privilege of mounting the same steed as the royal O'Connor. Further west at Errew on the shore of Lough Conn was another erenagh family of O'Flynn. Another sept of Ó Floinn was at one time famous in Ulster. They possessed a territory in southern Antrim between Lough Neagh and the sea and were the senior branch of Clanna Rury of Ulidia, tracing their descent back to Colla Uais, King of Ireland in the fourth century. The F of Ó Floinn was aspirated in modern Ulster Irish, with the result that the name became Ó Loinn and the anglicized form O'Lynn in the north.

Numerous though they are and were, few O'Flynns have found a place in the pages of Irish history. Fiacha O'Flynn (also called MacFlynn), Archbishop of Tuam, was the emissary of the Irish Church to England in 1255. Among the Irish in France, however, they have been prominent both as ecclesiastics and as officers of the Irish Brigade. In modern times Rev. Jeremiah O'Flynn (1788–1831) was a Franciscan friar whose interesting and stormy career relates chiefly to the early church in Australia and later in the U.S.A. Edmund James Flynn (b. 1847) was Premier of Quebec and William James Flynn (1867–1928) was a famous American detective.

Of the O'Lynns the most noteworthy was Father Donough O'Lynn, O.P., who was martyred in 1608 at the age of 90.

"Father O'Flynn," of the ever popular song, was a fictitious character. The northern form of the name is also popularized in a well known Irish song, "Brian O'Lynn."

Arms illustrated on Plate XI.

O'FOGARTY.

The sept of O'Fogarty was of sufficient importance to give its name to a large territory, viz. Eliogarty, i.e. the southern part of Eile or Ely, the northern being Ely O'Carroll. Eliogarty is now the name of the barony of Co. Tipperary in which the town of Thurles is situated. Eliogarty is a phonetic rendering of the Irish Eile ui Fhógartaigh, the nominative case of the surname being Ó Fógartaigh. Though located outside the area associated with the Dalcassian septs the O'Fogartys are counted as of Dalcassian origin. Woulfe states that the name is derived from the word *fógartach* meaning exiled : the modern Irish word *fógartha* does mean outlawed, but such facile derivations must be accepted with reserve. The "Annals of Ulster," under date 1072, describe the chief of the sept as O'Fogarty, King of Ely. In modern times the name is seldom found in English with its prefix O. The majority of Fogartys come from County Tipperary but their ancient seat, Castle Fogarty, is no longer in their hands. The most remarkable of these were Malachy O'Fogarty (fl. 1700), born at Castle Fogarty, of the University of Paris, and Archbishop Fogarty (1858–1955), who was for 51 years Bishop of Killaloe : he is best known for his fearless championship of the Irish cause during the "Black and Tan" scourge in the War of Independence.

The well known surname Gogarty is of cognate origin : it is Mag Fhógartaigh in Irish.

Arms illustrated on Plate XII.

O'FOLEY, (MacSharry).

Foley is an old Irish surname about which some confusion has arisen because there is an important family of Worcestershire called Foley, which is usually regarded

149

as English, though Bardsley thinks it was originally Irish. For example it is the arms of this English Family which are often erroneously ascribed to Gaelic Foleys. In this article these English Foleys can be disregarded, though it is not unlikely that a few of them came to Ireland at various times as settlers. The Irish Foleys are very numerous and this name is among the sixty most common in Ireland with an estimated population of about ten thousand souls. Most of these are found in the original habitat of the sept, viz. Co. Waterford, and they have spread across the southern part of the country to Counties Cork and Kerry. The name is presumably derived from the Irish word *foghladha*, meaning a plunderer, and is written Ó Foghladha, being anglicized more phonetically than the usual Foley as Fowloo in some places in Co. Waterford, and sometimes grotesquely as Fowler. The name is never seen with its prefix O nowadays. The surname MacSharry has been anglicized Foley in some parts of Ulster in the mistaken belief that it is derived from the word *searrach*—a foal.

John Henry Foley (1818–1874), sculptor, many of whose statues adorn the streets and squares of Dublin, attained international fame in this sphere; his brother Edward Foley (1814–1874) was also a talented sculptor. Rev. Daniel Foley (1815–1874), of Dublin University, compiled and published an Irish Dictionary. Samuel Foley (1655–1695) was another prominent Protestant ecclesiastic. The Catholic Church had an eminent bearer of the name in Maoliosa O'Foley, Archbishop of Cashel, who died in 1131. In modern times Alan James Foley (1835–1897) made a name as a singer under the pseudonym of Signor Foli.

FORDE, MacKinnawe, (Foran).

It is impossible for any Irishman called Forde or Ford to know the origin of his people unless there be a firm family tradition to aid him or alternatively he knows that they have long been located in a certain part of the country. The reason for this is that at least three Irish septs with entirely different surnames in Irish became known in English as Forde or Ford; there is also the not inconsiderable number of English planters and traders called Ford who from time to time settled in Ireland. The most notable of these came from Devonshire and became landowners in Co. Meath in the fourteenth century. Of the Gaelic septs the two which belonged to Connacht are the most important. One is Macgiollarnath, which is a corruption of Mac Giolla na Naomh (son of the devotee of the saints) and became Ford through a mistranslation of the corrupted form. They were located in southern Connemara. The earlier anglicized form of this name is MacAneave. The other Connacht sept is Mac Consnámha, (possibly meaning son of swimming hound) which, when not absurdly anglicized Forde, is MacKinnawe in English. In the " Composition Book of

Connacht " (1585) it appears as MacEnawe and in the census of 1659 as MacEnaw. The form Forde was then unknown in this connexion. The MacKinnawes were chiefs of Muintir Kenny, possessing a territory between Lough Allen and the river Arigna. One of this sept, Cornelius MacConsnamha (d. 1355), was Bishop of Kilmore. A third Gaelic sept to be noticed is that of Ó Fuartháin or Ó Fuaráin, properly anglicized Foran but commonly made Forde in Co. Cork where this sept originated.

No doubt the best known of all Fords is Henry Ford, of motor car fame, a man of Irish stock. Patrick Forde (1835–1913), founder of *The Irish World* and a force in American journalism, was born in Co. Galway. Others of some note were Francis Forde (lost at sea 1760), a fine soldier, and Samuel Forde (1805–1828), whose career as a very promising painter was cut short by his early death.

FOX.

In this note we may disregard English settlers of the name Fox, one family of whom became extensive landowners in Co. Limerick and are perpetuated there in the place name Mountfox, near Kilmallock. The Irish Foxes got their name as a sobriquet : Tadhg Ó Catharnaigh (*anglice* O'Caherny—mod. Carney or Kearney), Chief of Teffia, Co. Meath (d. 1084) was called Sionnach, i.e. The Fox, and in due course this branch acquired the name Fox as a distinct surname. (For Kearney see p. 192 *infra*). A report of the Registrar-General gives a list of alternative forms of surnames used by persons registering births, deaths, marriages. Few are so lengthy as that of Fox, the synonyms for which are MacAshinah (Co. Tyrone), MacShanaghy (Co. Louth)—from the Irish Mac a'tSionnaigh, son of the fox, Shanahy (Co. Westmeath), Shinagh (Co. Mayo), Shunny (Co. Louth), Shinnock (Co. Kilkenny), Shonogh (Co. Galway) and others, with Ó Sionnaigh in Irish in general use. It will be seen that these synonyms cover a wide stretch of country in three provinces. The name, as Fox, is found in every county, though nowhere in very large numbers : it is most numerous in Dublin, Longford, Tyrone and Leitrim. The head of the sept has for centuries since the English language was first introduced into Ireland been known as " The Fox " and this designation, still used to-day, is admitted as authentic by the Irish Genealogical Office—it cannot be called a title for titles are not recognized under the Irish Constitution.

Among interesting bearers of the name we may mention Sir Patrick Fox of Moyvore, Co. Westmeath, who was State Interpreter (of Irish) in 1568, and Charlotte Milligan Fox (1864–1916), a collector of folk songs and founder of the Irish Folk Song Society.

Arms illustrated on Plate XII.

FRENCH, de Freyne.

The use of the initial ff in spelling this name has become established with several families, but actually it arose through ignorance of the fact that in sixteenth and seventeenth century caligraphy capital F was written ff. Originally Norman, the name was de Freynes, from Latin *fraxinus*—an ash tree. The ancestor of the family now under consideration went from France to England with William the Conqueror in the person of Theophilus de French. One line of his descendants settled in Co. Wexford about 1300. A century later a branch of the Wexford Frenches migrated to Galway (in 1425), where his family prospered and multiplied, soon becoming accepted as one of the " Tribes of Galway "—Walter French being Sovereign of Galway (equivalent to mayor) in 1444. A branch of this branch moved into Co. Roscommon, circa 1620, and became the Frenches of French Park, and from this family came Field Marshal Sir John French (1852–1925). Two of these Galway Frenches were members of the Supreme Council of the Confederate Catholics at Kilkenny (1642–1649). Another Galway born French of that century was Rev. Peter French, O.P. (d. 1693), who for thirty years worked as a missionary among the Indians in Mexico. Most Rev. Nicholas French (1604–1678), Bishop of Ferns and author of *The Unkind Deserter*, was a Wexford man. In our own day Percy French (1854–1922), was well-known as the author of many popular comic Irish songs.

The name de Freyne is of the same origin as French. There is an Irish peerage of the de Freyne extant to-day, as well as one of ffrench.
Arms illustrated on Plate XII.

O'FRIEL.

O'Friel is a Donegal name. In Irish it is Ó Firghil (from Feargal) ; it is pronounced, and often written, Ó Frighil, i.e. in English phonetics O'Freel. The sept has a distinguished origin, being descended from Eoghan, brother of St. Columcille, and the leading family were hereditary co-arbs of Kilmacrenan, Co. Donegal. The Chief of the Name possessed the hereditary right of inaugurating O'Donnell as lord of Tirconnell. Not being a powerful or numerous sept they do not appear very frequently in the national records ; wherever they do they are of Tirconnell (Donegal). The records of the Diocese of Raphoe have many references to distinguished ecclesiastics of the name, both as O'Friel and Friel, including one Bishop Florence or Feargal O'Friel (d. 1299). Awley O'Friel was one of the many clergy from Raphoe and Derry who went to Iona—he was elected Abbot of Iona in 1203.

Statistics relating to the modern distribution of the population indicate that the name is seldom met with outside Co. Donegal and contiguous areas.
Arms illustrated on Plate XII.

GAFFNEY, (Caulfield, O'Growney, Keveney, MacCarron).

Gaffney is one of those quite numerous Irish surnames about which much confusion arises. Not only is it used as the anglicized form of four distinct Gaelic names, but Gaffney itself has for some obscure reason become Caulfield in many places. It never appears to-day with either Mac or O as prefix : of the four patronymics referred to above two are O names and two are Mac. The principal sept in question was Ó Gamhna of Ossory, but there Caulfield is the normal modern form. In the same area Gaffney is sometimes found as the anglicized form of Ó Caibheanaigh, *recte* Keveney in English. Then we have Mac Conghamhna, a sept of the Ui Fiachra Aidhne in South Galway : there again Caulfield is found as an equivalent as well as Gaffney. Finally Mac Carrghamhna, sometimes MacCaron in English, is usually made Gaffney in Cavan and Roscommon, where the name Gaffney is most commonly found to-day. Mac Cearáin, however, the name of a small Tirconnell sept, is the most usual original of MacCarron. To add to the confusion Mac Carrghamhna has been corrupted to Ó Gramhna, whence O'Growney in English, a name very familiar to all Gaelic Leaguers through the Irish language primers of Father Eugene O'Growney (1863–1899). Richard Caulfield (1823–1887), did much antiquarian and historical research for Co. Cork.

O'GALLAGHER.

The name of this sept, Ó Gallchobhair in Irish, signifies descendant of Gallchobhar or Gallagher, who was himself descended from the King of Ireland who reigned from 642–654. The O'Gallaghers claim to be the senior and most royal family of the Cineal Connaill. Their territory extended over a wide area in the modern baronies of Raphoe and Tirhugh, Co. Donegal, and their chiefs were notable as marshals of O'Donnell's military forces from the fourteenth to the sixteenth centuries. The principal branch of the sept were seated at Ballybeit and Ballynaglack.

Gallagher, usually without its prefix O, is one of the commonest names in Ireland being fourteenth in the statistical list compiled from birth registrations. Most of these were recorded in the north-western counties of Ulster and Connacht, the majority being from Co. Donegal, the original homeland of the sept.

The national records show them to have been even more intimately connected with ecclesiastical than with military activities. No less than six O'Gallaghers were bishops of Raphoe in the fifteenth and sixteenth centuries and one in the eighteenth. One of these, Laurence O'Gallagher, who held the see from 1466–1477, was anything but a saintly prelate, while on the other hand Most Rev. Redmond O'Gallagher (1521–1601), Bishop of Derry, the prelate who befriended the survivors of the Spanish

Armada and was forced to disguise himself as a shepherd in order to escape the prevailing religious persecution, was eventually captured and became one of our Irish Catholic martyrs. A later Bishop of Raphoe, and afterwards of Ossory, Most Rev. James O'Gallagher (1681–1751), was famous for his sermons (usually preached in Irish), which, when published, ran to twenty editions. In America Father Hugh Gallagher (1815–1882), had a most colourful career as a " frontier priest." William Davis Gallagher (1808–1894), American poet, was the son of an Irish refugee who took part in Robert Emmet's Rebellion.

Arms illustrated on Plate XII.

O'GALVIN.

The O'Galvins are a sept of Thomond and are mentioned among the Co. Clare septs which took part in the Battle of Loughraska, otherwise called the Battle of Corcomroe Abbey, in 1317. They do not appear prominently in any branch of Irish public life since that time, but representatives of the sept have remained continuously in their original homeland and are still found in Co. Clare and, in greater numbers to-day, in Co. Kerry. A branch located in Co. Roscommon was strong enough to be included among the more numerous names in the barony of Athlone in the 1659 census. The name is Ó Gealbháin in Irish, possibly a compound of *geal* (bright) and *bán* (white). The prefix O is not used with this name in modern times but O'Galvan and O'Gallivane are old forms of it in English.

The most famous comedian in England at the end of the last century was Dan Leno. His real name was George Galvin (1860–1904) : he was born in London of Irish parents.

Arms illustrated on Plate XII.

MacGANNON.

The name of the old Erris (Co. Mayo) family of Mag Fhionnáin is usually anglicized Gannon, without the Mac : in the spoken language in Irish it is often called Ó Geanáin but the equivalent O'Gannon is not used in English. Gannons are still more numerous in their original homeland in Co. Mayo than elsewhere. Father Michael Gannon, who took part in the 1798 insurrection, was earlier prominent on the side of the aristocracy in the period of the French Revolution. The American comedy actress Mary Gannon (1829–1868), is said to have been of Irish parentage. Nicholas John Gannon (1829–1875), the poet, was born in Co. Kildare.

O'GARA, (Geary).

The sept of O'Gara, Ó Gadhra in Irish, is closely associated with that of O'Hara. They have a common descent down to the tenth century, Gadhra, the eponymous ancestor of the O'Garas, being nephew of Eadhra (*a quo* the O'Haras). From this on they established separate chieftainries, O'Gara taking the territory to the south of the barony now known as Leyney, Co. Sligo, the O'Haras being to the north of them. The association remained close and the chiefs of the two septs frequently alternated as rulers of Luighne. By the thirteenth century the O'Garas had possessed themselves of the eastern part of the barony of Costello, Co. Mayo. However the Jordans drove them out in the next century, pushing them not westwards but eastwards and between 1450 and 1550 they appear as lords of Coolavin.

They have left their mark on the country historically, geographically and culturally. Their castle was Moygara on the shore of the lake still called Lough Gara. Two Archbishops of Tuam were O'Garas. Fergal O'Gara (fl. 1630), was the patron of the Four Masters ; Friar O'Gara, O.S.A. (fl. 1670), an exile in Belgium, left a notable collection of Irish poems ; Col. Oliver O'Gara commanded the regiment of infantry known by his name in the Irish Brigade in the service of France. Count Charles O'Gara was a millionaire Irishman in Brussels at the time of the French Revolution.

The name has become rather scarce in Ireland in modern times. Most of the survivors of the sept belong still to North Connacht. A branch of it migrated to West Munster in the fifteenth century: there the name Ó Gadhra became differently anglicized and, disguised under the synonym Geary, is still quite common in Counties Limerick and Kerry.

Arms illustrated on Plate XII.

MacGARRY, Garrihy, (O'Hehir, Hare).

MacGarry, found also not infrequently as Garry without the Mac, is one of those names which in the anglicized form takes its initial letter from the end of the prefix— in this case Mag (a variant of Mac often used with names beginning with a vowel or fh). In Irish MacGarry is Mag Fhearadhaigh. Garrihy, another form used in English, is phonetically nearer the original Irish than the commoner Garry. The sept, which was never very widespread or influential, is said to be of the same stock as the MacHughs of East Connacht. It certainly belongs to that province and to-day, apart from immigrants to Dublin and Belfast, it is mostly to be found in Counties Roscommon and Leitrim. The "Composition Book of Connacht" mentions the Chief of the Name in 1585 as of Moygarry, Co. Sligo.

This surname also presents an example of anglicization by erroneous translation, for Hare, and even O'Hare, is used as a synonym.

Hare and O'Hare are sometimes also used for O'Hehir. This important family, though by origin it belongs to the Ui Fidhgheinte group, has for so many centuries been established in Co. Clare in the heart of Thomond that it is usually counted as Dalcassian. Its main stronghold to-day is Co. Clare.

Arms illustrated on Plate XII.

O'GARVEY, MacGARVEY, (Garvin).

Garvey is one of those surnames which in Irish have both the Gaelic prefixes, Mac and O. Mac Gairbhith belongs to Co. Donegal where it is numerous : it is Mac-Garvey in English, the prefix being retained. The O, on the other hand, has been almost entirely discarded. The principal sept of Ó Gairbhith, now Garvey, is of the same stock as the O'Hanlons, their ancient territory being in the barony of Oneilland East, Co. Armagh, until largely dispossessed by the MacCanns. Nearby in the MacGuinness country another sept of O'Garvey dwelt, and as might be expected the name Garvey is not uncommon to-day in Co. Down. Most Rev. Anthony O'Garvey was Bishop of Dromore from 1759 to 1780. However it is in Co. Mayo Garveys are chiefly found in modern times ; but these are really Garvins (in Irish Ó Gairbhín), that name having been corrupted to Garvey in Connacht. That sept was of the Southern Ui Neill : they migrated from their original homeland in Co. Meath to Connacht after the Anglo-Norman invasion and settled near Crossmolina.

The most prominent family of Garvey in Co. Mayo is that of Murrisk Abbey. John Garvey (1527–1595), who was one of the more notable Protestant Archbishops of Armagh, though born in Co. Kilkenny, was eldest son of John O'Garvey of Murrisk : he took out letters of denization in 1561 and espoused the English cause, as did his brother James who possessed the Murrisk property.

Garvey, as well as Garvan, is a well known name in Counties Cork and Kerry. The ancient sept of Ó Garbháin of Munster was of the same stock as the O'Moriartys. No doubt the Munster Garveys are properly Garvan just as the Connacht Garveys are Garvin.

Other notable Garveys of Irish parentage were the artists Edmund Garvey, R.A. (1740–1813), and Michael Angelo Garvey (1820–1877).

Callaghan Garvan (1644–1735) was physician to the "Old Pretender" and to Queen Mary of Modena. The best known of the Garvins was probably James Louis Garvin (1868–1947), editor of the *Observer* newspaper.

Arms illustrated on Plate XII.

MacGEE.

MacGee is an Ulster name which is more usually written Magee (cf. MacGuire—Maguire; MacGuinness—Magennis, etc.). In Irish it is Mag Aodha, i.e. son of Aodh or Hugh, the Mac, as is often the case when the prefix is followed by a vowel, becoming Mag. It has been stated that our Ulster MacGees are of Scottish extraction, having come to Ireland during the Plantation of Ulster in the early seventeenth century. There certainly is a numerous Scottish family so called, who are akin to the MacDonnells and claim descent from Colla Uais and so an Irish origin. There are Gaelic Irish MacGees also. They belong to the country on the borders of Counties Donegal and Tyrone. The name is more usually associated with Co. Antrim because the large isthmus on the east of Lough Larne is called Island Magee and this territory was at one time in the possession of the Magees. In early mediaeval times a MacGee was chief of a sept in Co. Westmeath but these were dispersed after the Anglo-Norman invasion. The early history of the MacGees is thus rather obscure, but people of the name were prominent in various phases of Irish life in the eighteenth and nineteenth century. Most of these were northern Protestants, among whom were Most Rev. William Magee (1766–1831), Archbishop of Dublin and mathematician, his grandson William Connor Magee (1821–1891), strong opponent of Gladstone's Irish policy, rector of Enniskillen, Dean of Cork and finally Archbishop of York. Martha Magee (c.1755–1846), was the founder of Magee University College at Derry; two John Magees (1750–1809 and 1780–1814), father and son made history by their fearless journalism in their paper *The Dublin Evening Post*. Two others (Catholics) the brothers Thomas D'Arcy MacGee (1825–1868), and James E. MacGee (1830–1880) were associated with the Young Ireland movement and wrote many patriotic works: both went to America and the former was shot by one of the Fenians whose activities he had denounced. Three prominent American citizens whose names illustrate various spellings thereof, viz. William John McGee (1853–1912), geologist, Charles McClung McGhee (1828–1907), financier, and Christopher Lyman Magee (1848–1901), politician and philanthropist, were all of Irish extraction.

MacGENIS, Guinness, Magennis.

The modern spelling of this name is usually MacGuinness or MacGenis but in the historical records in English they are called as a rule Magennis, a form still to be found in some places to-day. In Irish the name is MagAonghusa, i.e. son of Angus. They are descended from Saran, chief of Dal Araidhe in St. Patrick's time and thence to Eochaidh Cobha of Iveagh. From the twelfth century the Magennises were the principal territorial lords of Iveagh, Co. Down. Like the chiefs of many of the great

Irish septs Magennis took advantage of the English policy of " surrender and regrant " early in the seventeenth century ; earlier they were often at loggerheads with the ecclesiastical authorities and they showed a tendency to accept the tenets of the Reformation : conforming bishops include two Magennises—one of the diocese of Down, the other of Dromore. However, by 1598 the Magennis chief of the time, whose father was officially regarded as " the civillest of all the Irish in these parts," had joined Tyrone (who was his brother-in-law) and thus " returned to the rudeness of the country." A generation later their loyalty to Ireland and the ancient faith was undoubted. The Franciscan Bishop of Down and Connor, Hugo Magennis (d. 1640), was closely related to Viscount Iveagh and many of the Gaelic nobility of Ulster. They were consistently on the Irish side during the resistance to English aggression in that century and after the disasters following the battle of the Boyne they were finally dispossessed of their wide patrimony in Co. Down, much of which had been planted with English (not Scottish) settlers after the Cromwellian war. Many of them took service as Wild Geese. The best known of these was Brian Magennis, second Viscount Iveagh, who was colonel of Iveagh's Regiment in the Austrian Imperial Army and was killed in action in 1703. His brother Roger Magennis, third Viscount (d. 1709) served both France and Spain with distinction. The present Lord Iveagh (of the second creation), head of the largest brewery concern in the world—Guinness of Dublin—though not a direct descendant of the lords of Iveagh mentioned above, belongs to a cognate family of Co. Down. This family spent very large sums on improvement of housing and social conditions in the city of Dublin as well as on the upkeep of St. Patrick's Cathedral and its surroundings.

General John R. MacGuinness (b. 1840), the American soldier, was born in Dublin.

Arms illustrated on Plate XIII.

MacGEOGHEGAN.

Geoghegan, usually nowadays without the prefix Mac, is a name which no non-Irish person will attempt to pronounce at sight ; it has many synonyms, and one of these, Gehegan, is a phonetic approximation of the longer and common form. In Irish it is Mag Eochagáin, from Eochaidh, i.e. the now almost obsolete, but once common, christian name Oghy. It will be observed that the initial ' G ' of Geoghegan comes from the prefix Mag, a variant of Mac—the anglicized form Mageoghegan was formerly much used.

The sept of the MacGeoghegans is of the southern Ui Neill and of the stock of the famous sixth century King Niall of the Nine Hostages ; it was located in the present barony of Moycashel, Co. Westmeath, with the chiefs' seat near Kilbeggan. These were of considerable importance up to the time of Cromwell when they suffered severely through war and confiscation. Fifteen MacGeoghegans, chiefs of Cinel Fiachach or Kinalea, sometimes called lords thereof, are mentioned in the " Annals of the Four Masters " between 1291 and 1450, besides many others of the name, the last of these being Richard MacGeoghegan, who, after fighting with great gallantry, was killed at the siege of Dunboy in 1602. The military tradition was long maintained. Five of the sons of Charles MacGeoghegan of Sinan, Co. Westmeath, were killed during the Jacobite War in Ireland ; and in the eighteenth century MacGeoghegans appear as soldiers on the Continent, mostly in the service of France.

The MacGeoghegan estates in Co. Westmeath were very extensive and were held by a number of different branches of the chiefly family. The most important of these properties was at Castletown, now called Castletown-Geoghegan. By the end of the seventeenth century the bulk of these vast estates had been confiscated or their owners, who ranked among the leading gentry of the county, outlawed. There have been many other distinguished MacGeoghegans—notably Ross, alias Roch, MacGeoghegan (1580–1644), the much persecuted Dominican, " saintly and enterprising " Bishop of Kildare ; Conal MacGeoghegan, Chief of the Sept, translator of the " Annals of Clonmacnois " into English in 1627 ; another well-known historian, the Abbé James MacGeoghegan (1702–1764) ; and Anthony Geoghegan (1810–1889), poet ; there were also three other lesser nineteenth century poets of the name. St. Hugh of Rahue (which lies between Tullamore and Tyrrell's Pass in Co. Westmeath) was of the family which became MacGeoghegan when surnames were adopted. The saint's crozier was in the possession of the MacGeoghegan family for many centuries—it passed from them to the Nagles of Jamestown House, Co. Westmeath, a family now extinct.

A branch of the MacGeoghegan sept settled at Bunowen, Co. Galway, and the name is found in that county as well as in their original territory. In the West it has been often shortened to Geoghan and even Gegan ; and Houghegan is a synonym of it in Connemara.

The brothers Lawrence and Sebastian Gahagan, who were sculptors of note in London between 1760 and 1820 were Irishmen called Geoghegan at home.

Arms illustrated on Plate XIII.

MacGERAGHTY, Gerty.

Geraghty is a Mac name, being Mag Oireachtaigh in Irish. Mac usually becomes Mag before a vowel so the initial G of Geraghty is really the last letter of the prefix Mac or Mag. There are no less than seventeen different synonyms of Geraghty in English, including MacGerity, Gearty and even Jerety. The surname arose in rather an unusual way. At first it was Ó Roduibh ; at the end of the twelfth century one of these was Oireachtach Ó Roduibh and it is from this Oireachtach their present surname is taken. They were a Hy Many sept in Co. Roscommon and Co. Galway in O'Kelly's country. Its head was one of the " four royal chiefs " under O'Conor, being of the same line of descent as O'Conor himself. They are prominent in Connacht records up to the year 1300 and there were several mediaeval bishops of the name. The Chief of the Name, called MacGiriaght in the " Composition Book of Connacht " was seated in the barony of Athlone in 1585. The analysis of the present population distribution indicates that Geraghtys are (disregarding the metropolitan district in which names from all provinces are numerous) mainly found in Co. Galway. Except for Father Bryan Geraghty, Dean of Elphin in 1744, I have not found any outstanding person of the name in modern Irish historical records. In the Argentine Monsignor Richard Joseph Gearty (c. 1864–1938), an Irishman, was an outstanding priest.

Arms illustrated on Plate XIII.

MacGILFOYLE, Powell.

Guilfoyle is Mac Giolla Phóil in Irish, i.e. son of the follower or devotee of St. Paul. It is sometimes disguised under the form Powell, an English surname adopted in its stead during the period of Gaelic depression. The prefix Mac, which properly belongs to it, is very seldom used with this name in modern times. The Guilfoyles were once a sept of some importance, their chiefs being seated in the vicinity of Shinrone, Co. Offaly, which lies in the Ely O'Carroll territory. Nichol and Owen MacGilfoil are the two first signatures on an indenture dated 1576 wherein Sir William O'Karrell (O'Carroll) agrees to the incorporation of the territory of Ely O'Carroll which, it is of interest to note, was originally in Munster, in the King's County (now Offaly). Some Guilfoyles are still found there and the name is also well known in East Clare. The spelling Guilfoyle has now quite superseded the older Gilfoyle.

Arms illustrated on Plate XIII.

MacGILLYCUDDY, (Archdeacon, Cody).

This name is well known to everyone who has made a visit to Killarney or even studied a map with the idea of doing so, because the picturesque MacGillycuddy's Reeks are the highest mountains in Ireland and are named from the Kerry sept who dwelt at their western base. This is one of the few septs whose present-day representative is officially recognized as Chief of the Name—MacGillycuddy of the Reeks. Nevertheless, the surname MacGillycuddy is not old : in fact it only dates from the sixteenth century. Previous to that they were O'Sullivans, a branch of O'Sullivan Mór, which at that comparatively late date became established as a sept distinct from the parent stem. At first the name MacGillycuddy was only used by the chief's family, the others still calling themselves O'Sullivan; for a while they were often described as O'Sullivan alias MacGillycuddy, but eventually the latter was adopted by the whole branch. By the end of the sixteenth century MacGillycuddys are recorded, e.g. in the Lambeth Library maps, as principal proprietors in the baronies of Dunkerron and Magunihy.

The name is by no means numerous and is not found outside Kerry, except of course in the case of Kerry families which have migrated to Dublin and elsewhere in recent times. Col. Denis MacGillycuddy was in command of a regiment in the Irish Brigade of the French Army in the seventeenth century.

A curious example of the way in which Irish surnames have often become confused is presented in the case of that remarkable Jesuit Richard Archdekin (1618–1693), author of a book on miracles, published in 1667 in the Irish and English languages. He was better known as Richard MacGillacuddy. The Norman family of Archdeacon of Co. Kilkenny (to which he belonged), early adopted the Gaelic patronymic Mac Oda, later anglicized Cody. Thus the variant MacCuddy became in this case Mac-gillacuddy by an erroneous extension. Like so many Irish families who were ruined by the defeat of James II several of the name Archdeacon settled in France. Nicholas Archdeacon, Bishop of Kilfenora from 1800 to 1824, spent much of his life in France, but he was born in Ireland.

Arms illustrated on Plate XIII.

O'GLISSANE, Gleeson.

In spite of its English appearance in its anglicized form the name Gleeson, never found with the prefix O in English, is that of a genuine Gaelic Irish family. In modern Irish it is Ó Gliasáin, earlier Ó Glasáin and originally Ó Glesáin. They belong to the Aradh and their original habitat was Mac Ui Briain Aradh's country, that is the country in Co. Tipperary between Nenagh and Lough Derg; but it should be emphasized that the Gleesons are not Dalcassians; they are of the same stock as the O'Donegans, of the barony of Ara, Co. Tipperary, who were originally of Muskerry, Co. Cork. In the census of 1659 the name is very numerous in north Munster (Counties Tipperary, Clare and Limerick) being then given many spellings, e.g. Glisane, Glison, Glyssane, O'Gleasane, O'Glassane etc. They are still fairly numerous in their home country but are not found much outside Munster. Prior to 1641 the O'Glissanes were very extensive landowners in Co. Tipperary but as such they disappear in the Cromwellian settlement.

Persons of the name have not been prominent in Irish history or literature, but three Irish Gleesons are well known in America, viz. Father William Gleeson, called the " founder of the Church in California " ; Edward Blakeney Gleeson the Rochester millionaire ; and Frederick Grant Gleason (1848–1903), the composer.

MacGORMAN, O'GORMAN.

This name is of particular interest philologically because although it is (with rare exceptions) really a Mac name it is almost always found to-day—when not plain Gorman—as O'Gorman. This can be accounted for by the fact that in the eighteenth and early nineteenth centuries, when the native Irish were in complete subjection, the Gaelic prefixes Mac and O were universally allowed to fall into disuse, particularly in the case of some names like Gorman ; then, when the spirit of the nation revived, these prefixes were gradually restored, but so completely had the form MacGorman fallen into oblivion that its rightful bearers when resuming a prefix assumed the wrong one and became O'Gorman, with the result that MacGormans are hardly to be found at all in Ireland to-day except in Co. Monaghan. O'Gormans are found chiefly in Co. Clare, while plain Gorman is more usual in Co. Tipperary. The Irish form is Mac Gormáin (derived from *gorm*, blue). Originally this sept inhabited the barony of Slievemargy in Co. Leix near the town of Carlow, of which their chief was lord, but they were driven out at the Norman invasion and settled in Ibrickan, West Clare, and in Co. Monaghan. In the former they attained considerable influence and the head of the sept became hereditary marshal to O'Brien of Thomond. The Mac-Gormans of Ibrickan were noted especially in the fifteenth century for their wealth, hospitality and for their patronage of the Gaelic poets.

Probably the man chiefly responsible for the substitution of O for Mac in the name was the celebrated gigantic Chevalier Thomas O'Gorman (1725–1808), exile vineyard owner in France, who, after being ruined by the French Revolution, became a constructor of Irish pedigrees. Several O'Gormans were prominently associated with Irish politics, notably Nicholas Purcell O'Gorman (1778–1857), secretary of of the Catholic Association, and Richard O'Gorman (1820–1895), the Young Irelander. The original name has a place in the roll of distinguished Irishmen, in the early days before the prefix was dropped, in the person of Finn MacGorman who was bishop of Kildare 1148–1160 and is famous as the compiler of " The Book of Leinster."

Arms illustrated on Plate XIII.

O'GORMLEY, (Grehan, Grimes).

Like many of the smaller independent septs of north-west Ulster the O'Gormleys sank into obscurity after the Plantation of Ulster about the year 1609. In the fourteenth century they were driven by the O'Donnells from their original territory, known as Cinel Moen (their tribe name), which was in the modern barony of Raphoe, Co. Donegal ; but their survival in their new country on the other side of the Foyle, between Derry and Strabane, whence they continued to fight the O'Donnells, is evidenced by the frequent mention of their chiefs in the " Annals of the Four Masters " up to the end of the sixteenth century. Reeves states that their chiefs were usually styled *taoiseach* (or *capitanus*), not *tighearna,* indicating that the sept was one of minor importance. In the " Four Masters " and in the " Topographical Poems " of O'Dugan and O'Heerin, the name is spelt Ó Gairmleadhaigh ; the " Annals of Loch Cé " write it Ó Gormshuil and Ó Gormshuiligh : the editor (William Hennessy) writing in 1871 states that the latter was then anglicized O'Gormooly, but Gormley is universal to-day. O'Donovan says that the O'Gormalys of Lough Key, Co. Roscommon (Ó Garmghaile) are quite distinct from the O'Gormleys of Co. Tyrone (Ó Gairmleadhaigh). In seventeenth century records they are found both as O'Gormley and MacGormley, located chiefly in counties Armagh and Derry, but also in Roscommon and Westmeath. In modern times some families of Gormley in Counties Cavan and Longford have changed their name to Gorman, the others in Co. Tyrone, nearer to their homeland, have become Grimes. Grimes, however, is also used as the anglicized form of several other Gaelic surnames particularly Ó Gréachain in Munster, which is Grehan and even Graham elsewhere. Gormleys to-day are chiefly found in Co. Tyrone and surrounding areas.

Arms illustrated on Plate XIII.

MacGOVERN, Magauran.

The MacGoverns are better known in history as Magauran. Both forms are phonetic approximations of the Irish Mag Shamhradhain, since MH is pronounced V in some places and W in others. The G of Govern thus comes from the last letter of the prefix Mag, which is used before vowels and aspirates instead of the usual Mac. The eponymous ancestor was Samhradhan, who lived circa 1100 at the time surnames came into being. This man was descended from Eochadh (fl. eighth century) whence the territory of the MacGoverns or Magaurans was called Teallach Eochaidh—now Tullyhaw—in north-west Cavan. There is a village called Ballymagauran in that area. The leading families of the sept were allied by marriage to the Maguires, O'Rourkes and other powerful families of that part of Ireland and are frequently mentioned in the Annals during the thirteenth to sixteenth centuries. Ballymagauran in Tullyhaw was burned by Maguire in 1481 for an allegedly dishonourable act by the Magauran of the day. " The Book of the Magaurans " is one of the famous old Gaelic manuscripts. Though the form Magauran is still used to some extent, MacGovern is much more numerous nowadays. It is chiefly found in its original habitat, north Cavan, and the adjacent counties of Leitrim and Fermanagh. Edmund Magauran, who was Archbishop of Armagh from 1588 to 1595, was one of the earlier Catholic martyrs in Ireland. Two Magaurans were Bishops of Ardagh—1445–1460 and 1815–1829. Hugh Magauran (alias MacGovern) was one of the Gaelic poets belonging to the O'Naghtens' circle in the eighteenth century. In modern times few MacGoverns have attained fame. The best known is probably John McGovern 1850–1917), the American novelist. The MacGoverns of Argentina, an important family in that country, are of Irish origin.

Arms illustrated on Plate XIII.

MacGOWAN, O'GOWAN, Smith, (MacGuane).

The Irish surname MacGowan (not to be confused with the Scottish MacGoun) is more often than not hidden under the synonym Smith. In Irish it is Mac an Ghabhain, i.e. son of the smith, and its translation to Smith (commonest of all surnames in England) was very widespread, particularly in Co. Cavan where the MacGowan sept originated. It is included by the chroniclers as one of the principal septs of Breffny. On the borders of Breffny, in Co. Leitrim, and to the north west in Counties Donegal and Sligo, the true form in English, MacGowan, is still used in preference to Smith. There was, too, in east Ulster a distinct sept of O'Gowan, a name which was also anglicized Smith. A very prominent member of this family, long resident in Co. Cavan, has recently, with the full approval of the Irish Genealogical Office, resumed the name O'Gowan. They came originally from a place called Ballygowan in Co. Down. O'Gowan, however, is very rarely met with in modern times. It is, however, to be found in the census of 1659 as one of the principal Irish names in the counties of Monaghan and Fermanagh.

Two MacGowans of Irish ancestry have distinguished themselves abroad: in the U.S.A. Samuel MacGowan (1819–1897), a Presbyterian, jurist and Confederate soldier; and in New Zealand, James MacGowan (1841–1912), statesman. Among the many alternative forms of the name recorded in the statistical returns of the Registrar-General, the most usual, apart from Smith, are Mageown and Magown.

Further confusion arises from the fact that the Gaelic surname MacDhubháin, a family of Raphoe, Co. Donegal, and also of Co. Clare, where the anglicized form is MacGuane, has become MacGowan in Co. Mayo ; while Mac Gamhna (normally Gaffney—*vide* p. 153 *supra*) is also rendered MacGowan in some places.

164

O'GRADY.

The O'Grady sept originated in Co. Clare and may be classed as Dalcassian, though the seat and territory of the Chief of the Name has for several centuries been at Kilballyowen, Co. Limerick. The present holder of that dignity (i.e. in popular parlance " The O'Grady ") is one of the very few the authenticity of whose claim to chieftainship is officially recognized in Ireland. The name in Irish is Ó Grádaigh or more shortly Ó Gráda, so that the anglicized form approximates closely to the original. A peculiarity about it is that its leading family in Co. Clare, who favoured the English invaders in the time of Henry VIII, gradually changed their name from O'Grady to Brady, being described in legal documents of the sixteenth century as " O'Grady alias Brady " or vice versa. Thus the Bradys around Tuamgraney in East Clare are really O'Gradys, though Brady is itself a common name in Ireland (especially in north Leinster and south Ulster) having no affinity with O'Grady at all. The ancestor of the present chief, though known at the time of his migration to Co. Limerick as John O'Grady alias Brady, dropped the latter and his descendants have ever since used the ancient and correct form of their name. If we examine the distribution of the name in modern times we find that, combining the separate returns for O'Grady and Grady (which are of course the same name), the total is not inconsiderable amounting to some four thousand all told. The majority of these hail from Co. Clare as might be expected. This is followed by Mayo which is of interest because it has been stated, on what authority I cannot say, that there was a distinct O'Grady sept originating in Mayo—more probably it was an offshoot of the Dalcassian stock.

John O'Grady was Archbishop of Tuam from 1364 to 1372. In modern times several members of the Co. Limerick O'Gradys have distinguished themselves in the service of Britain, one Standish O'Grady (1768–1840) being created Viscount Guillamore. The forename Standish with O'Grady is perpetuated by Standish Hayes O'Grady (1832–1915), who has been called " the last of the grand old scholars of Ireland."

Arms illustrated on Plate XIII.

MacGRATH.

Like several other names beginning with McG, MacGrath is often written Magrath (cf. MacGee—Magee ; MacGennis—Magennis, etc.). In Irish it is Mac Craith, the earlier form of which is Mac Raith or Mag Raith. Other synonyms still in use, especially in Ulster, are MacGraw, Magraw, MacGra etc. while the same Gaelic surname is found in Scotland as MacCrea, MacRae and Rae. There are two main septs of MacGrath in Ireland. One was located at Termon MacGrath on the borders of Donegal and Fermanagh, its head being co-arb of St. Daveog ; the other in County Clare where the family supplied ollamhs in poetry or hereditary poets to the O'Briens of Thomond. MacGraths are still found in Co. Clare, but the present day descendants of the Thomond MacGraths are mostly in Co. Tipperary and Co. Waterford. They were established there in the sixteenth century, for in Geoffrey Keating's boyhood the bardic school at Cahir was under their hereditary guidance ; and in Waterford City the ruins of Magrath's Castle are still to be seen. The Fermanagh MacGraths are now more numerous in the adjacent county of Tyrone. They are found, however, in every county and in all they are estimated to number ten thousand persons, thus constituting one of the hundred commonest names in Ireland, being placed fifty-fifth in the list.

The most remarkable and notorious man of the name was Miler MacGrath (1523–1622). Born in Co. Fermanagh he was first a Franciscan friar ; later, having become a Protestant, he rose to be Archbishop of Cashel though still holding the Catholic bishopric of Down ; in 1604 he held four bishoprics and seventy livings and was twice married. Another Franciscan, Miler MacGrath, was martyred for the faith in 1650. A brilliant if unstable character was Andrew MacGrath (d. 1790), described by Douglas Hyde as " a very melodious poet but frailest and wildest of the bards ". He was of Thomond ancestry and is known as An Mangaire Súgach. John MacRory MacGrath, eleventh century " chief historian of Dail Cais " and John McCraith or MacGrath author of " Caithreim Toirdhealbhaigh " (The Wars of Turlough) are the most distinguished of that time. Later, between 1391 and 1463, four of the Clare sept were Bishops of Killaloe. Two at least of the name were men of note in America : the Rev. James MacGrath (1835–1898), who became Provincial of the Oblates in that country ; and Andrew Condon Magrath (1813–1893), judge, Governor of Carolina and prominent Confederate in the Civil War, the son of John Magrath who took part in the 1798 Rising and, though captured, escaped to America. Joseph McGrath, veteran of the 1916–21 War of Independence, is well known now as a leading racehorse owner and as the organizer of the world-famous Irish Hospitals Sweepstakes.

Arms illustrated on Plate XIV.

O'GRIFFY, Griffin, (Griffith).

Ó Gríobhtha (pronounced O Greefa) is one of the many Gaelic surnames which have assumed in their anglicized forms those of British families of somewhat similar sound : in this case the earlier O'Griffy has been almost entirely superseded by Griffin. Here some confusion arises because a Welsh family of Griffin did actually settle in Ireland soon after the Anglo-Norman invasion. There is no doubt, however, that the great majority of Irish Griffins are really O'Griffys of Gaelic stock and not descendants of the Welsh settlers. They are very numerous and the name, with an estimated population to-day of over eight thousand persons, stands seventy-fifth in the list of commonest Irish surnames. These are chiefly found in Munster—Counties Clare, Limerick, Kerry and Cork. There was a minor sept of O'Griffy situated south of the Kenmare river, whose existence is recorded as late as the sixteenth century, their location being indicated by the placename Ballygriffin : little is known of them and they appear to have been absorbed by their powerful neighbours the O'Sullivans. It is possible that some of the Kerry and Cork Griffins are descended from that sept ; but Griffin is predominantly a Thomond name. The head of the O'Greefa, or O'Grifee, sept (so it was first spelt in English) was chief under the O'Deas of a territory in the south-eastern part of the barony of Inchiquin, Co. Clare, their seat being the castle of Ballygriffy, in the parish of Dysart, near Ennis. Gerald Griffin (1803–1840), best known as the author of that great Irish novel *The Collegians*, was of this leading O'Griffy family. Also in the literary sphere the Gaelic poet Muiris Ó Griofa, or Maurice Griffin (d. c. 1778) may be mentioned. The name is occasionally anglicized Griffith, but most Griffiths in Ireland are of Welsh origin. That name has been made illustrious in Irish affairs by several outstanding men, particularly by Sir John Griffith (1784–1878), the geologist and civil engineer, and by Arthur Griffith (1872–1922), founder with Edward Martyn of Sinn Féin, and first president of the Irish Free State.

Arms illustrated on Plate XIV.

MacGUIRE, Maguire.

These are spelling variants of the Irish Maguidhir. *Uidhir* is the genitive case of *odhar* meaning dun-coloured ; mag is a form of mac used before vowels. This is one of those names definitely associated with one county. The Maguires belong to Co. Fermanagh. The name first appears in the Annals in the year 956, but the predominance of the sept in Co. Fermanagh dates only from the fourteenth century ; for the next three centuries their chief was one of the most important in Ulster. They were not entirely dispossessed by the Plantation of Ulster, but they suffered very severely by the Cromwellian and Williamite confiscations. Maguire, Baron of Enniskillen, had a regiment of infantry in James II's army in Ireland. After the final defeat the Maguires are found prominently among the Wild Geese in the service of France and Austria. Later Barons of Enniskillen were accepted as nobility at the Court of France until the title became extinct about 1795. Of the many prominent soldiers of the name in Ireland the most noteworthy was Hugh Maguire who commanded the cavalry at the battle of the Yellow Ford where he slew Warham St. Leger ; he himself died of wounds received in action in 1600. There have been many other distinguished Maguires in Irish history, including the famous Bishop of Leighlin, Nicholas Maguire (1460–1512), and two fifteenth century bishops of Clogher, Cathal MacManus Maguire (1439–1498), historian, Conor Maguire (1616–1645), executed for his part in the 1641 Rising, the controversialist Father Tom Maguire (1792–1847), and Thomas Maguire (1831–1889), the first Catholic to be elected to a fellowship at Trinity College, Dublin.

At the present day the great majority of those who use the spelling Maguire hail from Co. Fermanagh; the MacGuires are mostly Connacht men (Mayo and Roscommon). This usage is in common with other cases where the Mac has become absorbed (e.g. MacGee—Magee) the distinct prefix being retained in the western counties. Counting the two forms together the name occupies thirty-ninth place in the list of most numerous surnames in Ireland: it holds first place in Co. Fermanagh and is high in the adjoining county of Cavan. A hundred years ago O'Donovan found the direct descendants of the great Hugh Maguire, mentioned above, working as sailors in cross-channel coal ships.

Arms illustrated on Plate XIV.

HACKETT.

The surname Hackett is of Norman origin, Haket being a common Norman personal name. The Hacketts came to Ireland at the time of the Anglo-Norman invasion at the end of the twelfth century, and people of that name were soon after settled in several places in the area covered by the modern counties of Kilkenny, Carlow and Kildare. Hacketstown, in Co. Carlow, is called after them. The Fiants of Henry VIII and Edward VI indicate that there were in the sixteenth century Hacketstowns, alias Ballyhackett, also in Counties Dublin and Kildare. A branch of this family moved into Connacht where they in due course became hibernicized and, like other Norman families in that province, formed a distinct if small sept which was known as MacHackett, their seat being Castle Hackett, six miles south-east of Tuam; but there is little trace of the name Hackett in Connacht to-day. It is still strong, however, in and around Counties Tipperary and Kilkenny, as it has been through the centuries. Hacketts and Hakets appear in the lists of sheriffs of Counties Tipperary, Cross Tipperary and Waterford and as members of parliament for Fethard in 1560, 1585 and 1613. Peter Hackett was Archbishop of Cashel from 1385 to 1407 and David Hacket Bishop of Ossory from 1460 to 1479; and Rev. John Baptist Hacket, O.P. (d. 1676), who was the intimate friend of Pope Clement X and a man of great influence in Rome, also came from that part of Ireland. Another Dominican, almost contemporary with him and also from Co. Tipperary, was Father Pádraigín

Hackett (c. 1600–1654), author of one of the best known poems in the Irish language " Múscail do mhisneach, a Bhanba."

In the last century Thomas Hacket (1805–1876), secretary of the Astronomical Society, and, in our own day, Rev. William P. Hackett, S.J. (1877–1949), and his brother Francis Hackett, the author, were Co. Kilkenny men of note.

Arms illustrated on Plate XIV.

O'HAGAN, Aiken.

This is one of the Gaelic names which was less affected than most by the widespread dropping of the prefix O during the centuries of Gaelic depression and submergence, for the form O'Hagan is much commoner than plain Hagan. In Irish it is Ó hAodhagáin, descendant of Aodhagán (diminutive of Aodh or Hugh). There are many variants of the name in English such as Hegan, Aiken etc. In this connexion I may mention a curiously inelegant synonym recorded by the Registrar-General as being used by an O'Hagan family, viz. Hogg! The O'Hagans are essentially Ulster people—but Catholic and Gaelic Ulster. The sept was located in Co. Tyrone with the seat of its chief at Tullahogue, where he exercised the hereditary right of inaugurating O'Neill as King or overlord of Ulster. O'Hagans were also connected with other parts of Ulster: as territorial magnates in mediaeval times with Monaghan and Armagh; and after the general dispossession of the old Irish families in Ulster as rapparees—two Antrim O'Hagans were hanged as such at Carrickfergus in 1722. Two places in Ulster are called Ballyagan, one in Co. Derry the other in Co. Antrim.

Of individual members of the sept perhaps the best remembered is Turlough O'Hagan, Chief of the Name, who journeyed to Co. Wicklow to bring back Hugh O'Neill to Ulster after the latter's dramatic escape from prison in Dublin Castle in 1590. Three O'Hagans from Co. Tyrone and two from Co. Derry were with O'Neill at the battle of Kinsale and several of these were attainted in 1612. Ivor O'Hagan, the tutor of St. Malachy (c. 1100) belonged to the Armagh O'Hagans. In the last century three people of the name were outstanding in Ireland. John O'Hagan (1822–1890), patriotic poet and judge; Thomas O'Hagan (1812–1885), the first Catholic Lord Chancellor of Ireland since the time of James II; and Mary O'Hagan (1823–1876), foundress and abbess of the Convent of Poor Clares. All these were Ulster born.

Arms illustrated on Plate XIV.

169

MacHALE.

Few names are more exclusively associated with one Irish county than MacHale of Mayo. Those of the Gaelic sept Mac Céile were erenaghs of Killala. The surname MacHale was also adopted by a Welsh family which settled in the barony of Tirawley, Co. Mayo, in the thirteenth century : it derives from the forename Howell. Being located in the same county the descendants of these cannot now be distinguished from their namesakes of Gaelic origin : in any case centuries of Connacht inter-marriages have made the one just as Irish in blood as the other. Outstanding personality of the name was that uncompromising protagonist of Irish-Ireland, John Mac-Hale (1791–1881), who was for forty-seven years Archbishop of Tuam.

O'HALLORAN.

O'Halloran, in Irish Ó hAllmhurain, is the name of two distinct septs. These were located in adjoining counties, Clare and Galway, where their present day descendants are numerous, though seldom found in Leinster or Ulster. The propinquity of these two counties makes it a matter of doubt to which sept dwellers on their border belong, except in cases where a pedigree or family tradition exists. The Co. Galway sept, whose slogan was " Clann Fearghaile abu," were chiefs of Clann Fearghaile, an extensive territory near Lough Corrib : they were the original proprietors of the lands on the western boundary of Galway City. They retained their leading position in Iar-Connacht to the end of the sixteenth century for they appear as such in the " Composition Book of Connacht " (1585). The Clare sept is of the same stock as the MacNamaras of Thomond ; they were located in Ogonnelloe on the shore of Lough Derg and spread southwards into Co. Limerick. Though originally of less importance than their Galway namesakes, they have, however, produced all the notable men of the name. Sylvester O'Halloran (1728–1807), surgeon and eye-specialist, historian, antiquary and Irish language enthusiast, and his brother Rev. Joseph Ignatius O'Halloran, S.J., (1718–1800), Professor of Philosophy at Bordeaux were born and bred in Limerick ; as was Sir Joseph O'Halloran (1763–1843), who, though he served for fifty years with distinction in the British army, retained his association with Limerick till his death. He had eight sons in the same service, two of whom, Thomas and William, subsequently became prominent in Australia. Another of the name, Laurence Hynes O'Halloran (1766–1831), after an adventurous life as poet, sailor, teacher and wanderer, was transported to that country and ended as the headmaster of a school in Sydney.

Arms illustrated on Plate XIV.

O'HANLON.

O'Hanlon is a name which is always associated with Co. Armagh. The sept was located in the baronies of Oneilland and Orior. For centuries their chiefs were known as lords of Orior. Ulster, of course, was the last of the four provinces to feel the calamitous effects of English invasions, but the O'Hanlons were not without experience of war against the invader : in 1493, for example the celebrated Poynings led an expedition against the most important chiefs of east Ulster—MacGennis and O'Hanlon. In 1537 Sir Oghie O'Hanlon, then Chief of the Sept, fell in with their policy of "surrender and regrant". On several occasions, indeed, their chiefs adopted a policy of conciliation, and this saved them from complete ruin at the time of the Plantation of Ulster, but later in the seventeenth century they suffered the normal fate of the Gaelic Catholic aristocracy. By 1675 we find the most noteworthy O'Hanlon of his time, not in the proud position of a chief, but as a rapparee : Redmond O'Hanlon (d. 1681), called "Count" by courtesy (though actually when in French service he received no such title), was, perhaps, the most celebrated of the many picturesque tories, or highwaymen, to be found in the pages of Irish history. Best known of the name, in modern times, was the Rev. John Canon O'Hanlon (1821–1905), author of *Lives of the Irish Saints* (nine vols.), *Irish American History* and many other works.

It should be mentioned that O'Hanlons are now numerous in Co. Cork, but southern branches of the Ulster sept appear to have been established there only in comparatively recent times.

Arms illustrated on Plate XIV.

O'HANLY.

The surname Hanley or Hanly is the anglicized form of the Irish Ó hAinle, which is possibly derived from the Gaelic word *áluinn*, beautiful (we may also note that in modern Irish *ainle* means a swallow). It is found to-day principally in, indeed it is almost confined to, two areas, viz. in Connacht to Counties Roscommon and Galway, where it is usually spelt Hanly, and in Munster to Co. Cork and adjacent districts where the spelling is Hanley. The ancient sept of O'Hanly originated on the banks of the Shannon in Co. Roscommon where the place-name Doohyhanly perpetuates their connexion with that district. These O'Hanlys were tributaries of the royal house of O'Conor. Their establishment in Co. Cork was comparatively late : the name is almost entirely confined to Co. Roscommon in the census of 1659 and in earlier records. A family closely allied to the O'Hanlys of Connacht are the Hallys of Co. Clare whose name has a similar derivation.

Donal O'Hanley was Bishop of Dublin from 1085–1096 and Samuel O'Hanley the same from 1096–1211 when the bishopric became an archbishopric.

Arms illustrated on Plate XIV.

O'HANNON, (Hanneen).

Although there are many substantial families of Hannon in Munster and Connacht, the Annals and other sources of information regarding the septs of mediaeval Ireland seldom mention the name O'Hannon. The death of Maelisa O'Hannen (Ó hAnáin), prior of Roscommon, in 1266 is one of the few such. According to the census of 1659 the name was then numerous in the barony of Athlone, Co. Roscommon ; while Haneens were found in considerable numbers in the barony of Bunratty, Co. Clare. The prefix O, dropped in the submergence of Gaelic Ireland, has not been resumed. Strictly speaking Hannon is the anglicized form of the Gaelic Ó hAnnáin. This name is chiefly associated with Co. Limerick. Another Gaelic surname, Ó hAinchín, that of a family of Síol Anmchadha belonging to south east Galway, nominally anglicized Hanneen, has, by attraction, become Hannon in most cases, though Hanneens are also found in western counties. It is of interest to note that older people in Clare and Galway call this name Hanheen thus keeping close to the Irish pronunciation of Ó hAinchín. Further there is Ó hAnnacháin which is called Hannon rather than Hanahan in Co. Limerick. The name Hannon to-day is principally found in Co. Limerick and in Counties Galway and Roscommon.

Arms illustrated on Plate XIV.

O'HANRAHAN, Hourihane.

The O'Hanrahans are a Dalcassian sept : for the most part they are still found in their original habitat—Counties Clare and Limerick. Their name in Irish is Ó hAnracháin. This is stated to be a variant of Ó hAnradháin which has been anglicized O'Hourihane in Co. Cork, where a sept of the name were erenaghs of Ross. (See also O hArracháin, *sub* O'Horan, p. 183 *infra*.)

O'HANRAGHTY, Enright, (Hanvey).

O'Hanraghty is an earlier, and now obsolete form of Ó hAnrachtaigh—the modern anglicized form being Hanratty. The name is still rarely found outside its original habitat. The sept, a comparatively small one descended from Ionrachtach, a scion of the great Maguires, was of Oriel, and the latest available statistics show that apart from the city of Dublin, in which, of course, there are migrant families from all parts of Ireland, nearly all the births registered for the name took place in the Counties Louth, Armagh and Monaghan. The chiefs of the O'Hanraghtys, of whom several are mentioned by the Four Masters between 1019 and 1161, under the style of Lords of Ui Meith, held a considerable territory in the northern part of the modern Co. Louth. The " Annals of Loch Cé " mention Aodh O'Hanratty as " King of Ui Meith " in 1107, and under the same date Donal O'Hanfey is also so described. O'Hanfy, or O'Hanify or Hanvey, is, however, quite a distinct name—Ó hAinbhith in Irish. Their territory was in the same part of the country. The pressure of the Anglo-Norman invasion pushed the O'Hanraghtys westwards into Co. Monaghan, and in the twelfth century they settled near the modern town of Castleblaney. Father Patrick Hanratty, a Franciscan of note in the first half of the seventeenth century, was a native of Co. Louth. The Four Masters use the form Ó hIonrachtaigh, while O'Dugan in the " Topographical Poem ", spells it Ó hInnrechtaigh, of which the Gaelic version, given above, is a modern variant. A branch of the family settled in France : one of these was among the aristocratic prisoners in the French Revolution.

The Mac form of the name Mac Ionnrachtaigh, now anglicized Enright, appears as MacKenraght and MacEnraghty in old records : it belongs, almost exclusively, to West Munster, the great majority of Enrights to-day coming from Co. Limerick.

Arms illustrated on Plate XV.

O'HARA.

The O'Haras are an important Irish sept of distinguished origin. They are descended from Eaghra (pronounced Ara), who was chief of Leyny in Co. Sligo, a scion of the family of Olioll Ollum, King of Munster. In Irish the name is Ó hEaghra, of which the anglicized form O'Hara is a phonetic rendering. About 1350 this sept formed two divisions, the chiefs of which were called respectively O'Hara Boy (i.e. *buide*, tawny) and O'Hara Reagh (i.e. *riabhach*, grizzled). In the " Composition Book of Connacht " (1585) O'Hara Boy is seated at Collooney and O'Hara Reagh at Bally-harry : the latter is a contemporary English attempt at writing Baile ui Eaghra or Ballyhara. A branch migrated to the Route, Co. Antrim. As might be expected, therefore, the O'Haras of to-day are chiefly found in Counties Sligo and Antrim. The famous manuscript known as " The Book of O'Hara " is still in existence : it contains a very full record of chiefs of the name. Boswell in his *Tour to the Hebrides with Dr. Johnson* (Sep. 28, 1773) tells an interesting anecdote which illustrates the respect in which the O'Haras and other ancient Gaelic families were held by the native Irish in the eighteenth century. A century later they were very extensive landlords : in Co. Sligo the O'Haras of Cooper's Hill and Annaghmore possessed more than 21,000 acres, and this family is still of importance in that county.

Among many distinguished O'Haras the most notable, in addition to three bishops of Achonry, were Kane O'Hara (1712–1782), author of the popular burlesque *Midas*, a Sligo man ; James O'Hara (1752–1819), American revolutionary, son of John O'Hara, an Irishman ; Theodore O'Hara (1820–1867), whose father Kean O'Hara escaped from Ireland after participating with Lord Edward Fitzgerald in the 1798 insurrection ; Most Rev. William O'Hara (1816–1899), first bishop of Scranton. The Sligo O'Haras who took the side of England were rewarded with a title (Baron Tyrawley) in the year 1706. One of the founders of Pittsburg, U.S.A., was an O'Hara. Maureen O'Hara, the Irish actress, has made the name well known all over four continents.

Arms illustrated on Plate XV.

HARRINGTON, O'Harraughton.

Harrington itself is a well-known English name, common in England, but very few indeed of our Irish Harringtons are of English stock. This name is an example of that slavish tendency, much in evidence during the centuries of Gaelic submergence, whereby good old Gaelic Irish surnames were transmogrified into common English ones having more or less the same sound. In this case, so far as the majority of Harringtons are concerned, the anglicized form was only remotely similar to the original phonetically. Formerly Harrington was O'Hungerdell in English which was an approximate pronounciation of the Gaelic original Ó hIongardail, but the form O'Hungerdell, which is found in documents about the time when English came to be used for legal business, is now quite obsolete. The Harringtons of this sept are numerous in south-west Cork and Kerry—almost ninety per cent of the births registered for Harrington were from that area fifty years ago and a comparison with voters' lists and directories of to-day shows that this is still substantially the case. There are two other Gaelic surnames which are sometimes also anglicized as Harrington. One is Ó hOireachtaigh, properly anglicized as Heraghty, which belongs to Counties Galway and Mayo. The third is Ó hArrachtain, *anglice* Harraughton. This is recorded as a synonym or alias of Harrington in the Tralee-Dingle area of Kerry, which suggests that the Harringtons of that part are not of the main family of Ó hIongardail but migrants from the Hy Many country to which the minor sept of Ó hArrachtain belonged. However, Harrington may be regarded as essentially a West Cork name. There, at Castletownbere, was born Timothy Harrington (1851–1910), who was probably the best known Irishman of that name : he was secretary of the Land League, M.P. and Lord Mayor of Dublin. Harrington is to-day a very prominent name in the industrial life of Cork City. Sir Henry Harrington, a leading figure in Elizabethan Ireland, was an Englishman.

O'HART.

Hart is a native English name, numerous in that country; but in Ireland the Harts (usually spelt Harte in Connacht) are nearly all of the sept O'Hart. Some families have always retained, others have recently resumed, the prefix O. In Irish the name is Ó hAirt, i.e. descendant of Art, who was son of King Conn of the Hundred Battles. The O'Harts were of the southern Ui Neill and were one of the Four Tribes of Tara: in early times their chiefs were lords of Teffia (Co. Meath), but after the Anglo-Norman invasion they were pushed westwards and settled in the territory now known as the barony of Carbury, Co. Sligo. O'Hart is included among the sixteenth century Sligo chiefs in the "Composition Book of Connacht." Sligo, with the adjacent counties of Leitrim and Roscommon, is their principal home to-day, though the name is also found in considerable numbers in Co. Cork. The O'Harts of Newtown, Ardtarmon, and other extensive estates in Co. Sligo, were, until the seventeenth century, one of the leading families in north Connacht, but like other Catholic proprietors, were reduced to straightened circumstances by the two great confiscations of land in that century.

The best known man of the name was John O'Hart (1824–1870), author of *Irish Pedigrees : the Original Stem of the Irish Nation*, a laboriously compiled and voluminous, but not always reliable, work. Therein will be found much information regarding the O'Harts of Co. Sligo.

Arms illustrated on Plate XV.

O'HARTIGAN.

The O'Hartagans, or O'Hartigans, are a Dalcassian sept located in Thomond and still well known around Limerick, though nowhere very numerous. The name is Ó hArtagáin in Irish, probably derived from the well-known christian name Art. Dunlaing O'Hartigan was one of the heroes of Clontarf. The best known of all the sept was born in Ulster far from the home of his ancestors, viz. Cineth O'Hartagan, the Gaelic poet who died in 975.

Father Matthew O'Hartigan, S.J., of Limerick, who did so much to spread the Society in Ireland, was an emissary of the Catholic Confederation to France in 1643. He is also noteworthy for his efforts on behalf of the Irish exiles in the West Indies. Another Father Hartegan was an Irish-Australian poet at the beginning of the present century.

Arms illustrated on Plate XV.

O'HEA, Hayes, Hughes.

O'Hea is one of the anglicized forms of the very common Gaelic surname Ó hAodha, which has at least a dozen different and distinct origins in Ireland and is usually anglicized Hayes, except in Ulster where it has become Hughes. Ó hAodha simply means descendant of Aodh, *anglice* Hugh. The sept so named, which is located in Corca Laoidhe—i.e. the south-western part of Co. Cork—is the only one which is called O'Hea in English and this form is invariable in that area. Murrough O'Hea was Bishop of Cork in 1205, and Maurice O'Hea was Bishop of Ross in 1559. In Co. Cork only is the name found in directories to-day (apart from a few migrants to Dublin). John Fergus O'Hea (1850–1912), artist and cartoonist, was a Cork man, and Captain William O'Hea, an officer in Nicholas Browne's infantry in King James the Second's army, was of Aghamilly Castle in Pobble O'Hea, a district retained by the sept under the overlordship of the Barrys. This name, by the way, was also known as Heas which is identical in pronunciation with Hayes.

Hayes is a very common name in England but, apart from a family of the name in Co. Wexford, Irish Hayeses are almost invariably scions of one of the Ó hAodha septs. The most considerable of these was the Dalcassian sept of Thomond, now chiefly associated with Counties Limerick and Tipperary, whence came Catherine Hayes (1825–1861), singer, and the two painters Edward Hayes (1797–1864) and Michael Angelo Hayes (1820–1887). In the seventeenth century the form O'Hea, not Hayes, was used in Co. Clare as is evidenced by the number of O'Heas in Petty's census of 1659. Woulfe gives no less than twelve distinct septs of Ó hAodha, including, as well as those mentioned above, others located around Ardstraw (Co. Tyrone), Ballyshannon (Co. Donegal), Farney (Co. Monaghan), Navan (Co. Meath), Gorey (Co. Wexford), Ballintobber and Templemurray (Co. Mayo), Dromard (Co. Sligo), and one of the Uí Máine.

Arms illustrated on Plate XV.

O'HEALY, Hely, (Kerrisk).

Though a genuine Gaelic name, Healy is very rarely found nowadays with its proper prefix O; there is no entry in current directories under O'Healy, O'Hely or O'Haly, forms which were quite usual up to the end of the seventeenth century. Healy, however, is one of the commonest names in Ireland having forty-seventh place in the list of the hundred commonest surnames, with a total number of persons so called of nearly thirteen thousand. One sept, in Irish Ó hElidhe, derived from *éilidhe* (claimant), possessed a territory at the foot of the Curlew Mountains on the western shore of Lough Arrow, i.e. the corner of County Sligo lying between Counties Mayo and Roscommon. The first of the frequent references to the family by the Four Masters is to Dermot O'Healy who died in 1309—he is described as " a princely farmer, the best of his time." A greater number, however, belong to the Munster sept. In Munster it is Ó hÉalaighthe, possibly from the word *ealadhach* (ingenious). This name was formerly correctly rendered as O'Healihy in English, and it so appears in the seventeenth century records, e.g. those reciting the transfer of their estates to the Earl of Clancarty after the Restoration. Though dispossessed, the O'Healihys remained on the lands and it was one of these who, having become a Protestant, was created Earl of Donoughmore. This title was taken from the place Donoughmore in the barony of Muskerry, Co. Cork, which was the centre of the territory possessed by the sept. The influential family of Hely d'Oissel of Normandy, ranked among the nobility of France, is descended from Peter O'Hely a Jacobite exile.

Several places in Ireland perpetuate the name Healy : Ballyhely in Co. Sligo was the seat of the O'Healys of Lough Arrow, mentioned above. It is curious that four such place names (three Ballyhealys and one Healysland) are to be found in Wexford, a county not specially associated with the septs of O'Healy, either traditionally or by reason of present population distribution. No less than five of the Donoughmore Helys (who assumed the additional name of Hutchinson) were considered worthy of a place in the *Dictionary of National Biography*, but though one of these, Richard Healy-Hutchinson, first Earl (1754–1825), was indeed an advocate of Catholic Emancipation, they distinguished themselves in the service of England rather than of Ireland. Four Healys have a lasting place in Irish history ; Patrick O'Healy, Franciscan, last Bishop of Mayo before it was united to Tuam, who in 1579 was tortured and martyred ; John Healy (1841–1918), Archbishop of Tuam, author of *Insula Sanctorum*, etc. ; the famous humorist, Father James Healy (1824–1894) ; and Timothy Healy (1855–1931), universally known as Tim Healy, the irrepressible Irish Nationalist M.P., who finally became a most successful first Governor-General of the Irish Free State.

The surname Kerrisk, which is found in Kerry to-day and is peculiar to that county, is believed to be O'Healy by origin, the first to be so called being the son of one Pierce O'Healy : in Irish the name is Mac Fhiarais, i.e. the son of Pierce.

O'HEFFERNAN.

The sept of Heffernan originally inhabited a territory near Corofin, Co. Clare, called Muintirifernáin after them. Very early, however, they established themselves in eastern Co. Limerick on the Tipperary border and were chiefs there of Owneybeg, whence they were in due course displaced by the Ryans. The principal families of the name did not migrate very far since Carew tells us that they were among the most important in the barony of Clanwilliam in 1600. The rank and file remained undisturbed and it is in Counties Tipperary and Limerick they are most numerous to-day. The old manuscripts, such as the " Book of Rights ", describe the O'Heffernans as one of the " four tribes of Owney ", the others being MacKeogh, Ó Loingsigh (Lynch) and O'Cahalan. The two most distinguished members of the sept were Aeneas O'Heffernan, Bishop of Emly, 1543–1553 and William Dall O'Heffernan (1715–1802), Gaelic poet. The prefix O, discarded during the period of Gaelic submergence, has not been resumed in modern times except in very few cases. Hiffernan is an alternative spelling of the name. The most notable so called was Dr. Paul Hiffernan (1719–1777), the dramatist.

Arms illustrated on Plate XV.

O'HEGARTY.

Hegarty, sometimes O'Hegarty but seldom Haggerty in Ireland (a form of the name found among Irish-Americans), is in Irish Ó hÉigceartaigh (*éigceartach* means unjust). Though now associated principally with Co. Cork, the Hegartys of Munster are in fact a branch of the main O'Hegarty sept of the Cinel Eoghan which was located on the borders of the present counties of Donegal and Derry. In the fourteenth century the barony of Loughinsholin (Co. Derry) was their principal habitat ; in the seventeenth they were more numerous in Tirkeeran (Co. Derry) and Inishowen (Co. Donegal) in the north, and in the baronies of Barrymore and Carbery West in Co. Cork. As is usually the case the present representatives of the sept are to be found in their traditional homeland and are to-day most numerous in Counties Cork, Donegal and Derry. The Ulster sept were subfeudatory to O'Neill : Maolmuire O'Hegarty fell at Kinsale in O'Neill's army. The 1691 attainders of O'Hegartys relate to those of Ulster. The records of persecuted priests in the seventeenth century also indicate the Ulster character of the sept up till modern times. The name appears very frequently in the annals of the Irish Brigades and among those who distinguished themselves particularly in this field of action was Lt.-Col. Hegarty of Lally's Regiment, who for his services was rewarded in 1747 by Louis XV of France, while Peter O'Hegarty was made Governor of the Isle of Bourbon. Another Irish Hegarty in eighteenth century France, Daniel O'Hegarty, shipbuilder of Dunkirk, a Catholic, strange as this seems to us now, founded the first Freemason lodge in that country in 1721. According to Dr. Richard Hayes the main object of these lodges, which were largely composed of Jacobite exiles, was the restoration of the house of Stuart.

In recent times the name has been less distinguished, though several Hegartys were prominent in the struggle for Irish Independence 1916–1921 : of these P. S. O'Hegarty (1879–1955), who was an author of repute, is the best known. The place, name Hegarty's Rock at Killygarvan near Lough Swilly commemorates the barbarous and treacherous murder of Father James Hegarty there in 1715.

Arms illustrated on Plate XV.

O'HENNESSY, Henchy.

Hennessy is a name from which the prefix O has been entirely dropped in modern times, though O'Hennessy was still widely used in the seventeenth century. In Irish it is Ó hAonghusa, i.e. descendant of Aonghus or Angus. The principal sept of this name was located near the town of Kilbeggan and the hill of Croghan, their territory being chiefly in the northern part of Co. Offaly, where they shared with O'Holohan the lordship of Clan Cholgain ; a branch of this was located nearer to Dublin, the head of it being chief of Gailenga Beg on the north side of the River Liffey on the borders of Counties Meath and Dublin. The latter were displaced by the Anglo-Norman invasion. The Offaly O'Hennessys spread into Tipperary and Clare—in the latter county they are now called Henchy, formerly Hensey. Dr. Florence Hensey (b. 1715), whose trial in London as a secret agent of France in 1758 was a *cause célèbre*, was one of these. Another distinct sept of O'Hennessy was of Corca Laoidhe, located near Ross Bay in South-west Cork. At the present day the name is principally associated with Counties Cork, Limerick and Tipperary. There are places called Ballyhennessy in Co. Clare, Co. Cork and Co. Kerry (near the Limerick border).

To most people the name Hennessy suggests brandy rather than Ireland. The French Hennessys, famous for their cognac, are of Irish stock. Richard Hennessy (b. 1720), of Ballymacmoy, Co. Cork (Mallow area), joined his Wild Geese relatives in France and became an officer in Dillon's Regiment : he fought at Fontenoy in 1742 and later settled in Cognac. His son James was a member of the French Chamber of Deputies and became a peer of France, though an Irishman and never naturalized. He married a Martell, another name intimately associated with cognac or brandy.

Other Hennessys worthy of mention are Nicholas O'Hennessy, the Cistercian Bishop of Waterford and Lismore from 1480 to 1482, Henry Hennessy (1826–1901), scientist, Professor of Engineering in Newman's Catholic University (Dublin), and Sir John Pope Hennessy (1834–1891), first Catholic Conservative Irish M.P. at Westminster, both Corkmen ; and the Kerryman William Hennessy (1828–1889),

179

Gaelic scholar; while Irish-Americans of note were Most Rev. John Hennessy (1825–1900), Archbishop of Dubuque, and William John Hennessy, painter, son of John Hennessy, the Young Irelander.

Arms illustrated on Plate XV.

O'HEYNE, Hynes.

The rather commonplace surname Hines or Hynes is a modern form in English of the very distinguished name O'Heyne, in Irish Ó hEidhin. Descended from Guaire the Hospitable, King of Connacht, from the seventh century to the destruction of the Gaelic order nearly a thousand years later the head of the O'Heynes was chief of a territory in south Galway, barony of Kiltartan. This family shared with their kinsmen the O'Shaughnessys the Lordship of Aidhne, which comprised the country stretching from Gort to Oranmore. Mulroy O'Heyne, who was father-in-law of Brian Boru, was styled Lord of Aidhne. O'Heyne and O'Kelly commanded the forces of Connacht at the Battle of Clontarf in 1014. The abbey of Kilmacduagh is called O'Heyne's Abbey. When the Anglo-Normans occupied considerable portions of Co. Galway in the thirteenth century the O'Heynes and the O'Shaughnessys were left in possession of large tracts of their ancient patrimony, and as late as 1878 the head of the family was in possession of 4,169 acres, near Ballinasloe, where his residence then was. In 1608 the O'Heynes are recorded as owning 8,640 acres in the northern part of Aidhne around Kinvarra. As might be expected the name is still found most plentifully in Counties Galway and Clare. Since the middle of the seventeenth century the O'Heynes have been chiefly notable as missionary priests. The most remarkable was Father John O'Heyne, O.P. (d. 1715), historian of the Dominican Order.

Arms illustrated on Plate XV.

O'HICKEY.

Hickey, also spelt Hickie, is the anglicized form of the Irish Ó hIcidhe (pronounced O Hickee), *iceadh*, from which it is derived, meaning a physician or healer. The Hickeys are closely identified with Co. Clare and north Tipperary, being Dalcassian in origin and hereditary physicians to the ruling O'Briens of Thomond. In course of time they have spread to adjoining counties and at present are as numerous in Limerick as in Clare and Tipperary.

Of distinguished Irish Hickeys, the Franciscan Professor Anthony Hickey (d. 1641), of St. Isidores, Rome and Louvain, John Hickey (1756–1795), sculptor, his brother Thomas Hickey (1760–1822), portrait painter, Thomas O'Hickey (fl.1820), one of the best of the traditional Irish scribes, and William Hickey (c. 1787–1875), who was a pioneer in the field of agricultural education, as well as Father Patrick O'Hickey (1861–1916), champion of essential Irish in the National University of Ireland, may be specially mentioned. William Hickey (1749–1830), whose auto-biography is a classic, was the son of a Cashel man.

Arms illustrated on Plate XVI.

O'HIGGIN.

Despite the very English appearance of the surname Higgins, as it is usually anglicized, it is in fact a purely native Irish Gaelic name which should normally have been O'Higgin in English, the Irish form being Ó hUigín, pronounced O'Higgeen. The name, according to modern scholarship, is derived from the old Gaelic word *uiging*, akin to the Norse Viking, not from the word *uige*. Originating as a branch of the O'Neills of the midlands of Ireland (not the Ulster O'Neills) this sept spread westwards as far as Co. Sligo where they held large estates. They were still extensive landowners in 1878 having estates in nearly all the western counties. The really remarkable fact about them is the number of distinguished poets they produced during three centuries, beginning with Tadhg Mór Ó hUigín who died in 1315 to Tadhg Dall (d. 1617). Another Tadhg, called Óg, flourished in the first half of the fifteenth century. The sixteenth century saw five more poets of the name, one of whom, Maolmuire (d. 1591), was also Archbishop of Tuam. A poem by one of these, Pilib Bocht Ó Huigín, was the first to be printed in the Irish language. With the destruction of the Gaelic order in the seventeenth century the O'Higginses lost their pre-eminence in the literary sphere, but not their prominence in the world of affairs : John Higgins (1676–1729), of Limerick, was a famous physician in Spain ; Don Ambrosio O'Higgins (1721–1801), of Ballina, who became Marquis of Osorno and Viceroy of Peru, had a most interesting and distinguished career in South America, while his son Bernardo O'Higgins (1780–1846) is known as the Liberator of Chile, in which country a province is called O'Higgins in memory of these men. Four of the name were martyred for the faith during the Cromwellian régime. William Higgins (1763–1825) was a chemist of international fame. In our own time one family of the name has produced four Irish cabinet ministers including Kevin O'Higgins (1892–1927), whose brilliant career was cut short by his assassination.

As a slight set off against this galaxy of distinguished men we may mention the notorious Francis Higgins (1746–1802), commonly known as the " Sham Squire ", and another Francis Higgins (1669–1728), a notorious and somewhat disreputable Protestant preacher.

At the present time the name is chiefly found in Connacht (more than fifty per cent are in that province, especially Counties Mayo and Roscommon). It is estimated that there are some eight thousand persons of the name in Ireland to-day, very few of these using the prefix O.

Arms illustrated on Plate XVI.

O'HOGAN.

The Hogans are a Dalcassian family, their eponymous ancestor being Ógan who was descended from an uncle of Brian Boru, the most celebrated of all the Kings of Ireland. The Dalcassian territory extended well beyond the boundaries of Co. Clare which was the heart of Thomond, their country. The Hogans occupied the extreme north-eastern part of it and their chief lived at Ardcrony, near Nenagh, Co. Tipperary. The name is numerous in Ireland, being among the hundred commonest surnames. The great majority of the eight thousand or so persons so called (which is the estimate of the present Hogan population) belong to their original native habitat, being found to-day in Counties Tipperary, Clare and Limerick. There are also a number in Co. Cork, whose origin is stated by O'Donovan to be different from the Dalcassian Hogans. One of the minor Corca Laidhe septs was O'Hogan. In Irish the name is Ó hÓgáin but the prefix O is only occasionally met with in the modern form in English. In the seventeenth century the name was often written Ogan. There is a placename Ballyhogan in the parish of Dysart, Co. Clare.

The most famous Hogan is probably John Hogan (1800–1858), an Irish sculptor of international repute ; but to Irishmen the romantic figure of " Galloping Hogan " (the date of whose birth and death I cannot trace), the hero of Sarsfield's exploit at Ballyneety (1690), makes the most appeal. Maurice O'Hogan was a notable Bishop : he held the see of Kildare from 1281 to 1298. Rev. Edmund Hogan, S.J. (1831–1917), did much work as an editor of manuscripts and produced his best known book *Onomasticon Gaedelicum* at the age of seventy-two. The first Minister of Agriculture in the Irish Free State Patrick Hogan (1891–1936), was one of three brothers who have distinguished themselves in various national activities in our own time.

Arms illustrated on Plate XVI.

O'HOLOHAN, Holland, (Mulholland, Hyland).

O'Holohan—Ó hUallacháin in Irish—is the name of at least two septs originally located in Offaly and in Thomond. In the course of time they spread southwards in both cases, but in the census of 1659 the great majority of the name were living in Co. Kilkenny : at the present time it is chiefly found in that county with the spelling Holohan, and in the western part of Munster with the spelling Houlihan. No less than seventeen variant spellings of the name are recorded by the Registrar-General, including Oolahan and Whoolehan. In Offaly the O'Holohans shared the leadership of the Clan Colgan with the O'Hennessys. It was one of these, Dermot O'Holohan, who constructed the curragh bridge across the Shannon above Portumna which enabled O'Sullivan Beare to cross into Connacht on his epic march from Kinsale in 1602. The southward movement both from Offaly and Clare brought them to Co. Cork where many families of Houlihan adopted the name Holland as the English form of their surname. This was also done to some extent in their original Thomond homeland : John Holland (1841–1914), the noted American inventor, was a native of Co. Clare.

The name Holland may also be an abbreviation of Mulholland (once Ó Maolchal-ann, devotee of St. Callan) a sept located in the northern part of Co. Limerick : the Ulster Mulhollands, however, never abbreviated their name to Holland.

Finally it may be mentioned that Holland is found in Ulster as the anglicized form of O hAoláin, which in Leinster is Hyland and in Munster Heelan.

In mediaeval times the most notable man of the name was Donal O'Hoolahan, Archbishop of Cashel from 1171 to 1182.

A curious anglicization of Ó hUallacháin is mentioned in the article on Nolan (q.v. p. 242 *infra*).

Arms illustrated on Plate XVI.

O'HORAN, Haren.

The true sept of O'Horan (Ó hOdhráin in Irish) originated in Co. Galway whence they spread into Co. Mayo and are now fairly numerous in those Connacht counties. Another Gaelic surname, Ó hArracháin, which is a corruption of Ó Hanradhain (*anglice* Hanrahan) is commonly anglicized Horan, though in Thomond (Co. Clare), where this minor Dalcassian sept originated, it is usually pronounced, and sometimes written, more phonetically Harhan. Other anglicized forms recorded in Co. Clare are Haren and Haran. Even when written Horan it is pronounced with an internal aspirate which is more accurately represented by the form Haughran, found in the birth registers of Co. Offaly as a synonym of Horan. Yet another variant, in this case peculiar to Co. Cork, is O'Hourahan or O'Horahan, a rare name but one familiar formerly to readers of *The Nation* on account of its regular contributor M. J. O'Horahan. This family, quite distinct from the Thomond one, belonged to Co. Cork and were erenaghs of Ross. The Horans now found in not inconsiderable numbers in Co. Cork are of this stock. The distinguished Admiral Horan of the British Navy is the son of a Co. Limerick man, presumably of Thomond lineage. The name has not been prominent in Irish cultural or political history.

Arms illustrated on Plate XVI.

O'HOSEY, Hussey.

It is very usual for Gaelic names to be given common English surnames of somewhat similar sound as their anglicized equivalent ; Hussey is one of the few examples of a Norman name being so adopted. It is not very common in Ireland to-day: the counties with which it is mostly associated are Kerry and Roscommon. The Kerry Husseys are a branch of the Norman family of Houssaye in France, first called de Hosé and de Hosey here and later Hussey. The first of these to settle in Ireland came with Strongbow and acquired through Hugh de Lacy extensive lands near Dublin, including Galtrim in Co. Meath whence comes the Palatine title of Baron of Galtrim : Sir Hugh Hussey, Kt., was summoned to the Irish Parliament of 1294, as such and his heirs for many generations were so styled, but it was not recognized as a peerage by the English crown. In 1878 large estates were owned by Husseys in Co. Meath and Co. Kerry, but the only line of this family which has survived in any considerable numbers is that which migrated to Dingle about 1550. The Husseys of Connacht are presumably of the sept Ó hEodhusa, hereditary bards to the Mac-Guires of Fermanagh. The last of these was Eochaidh O'Hussey (c. 1574–c. 1630). Another distinguished Gaelic writer was Bonaventura O'Hussey, O.F.M. (d. 1614), born at Clogher and died at Louvain where he was an original member of the Franciscan College. The name Ó hEodhusa presents an example of the absurdity of the anglicized equivalents sometimes adopted during the period of Gaelic submergence : even the Norman name Hussey was not English enough for some families who became Oswell, and their descendants are still in Ulster under that guise.

In the eighteenth century Philip Hussey (1713–1783), who was born in Cork and died in Dublin, was a foremost portrait painter, and Most Rev. Thomas Hussey (1741–1803) was Bishop of Waterford and Lismore.

O'HOUNEEN, MacGlashan, Greene.

Although Green is one of the commonest indigenous surnames in England and no doubt many of our Irish Greenes are of English extraction, nevertheless the majority of those who hail from Connacht and west Munster are native Irish in origin. There the name is almost always spelt with a final E. In Co. Clare where the name is well known, it is a synonym, by translation of the word *uaithne* (green), for Ó hUaithnín, formerly anglicized phonetically as Huneen and Houneen : this is a genuine Dalcassian family. A similar metamorphosis has occurred in Co. Cork, where however Hooney was commoner as an alternative than Hooneen. Then again, there are Gaelic Greenes in Ulster to be found in every county from Derry to Armagh and into Louth. These are usually Mac Glasáin (alternatively MacGlashan) from the word *glas* which denotes a greyish green colour. Ó Fathaigh, normally Fahy, has sometimes been anglicized as Green by mistranslation, *faithche* meaning a green or lawn. In some parts of Ulster the Irish forms Ó Griana and MacGriana are found. These would not appear to be of any antiquity, but the latter was in existence two centuries ago, the name Nial Magreena appearing in a list of parishioners of Stranorlar in 1751. The present distribution of the name Greene in Ireland, as revealed in the returns of the Registrar-General, is widespread throughout the country, with the adjoining counties of Clare, Galway and Tipperary predominating.

No Irishman or woman called Greene is famous unless we count Alice Stopford (Green) the Irish historian who married the English historian J. R. Green. Plunket Greene (1865–1936), was a singer and composer of some note. Daniel O'Huonyn, of the family of Greenes of Co. Clare, became an Admiral of the Spanish Navy about 1750.

MacHUGH.

The Gaelic surname MacAodha, signifying the son of Aodh, i.e. Hugh, has acquired in the process of anglicization a great number of variants. These include MacKay, MacKee, MacCoy, Hughes, Hewson, Eason, etc., and also MacHugh—the name now under consideration. MacHugh is the form used by the Connacht sept which is of the same stock as the O'Flahertys : they were chiefs of the territory known as the barony of Clare in Co. Galway. In 1585, the date of the " Composition Book of Connacht," the MacHughs were not only there but in the barony of Athlone, Co. Roscommon, also. Nearly a century later the records of the Cromwellian settlement show that they were landowners in Co. Galway. To-day they are found all around that area and even beyond it—as far north as Leitrim and Fermanagh. Malachy MacHugh, Archbishop of Tuam (1313–1348), was of this branch of the sept.

He is called Molassie MacHugh in the " Annals of Clonmacnois," and in the " Annals of Loch Cé " we find an interesting entry indicating that he only became Bishop of Elphin in opposition to the nominee of the diocesan chapter.

MacHugo, a name not uncommon in Co. Galway, is not a variant of MacHugh, but one of the many gaelicized branches of the Burkes.

Arms illustrated on Plate XVI.

O'HURLEY, O'Murhila, Murrily, (O'Herlihy).

The well known surname Hurley is used as the anglicized form of two distinct Gaelic patronymics. The Thomond sept Ó hUirthile descends from one Uirthile or Urley (an obsolete christian name) who was of the race of Blod, son of Cas, the progenitor of the Dalcassians. O'Hurley was one of the principal chiefs of Thomond in 1309, but after that they are mainly met with in Co. Limerick, in the Kilmallock area, and in north Tipperary where there is a place-name Rathurley in the parish of Kilruane. Kilmallock was represented in the parliaments of 1585 and 1689 by an O'Hurley of Knocklong Castle, and Sir Maurice O'Hurley of the same family was prominent in the activities of the Confederate Catholics in 1646. Two were Bishops of Emly in the stormy seventeenth century, and one of the most famous prelates of the first persecution era was Dermot O'Hurley (1519–1584), Archbishop of Cashel, who for his part in the struggle against English aggression in Ireland was first tortured and then hanged. One of the most remarkable characters of late seventeenth century Ireland was the informer Patrick Hurley of Co. Clare, self-styled Count of Mount-callan, whose adventurous and infamous career was finally brought to a close by his trial and conviction in 1700.

It may here be mentioned that some Clare Hurleys have acquired the name Commane by a process of erroneous translation, *camán* being the Irish word for a hurley (stick).

The great majority of present day Hurleys are from Co. Cork. This was the case, too, in the seventeenth century when the name was also recorded as numerous in Counties Limerick and Clare. To Co. Cork belonged the second sept referred to above. These in Irish are Ó Muirthile, sometimes phonetically anglicized as Murhilla and shortened to Murley, but nearly always Hurley, for no obvious reason. They were located in the neighbourhood of Kilbritain (in Carbery East): one of them, who became Bishop of Ross in 1517, is recorded as John O'Murily or O'Murhila. In early records confusion is caused by reason of the fact that the Co. Limerick O'Hurleys sometimes appear as Murilly. Further confusion in the case of the Co. Cork O'Hurleys arises because the name of the sept Ó hIarhatha, normally anglicized O'Herlihy, has become Hurley in some places. This family were erenaghs of St. Gobnait's Church, Ballyvourney. One of them, Thomas O'Herlihy, was Bishop of Ross from 1562 until 1570 when he was forced to abdicate and was incarcerated in the Tower of London until his death ten years later.

Brother Donogh O'Muirhily (d. 1586) was one of the many Franciscans who suffered martyrdom in Ireland in the sixteenth and seventeenth centuries.

Arms illustrated on Plate XVI.

MacINERNEY, Nerney, Kinnerk.

In Irish this name is Mac an Airchinnigh, i.e. son of the erenagh. The word erenagh denotes steward of church lands, originally an ecclesiastical office but later in the hands of laymen and hereditary. As might be expected, therefore, the surname in question came into existence in a number of unrelated families in different parts of the country. The erenaghs of St. Patrick's, Elphin, and of Tuam thus acquired the surname Mac an Airchinnigh. The descendants of the former are still to be found in Co. Roscommon, but their name is now anglicized Nerney. Much more numerous is the sept of Thomond; indeed the name MacInerney is now almost exclusively associated with County Clare where it is now one of the most numerous surnames. Their origin as erenaghs there is obscure, but they were established as a sept of the same stock as the powerful Macnamaras at least as early as 1300. They are centered in the old parish of Kilconry, barony of Bunratty (between Ennis and Quin), but their ancestral estate at Ballycally was lost at the time of the Cromwellian confiscations. Nevertheless the sept as a whole remained undisplaced, for the 1659 census shows that there were then some thirty families of MacInerney in Clare, all in the barony of Bunratty. An alternative form of the name found in Clare, though not common, is Kinnerk; and in this connexion it may be mentioned that the local pronunciation of MacInerney is—or was until recently—MacInerheny (almost MacInerkney). Father Laurence MacInerheny, the priest who was martyred by the Cromwellians in 1642, so spelt his name.

Few of the name have been prominent in Irish history. In modern times the most distinguished was Father M. H. MacInerny, O.P., author of *The History of the Irish Dominicans*. To most people in Ireland to-day it connotes Clare hurling and large scale building.

Arms illustrated on Plate XVI.

JENNINGS.

The name Jennings is the modern anglicized form of Mac Sheoinín, pronounced MacKeoneen, and written MacIonyn, MacJonine etc. in the records up to the middle of the seventeenth century. It is not, however, of true Gaelic origin being a surname adopted by a branch of the Burkes of Connacht, descended from Seoinín (or Little John) Burke. Jennings, of course, is itself a common indigenous English surname and some people in Ireland so called may well be of English origin ; but it is safe to say that in Connacht, where the name is chiefly found to-day, they are of the Burke stock. At the time of the Composition of Connacht (1585) they held extensive lands in the baronies of Dunmore, Co. Galway, and Kilmaine, Co. Mayo. One of the family John Jennings, alias Burke, was Archbishop of Connacht (i.e. Tuam) 1441–1450. The family produced a number of distinguished soldiers. Charles Jennings (1744–1799), who assumed the name of Kilmaine from his ancestral home, is regarded as the greatest Irish soldier of the French revolutionary period ; his brother Father James Jennings suffered a long imprisonment during the French Revolution ; and two others David and Patrick Jennings were officers in the Irish Brigade. Sir Patrick A. Jennings (1830–1897), Governor of New South Wales, was born at Newry.

JORDAN.

Though Jordan is quite a common English name very few of Irish Jordans are of English descent. Mac Siurtáin was a surname of the Gaelic type adopted by one of the hibernicized Norman families which acquired extensive territory in Connacht after the invasion of 1172. It signifies descendants of Jordan, i.e. Jordan d'Exeter, and this sept, for such it was in effect, in due course became in the sixteenth century phrase " wild Irish ". In the " Annals of Connacht," in which the name appears frequently between the years 1336 and 1470, it is spelt MacSiurtan. This origin was by no means forgotten, for one of them who was killed in 1422 is described by the annalist as " the strongest hand and the bravest heart of all the d'Exeters of his time." In English they were usually called MacJordan in Mayo, while in Clare, where they were also settled, the Fiants give them variously as MacShurtan, MacShurdane, MacShurton etc. Nowadays the form always used is simply Jordan. The modern barony of Gallen in Co. Mayo was long known as MacJordan's country, and it is so described both in the Fiants and in the " Composition Book of Connacht." In the latter the chief is called MacSurtaine alias Jordan.

Dorothea Jordan (1762–1816), actress and mother of the FitzClarences (she was the mistress of William IV), was actually Dorothea Bland, from Derryquin, Co. Kerry, Jordan being a stage name. Kate Jordan (1862–1926), American novelist and playwright, was also born in Ireland. Father Fulgentius Jordan, martyred in 1652, was a member of the Augustinian Order.

At the present time the name is chiefly found in Counties Galway and Mayo.
Arms illustrated on Plate XVI.

JOYCE.

Though not Gaelic and sometimes found in England of non-Irish origin, Joyce may certainly be regarded as a true Irish name, and more particularly a Connacht one. The first Joyce to come to Ireland of whom there is authentic record was Thomas de Jorse or Joyce, stated by MacFirbis to be a Welshman, who in 1283 married the daughter of O'Brien, Prince of Thomond and went with her by sea to Co. Galway ; there in Iar Connacht, which runs over the Mayo border, they were at first tributary to the O'Flahertys but they established themselves so firmly and so permanently that the territory they inhabited became known as Joyce's Country and they had a recognized Chief of the Name in the Irish way : the " Composition Book of Connacht " places that chief in the barony of Ross (Co. Galway). Statistics of births, deaths and marriages show that this is still their stronghold : over eighty per cent of the Joyces in Ireland come from Galway or Mayo. In Ballinrobe, Co. Mayo, the Joyces are sometimes called Shoye which is clearly a phonetic spelling of the form of the name used in the Irish language, viz. Seoighe. A very curious synonym for Joyce, found at Claremorris, is Cunnagher. Before coming to the matter of distinguished individuals of the name in Irish history the fact that the Joyces have always been noted for their exceptional stature should be mentioned. William Joyes, or Joyce, was Archbishop of Tuam from 1487 to 1501, and two of the name were Archbishops of Armagh from 1307 to 1324. Three Joyces of Galway, two of them priests, were instrumental in establishing the Dominican College at Louvain in 1648 which was soon afterwards incorporated in the University. Several were mayors of Galway City of which the Joyces were one of the " Fourteen Tribes." The most notable of modern times were James Joyce (1882–1941), author of *Dubliners*, *Ulysses* etc., Patrick Weston Joyce (1827–1914), historian and author of *Irish Names of Places*. His brother Robert Dwyer Joyce (1830–1883) was well known in the U.S.A. as a physician and poet, while Isaac Wilson Joyce (1836–1905), an American citizen of Irish descent, made a name in a different field, for he was a Methodist revivalist preacher.

Arms illustrated on Plate XVII.

KAVANAGH, (Keevan).

Kavanagh is one of the very few ancient Gaelic Irish surnames which has neither the prefix Mac or O : it is wrong to call it Ó Caomhánach in Irish as is sometimes erroneously done. In Irish it is simply Caomhánach which is an adjective denoting association with Caomhán, in this case St. Caomhán, the first Kavanagh having been fostered by a successor of that saint. It was not customary for such epithets to be perpetuated, as happened with this branch of the MacMurroughs. The first Kavanagh was Donal son of Dermot MacMurrough, King of Leinster, who was one of the prominent figures in Irish history, being the immediate cause of the Anglo-Norman invasion. The Kavanagh territory lay then in Counties Wexford and Carlow and they continued to be extensive landowners there up to recent times. The name is very numerous in and around Co. Wexford in all classes of society, so much so indeed that there are enough Kavanaghs in the south-eastern counties of Leinster by themselves, without counting the scattered Kavanaghs in the rest of the country, to put the name in the list of the eighty commonest surnames in the country : all told they hold fifty-third place in that list. The agnomen Kavanagh was long associated with the MacMurroughs, Art Mac Murrough, the King of Leinster who put up so determined a resistance to Richard II of England, being styled Kavanagh. The Kavanaghs themselves have produced a number of notable figures, none more picturesque than Arthur MacMurrough Kavanagh (1831–1889), who, although he had only stumps of arms and legs, overcame the disability and became an expert horseman and fisherman, learned to write and draw and was for many years a Member of Parliament. In the same century Morgan Peter Kavanagh (1800–1874) and his daughter Julia Kavanagh (1824–1877) were well-known authors in their day. Going back to the sixteenth century there was Cahir Mac Art Kavanagh (1500–1554), who took part in the Geraldine rebellion, and Art Kavanagh, who was Hugh O'Neill's companion in the dramatic escape from Dublin Castle in 1590. In the next century we find Brian Kavanagh, one of the many Kavanaghs who fought for the Stuart cause, described as the tallest man in King James's army ; while among the Wild Geese of the name Morgan Kavanagh, who rose to be Governor of Prague in 1766, was said to be the biggest man in Europe. Several Kavanaghs were officers in the Irish Brigade in the army of France and a branch of the family settled in that country, but it was in Austria they chiefly distinguished themselves. Two were prominent in 1798—Rev. Francis Kavanagh, who was one of the leaders of the insurrection in Co. Wexford, and Walter Cavanagh of Borris, Co. Carlow, nicknamed by the people " the monarch ", whose house was burned down by the insurgents. The well-known song " Eileen Aroon ", said to have been composed by Carol O'Daly in the thirteenth century, should be mentioned in connexion with this family, the Eileen invoked being the daughter of the Kavanagh chief of the time.

Kavanagh is sometimes used as a synonym for two often quite distinct surnames, affording an example of the not uncommon process of attraction whereby some well-known patronymic of somewhat similar sound is assumed in place of the original name. Ó Caomháin, *anglice* O'Keevan and Kevane, once an important sept in Mayo, where it has also been maladroitly turned into Cavendish, is one ; the other is Ó Caibhdeanigh of Ossory, an obsolete form of Gaffney.

Arms illustrated on Plate XVII.

KEANE, O'KANE, O'Cahan, (MacCloskey, MacEvinney).

There were two great septs of Ó Catháin. The earlier anglicized form of this name was O'Cahan, and even as late as the beginning of the present century, O'Cahans were still found in Co. Derry ; but in modern times the forms Keane, Kane, and some-times O'Kane, are almost universally used, Keane in Munster and Connacht, Kane in Ulster. The two septs were quite distinct originally, but if the belief that the Keanes of Thomond are a minor branch of Ó Catháin of Ulster is true, as the best authorities assert, the propinquity of Clare to Galway must necessarily lead to un-certainty in the west of Ireland in cases where no pedigree or reliable family tradition exists. In this connexion it should be added that the Cahanes of west Clare, who were co-arbs of St. Senan, wrote their name MacCahan and are thought to be quite distinct from the O'Cahanes.

The O'Kanes of Keenaght and Coleraine (Co. Derry) were a powerful and important sept, though not of much account before the twelfth century when they ousted the O'Connors of Glengiven (mod. Dungiven) from their territory. Once established there they retained their ascendancy in the country which is now Co. Derry until they were ruined by the Plantation of Ulster. Many of this sept appear in the Annals from the year 1170 onwards. According to Keating, O'Cahan was one of the inaugurators of O'Neill. In 1598 the last of their regularly inaugurated chieftains, Donnell Ballagh O'Cahan (d. 1617) was formally installed as such. He joined Tyrone (O'Neill) in the great war against the English but later, having submitted with the loss of much of his estates, he so far changed his allegiance as to be knighted by James I ; never-theless, he spent his last years as an untried prisoner in the Tower of London. A century later, Sir Richard Kane (1666–1736) distinguished himself as a soldier in the British army and as a writer on military subjects. Echlin O'Kane (1720–1790), an Ulsterman though born in Drogheda, was one of the most famous Irish harpers of the eighteenth century, playing as he did in several European courts. Sir Robert John Kane (1809–1890) was a leading Dublin scientist, best remembered for his book *The Industrial Resources of Ireland*. O'Donovan says he was of the Derry sept. The MacCloskeys of Co. Derry are a branch of the O'Kanes, being descended from Bloskey O'Kane, slayer of Murtagh O'Loughlin—heir to the throne of Ireland in 1196. The best known of these in modern times was Dr. MacCloskey, Archbishop of New York, who was created Cardinal in 1875.

Another branch became MacEvinney or MacAvinny (Mac Aibhne in Irish), the eponymous ancestor being Aibhne Ó Catháin. It must be remembered, however, that MacEvinney is also the anglicized form of the Breffny surname Mac Dhuibhne.

Apart from the prowess of the O'Cahans of Ulster in mediaeval times, the Tho-mond O'Cahans, or O'Keanes as they were usually called on the continent, supplied many distinguished officers to the armies of France and Spain in the eighteenth century, notably Eugene O'Keane (killed in action 1693), one of fourteen brothers four of whom served in France.

The other sept was of the Ui Fiachrach, located in Co. Galway. Though numerous they were not of great prominence in Connacht in the history of the province, where, however, they are still to be found in large numbers.

Finally, the name Kean, usually nowadays without the final e, is that of a Co. Waterford sept quite distinct from O'Cahane, the surname being Ó Céin in Irish. This sept, situated in the territory between Kilmacthomas and Bunmahon, is mentioned by O'Heerin and is still represented there. Several notable Keanes came from Munster, such as August Henry Keane (1833–1912), the anthropologist ; John Lord Keane (1781–1844), a soldier of renown. Charles Kean (1811–1880), the actor, was born in Waterford, and his father, Edmund Kean (1787–1833), a still more famous actor, is stated by O'Donovan to be of the O'Cein sept.

Arms illustrated on Plate XVII.

O'KEARNEY, Carney.

The name Kearney is evenly distributed throughout the four provinces of Ireland ; the alternative spelling Carney, however, is almost confined to Connacht, particularly Co. Mayo. The latter are Ó Cearnaigh in Irish (presumably from *cearnach*, victorious) and arc a branch of the Ui Fiachrach whose territory was around Moynulla and Balla in Co. Mayo. The Dalcassian O'Kearneys, who migrated to Cashel in early times, are also Ó Cearnaigh. The most important Kearney sept in history are of different origin. In Irish their name is Ó Catharnaigh. They were chiefs of Teffia, Co. Meath, and even when their influence diminished they retained a considerable territory in Kilcoursey in Co. Offaly. One of them became Baron Kilcoursey. The Meath Kearneys are usually known as Fox, the head of the family being styled " The Fox." This arose from the fact that the cognomen Sionnach (fox) was applied to their eleventh century ancestor. For further particulars see p. 151 *supra sub* Fox. Quite a number of alternative forms are used in English besides Carney, including Keherney, O'Caherney and (in Co. Cavan) McCarney. There is a townland called Ballymacarney in Co. Meath.

Five Kearneys of Irish origin appear in the *Dictionary of American Biography* in the spheres of politics, literature and war. Seven notable ecclesiastics called Kearney lived and worked in Ireland, of whom Rev. Barnabas Kearney, S.J. (1567–1640), David Kearney, Archbishop of Cashel from 1603 to 1625, and the Protestant Rev. John Kearney (1542–1600), author of a Catechism in the Irish language, may be specifically mentioned. In France the Abbé Charles Kearney (c. 1745–1820) was a prominent anti-revolutionary at the time of the French Revolution.

The family of John Kearney of Fethard, who was secretary to James II, were very prominent in French court and legal circles during the eighteenth century.

Arms illustrated on Plate XVII.

KEATING, (Keaty).

Though it is still found indigenous in England, Keating is a name which may be regarded as hibernicized. The Keatings of Norman origin themselves first came to Ireland with the Anglo-Norman invaders at the end of the twelfth century, when they settled in Co. Wexford. With that county they have since been most prominently associated ; but branches of the family soon established themselves in Leix and other parts of South Leinster. Writing of Queen's County in 1613 the Lord Deputy describes the Keatings as a " great sept of people " there. In 1579 Sir Nicholas Malby, in his description of Ireland and its septs, calls them ill-disposed rebels (of Co. Carlow). From the year 1302 onwards Keatings held many positions of importance as sheriffs, members of parliament etc. The best known of these was John Keating (1635–?1695), who was Lord Chief Justice and a notable figure in the parliament of 1689. At that time also several served in King James's Irish army. The name appears among the attainders following the defeat of James II, one family so dispossessed being as far north in Leinster as Co. Meath. They do not seem to have been so closely identified with the national cause in the previous generation, as none was attainted in 1642. However, the most famous and most patriotic of all Keatings lived then, viz. Seathrún Céitinn or Dr. Geoffrey Keating (1570–1644), hunted priest, gifted preacher and author of *Foras Feasa* and other important works in the Irish language. During the eighteenth and nineteenth centuries the name was not prominent in Ireland, though General Thomas Keating (1748–1796) was a notable figure in revolutionary France ; but in our own day we have Seán Keating, the outstanding artist, who is President of the Royal Hibernian Academy.

The name Ó Céatfhadha, usually anglicized Keaty, belonging to a minor Dalcassian sept located near the city of Limerick, has in some cases assumed the form Keating. MacKeatings are found in Ulster : I have not traced their origin.

Arms illustrated on Plate XVII.

O'KEEFFE.

The O'Keeffes not only originated in Co. Cork, but they also stayed there. It is still an out-and-out Co. Cork name, judging by birth registrations, voters' lists, directories and such like tests. It is true that, like so many powerful native Irish septs, they were forced out of their original territory by the invading Normans early in the thirteenth century, but in their case it was only a trek westwards within the bounds of what is now Co. Cork. So firmly did they establish themselves on the lands they then acquired in the Duhallow country that their new territory got and kept the name of Pobal O'Keeffe. O'Keeffe, in Irish Ó Caoimh, is derived from the personal name Caemh. The eponymous ancestor of the sept was Art Caemh whose father, slain in 902, was King of Munster. Unlike most O names, O'Keeffe is one which has retained the prefix fairly consistently : even in the 1880's, when Gaelic ideals were at their nadir, registration of O'Keeffes and Keeffes was about equal and to-day the O'Keeffes largely predominate. Though, as already stated, not numerous outside Co. Cork, they total enough to be included in the list of the hundred most common names in Ireland. The two most famous O'Keeffes in the story of Ireland were Father Eoghan (or Owen) O'Keefe (1656–1726), who was president of the bards of north Co. Cork, and John O'Keeffe (1747–1833), the playwright; the latter's daughter Adelaide O'Keeffe was a well-known authoress in her day. Exiled O'Keeffes, from Pobal O'Keeffe, were prominent in France, particularly the family of the intrepid Irish Brigade officer Constantine O'Keeffe (1671–1745) which was admitted into the nobility of France; General Patrick O'Keeffe (1740–1809) of a later Irish Brigade, continuously on active service for forty-seven years and four times severely wounded, is also worthy of mention.

Arms illustrated on Plate XVII.

O'KEENAN.

The sept of O'Keenan—Ó Cianáin in Irish—is chiefly remarkable for the number of distinguished ecclesiastics and historians it produced in the middle ages. Between 1345 and 1508 no less than eight are mentioned by the Four Masters as historians to the Maguires of Fermanagh. The most famous of these was Adam Ó Cianáin, Canon of Lisgool, while one Rory O'Keenan was chief scribe of the " Book of Magauran." The Abbey of Lisgool is in Co. Fermanagh and this, running through Co. Monaghan into Louth, and comprising the territory formerly known as Oriel, is the home country of the Keenans nowadays as in mediaeval times. The name Keenan is not to be confused with Keenahan which is quite distinct from it. The best known Keenans are Frank Keenan (1858–1929), American actor, son of an Irish emigrant, Sir Norbert Keenan (b. Dublin 1866), Australian statesman, Sir Patrick Keenan (1829–1894), Chief Commissioner of National Education in Ireland and Joseph Henry Keenan (b. 1900) the authority on thermodynamics. The form MacKeenan appears in the census of 1659 as numerous in Leitrim and elsewhere, but the prefix Mac is now quite obsolete and may be due to a mistake on the part of the seventeenth century non-Irish officials who were often confused between O and Mac. It is always O in the native Irish Annals.

O'KELLEHER.

The Kellehers are a Dalcassian family, in Irish Ó Céileachair, i.e. descendant of Céileachar or Kelleher, who was a nephew of the famous Brian Boru. They left their original habitat in Co. Clare in the fourteenth century and migrated to Co. Cork. The name is now seldom found outside that part of Munster: of 148 births recorded in one year for that name 92 were in Co. Cork and 23 in Co. Kerry. According to the extracts made from the census of 1921 by Jeremiah King, the Kerry historian, there were 165 families of Kelleher in the county at that date. The name is sometimes abbreviated to Keller, but most Kellers are of German or Austrian origin—though Alderman Keller of Cork, who was well known in that city in the eighties, was really a Kelleher, as was Monsignor Keller, of Cloyne, another prominent figure in Co. Cork about the same time. Maolmuire Mac Ceileachair, the compiler of the " Book of the Dun Cow," belongs to the pre-surname period and his name merely indicates that he was the son of a man called Ceileachar (Kelleher).

O'KELLY, Queally, (O'Keily).

There are approximately 50,000 Kellys and O'Kellys in Ireland to-day. It is the second commonest Irish surname, not far behind Murphy in numerical strength. This name presents a remarkable example of the extent to which the prefixes O and Mac, so widely dropped during the period of Gaelic submergence, have been resumed. In the year 1890 there were 1,242 births registered as Kelly (distributed all over the country), while only nine were registered as O'Kelly. To-day the proportion has risen from one in 130 to approximately one in twenty. The universally respected President of Ireland, Mr. Seán T. O'Kelly, is a case in point.

There is a fairly widespread but quite erroneous belief that all persons of the name descend from members of the great O'Kelly sept of Ui Máine. The fact is that this surname came into being independently in at least seven widely separated places. Up to the thirteenth century the O'Kellys of Breagh (Co. Meath) were equal in importance to those of Ui Máine, but the impact of the Anglo-Norman invasion dispersed them. The Kellys of Ulster to-day are, no doubt, mostly of the O'Kelly of Cinel Eachach sept (Counties Antrim and Derry) ; those of the midlands come probably from one of the O'Kelly septs of Leix who were still strong in their homeland in 1543, when they were specifically mentioned in an order relating to martial law in Queen's Co. ; the atrocious murder of Fergus O'Kelly of Leix by the Earl of Kildare later in the same century, and the subsequent transfer of O'Kelly's estates to the Fitzgeralds makes a black page in the history of the latter family ; north Connacht Kellys are more likely to be of the Templeboy (Co. Sligo) sept than of that of Ui Máine ; while Dublin Kellys can either be from a north Wicklow family of the name, or migrants from any of the above septs. In each case the eponymous ancestor was called Ceallach, a personal name, from the genitive case of which we get Ó Ceallaigh, the Irish form of the surname. The Kellys of Kilkenny and Tipperary, however, are Ó Caollaidhe, not Ó Ceallaigh, some of whom retain the older form Kealy, which is Queally in Co.

Waterford. Queally is also found as a synonym of Ó Cadhla, usually O'Keily in English. Most Rev. Malachy Queally, who was among the most distinguished of the Archbishops of Tuam (1630–1645), was born in the diocese of Killaloe which includes a great part of Tipperary.

O'Kelly of Ui Máine was, and is, outstanding among all these. There is an authentic pedigree of their chiefs from the earliest times until the present day, and O'Kelly of Gallagh is one of the few whose claim to the designation Chief of the Name is officially recognized : in popular parlance he is The O'Kelly. The arms illustrated in plate XVII are those of O'Kelly of Ui Máine and, it should be understood, do not appertain to O'Kellys of other septs. Ui Máine, often called Hy Many, covers east Co. Galway and the southern part of Co. Roscommon. The Four Masters and the other Annals are full of their exploits and obituaries. Four of them have been Bishops of Clonfert, which is the diocese comprising much of the O'Kelly country. In 1518 the O'Kellys were one of the dangerous Irish septs named by the Corporation of Galway (see p. 66 supra). In the next century the O'Kellys of Co. Galway were very prominent, as indeed were those of the Pale, too, for no less than ten of the name in Counties Dublin, Kildare and Meath were attainted in 1642. The most famous was Col. Charles O'Kelly (1621–1695), who first appears in the 1641 war, was a commander under Sarsfield in 1690, and represented Co. Roscommon in the Parliament of 1689 ; he is best known, however, as the author of the very valuable contemporary history *Excidium Macariae*. It is of interest to note that the estate of this leading Catholic family was secured to them under the Treaty of Limerick. Twenty-five O'Kelly proprietors, nearly all of them of the Hy Many sept, were attainted in 1691. In modern times they have been less prominent. Dennis O'Kelly (1720–1787) had a remarkable career : emigrating from Ireland he started as a billiard-marker in London, was part owner of the famous Derby winner " Eclipse," and became a colonel. Patrick O'Kelly (1754–1835) was a well-known character— poet and eccentric. James O'Kelly (1845–1916), had a varied and adventurous career as war correspondent in three continents and Parnellite M.P. Seumus O'Kelly (1881–1918), playwright, was another man of note hailing from east Galway.

Many O'Kellys have distinguished themselves in America. Eugene Kelly (1808–1894), banker and philanthropist, a strong Irish nationalist and Catholic, and John Kelly, the missionary, were of the Derry-Tyrone sept. William Kelly (1811–1888), the inventor, and, in a very different sphere, Michael Kelly (1857–1894), the idol of baseball fans, and also Col. Patrick Kelly, commander of the Irish Brigade at Gettysburg, may be mentioned.

In France Father Malachy Kelly (d. 1684) was the founder of the Irish College, Paris. One branch of the Hy Many sept settled at Guyenne and was ranked among the nobility of France.

It should be added that some Kellys are MacKelly, not O'Kelly. This was a minor sept also of east Connacht, but the Mac prefix is now entirely lost and any surviving modern representatives are thus indistinguishable from O'Kellys. Daniel MacKelly, Archbishop of Cashel from 1238–1253, was the first Dominican to become an Irish bishop. The well-known Kelly family of the Isle of Man is also MacKelly.

Arms illustrated on Plate XVII.

MacKENNA.

MacKenna is one of the few names from which the old Gaelic prefixes of Mac and O were not generally dropped in the dark period of the eighteenth and nineteenth centuries. Though almost always written MacKenna, in the spoken language Kenna is quite common and in some places, notably Clare and Kerry, the emphasis is on the final A, with the result that births have been from time to time registered under many synonyms—such as Kennagh, Ginnaw and even Gna. These forms are peculiar to Co. Kerry. By origin, however, the MacKennas do not belong to Munster. They are a branch of the southern Ui Neill but, nevertheless, they are seated in south Ulster, their territory being Truagh (the modern barony of Trough in the northern part of Co. Monaghan). A branch of this sept settled in the parish of Maghera, Co. Down in the seventeenth century.

The MacKennas, though "lords of Truagh," were not prominent in mediaeval times. O'Dugan in the "Topographical Poems" says that they were originally Meathmen before they settled in Truagh. In our modern history nearly all the MacKennas of note, have made their name in the field of literature. Niall MacKenna (b. c. 1710) was a Gaelic poet and harper; Theobald MacKenna (d. 1808), secretary of the Catholic Committee in 1791, was a prolific pamphleteer; Andrew MacKenna (1833–1872), was a leading editor and writer in Belfast; Stephen MacKenna (1837–1883), was a novelist; better known as a novelist is another Stephen MacKenna (b. 1888), while a third Stephen MacKenna (1872–1934), was translator of Plotinus and an Irish language enthusiast; Father Lambert MacKenna, S.J. (1870–1956), known for his English-Irish Dictionary, has many Gaelic language publications to his credit. Nearly all of these were of families belonging to the country around Trough, as also was General John MacKenna (1771–1814), who, after a period of service in the Spanish army, joined Bernard O'Higgins, the "Liberator of Chile," and became an outstanding figure in South America. Patrick MacKenna (b. c. 1765), of Maghera, was an active associate of Wolfe Tone and Napper Tandy: he became a successful shipbuilder at Boulogne. Father Charles MacKenna, P.P. of Donagh, which is in the barony of Trough, was chaplain to the Irish Brigade at Fontenoy in 1745. At the present time probably the best known bearer of the name is Siobhan MacKenna, the Irish actress.

Arms illustrated on Plate XVII.

O'KENNEDY, Minnagh.

The eponymous ancestor of the O'Kennedys was Kennedy, nephew of Brian Boru, or Cinnéide in Irish, the resultant surname being Ó Cinnéide. They are thus a Dalcassian sept, and at first their territory was around Glenomra near Killaloe, and their occupation is perpetuated by the name of the civil parish comprising that area, viz. Killokennedy, but pressure from the powerful O'Briens and MacNamaras caused them to cross the Shannon and settle in Upper and Lower Ormond. There they soon increased in power and importance, and from the eleventh to the sixteenth century they were lords of Ormond. The sept divided into three branches, the chiefs of which were distinguished by the epithets Don (brown), Fionn (fair) and Rua (red). The Four Masters record the martial exploits of many of these chiefs. According to Keating, St. Ruadhan of Lorrha was the special protector of the O'Kennedys of Ormond. A branch of the sept emigrated to Antrim about the year 1600, and the name is found in that county now, though, no doubt, some of the Ulster Kennedys are of Scottish origin, for Kennedy is also a Scots name. Kennedy, indeed, is one of the commonest names in Ireland, being widely distributed over all the provinces, with a preponderance in Co. Tipperary : it is placed sixteenth in the statistical list of Irish surnames with an estimated present day population of some eighteen thousand persons.

Unlike most Irish surnames Kennedy has few synonyms in English : one, however, still found in Co. Leitrim is interesting, viz. Minnagh, i.e. Muimhneach—or the Munster man (cf. Donlevy—Ultagh). Kennedy became Quenedy in Spanish, for, like all the great Irish families, many of the sept found their way to the continent. Matthew Kennedy (1652–1735), who went to France after the capitulation of Limerick in 1691, was a notable literary figure in Paris : he was remarkable for his life-long enthusiasm for the Irish language. At home the O'Kennedys, though remaining Catholic, were not entirely submerged as a result of the successive conquests and confiscations of the seventeenth century : an Order of the Lord Lieutenant, dated 30th March, 1705, granting permission to a few selected papists to carry arms, included eight gentlemen of Co. Tipperary, and among them is John Kennedy of Polnorman. In more modern times the name has been less prominent than might be expected having regard to its numerical strength. It furnished sensational news in 1779 through the famous abduction case of the two Miss Kennedys of Co. Waterford. In the same century Rev. John Kennedy, a Presbyterian minister, made a useful contribution to social history by keeping an interesting diary (1724–1730) describing his many duties in Ulster. Another author was Patrick Kennedy (1801–1873) ; while, also in the field of literature, Patrick John Kennedy (1843–1906), was a well-known Irish-American Catholic publisher. In our own day a brilliant lawyer, Hugh Kennedy (1879–1936), was first Chief Justice of the Irish Free State.

Arms illustrated on Plate XVII.

O'KENNY.

The name Kenny is numerous in Ireland : it has seventy-sixth place in the list of commonest surnames. The majority of the people so called belong to families located in Counties Galway and Roscommon. This is the homeland in early times, as well as to-day, of the O'Kenny sept which in Irish is Ó Cionnaoith : it is of the Ui Máine (Hy Many) and the same stock as the O'Maddens. Another sept of the same name was in early times in Co. Tyrone, but there is little trace of it left there now. When Kennys are found of long standing connexion with Co. Down, they are probably of the minor Ulster sept of Ó Coinne.

The situation with regard to the main body of the Kennys, i.e. of Galway and Roscommon, is unusual because by a coincidence it is also the name of a prominent English family from Somerset who, through intermarriage with Co. Galway families, became extensive landowners in that county and in Roscommon. These descend from Nicholas Kenny, Escheator General for Ireland under Elizabeth I, whose family was then established in Co. Wexford. Thus the leading families of the name in the Hy Many country, to which the O'Kenny sept belongs, are in fact of English origin. Rev. Arthur Kenny (1776–1855), the anti-Catholic controversialist, was probably one of these. On the other hand Rev. Peter James Kenny, S.J. (1779–1841), founder of Clongoweswood College, was one of the most distinguished Catholic preachers and theologians of the nineteenth century. James Kenny (1780–1849), the dramatist, was born in Dublin and his, perhaps better known, son, Charles Lamb Kenney (1821–1881), was born in Paris. James F. Kenney (b. 1884), was the author of the standard work *Sources for the Early History of Ireland*.

MacKEOGH, Kehoe ; O'Hoey, Hoy.

Keogh, including Kehoe and MacKeogh, almost equally common forms of the same Irish surname—Mac Eochaidh—just misses a place in the hundred most numerous names in Ireland. It is chiefly found in the province of Leinster, the spelling Kehoe being usual in Co. Wexford. Outside Leinster MacKeoghs are mainly located in the neighbourhood of Limerick : the place name Ballymackeogh is in Co. Tipperary a few miles from that city. This was the homeland of one of the three distinct septs of MacKeogh. The second was in the Ui Máine group. Their eponymous ancestor was Eochaidh O'Kelly ; they were lords of Magh Finn and their territory of Moyfinn in the barony of Athlone, Co. Roscommon, long known as Keogh's Country, was popularly so-called even in quite recent times. The place Keoghville in the parish of Taghmaconnell took its name from them. The third and historically the most important sept were the MacKeoghs of Leinster. These are of the same stock as the

O'Byrnes and were hereditary bards to that great family. With them they migrated in early mediaeval times from north Kildare to Co. Wicklow, whence they spread later to Co. Wexford. The Four Masters describe Maolmuire MacKeogh as chief professor of poetry in Leinster in 1534, and several fine poets of the name are cited by Douglas Hyde in his *Literary History of Ireland*. In a different field of literature two eighteenth century Protestant clergymen called Keogh are remembered : John Keogh (1653–1725), as a mathematician and another John Keogh (1681–1754), as a botanist and zoologist. In the political sphere Keoghs have produced three notable figures the third of whom, however, sheds no lustre on the name : Matthew Keogh (1744–1798), hanged for his prominent part in the '98 Insurrection ; John Keogh (1740–1817), Catholic leader in the depressed days before O'Connell ; and William Keogh (1817–1878), M.P. and judge, and associate of the swindler Sadlier —of whom the less said the better. Mention should also be made of Capt. Myles Walter Keogh (1840–1876), a distinguished officer of the Federal Army in the American Civil War, who lost his life in the memorable battle of Little Bighorn in the Indian war, in which the only survivor on his side was Keogh's horse.

The cognate patronymic Ó hEochaidh is anglicized O'Hoey and Hoy. The sept so named, which was of the same stock as the MacDonlevys, was of such importance in early times that its chiefs were Kings of Ulster until the end of the twelfth century when their kinsmen the MacDonlevys superseded them in that dignity. John Cashel Hoey (1828–1893), editor of the *Nation* after Gavan Duffy, later became a man of note in Australia ; his wife Frances Sarah Hoey (1830–1908), was a successful and prolific novelist.

Arms illustrated on Plate XVIII.

MacKEON, MacKeown, (Owens, Hone).

Though it originated in Co. Sligo the sept of MacKeon may be regarded as belonging to the adjacent county of Leitrim, as it is there they are found located both in mediaeval and modern times. The name, in Irish Mac Eoghain, simply means son of John or Owen (in the Tuam area it is sometimes anglicized as Johnson). This sept had an important branch in Co. Galway : the sixteenth century " Composition Book of Connacht " refers to lands in the barony of Kiltartan then called Termon Brian MacOwen.

Another common spelling is MacKeown but, while some people so called are no doubt of the MacKeon sept referred to above, most of them, especially in the Six Counties of Northern Ireland, are the descendants of Scotsmen, originally called Bissett, who settled in the Glens of Antrim as early as the thirteenth century and became very numerous. Their name in Irish is MacEoin, Eoin (pronounced Owen) being one of the alternative forms of John in Irish. What has been said above is illustrated by two place names: Keonbrook is in Co. Leitrim and Ballymakeown near Belfast. It will be observed that the initial K in Keon or MacKeon is actually formed from the final letter of the prefix Mac. The name MacKeon is best known in Ireland in the person of General MacEoin, twice a minister in the Government of the Republic, who as " the blacksmith of Ballinalee " made an undying name for himself in the War of Independence (1916–1921). Miles Gerald Keon (1821–1875), the novelist, and Miles Keon who devised a new constitution for the Catholic Committee in 1792, were both Co. Leitrim men.

Irish families of Owens may be Mac or O. MacEoghain is dealt with above. Ó hEoghain is of dual origin: a Clare sept of the same stock as the O'Neills of Thomond (quite distinct from the famous Ulster O'Neills), and an ecclesiastical family from the Lough Erne area. Members of the latter are usually called Owens in English speech. This is also true to a less extent of Co. Cork. The surname MacOwen (*sic*) was in 1659, when Petty's census was taken, one of the commonest names in Counties Cork and Limerick, being very numerous in almost every barony in both those counties and also to some considerable extent in Kerry. Yet to-day MacOwen scarcely exists as a surname there. Such of their descendants as survive are probably known as Owens now. They did not become McKeon. In this connexion, however, it must be remembered that many ephemeral surnames, formed by prefixing Mac to the father's christian name, were still common among the cottiers and small farmers of the mid seventeenth century. In most parts of the country the two Gaelic surnames noted above have several forms in English: the O families have become Hynes as well as Owens, and the Mac families MacKeown, MacKeon, MacOwen etc. The sum total of all these makes a considerable section of the population, but those actually using the form Owens are little more than three thousand persons, some at least of whom are of Welsh descent. They are widely distributed.

Although not actually called Owens we may mention Robert Owenson (1744–1812), in his day a famous actor both in Dublin and London, because his real name was MacOwen. His daughter was Lady Morgan (1783–1859), poetess and patriotic Irish novelist. Another notable Irish actor was John Lonnergan Owens who flourished in Dublin at the time of Grattan's Parliament.

Finally it may be mentioned that in 1659 Ó hEoghain was anglicized O'Howen and O'Hone in Co. Fermanagh. A different origin, however, is ascribed to the well known Hone family of modern times which produced the artists Nathaniel Hone (1718–1784), and his two sons, and in our own day Evie Hone (1894–1955), of stained glass fame. (I am informed by a member of the family that they came to Ireland from Holland).

Arms illustrated on Plate XVIII.

O'KIERAN, O'Kerin, Kearns, Kerrane.

The sept known in Irish as Ó Céirín was in early times in possession of the greater part of the present barony of Costello, Co. Mayo, of which their chiefs were paramount. During the mediaeval period they gradually became reduced in importance, though they remained in their native habitat in a more or less subordinate position and also spread into the neighbouring counties. An inquisition of 1609 describes them as then erenaghs of Killaghtee, in the diocese of Raphoe ; and in the census of 1659 we find them in Co. Sligo. It is in Co. Mayo they are still most numerous to-day. This Mayo sept anglicized their name Kearns. In Donegal it is sometimes Kerr to-day. An influential branch of it settled in Co. Clare about the year 1420. They prospered in their new home and have been prominent in Co. Clare since then. The anglicized form of the surname of this branch is Kerin or O'Kerin. The tomb of Teige O'Kerin (1685) is still to be seen in Ennis Abbey. Kearon in Wicklow and Kerrane in Mayo are other variants of the name. The three best known men of the name were in fact none of them from Co. Mayo or Co. Clare. Father Moses Kearns, the intrepid leader in Co. Wexford in 1798, was executed in that year ; a decade earlier he had been hanged from a lamp post in Paris by the revolutionary mob, but survived through the breaking of the rope and the fortunate presence of an Irish doctor. William Henry Kearns (1764–1846), a Dublin man, was a noted violinist, organist and composer. Richard Kerens (1842–1916), American railroad builder, was the son of a Kearns from Co. Meath.

Arms illustrated on Plate XVIII.

O'KINNEALLY, (Quinnelly).

The original Gaelic form of this name is Ó Cinnfhaelidh ; there are several anglicized forms of it—Kinneally, Kennelly, etc. The last mentioned is also used as a synonym for Quinnelly, a west Cork surname, so that confusion may arise in this case. The name now under consideration is that of a sept living in the territory known to-day as the barony of Connello in Co. Limerick. They do not appear in the Annals after the end of the twelfth century, having been subdued and dispersed by the Fitzgeralds after the Anglo-Norman invasion ; but their descendants are still found in Munster in many places between Limerick and Waterford. One of these was a lieutenant in King James II's own Regiment of infantry at the Boyne, and another was a brigadier in the Irish Brigade in France in the next century.

In more recent times the best known of the name was Edmund Vaughan Kenealy (1819–1880), a Cork barrister who was a public figure in England, coming into particular prominence for his part in the notorious Tichborne case, for which he was disbarred. He was a poet of some note, as was another Cork man, William Kenealy (1828–1876), who was closely associated with Kilkenny, of which town he was Mayor. Dr. Kenealy, O.S.F.C., was first archbishop of Simla (India).

Arms illustrated on Plate XVIII.

KINSELLA.

This is one of the few genuine native Gaelic surnames without the prefix Mac or O. It is true that the form O'Kinsellagh is sometimes found in old documents, and a few present-day Kinsellas have " resumed " an O, but to do so is incorrect, as Kinsella, or Cinnsealach in Irish, is, like Kavanagh, an agnomen which has supplanted the original name. Kinsellas and Kavanaghs descend from Dermot Mac-Murrough, ill-famed King of Leinster from 1134–1171 ; and the names are derived from Enna Cinnsealach and Domhnall Caomhánach, sons of that king. The territory of the Kinsella sept comprised most of the barony of Gorey in the northern part of the modern Co. Wexford, and it is in that part of Leinster they are chiefly found to-day. This district was formerly called The Kinsellaghs. Many of the sept acquired the name MacEdmund, but this is now obsolete.

The Kinsellas are much less numerous than their kinsmen the Kavanaghs, and have produced less men of note. One, Aeneas Kinsella, was a member of the Supreme Council at Kilkenny in 1646, and another, Bonaventure Kinselagh, was an officer in Kavanagh's infantry regiment in King James II's army in Ireland ; but none, strangely enough, took a leading part in Co. Wexford in the insurrection of 1798. One notable Wexford-born Kinsella was well known in America as the editor of the *Brooklyn Daily Eagle*, viz. Thomas Kinsella (1822–1884), who has been described as " a splendid example of an emigrant Irish boy, rising to wealth and honoured position in the country of his adoption."

Arms illustrated on Plate XVIII.

O'KIRWAN.

The Kirwans—the O is never used with this name nowadays—are best known as one of the " Tribes of Galway " ; they are second only to the Lynches as a leading family of that city. Like the Darcys and unlike the other twelve " tribes " they are of Gaelic origin. They are first recorded in history as erenaghs in Co. Louth, and were not connected with Galway until the fifteenth century. In Irish the name is Ó Ciardubháin, the sept being of the race of Heremon. Early forms in English are Kerovan,

Kyrvan and O'Quirivan, whence the Co. Clare placename Craggykerrivane. It was not until they went to Galway that they made their mark in Irish history. Since then there have been many Kirwans of note. Most Rev. Francis Kirwan (1589–1661), Bishop of Killala, was a prominent supporter of Rinuccini—he was driven into exile and ended his days in France. A generation later, John Kirwan is noteworthy as the only Catholic mayor of Galway (1686) between 1654 and the passing of the Catholic Emancipation Act in 1829. Richard Kirwan (1708–1779), of Cregg, Co. Galway, was especially remarkable in an age of fine soldiers for his valour in the service of France and Austria and as a successful duellist. An Irish family of Kirwan established in Dauphiny was ranked among the nobility of France. Two remarkable men who began their careers as Jesuits and became Protestants, were Walter Blake Kirwan (1754–1805), Dean of Killala and famous preacher, and Richard Kirwan (1734–1812), chemist, linguist, philosopher, patron of Bunting and President of the Royal Irish Academy. Of the former, his uncle, the Catholic Archbishop of Tuam, on hearing his nephew, a devout Catholic parish priest, bewail his apostate brother's change of religion, is said to have remarked, " Tut, man, he had no religion to change " ! Another Kirwan should also be mentioned, for Owen Kirwan was hanged with Robert Emmet in 1803.

Arms illustrated on Plate XVIII.

LACY, de Lacy.

The De Lacys of Ireland, more commonly now called Lacy or Lacey, came to this country at the time of the Anglo-Norman invasion, having gone to England from Lascy in Normandy in the previous century with William The Conqueror. In the Annals the name is written de Léis in Irish. The first and most famous of them was Hugo de Lacy (killed 1186) to whom was " granted " the whole of O'Melaghlin's territory, the Kingdom of Meath (of much greater extent than the modern county of Meath). Twice married, his second wife was a daughter of Roderick O'Connor, King of Ireland. The vast Meath possessions went out of the family through the failure of the male line. The de Lacys of Co. Limerick, a family which produced many famous men, to some of whom reference will be made in this note, claim descent from the O'Connor marriage, but, though this is accepted by O'Donovan, some doubt is cast upon its authenticity in a closely reasoned article on the subject by N. J. Synnott (*J.R.S.A.I.* 1919), who suggested that the Limerick families may be Lees, a name of frequent occurrence in Limerick records from the twelfth to the fifteenth century; he points out that in the sixteenth century the Lacys of Bruff and Bruree spelt their name Leash, as well as Lacy ; and Leash, of course, is phonetically equivalent to the Irish form Léis. Be that as it may, the Lacys are undoubtedly of

Norman origin and are historically intimately connected with Co. Limerick. Most Rev. Hugh Lacy, Bishop of Limerick from 1557 to 1581, is a case in point, as his name appears in records as Lacy alias Lees. He was "deprived" of his bishopric by Queen Elizabeth in 1571, and died for his faith in gaol ten years later. Pierce Lacy of Bruff, who took a prominent part in the Elizabethan wars, was executed in 1607. Col. John Lacy was a member of the Supreme Council of the Confederate Catholics in 1647 and was expressly excluded from the amnesty after the Siege of Limerick in 1651. At the second Siege of Limerick in 1691 another Pierce, or Peter, Lacy of the Ballingarry family took a prominent part though then only thirteen years of age. He is better known as Count de Lacy (1678–1751) for, having gone into exile with Sarsfield, he took service with Peter the Great of Russia and became one of the most famous soldiers of the eighteenth century. Indeed no Irish family has attained greater fame in the military history of Europe. The most renowned of these besides Count Peter, already mentioned, were his son Marshal Francis Maurice de Lacy (1725–1801), who was an Austrian field-marshal, and another Maurice de Lacy (1740–1820), who was a celebrated general of the Russian army; and Count Francis Anthony de Lacy (1731–1792), who was a distinguished general and diplomatist in the Spanish service at the same period.

Though the name is still found in Co. Limerick and other parts of Munster, the ancestral estates of the de Lacys, which were at Ballingarry, Bruff and Bruree, have long since passed into other hands, and even a century ago there was no large landed proprietor of the name in Ireland.

It should be added that the Gaelic surname Ó Laitheasa, a Co. Wexford family, is Lacy in English.

Arms illustrated on Plate XVIII.

LALLY, O'Mulally.

The name Lally is a contraction of O'Mullally, which was formerly the normal form in English of the Gaelic Ó Maolalaidh. This sept, a branch of the Ui Máine of the same stock as the O'Naghtens, was of some importance in Connacht, where, after the coming of the Anglo-Normans, they were at constant feud with the de Burgos or Burkes. Through this, and other causes, they were obliged to move northwards, but only a short distance, as they remained in the area subsequently formed into the county of Galway, settling in the neighbourhood of Tuam. Two O'Mulallys became Archbishops of Tuam, and two others Bishops of the adjacent dioceses of Clonfert and Elphin between 1211 and 1611. Those who did not go abroad have remained there or thereabouts ever since: of the thirty-four births recorded for Lally in one year, thirty were in Connacht.

After the siege of Limerick, however, it is among the Wild Geese and other exiles that we must look for Lallys of note. The most famous of these, was Thomas Arthur O'Mullally (1702–1766), better known as Count Lally de Tolendal, who, after a most distinguished and romantic career in the French army, was executed through the machinations of his enemies. His trial has since been officially declared a travesty of justice and the decree finding him guilty solemnly reversed. Tolendal was the French equivalent of Tullaghnadaly, which the historian of the family, Denis Patrick O'Mullally, on the authority of William Hawkins, Ulster King of Arms, asserts should be Tullagh O'Mullally—an assertion clearly disproved by John O'Donovan in his edition of *The Tribes and Customs of Hy Many*. It was in English written Tullindaly in 1689, for James O'Mullally, ancestor of Count Lally and member of the James II Parliament of that date, is recorded as of Tullindaly. The book referred to—*History of the O'Mullally and Lally Clann* (Chicago 1941)—though an uncritical and amateurish work marred by the inclusion of much high-falutin padding, is, nevertheless, a mine of information on the activities of the sept and its members.

Arms illustrated on Plate XVIII.

O'LALOR, Lawlor.

This name in modern times is spelt in three different ways—Lawlor, Lalor, Lawler —the first of these being slightly more numerous than the others. In Irish it is Ó Leathlobhair, which would appear to denote descendant of the half leper, no doubt a nickname arising from some physical defect and not to be taken literally. The prefix O, it may be noted, which was discarded during the period of Gaelic submergence, has not been resumed in modern times. The O'Lalors, like their kinsmen the O'Mores, were one of the Seven Septs of Leix. They were located near the famous Rock of Dunamase in Co. Leix, but were driven from this territory by the English invaders under Queen Elizabeth I. The scene of the making of the treaty, as a result of which the leading men of the Seven Septs were transplanted to Co. Kerry in 1609, is still called Lalor's Mills. The peasants and workers of the O'Lalor sept remained in their old territory, a fact which is borne out by the prevalence of the name there to-day: nearly all the Lalors, Lawlors and Lawlers in Ireland are to be found in Leinster, either in Leix or in the counties lying to the east of it. The name of one Harry Lalor is traditionally preserved as the hero of the massacre of Mullaghmast in 1577 in which many innocent and unsuspecting Lalors, O'Mores and other inhabitants of Leix were treacherously done to death by the O'Dempseys in conjunction with the English planters of the district. The fall of the O'Dempseys as a great family was, according to John O'Donovan, locally attributed to this disgraceful event.

Rev. James O'Lalor (or Lawler), a Co. Kilkenny Parish Priest, wrote in 1764 a notable elegy in Irish on one of the Kavanaghs, which was published by John O'Donovan some 90 years later. The editor in his introduction mentions several distinguished Lalors all of Leix or Kilkenny. He does not, however, refer to the most remarkable man of the name, the revolutionary James Fintan Lalor (1817–1849), son of Patrick Lalor a strong Leix farmer and sometime M.P. for that county; his brother Peter Lalor (1823–1889), led the insurgent miners at Eureka, Australia, in 1854 and subsequently became a minister and speaker of the Legislative Council of Victoria. John Lawlor (1820–1901), the sculptor, is remembered by his statues in London, Cork and Limerick. Alice Lalor (1766–1846), better known as Mother Teresa, was a prominent figure in the religious life of America.

Arms illustrated on Plate XVIII.

O'LEARY.

O'Leary is and always has been essentially a Co. Cork surname. Like many Gaelic septs they were driven from their original habitat at the time of the Anglo-Norman invasion at the end of the twelfth century, but they did not migrate far— only from Corca Laoidhe in south-west Cork to Inchigeela in the same county, a remote territory with the lofty Kerry mountains in sight to the west of them. Here they long ruled as chiefs under the paramount Muskerry MacCarthys. Out of one hundred and three landowners recorded in the Civil Survey (1654) of the barony of Muskerry no less than thirty-four were O'Learys, while MacCarthys numbered forty-one and O'Herlihys ten. The name is to-day very numerous being sixty-second in the list of the hundred commonest names in Ireland with an estimated population figure of almost ten thousand persons. It is remarkable, what a large proportion of these, as indicated by vital statistics, were born in that part of the country to which the sept traditionally belongs—no less than eighty per cent. In this connexion it may be added that there are two places called Ballyleary in Ireland, both in Co. Cork. The O'Learys took a prominent part in the Irish wars against the English invader when these affected Munster. They suffered much in the Desmond Wars; one Mahon O'Leary was a forerunner of the Wild Geese as he went to Spain with d'Aquila after Kinsale; fifteen were attainted in 1642; the name is found in the 1691 attainders and also in the Irish regiments of France in the eighteenth century. Indeed almost every aspect of Irish life has been enriched by an O'Leary. Literature has Ellen O'Leary (1831–1889), patriotic poetess, Joseph O'Leary (1795–1855), song writer and, most notable of all, Father Peter O'Leary (1839–1919), better known as Peadar Ó Laoghaire, called in his day " the greatest living master of Irish [Gaelic] prose." Law has Joseph O'Leary (1792–1857), author of many standard legal works ; William Hegarty O'Leary (1836–1880) made his name as a surgeon ; while the most famous of all was John O'Leary (1830–1907), the Fenian. In the field of athletics Daniel O'Leary (1846–1933) performed amazing feats in America and long held the world record for long distance walking. The town of Dunlaoghaire, formerly Dunleary, a suburb of Dublin, is named after Laoghaire who was King of Ireland at the time of St. Patrick in the fifth century ; but this, of course has no connexion with the surname formed some six centuries later. In Irish O'Leary is Ó Laoghaire.

Arms illustrated on Plate XIX.

O'LEE, MacAlee.

Lee is a fairly widespread name in Ireland, but as it is also a very common indigenous surname in England it is impossible to say in the absence of a pedigree, or at least a well-established tradition, whether a family of the name in Ireland is Gaelic in origin or of planter stock. The latter were well established in Co. Tipperary and elsewhere at the beginning of the seventeenth century. Confining our attention to the former it may first be stated that there are four distinct septs to be considered, two O's and two Macs, so that in English we find occasional O'Lees and MacLees side by side with the simple form Lee. Ó Laidhigh is the Connacht form, centered in Co. Galway ; and Ó Laoidhigh the Munster, chiefly associated with Counties Cork and Limerick. MacLaoidhigh belongs to Leix and is written Lea in the census of 1659 ; and Mac an Leagha to Ulster, anglicized as Lee, MacAlee and MacAlea. Laoidhigh is the genitive case of *laoidheach* the adjective formed from *laoidh* (a poem).

The most important of these septs were the O'Lees of West Connacht, best known as a medical family, not only chiefs in their own right but also hereditary physicians to the powerful sept of O'Flaherty. The Lees, indeed, were traditionally doctors by profession, for in addition to the family just mentioned a number of mediaeval medical treatises in Irish and Latin were written by MacLees. The form MacLee was sometimes used by the O'Lees of Connacht, who were also erenaghs of Annaghdown : among the many ecclesiastics of this sept was John O'Lee, notable Dominican Bishop of Killala from 1253 to 1275. Another Father John Lee (b. c. 1560) was an Irish priest prominent in the educational sphere in Paris. He came from a leading family in Waterford, of which city another member of it was Sheriff from 1575 to 1580. Andrew Lee (1650–1734), colonel successively of Clare's and Mountcashel's Regiments, was one of the very greatest soldiers ever to fight for France in the Irish Brigade.

O'LENAGHAN, Linehan.

A Roscommon family of this name, in Irish Ó Léanacháin, appears in early records, the most notable of whom was Maelciaran O'Lenechan of Tuamna, in Boyle barony, a priest very highly praised in the " Annals of Loch Cé " and by the Four Masters for his numerous good qualities : he died in 1249. Little is heard of them in modern times. Linehan, or Lenihan as it is also spelt, is now regarded as belonging primarily to Counties Limerick and Tipperary. Maurice Lenihan (1811–1895), author of the *History of Limerick*, is the most notable bearer of the name.

O'LENNON, LINNANE, Leonard, (Linnegar ; MacAlinion).

The normal form of Lennon in Irish is Ó Leannáin, or Ó Lionnáin, but confusion arises because these Gaelic names have been anglicized Leonard and Linnane, while the Irish surnames Ó Lonáin (Lenane) and even Ó Luinín (Linneen) are also sometimes Lennon or Leonard in English. Of these Lennane, or Linane, belongs to the Corca Laoidhe group and was situated near Glandore Harbour. Ó Leanáin in, but not of, Hy Many, is still found in Co. Galway as Lennon, while the same name belonging also to a Hy Fiachra sept of Co. Mayo is now usually called Leonard : their position is shown on the folded map at the end of this book. Historically O'Lennon of Fermanagh is the only Lennon sept of importance. They were erenaghs of Lisgoole near Enniskillen and produced many distinguished ecclesiastics : no less than six of them are mentioned by the Four Masters as priors or canons of Lisgoole between 1380 and 1466 ; while to-day the name is closely associated with the church, an unusually large proportion of persons of the name being priests. Apart from these the most noteworthy are John Lennon (1768–1846), a sailor famous for his daring feats, and John Brown Lennon (1850–1923), the American Labour leader. Ó Luinín, mentioned above, also belongs to Co. Fermanagh and is now almost indistinguishable from Ó Leannáin, except where, strangely enough, it has been anglicized Linnegar.

Leonard, itself a well-known indigenous English surname, is remarkable in Ireland for the fact that it is used as the synonym or anglicized equivalent of a greater number of quite distinct Gaelic surnames than almost any other. In addition to the three distinct sept names mentioned above, there is the royal family of Mac Giolla Fhinnéin—son of the follower of St. Finnian—also anglicized as McAlinion. From this stock come many of our Irish Leonards, at any rate those associated with West Ulster (Donegal and Fermanagh). They are descended from Giolla Finnéin O'Muldory, as are the once powerful family of O'Muldory whose head was chief or lord of Lough Erne. Another family which sometimes, rather strangely, anglicized their name as Leonard was that of Mac Giolla Seannáin (the saint in this case is St. Senan, not St. Finnian) this name being corrupted in Irish to Maguinnseanáin and usually anglicized as Nugent. The Registrar-General's returns show that, in addition to the foregoing, Lenaghan and even Nanany are found as synonymous with Leonard in English.

No person of the name Leonard has distinguished himself in the political, military or cultural life of Ireland (or for that matter in England either).

O'LONERGAN.

In pre-Norman times the O'Lonergans inhabited north-east Thomond, i.e. that part of Tipperary which lies on the east side of Lough Derg, but the pressure exerted by the Anglo-Norman Butlers forced them southwards to the country around Cashel and Cahir, where they have remained in considerable numbers up to the present day. The name, in Irish Ó Longargain, is usually anglicized Lonergan, without the prefix O, but sometimes takes the form Londrigan. The Chief of the Sept resided near Cahir, but little is heard of them in the stormy military and political history of Ireland. Their claim to fame lies in the number of leading ecclesiastics they gave to the Church from the twelfth to the fifteenth century, no less than six of these being archbishops or bishops, two of Killaloe and three of Cashel, i.e. in the two homelands of the sept. The most distinguished of these was Donnell (not Donat as sometimes stated) O'Longargan or O'Lonergan, Archbishop of Cashel, who took a prominent part in the Council of Kells in 1152. Mention should be made, too, of the family of O'Lonergan which supplied harpers to the O'Kellys of Ui Máine. They possessed a small patrimony at Ballynabanaby in the parish of Kilgerril (south-east Galway) at the time that the Book of Lecan was compiled, i.e. at the beginning of the fifteenth century. In modern times the only Lonergans of any note were Thomas S. Lonergan (b. 1861), Irish born American poet and politician, and Anne Lonergan, the Irish nun who was imprisoned during the French Revolution.

Arms illustrated on Plate XIX.

O'LORCAN, Larkin.

The prefix O has been entirely dropped from this old and distinguished Gaelic surname. It was borne by a number of distinct and unrelated septs. The most important of these was Ó Lorcáin of Leinster, of royal blood in that province but dispossessed of their patrimony in the barony of Forth (Co. Wexford) by the Anglo-

Norman invaders : the lesser families, however, remained on the lands and the name is still fairly numerous in Leinster. The other counties in which it is chiefly found to-day are Armagh, Galway and Tipperary ; and each of these is the homeland of one of the several septs referred to above. Those of Armagh descend from the Oriel Ui Lorcáin, chiefs of Farney and of West Ui Breasail ; the Galway Larkins are of the same stock as the O'Maddens ; and in Co. Tipperary the head of the family was erenagh of Lorrha. James Larkin (1876–1947) was a notable Labour leader particularly in the great Dublin strike of 1913.

O'LOUGHLIN, (Loughnane).

The sept of O'Loughlin is entirely distinct from those of MacLoughlin (q.v.), though come confusion arises outside Munster due to the dropping of the prefixes Mac and O in the eighteenth and nineteenth centuries. It should also be remembered that the MacLoughlins of Cineal Eoghan or Kinel Owen, in the days when they were a royal family, were first called O'Loughlin, but about the year 1200 they became MacLoughlin. O'Loughlin as we know it, however, is by origin a Clare name and in Co. Clare it is chiefly found to-day. A Dalcassian sept, the O'Loughlins were the most powerful of those in the north-western part of the county on the shores of the Atlantic and Galway Bay. Their chief was Lord of Corcomroe in early times, but later their territory was restricted to the present barony of Burren. As late as seventy years ago the head of the O'Loughlins was known locally as "The King of Burren." Corcomroe is so called because the clan-name of the O'Loughlins and O'Connors was Corca Modhruaidh ; when the division came the latter took Corcomroe and the former Burren. Even when Lord of Corcomroe, O'Loughlin was usually styled O'Loughlin Burren. In 1585 the chief of the name was seated at Craggans, Co. Clare. Ballyvaughan and Kilfenora are still the heart of the O'Loughlin country. One Conghalach O'Loughlin was bishop of Corcomroe from 1281–1300 : this see was subsequently called Kilfenora. Three Clare O'Loughlins made a name for themselves in the nineteenth century : Sir Michael O'Loghlen (1789–1842), Master of the Rolls and supporter of Daniel O'Connell, and his two sons Sir Colman O'Loghlen (1819–1877), M.P. for Clare and Catholic protagonist, and Sir Bryan O'Loghlen (1828–1905), who was Prime Minister of Victoria, Australia.

The O'Laughnans, Ó Lachtnain in Irish and normally anglicized O'Laughnan and Loughnane, present an example of the tendency for scarce Gaelic surnames to be changed into a well-known name of somewhat similar sound. Thus O'Loughnan has in some places become O'Loughlin. It has also been atrociously anglicized Loftus in Connacht and Lawton in Co. Cork. There were several septs of O'Lachtnain. The numerous mediaeval bishops and abbots of the name were all Connacht men.

Arms illustrated on Plate XIX.

MacLOUGHLIN.

The surname MacLoughlin, also spelled MacLaughlin, is used in modern Ireland as the anglicized form of that of two entirely distinct Gaelic septs, both of considerable importance. One indeed which was of royal status, is not a Mac name at all but an O name, being Ó Maoilsheachlainn in Irish, and up to the end of the seventeenth century always anglicized O'Melaghlin (with some slight variants). They are descended from Maoilsheachlainn, better known as Malachy II, King of Ireland from 980 to 1002, when he was dethroned by the great Brian Boru. Maoilsheachlainn signifies servant or follower of Seachlainn, i.e. St. Secundinus. Malachy was of the race of Niall of the Nine Hostages. After the Anglo-Norman invasion the O'Melaghlins, like all the Gaelic princes and chiefs of Meath and central Ireland, were greatly reduced in power. In 1543 they were still strong enough to be named in an Order establishing martial law in the midland counties (see note *sub* Dunn p. 132 *supra*), but in each of the successive waves of invasion, especially in the seventeenth century, they further declined, till after 1691 they disappear altogether as O'Melaghlins, and the remnant of the sept remaining in their ancestral territory were thereafter known as MacLoughlin. One of their descendants has of late years done a great deal of research on the O'Melaghlin genealogy and the pedigrees of their present day MacLoughlin representatives : the results of his work are deposited in the Genealogical Office (Office of Arms), Dublin Castle.

Turning to the MacLoughlins proper, we have another powerful and important sept, or at least one which can be so described up to the thirteenth century, when they too declined in influence. This sept was called Mac Lochlainn in Irish, i.e. son of Lochlainn, a forename of Norse origin, which does not, however, imply that the family was itself of Norse stock : the MacLoughlins of Ulster were, in fact, a senior branch of the northern Ui Neill and their territory was in Innishowen (Co. Donegal). At the present time the name, which is very numerous, is found chiefly in Counties Donegal and Derry. In Dublin the name appears as MacGloughlin, presumably from the variant form in Irish, Mag Lochlainn.

Up to 1241, when the MacLochlainn ascendancy in Ulster was finally ended at a battle of that date, the leading men of this sept are mentioned continuously in the Annals of our mediaeval history, as are the O'Melaghlins of Meath ; but subsequently no outstanding figure of the name appears in any phase of national activity, though the branch of the Ulster sept, which had settled in Co. Leitrim under the O'Rourkes, was sufficiently established there to be included among the chieftains of that county in the Composition Book of Connacht (1585). In modern times the most notable person of the name was John MacLoughlin (1784–1857), of Hudson Bay Company fame.

Arms illustrated on Plate XIX.

O'LOWRY, LAVERY.

The Irish surname Ó Labhradha is in English Lowry and Lavery, both these forms being found in almost equal numbers in north-east Ulster where the sept originated. Their territory in mediaeval times was in the neighbourhood of Moira, Co. Down. Branches of the sept were called Baun-Lavery, Roe-Lavery and Trin-Lavery, these eipthets being the Gaelic adjectives *bán* (white), *rua* (red) and *tréan* (strong). Trin-Lavery became Armstrong in some cases—one of the numerous examples of mistranslation.

Sir John Lavery (1856–1941), famous landscape and portrait painter was born in Belfast. He designed the Irish bank-notes, the head engraved thereon being that of Lady Lavery, his wife.

LYNCH.

It must be emphasized at once that the name Lynch, which is among the hundred commonest surnames in Ireland, is of dual origin. Lynch is used as the anglicized form of the native Gaelic name Ó Loingsigh, and also of the Norman de Lench.

The Norman family of Lynch, though far less numerous than their Gaelic name-sakes, have been more prominent on account of their predominance in the affairs of Galway city, where they were the most influential of the " Tribes ". In the hundred and seventy years which elapsed between 1484, when Dominick Lynch procured the city's charter from Richard III, and 1654, when Catholics were debarred from civic offices, no less than eighty-four mayors of Galway were of the family of Lynch. Dominick's son, Stephen Lynch, was in turn responsible for obtaining from Pope Innocent VIII the Bull which established that unique ecclesiastical institution, the Wardenship of Galway. Many of the Wardens were Lynches. The Galway family also produced a number of distinguished ecclesiastics, the most famous of whom were Most Rev. John Lynch (1599–1673), the author of *Cambrensis Eversus ;* the centenarian Archbishop of Tuam, Most Rev. James Lynch (1609–1713), who despite persecution and imprisonment, continued to administer his diocese ; Rev. Richard Lynch, D.D. (1611–1676), the author of many works in Spanish ; and Rev. Dominick Lynch (d. 1697), the Dominican philosopher. Of all the Galway Lynches the one most likely to be remembered by any visitor to that city is James Lynch, the stern mayor who in 1493 felt it his duty to hang his own son for an offence for which the penalty was death : the spot where this event took place, known as the gate of the Old Jail, with its tragic inscription, is still pointed out and the story retold. It should be noted, however, that some modern Galway historians have suggested that this story may be apocryphal. Nearby is Lynch's Castle which was built in 1320.

After the coming of the Normans, the Leyns (Lynch) family was first settled in Meath, where Lynch's Knock, the site of a battle in 1647, perpetuates their occupation. It was a branch of this family that migrated to Galway in the early fifteenth century. The arms illustrated in Plate XIX are those of the Lynches of Galway. Branches of this family have been prominent among the modern landowners in Co. Galway under the hyphenated names Lynch-Blosse and Blosse-Lynch.

The Gaelic Lynches, formerly often called O'Lynch, comprise a number of quite distinct and independent septs, most of which were submerged as such after the Anglo-Norman invasion but whose descendants are still to be found in their several places of origin. The Thomond sept produced Clare-born Patrick Lynch (1757–1818), linguist and Gaelic scholar. The Sligo sept has Alan O'Lynch, noted Dominican Prior of Killaloe (1411), to its credit. From that of Breffny came Dr. John Joseph Lynch (1816–1888), Bishop of Toronto, the first Catholic ecclesiastical dignitary to attend a British royal levée since the time of James II. Col. Charles Lynch (1736–1796), from whose name the American word to lynch, or "lynch law," was coined, was son of another Charles Lynch, scion of the northern sept whose head in early mediaeval times was chief of Dalriada. The Lynches of Co. Donegal are properly Mac Loingseacháin (Lynchehaun); those, Ó Loingsigh (or Lynch), now numerous in Cork, Kerry and Limerick, probably stem from the septs of the name located in Corca Loaidhe and in Owney. Thomas Lynch (1749–1779), the youngest of the signatories of the American Declaration of Independence, was of an Irish family which had then been three generations in America. Count John Baptist Lynch, a peer of France, was grandson of an officer who went to that country with James II: he lost all in the French Revolution but later recovered some of his property. General Isodore Lynch, who joined the revolutionary army, had a distinguished military career in the French service. Patrick (Patricio) Lynch (1824–1886), "son of a wealthy Irish merchant," who first saw service in the British navy, has been described as "the foremost Chilean naval hero." Finally we may mention Hannah Lynch (1862–1904), a leading figure in the Ladies' Land League.
Arms illustrated on Plate XIX.

O'LYNE, LYONS, LEHANE, LANE.

The four surnames given above are the anglicized forms of two distinct Gaelic surnames. Lehane is peculiar to Co. Cork, while Lyne to-day is found chiefly in Co. Kerry, though formerly well known in Co. Galway where Lyons has superseded it. Lyons is the most numerous: 210 births are recorded by Matheson as being registered in a year, of which 85 were in the Cork-Kerry-Limerick area and 71 in Co. Galway. Over seventy per cent of the Lane births were in Counties Cork and Limerick.

Lyons, it should be added, is quite distinct from the Scottish name Lyon. It will thus be seen that much confusion arises in connexion with these names.

The two Gaelic surnames referred to above are Ó Liatháin and Ó Laighin. Ó Liatháin, said to be originally of the Ui Fidhgheinte of the modern Co. Limerick, were settled in the barony of Barrymore, Co. Cork, but are more closely associated with the country north of Youghal, called Ui Litháin by the Four Masters, wherein lies the village of Castle Lyons. The same Gaelic name, anglicized Lehane, is found in the Courtmacsherry area. Ó Laighin belongs to Co. Galway. They were centred around Kilconnell, but though dwelling in the Hy Many country they were, according to O'Flaherty's *Ogygia*, not of it, but of Firbolg origin. O'Donovan states that the Lanes of Trughanacmy (Co. Kerry) are of a different origin again, their name in Irish being Ó Laoghain.

Among notable Irishmen called Lyons we may mention Rev. John Lyons (1708–1790) and John Charles Lyons (1792–1874), two distinguished antiquarians, and Dr. Robert Lyons (1826–1886), Professor of Medicine in the Catholic University medical school, Dublin. We may also include Matthew Lyon (1746–1822), a Co. Wicklow man who from being a poor emigrant to the U.S.A. became a colonel in the American army in the War of Independence and a member of Congress much in the public eye. Sir Hugh Lane (1875–1917), the famous collector of pictures, who was drowned in the torpedoing of the " Lusitania ", is the best known Irishman of that form of the name. Some Kerry families, especially around Dingle, spell the name Leyne, and are particular about this. Father Matthew O'Leyn (d. 1599) was one of the many Irish Franciscan martyrs.

MacLYSAGHT, (MacAleese).

The MacLysaghts, like the Considines, are a sub-sept of the leading Dalcassian sept of O'Brien of Thomond. The name, in Irish Mac Giolla Iasachta, is of obscure origin. It is believed to indicate that the eponymous ancestor was loaned by the O'Briens as a fighting man or in some other capacity. It is not, as some have stated, " son of the servant of Jesus," which is Mac Giolla Iosa, *anglice* MacAleese, a well known surname in Co. Derry. To that family belonged the famous painter Daniel MacLise (1806–1870). The sept of MacLysaght was originally located in the neighbourhood of Ennistymon, Co. Clare, and the name, though nowhere very numerous, is still to be found chiefly in Counties Clare and Limerick, with a branch in Co. Cork. The latter was established by a younger son who early in the seventeenth century became a Protestant ; this particular family was consistently pro-English and his descendant was created a peer, thus becoming one of the very few members of the eighteenth century Irish House of Lords who was of Gaelic Irish Stock. His ancestor fought in William III's army, but at the same time William MacLysaght, or Lysaght, distinguished himself by his valour on the Jacobite side as an officer in Clare's Dragoons at the Boyne, Aughrim and Limerick. One or two of the Clare sept conformed in the penal times, but the great majority of the MacLysaghts remained Catholic and obscure. It would be more accurate in this connexion to say Lysaghts than MacLysaghts because, as in the case of so many native Irish names, the prefix had fallen almost entirely into disuse until early in the present century. In the sixteenth century Fiants the name, always in Co. Clare, appears very frequently, with many variations in these early attempts to spell this difficult name in English, as for example MacGillesiaghtie, MacGillisiachta and MacGyllysaghta : the last of these shows clearly how it eventually became Lysaght. In a list of priests of the diocese of Kilfenora sent to Pope Urban VIII in 1629 the spelling is MacGilliesaghta. The restoration of the Mac is in this case noteworthy, because it was not done gradually and haphazard as has happened with other surnames, but the resumption was made about forty years ago by the concerted and formal action of some hundred or more Lysaghts (organized by William MacLysaght of Doon, Co. Limerick). We thus find certain members of the sept in modern times known indifferently as Lysaght and MacLysaght. Of these the most distinguished was S. R. Lysaght (1856–1941) the poet and novelist. Edward Lysaght (1763–1811), known as " Pleasant Ned ", wit, duellist and poet in both the English and Irish languages, was one of the celebrated characters of Dublin at the time of Grattan's Parliament. His namesake, and a Clareman but no traceable relation, Edward MacLysaght, was first Chief Herald of Ireland in succession to the Ulster Kings of Arms. Two of the latter's forbears were sheriffs of Limerick City in the seventeenth century, one being concerned in the famous " Battle of the Mayors ". This family, as well as others of the name, was transplanted in the Cromwellian Settlement as Irish papists, thus returning from Co. Limerick to Co. Clare, the county of their origin. The following curious and unusual inscription can be read on the tomb of Patrick Lysaght (1656–1741) at Kilfenora :

> Non quemquam defraudavi, me saepe fefelli
> Et Marti et Baccho saepe tributa dedi.*
>
> *Arms illustrated on Plate XIX*

O'MADDEN, (MacAvaddy, Madigan).

Madden is one of those Gaelic Irish surnames from which the prefix O was dropped during the centuries of Gaelic eclipse, but which did not share in the widespread resumption of O's and Macs since the Gaelic revival. In Irish it is Ó Madáin, the earlier form being Ó Madadháin. This sept was a branch of the Ui Máine (Hy Many)

* I have defrauded no one, I have often deceived myself, and I have often paid tribute to Mars and to Bacchus.

living in that part of Co. Galway which lies beside the Shannon and extending over that river into Offaly. Their chief was the recognized lord of that area in early times, and after the occupation of Connacht by the Anglo-Normans retained his lordship under the de Burgos. That is the part of the country in which the Maddens are still most numerous. Referring to the supposed derivation of the name from the word *mada*, it is interesting to note that in Co. Mayo the name Mac a' Mhadaidh (which literally means "son of a dog") is indifferently anglicized MacAvaddy and Madden, the former being a close approximation phonetically to the Irish form. It should also be mentioned that the Madigans of Counties Antrim and Derry, especially in the Magherafelt district, often shorten their name to Madden. The Madigans, however, who may now be regarded as almost exclusively a Clare-Limerick family, are a branch of the Co. Galway Maddens using an otherwise obsolete form of the name. A Madden family of English origin is also found in Ireland, who gave their name to the village of Maddenton in Co. Kildare. The Maddens of Athgarret in the same county, however, are O'Maddens from Co. Galway. In the heyday of landlordism, prior to the Land Acts, the Madden estates, principally in Mayo, Leitrim and Fermanagh, comprised some 25,000 acres.

The Rev. Samuel Madden (1686–1765) the philanthropist, belonged to the Maddenton family; Richard Robert Madden (1798–1886), author of *The United Irishmen, their Lives and Times*, was of Gaelic stock. Two other Irish Maddens distinguished themselves in the field of literature, viz. Daniel Owen Madden (1815–1859), and Thomas More Madden (1844–1902), the latter a son of Richard Robert mentioned above.

Arms illustrated on Plate XIX

MacMAHON, (Mohan, Vaughan).

MacMahon is one of the best known and most distinguished names in Ireland. In Irish Mac Mathghamha, or in ultra-modern spelling MacMahúna, it is said to be derived from the Irish word for a bear. It is borne by two quite distinct septs. The more important of the two belongs to Co. Clare, in which county it is now the most numerous name. These descend from Mahon, son of Murtagh Mór O'Brien, King of Ireland (d. 1119), and the last inaugurated Chief of the Name fell at the battle of Kinsale in 1602. Their territory was Corcabaskin in West Clare. The Ulster sept of MacMahon in the thirteenth century became lords of Oriel on the decline of the O'Carrolls. It is associated chiefly with Co. Monaghan, where the name holds third place in the county list. In fact, as is usually the case with old Gaelic families, their present-day representatives in Ireland (who are about ten thousand in number) are still to be found chiefly in their original territories—in this case Clare and Monaghan.

There have been very many distinguished bearers of the name MacMahon. Bernard MacMahon (1680–1747), his uncle Hugh MacMahon (d. 1737) and his brother Ross Roe MacMahon (1698–1748) were all Archbishops of Armagh, having previously been bishops of their native Clogher. Of the five bishops who held the see of Clogher in the eighteenth century, three were MacMahons and two O'Reillys. Another earlier and very famous Bishop of Clogher was Heber MacMahon (1600–1650), a leader of the Confederate Catholics who actually commanded the Ulster army and died on the scaffold. Prominent in the same cause were Hugh McMahon, last chief of the Ulster sept, who was also beheaded, having been betrayed by Owen O'Connolly in 1641, and Col. Brian MacMahon, who fought at Benburb (1646) and was a member of the Supreme Council of the Confederate Catholics. A generation later the name appears frequently in King James's Irish Army, in which Col. Art MacMahon's infantry regiment was notable. Subsequently many of these officers distinguished themselves in the service of France in the Irish Brigade. Later in that country there was John MacMahon (1715–1780), who was ennobled as Marquis d'Eguilly, of the Clare MacMahons, and his grandson Patrick MacMahon (1808–1893) who was President as well as Marshal of France. It is probable that Charles Patrick Mahon (1800–1891), better known as " The O'Gorman Mahon ", was a descendant of the Clare MacMahons.

Mahon, however, though sometimes used as an abbreviated form of MacMahon, is as a rule a distinct name, being that borne by two septs located in Connacht, one in the diocese of Kilmacduagh (south Galway) and the other an erenagh family of Killaraght, Co. Sligo, who were hereditary custodians of the Cross of St. Attracta. This surname, Ó Mocháin in Irish and properly Mohan in English, spread into Munster, where it was usually anglicized Vaughan. Though Vaughan is, of course, a common Welsh name most of our Irish Vaughans are in fact of this Gaelic stock.

Arms illustrated on Plates XIX and XX.

O'MAHONY.

There are a great many O'Mahonys in Ireland—the name is included, usually without the prefix O, among the hundred commonest surnames. It belongs almost exclusively to West Munster, the great majority of Mahony and O'Mahony births being registered in Co. Cork, particularly in the area associated historically with the O'Mahony sept. Their chieftains were powerful, being often described as princes. Their principal territory comprised the modern barony of Kinelmeaky and extended to the sea, with a fortified castle called Rosbrian off the coast of south-west Cork. The name Ó Mathghamhna—in modernized spelling O'Mahúna—is derived from their ancestor Mathghamhan, whose mother was a daughter of Brian Boru. *Mathghamhan* is the Irish word for a bear. He was killed, with many more of the Desmond fighting men, at the Battle of Clontarf in 1014. Another famous soldier of the name was Count Daniel O'Mahony (d. 1714), general in the Irish Brigade in the service of France and hero of the battle of Cremona, the best known of the many O'Mahonys who served with distinction in the French and Spanish armies. John O'Mahony (1816–1877) of Kilbeheny near Mitchelstown, was the celebrated Fenian leader. In the literary sphere the best-known is Sylvester Mahony (1804–1866), who under the pseudonym of Father Prout was the author of " The Bells of Shandon " and other poems associated with Cork. Father Francis O'Mahony, Provincial of the Irish Franciscans from 1626 to 1629, was also known as Father Francis Matthews. Matthews is rare as an anglicized form of O'Mahony, but not unusual in Ulster as a synonym of MacMahon.

Arms illustrated on Plate XX

O'MALLEY.

O'Malley may well be said to be Irish of the Irish. It is one of the few O names from which the prefix was never widely dropped. It is not specially numerous, but it is very well known. It belonged exclusively in the past to Co. Mayo, and this is almost equally true of the present day : over eighty per cent of the births recorded are in Connacht and most of these are in Co. Mayo. Their particular territory is in the baronies of Burrishoole and Murrisk in that county. Unlike the majority of septs located on the coast the O'Malleys were famous for their naval exploits and their prowess at sea is enshrined in their motto " *terra marique potens* ". Outstanding in this connexion was Grace O'Malley, the subject of so many romantic tales. These "tales" are based on fact, for she has been variously described by responsible contemporary writers as " a most famous sea captain " and " nurse of all the rebellions in the province [of Connacht] for forty years ". She is still known as Graine Mhaol: in Irish her name is Gráine Ní Mháille, O'Malley being Ó Máille. Locally in Co. Mayo it is often anglicized Melia, the variant in Irish being Ó Maele. It may be of interest to notice here that the well-known Sir Owen O'Malley, diplomat and author, who claims to be Chief of the Name, insists on his name being pronounced O'Mailey. In addition to Grace O'Malley (1530–1600)—*vide supra*—we may mention Austin O'Malley (c. 1760–1854), United Irish leader, who fought with Humbert at Castlebar in 1798, while at the same time George O'Malley (1780–1843) at the age of eighteen took the English Government side on the occasion of the French invasion of Co. Mayo and subsequently distinguished himself at the battle of Waterloo. The former was father of General Patrick O'Malley (d. 1869) of the French army. Also notable were Rev. Thaddeus O'Malley (1796–1877), the priest who got into trouble frequently for his unorthodox ecclesiastical and political views ; and Frank Ward O'Malley (1875–1932), well-known Irish-American wit and writer. Perhaps I might add Lever's celebrated fictional character Charles O'Malley, the typical divil-may-care Irishman.

Arms illustrated on Plate XX

O'MALONE.

Although Malone is a genuine O name, being in Irish Ó Maoileoin (meaning descendant of the follower of St. John), it is never met with in English with its prefix. The Malones are an ancient sept, being a branch of the O'Connors of Connacht, and their principal family was for centuries associated with the Abbey of Clonmacnois, to which they furnished many abbots and bishops, for Clonmacnois was for a time an independent see before being united with Ardagh. Unlike most old Irish septs its modern representatives are not found in any considerable numbers in the territory of their origin : Counties Clare and Wexford—in quite different parts of the country—now have more Malones than other areas. The Clare Malones are probably descendants of the Clonmacnois sept, but the origin of those of Wexford is obscure. The Rev. Sylvester Malone (1822–1906), author of the *Church History of Ireland*, was a Clare priest. Another notable priest of the name was Rev. William Malone (1586–1659), Superior of the Jesuit Mission to Ireland. Three Malones sat in the Parliament of 1689, three served in King James II's army in Ireland and eight were attainted after 1691. One family of Malones was outstanding in the eighteenth century in Ireland. They had conformed, but were nevertheless prominent in their advocacy of Catholic emancipation. Anthony Malone (1700–1776) was Chancellor of the Exchequer ; his brother Edmund Malone (1704–1776) was an Irish M.P. and judge, and the latter's sons were noteworthy—Edmund Malone (1741–1812) as friend of Johnson, Boswell etc. and Shakespearian critic while Richard Malone (1738–1816) was another prominent Irish M.P.

Arms illustrated on Plate XX.

MANGAN, O'Mongan.

The normal form of Mangan in Irish is Ó Mongáin, which is more phonetically anglicized as Mongan in parts of Connacht ; but even in Mayo, the original homeland of one of the septs so called, it is more usually Mangan nowadays. The Munster Mangans, originally of Co. Cork, are now found more in Co. Limerick. James Clarence

Mangan (1803–1849), the poet, came from Shanagolden, Co. Limerick, where the family to which he belonged still live. Rev. Edward Mangin (1772–1852) was also a poet and essayist of note.

Mangan is also found as a synonym of Manahan (a form of Monahan, q.v. p. 227 *infra*) and of Mannion (q.v. *infra*).

MANNION, O'Mannin, Manning.

The sept of Ó Mainnín was located in the barony of Tiaquin, Co. Galway, their chief's residence being the castle of Clogher. They were an important sept in the Hy Many country but were not of that group by descent, as their ancestors were the ancient pre-Gaelic Pictish rulers of that area. Their territory was much reduced by the O'Kellys, and their estates were largely lost in the seventeenth century confiscations, but the Mannions (as they are called in Connacht) remained in their homeland where they are numerous to-day. The name has also been anglicized Manning: Cornet John Manning of O'Neills Dragoons in King James II's Irish Army was an O'Mannin. Manning, of course, is a fairly common name in England, and some of the Mannings of Dublin and Cork are of English descent. Frederick Maning (1812–1883), who became a Maori chief in New Zealand, was a Dublin man.

MANNIX, O'Mannis, O'Manihan, (MacNeice).

Mannix is the usual form in English of the Gaelic surname Ó Mainichín (derived from *manach*—a monk), a minor sept of Corca Laoidhe in the south-west of Co. Cork: it is placed in the " Book of Lecan " and other mediaeval manuscripts in the O'Hennessy territory at the head of Ross Bay. An obsolete anglicized form of this is O'Mannis, which is that used in the record of the sept arms illustrated in Plate XX. The name was never numerous and is now scarce, being rarely found outside the counties of south-west Munster; it is well-known throughout the world in our own time on account of the uncompromising pro-Irish political opinions of Most Rev. Daniel Mannix (b. Co. Cork 1864), Archbishop of Melbourne, Australia.

This name is also sometimes anglicized Mannihan or Manahan, but not Manning, which is a synonym of Mannion (q.v.). Mannix, it should be added, is an occasional synonym of MacNeice (MacNaois in Irish), an Ulster surname, which is itself a variant of MacAonghnis, *anglice* MacGenis.

Arms illustrated on Plate XX.

MacMANUS.

This name is often stated to be Norse in origin but in fact it is as thoroughly Irish as any ancient Gaelic name. MacManus is Mac Maghnuis in modern Irish, i.e. son of Magnus. Magnus (Latin: great) as a christian name came to Ireland from northern Europe it is true, but its combination with Mac as a surname originated in Ireland. In two separate cases it designated descent from individual persons called Maghnus. The first is descended from Maghnus (d. 1181), son of Turlough O'Connor, King of Ireland, and was seated in the parish of Kilronan, Co. Roscommon; the other, a distinguished Fermanagh family, lived on the shores of Lough Erne. The island of Belle Isle in that lake was formerly called Ballymacmanus. These are a branch of the Maguires. As is frequently the case, the present-day bearers of the name are found in greater numbers in their original habitat than elsewhere: it holds second place in the list of most numerous names in Co. Fermanagh, but does not so appear in any other county. It is one of those few names from which the prefix Mac has not been widely dropped. It is, however, in some parts of Ulster disguised under the English form Mayne. It is very seldom met with in Munster. In Connacht, Mayo is its main stronghold. The most famous of the MacManus sept in Irish history, Terence Bellew MacManus (1823–1860), hailed from Co. Fermanagh. He fought beside William Smith O'Brien at Ballingarry, and was sentenced to death and transported, but escaped and went to America. His funeral in Dublin was the occasion of the greatest Fenian demonstration ever seen.

Arms illustrated on Plate XX.

MARTIN, GILMARTIN.

Martin is among the fifty most numerous surnames in Ireland; in fact it has thirty-eighth place. The thirteen thousand persons of the name in Ireland are widely distributed over the country, being found most frequently in East Ulster and, of course, in Dublin which, being the metropolis, contains families from all the provinces. Martin is also a common name in Great Britain: it has thirty-first place in England and forty-eighth in Scotland.

The best known families of Martin are those of Galway city and county: they were one of the celebrated "Tribes of Galway". These Martins are not Gaelic in origin. Their pedigree states that they came to Ireland with Strongbow. An interesting fact relating to the Martyns of Tullyra, Co. Galway, should be mentioned here. A special clause was inserted in the penal act 8 Anne, chap. 3, providing that the prohibition of gavelkind in Catholic families should not apply to Oliver Martin of Tulliry on account of his assistance to Protestants during the brief period of Catholic ascendancy in the seventeenth century—an example of clemency very unusual in the ferocious Penal Code.

Our native indigenous Martins may be either O's or Macs. The O'Martins were of some importance in the mediaeval period : Giolla Earnáin Ó Martain who died in 1218 is described in the various Annals as chief brehon or chief professor of law in Ireland—chief poet etc., in " Loch Cé " ; and in 1431 the death of the Bishop of Clogher, who was also an O'Martin, is recorded. MacMartin was the surname assumed by a branch of the O'Neills in Co. Tyrone. Survivors of these minor septs are now plain Martin without either prefix. Co. Tyrone is also the original homeland of another sept whose present-day representatives are sometimes called Martin : this is the important sept of Mac Giolla Mhártain, anglicized MacGilmartin in the seventeenth century and now usually Gilmartin. Their forbears were chiefs in the barony of Clogher, Co. Tyrone, but, though they were still numerous in the adjoining county of Fermanagh at the time of the 1659 census, they were gradually forced westwards to the territory in which they are now chiefly found, i.e. Counties Leitrim and Sligo. Fergal MacMartin (d. 1431), Bishop of Killala, was probably of this sept.

A number of distinguished men and women of the name have adorned the annals of Ireland, especially in the nineteenth century. The most notable of these were : John Martin (1812–1875) the Young Irelander and brother-in-law of John Mitchel ; Richard Martin (1754–1834) that romantic character known as " Hair Trigger Dick " and " Humanity Dick " (the originator of legislation against cruelty to animals), who could boast that his Connacht avenue was thirty miles long ; his daughter Harriet Letitia Martin (1801–1891), the novelist ; his grand-daughter Mary Letitia Martin (1815–1850), the " Princess of Connemara ", owner of 200,000 acres, who ruined herself relieving sufferers at the time of the Great Famine. In recent times we have had Miss Martin of Ross (1862–1915), of the famous literary partnership Somerville and Ross ; and finally, not to mention various distinguished churchmen and colonial statesmen, Edward Martyn (1859–1923) another remarkable Co. Galway man, the co-founder of Sinn Féin and a pioneer of the Irish dramatic movement.
Arms illustrated on Plate XX.

O'MEAGHER, Maher.

Maher, also written Meagher, is in Irish Ó Meachair, derived from the word *meachar*, meaning hospitable—Maher is a word of two syllables, not pronounced Marr. Of the same stock as the O'Carrolls of Ely it belongs to the barony of Ikerrin in Co. Tipperary where it originated and where it is still more common than anywhere else in Ireland—in fact fifty per cent of the eight thousand people of the name come from Co. Tipperary. Their territory was near Roscrea, at the foot of the famous Devil's Bit Mountain and, unlike some Gaelic septs, they were not ousted by Norman invaders but remained in possession side by side with the Ormond Butlers. Though this is a genuine Gaelic O name it is rarely, if ever, met with in its English form with the prefix.

One of the adventurous and ill-starred rapparees of the seventeenth century was Capt. John Meagher, who was captured and hanged in 1690. Father Maher (1793–1874) was a distinguished ecclesiastic ; and Thomas Francis Meagher (1823–1867), known as " Meagher of the Sword," was one of the most prominent of the Young Irelanders. He was later leader of the Irish Brigade in the Federal Army in the American Civil War.

Arms illustrated on Plate XX.

O'MEARA, O'Mara.

In Irish this name is Ó Meadhra and both the spellings given above are used as the ordinary anglicized form, O'Meara being slightly more numerous than O'Mara. It is of interest to note that, while sixty years ago the records show that less than one third of the people of the name used the prefix O, to-day it is very rare in Ireland to find plain Mara or Meara, without it. The O'Mearas are now and always have been Co. Tipperary people : they belong by origin to the north of that county, the centre of their territory being Toomevara, a place-name which embodies their surname—Tuaim ui Mheadhra in Irish. Dermod O'Meara, physician and poet, author of the first medical work printed in Dublin (1619), his son Edmund O'Meara (d. 1680), another medical author, and Barry O'Meara (1786–1836), also a surgeon and author, famous for his association with Napoleon at St. Helena, were all Tipperary men. Kathleen O'Meara (1839–1888), grand-daughter of the last named, wrote many novels and biographies. Also of Tipperary stock were the brothers Count Thomas O'Meara (1750–1819), Baron William O'Meara (1764–1818) and Col. Daniel Ó Meara (b. 1764), all of whom had distinguished service in the Irish Brigades in France. In our own time the O'Maras of Limerick have been very prominent in the industrial and political activities of that city ; and one of them, Joseph O'Mara, was the founder and also the star of the well-known O'Mara Opera Company.

Arms illustrated on Plate XX.

O'MEEHAN, Meighan.

O'Meehan, in Irish Ó Miadhacháin, is the name of a sept belonging to Co. Leitrim : this sept (also called O'Meighan) is of the same stock as the MacCarthys of south Munster, but by the end of the eleventh century they had migrated and established themselves in their new country, their association therewith being perpetuated by

224

the place name Ballaghmeehin, or Ballymeighan, in the parish of Rossinver, Co. Leitrim. Thence they spread into adjacent counties and are now fairly numerous in all east Connacht, and in Co. Clare where they are mentioned in 1317 as one of the Thomond septs which rallied to O'Brien; they also appear in the 1659 census as more numerous in Co. Clare than elsewhere.

Thomas and Denis O'Miachan (O'Meehan) were successively bishops of Achonry between 1251 and 1285, and another bishop, Edru O'Meighan, held the see of Meath from 1152, when he attended the Council of Kells, until 1173. Another distinguished ecclesiastic was the historian Rev. Charles Patrick Meehan (1812–1890). Two of the sept distinguished themselves in France: Count James Anthony Mehegan (alias Meehan) (1719–1792), son of Chevalier O'Mehegan, as a soldier, and his brother, Chevalier William Alexander Mehegan (1721–1766) as a French author.

The most notable fact relating to the sept is of a religious character: a metal case containing a manuscript of St. Molaise of Devenish (sixth century) was for over a thousand years preserved by successive generations of O'Meehans, and is now in the National Museum of Ireland.

Arms illustrated on Plate XXI.

O'MOLLOY, (Miley).

The O'Molloys, now always simply Molloy or occasionally Mulloy, are of very distinguished origin. They are of the southern Ui Neill, traditionally descended from the famous Niall of the Nine Hostages, King of Ireland A.D. 371 The head of this important sept was O'Molloy chief or lord of Fercal, a district covering several baronies of the county of Offaly (alias King's County). In Irish this name is Ó Maolmhuaidh, which, according to O'Donovan, signifies noble or venerable chieftain. A quite different origin is traced for the Molloys of Connacht, who are called Ó Maoil Aoidh (servant of St. Aedh), a name which has many anglicized forms such as Millea, Miley and Mullee, the most usual being Molloy. The origin of the Offaly sept is evidenced by the fact that in early records in English the name is often given as O'Mulmoy. Many of this distinguished family had friendly relations with the English crown. In 1189 Albin O'Molloy (d. 1223), then Bishop of Ferns, was one of the officiating prelates at the coronation of Richard I and, notwithstanding the efforts of several prominent O'Molloys to withstand Tudor aggression in Ireland, their chief was appointed hereditary bearer of the English standard in Ireland, an office he exercised at least within the Pale. An important branch of this sept, whose head was known as the Green Molloy, is said to have migrated to Co. Roscommon, though one eminent authority, John O'Donovan, considered them a distinct sept. The fact remains that east Connacht and Offaly are the main habitats of Molloys in modern times. Many distinguished O'Molloys and Molloys may be mentioned.

Albin O'Molloy (*vide supra*) was a Cistercian monk before he became Bishop of Ferns ; he is remembered for his reply to Geraldus Cambrensis, attributing the ills of Ireland to English and Welsh clerical intruders, and for his excommunication of the Earl of Pembroke. Two other priests were notable, viz. the Franciscan, Rev. Francis Molloy, author of *Lucerna Fidelium* (published 1676) and the first printed Irish grammar, and Monsignor Gerald Molloy (1834–1906), theologian and scientist. James Lynam Molloy (1837–1909), composer of " Love's Old Sweet Song " and many popular ballads, Joseph Fitzgerald Molloy (1858–1908), novelist and poet, Charles Molloy (1690–1767), dramatist, and Charles Molloy (1646–1690), author of a standard treatise on maritime law, were other contributors to the literature of their country. Most of these were Offaly men. There were two distinguished officers of the name in King James II's army in Ireland and one, a relative, in that of King William.

Arms illustrated on Plate XXI.

O'MOLONY, (Maloughney).

Molony or Moloney is Ó Maoldhomhnaigh in Irish, which denotes descendant of a servant of the Church. It is seldom if ever found to-day with the original prefix O, though it is one hundred per cent Gaelic with no similar name to be found in England. Molony is a Dalcassian sept belonging to Kiltanon near Tulla in East Clare, where they are very numerous to-day, though also found in equal numbers in the adjoining counties of Limerick and Tipperary. An interesting example of the vagaries of Irish nomenclature is afforded by this name Molony. Some families in north Co. Tipperary now called Molony are not Ó Maoldhomhnaigh, but Ó Maolfhachtna, which, however, is also in rare cases anglicized as Maloughney and MacLoughney, thus giving the impression that it is a Mac and not an O name.

A number of Molonys have done good work in the field of historical and genealogical research. Two O'Moloneys of the Kiltanon sept were successively Bishops of Killaloe for a period of more than seventy years. The younger John O'Moloney (1617–1702), nephew of the elder, was remarkable both for his intellectual attainments as a University professor in Paris and later for his stout resistance to the persecution of his fellow Catholics in Ireland. Father Donogh O'Moloney, V.G. of Killaloe, was tortured to death in 1601. Col. Sir James Stacpoole Moloney was one of those intrepid soldiers who took part in the forlorn hope attack on Montreal in 1786, in which ninety-three of the one hundred participants were killed. In America the name of Irish-born Martin Molony (1847–1929), self-made millionaire, is still well remembered on account of his munificence in Catholic causes.

Arms illustrated on Plate XXI.

O'MONAHAN, Monks.

The name Monahan or Monaghan (the latter is the more usual spelling in Ireland) is chiefly to be found in the counties of Galway, Mayo and Fermanagh, all of which are not far from the original habitat of the O'Monaghans, viz. that part of the Co. Roscommon which lies between Elphin and Jamestown. The Four Masters record O'Monaghan (Ó Manacháin in Irish) as Lord of the Three Tuathas of Roscommon in 1287, about the time they were displaced from the lordship by the O'Hanlys. The Manachán from whom the family takes its name was a famous Connacht warrior of the ninth century. *Manachán* denotes a monk, hence the synonym Monks used in some places as the anglicized form of the name. Dick Monk, who fought with the rebels at the battle of Arklow in 1798, was also known as Richard Monaghan. There is a remarkable Monaghan tomb in the Dominican Church at Athenry, Co. Galway, dated 1686. The name has not been very prominent in Irish history or literature. The Irish-American poet James Monaghan was born in Co. Westmeath (1862); James Henry Monaghan (1804–1878), b. Co. Galway, was notable as the prosecutor (in his capacity of Attorney-General) of William Smith O'Brien, T. F. Meagher, Gavan Duffy, John Mitchel etc. and later as the Catholic Chief Justice who tried the Fenian prisoners.

Arms illustrated on Plate XXI.

O'MOONEY, Meeny, Mainey.

This name, Ó Maonaigh in modern Irish, is derived, according to Professor M. A. O'Brien, from the Old Irish word *moenach* meaning dumb. It is a surname adopted by several unrelated septs. The eponymous ancestor of the O'Mooneys of Ulster was Monach, son of Ailioll Mór. His descendants became erenaghs of Shanaghan in the parish of Ardara, diocese of Raphoe. More numerous to-day and better known in history are the Mooneys of Offaly, where they have given their name to the townland of Ballymooney—there is also another townland Ballymooney in the adjoining county of Leix. The Mooneys of the parish Lemanaghan, near Clara, were for centuries the custodians of the shrine of St. Monahan. Thirdly there was a sept of Ó Maonaigh located in the barony of Tireragh, Co. Sligo. Their present-day representatives are usually called Meeny: four townlands called Ballymeeny in the parish of Easky indicate their territory. Finally, there was the Munster sept of the same name in Irish: the form used there in modern times is Mainey, in accordance phonetically with the Munster pronunciation of Irish.

A notable person of the name was Father Donagh Mooney, Provincial of the Irish Franciscans from 1615 to 1618, who was guardian of the young Earls of Tyrconnell and Tyrone at Louvain in 1626. Thomas Mooney (1815–1888), the Dublin man who edited a Fenian newspaper in San Francisco, was in his latter years a very controversial figure in London.

Arms illustrated on Plate XXI.

O'MORAN.

Though numerous enough to be included among the sixty commonest names in Ireland and now to be found in every county, Moran is essentially a Connacht name and the majority of the population so called belong to the Connacht counties of Mayo, Galway, Roscommon and Leitrim. This might be expected, because the two quite distinct septs Ó Móráin and Ó Moghráin, now both anglicized Moran, held their territory in that province. Ó Móráin (possibly derived from the word *mór*, big) was a chief in Co. Mayo and resided near Ballina ; Ó Moghráin, earlier Ó Mughráin, of Ui Máine was chief of Criffon in Co. Galway and another was head of a powerful family in Co. Roscommon, seated near Ballintober.

Among distinguished bearers of the name were General James O'Moran (1739–1794), of Dillon's Irish regiment in the army of France, who was guillotined, though he was a brilliant soldier and continued to serve France loyally after the Revolution : Michael Moran (1794–1871), the Dublin street singer and public character known as " Zozimus " ; Most Rev. Patrick Moran (1823–1895), bishop in South Africa and New Zealand ; and Cardinal Patrick Moran (1830–1911) of Australia, author of *The Life of Blessed Oliver Plunket*. David Patrick Moran (1870–1936), founder of the weekly review, *The Leader*, had a considerable influence on public opinion (especially in the early days of the " Irish-Ireland " movement) through his writings in that journal, which is still flourishing after nearly sixty years of continuous publication.

Arms illustrated on Plate XXI.

O'MORE, MOORE.

Moore is a very numerous name in Ireland : with some 16,500 of the population so called it holds twentieth place in the list of commonest names. The great majority of these (apart from the metropolitan area) are in Munster and Ulster. It is practically impossible to say what proportion of these are of Gaelic Irish origin and what proportion of English extraction, for Moore is also indigenous in England and very common there (it has thirty-ninth place in their list). It would perhaps be better to say Anglo-Norman rather than English, since Anglo-Norman Moores established themselves in Munster soon after the invasion. These Moores are called de Móra in Irish, a phonetic rendering of the English name which is derived from the word moor (heathy mountain). The old Irish Moores are Ó Mórdha, from the word *mórdha* (stately, noble). The eponymous ancestor Mórdha was twenty-first in descent from Conal Cearnach, the most distinguished of the heroes of the Red Branch. The O'Mores were the leading sept of the Seven Septs of Leix, the other six being tributary to them. According to Keating the O'Mores have St. Fintan as their protector. Of thirteen families of Moore recorded in Burke's *Landed Gentry of Ireland* (1912), twelve claim to have come to Ireland as settlers from England or Scotland and only one to be an offshoot of the O'Mores. Judged by the test of resistance to English aggression the O'Mores may be described as one of the foremost Irish septs. In this connexion particular mention may be made of Rory O'More (d. 1557) and his son Rory Óg O'More (d. 1578), both of whom were distinguished Irish leaders in the wars against the Tudor sovereigns, and another Rory O'More, a member of the Leix sept, the head of the 1641 Rising and a staunch ally of Owen Roe O'Neill in the subsequent war. It is of interest to note that he was known in English as Moore as well as O'More.

Of the many Moores who have distinguished themselves in various phases of Irish life the most famous was, perhaps, Thomas Moore (1779–1852), the poet : he was of a Co. Wexford family. The Moores of Moore Hall, Co. Mayo, produced George Henry Moore (1810–1870), the politician, and his two sons George Moore (1852–1933) the novelist, and Col. Maurice Moore (1854–1939), author and ardent worker in the Nationalist cause in the present century. The Moores of Moore Hall descend from the Moores of Alicante, Spain, who were English in origin. Father Florence O'More, alias Moore (1550–1616) was a noted Irish Jesuit in Austria. Rev. Michael Moore (1640–1726) was the only Catholic provost of Trinity College (Dublin University). Others were noted as economists, architects etc., and one Rev. Henry Moore (1751–1844) was friend and biographer of John Wesley.

A number of O'Mores of the Leix sept were officers of the Irish Brigade in France in the eighteenth century. The descendants of one of them, Murtagh O'More, (who went to France in 1691) ranked among the nobility of France as lords of Valmont.

The family name of the Earls of Drogheda is Moore : their ancestor came to Ireland under Queen Elizabeth I. The Moores of Barmeath have been settled there since the fourteenth century. The grandson of Saint Thomas More claims in his *Memoir* that the family of More in England was a branch of the O'Mores of Ireland : subsequent research suggests that, though they did indeed come from Ireland, they were of the Barmeath line.

St. Malachy, who was Archbishop of Armagh from 1132 to 1148, is described by Gams and other ecclesiastical authorities as Malachy O'Moore. His surname, however, was O'Morgair (now obsolete), which is not, in fact, an early form of Ó Mórdha.

Arms illustrated on Plate XXI.

O'MORIARTY; Murtagh.

Moriarty is Ó Muircheartaigh in Irish, but nowadays the prefix is never attached to this name, though the form O'Moriarty (and indeed occasionally MacMoriarty) is found in old records. The sept, which is of the same stock as the O'Donoghues and the O'Mahonys, has always been associated with Kerry. Their original territory lay on both sides of Castlemaine Harbour, but after the Anglo-Norman invasion their influence was reduced by the uprise of the Fitzgeralds, in spite of an early alliance by marriage—O'Moriarty, Chief of the Name, married the daughter of a leading Fitzgerald about the year 1210. Nevertheless the rank and file of the sept remained in the homeland throughout the centuries and in our own time statistics indicate that ninety per cent of the births registered in the name of Moriarty take place in Co. Kerry.

The Most Rev. David Moriarty (1814–1877), Bishop of Kerry, was remarkable for his opposition not only to the Fenians but also to Home Rule. Another notable ecclesiastic was Rev. Patrick Eugene Moriarty (1804–1875), born in Dublin of Kerry stock, and Augustinian Superior in the U.S.A., who was famous as a preacher and temperance reformer. Henry Augustus Moriarty (1815–1906), whose family lived on Dursey Island at the mouth of the Kenmare River, made his name as a seaman and particularly by his success in recovering the broken Atlantic cable in mid-ocean in 1866. Four priests named Moriarty were among those from Kerry who were proscribed under the Penal Code in 1714. In the previous century Father Thady MacMoriarty, a noted Dominican of Tralee, was martyred in 1653.

Ó Muircheartaigh is also the name of a sept located near Kells, Co. Meath. Like other minor septs in that part of the country they were soon submerged after the Anglo-Norman invasion; but their descendants have survived, not however as Moriarty, but as Murtagh, and this name is fairly numerous in the midlands. The Murtaghs of Ulster and North Connacht, where the name is also found, are in many cases of Scottish origin—in Scotland the form Murdoch is more usual.

Arms illustrated on Plate XXI.

O'MORONEY, Mulrooney.

The Irish surname Ó Maolruanaidh (i.e. descendant of the follower of Ruanaidh or Rooney) was that of several septs in mediaeval times. That of Fermanagh, where they were powerful before the rise of the MacGuires, survives to-day in small numbers under the name of Mulrooney. West of the Shannon the name has become Moroney. As such it is almost exclusively a Co. Clare surname, though formerly they were to be found also in the north-east of Co. Galway.

Arms illustrated on Plate XXI.

MORRIS, FITZMAURICE, (Morrison).

Though the name Morris is essentially English, it has been used, as also has Morrison, as an anglicized form of Ó Muirgheasa, a sept of the Ui Fiachrach (Co. Sligo), where, however, the normal form Morrissey is now rarely met with. Ó Muirghis is an abbreviation of this ; Morris is also used as an abbreviation of Fitzmaurice (in Irish Mac Muiris), the Fitzmaurices being celebrated as a branch of the Geraldines and lords of Lixnaw in Kerry. Fitzmaurice was also the surname adopted by a branch of the Prendergasts in Co. Mayo.

The family of Morris whose arms are illustrated in Plate XXII are of Norman origin. When they first came to Ireland they were known as de Marreis, or by its Latin equivalent de Marisco (*vide* Morrissey *infra*). In 1485 a branch of this stock settled in Galway City where they became one of the " Tribes of Galway," and from that date until the submergence of Catholic Ireland in Cromwell's time, they were prominent in the commercial and social activities of Galway, though surprisingly few of them held municipal office : those who did so are recorded as Mares, Mareis and Maries, but in no case in the modern form Morris up to 1654, when the Catholic Corporation was suppressed.

The Fitzmaurices of Kerry were very prominent in the wars against the Elizabethan invaders in the sixteenth century, notably James Fitzmaurice (1530–1579), two Thomas Fitzmaurices (1502–1590 and 1574–1630), and Patrick Fitzmaurice (1550–1600). Of men called Morris the best known is Rev. Francis Orpen Morris (1810–1893), author of *British Birds* and other standard works on natural history, who was born in Co. Cork. Hervey Montmorency Morres (1767–1839), Tipperary-born officer in the Austrian and the French armies, was a United Irishman and took a leading part in the 1798 insurrection. From Galway there was Michael Morris (1827–1901) the judge, who was created a peer in his old age. His grandnephew, the well-known Lord Killanin, is the present head of the Morris family of Galway.

Arms illustrated on Plate XXII.

MORRISSEY.

As in the case of Morris, the bearer of the name Morrissey anxious about his forbears, is faced with many problems, unless he has a reliable pedigree of, or at least a well recognized tradition about, his own family.

The only native Gaelic Irish sept whose name has been anglicized as Morrissey is Ó Muirgheasa, a branch of the Ui Fiachra : their territory was at the southern side of Sligo Bay. These are of MacDermot stock, being descended from Muiris, the grandson of a famous MacDermot, viz. Donogh na mainstreach (i.e. of the monas teries). It may be mentioned that Mac Muirgheasa was the Gaelic form of their name used by the Fitzmaurices of Mayo. However, Morrissey is a name which is only very rarely to be found in any part of Connacht to-day : in fact it is chiefly confined to Munster, particularly Counties Waterford, Limerick and Cork. There is, it may be added, a place called Morrisseysland near New Ross. No Gaelic sept of Morrissey is associated with Munster or Leinster. There was, however, a very powerful family called de Marisco, whose first representatives in Ireland were Normans, attached to the house of Ormond, through which they obtained extensive grants of land. As is well known, many of the Norman families became thoroughly hibernicized, like the Powers, the Roches, the Purcells, the Walshes etc. of that region. The de Mariscos adopted the patronymic MacMuiris and in due course this became in many cases Morrissey. An early form of the name in English is de Marecy. In other parts of the country genuine Irish Morrisseys (i.e. O'Morrissey, but in fact the O is never seen in English in this name) allowed themselves to be called Morris and Morrison. Morris, indeed, is a commoner name in Ireland than Morrissey (the proportion is eleven to nine). Here I must mention a further difficulty : Morrissey is also an indigenous English surname. It is nevertheless reasonably certain that the great majority of Irish Morrisseys are of hibernicized Norman Marisco stock.

O'MULCAHY, (Muckley).

This is Ó Maolchathaigh in Irish—*cathach* means warlike. The prefix O is seldom if ever used nowadays. Mulcahy is a fairly common name in south Munster but not elsewhere. It is said to have originated in south Tipperary. The census of 1659 shows that it was numerous in Counties Waterford and south Tipperary, and also Limerick and Cork in the seventeenth century. It is remarkable how little is heard of this sept in mediaeval records or of its modern representatives. General Richard Mulcahy (b. 1886), close associate of Michael Collins in the War of Independence and subsequently a minister in several Irish governments, is the best known bearer of the name. Others worthy of mention are Denis Dowling Mulcahy (1833–1920), Fenian and author ; Jeremiah Hodges Mulcahy (d. 1889), painter ; and Hon. Edward Mulcahy (b. 1883), New Zealand cabinet minister : all these were born either in Co. Tipperary or Co. Limerick.

An example of the absorption by attraction of a rare name in a well-known one is to be seen in Mulcahy, which has been used as a synonym of Mulclohy. This name, Ó Maolchloiche in Irish, belongs by origin to Inishmulclohy, Co. Sligo, where it is now usually anglicized Stone (by a mistranslation). In Munster, when not made Mulcahy, it is Muckley.

O'MULLAN, (O'Mellan, Mullen).

The name Mullen originated from several very distinct sources. It can be an abbreviation of MacMullen, a Scottish surname borne by many of the seventeenth century settlers in Ulster ; it can be one of the anglicized forms of the Irish Ó Maoláin, which is possibly derived from the Gaelic word *maol* (bald). Other forms besides Mullen are Mullin and Mullan in Connacht, and Mullane and Mullins in Cork, Limerick and Clare. If all these forms, excluding MacMullen, were counted as one the name may be included among the fifty commonest surnames in Ireland. As a historic sept O'Mullan belongs to Co. Galway. The eponymous ancestor, Mullan, was descended from a King of Connacht and was of the same stock as O'Concannon. Another sept of O'Mullan or O'Mullen existed in Ulster (Tyrone and Derry), not to be confounded with the planter MacMullens. Chichester, writing in 1608, mentions O'Mullane as one of the principal septs under the O'Cahanes. The most famous of this sept was Shane Crosagh O'Mullan, the Derry rapparee, who, having been evicted from his property about the year 1729, took to the mountains and for several years led a fabulous Robin Hood type of existence, but was eventually hanged with his two sons at Derry jail. A third sept of Ó Maoláin is that of Co. Cork. The name in this case is usually anglicized as Mullane. The mother of the Liberator, Daniel O'Connell, was an O'Mullane and he is said to have inherited his distinctive and so-called typical Irish face from her people, not from his father's family. John Mullan (1830–1909), the American explorer and pioneer, was the son of an Irish emigrant. Dr. James Mullin (1846–1920) was probably the most remarkable man of the name : born in extreme poverty, he worked on a farm at the age of eleven and later as a carpenter, was entirely self-taught, yet became an M.D. and also wrote many notable books including *A Toiler's Life*. Most Rev. John MacMullen (1833–1883), Bishop of Davenport, the Chicago educator and churchman, was born in Co. Down. Finally, it should be noted that Ó Mealláin, in English O'Mellan, has to a large extent become, by attraction, Mullen : this is a sept of Co. Tyrone, keepers of St. Patrick's bell, of whom the best known is the Franciscan friar Terlagh O'Mellan whose journal (1641–1647) is a most valuable source of seventeenth century history.

Arms illustrated on Plate XXII.

O'MULLIGAN.

The name Mulligan has in our day acquired a comic connotation on account of Jimmy O'Dea the Irish comedian's inimitable sketches of " Mrs. Mulligan the Pride of the Coombe." The sept of O'Mulligan (in Irish Ó Maolagáin), however, is of distinguished origin, its chiefs being lords of a territory called Tír MacCarthain (in the baronies of Boylagh and Raphoe, Co. Donegal). They were dispossessed in the Ulster Plantation of the early seventeenth century. To-day the Mulligans are chiefly located in Counties Mayo and Monaghan. In 1659 the Mulligans were found in considerable numbers in the last-named county and in Fermanagh, and also in the Longford-Westmeath area. In Donegal their name was sometimes changed to Molyneux, but this is rare there now. Of this sept was Charles J. Mulligan (1866–1916), the American sculptor, who was born in Co. Tyrone. John O'Mulligan, who was Bishop of Leighlin and died in 1431, is also said to be of this line. Another Ulster Mulligan of some note was Rev. William Mulligan (d. 1883), professor of mathematics in Queen's College, Belfast. Col. James Mulligan (1830–1864), a renowned officer who commanded the Western Irish Brigade on the Federal side in the American Civil War and was killed in action, was of Irish parentage. Father Edmund Mulligan, who was executed in 1643, was a noted Cistercian.

O'MULVIHIL, Melville, Mitchell.

O'Mulvihil is the anglicized form of Ó Maoil Mhichil, the eponymous ancestor being so called on account of his devotion to St. Michael. The sept was of some importance in mediaeval times, being of the same stock as the MacBrannans, and located with them on the west bank of the Shannon in the modern county of Roscommon ; both were styled chiefs of Corca Sheachlainn, or Corcachlann. O'Mulvihil and MacBrannan are eulogized together in O'Dugan's famous " Topographical Poem," written in the fourteenth century, but the O'Mulvihils disappear from history at an early date—the last to find a place in the " Annals of the Four Masters " being Gillananaev O'Mulvihil, who was one of the leading men responsible for the assassination of the son and heir of the King of Connacht in 1189. In the census of 1659 the O'Mulvihils are recorded as among the most numerous families in Co. Longford. In modern times the representatives of this sept are scattered, being found in places so widely separated as Kerry, Donegal and Wicklow, but nowhere in large numbers. The arms illustrated in Plate XXII are those of the chief representative of the sept in 1874, who was then seated at Knockanira, Co. Clare. The family acquired that property in 1712 from the Earl of Thomond. Doon, formerly Doonmulvihil, is a place in the civil parish of Inchicronan near Ennis, which indicates that the Mulvihil family of Knockanira, just referred to, were established in Co. Clare long before that date. Mulvihils are still in Co. Clare. In some places the name Mulvihil has been anglicized Mitchell, and in others Melville.

Arms illustrated on Plate XXII

234

O'MURPHY, O'Morchoe.

Murphy is much the commonest surname in Ireland : birth registration statistics indicate that of, a population of $4\frac{1}{4}$ millions, no less than approximately 55,000 are Murphys. The name, with which the prefix O is never used nowadays, may be either Ó Murchadha or Mac Murchadha in Irish (see MacMurrough p. 236). It arose independently in several parts of Ireland : there are, for example, indigenous septs so called in Counties Tyrone and Sligo, but these are unimportant in comparison with the great Murphy clan of Leinster. This was centred in Co. Wexford. The Chief of the Name is O'Morchoe, an otherwise obsolete form in English. Birth statistics indicate that Murphy is the commonest name in Co. Wexford and it also has first place in Co. Carlow. The surname, however, is even more numerous to-day in Munster than in Leinster, particularly in Counties Cork and Kerry. This Munster sept, which is associated particularly with the barony of Muskerry, Co. Cork, is said to be a branch of the Kinsella section of the Wexford clan. Their arms, however, are quite different from those of the Wexford Murphys. The Ulster sept of Murphy, mentioned above as belonging to Co. Tyrone, is still numerous but is now more common in the adjacent county of Armagh, where in fact it is first in the statistical list. A chief named Flaherty O'Murphy is recorded in the Annals of Tir Boghainne, i.e. the modern barony of Banagh in Co. Donegal, so that it will be seen that the Murphys were and are widespread in Ulster also.

As might be expected in the case of a name as numerous as Murphy the references to prominent persons of the name in the Annals are frequent throughout the centuries, both of the Leinster and the Ulster septs, for the most part to chiefs and soldiers ; but there are others, e.g. Domhnall Dall Ua Murchadha " chief sage of Leinster " who died in 1127. Passing on to more modern times a few names may be selected to illustrate the extent to which the Murphys have contributed to the political and cultural history of the nation. Wexford produced the best known of these : the two Catholic priests who lost their lives in the 1798 Rising—Rev. John Murphy (1753–1798) and Rev. Michael Murphy (1767–1798). Of the many Co. Cork Murphys who have distinguished themselves we may mention John Murphy (1700–1770), better known as Seán Ó Murchadha na Raithíneach, last chief of the Blarney bards ; Canon Jeremiah Murphy (1848–1915) and Most Rev. John Murphy (1772–1847), Bishop of Cork, both of whom were remarkable not only for their scholarship but also for the extraordinarily fine libraries, including Irish manuscripts, which they possessed. Marie Louise O'Murphy (1737–1814), beautiful daughter of an Irish soldier settled at Rouen, was an influential mistress of Louis XV. Her features are immortalized in many paintings by Boucher, whose model she was. John Murphy (1755–1836), was a famous sea captain ; James Cavanagh Murphy (1760–1814), first a bricklayer, later an architect, was a leading authority on Spanish, Moorish and Portuguese architecture ; and finally there was William Martin Murphy (1844–1921), business magnate and leader of the employers in the great Dublin strike of 1913. The Ulster

Murphys have been less prominent : Arthur Murphy (1727–1805) was an actor and dramatist of some note ; Rev. James Gracey Murphy (1808–1896) was a Hebrew scholar ; and Patrick Murphy (1834–1862) was remarkable for his immense height, being eight feet one inch tall. Many Murphys of Irish emigrant families have also been outstanding in various phases of life in America and Australia ; and many appear in the regimental lists of the Irish Brigade in the service of France.

Arms illustrated on Plate XXII

MacMURROUGH.

The name MacMurrough is one of the most illustrious in Ireland. It is, of course, best known as that of the royal house of Leinster—not too happily in the case of Dermot MacMurrough (1110–1171), King of Leinster, the abductor of Dervorgilla the wife of O'Rourke, Prince of Breffny: it was MacMurrough who sought help from Henry II and thus was the immediate cause of the Anglo-Norman invasion. His descendant Art MacMurrough (1357–1417), also King of Leinster, did much to remove the opprobrium consequently attaching to the name by his continuous and successful resistance to English aggression. Art MacMurrough was styled Kavanagh. This important sept became divided into several sub-septs. The MacMurroughs, the Kavanaghs and the Kinsellas descend from Murchadha (Murrough), grandfather of King Dermot MacMurrough ; and from his brothers came the O'Morchoes and MacDavie Mores. The latter, except in the case of the Chief of the Name, who is now styled O'Morchoe, all became Murphys and Davises respectively. They all belong to County Wexford and adjacent counties. The country south-east of Enniscorthy is still known locally as "The Murroughs" and the MacDavie More district near Arklow is colloquially called "The Macamores." The original surname is now rare, MacMurrough being seldom found to-day outside Co. Dublin. In Irish it is written Mac Murchadha, i.e. son of Murrough. The arms illustrated (Plate XXII) are those of the Kings of Leinster, but they are not borne by any family now, the various branches (Kavanagh, etc.) each having its own distinct coat of arms. MacMorrow (q.v. *infra*) is a name of different origin.

Arms illustrated on Plate XXII

O'MURRY, MacMurry, Murray, MacMorrow, (Gilmore).

A considerable proportion of the Murrays now living in Ireland are of Scottish extraction, particularly in Ulster, where they are more numerous than in the other provinces. The old Irish surname Ó Muireadhaigh, formerly anglicized O'Murry is now almost always Murray. There were several septs so called, of which the only one of importance after the Anglo-Norman invasion was that of Ui Máine. The Chief of the Name as recorded in the " Composition Book of Connacht " (1585), was seated at Ballymurry, their territory being in the barony of Athlone (Co. Roscommon). These are mentioned about the same time by Carew, who also refers to O'Murrihie of Ballywiddan in the barony of Carbery, Co. Cork : this is a local variant of the name usually anglicized Murray. Donogh O'Murry, Archbishop of Tuam from 1458 to 1484, a member of this sept, was responsible for the establishment of that unique ecclesiastical jurisdiction, the Wardenship of Galway ; and Bartholomew Murray (1695–1767), of Co. Clare, is memorable for his benefactions to the Irish College in Paris. In the nineteenth century there were two leading Irish architects called William Murray : the elder was nephew and associate of Francis Johnston (1761–1829) of Armagh, greatest of Irish-born architects.

The " Composition Book of Connacht " also mentions MacMurry of Co. Leitrim, the Chief of the Name being of Loghmoyltagh in that county. The present day representatives of that sept, who mostly come from this area, use the name MacMorrow. There is another Gaelic name which has been sometimes anglicized Murray, viz. Mac Giolla Mhuire, of the barony of Castlereagh in Co. Down : Murray is here an abbreviation of MacIlmurray ; but the usual form of this in English is Gilmore.

O'NAGHTEN, (MacNaughton).

There are a great many synonyms for O'Naghten (Ó Neachtain in Irish) in modern Ireland, including Naughtan, Naughton, Nochtin, Nocton, Knockton and even sometimes Connaughton (which is actually a different surname) ; while, very strangely, some families of Naughten in Kerry have become Behane. The English name Norton is grotesquely also so used : the Nortons of Athlone, for example, are descended from Feradach O'Naghten (fl. c. 1790).

The sept of O'Naghten has, however, no historical connexion with Kerry or with any part of Ireland outside Connacht, except Co. Clare, and indeed practically all the O'Naghtens, Naughtons etc. of the present day come from the West. The O'Naghtens of Clare are a Dalcassian sept of the same stock as the O'Quinns located in the district north of Corofin : one of them was elected Bishop of Limerick in 1581. Though still found in Thomond this sept was of comparatively minor importance. The important sept of the name was of Ui Máine and akin to the O'Mulallys. Up to the time of the Anglo-Norman invasion they were chiefs of a territory near Loughrea ; after the upheaval they settled not far north of this in the Fews (barony of Athlone, Co. Roscommon). O'Naghten appears as Chief of the Fews in several sixteenth century manuscripts, and as late as the eighteen eighties the Naughtons of

Thomastown Park possessed an estate of 4,829 acres between Athlone and Ballinasloe in the historic O'Naghten country.

John O'Neachtan (c. 1655–1728), a fine Gaelic scholar and poet, was of this sept, though his life was spent in Co. Meath. He and his son, Teig O'Neachtan, or O'Naughton, were the principal figures in a Gaelic literary circle in the Dublin of the 1720's. Some families there use the form MacNaghten instead of O'Naghten. MacNaughton, as it is usually spelt in the north of Ireland, is however, a surname of quite different origin : it is that of a Scottish family settled in Co. Antrim.

Arms illustrated on Plate XXII.

NAGLE, Nangle.

Nagle, or Neagle, is the form used by the Cork branch of the de Angulos who are called Nangle in north Connacht where, after the invasion at the end of the twelfth century, that famous Norman family became possessed of vast estates. The leading de Angulos adopted the surname MacCostello (q.v. p. 95 *supra*). This does not apply to the Cork branch, which, as noted above, retained an anglicized form of de Angulo, viz. Nagle, and this was written de Nógla in Irish. Sir Richard Nagle (d. 1699), who was Attorney General and Speaker of the Irish Parliament in 1689, is called Nangle by Clarendon—he was a leading man in the temporary Catholic revival under James II. Another Co. Cork Nagle, Admiral Sir Edmund Nagle (1757–1830), captivated King George IV by his " rollicking Irish humour " and ability to tell a good story, and became a great favourite of that monarch. Nano Nagle (1719*– 1784), who devoted her life to the service of the poor in her native Co. Cork, was foundress of the Presentation Order of nuns. Nagle's Mountains near Ballyhooly, Co. Cork, are named after this family.

Thomas Patrice Nagle, son of Gerrard Nagle of Cambrai, both of the Irish Brigade, having accepted the Revolution, was in 1809 created Baron by Napoleon. General James Nagle (b. 1822), was distinguished for his bravery in the American Civil War on the Federal side. The only Nangle prominent in history was Richard Nangle (d. 1541), Provincial of the Austin Friars, whose appointment as Bishop of Clonfert at different times by Henry VIII and the Pope was the occasion of much controversy and of his own abduction by a rival. Edward Nangle (1799–1883), zealous Protestant, was termed " the apostle of Achill ".

There is a rare Gaelic surname Mac an Óglaoich which belongs to Co. Sligo and was anglicized MacNogly in sixteenth century records. Woulfe suggests that this may still be extant in the form of Nagle. This is doubtful : the name Nagle is almost entirely confined to Co. Cork, but it is a fact that there are Nangles in north Connacht.

Arms illustrated on Plate XXII.

* 1719 is the correct date not 1728 as given in Dictionary of National Biography and elsewhere.

MacNALLY, MacAnally.

The usual form of this name in Irish is Mac an Fhailghigh, the derivation of which is obscure (in modern Irish *failgheach*, genitive as above, means a person having wreaths but it does not necessarily follow that this is the derivation). These words are pronounced approximately MacAnally and this is quite a common alternative form of the name in English. In Connacht, where the name is found in Mayo and Roscommon, the prefix Mac is usually dropped, the simple form Nally being in use. Woulfe says that the family is of Welsh or Norman origin and that—settled in Co. Mayo—they acquired the Gaelic name now borne by them. This may be true of the Mayo Nallys ; but it is certain that in Ulster, where the name is chiefly found, it is often used as an English synonym of the Gaelic Mac Con Uladh, i.e. son of the hound of Ulidia (eastern part of Ulster). In this connexion it is worthy of note that the majority of modern bearers of the name MacNally or MacAnally (outside the two large cities of Dublin and Belfast) are found in Counties Armagh and Monaghan, which are in East Ulster, and this was the case in 1659 when Pettys' census was taken.

The only well-known character in Irish history, political, cultural or military, of the name is of little credit to it, for that was Leonard MacNally (1752–1820), friend and associate of the '98 men, who betrayed them to the British Government. On the credit side we may place Most Rev. Dr. John MacNally (b. 1871), illustrious Archbishop of Halifax, Canada, who was of Irish descent, and Most Rev. Charles MacNally, Bishop of Clogher (1843–1864). David Rice MacAnally (1810–1895), who was a Methodist clergyman, educator, sheriff and local preacher, is said to have weighed no less than three hundred and sixty lbs. !
Arms illustrated on Plate XXII.

MacNAMARA.

In Co. Clare, the homeland of the MacNamaras, the name is very numerous. In fact in everyday speech it is usually abbreviated to simple Mac : this is interesting, because another Mac name, MacMahon, comes first in the numerical list of Co. Clare names, considerably ahead of MacNamara, which has second place, yet the abbreviation is never applied to MacMahon. The sept of MacNamara was, after the O'Briens, the most important and powerful of the Dalcassians of Thomond. They were hereditary marshals to the O'Briens and had the privilege of inaugurating the chief of the O'Briens who was, of course, often a king. The sept was originally confined to a small territory, but by the end of the eleventh century they had become lords of Clancullen (which comprises a great part of East Clare) and they are so described by the Four Masters many times at various dates between 1099 and 1600. The sept in due course became two—the chief of West Clancullen (barony of Bunratty) being MacNamara Fyne (i.e. *fionn*, fair), and the chief of East Clancullen (baronies of Upper and Lower Tulla) MacNamara Reagh (i.e. *riabhach*, swarthy or grizzled). They were to a great extent dispossessed in the Cromwellian débâcle, but one family, resident until quite lately at Ennistymon, became Protestants and were extensive landlords up till the Land Act of 1903. The history of Clare is full of the name MacNamara : among other notable acts they founded the Franciscan Abbey of Quin in 1402.

After a period of obscurity they emerged into fame or notoriety in the eighteenth century. Donough MacNamara (d. 1814), better known by the Gaelic form of his name—Donnchadha Rua Mac Conmara—was born at Cratloe in East Clare, educated as a priest, expelled, led a wild life and is one of the best known of the Gaelic poets. His contemporary, another Clareman, Admiral James MacNamara (1768–1826) was tried for murder following a duel over a dog and was acquitted. Thomas " Fireball " MacNamara was a duellist *pur sang*, whose career in France is reminiscent of the " Three Musketeers " ; he eventually became a highwayman as well as a Clare rebel and ended on the scaffold about the year 1710. Two other MacNamaras were noteworthy in France at the time of the French Revolution, particularly Count MacNamara, naval commander and diplomatist, who was assassinated in 1790 on account of his royalist sympathies. For a note on the name of the well-known playwright Brinsley MacNamara see page 47.

Mac Conmara, the Irish form of this name, is derived from the words *cu* (hound) and *na mara* (of the sea). The forename Cumara was at one time found in connexion with the surname Mac Conmara, and was the name of the eponymous ancestor of the sept, who was twenty-third in descent from Cormac Cas.

Arms illustrated on Plate XXIII.

O'NEILAN, Neylan.

This name is seldom found with the O nowadays. It is usually spelt Neilan in Connacht and Neylan in Co. Clare—the O'Neilans being the original owners of Ballyally Castle. It originated in Thomond (Co. Clare) : three of the name are listed as persons of importance in Co. Clare in the " Composition Book of Connacht " in 1585, though they are not described as chiefs. (Clare being west of the Shannon was included with Connacht for the purpose of that survey). In 1659 they were very numerous in Co. Clare and scarcely met with elsewhere. They are still found chiefly in Connacht and Clare.

The O'Neilans—Ó Nialláin in Irish—have not been prominent in Irish history. One was tanist abbot of Clonmacnois (d. 1093). They are seldom heard of again till the sixteenth century when John O'Neylan was Bishop of Kilfenora from 1541 to 1572, James O'Neylan was (according to the Clongowes Manuscript), one of the principal gentry of Co. Clare in 1598 and two others are also mentioned by the Four Masters, all being Claremen. Nicholas O'Nelan, abbot of the Augustinian Order in Co. Clare, is recorded as living in the diocese of Killaloe in 1613—seventy years after their house was officially suppressed. Two priests of the name appear in the roll of martyrs for the Faith—Father Daniel O'Neilan, O.F.M. (d. 1580) and Father Denis O'Neilan (d. 1651). Baron Patrick O'Neillan was a distinguished general in the Austrian Imperial army, having become colonel in 1717. Fifteen of the name are mentioned in Frost's *History of Co. Clare*, and many families of the name appear in the 1659 census of Co. Clare. It is thus essentially a Clare name even though it is now rather more numerous in the Connacht counties to the north of it.

Arms illustrated on Plate XXIII.

O'NEILL, Nihill.

As has already been remarked under the headings O'Brien and O'Connor, it is impossible to do justice to these great septs within the limits of this work. The following is a very brief summary of the origin and achievements of the O'Neills.

First it should be made clear that although the name O'Neill is inseparably associated with Ulster (the Red Hand of Ulster was taken from their arms), there are several other quite distinct septs of O'Neill which may be mentioned before the Ulster septs are dealt with. The O'Neills of Thomond were chiefs of a territory in the modern barony of Bunratty: to-day O'Neill is not a common name in Co. Clare, but the Nihills and the Creaghs of that county claim to be of Thomond O'Neill stock. Dr. Richard Hayes, however, states that the Nihills were originally Ulster O'Neills who settled in Co. Clare after the battle of Kinsale. The name O'Neill is quite numerous in and around Co. Carlow, where an O'Neill sept was situated in the barony of Rathvilly. Another O'Neill sept was located in the Decies and its present day representatives are found in Co. Waterford and south Tipperary.

The first of the great Ulster sept to bear the surname O'Neill was Donell O'Neill, the eponymous ancestor being his grandfather Niall, King of Ireland, who was killed in a battle with the Norsemen in A.D. 919, not, as might be supposed, the famous Niall of the Nine Hostages, though that somewhat legendary and heroic character was also a remote ancestor. From that time until the end of the seventeenth century, when Ulster ceased to be the leading Gaelic province of Ireland, the O'Neills figure prominently among the great men of Irish history.

The O'Neills were the chief family of the Cinel Eoghan, their territory being Tir Eoghan. Tir Eoghan (modern Tyrone) in early times comprised not only that county but most of Derry and part of Donegal. Down to the time of Brian Boru, who reigned from 1002 to 1014, the Ui Néill, i.e. descendants of Niall of the Nine Hostages, were, almost without interruption, High Kings of Ireland. Their race formed two main branches—the northern Ui Néill of Ulster and the southern Ui Néill, as those who established themselves in Meath were called. The latter did in fact occupy also part of southern Ulster contiguous with Meath. In the fourteenth century a branch of the Tyrone O'Neills migrated to Antrim where they became known as Clann Aodha Bhuidhe, from Aodh Buidhe (or Hugh Boy) O'Neill, who was slain in 1283, the term being perpetuated in the territorial name Clannaboy or Clandeboy. The attempts made by the English in the sixteenth century to exterminate them, which were carried out by Essex and others with a ferocity and perfidy seldom equalled even in that violent age, were unsuccessful, and O'Neills are numerous there to-day, as they are also in West Ulster. The sixteenth and seventeenth centuries produced the most famous of the O'Neills : among them Con Bacach O'Neill (1484–1559), first Earl of Tyrone ; Shane O'Neill (1530–1567) ; Hugh O'Neill (1540–1616), second Earl of Tyrone ; Owen Roe O'Neill (1590–1649) ; Sir Phelim O'Neill (1604–1653) ; and Hugh O'Neill (d. 1660)—names too well known in the history of Ireland to require description here. Less famous but worthy of mention, even in so cursory a sketch as this, is Sir Nial O'Neill (1658–1690), whose regiment of dragoons distinguished itself at the battle of the Boyne, where he was mortally wounded. In the century following that disaster many O'Neills were to be found among the outstanding officers of the Irish Brigades in the French army. Arthur O'Neill (1737–1816), the blind wandering harper may be regarded as the precursor of Bunting in the field of Irish traditional music ; and John O'Neill (1834–1878), was leader of the Fenian invasion in Canada in 1867. All these were Ulstermen. The only man of the other septs, referred to at the beginning of this section, to make much mark was John O'Neill (c. 1777–c.1860), who began life as a shoemaker in Co. Waterford, whence he went to London and became a successful dramatist. Eugene O'Neill (1888–1953), the American dramatist was son of the American actor James O'Neill (1849–1920), who was an Irish emigrant. In that field we may also mention the actress Peggy O'Neill (1796–1879).

It may be remarked in conclusion that O'Neill is one of the very few surnames the spelling of which is identical in both the Irish and English languages. In Irish, however, the E is accented.

Arms illustrated on Plate XXIII.

O'NOLAN.

Nolan, seldom found nowadays with its legitimate prefix O, is the name of a sept of great antiquity which has always been associated with that part of Ireland which lies around the barony of Forth in Co. Carlow (not to be confused with the better known Forth in Co. Wexford). In pre-Norman days their chiefs, who held high hereditary office under the Kings of Leinster, were known as Princes of Foharta (modern Forth). After the invasion, though their power declined, they retained considerable influence.

In the sixteenth century a branch of the Nolans migrated to Connacht and became extensive landowners in Counties Mayo and Galway, in which counties the name is not uncommon to-day. Nolan is among the forty most numerous names in the country as a whole, the great majority of persons so called being found, as might be expected, in Carlow and the adjacent counties. In 1878, however, Connacht landlords named Nolan possessed over 12,000 acres ; but there was no extensive landowner of the name in or near Co. Carlow. There was also a small sept of O'Nuallain belonging to the Corca Laidhe group. (Possibly the Nolans of west Munster to-day stem from them). These, however, for some reason not apparent, were often called O hUallacháin—thus in Lynch's *De Praesulibus* (1672) the two names are treated as interchangeable. In this connexion it may be mentioned that, according to Woulfe, Ó hUallacháin is anglicized Nolan in north Connacht.

In Irish the name is Ó Nualláin, i.e. descendant of Nuallán. The derivation of the name is obscure. The word *nuallan* in modern Irish means a shout or cry, but it does not follow that the name comes from that.

In recent centuries few Nolans stand out as being particularly distinguished but several not unimportant persons of the name may be mentioned. Philip Nolan (1771–1801), an Irish emigrant to America, was one of the most notorious frontiersmen and contraband traders of those early days in the West ; Most Rev. Edward Nolan (d. 1859), was Bishop of Kildare and Leighlin ; two Nolans had some success in the literary field, viz. Rev. Frederick Nolan (1784–1864) as a Protestant theologian and Michael Nolan (d. 1827) as a legal writer ; John Philip Nolan (1838–1912), of the Co. Galway Nolans, is remembered not so much as a soldier as for his political career during which he came into conflict with the notorious Judge Keogh and took the part of Parnell at the split of the Irish Parliamentary Party.
Arms illustrated on Plate XXIII.

NUGENT, (Gilsenan).

Though not an indigenous Irish surname Nugent may be regarded as completely Irish to-day, since the Nugents have been important people in Ireland since the twelfth century when they came at the time of the Anglo-Norman invasion, their home country being France. They were then called de Nogent, i.e. of a place called Nogent in France, where they can trace their descent back to A.D. 930. The Nugents were one of the Norman families which got extensive grants of land in Ireland : theirs was in Meath and Westmeath, with which they have been identified ever since. The head of the family was created Baron Delvin (a place in Co. Westmeath) in

1486 and in 1621 Earl of Westmeath. Their descendants are found to-day in every walk of life and the name is frequently met with in all the provinces except Connacht.

They are now numerous in Co. Cork, where a branch of the family established themselves and formed a sept in the Irish fashion : their chief resided at Aghavarten Castle, near Carrigaline.

In Irish history the Nugents have chiefly distinguished themselves as soldiers. In the *Dictionary of National Biography* and similar works of reference no less than twelve appear as such between the years 1444 and 1862 : four of these were upholders of the English interest ; and eight were either rebels or supporters of the Stuart cause. Perhaps the most outstanding of these was Christopher Nugent (d. 1731), who after the siege of Limerick in 1691 took service with the French and commanded Sheldon's regiment, later known as Nugent's regiment. He took part with James III in the 1715 expedition to Scotland. In the course of his distinguished military career he was wounded at least twelve times. John Nugent (1672–1754), fifth Earl of Westmeath, who also served with distinction in James II's Irish army and in that of France, was the last Catholic holder of the title. Many other Nugents were prominent among the Wild Geese in France and Austria.

The Gaelic name Mac Giolla Seanáin, normally anglicized Gilsenan, that of a sept belonging to Meath and Cavan, has also in some cases curiously taken the form Nugent in English. The great majority of Nugents, however, are of the stock referred to above.

Arms illustrated on Plate XXIII.

MacNULTY.

The derivation of many Irish surnames is open to doubt, but there is none about that of MacNulty : in Irish it is Mac an Ultaigh, i.e. son of the Ulsterman. An older anglicized form of the name, now rare, is MacAnulty. The MacNultys belong to-day, as they have done since the inception of surnames, to north-west Ulster—to Donegal, which claims to be the most Irish part of Ireland. As might be expected from the location of this sept they were overshadowed by the O'Donnells, sometimes in association with them, as in the battle of Desertcreagh in 1281 (a MacNulty was among the " distinguished slain " there), sometimes against them as on the occasion in 1431 when the O'Donnells are recorded by the Four Masters as making a predatory expedition against the MacNultys of Tirhugh (Co. Donegal). From Derry, on the border of Co. Donegal, came Frank Joseph MacNulty (1872–1926), American labour leader, whose father Owen MacNulty was a veteran of the Civil War.

The name is also found in Co. Meath but always it is shorn of its prefix Mac there. I presume these Nultys are an offshoot of the Donegal MacNultys. Bernard MacNulty (d. 1892), friend of John Boyle O'Reilly, was the founder of the first branch of the Fenian Brotherhood in the U.S.A.

O'NUNAN, Noonan.

The name Noonan, which is also, but less frequently, spelt Nunan (the prefix O has not been resumed), belongs almost exclusively to the province of Munster and particularly to Co. Cork, where it originated. In modern Irish it is Ó Nuanáin : this is a corrupt or contracted form of the older Ó h-Ionmhaineáin, of which the anglicized form O'Hinunane, now obsolete, is approximately a phonetic rendering. In early times O'Noonan was chief of a sept in Duhallow and the O'Noonans were also connected with the Church as erenaghs of the church of St. Beretchert at Tullylead, in the barony of Duhallow.

The most notable man of the name in modern times was James Patrick Noonan, (1878–1929), American labour leader, son of an Irish emigrant. In the middle ages William O'Noonan, alias Ouhynaunen, was remarkable inasmuch as at a time when the native Irish were officially outlaws in English law he was " the King's surgeon " and in 1341 he cured Lionel Duke of Clarence, son of King Edward III, then Viceroy of Ireland.

O'PHELAN, Whelan.

The name Whelan must be dealt with in conjunction with Phelan, as they are anglicized variants of the same Gaelic surname, viz. Ó Faoláin, which itself has variant forms such as Ó Faoileáin and Ó hAoláin. Whelan is more numerous than Phelan : it alone stands seventy-ninth in the list of the hundred commonest names in Ireland ; with Phelan added the name takes forty-fourth place, with an estimated population of about twelve thousand persons. In the last year for which such statistics are available 214 births were registered for Whelan and 93 for Phelan. Eighty per cent of the latter belonged to Counties Waterford, Kilkenny and adjacent areas ; while Whelans extended further into Wexford and Carlow. Many, of course, were born in Dublin, but in considerations of this kind the metropolitan area can be disregarded. It is natural that the present day representatives of the sept of Ó Faoláin should be found in the places mentioned, because their chiefs were Princes of the Decies before the Norman invasion, while a branch of the sept was settled a little further north in the south-west part of Co. Kilkenny. One of these, John Phelan, was Bishop of Ossory at the time of the Catholic resurgence under James II. The gentleman who styles himself " O'Phelan, Prince of the Decies " (a claim not allowed by the Genealogical Office), was born Whelan ; the well-known writer Séan O'Faolain is the son of Denis Whelan. Another distinguished Whelan was Leo Whelan, R.H.A. (1892–1956), the portrait painter. Of those using the form Phelan the best known are Edward Joseph Phelan, the Director-General of the

International Labour Office, formerly of Dublin, and Frederick Ross Phelan, a distinguished Canadian soldier. In the United States, Phelans have been prominent, notably James Phelan (1824–1892), Leix-born pioneer, and his son James Duval Phelan (1861–1930), senator and mayor of San Francisco.

Arms illustrated on Plate XXIII.

PLUNKETT.

The name Plunkett or Plunket is of French origin, not Danish as has often been stated : it is a corruption of *blanchet*, derived from *blanc*, white. Though not an indigenous Gaelic surname it is one of those introduced into Ireland at the time of the Anglo-Norman invasion which have become exclusively Irish, for Plunkett is not found elsewhere except in the case of exiles of Irish stock. It may fairly be said that it is one of the most distinguished names in our history. From the year 1316, when Thomas Plunkett of Louth was Chief Justice of the Common Pleas, down to our own time there has scarcely been a generation in which one or more Plunketts have not been prominent in the life of the country, either in the Church or the law or in politics or literature. Taking the Church first we may observe that one of the most notable Protestant Archbishops of Dublin was William Conyngham Plunket, who was also Baron Plunket. There are, it may be mentioned here, no less than three other old peerages in the various branches of the Plunkett family, viz. Fingall, Louth and Dunsany. One of the greatest Irishmen of all time was also an Archbishop— Blessed Oliver Plunket (1629–1681), whose labours in his diocese of Armagh and further afield were tireless, though he lived at a time when to be a Catholic prelate in Ireland was to be a hunted man : it is hardly necessary to add that his life ended on the scaffold, for, after a mockery of a trial in London, he was hanged, drawn and quartered. The great majority of the Plunketts, including the Earls of Fingall and the Barons of Louth, remained steadfastly Catholic through successive generations of Penal Code and persecution ; they are indeed remarkable inasmuch as they retained their aristocratic status, though a number of them were attainted for their activities on the Irish side in 1642 and 1691. In this brief summary it is not possible to enumerate the many Plunketts who distinguished themselves in the service of their country. The best known, in addition to those already mentioned, are Nicholas Plunket, seventeenth century historian ; Thomas Plunket (1716–1779), successful general in the Austrian army ; Patrick Joseph Plunkett (1738–1827) French university professor and later Bishop of Meath ; John Hubert Plunkett (1801–1869), Roscommon-born Australian statesman and protagonist of Catholic Emancipation (as indeed were many of his namesakes, including the first Baron Plunket, a Protestant and Lord Chancellor of Ireland) ; Sir Horace Plunkett (1854–1932), founder of the

co-operative movement in Ireland ; and Joseph Mary Plunkett (1887–1916), poet and revolutionary soldier who paid with his life for his signature of the republican proclamation of Easter 1916. All these, with one exception, came from the Dublin-Meath-Louth area with which the Plunketts have been identified for seven centuries.
Arms illustrated on Plate XXIII.

POWER.

Though not Gaelic in origin, Power is one of that class of hibernicized names (like Burke and Walsh) which may be regarded as one hundred per cent Irish. The name, now one of the most numerous in Ireland—it is estimated that there are about eleven thousand Powers in the country to-day—came with the Normans in Strongbow's twelfth century invasion. It is derived from the old French word *povre* (Latin *pauper*, poor) and was first written le Poer, a form still retained by one or two families. The poverty implied was rather that of a voluntary vow than of destitution. The Norman Powers settled in Co. Waterford where they are still more numerous than anywhere else : in fact nearly half their total is in that county and Power heads the statistical list for Co. Waterford. The remainder, apart from the city of Dublin, which contains people from all the provinces, are for the most part in the counties which adjoin Waterford, viz. Cork, Tipperary, Kilkenny and Wexford. Baron le Poer was among the great Norman lords who took part in the thirteenth century occupation of Connacht, and Powers remained in that province under the Burkes. The name, however, does not survive in Connacht.

Though few individuals are actually outstanding, many of the name have held positions of importance in the Church, notably as Bishops of Waterford ; and many are recorded as participating in the age-long struggle against English aggression, particularly in the seventeenth century when two Powers were members of the Supreme Council of the Confederate Catholics in 1646 and later when a number of them fought in the Irish army of James II. Notwithstanding this fact the leading families of Power succeeded in retaining a much greater portion of their estates than most of their fellow-Jacobites.

In the last century Tyrone Power (1797–1841) was a celebrated Irish comedian ; Marguerite Power (1789–1849), better known as Countess of Blessington, was a popular novelist in her day. Frank Power (1858–1884), artist and journalist, was well known during his lifetime on account of his adventurous association with Gordon at Khartoum. In our own time Father Patrick Power (1862–1951), author of *History of the Diocese of Waterford* etc., was a notable historian and antiquarian. Power's distillery produces a famous Irish whiskey.
Arms illustrated on Plate XXIII.

PRENDERGAST, Pender.

Maurice de Prendergast, whose name was taken from a village in Pembrokeshire, came to Ireland with Strongbow and was one of the leading Anglo-Norman invaders who obtained extensive grants of land in various parts of the south and west of the country. His descendants were seated near Waterford and in south Mayo, districts in which the name has always subsequently been found. In 1598 they are listed as among the leading gentry of Counties Waterford, Wexford and Tipperary. Some families of Prendergast assumed the name Fitzmaurice at an early date.

The most distinguished man of the name was John Patrick Prendergast (1808–1893), author of *The Cromwellian Settlement of Ireland* and other historical works. Two Sir Thomas Prendergasts (1660–1709 and 1698–1760), father and son, are noteworthy, though not praiseworthy from the Irish point of view : the first was a Jacobite who betrayed an anti-William plot in which he was concerned and subsequently became a brigadier in the English army, being killed at the battle of Malplaquet ; the son who became a Protestant was noted for his virulent anti-clericalism. After the defeat of James II these Prendergasts obtained extensive grants of O'Shaughnessy lands in Co. Galway, litigation regarding which dragged on till 1755.

The name Prendergast has been widely corrupted to Pender.

PURCELL.

Purcell is usually regarded as an Irish name, though the most famous man so called, Henry Purcell, the composer, was an Englishman. Both English and Irish Purcells are of Norman descent, the latter being found mostly in the contiguous counties of Kilkenny and Tipperary. The picturesque ruined castle of Loughmoe, the seat of the head of the family, is a well-known landmark near Thurles, to be seen from the main line railway halfway between Dublin and Cork. He was known as Baron of Loughmoe, a title conferred by the First Earl of Ormond as Lord of the Palatinate, but this title was not offically recognized by the Crown. The name is derived from the Norman-French word *porcel*, which in turn comes from the Latin *porcus*. Though Norman, the Purcells did not come to Ireland until some years after the Anglo-Norman invasion of 1172, when they became adherents of the great Butler (Ormond) family. In Irish the name is written Puirscíl. The Purcells are a good example of the saying " *hiberniores Hibernicis ipsis* ", for not only are they found as Bishops of Ferns and of Waterford and as Abbots of Holy Cross and St. John's, Kilkenny, but also as staunch fighters in the Irish cause : one, Major-General Purcell, though unsuccessful as a military strategist in earlier engagements, was so prominent in the defence of Limerick in 1651 as to be excluded from the favourable terms granted to the defenders generally ; and another, Col. Nicholas

Purcell, was one of Patrick Sarsfield's right hand men. This Purcell was one of the negotiators of the Treaty of Limerick in 1691. Subsequent to this they were active as Wild Geese both in the regiment known as Purcell's Horse and in Clare's Dragoons etc. Other Purcells worthy of mention are Richard Purcell (c. 1720–1766), who in his day was a celebrated engraver, and John Baptist Purcell (1800–1883), Archbishop of Cincinnati, who was born at Mallow. In connexion with him may be recalled his brother Father Edward Purcell and the dramatic story of the failure of the " Purcell Bank ".

Arms illustrated on Plate XXIII.

MacQUAID.

The origin of the name MacQuaid, of which Mac Uaid is the form used in Irish, is obscure. It has long been well known in Co. Monaghan which is its principal location to-day. It has been borne by two notable churchmen : Bernard John MacQuaid (1823–1909), first bishop of Rochester, U.S.A., whose parents, Irish emigrants, were murdered ; and Most Rev. John Charles McQuaid, the present Archbishop of Dublin.

O'QUIGLEY, Cogley.

This name is Ó Coigligh in Irish, denoting descendant of Coigleach, a forename which suggests that its first bearer was an untidy person. Although even as late as the year 1800 the form O'Quigley was used as its English equivalent, it is seldom if ever found nowadays with its prefix O. Synonyms recorded by the Registrar-General for different places in Ireland are Twigley, Kegley and Cogley, but Quigley is the usual spelling. The sept belongs to the northern Ui Fiachra and was located in Co. Mayo (barony of Carra). It became dispersed by the end of the sixteenth century and is now widespread, most of the name belonging by birth or recent family ties to the Derry-Donegal-Sligo area, its main habitat also in the seventeenth century, with others in Counties Galway and Louth. Two very notable Quigleys, both priests, should be particularly mentioned : Father James O'Coigley or Quigley of Armagh, who after many exciting adventures in France at the time of the French Revolution was hanged in England on unquestionably tainted evidence in 1798, and Dr. James Edward Quigley, Bishop of Buffalo, whose support of trade unionism in America and success in the settlement of strikes there up to the time of his death in 1915 made him a prominent figure in the U.S.A.

Arms illustrated on Plate XXIV.

MacQUILLAN.

Though MacQuillan is not a name of Gaelic origin it came into existence in Ireland and is not found elsewhere except among emigrants from Ireland. The MacQuillans are of Norman-Welsh descent : they settled soon after the invasion in the territory called the Route (Co. Antrim), and were known as Lords of the Route with their chief residence at the Castle of Dunluce until, following their major defeat at the battle of Ora in 1563 and again in 1580 by Sorley Boy MacDonnell, they were finally dispersed by the MacDonnells. In 1315 the MacQuillan chief of the day joined Edward Bruce. By that time they had become indistinguishable from any native Gaelic sept— in the words of a contemporary " they were as Irish as the worst ". They were described as Princes of Dalriada and ranked, at any rate in the fourteenth century, as hereditary High Constables of Ulster. Their predominant position was consolidated by Sincin Mór MacQuillan, who ruled as Chief from 1390 to 1449. As such they are prominent in the warlike activities of the O'Neills, O'Donnells and O'Cahanes in that province up to the date of the battle of Ora, mentioned above. Rory Óg MacQuillan, then Chief of the Name, in 1541 declared that no captain of his race ever died in his bed. The last of the family of note in Ireland were Edward MacQuillan (1503–1605), whose remaining estate was confiscated in the Plantation of Ulster, and Rory Óg MacQuillan (d. 1634), to whom some of the estate was regranted. He was the last to be known as the " Lord of the Route ". Subsequently members of the sept are chiefly met with in France and Spain, in the Irish Brigades. One, Capt. Rory MacQuillan, was an officer in O'Neill's infantry in King James II's army in Ireland. Father Peter MacQuillan (c. 1650–1719) from Co. Derry became a leading Dominican in France, and later prior at Louvain. Many of the rank and file of the sept remained in Ulster as is evidenced by the prevalence of the name in Counties Antrim, Armagh etc., in the Inquisitions, Hearth Money Rolls, 1659 census etc., as well as modern birth indices, voters' lists and so forth. John Hugh MacQuillan (1826–1879), a Quaker, was a pioneer of modern dentistry in America.

There is some doubt as to the derivation of the name. It is usually given as either son of Hugelin (diminutive of Hugh), or son of Hudelin (diminutive of Hud), the Irish forms being Mac Uighilín and Mac Uidhilín. MacFirbis describes the sept as Clan Uighilin. Some authorities, however, make the name a gaelicized version of son of Llewellyn, but Prof. Curtis, in a critical examination of the subject, rejects this and is convinced that the eponymous ancestor was Hugelin de Mandeville.

Arms illustrated on Plate XXIV.

MacQUILLY, Cox.

Although Cox is a common English name the great majority of our Irish Coxes are of native Irish stock, Cox (i.e. Cocks) being derived by translation from the

Gaelic Mac an Choiligh (son of the cock), the alternative form in English being the phonetic MacQuilly. This sept is still most numerous in the county of its origin, viz. Co. Roscommon : they were co-arbs of St. Barry of Kilbarry in that county. There is another indigenous Irish surname Mac Conchoille, which has also been anglicized Cox in some parts of the country through a mistranslation—it is more often rendered as Woods meaning, as it does, son of the hound of the wood.

Sir Richard Cox (1650–1733), though Irish, was an aggressive Protestant who espoused the Williamite cause : he was a judge and Governor of Cork, but was removed from the Privy Council because, in spite of his Protestantism, he opposed the violation of the Treaty of Limerick. He later became Lord Chancellor of Ireland. The only other Irish Cox of much note was Walter Cox (1770–1837), gunsmith and editor of extremist newspapers ; he was resident for a time in New York.

O'QUINLAN, Quinlevan, Kindellan.

Quinlan is the Munster form of the Gaelic Ó Caoindealbháin which, in Leinster, where the sept originated, was usually anglicized as Kindellan, and in modern times as Conlan and Connellan (*vide* p. 86 *supra*). They were of distinguished origin, being of the southern Ui Neill, and the senior line of the descendants of Laoghaire, King of Ireland in St. Patrick's day. The sept, originally located in north Meath, was much reduced by the Anglo-Norman invasion, but they retained property there until the defeat of James II. At that time the form of the name in use in Co. Meath was Kindellan and this has been retained in Spain, the country in which they settled as exiles. The Kindellans have been prominent in Spain since then. John Ambrose Kindellan (1750–1822) was a noted general in the Spanish army and in our own time General Alfredo Kindelan has been an important member of Gen. Franco's Cabinet in that country. The branch which settled in north Tipperary became Quinlan in English. The Quinlans are among the more numerous Irish families in Co. Tipperary in the 1659 census and do not appear as such elsewhere in it. Timothy Francis Quinlan (b. 1861), the Australian politician, was born in Co. Tipperary. The name is now almost confined to Munster, particularly Counties Cork, Limerick and Tipperary ; in Clare it is also found but under the synonym Quinlevan.
Arms illustrated on Plate XXIV.

O'QUINN.

Quinn is one of the most numerous Irish surnames, the number of people in Ireland so called at the present day being estimated at seventeen thousand : in the list of commonest surnames it occupies twentieth place in the country as a whole and first place in Co. Tyrone, though widespread in many counties. Tyrone is the place of origin of one of the five distinct septs of this name. The most notable were the Dalcassian sept of Thomond, whose territory lay around Corofin, in the barony of Inchiquin, Co. Clare; and that of Antrim, where the Quinns have long been associated with the Glens of Antrim. The O'Quinns of Co. Longford were also an important sept, being of the same stock as the O'Ferralls of Annaly. It will be noticed that the place names Inchiquin, Ballyquin etc., are spelt with only one final N. There are two in Irish—Ó Cuinn—which surname is formed from the personal name Conn. At the present time as a rule Catholic families use two Ns and Protestants one; but this practice is not invariable now, and was less so in the past. The first of the Dalcassian sept to bear the surname was Niall Ó Cuinn, who was killed at the battle of Clontarf in 1014.

Among prominent men of the name James Quin (1693–1766), the famous actor, and Walter Quin (1575–1634), the Dublin born poet who was tutor and lifelong associate of Charles I, and his son James Quin (1621–1659), noted singer, may be specifically mentioned. The Franciscan Thomas O'Quinn was Bishop of Clonmacnois from 1252 to 1279, and John Quinn, a Dominican, was Bishop of Limerick from 1522 to 1551. Thady Quin (1645–1726), of Adare, who was a descendant of the Thomond O'Quins, was the grandfather of the first Earl of Dunraven: this peerage is one of the few held by old Gaelic families, others being O'Brien, O'Callaghan, O'Daly, O'Grady, MacLysaght and O'Neill.

Families of O'Quinn settled in France and became leading citizens both in Bordeaux and Pau. There is a street called Rue O'Quinn in Bordeaux, indicating the importance of the family, which is still extant in that part of France.

Arms illustrated on Plate XXIV.

O'RAFFERTY, Roarty, (Raftery).

Originally belonging to the adjacent counties of Donegal and Sligo, the O'Raffertys are now found in many parts of Ireland, though nowhere in large numbers. They are still associated with Co. Donegal where they were co-arbs of St. Columcille in Tory Island. In Sligo the sept was one of the " seven pillars of Skreen," but the descendants of these have become scattered. At no time have they played a prominent part in the political, military or cultural life of the country: only one is mentioned by the Four Masters—he was abbot of Durrow in 1090, far away from the homeland of his sept.

The usual form of the name in modern Irish is Ó Raithbheartaigh, but this is actually a variant of the older Ó Robhartaigh, the sound of which is preserved in the anglicized form Roarty. This surname, though rare, is still extant in the north-western counties.

Raftery, sometimes confused with Rafferty, is quite a different name : it is Ó Reachtaire in Irish and belongs exclusively to Connacht. It is notable on account of the blind Mayo folk-poet Anthony Raftery (1784–1835).

Arms illustrated on Plate XXIV.

MacRANNALL, Reynolds, Grannell.

In Reynolds we have an example of a fine old Gaelic Irish surname which has been given as its usual anglicized form a common English one. In Irish it is Mac Raghnaill, Raghnall being the Gaelic equivalent of Randal and Reginald. The forms MacRannal and Grannell, also used in English, are of course, nearer the original. The sept belongs to Co. Leitrim : their territory was Muintir Eolais in the southern half of that county. They remained influential as long as the Gaelic order survived and indeed up to the end of the seventeenth century, in spite of continual rivalry and feuds with their powerful Breffny neighbours the O'Rourkes (with whom, however, they were at times allied). The " Composition Book of Connacht " calls the Chief of the Name Magranill of Moynish (Co. Leitrim) and thirty years later Camden, writing of Counties Leitrim and Longford in 1617, includes them, under the name of MacGrannell, with the O'Rourkes as " downright Irish." O'Dugan's fourteenth century " Topographical Poem " shows that they were equally prominent in the mediaeval period. Modern statistics indicate that Co. Leitrim is still the principal stronghold of the name, nearly half the people in Ireland so called hailing from that area.

An excellent memoir on the MacRannals in the *Journal of the Royal Society of Antiquaries* (vol. xxxv) gives much valuable information, particularly about the family of Lough Scur Castle, whence came several notable members of parliament as well as James Reynolds, whose diary (1658–1660) is of great interest. The Elizabethan Mac Rannal of this line who was the first to change the name to Reynolds was known in consequence as Mac Raghnaill Gallda (i.e. the English MacRannal). Their estates were very extensive : after the Restoration and the Act of Settlement they were in possession of no less than 6,660 acres in Co. Leitrim and 1,000 acres in Co. Roscommon.

Quite a number of Irishmen called Reynolds have distinguished themselves in various fields of activity. To the Church they have given Most Rev. Christopher Augustine Reynolds (1834–1893), first Catholic Archbishop of South Australia. (Richard Reynolds, Catholic martyr, was not Irish). In science there were Osborne Reynolds (1842–1912), famous for his original investigations on mechanical and physical subjects, and James Emerson Reynolds (1842–1920), discoverer of various chemical substances. In literature the father of the last named, Dr. James Reynolds (d. 1866) was a novelist and playwright, while George Nugent Reynolds (1770–1802) was a noted ballad writer and probably the author of " The Exile of Erin." We must also mention Thomas Reynolds (1771–1832), brother-in-law of Wolfe Tone, whose betrayal of the United Irishmen was largely responsible for the failure of their plans to free Ireland from British domination. On the other hand it should be mentioned that the Reynoldses, especially those of Lough Scur, were strong supporters of James II and figured largely in the attainders and forfeitures which followed his defeat.

Arms illustrated on Plate XXIV.

REDMOND.

Redmond is a name of Norman origin : the first in Ireland was Alexander Raymond, who was of the same stock as Raymond le Gros, one of the best known of the Anglo-Norman invaders. The name soon became Redmond. The family obtained considerable grants of land in Co. Wexford, and throughout the 780 years since they settled in Ireland they have always been associated with that county and prominent in its affairs. The Ortelius map marks them as a sept in the barony of Forth, Co. Wexford. They are found on the Irish side in the seventeenth century, several of the name being attainted after 1691. Two were Wexford rebels in 1798 : Rev. John Redmond and Michael Redmond ; and the four Redmonds, notably Chevalier Gabriel Redmond (1713–1789), who served with distinction on the Continent with the Irish Brigade were all of Wexford families. In the present century John Edward Redmond (1855–1918), a Co. Wexford landlord, was leader of the Irish Party in the British House of Commons up to its extinction on the rise of Sinn Féin, and his brother, William Redmond (1861–1917), killed in the first Great War, was also a leading member of that party. At the present time the Redmonds are almost entirely concentrated in the three eastern counties of Wexford, Wicklow and Dublin.

" The Composition Book of Connacht " (1585) includes the name MacRedmond among the leading men of Co. Mayo. These MacRedmonds were also of Norman stock but had no connexion with the Redmonds of Wexford, MacRedmond being the name assumed by a branch of the great family of Burke. They are extinct now, or have reverted to the surname Burke.

Arms illustrated on Plate XXIV.

O'REGAN.

Regan is listed among the hundred most numerous Irish surnames : it holds sixty-sixth place with a total estimated population of nine thousand two hundred and fifty persons at the present time. Fifty years ago few bearers of the name made use of their prefix O, but it has been resumed by many families and the voters' lists, directories etc., now indicate that nearly forty per cent are listed as O'Regan. Like most of the widespread Irish surnames O'Regan originated independently in more than one place. As regards origin, the more important of these was Ó Riagáin of Counties Meath and Dublin, one of the Four Tribes of Tara, and very prominent in the wars against the so-called Danes. They were dispersed after the Anglo-Norman invasion and their descendants have largely disappeared except in Co. Leix, to which area they migrated. The other O'Regan sept, Dalcassian in origin, descends from Riagan, nephew of the famous Brian Boru : they were seated in the Limerick area of Thomond. In modern times Regans and O'Regans are found more in Co. Cork than in Co. Limerick. Fineen MacCarthy, writing in 1595, claims several families of O'Regan, living in Carbery, as his kinsmen. Keating, Terry and other seventeenth century authorities state that some families in Co. Limerick stem from the Co. Leix O'Regans ; and it is a fact that the arms borne by families located in both those areas are the same.

Riagan being pronounced Reegan, the tendency in speech to call it Raigan (it is even spelt Ó Raogáin in Co. Waterford Irish-speaking districts) can only be explained by the influence of the written word Regan (cf. Egan correctly pronounced locally Aigan).

While there have been surprisingly few outstanding figures in Irish life called Regan, two are worthy of individual mention : Maurice O'Regan who wrote a contemporary account of the Anglo-Norman invasion under Strongbow ; and Teige O'Regan, the faithful follower of James II, who greatly distinguished himself at the siege of Limerick.

Arms illustrated on Plate XXIV.

O'REILLY, (O'Rahilly).

O'Reilly, in Irish Ó Raghailligh, i.e. descendant of Raghallach, was until recently much more commonly found without the prefix O. Reilly and O'Reilly constitute one of the most numerous names in Ireland, being among the first dozen in the list. The bulk of these come from Cavan and adjoining counties, the area to which they belong by origin, for they were for centuries the most powerful sept in Breffny, their head being chief of Breffny-O'Reilly and for a long time in the middle ages his influence extended well into Meath and Westmeath. At the present time we find them very numerous still in Breffny, heading as they do the county list both in Cavan and Longford. In 1878 O'Reilly landlords possessed over 30,000 acres.

Five O'Reillys have held the Primacy as Archbishops of Armagh, notably Edmund O'Reilly (1606–1669) and Hugh O'Reilly (1580–1653) ; five were Bishops of Kilmore, two of Clogher and one of Derry ; and another famous churchman was Edmund Joseph O'Reilly, S.J. (1811–1878). Edward O'Reilly (d. 1829) compiled a pioneer Irish-English Dictionary in 1817. In the field of patriotic endeavour we have John Boyle O'Reilly (1844–1890) the Fenian ; Myles O'Reilly M.P. (1825–1880), who commanded the Irish Brigade in the Papal service; and Philip McHugh O'Reilly (d. 1657), who, having been largely responsible for organizing the rising of 1641 in his own county of Cavan, fought under Owen Roe O'Neill and died in exile. In King James II's Irish army Col. Edmund O'Reilly's regiment of infantry included thirty-three officers and Col. Mahon's regiment sixteen officers called Reilly or O'Reilly. Many of these became Wild Geese. Count Don Alexander O'Reilly (d. 1797), after a distinguished military career in the French, Austrian and Spanish service ended his days as Governor of Louisiana in America. A good deal of unreliable material is to be found in print on the subject of the O'Reillys. It is therefore advisable to mention that an authoritative article on them appeared in the *Irish Ecclesiastical Record* (Vol. 45—1935, Part 2), from the pen of Father Paul Walsh. In it that famous and almost legendary seventeenth century figure " Myles the Slasher " finds a correct place.

O'Reilly is occasionally found as a synonym of O'Rahilly, but this is merely an example of careless registration since O'Rahilly, which is Ó Raithile in Irish, has no connexion with Breffny. It is true that the sept originated in Ulster but they have so long been associated with Co. Kerry that they must be regarded as Munstermen, especially as Egan O'Rahilly (1670–1726), greatest of Munster poets—by many regarded as greatest of all Gaelic poets—was of a family long established near Killarney.

Arms illustrated on Plate XXV.

RICE, (O'Mulcreevy).

The name Rice in Ireland is of two very different origins. The Rices of Oriel, now found chiefly in Louth and Armagh—counties comprised in that area—are Gaelic, being called Ó Maolcraoibhe in Irish. The anglicizing of this surname as Rice is curious : the word *craobh* from which the name is derived means a branch. In Co. Down in O'Donovan's time families of the name were known both as Mulcreevy and Rice, not, he adds, as might be expected Bushe. In Munster a few families originally Ó Maolcraoibhe became more naturally Creagh in English, though of course most of the Munster Creaghs are of quite different descent (see p. 98 *supra*). The Rices of Munster are Welsh in origin, Rhys being their name in Wales. Though never numerous, from the fourteenth century onwards they were influential in Counties Limerick and Kerry; many appear in town life as provosts, mayors and sheriffs of Limerick, Cork and Waterford and as landed proprietors in Counties Limerick and Kerry, where they settled near Dingle. Sir Stephen Rice was among the prominent Jacobites who suffered for their adhesion to the cause of James II. In Co. Limerick the best known family were the Spring-Rices of Foynes, who have provided several prominent members of the British diplomatic service: the first Lord Monteagle, Thomas Spring-Rice (1780–1866), M.P. for Limerick and Chancellor of the Exchequer, was one of these. The national record of the Rices of Co. Kerry in the seventeenth century can be judged by the fact that no less than twenty of them lost their lands as a result of the Cromwellian forfeitures. Of this family were James Louis Count Rice (b. c. 1730) soldier in the Austrian army and close friend of the Emperor Joseph II and also renowned as a duellist. Some of the exiled Rices of Kerry settled in France where they became successful bankers. The most distinguished Irish Rice in modern times in Ireland was Edmund Ignatius Rice (1762–1844), founder of the Christian Brothers.

The name Rice has also associations with the city of Galway. The pilot traditionally believed to have accompanied Christopher Columbus on his voyage of discovery and even to have sailed to America on his own, was Rice de Galvey alias Penrise.

O'RIORDAN, Rearden.

The sept of O'Riordan originated in Co. Tipperary, but they migrated to Co. Cork at such an early date that they can be regarded as belonging to that county, where they are now far more numerous than anywhere else. The vital statistics are indeed quite remarkable in this respect: of 170 births recorded for a given year 100 were in Co. Cork and 54 in the counties (Kerry and Limerick) adjoining their territory in north-west Cork, where they were " followers of the Lords of Muskerry." The place name Ballyreardon in East Cork indicates that they were also influential in that part of the county. The spelling of this place-name will be noted: Reardon is an alternative form of Riordan, which in Irish is Ó Ríordáin. The O prefix is frequently used in English, having been very widely resumed in the present century: sixty years ago there were sixteen Riordans for every one O'Riordan, now the numbers are approximately equal. The sept did not produce any outstanding figure in Irish history, literature or art, though several Co. Cork O'Riordans appear as Irish soldiers in the seventeenth century. MacFirbis mentions a family of O'Riordan who were historians of Eile but little is known of these. Rev. Dr. M. O'Riordan was the author of *Catholicity and Progress in Ireland*, a book which was much discussed when it appeared in 1906. Professor Seán P. O'Riordan (1905–1957), of Cork, was an archaelogist, whose excavations at Tara and elsewhere earned him an international reputation. A branch of the O'Riordans, long seated at Derryroe, Co. Cork, settled at Nantes in 1753 and later became Peers of France.

Arms illustrated on Plate XXV.

ROCHE, (Rochfort).

Although Roche is not an indigenous Gaelic Irish surname it can nevertheless be regarded as exclusively Irish to-day, being found in England only in Irish, and more rarely French, emigrant families. It is French in origin—*de la roche* (of the rock)—and came to Ireland at the time of the Anglo-Norman invasion in the twelfth century. Like Barry, Burke, Power and Walsh, which are in the same category it became one of the commonest names in Ireland, especially in Munster and Wexford, where most of the original Roche settlers were located. They are particularly associated with Co. Cork on account of the predominance of a powerful family of Roches in the neighbourhood of Fermoy where a large area of territory was long known as Roche's Country. The head of this family is Baron Fermoy. Roche of Rochesland is listed as one of the principal gentlemen of Co. Wexford in the sixteenth century. In the Irish language the name is de Róiste.

Two Roches are especially well remembered. Father Philip Roche of Co. Wexford, hanged for his prominent part in the 1798 Rebellion—in which one Edward Roche also participated with distinction—and Sir Boyle Roche (1743–1807), famous for his wit and " bulls." Several were noted in their days as writers. One of these, James Jeffry Roche (1847–1908), the poet, went to the United States and became American minister to Switzerland ; another James Roche (1770–1853), author of *Essays of an Octogenarian*, had a varied and interesting career in business and politics in Paris, Bordeaux and Cork.

In the mediaeval period the name was often written de Rupe (Latin *rupes*, a rock). In the same way de Rupefort is equivalent to Rochfort, the name of a Hiberno-Norman family whose long association with Co. Westmeath is perpetuated in the village of Rochfortbridge.

Arms illustrated on Plate XXV.

O'ROONEY.

In modern Ireland this name is seldom if ever found with the prefix O to which it is entitled, since it is Ó Ruanaidh in Irish. The O'Rooneys were a sept of Dromore (Co. Down) and to-day they are principally to be found in Ulster and the neighbouring county of Leitrim. Several notable ecclesiastics of the name appear in the history of the diocese of Dromore ; Felix O'Rooney, Archbishop of Tuam, was a famous character who fell foul of the ruling O'Connors in Connacht, but in spite of imprisonment by them lived on till 1238, having resigned the episcopate and become a monk. The O'Rooneys were a literary family : Ceallach O'Rooney (d. 1079), was called chief poet of Ireland and Eoin O'Rooney (d. 1376) was chief poet to MacGuinness of Iveagh. This tradition was maintained by John Jerome Rooney (b. 1866), the Irish-American Catholic poet, and by the better-known William Rooney (1873–1901), poet and Gaelic revivalist. There is a place called Rooney's Island in Co. Donegal.

MacRORY, Rogers, MacCrory.

In the sixteenth and seventeenth centuries, as evidenced by the Tudor Fiants, by the census of 1659 and other records, the name MacRory was both numerous and ubiquitous ; now it is rare. This is no doubt partly due to the fact that in the southern half of the country it has been turned into the common English name Rodgers or Rogers ; it can also be ascribed to the ephemeral nature, outside its own proper territory, to which reference will be made hereunder, of the surname MacRory, i.e. Mac Ruaidhri, son of Rory. This, like MacTeige and MacCormac, was, at least up to the middle of the seventeenth century, frequently used for one generation only. In Co. Clare, for example, many of the people who appear in the records as MacRory were O'Briens, MacNamaras or MacMahons. Later some resumed their real patronymic but a larger number became Rodgers, thus obscuring their Dalcassian origin.

The true Gaelic sept of MacRory belongs properly to Co. Tyrone. A branch of this was established in Co. Derry where they became erenaghs of Ballynascreen in the barony of Loughinsholin. Cardinal MacRory (1861–1945) was of this sept. MacRorys are still found in Counties Tyrone and in the Connacht county of Leitrim, while MacCrory and MacGrory are synonyms in parts of Ulster.

In the fourteenth century some families of MacRory came to Ulster from Scotland as gallowglasses. If any descendants of these are left they are now indistinguishable from the native Ulster MacRorys.

O'ROURKE.

In mediaeval times the O'Rourkes were one of the great princely families of Ireland, being Lords of Breffny and providing more than one King of Connacht in the period prior to the Norman invasion. At various times their territory expanded or contracted largely because of the long standing rivalry between the O'Rourkes and O'Reillys in Breffny. At its widest it extended from Kells, in Co. Meath, to Sligo. After Cromwell, like all great Gaelic families its star declined. Many of its ablest members left the country to become valued leaders, particularly military leaders, in European countries : their descendants are still (or were till Russian Communism upset the old order) among the important families in Russia and Poland. Joseph O'Rourke, Prince O'Rourke in the Russian aristocracy, was General-in-Chief of the Russian Empire in 1700 and Patrick Count O'Rourke was a distinguished member of the same service in the middle of the last century, while two Owen O'Rourkes, both Counts, served Maria Teresa of Austria between 1750 and 1780. Of those who went to France the most noteworthy were Col. Count John O'Rourke (c. 1705–1786) and Father Manus O'Rourke (1660–1741) who during a lifetime as an exile wrote voluminously in the Irish language. With a great sept like this, of course, such emigration, though it impoverished their prestige at home, had little effect on numbers, and the Rourkes and O'Rourkes (including such variant spellings as Rorke and Roark) constitute a body of population sufficiently large to find a place in the one hundred most numerous names in Ireland. The bulk of these, as might be expected, are to be found in the counties comprising the old territory of Breffny (i.e. Cavan, Leitrim and part of the adjoining counties).

Apart from those O'Rourkes who distinguished themselves in continental armies and other forms of foreign service, there have been many notable Irishmen of the name. Earliest of these is Tiernan O'Rourke, Prince of Breffny (killed in battle 1172), who is best known on account of the epoch-making events which followed the carrying off of his wife Dervorgilla by Dermot MacMorrogh ; Brian O'Rourke, inaugurated Chief of the Name in 1564, had a most romantic career, ending, still without knowing a word of the English language, on the scaffold in London ; his son Brian O'Rourke, also Chief of the Name, was equally hostile to the English but died a natural death in 1604. In a very different sphere Edmund O'Rourke (1814–1879) may be mentioned: he was in his day famous under the pseudonym of Edmund Falconer, as a dramatist and actor-manager. It is probable that William Michael Rooke (1794–1847), the Dublin-born composer, came of a family of Rourkes whose name had been corrupted to Rooke.

Arms illustrated on Plate XXV.

RYAN, O'Mulrian.

Ryan is amongst the ten most numerous surnames in Ireland with an estimated population of twenty-seven thousand five hundred. Only a very small proportion of these use the prefix O. Subject to one exception, to be noticed later in this section, it is safe to say that the great majority of the twenty-seven thousand five hundred Ryans are really O'Mulryans—this earlier form of the name is, however, now almost obsolete : even in the census of 1659 in Co. Limerick Ryan outnumbers Mulryan by about four to one, and to-day there is not one O'Mulryan or Mulryan in the Telephone Directory. The sept of Ó Maoilriain was located in Owney, formerly called Owney O'Mulryan, which forms two modern baronies on the borders of Limerick and Tipperary, in which counties the Ryans are particularly numerous to-day. They do not appear in the records in this territory (formerly belonging to the O'Heffernans) until the fourteenth century, but after they settled there, they became very powerful. Nevertheless they did not produce any really outstanding figures in Irish history or literature, except the romantic character known as Eamonn a 'chnuic, or Ned of the Hill, i.e. Edmond O'Ryan (c. 1680–1724), Gaelic poet, gentleman, soldier and finally rapparee, beloved of the people, though he met his death through the treachery of one of them. Two abbés called O'Ryan were executed during the French Revolution. Luke Ryan (c. 1750–1789) first an officer in the Irish Brigade, made a huge fortune as a privateer, was condemned to death and four times reprieved, and having been cheated out of his money died in a debtor's prison.

Many Ryans have distinguished themselves in the United States. Father Abram Joseph Ryan (1838–1886), of a Clonmel family, was poet of the Confederates in the Civil War ; another Tipperary man, Patrick John Ryan (1831–1911) was Archbishop of Philadelphia, and Stephen Vincent Ryan (1825–1896) from Clare, was Bishop of Buffalo. In other walks of life the most noteworthy Irish-American of this name was Thomas Fortune Ryan (1851–1928), a millionaire who began life as a penniless youth.

The Ryans of Co. Carlow and other counties in that part of Leinster, are distinct from those dealt with above, though both are of the race of Cathaoir Mór, King of Leinster in the second century. These are Ó Riain, not Ó Maoilriain : the chief of this sept was lord of Ui Drona (whence the name of the barony of Idrone in Co. Carlow).

Arms illustrated on Plate XXV.

SARSFIELD.

This name is dear to all Irishmen on account of the picturesque career of one of our national heroes, Patrick Sarsfield (1650–1693), the highlights of whose distinguished military career were the destruction of the Williamite siege train at Ballyneety, the defence of Limerick and his death from wounds at Landen ; the year before he had been made a marshal in the French Army. It is interesting to note that the great popularity of the christian name Patrick dates from the time of Patrick Sarsfield.

There were two main branches of the Sarsfield family seated in Counties Dublin, Cork and Limerick. Patrick Sarsfield, who was Earl of Lucan, belonged to the former. The first record of the name in Ireland is Willielmus de Sharisfeld who appears in the Pipe Roll of Cloyne (Co. Cork) in 1252, though it is claimed that Thomas de Sarsefeld, chief standard-bearer to King Henry II, was in Ireland in 1172. Unquestionably they obtained grants of land in Co. Cork about 1300 if not earlier, (branching to Lucan in Co. Dublin somewhat later), and they are represented to-day by a leading family in Co. Cork, whose archives are lodged in the National Library. The Chevalier Col. Edmund Sarsfield (b. 1736), an Irish Brigade officer who adopted the unusual course of embracing the principles of the French Revolution, was one of this branch. Field-Marshal Jacques Hyacinthe Viscount de Sarsfield (1717–1787), and Col. Guy Claude Comte de Sarsfield (1718–1789), were of the Munster branch which, it should be added, had a seat at Killmallock, Co. Limerick. A family of this branch settled at Nantes in 1653. In 1746 five of the six sons of Francis Sarsfield, of Doolin, Co. Clare, were serving in the French army. Patrick Sarsfield's only son, Col. James Francis Sarsfield (d. 1719), was an officer in the Spanish army and later in that of France.

A large rock at Cullen near Ballyneety is still known as Sarsfield's Rock in commemoration of the exploit mentioned above.

Arms illustrated on Plate XXV.

O'SCANLAN, O'Scannell.

There are at least two quite distinct septs whose descendants are now known as Scanlan. One is Ó Scannláin of Munster and the other Mac Scannláin of Oriel (Louth), neither of which has retained the prefix O or Mac in modern times. The latter are perpetuated in the place name Ballymascanlon near Dundalk. The widespread distribution of the O'Scanlans is indicated by the fact that there are six Ballyscanlans in Ireland as well as a Scanlansland and a Scanlan's Island. Two of these are in Co. Clare and one in Mayo, which lends colour to the statement that there was also a north Connacht sept of O'Scanlon. Further evidence in support of this is supplied by the records of the Registrar-General, which show that after the Kerry-Limerick-Cork area most Scanlan births are reported from Clare and Sligo. In this connexion the returns of the 1659 census are interesting : in that year the majority of people called O'Scanlon and O'Scannell were located in those very areas. At that time it would appear that O'Scannell was often used as a synonym of O'Scanlon even in Munster. The " Composition Book of Connacht " (1585) uses the form Scanlan in its survey of Co. Sligo. The MacScanlans appear to have almost died out as hardly any Scanlan births were reported from the provinces of Leinster and Ulster. The

Scanlans belonging to Co. Sligo and Co. Donegal are really O'Scannells—an instance of a common name absorbing a rarer one—for example Most Rev. Patrick O'Scanlan, Bishop of Raphoe, (afterwards Archbishop of Armagh 1262–1272), was also called O'Scannell. A Tipperary-born bishop of modern times Dr. Lawrence Scanlan (1843–1915), Bishop of Salt Lake City, is remembered in America on account of his amicable relations with the Mormons of that place. In Ireland the name is chiefly associated with a most tragic event, the Scanlan murder in Co. Limerick in 1819, which was the theme of several novels and plays, the best known of which is *The Colleen Bawn*. There were three Irish-American authors of note, viz. John F. Scanlan (b. 1839), Co. Limerick Fenian and poet, his better-known brother Michael Scanlan (b. 1836, Co. Limerick), author of *Jackets Green*, *The Fenian Men* etc.; and William J. Scanlan (1855–1898), actor, singer and song writer. Rt. Rev. Mgr. James Donald Scanlan (b. 1899) is Bishop of Dunkeld and Vicar Delegate to the U.S. Forces in Britain.

Arms illustrated on Plate XXV.

O'SCULLY.

Though originally a Westmeath sept, as early as the twelfth century the Scullys (in Irish Ó Scolaidhe) were driven by Anglo-Norman pressure to Co. Tipperary and may be regarded as belonging to Munster—birth statistics place them chiefly in Co. Cork to-day. A branch of the family retained its lands in Co. Dublin up to 1256 when the property of William O'Scully passed into ecclesiastical possession. On leaving Delvin (Co. Westmeath), one branch settled at Lorrha in north Tipperary where they became erenaghs of the church of St. Ruan. It was no doubt an offshoot of these which gave its name to Ballyscully, a place on the other side of the Shannon. Another branch of the same sept settled near Cashel in south Tipperary in the seventeenth century. Scully's Cross, unlike many family memorials, may be said to add to the beauty of the Rock of Cashel, in which famous ecclesiastical ruin the Scullys have the privilege of interment. The best known Scullys were Tipperary men. James Scully was proprietor of Scully's Bank at Tipperary, one of the few private banks to weather the financial crises of 1820 and 1825. It is of interest to record that this very reputable institution was acquired by John Sadlier of scandalous and notorious memory. Denis Scully (1773–1830), political writer and Catholic advocate, and his son Vincent Scully (1810–1871), well-known Irish politician and author, were of the same Kilfeacle family. James Scully (b. 1865), American poet, was born in Co. Cork. Vincent Scully (b. 1900), Canadian cabinet minister, was born and educated in Ireland.

O'SHANNON, O Shanahan, Gilshenan, Giltenan.

The Gaelic names of three distinct Irish families became anglicized as Shannon or O'Shannon. First there is Ó Seanáin (descendant of Senan, a personal name) of which we know little beyond the fact that it was associated with Counties Carlow and Wexford, where, however, the name is now rare. Another derivation from the same personal name is Mac Giolla t-Seanáin (son of the follower of St. Senan), which, though normally anglicized Giltenan, has become Shannon in Co. Clare. The cognate Mac Giolla Seanáin anglicized Gilshenan etc., the name of a Tyrone-Fermanagh sept, is not rendered Shannon in recent times; but the census of 1659 (in which prefixes Mac and O were often confused) gives O'Seanan as one of the principal Irish names in the district around Enniskillen, Co. Fermanagh, at that date. A further complication arises insomuch as in Co. Clare, where, with Belfast, the name Shannon is found most plentifully, it is a synonym of Shanahan (in Irish Ó Seanacháin). This is a case of contraction due to English influence: English surveyors and law clerks (being like many English of the present day inclined to silence an internal H) at the time of the Act of Settlement and again after the Williamite confiscations wrote down Irish names as nearly as they could phonetically, hence Shanahan was recorded Shannon. The O'Shanahans were a Dalcassian sept of sufficient importance to have a recognized chief in early times: of the clan Ui Bloid, his territory lay between Bodyke and Feakle in Co. Clare where the name still survives; but in the year 1318 he and his followers were dispossessed by the Mac-Namaras and in the fourteenth century they became dispersed all over Munster. Curiously enough, though one would expect less foreign influence in the west, the form Shannon is normal in Clare, but Shanahan is commoner in the other Munster counties. The total number of births recorded is approximately the same for Shannon and Shanahan (i.e. sixty per year each).

It should be noted that the surname Shannon is unconnected with the name of the principal river in Ireland.

The name does not appear frequently in the history of the country or among its notabilities in the cultural sphere. The well known London portrait painter Charles Shannon (1863–1937), was presumably of Irish extraction. A prominent Labour leader and writer in our own day is Cathal O'Shannon and, in America, Wilson Shannon (1802–1877), the governor of Ohio, made his mark as lawyer and diplomat.

MacSHANLY.

The prefix Mac of the name was dropped as early as the middle of the seventeenth century; occasionally, since that time, O has been prefixed to it, but quite erroneously, as it is truly a Mac name, Mac Seanlaoich in Irish. In modern Irish *sean-laoch* means old hero. The sept is of Co. Leitrim, the chief being known as MacShanly of Dromod. One Donncahy MacShanly is described in 1404 as a wealthy farmer of this place—his father, Murray, being " servant of trust " to the King of Connacht. They were often at war with their more powerful neighbours the MacRannalls, and in 1473 the latter destroyed their dwellings by fire and slew several of their leading men.

They remained steadfastly Catholic : one, Cormac Shanley, is among the priests enumerated in a Penal Law presentment for Co. Leitrim in 1714. Except for the Irish born Canadian poet, Charles Dawson Shanly (1811–1875), whose two brothers, Walter and Francis, were noted engineers in Canada, the name has seldom been prominent in modern times.

Arms illustrated on Plate XXV.

O'SHAUGHNESSY.

The O'Shaughnessys (in Irish Ó Seachnasaigh) were a sept of considerable importance in that part of Co. Galway known as the barony of Kiltartan ; indeed we may say are, rather than were, for around that area the greater number of persons of the name are still concentrated. They have an illustrious origin, being of the southern Ui Fiachrach, descended from the famous King Daithi, the last pagan King of Ireland. In the eleventh century they supplanted their kinsmen the O'Cahills and also the O'Clerys as the principal sept in Ui Fiachra Aidhne which was co-extensive with the diocese of Kilmacduagh : they are recorded as chiefs there from 1100 onwards and their territory is described in the " Composition Book of Connacht " (1585) as O'Shaughnessy's Country.

They do not figure very prominently in the history of the country until the seventeenth century. Sir Dermot O'Shaughnessy whose great-great-grandfather had, as Chief of the Name, so far forsaken the Gaelic order as to fall in with the policy of " surrender and regrant " and accept a knighthood from Henry VIII, joined the Confederation of Kilkenny. As a result his estates were confiscated under the Cromwellian régime. Though possession of a considerable portion was regained at the Restoration much of it was once more lost in the Williamite forfeitures, for the chief of the day was again found on the Irish side. However, the O'Shaughnessy influence remained strong in south Galway for at least another generation for we find in a case relating to O'Shaughnessy lands in 1731 their opponents appealing for a transfer of venue on the grounds that no jury in Co. Galway would give a verdict unfavourable to that family. As was the case in so many of the great Irish families the last Chief of the Name, William O'Shaughnessy (1674–1744), served in the Irish Brigade : he was colonel of Clare's regiment and died in France, having attained the rank of marshal after almost fifty years of active service, which began in King James's army at the Boyne.

A branch of the Kiltartan O'Shaughnessys settled in Co. Limerick in the sixteenth century where their descendants are still living. One family of this branch changed their name to Sandys. Sir John ("Big John") O'Shanassy (1818–1883), distinguished himself as an Australian statesmen and ardent Catholic; while Sir William Brooke O'Shaughnessy (1809–1889) of the Limerick branch, was a pioneer of telegraphy as well as an eminent surgeon.

The sacred crozier of St. Colman, reputed to be used as a means of inducing defrauders to give up illicitly acquired goods to their rightful owners, was in the possession of the O'Shaughnessy family from the time of Bishop O'Shaughnessy of Kilmacduagh (d. 1223) for several centuries: it is now in the collection of the National Museum of Ireland.

Arms illustrated on Plate XXV.

O'SHEA, Shee.

O'Shea is included in the list of fifty most numerous surnames in Ireland with an estimated number of nearly twelve thousand persons so called, if we include Shea, Shee and O'Shee, (variants of the same name) in the total. In Irish it is Ó Séaghdha, i.e. descendant of Séaghdha: this word means hawk-like and hence dauntless. The O'Sheas are primarily a Kerry sept. They were Lords of Iveragh but their power declined there from the twelfth century onwards, though not their numbers, for it is there that the great majority of O'Sheas are found even at the present day. Some of the leading members of the sept migrated to Co. Tipperary and we find Odoneus O'Shee recorded as Lord of Sheesland in Co. Tipperary in 1381. In the next century their sphere of influence moved to the adjoining county of Kilkenny: Robert Shee was Sovereign (i.e. chief burgess) of the city of Kilkenny in 1499, and the well known family, now represented by the Poer O'Shees of Gardenmorris and Sheestown, Co. Kilkenny, came into prominence there about that time. Of the so-called Ten Tribes of Kilkenny the Shees (the only one of Milesian blood), were the most influential; the Rothes and the Archers were next in importance.* The form Shee and O'Shee is based on an anglified pronunciation of Shea (cf. O'Dea and Dee) and is not met with often outside Co. Kilkenny. Sir William Shee (1804–1868), M.P. for Kilkenny was the first Catholic judge in Ireland since the Revolution of 1690. Capt. Robert O'Shea was a devoted follower of Prince Charlie and was with him at Culloden. He was an officer of the Irish Brigade in France. At least five others of the name (O'Shee in France) were distinguished officers. The son of one of them became a peer of France. Sir Martin Archer Shee (1769–1850) was the President

---

* The others were Archdekin, Cowley, Knaresborough, Langton, Lawless, Ley and Ragget.

of the Royal Academy (London) for twenty years. Daniel Shee (1777–1836) was an orientalist who was expelled from Dublin University for refusing to give evidence against his friends among the United Irishmen. John Dawson Gilmary O'Shea (1824–1892) was an American historian of note, whose father, a leader in Irish-American affairs, went to the U.S.A. in 1815. The murder of the twelve year old boy Denis Shea in 1851 is a shocking commentary on the evils of landlordism at that period. The name of O'Shea is of course intimately associated with the fall of Parnell.

Arms illustrated on Plate XXVI.

O'SHEEHAN, Sheahan.

Sheehan is one of Ireland's very numerous surnames : combining the alternative spellings Sheehan (eighty per cent) and Sheahan (twenty per cent), it holds the seventy-fifth place in the list thereof, with an estimated total population in Ireland to-day of about eight thousand five hundred persons of the name. Of these the great majority were born in Co. Cork or, on its borders, in the adjacent counties of Kerry and Limerick. The name should be Sheehan rather than Sheahan because in Irish it is Ó Siodhacháin, said to be derived from the word *siodhach* (peaceful) but Celtic scholars doubt this. The sept originated as a Dalcassian one, having a chief resident in Lower Connello, Co. Limerick, but, as stated above, the passing of the centuries finds their modern representatives somewhat south of this. It is seldom met in English with its prefix O.

Although the name has little present-day association with Connacht it should be stated that there was in mediaeval times a sept of the Ui Máine called O'Sheehan : they were hereditary trumpeters to O'Kelly, the O'Lonergans being the harpers to the same leading chief. O'Sheaghyn, mentioned in the Fiants of 1543 as Chief of His Nation in southern Co. Galway, was not, as might be supposed, an O'Sheehan : O'Sheaghyn is there the somewhat grotesque attempt of a foreign official to write down the name O'Shaughnessy.

The two most distinguished persons of the name in Irish life have both been Catholic priests, viz. Patrick Augustine Sheehan (1852–1913), universally known as Canon Sheehan, author of *My New Curate* etc., and Richard Alphonsus Sheehan (1845–1915), Bishop of Waterford, writer and champion of the Irish language.

Arms illustrated on Plate XXVI.

267

MacSHEEHY.

This name is now peculiar to Munster, though it is not found there before 1420 when the first of the family came to Co. Limerick, where they took service with the Earl of Desmond and established themselves near the town of Rathkeale. They are first heard of in Ireland as gallowglasses, and as such they fought with distinction in many battles, having come to Ireland in the fourteenth century from Scotland, (where they were a branch of the MacDonnell clan). The most spectacular of the engagements in which they took part was the sack of Kilmallock in 1591 when, with the MacSweeneys, under James Fitzmaurice, it took three whole days and nights to remove the treasures of that town. Later, when engaged in the 1642 war in Co. Limerick, they are noticeable for their savage treatment of their prisoners. The supposed derivation of their name Mac Sithigh, from the Irish adjective *sitheach* (peaceful) would thus seem to be inappropriate.

Though the census of 1659 shows that the name was then always written with the prefix, the Mac was subsequently dropped and the name is now always found simply as Sheehy, though a few isolated families have " resumed " an O, calling themselves O'Sheehy, which is a solecism. The Mac was still retained in the eighteenth century, especially among exiles. Seven MacSheehys were prominent in France. Dr. John MacSheehy (1745–1815) was physician to the French court, before the Revolution, and, a few years later, Brian (or Bernard) Mac Sheehy (1774–1807) went to Ireland in 1796 to prepare for Wolfe Tone's expedition : he was killed beside Napoleon, whose aide-de-camp he was, at the battle of Eylau. John's uncle, Patrick MacSheehy, was killed at the battle of Grenada in 1779 after distinguished service in the French army ; and another, chevalier John Desmond Louis MacSheehy (1783–1867), also attained high honours in the same service. Father Nicholas Sheehy (1728–1766) who was parish priest of Clogheen, Co. Tipperary, is noteworthy for the fact that he was singled out by the Ascendancy as champion of the Whiteboys, and was hanged for an alleged murder with which he cannot have been associated.
Arms illustrated on Plate XXVI.

O'SHERIDAN.

The Sheridan family originated in Co. Longford, being erenaghs of Granard, but later moved to the next county—Cavan—where they became devoted followers of the powerful O'Reillys. The name is Ó Sirideáin in Irish, i.e. descendant of Siridean, a personal name the derivation of which is uncertain. While Cavan is the county in which they are still to be found in greater numbers than elsewhere, the Sheridans are now dispersed widely throughout every province, though less in Munster than elsewhere. The prefix O has been entirely dropped since the seventeenth century.

The Sheridans have been chiefly notable for their achievements in the literary field. The most famous, of course, was Richard Brinsley Sheridan (1751–1816) the Dublin-born dramatist and orator, long a prominent member of the English parliament; his mother Frances Sheridan (1724–1766), was also a successful writer, as was his brother Charles Sheridan (1750–1806); and yet another member of this remarkable literary family was Thomas Sheridan (1719–1788) who was also one of the leading actors of his day. These do not complete the list of Sheridans prominent in the literary sphere, for Denis Sheridan (b.1612) assisted Bedell to translate the Bible into Irish and his son William Sheridan (1636–1711) was Protestant Bishop of Kilmore. We must also mention Rev. Thomas Sheridan (1687–1738), an author best remembered now as the intimate friend of Dean Swift; and another Thomas Sheridan (1647–1712), a close follower of James II; while his son, yet another Thomas Sheridan (1684–1746), was tutor in exile to Prince Charles, the " Young Pretender ", and took part with him in the "Forty-Five", as did his nephew Chevalier Michael Sheridan (1715–c. 1775). Lastly, we have General Philip Henry Sheridan (1831–1888) the well-known and successful commander in the American Civil War. He, like nearly all the others cited above, was a Co. Cavan man.

Arms illustrated on Plate XXVI.

O'SHIEL, Shields.

By origin and by the test of present-day distribution of population, O'Shiel is an Ulster name. In Irish Ó Siadhail, it is usually anglicized as Shiels, Sheils, Shields or Sheilds rather than O'Shiel, and these forms are chiefly found in Counties Donegal, Derry, Antrim and Down. Though claiming descent from Niall of the Nine Hostages, the O'Shiels were known as a medical family, rather than as a territorial sept. They became physicians to several great chiefs in various parts of the country. The most famous of these was Murtagh O'Shiel, hereditary physician to MacCoughlan, who was killed in 1548. An important branch of the family was settled in MacCoughlan's country with a seat at Ballysheil (in the parish of Gillen, Offaly). The two most notable men of the name were of this branch : Richard Lalor Sheil (1791–1851), founder of the Catholic Association and second only to Daniel O'Connell in the struggle for Catholic Emancipation ; and his brother, Sir Justin Sheil (1803–1871), soldier, diplomatist and staunch Catholic. Two others prominently identified with the Catholic cause in America were Senator James Shields (1806–1879), a Tyrone man, and Father Thomas Edward Shields (1862–1921). Three centuries earlier Connach O'Shiel, Abbot of Ballysodare, who was appointed Bishop of Elphin by Henry VIII in 1545, rejected the new doctrines till his death in 1552. After the Jacobite defeat several families of O'Shiel settled in France. One of these (of Nantes) was admitted to the ranks of the French nobility in 1775.

To-day the name is intimately associated with the stage and particularly the Abbey Theatre—George Shields being one of its most prolific playwrights. His brother (better known as Barry Fitzgerald) before going to Hollywood made his name as an actor in that Dublin theatre.

Arms illustrated on Plate XXVI.

SKERRETT.

The Skerretts of Ballinduff, Co. Galway, and Finvarra, Co. Clare, have now died out in the male line—the last representative being Rev. Hyacinth Heffernan Skerrett, a priest. They were extensive landowners in both those counties eighty years ago. Some junior lines survive elsewhere, but the name is now very rare. It is included here because the family was one of the " Tribes of Galway." Of English origin it appears under the guise of Huscared, and subsequently Scared, as early as 1242, when they held lands in Connacht under Richard de Burgo. In 1378 we find the name as Scared, alias Scaret : in that year one of them was Provost of Galway ; by 1414, when another of the name held that office, it had become Skeret. After that it occurs intermittently in the lists of mayors and sheriffs up to 1642, and they were listed as Irish Papists in the return made under the Act of Settlement of proprietors in 1640. Twelve years after that date, two Skerretts were among those townsmen who refused to sign the articles of capitulation at the end of the siege of Galway. Two of the "tribe" were Archbishops of Tuam : Nicholas Skerrett, who was expelled from the see in 1583, and Mark Skerrett, who held it from 1756 to 1775.

O'SULLIVAN.

In Irish O'Sullivan is Ó Súileabháin. The derivation of the name is in dispute among scholars. There is no doubt that the root word is *súil* (eye), but whether it is to be taken as one-eyed or hawk-eyed must be left an open question. While not quite as numerous as Murphy and Kelly, Sullivan, which is by far the commonest surname in Munster, comes third in the list for all Ireland. Almost eighty per cent of the Sullivans (or O'Sullivans) in Ireland to-day belong to the counties of Cork and Kerry, the remainder being mostly of Co. Limerick, or of the city of Dublin, in which, of course, families from all the four provinces are found. Thus the O'Sullivans, as is almost always the case with the great Gaelic septs, are still concentrated in or near their ancient homeland.

It was not until after the Anglo-Norman invasion that the O'Sullivans came to the fore. Their origin, however, is illustrious : descended from Eoghan (Owen) Mói, the father of the famous Oilioll Olum, they were, with the O'Callaghans, the

MacCarthys and the O'Keeffes, one of the leading families of the Munster Eoghanacht. Some at least of them were lords of a territory near Cahir prior to the invasion : from 1200 onwards, however, they are to be found in the extreme south-west of Munster. There they became very numerous and powerful, dividing into a number of branch septs of which O'Sullivan Mór and O'Sullivan Beare were the most important. The former had his principal castle at Dunkerron on the shore of Kenmare Bay, the latter was lord of the modern baronies of Beare and Bantry.

Though seldom appearing in any of the Annals before the year 1400, they were prominent in the sixteenth century. Outstanding at that period was Donal O'Sullivan Beare (1560–1618), hero of the siege of Dunboy and particularly famous for his almost incredibly hazardous march to Ulster after the disasters of the battle of Kinsale and the capture of Dunboy. His nephew, Philip O'Sullivan Beare (1590–1660), was a soldier in the Spanish army, but is better known as a historian : his *Historiae Catholicae Iberniae Compendium* recounts the events of the Elizabethan wars as told to him by his uncle and other participants. From a junior branch came Col. John William O'Sullivan (b. 1700), close companion of " the Young Pretender " in his Rebellion of 1745. Since his time the name has been made famous by many O'Sullivans and Sullivans. In the field of literature Owen Roe O'Sullivan (1748–1784) and Tadhg Gaolach O'Sullivan (d. 1800) were two of the best of the eighteenth century Gaelic poets ; Humphrey O'Sullivan (1780–1837) kept a most interesting diary in Irish which has been partially published by the Irish Texts Society ; the brothers A. M. Sullivan (1830–1884), and T. D. Sullivan (1827–1914), as well as being authors of note, were leading Nationalist M.P's, the former being a Young Irelander in 1848. On the stage Barry Sullivan (1821–1891), and Charles Sullivan (1848–1887), were celebrated actors, and Maureen O'Sullivan is famous to-day in the same sphere, while Sir Arthur Sullivan (1842–1900), of the Gilbert and Sullivan operas, was of Irish descent. If we add, from a very different sphere, John L. Sullivan (1858–1918), perhaps the best known pugilist of all time, we have recorded but a tithe of the O'Sullivans of note to be found not only in Ireland itself but also in the Irish Brigades, in the French Revolution (on both sides) and in the history of the United States.

Arms illustrated on Plate XXVI.

MacSWEENEY.

The statement that the MacSweenys are of the race of O'Neill is somewhat misleading because, though it is true that their eponymous ancestor was Suibhne O'Neill, this man was a chieftain in Argyle, and the MacSweenys who later established themselves as three great septs in Tirconnell (Donegal) did not do so until the fourteenth century—there is no mention of them in the Annals before 1267 when both the Four Masters and the " Annals of Connacht " record the death of Murrough

MacSweeny, who was grandson of Suibhne. (The name is Mac Suibhne in Irish). He was the first of the famous MacSweeny gallowglasses. This word (*gallóglach*) denotes a paid fighting man retained permanently as such by an Irish chief, often (though not necessarily) brought over in the first instance from Scotland. Although soldiering was their regular occupation this did not prevent them becoming an Irish sept in the usual sense, or rather in this case, three kindred septs, viz. MacSweeny Fanad, MacSweeny Banagh and MacSweeny na dTuath, commonly called MacSweeny of the Battleaxes, though the words na dTuath actually mean " of the Districts " (in Tirconnell). A branch of the first of these migrated to Munster, where about the year 1500 they followed their hereditary profession under the MacCarthys, and became possessed of territory and fortified castles in Muskerry (Co. Cork).

MacSweeny (also spelt MacSweeney and MacSwiney, often without the prefix Mac) is now regarded almost more as a Cork-Kerry surname than as a Donegal one, for though still common in its original territory in Ulster, it is to-day more numerous in the south. To this branch belonged Terence MacSwiney (1879–1920),[*] Lord Mayor of Cork, whose death in prison after a seventy days hunger strike did much to focus world attention on the struggle for Irish independence. Many of the Tirconnell MacSweenys had a place in Irish military history from the fourteenth century till the early seventeenth, when Ulster, up to that time the most Irish and independent province of the country, was subdued. In modern times up to 1916 Irish professional soldiers have had to find scope for their talents abroad. There were, it is true, no less than eleven officers called MacSweeny in James II's army in Ireland, but after this brief opportunity of fighting on their native soil we have to look for them in the Irish Brigades in the service of various continental powers. Both Ulster and Munster MacSweenys contributed their quota. Thomas William Sweeny (1820–1892), leader of the Fenian raid into Canada, was born in Co. Cork.

The MacSweenys do not figure prominently in the literary or ecclesiastical history of the country. One of the nineteenth century Connacht poets mentioned by Hyde was a MacSweeny, and Terence MacSwiney (*vide supra*), as well as some plays, wrote *Principles of Freedom*, which was published posthumously.

Arms illustrated on Plate XXVI.

TAAFFE.

Taaffe was originally a Welsh name signifying David (cf. the modern pet name Taffy). In Irish it is rendered Táth, pronounced Taa and, according to O'Donovan, often so spelt. Settling in Co. Louth soon after the Anglo-Norman invasion, the

---

[*] This date (1879) is correct. The date 1883 usually given for the birth of Terence MacSwiney actually refers to another man of the same name.

Taaffes rapidly attained a position of considerable importance in the country and, though they never became numerous like so many of the Norman immigrants, they continued to be one of the most influential families in Ireland. The ancestor of most of the Taaffe lines was Sir Nicholas Taaffe whose grandson, Richard Taaffe, was Sheriff of Dublin in 1295, and in 1315 Sheriff of Co. Louth. His son, John Taaffe —a Franciscan—was Archbishop of Armagh. Several other descendants of Sir Nicholas were Sheriffs of Louth in the fourteenth, fifteenth and sixteenth centuries. Their principal property at Ballybragan was forfeited in the confiscations which followed 1641 : before that time a branch of the family had migrated to Co. Sligo where their descendants are still living. The Taaffes were consistent supporters of the Stuart cause and the head of the Sligo branch was ennobled as Viscount Taaffe and later Earl of Carlingford. Nine of the name were in the army of James II in 1690, two of them being killed ; one at the siege of Derry, the other at the battle of the Boyne. The third Earl of Carlingford and fourth Viscount, Francis Taaffe (1639–1704), was the celebrated Count Taaffe of the Austrian Empire in which service he became a field-marshal and received many honours. His nephew Nicholas Count Taaffe (1677–1769), also an Austrian field-marshal, was even more famous as a military commander. This illustrious branch of the family remained in Austria. The tenth Viscount was Chamberlain to the Empire and in 1860 established before the British House of Lords his right to the Irish title. His brother Edward (1833–1912), the eleventh Viscount, was Imperial Prime Minister and one of the very few persons of Irish name to be a Knight of the Golden Fleece (the most exclusive order in Christendom). The name of his son Heinrich was removed from the roll of Viscounts on account of his having fought against Britain in the first World War. His only son and heir uses his Imperial title of Count only.

Two Co. Louth Taaffes are notable in the literary field. Rev. Denis Taaffe (1753–1813), as well as being a prolific author, was a co-founder of the Gaelic Society ; he was excommunicated in 1790, became a Protestant clergyman, fought on the side of the United Irishmen and was wounded in 1798, and finally returned to the Catholic Church. John Taaffe (1787–1862), poet and commentator of Dante, was of the circle of Byron and Shelly.

Arms illustrated on Plate XXVI.

MacTIERNAN, MacKiernan.

No less than thirty-three MacTiernans are mentioned in the " Annals of the Four Masters ", practically all of them Chiefs of Teallach Donnchadha (modern Tully-hunco, in the county of Cavan) or their relatives. Though not much information is given about their exploits, the mere recording of so many obituaries indicates the importance of the sept throughout the three centuries from 1250 to 1550. The name is still found chiefly in the Cavan-Leitrim area but generally without the prefix Mac; when the Mac is retained MacTernan is now the usual form. Another sept of MacTiernan held territory in the north-eastern part of Co. Roscommon in mediaeval times. Their origin is different from the Tullyhunco sept, being descended from Tiernan, grandson of Turlough Mór O'Connor, King of Ireland, while the Cavan sept is a branch of the O'Rourkes. This being so, it is of interest to note that the large estate of Hugh MacTernan of Heapstown House, Boyle, Co. Roscommon, in 1878 lay for the most part in Co. Leitrim.

The name in Irish is Mac Tighearnáin (derived from *tighearna*, a lord). It is also spelt with the T aspirated—MacThighearnáin—which was phonetically anglicized MacKiernan. The chiefs of Tullyhunco were occasionally called MacKiernan instead of MacTiernan. To-day the two names, including their variants with and without the Mac, are about equal in numbers, and Kiernan is numerous in the same area as Tiernan. The latter is sometimes confused with Tierney, but there is actually no connexion between them.

In modern times the two best known people of these names are associated with America: Frances Christine Fisher Tiernan (1846–1920), wife of James Tiernan, Catholic novelist and devoted supporter of the Confederates in the Civil war; and Francis Kiernan (1816–1892), Democratic senator. At home Most Rev. Edward Kernan (d. 1844) was Bishop of Clogher for over twenty years.
Arms illustrated on Plate XXVII.

O'TIERNEY, (Tiernan).

The most important of the original O'Tierney septs was that of Co. Mayo, where their chiefs were lords of Carra. The name is now very scattered, being found in every county of Munster and Connacht, while it is rare in Ulster, outside Donegal. In Mayo, Tierney and Tiernan have been used as synonyms and cases of this are also reported from Co. Clare. Both O'Tierney (Ó Tighearnaigh) and O'Tiernan (Ó Tighearnáin) are derived from the Irish word *tighearna*, lord. Many examples of the remarkable family pride of the O'Tiernans of Co. Mayo are recorded. Tierney is much more numerous than Tiernan: 78 births were recorded for the former compared with 26 for the latter in the last year for which statistics are available. While Tierneys cannot be assigned definitely to a particular area in the way most Gaelic families can be placed, it may be said that the name is chiefly associated with the Counties Galway, Limerick and Tipperary. They were undoubtedly firmly established as a territorial family, if not an indigenous sept, in Upper Ormond, for in the Ormond Deeds Fearnan O'Tyernie (i.e. O'Tierney's country) is several times mentioned. As early as 1273 there was a Florence O'Tierney, Bishop of Kilfenora, and in 1372 Cornelius O'Tierney became Bishop of Kerry. An O'Tierney monument in St.

Nicholas Church, Galway, is dated 1580. The only Tierney in the 1691 attainders was of Galway. The arms illustrated in Plate XXVII were confirmed in 1748 to a Co. Limerick family of Tierney stated in the patent to have had " long user thereof ". The best known Tierney was George Tierney (1761–1830), the English statesman, whose father was a Limerick man. The most remarkable were the brothers Matthew Tierney (1776–1845), and Edward Tierney (1780–1856). The sons of a small farmer in Co. Limerick, both attained astonishing success in their respective careers : Sir Matthew, beginning as an apothecary's apprentice at Rathkeale, rose to be one of the leading doctors in England and Physician in Ordinary to the King ; Sir Edward, who inherited his brother's baronetcy by special patent, remained in Ireland, where he not only obtained the lucrative appointment of Crown Solicitor for Ulster but also acquired under the will of Lord Egmont, whose agent he was, the extensive Egmont estates in Co. Cork. The extraordinary finale of this story, which is full of dramatic incidents and reads more like romantic fiction than fact, was that some years after Sir Edward's death the will in his favour was challenged, and eventually the estates reverted to the Egmont family. Father Richard Henry Tierney, S.J. (1870–1928), editor of *America*, belonged to a Co. Tipperary family ; Dr. Michael Tierney, President of University College, Dublin, comes from Co. Galway. The famous annalist Tighearnach was not an O'Tierney, but of the race of the O'Breens.

Arms illustrated on Plate XXVII.

TOBIN.

Though Tobin is not an indigenous Gaelic Irish name the family may be regarded as completely hibernicized. Originally of Aubyn in France, they were first called de St. Aubyn. They came to Ireland in the wake of the Norman invasion and by 1200 they were settled in Counties Tipperary and Kilkenny, whence they spread in course of time to the neighbouring counties of Waterford and Cork. While not really numerous compared with some others in the same category, such as Walsh, Roche and Power, they are still to be found to-day in considerable numbers in the counties mentioned above, but very few in any other part of the country. The Tobins became so influential in Co. Tipperary that in mediaeval times the head of the family was known as Baron of Coursey, though this was not an officially recognized title. Clyn in his Annals states that in the fourteenth century the Tobins were a turbulent sept more dreaded by the English settlers than the native Irish. The place Ballytobin near Callan (Co. Kilkenny) took its name from them. No outstanding person of the name appears in the pages of Irish political, military or cultural history, but James Tobin represented Fethard in the Parliament of 1689. Tobin appears frequently as a name in the Ormond archives and there have been also one or two minor poets in the family.

Several Tobins were among the Wild Geese. A branch of the family, returning to the country of its origin, became established at Nantes where so many Irish emigrant families settled. The best known of this branch was Edmund, Marquès de Tobin (1692–1747), who was killed in action in the War of Austrian Succession while in the service of Spain. Another branch of the Irish Tobins settled in Newfoundland and have prospered there.

Arms illustrated on Plate XXVII.

O'TOOLE, (Toal).

The O'Tooles are remarkable for their unremitting resistance to English attempts to conquer Ireland from the late twelfth century, when the Anglo-Norman invasion took place, down to the end of the seventeenth century, when the country was finally subdued. Nor is the name absent from the Roll of Honour in 1798. Their territory, though near Dublin, the seat of government, was admirably suited to resistance on account of its wooded and mountainous nature : they possessed an area co-extensive with the small diocese of Glendalough, and it is of interest to recall the fact that their chiefs exercised what practically amounted to the right of nominating the Abbots of Glendalough and the bishops of that diocese up to the time it was united to the Archdiocese of Dublin. Laurence O'Toole, who was afterwards canonized, was one of these abbots. In 1171, though he was Archbishop of Dublin at the time, he took up arms against the Anglo-Norman invaders. Individual O'Tooles who distinguished themselves in the wars against England are too numerous to particularize, and this is also the case with officers of the Irish Brigades in the service of France. O'Tooles also served other European powers in the eighteenth century. One of the latter may, however, be specially mentioned for his part in the dramatic abduction—or rescue—of Maria Clementina Sobieski of Poland prior to her marriage to James III (the " Old Pretender "), for which exploit Capt. Luke O'Toole and his companions were personally decorated by Pope Clement XI. Most of the O'Tooles of the present day are found in Dublin city and county and the adjacent county of Wicklow. There are also an appreciable number in Counties Galway and Mayo, where a branch of the O'Tooles was established at an early date—some authorities regard these as a separate sept. In Irish the name is Ó Tuathail. A minor sept in southern Ulster so called have anglicized it as Toal, a well known surname in Co. Monaghan.

Apart from St. Laurence O'Toole (1132–1182) and the twelfth to eighteenth century soldiers noticed above, one member of the sept, though not a credit to it, had an interesting career, viz. Adam Duff O'Toole, who ended by being burned alive in Dublin in 1327, having been condemned to that death for his advocacy of blasphemous doctrines. It was with Felim O'Toole that Hugh O'Neill took refuge at Glendalough after his escape from captivity in Dublin Castle in 1590. Capt. Luke O'Toole was one of the Irishmen who were guillotined as aristocrats during the French Revolution terror. Laurence O'Toole (b. 1722), of Fairfield, Co. Wexford, an officer in the Irish Brigade in France, had eight sons, all of whom served in the French army. The eldest of these, Col. John O'Toole (d. 1823), was created a Count and he is the ancestor of the present Count O'Toole of Limoges.

Arms illustrated on Plate XXVII.

O'TRACY.

It is easy to be misled in dealing with the surname Tracy, for it is borne by an ancient and noble English family (Barons Sudeley), who are descended from Saxon ancestry. Their surname, however, is not Saxon, having been acquired from a female Norman line who were called after Traci, a place in France. The English place Bovey Tracy derives its name from that family. There were also Anglo-Irish Tracys— Viscounts Rathcoole, and baronets in Co. Limerick.

So far as modern Ireland is concerned it is safe to say that few if any of the people called Tracy (Treacy being a common alternative spelling in Ireland but not elsewhere), are of English origin. There are three distinct families of Ó Treasaigh (*anglice* Tracy etc.) recorded in the old genealogical manuscripts. Of these, that of south-east Galway, akin to the O'Maddens, was dispersed as a sept at an early date but scattered families of the name have remained in that area till the present day. The Tracys of Co. Cork were descended from a younger branch of the royal house of Munster and are of the same stock as the O'Donovans of west Cork, where, as in the former case, they are still to be found. A branch of these settled in Co. Limerick. Finally, in Co. Leix, Tracys were Lords of Slievemargy until dispersed by successive invasions : traces of these are to be found no doubt in the place-names Ballytracy and Tracystown in Co. Wexford, but the name is not common there now. Rory O'Trassy was Bishop of Ferns in the twelfth century. The name O'Tressy occurs as of Cloncurry (Co. Kildare), in the " Red Book of Ormond " under date 1304.

Two Tracys made their mark in America, viz. Nathaniel Tracy (1751–1796), son of an Irish emigrant, who was one of the chief financiers of the Revolution, and Benjamin Franklin Tracy (1830–1915), lawyer, soldier and secretary of the Navy, who was also of Irish descent. At home two writers, Thomas Tracy (b. 1820), poet, and Father William Tracy, S.J. (b. 1840), author of *Irish Scholars of the Penal Days*, and also John Joseph Tracey (1813–1873), painter, may be mentioned.

TRAYNOR.

The Gaelic Ulster surname Mac Thréinfhir—son of the strong man, or champion—is anglicized Traynor, also spelt Treanor and Trainor, without the Mac, though the prefix is retained in the variant MacCrainor, which is phonetically more correct, since the T is aspirated in the Irish form of the name. Apart from Dublin city, Traynors are chiefly found in the districts between Monaghan, Armagh and Dungannon. Sometimes the English surname Armstrong is used (by quasi-translation) as a synonym for Traynor.

O'TREHY, Troy.

Though not numerous in Ireland the name Troy is not uncommon in Co. Tipperary and surrounding areas. The location of this small sept (which originated in Co. Clare but did not remain there) was in the Clogheen district of Co. Tipperary : their association with that part of the country is perpetuated in the place-name Ballytrehy. O'Trehy is an older anglicized form of the name in use as late as the seventeenth century, but now obsolete : O'Trehy is a phonetic rendering of the Irish Ó Troighthigh, presumably derived from the Irish word *troightheach* meaning a foot-soldier. The name in the 1659 census is spelt Trohy and it appears among the more numerous names in the baronies of Eliogarty and Ikerrin, Co. Tipperary. Another place-name is Castletroy, now a suburb of Limerick. The name was closely associated with that city and appears very frequently in its earlier records. Henry Troy was Provost of Limerick in 1197. In 1198 the first mayor and sheriffs were chosen : between that date and 1463 no less than twenty-one Troys held one or other of those offices.

The best known Irishman so called was Most Rev. Thomas Troy (1739–1823), Archbishop of Dublin : he was noted for his strong and forcibly expressed views in opposition to popular Irish sentiment, e.g. his censure of the priests who took part in the 1798 Rising, his denunciation of the Whiteboys and his advocacy of the Union ; he was also a co-founder of St. Patrick's College, Maynooth. The well-known American painter of horses was not of this stock : his father was a Frenchman called de Troye, and this family is also found in Ireland, where it has been gaelicized as de Treo.

Arms illustrated on Plate XXVII.

TULLY, MacAtilla, Flood.

This name is fairly common in Counties Galway and Cavan but rare elsewhere (except in the city of Dublin where, of course, names from all parts of Ireland are to be found). It was formerly MacTully, and the form MacAtilla is used to-day in some places which suggests that the name in Irish was MacTuile or Mac a'tuile, meaning son of the flood ; and it is a fact that the surnames Tully and Flood were at one time interchangeable and that what has been termed a mistranslation may indeed be a translation.

In the Elizabethan Fiants we find Dionysius Flood alias Donogh O'Multilly. O'Multilly, spelt O'Moltolle in another case, is Ó Maoltuile in Irish. It has been stated by usually reliable authorities that MacTuile is a corruption of Ó Maoltuile and that the latter is the real name of the celebrated medical family, but the form Mac Tuile appears in a seventeenth century manuscript which is a copy by a well-known scribe of a thirteenth century manuscript. The original, written by an eye witness of the inauguration of Cathal O'Connor, last King of Connacht, describes MacTully (Mac Tuile) who was present as O'Connor's physician. The MacTullys were in fact hereditary physicians not only to the O'Connors but also to the O'Reillys of Breffny. This accounts for the modern distribution of the name as given above. The place-name Tullystown near Granard is associated with the Breffny branch of the family. The Tullys listed in the 1691 attainders are all of Co. Galway and the leading family whose arms are illustrated on Plate XXVII are of that county. The same arms are used by the Floods of Co. Kilkenny.

The most noteworthy of the Tullys was Father Fiacre Tully, O.F.M., who in the years 1625–1631 was extremely active in Rome in the Irish interest. The Floods of Co. Kilkenny are said to be of English extraction. To this family belonged two notable politicians : Sir Frederick Flood (1741–1824) and Henry Flood (1732–1791), both prominent as Volunteers and opponents of the Union, the latter one of the out-standing personalities of eighteenth century Ireland. The distinguished Rev. Dr. Peter Flood (d. 1803), President of St. Patrick's College, Maynooth, on the other hand gave that measure some support. William Henry Grattan Flood (1867–1928), author of the *History of Irish Music* was a noted composer of liturgical music.

Tully, alias Tally, is also the anglicized form of the Irish surname Ó Taithligh borne by a sept located near Omagh, Co. Tyrone, of which, however, little trace remains to-day.

Arms illustrated on Plate XXVII.

O'TWOMEY.

The name Twomey, usually without the prefix O, is now, as always, predominantly associated with Co. Cork. When found elsewhere it is often spelt Toomey. In the census of 1659 O'Twomy appears as the second most numerous surname in the barony of Barretts, Co. Cork, Murphy being then the commonest there. The most distinguished man of the name, however, Seán Ó Tuama (1706–1775), was born and lived all his life at Croom, in the neighbouring county of Limerick : there he and his wife kept a publichouse which was the meeting place of the Maigue Gaelic poets, he himself—" O'Twomey the gay "—being the most distinguished of them.

WALL.

The name Wall is found in considerable numbers in that part of Munster which lies between Limerick and Waterford, and in the counties of Leinster which adjoin this. The name is common in England also. It is of Norman origin : its earliest form is du Val, i.e. of the valley, hence the form de Bhál in Irish. The Walls have been in Ireland since the thirteenth century and when they first appear in Irish records they were called de Vale, alias Faltagh ; O'Donovan states that Faltagh was the usual English equivalent in his day—a hundred years ago. An alternative of de Vale was de Wale. Wale, which we would now pronounce Wayle, was, up to the end of the seventeenth century pronounced Wall, just as the verb to fall was often written fale, and thus the present form of the name came into general use (c.f. Smale—Small, Sale—Saul). From the fourteenth century to the twentieth Irish Walls have made the name an honoured one. Three of them were bishops in the fourteenth century, notably Stephen de Wale, or Vale, Bishop of Limerick (1360–1369) and of Meath (1369–1379), and also Lord High Treasurer of Ireland. Richard Wall (1694–1778), Spanish war minister, son of Mathew Wall of Kilmallock, was a famous man in his adopted country ; Joseph Wall (1737–1802), who was born in Co. Leix, achieved notoriety in India and was hanged for his cruel conduct while British governor there ; Patrick Viscount Wall, one of the Carlow Walls, was a notable figure at the court of Louis XVI and was murdered in 1787. Four close relatives of his were outstanding officers in the Irish Brigade. At home, Edmund Wall (c. 1670–1755) was one of the Gaelic poets of the Jacobite period ; Rev. Dr. Charles William Wall (1780–1862) was famous as a Hebrew scholar ; Father Patrick Wall (c. 1780–1834) was the constant patron of the Co. Waterford Irish scribe Thomas O'Hickey ; and more recently, Fr. Thomas Wall was a popular figure of the War of Independence on account of his defiance of Sir John Maxwell, commander-in-chief of the British forces, in which he had the full support of Dr. O'Dwyer, Bishop of Limerick. Both Father Tom Wall and Rev. Charles Wall, mentioned above, belong to Co. Limerick.

Arms illustrated on Plate XXVII.

WALSH, Brannagh.

Only three surnames (Murphy, Kelly and Sullivan) exceed Walsh in numerical strength among the population of Ireland. It is found in every county and is particularly strong in Mayo, where it has first place, and also in Galway, Cork, Wexford, Waterford and Kilkenny. The last area is that most closely associated with the Walshes, where they have given their name to the Walsh Mountains in Co. Kilkenny. The name originated as a result of the Anglo-or, more properly, the Cambro-Norman, invasion, and simply means the Welshman, in Irish Breathnach, which was sometimes anglicized phonetically as Brannagh—not, however, as Brannock, a name of different though somewhat similar origin. The first to be so called is said to have been Haylen Brenach, alias Walsh, son of " Philip the Welshman ", one of the invaders of 1172. Unlike many of the Anglo-Norman families such as Burke, Fitzgerald, Roche etc., which have since become exclusively identified with Ireland, the Walshes did not all spring from one or two known ancestors, but the name was given independently to many of the newcomers and, perhaps in consequence of this, no clearly defined Hiberno-Norman sept of Walsh was formed on the Gaelic Irish model, as happened with a number of those other families. Nevertheless the Walshes of the south-eastern part of Ireland are mostly descended from the Philip mentioned above and from his brother David ; and the leading members of this family established themselves as landed gentry at Castlehowel (Co. Kilkenny), at Ballykileavan (Co. Leix), at Ballyrichmore (Co. Waterford) and also at Bray and Carrickmines near Dublin. References to men of the name are very numerous in both national and local records : they appear as sheriffs, judges, army officers etc., usually on the side of the King (which of course meant attainder in the seventeenth century) but not always—two for example were killed " in rebellion against Queen Elizabeth ".

The pedigree of the Tirawley (Mayo) Walshes was compiled by Lawrence Walsh in 1588. He states that they are descended from Walynus, a Welshman who came to Ireland with Maurice Fitzgerald in 1169 and that this man's brother Barrett was the progenitor of the Barretts of Tirawley (q.v. p. 51 *supra*).

The many famous bearers of the name include Rev. Peter Walsh (1618–1688), pro-Ormond opponent of Rinuccini and author of " The Loyal Remonstrance," for which he was excommunicated and expelled from the Franciscan Order ; John Walsh who in 1604 wrote the beautiful Gaelic " Lament for Oliver Grace " ; Edward Walsh (1805–1850), and John Walsh (1835–1881), both National School teachers and poets ; Most Rev. William John Walsh (1841–1921), one of the most distinguished of all the Archbishops of Dublin. The Churches have had many other Walshes of note : among them Most Rev. Thomas Walsh (1580–1654), the much persecuted Archbishop of Cashel whose active career occupies many pages of the Wadding (Franciscan) papers ; and Most Rev. John Walsh (1830–1898), Catholic Archbishop of Toronto, who promoted the Irish Race Convention after the Parnell Split, as well as several Protestant bishops, notably the Rt. Rev. Nicholas Walsh of Waterford, who was murdered in 1585 by a man whom he had rebuked, and is remembered as the man who introduced Irish type to the native printing press in connexion with his unfinished translation into Irish of the New Testament. The Walsh family of St. Malo and Nantes has had a distinguished history in France since its establishment there at the end of the seventeenth century, many of its members being notable in war, politics and literature. The first emigrant was Philip Walsh (1666–1708), shipbuilder and privateer, his father being the James Walsh, of Ballynacooly in the Walsh Mountains, Co. Kilkenny, who commanded the ship which brought James II to France after the Battle of the Boyne. Judge John Edwards Walsh (1816–1869), was the author of a well-known book *Ireland Sixty Years Ago*, published in 1847. Many Irish-American Walshes have also made their mark, of whom the best known were Blanche Walshe (1873–1915), actress, and Henry Collins Walsh (1863–1927), explorer.

The ubiquity of the Walshes in Ireland is illustrated by the place names Walshtown, Walshpark etc., of which there are twenty-four in thirteen counties as far apart as Down, Mayo and Cork, while the name, in more Irish guise, as Ballybrannagh and Ballinabrannagh, appears in Counties Carlow, Down, Cork and Kerry.

Arms illustrated on Plate XXVII.

MacWARD, Ward.

Although Ward is a very common English name, the great majority of Irish Wards are native Irish in origin, the Gaelic form of the name being Mac an Bháird, which means son of the bard ; the pronunciation of these words is closely reproduced in the alternative form in English, viz. Macanward, also written MacAward and McWard. The Wards, as their name implies, were professional and hereditary bards, one family being thus attached to the O'Donnells of Tirconnel (Donegal) and another to the O'Kellys of Ui Máine (Hy Many) : the latter, whose territory was near Ballinasloe are perpetuated in the Co. Galway place-name Ballymacward, the former by Lettermacaward near Glenties. Ward is included in the list of the hundred commonest names in Ireland. Like so many old Gaelic families the Wards are still found chiefly in the territories of their origin, the birth indexes showing Counties Donegal and Galway as their present strongholds. The Wards of Co. Down, the head of which family is Viscount Bangor, are of English origin. The arms often ascribed to Irish Wards belong to the Bangors and do not appertain to the Gaelic Wards (MacWards).

Maelisa MacAward was bishop of his native see, Clonfert, 1171–1173, but most famous Irishmen of the name were from Ulster. Greatest of these was Hugh Boy Macanward (1580–1635), the historian, first professor of Theology in the Irish College at Louvain. He was born at Lettermacaward. Eight Macanwards of this Donegal sept were notable poets in the seventeenth century. A remarkable Irishman in the French army was General Thomas Ward (1749–1794) who, though he continued to serve under the Republic and had many years distinguished service to his credit, was guillotined. He was born in Dublin. John Ward (1832–1912), son of Marcus Ward the Belfast publisher, was an artist of note. Though he cannot be described as distinguished we may also mention another John Ward (1781–1837), an uneducated Corkman who achieved much notoriety in England as a mystic of very extreme views. The popular theatre in Dame Street, Dublin, in the first half of the eighteenth century was known as Ward's Theatre.

WOULFE.

The Woulfes, or Wolfes, are a family of Norman origin who first came to Ireland at the time of the invasion at the end of the twelfth century. In Irish the name is usually written de Bhulbh, but *le* would be more fitting than *de* since the Norman form is Le Woulf (the wolf). Though both influential and fairly numerous they never actually formed a sept on the Irish model, as did several of the Anglo-Norman invading families. From the beginning they settled in two widely separated areas. In Co. Kildare they became so well established that their territory near Athy, was known as Woulfe's Country ; the Wolfes of Forenaughts, Co. Kildare were still extensive landowners in that county and also in Co. Limerick in 1880. In modern times their homeland is in Co. Limerick, the second of their original settlements. They held extensive lands in the modern Counties Cork and Limerick, much of which was lost as a result of their participation in the Geraldine War towards the end of the sixteenth century. Two generations later they were identified with the resistance to Cromwell, two of the name being expressly exempted from pardon after the famous siege of Limerick in 1651. The name also occurs frequently in the records of that city up to that date. One of these, Capt. George Woulfe, was the great-great-grandfather of General James Wolfe (1727–1759), the hero of Quebec, who was thus of Irish (Limerick) descent. Distinguished Irishmen of the name have been numerous, including Rev. David Woulfe, S.J. (1523–1578), Papal Legate, whose description of Ireland written in 1574 is of great interest ; Father James Woulf, O.P., hanged after the Siege of Limerick in 1651 ; Peter Woulfe (1727–1803), mineralogist and inventor of Woulfe's bottle ; Stephen Woulfe (1787–1840), advocate of Catholic Emancipation but later an opponent of Daniel O'Connell—all of the Limerick branch, as was Father Patrick Woulfe (d. 1933), author of *Irish Names and Surnames*. Arthur Woulfe (1739–1803), killed in the Emmet Rising, John Woolfe (b. c. 1740), a notable architect, and Rev. Charles Wolfe (1791–1823), author of the well-known poem

" The Burial of Sir John Moore ", were all from Co. Kildare. Irish Woulfes were also prominent in France at the time of the French Revolution both as military officers and churchmen.

While it can be said that Irish Woulfes to-day are of the Norman stock dealt with above it should be mentioned that there is a surname Ulf, *anglice* Wolfe, which according to Professor Edmund Curtis is of Norse origin and pre-Anglo-Norman. There is also an indigenous Gaelic surname Ó Mactíre, belonging to East Cork, which was anglicized as Woulfe or Wolfe, *mactíre* being the Irish word for wolf. A bishop Oonahan Ó Mactire, probably of Cloyne, died in 1099, and another Mactíre also appears in the Four Masters as tanist of Teffia in 1025, but there appears to be no record of this name in its Gaelic form since early mediaeval times.

Arms illustrated on Plate XXVII.

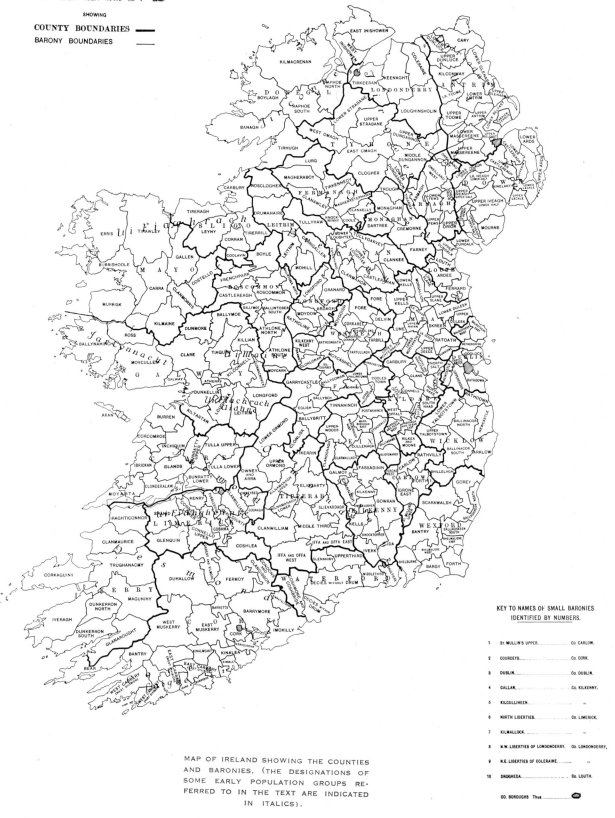

MAP OF IRELAND SHOWING THE COUNTIES
AND BARONIES. (THE DESIGNATIONS OF
SOME EARLY POPULATION GROUPS RE-
FERRED TO IN THE TEXT ARE INDICATED
IN ITALICS).

KEY TO NAMES OF SMALL BARONIES
IDENTIFIED BY NUMBERS.

1	ST. MULLIN'S UPPER	Co. CARLOW.
2	COURCEYS	Co. CORK.
3	DUBLIN	Co. DUBLIN.
4	CALLAN	Co. KILKENNY.
5	KILCULLIHEEN	"
6	NORTH LIBERTIES	Co. LIMERICK.
7	KILMALLOCK	"
8	N.W. LIBERTIES OF LONDONDERRY	Co. LONDONDERRY.
9	N.E. LIBERTIES OF COLERAINE	"
10	DROGHEDA	Co. LOUTH.

CO. BOROUGHS Thus

AHERNE

Vert, three herons argent.

Crest: A pelican in her piety proper.

MacAULIFFE

Argent three mermaids with combs and mirrors in fess azure between as many mullets of the last.

Crest: A boar's head couped or.

MacAWLEY

Argent a lion rampant gules armed and langued azure in chief two dexter hands couped at the wrist of the second.

Crest: A demi-lion rampant gules.

BARRETT

(Of Barretts Country, Co. Cork)

Barry of ten per pale argent and gules counterchanged.

Crest: A demi-lion rampant sable ducally crowned per pale argent and gules.

BARRY

Argent 3 bars gemels gules.

O'BEIRNE

Argent an orange tree eradicated and fructed proper, in base a lizard vert, in the dexter base point a saltire couped gules, on a chief azure the sun in his splendour or and a crescent of the first.

Crest: A dexter arm in armour embowed the hand grasping a sword all proper.

BLAKE

Argent a fret gules.

Crest: A leopard passant proper.

O'BOLAND

Argent a lion passant gules langued and armed azure, on a chief or an eagle displayed of the third.

Crest: A demi-lion rampant argent.

O'BOYLAN

Argent an eagle displayed sable armed or.

The blazons for arms depicted on Plate I (opposite)

AHERNE

Per ardua surgo

MacAULIFFE

MacAWLEY

BARRETT
(of Barrett's Country, Co. Cork)

BARRY

O'BEIRNE

BLAKE

O'BOLAND

O'BOYLAN

Plate I

O'BOYLE

Or an oaktree eradicated vert.

Crest: A sword point upwards proper and a passion cross or in saltire surmounted of a heart gules.

MacBRADY

Sable, in the sinister base a dexter hand couped at the wrist proper pointing with index finger to the sun in splendour in dexter chief or.

O'BRENNAN

(*Connacht*)

Argent a lion rampant azure, in chief two dexter hands couped at the wrist apaumée gules.

Crest: Out of a ducal coronet or a plume of five ostrich feathers alternately azure and or.

O'BRENNAN

(*Ossory*)

Gules two lions rampant combatant supporting a garb all or; in chief three swords two in saltire points upwards and one in fess point to the dexter, pommels and hilts of the second.

Crest: An arm embowed in armour grasping a sword all proper.

O'BRIEN

Gules three lions passant guardant in pale per pale or and argent.

O'BRODER

Per pale gules and sable, on a fess between three griffins' heads erased or as many lozenges ermines.

Crest: A demi-greyhound sable holding in the paws a dart gules feathered argent.

BROWNE

(*Galway*)

Or an eagle displayed with two heads sable.

BURKE

Or a cross gules, in the dexter canton a lion rampant sable.

Crest: A cat-a-mountain sejant guardant proper collared and chained or.

BUTLER

Quarterly: 1st and 4th, Or a chief indented azure; 2nd and 3rd, Gules three covered cups or.

Crest: Out of a ducal coronet or a plume of five ostrich feathers argent, therefrom issuant a falcon rising of the last.

The blazons for arms depicted on Plate II (opposite)

O'BOYLE

MacBRADY

O'BRENNAN
(*Connacht*)

O'BRENNAN
(*Ossory*)

O'BRIEN

O'BRODER

BROWNE

BURKE

BUTLER

Plate II

O'BYRNE

Gules a chevron between three dexter hands couped at the wrist argent.

Crest: A mermaid with comb and mirror proper.

MacCABE

Vert a fess wavy between three salmon naiant argent.

Crest: A demi-griffin segreant.

O'CAHILL

(*Munster*)

Argent a whale spouting in the sea proper.

Crest: An anchor erect cable twined around the stock all proper.

O'CALLAGHAN

Argent in base a mount vert on the dexter side a hurst of oak trees issuant therefrom a wolf passant towards the sinister all proper.

MacCANN

Azure fretty or, on a fess argent a boar passant gules.

Crest: A salmon naiant proper.

O'CARROLL

(*Ely*)

Sable two lions rampant combatant or armed and langued gules supporting a sword point upwards proper pommel and hilt of the first.

MacCARTAN

Vert a lion rampant or, on a chief argent a crescent between two dexter hands couped at the wrist gules.

Crest: A lance erect or headed argent entwined with a snake descending vert.

MacCARTHY

Argent a stag trippant gules attired and unguled or.

O'CASEY

Argent a chevron between three eagles heads erased gules.

The blazons for arms depicted on Plate III (opposite)

O'BYRNE

MacCABE

O'CAHILL
(*Munster*)

O'CALLAGHAN

MacCANN

O'CARROLL
(*Ely*)

MacCARTAN

MacCARTHY

O'CASEY

Plate III

O'CASSIDY

Per chevron argent and gules, in chief two lions rampant and in base a boar passant both counterchanged.

Crest: A spear broken into three pieces two in saltire and the head in pale proper banded gules.

MacCLANCY

Argent two lions passant guardant in pale gules. *Crest:* A dexter hand couped at the wrist erect holding a sword in pale pierced through a boar's head couped all proper.

O'CLERY
(*Aidhne*)

Or three nettle leaves vert.

O'COFFEY
(*Co. Cork*)

Vert a fess ermine between three Irish cups or.
Crest: A man riding on a dolphin proper.

MacCOGHLAN

Argent three lions passant guardant gules crowned or.

MacCOLGAN

Azure a lion rampant or between three pheons points down argent.

O'CONCANNON

Argent on a mount in base proper an oak tree vert, perched on the top thereof a falcon proper, two crosses crosslet fitchée in fess azure.

Crest: An elephant sable tusked or.

CONDON

Argent a lion rampant gules langued and armed azure.

O'CONNELL

Per fess argent and vert a stag trippant proper between three trefoils slipped counterchanged.

The blazons for arms depicted on Plate IV (opposite)

O'CASSIDY

Frangas non flectes

MacCLANCY

O'CLERY
(*Aidhne*)

O'COFFEY
(*Co. Cork*)

MacCOGHLAN

MacCOLGAN

O'CONCANNON

Con can an

CONDON

O'CONNELL

Plate IV

O'CONNOR DON

Argent an oak tree vert.

Crest: An arm embowed in armour holding a short sword entwined with a serpent all proper.

O'CONNOR FALY

Argent on a mount in base vert an oak tree acorned proper.

O'CONNOR KERRY

Vert a lion rampant double queued and crowned or.

Crest: A dexter arm embowed in mail proper garnished or the hand grasping a sword erect proper.

O'CONNOR SLIGO

Per pale vert and argent, in the dexter a lion rampant to the sinister or, in the sinister on a mount in base vert an oak tree proper.

Crest: An arm in armour embowed, holding a sword all proper.

O'CONNOR
(*of Corcomroe*)

Vert a stag trippant argent.

Crest: A hand in a gauntlet erect holding a broken dart all proper.

O'CONNOLLY
(*Co. Kildare*)

Argent on a saltire sable five escallops of the field.

O'CONRY
(*Offaly*)

Quarterly: 1st, Vert three goats passant argent; 2nd, Argent a lion rampant gules; 3rd, Gules three escallops argent; 4th, Vert a cock statant proper.

Crest: A blackamoor's head in profile couped at the shoulders sable and bound round the temples with a ribbon argent.

CONROY
(O'MULCONRY)

Azure an ancient book open indexed edged or, a chief embattled of the last.

Crest: A dexter arm vested or cuffed ermine grasping a wreath of laurel proper.

MacCONSIDINE

Per pale sable and gules, three lions passant guardant in pale per pale or and argent armed azure.

The blazons for arms depicted on Plate V (opposite)

O'CONNOR DON

O'CONNOR FALY

O'CONNOR KERRY

O'CONNOR SLIGO

O'CONNOR
(*of Corcomroe*)

O'CONOLLY
(*Co. Kildare*)

O'CONRY
(*Offaly*)

CONROY (O'MULCONRY)

MacCONSIDINE

Plate V

O'CORRIGAN

Or a chevron between two trefoils slipt in chief and in base a lizard passant vert.
Crest: Two battle axes in saltire in front of a sword proper point downwards pommel and hilt or.

MacCOSTELLO

Or three fusils azure.
Crest: A falcon proper belled and jessed or.

MacCOTTER

Azure three evetts in pale proper.
Crest: A lion passant reguardant proper.

CREAGH

Argent a chevron gules between three laurel branches vert, on a chief azure as many bezants.
Crest: A horse's head erased argent caparisoned gules in the headstall of the bridle a laurel branch vert.

O'CREAN

Argent a wolf rampant sable between three human hearts gules.
Crest: A demi-wolf rampant sable holding between the paws a human heart or.

O'CROWLEY

Argent a boar passant azure between three crosses crosslet gules.

O'CULLANE
(COLLINS)

Argent two lions rampant combatant proper.
Crest: A pelican vulning herself wings elevated proper.

O'CULLEN
(*Leinster*)

Gules on a chevron between three dexter hands erect couped at the wrist argent a garb of the first between two trefoils slipt vert.
Crest: A mermaid with comb and mirror all proper.

O'CULLINAN

Argent a stag springing gules attired and unguled vert, in base a dexter hand appaumée couped at the wrist proper.

The blazons for arms depicted on Plate VI (opposite)

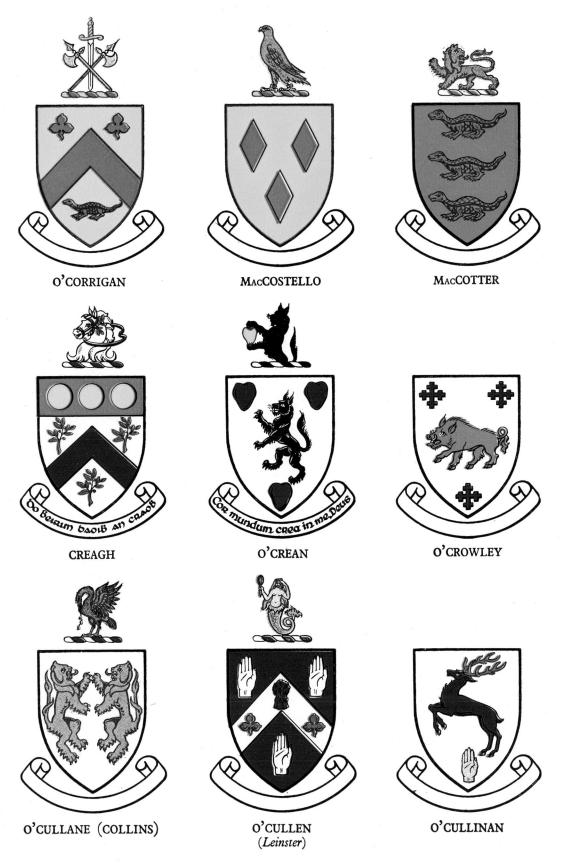

O'CORRIGAN

MacCOSTELLO

MacCOTTER

CREAGH

O'CREAN

O'CROWLEY

O'CULLANE (COLLINS)

O'CULLEN
(*Leinster*)

O'CULLINAN

Plate VI

MacCURTIN

Vert in front of a lance in pale or a stag trippant argent attired or between three crosses crosslet or, two and one, and as many trefoils slipt argent one and two.

Crest: In front of two lances in saltire argent headed or an Irish harp sable.

CUSACK

Per pale or and azure, a fess counterchanged.

DALTON

Azure a lion rampant guardant argent charged on the shoulder with a crescent sable between five fleur-de-lis or.

O'DALY

Per fess argent and or a lion rampant per fess sable and gules, in chief two dexter hands couped at the wrist of the last.

DARCY

(Galway)

Azure semée of crosses crosslet and three cinquefoils argent.

Crest: On a chapeau gules turned up ermine a bull sable armed or.

O'DAVOREN

Argent a sword erect in pale distilling drops of blood proper pommel and hilt or.

Crest: A hind statant proper.

O'DEA

Argent a dexter hand lying fessways couped at the wrist cuffed indented azure holding a sword in pale all proper, in chief two snakes embowed vert.

O'DEMPSEY

Gules a lion rampant argent, armed and langued azure between two swords points upwards of the second pommels and hilts or one in bend dexter the other in bend sinister.

MacDERMOT

Argent on a chevron gules between three boars' heads erased azure tusked and bristled or as many cross crosslets of the last.

Crest: A demi-lion rampant azure holding in the dexter paw a sceptre crowned or.

Motto over: Honor et virtus.

The blazons for arms depicted on Plate VII (opposite)

MacCURTIN

CUSACK

DALTON

O'DALY

DARCY
(*Galway*)

O'DAVOREN

O'DEA

O'DEMPSEY

MacDERMOT

Plate VII

DILLON

Argent a lion passant between three crescents gules.

Crest: A demi-lion rampant gules holding in the paws an estoile wavy or.

O'DINNEEN

Azure two swords in saltire points upwards argent pommels and hilts or between four roses or.

Crest: A stag's head proper.

O'DOHERTY

Argent a stag springing gules, on a chief vert three mullets of the first.

MacDONLEVY

Argent on a mount in base proper a lion gules and a buck of the second rampant combatant supporting a dexter hand couped at the wrist of the third.

Crest: A lion rampant gules.

MacDONNELL
(*Clare and Connacht*)

Azure an ancient galley sails set and flags flying argent between in chief a cross calvary in three grieces or, between in the dexter an increscent of the second and in the sinister a dexter hand couped at the wrist appaumée proper and in base a salmon naiant of the second.

Crest: A unicorn passant gules.

MacDONNELL
(*of the Glens*)

Quarterly: 1st, Or a lion rampant gules; 2nd, Or a dexter arm issuant from the sinister fess point out of a cloud proper, in the hand a cross crosslet fitchée erect azure; 3rd, Argent a lymphad sails furled sable; 4th, Per fess azure and vert a dolphin naiant proper.

Crest: A dexter arm embowed fesswise couped at the shoulder vested or cuffed argent holding in the hand proper a cross crosslet fitchée erect azure.

O'DONNELL

Or issuing from the sinister side of the shield an arm fessways vested azure cuffed argent holding in the hand proper a passion cross gules.

O'DONNELLAN

Argent an oak tree eradicated proper, on the sinister side a slave sable chained to the stem gules.

Crest: On a mount proper a lion rampant or.

O'DONNELLY

Argent two lions rampant combatant supporting a dexter hand couped apaumée gules, in base the sea therein a salmon naiant proper.

The blazons for arms depicted on Plate VIII (opposite)

DILLON

O'DINNEEN

O'DOHERTY
AR nDÚṫċAS

MacDONLEVY

MacDONNELL
(*Clare and Connacht*)
His vinces

MacDONNELL
(*of the Glens*)

O'DONNELL

O'DONNELLAN
Omni violentia major

O'DONNELLY

Plate VIII

MacDONOGH

(*Connacht*)

Per chevron invected or and vert, in chief two lions passant guardant gules in base a boar passant argent armed and bristled of the first langued of the third.

Crest: A dexter arm erect couped at the elbow vested azure cuffed argent holding in the hand a sword erect entwined with a lizard all proper.

O'DONOGHUE

Vert two foxes rampant combatant argent, on a chief of the last an eagle volant sable.

Crest: An arm in armour embowed holding a sword the blade entwined with a serpent all proper.

O'DONOVAN

Argent issuing from the sinister side of the shield a cubit dexter arm vested gules cuffed of the first the hand grasping a scian in pale the blade entwined with a serpent all proper.

Crest: A falcon alighting or.

O'DORAN

Per pale sable and argent a boar passant counterchanged, on a chief azure three mullets of the second.

Crest: Out of a ducal coronet or a lion's head proper.

O'DOWD

Vert a saltire or, in chief two swords in saltire points upwards the dexter surmounted of the sinister argent pommels and hilts or.

O'DOWLING

Argent a holly tree eradicated proper, on a chief azure a lion passant between two trefoils slipt or.

Crest: A lion's head erased azure collared gemelles or.

DOYLE

(*Co. Wicklow*)

Argent three bucks' heads erased gules attired or, within a border compony counter compony or and azure.

Crest: A buck's head couped gules attired argent ducally gorged or.

O'DRISCOLL

Argent an ancient galley sails furled sable.

Crest: A cormorant proper.

O'DUGGAN

Azure a decrescent argent between nine estoiles of eight points or.

Crest: A demi-lion rampant or langued and armed gules.

The blazons for arms depicted on Plate IX (opposite)

MacDONOGH
(*Connacht*)

O'DONOGHUE

O'DONOVAN

O'DORAN

O'DOWD

O'DOWLING

DOYLE
(*Co. Wicklow*)

O'DRISCOLL

O'DUGGAN

Plate IX

O'DUNN

Azure an eagle displayed or.

Crest: In front of a holly bush proper a lizard passant or.

O'DWYER

Argent a lion rampant gules between three ermine spots.

Crest: A hand couped at the wrist and erect grasping a sword all proper.

MacEGAN

Quarterly: 1st, Gules a tower argent supported on either side by a man in complete armour each holding in the interior hand a battle-axe all proper, in chief a snake fessways or; 2nd and 3rd, Or on a bend vert three plates; 4th, As first quarter but on the tower a swan proper.

Crest: A tower argent issuant from the top a demi-man in armour couped at the knees holding in the dexter hand a battle-axe all proper.

MacENCHROE
(CROWE)

Argent on a mount vert an oak tree proper, a canton gules charged with an antique Irish crown or.

Crest: On a mount vert an Irish wolfhound argent collared gules.

MacENIRY

Argent an eagle displayed vert.

Crest: A falcon close belled proper.

MacEvoy

Per fess azure and per pale or and ermine a fess gules issuant therefrom a demi-lion argent, in the dexter base a dexter hand couped at the wrist of the fourth.

Crest: A cubit arm erect proper vested gules cuffed erminois in the hand a sword proper.

FAGAN

Per chevron gules and ermine, in chief three covered cups or.

Crest: A griffin argent winged and tufted or supporting in the talons an olive branch vert fructed or.

O'FAHY

Azure a hand couped at the wrist fessways in chief proper holding a sword paleways argent pommel and hilt or point downwards pierced through a boar's head erased of the last.

Crest: A naked arm erect couped below the elbow holding a broken spear all proper point downwards or.

O'FALLON

Gules a greyhound rampant argent holding between the forepaws a tilting spear point to the dexter or.

Crest: A demi-greyhound salient argent.

The blazons for arms depicted on Plate X (opposite)

O'DUNN

O'DWYER

MacEGAN

MacENCHROE (CROWE)

MacENIRY

MacEVOY

FAGAN

O'FAHY

O'FALLON

Plate X

O'FARRELL

Vert a lion rampant or.
Crest: On a ducal coronet
or a greyhound springing
sable.

O'FINNEGAN

Gules two lions rampant
c o m b a t a n t argent
supporting a sword in
pale blade wavy point
upwards proper.
Crest: A falcon alighting
proper.

FITZGERALD

Argent a saltire gules.

FITZGIBBON

Ermine a saltire gules,
on a chief argent three
annulets of the second.
Crest: A boar passant
gules charged on the
body with three annu-
lets fessways argent.

FITZPATRICK

Sable a saltire argent,
on a chief azure three
fleur-de-lis or.
Crest: A dragon reguar-
dant vert surmounted
of a lion guardant sable
dexter paw resting on
the dragon's head.

O'FLAHERTY

Argent two lions ram-
pant combatant support-
ing a dexter hand couped
at the wrist all gules, in
base a boat with eight
oars sable.

O'FLANAGAN

Argent out of a mount
in base vert an oak tree
proper, a border of the
second.
Crest: A dexter cubit
arm in armour proper
garnished or and gules
holding a flaming sword
azure pommel and hilt
of the second.

FLEMING

Vair a chief chequy or
and gules.

O'FLYNN

Azure a wolf passant
argent, in chief three
bezants.
Crest: A dexter hand
erect couped holding a
serpent tail embowed
head to the sinister all
proper.

The blazons for arms depicted on Plate XI (opposite)

O'FARRELL

O'FINNEGAN

FITZGERALD

FITZGIBBON

FITZPATRICK

O'FLAHERTY

O'FLANAGAN

FLEMING

O'FLYNN

Plate XI

O'FOGARTY

Azure two lions rampant combatant supporting a garb all or, in dexter base a crescent argent, in sinister base a harp of second stringed of the third.

FOX

Argent a lion rampant and in chief two dexter hands couped at the wrist gules.

Crest: An arm embowed in armour holding a sword all proper.

FRENCH

(*Galway*)

Ermine a chevron sable.
Crest: A dolphin embowed proper.

O'FRIEL

Gules in dexter fess a garb or, in sinister fess a dexter hand couped at the wrist fessways proper grasping a cross calvary on three grieces argent, in chief three mullets of the second.

Crest: A garb or.

O'GALLAGHER

Argent a lion rampant sable treading on a serpent in fess proper between eight trefoils vert.

Crest: A crescent gules out of the horns a serpent erect proper.

O'GALVIN

Gules three salmon haurient argent.

O'GARA

Argent three lions rampant azure, on a chief gules a demi-lion rampant or.

Crest: A demi-lion rampant ermine holding between the paws a wreath of oak vert acorned or.

MacGARRY

Argent a lion rampant between four trefoils slipt vert, in chief a lizard passant vert.

Crest: A fox's head couped gules holding in the mouth a snake proper.

O'GARVEY

Ermine two chevronels between three crosses pattée gules.

Crest: A lion passant guardant gules.

The blazons for arms depicted on Plate XII (opposite)

O'FOGARTY

FOX

FRENCH
(*Galway*)

O'FRIEL

O'GALLAGHER

O'GALVIN

O'GARA

MacGARRY

O'GARVEY

Plate XII

MacGENIS

Vert a lion rampant or, on a chief argent a dexter hand erect couped at the wrist gules.

MacGEOGHEGAN

Argent a lion rampant between three dexter hands couped at the wrist gules.

Crest: A greyhound passant or.

MacGERAGHTY

Argent on a mount vert an oak tree proper, in chief two falcons volant gules.

Crest: On a mount vert an oak tree proper bent towards the dexter.

MacGILFOYLE

Azure two bars argent.

Crest: A demi-lion rampant argent holding between the paws a battle-axe erect gules blade of the first.

MacGILLYCUDDY

Gules a wyvern or.

Crest: MacGillycuddy's Reeks proper.

MacGORMAN

Azure a lion passant between three swords erect argent.

Crest: An arm embowed in armour grasping in the hand a sword, blade wavy, all proper.

O'GORMLEY

Or, three martlets gules, two and one.

MacGOVERN (MAGAURAN)

Azure a lion passant or, in chief three crescents of the last.

O'GRADY

Per pale gules and sable three lions passant per pale argent and or.

Crest: A horse's head erased argent.

The blazons for arms depicted on Plate XIII (opposite)

MacGENIS

MacGEOGHEGAN

MacGERAGHTY

MacGILFOYLE

MacGILLYCUDDY

Sursum corda

MacGORMAN

Cosac cača a's deine air

O'GORMLEY

MacGOVERN (MAGAURAN)

O'GRADY

Vulneratus non victus

Plate XIII

MacGRATH

Quarterly: 1st, Argent three lions passant gules; 2nd, Or, a dexter hand lying fessways couped at the wrist proper holding a cross formée fitchée azure; 3rd, Gules a dexter hand lying fessways couped at the wrist proper holding a battle-axe or; 4th, Argent an antelope trippant sable attired or.

O'GRIFFY (GRIFFIN)

Sable a griffin segreant or, langued and armed gules.

MacGUIRE

Vert a white horse fully caparisoned thereon a knight in complete armour on his helmet a plume of ostrich feathers his right hand brandishing a sword all proper.

HACKETT

(Co. Carlow and Co. Tipperary)

Azure three hake fishes haurient in fess argent, on a chief of the second three shamrocks proper.

O'HAGAN

Quarterly, argent and azure, in 1st quarter, a shoe proper, on a canton per chevron gules and ermine three covered cups or; in 2nd quarter, a flag of the first charged with a dexter hand of fourth; in 3rd quarter, a lion rampant of the sixth; and in 4th quarter, a fish naiant proper.

Crest: A cubit arm proper vested gules cuffed ermine the hand holding a dagger erect both proper.

O'HALLORAN

Gules a horse passant argent saddled and bridled proper, on a chief of the second three martlets azure.

Crest: A lizard or.

O'HANLON

Vert on a mount in base proper a boar passant ermine.

Crest: A lizard displayed vert.

O'HANLY

Vert a boar passant argent armed hoofed and bristled or, between two arrows barways of the second headed of the third, that in chief pointing to the dexter and that in base to the sinister.

Crest: Three arrows sable flighted argent pointed or one in pale the other two barways.

O'HANNON

Quarterly gules and or on a bend sable three crosses pattée argent.

The blazons for arms depicted on Plate XIV (opposite)

MacGRATH

O'GRIFFY (GRIFFIN)

MacGUIRE

HACKETT
(*Co. Carlow and Co. Tipperary*)

O'HAGAN

O'HALLORAN

O'HANLON

O'HANLY

O'HANNON

Plate XIV

O'HANRAGHTY

Azure a griffin passant wings elevated or.

Crest: On a helmet in profile visor closed a dolphin n a i a n t all proper.

O'HARA

Vert on a pale radiant or a lion rampant sable.

O'HART

Gules a lion passant guardant or, in base a human heart argent.

Crest: A naked arm couped below the elbow and erect grasping a s w o r d flammant all proper.

O'HARTAGAN

Azure a lion rampant or holding in each fore-paw a dagger argent pommels and hilts of the second.

Crest: A gauntlet erect grasping a sword proper pommel and hilt or.

O'HEA

Argent a dexter arm lying fessways couped below the elbow vested gules turned up of the first grasping in the hand a sword in pale entwined with a serpent descending all proper.

O'HEFFERNAN

Per fess vert and gules, on a fess or a lion passant guardant azure, in chief three crescents or.

Crest: A cubit arm erect in armour the hand gauntleted and holding a broken sword proper.

O'HEGARTY

A r g e n t an oaktree eradicated proper, on a chief gules three birds of the first beaked and legged sable.

Crest: An arm in armour embowed the h a n d grasping a scymitar all proper.

O'HENNESSY

Vert a stag trippant a r g e n t between six arrows two two and two saltireways or.

Crest: Between t h e attires of a stag affixed to the scalp or an arrow point downwards gules headed and flighted argent.

O'HEYNE
(HYNES)

Per pale indented or and gules two lions rampant combatant c o u n t e r-changed.

Crest: A dexter arm armed embowed the hand grasping a sword all proper.

The blazons for arms depicted on Plate XV (opposite)

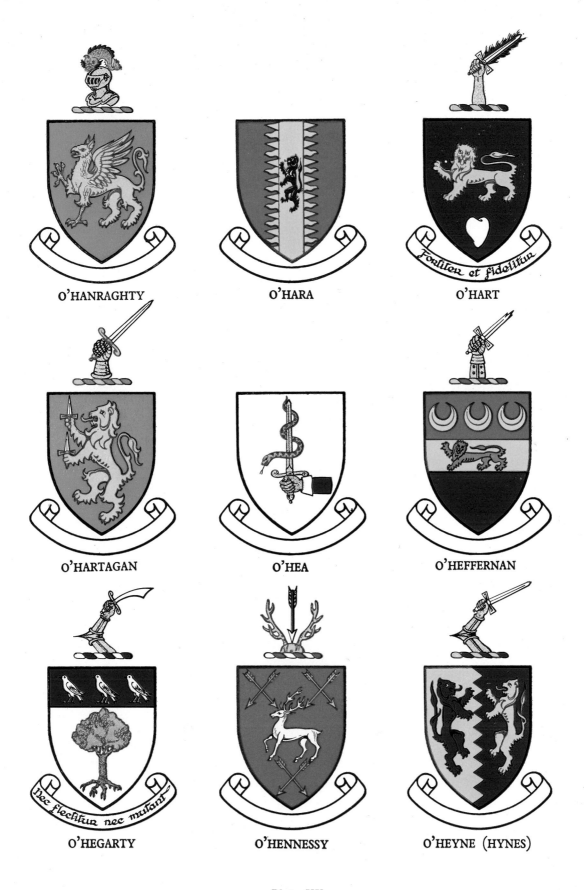

O'HANRAGHTY

O'HARA

O'HART

Fortiter et fideliter

O'HARTAGAN

O'HEA

O'HEFFERNAN

Nec flectitur nec mutant

O'HEGARTY

O'HENNESSY

O'HEYNE (HYNES)

Plate XV

O'HICKEY

Azure a lion passant guardant or, on a chief ermine a bend sable.

Crest: A hand in a gauntlet erect holding a baton all proper.

O'HIGGIN

Argent guttée de poix on a fess sable three towers of the first.

Crest: A tower sable issuant from the battlements a demi-griffin wings elevated argent holding in the dexter claw a sword proper.

O'HOGAN

Sable on a chief or three annulets of the field.

O'HOLOHAN

Azure a tower or supported by two lions rampant argent, in base two crescents of the last, on a chief of the third three annulets gules.

O'HORAN

Vert three lions rampant two and one or.

Crest: A demi-lion rampant or.

MacHUGH
(*Co. Galway*)

Argent a saltire vert between a dexter hand couped at the wrist in chief gules, two trefoils slipt of the second in fess and a boat with oars proper in base.

O'HURLEY

Argent on a cross gules five frets or.

MacINERNEY

Argent three lions passant in pale gules armed and langued azure.

Crest: A mermaid proper.

JORDAN
(MacSURTAIN)

Argent a fess sable, in base a lion passant of the last.

The blazons for arms depicted on Plate XVI (opposite)

O'HICKEY   O'HIGGIN   O'HOGAN

O'HOLOHAN   O'HORAN   MacHUGH
(Co. Galway)

O'HURLEY   MacINERNEY   JORDAN (MacSURTAIN)

Plate XVI

JOYCE

Argent an eagle with two heads displayed gules, over all a fess ermine.

Crest: A demi-wolf argent ducally gorged or.

KAVANAGH

Argent a lion passant gules, in base two crescents of the last.

KEANE
(O'CAHAN)

Azure on a fess per pale gules and argent between in chief out of the horns of a crescent a dexter hand couped at the wrist and apaumée surmounted by an estoile between on the dexter a horse counter-saliant and on the sinister a lion rampant each also surmounted by an estoile, and in base a salmon naiant all argent, on the dexter side three lizards passant in bend sinisterways argent and on the sinister an oak tree eradicated vert, over all an escutcheon argent charged with a cross calvary on three grieces proper.

Crest: A cat-a-mountain rampant proper.

O'KEARNEY

Argent three lions rampant gules, on a chief azure between t w o pheons of the first a gauntletted hand fessways or holding a dagger erect proper pommel and hilt or.

Crest: A gauntletted hand holding a dagger as in the Arms.

KEATING

Argent a saltire gules between four nettle leaves vert.

Crest: A boar statant gules armed and hoofed or holding in the mouth a nettle leaf vert.

O'KEEFFE

Vert a lion rampant or, in chief two dexter hands couped at the wrist erect and apaumée of the last.

Crest: A griffin passant or holding in the dexter claw a sword proper.

O'KELLY
(*Ui Máine*)

Azure a tower triple-towered supported by two lions rampant argent, as many chains descending from the battlements between the lions' legs or.

Crest: On a ducal coronet or an enfield vert.

MacKENNA

Vert a fess argent between three lions' heads affrontée or.

Crest: A salmon naiant proper.

O'KENNEDY

Sable three helmets in profile proper.

Crest: An arm embowed vested azure holding a scymitar all proper.

The blazons for arms depicted on Plate XVII (opposite)

JOYCE

KAVANAGH

KEANE (O'CAHAN)

Felis demulcta mitis

O'KEARNEY

KEATING

O'KEEFFE

Turris fortis mihi Deus

O'KELLY
(*Uí Máine*)

MacKENNA

O'KENNEDY

Plate XVII

MacKEOGH
(*Connacht*)

Argent a lion rampant gules, in the dexter chief a dexter hand couped at the wrist and in the sinister a crescent both of the second.

Crest: A boar passant azure.

MacKEOWN

Argent two lions rampant combatant sable supporting a dexter hand couped at the wrist gules, in chief four mullets of eight points gules, in base waves of the sea therein a salmon naiant all proper.

Crest: An arm embowed in chain armour the hand holding a sword blade wavy all proper.

O'KIERAN
(*Thomond*)

Vert on a c h e v r o n argent three leopards' faces gules.

Crest: A demi-lion rampant sable holding in the dexter paw a sword erect argent pommel and hilt or.

O'KINNEALLY
(*Munster*)

Gules a stag statant argent.

KINSELLA

Argent a fess gules between in chief two garbs of the last and in base a lion passant sable.

O'KIRWAN

Argent a chevron sable between three Cornish choughs proper.

Crest: A Cornish chough proper.

LACY
(DE LACY)

Or a lion rampant purpure.

LALLY
(O'MULLALLY) .

Argent three eagles displayed gules two and one each holding in the beak a sprig of laurel proper between as many crescents, one and two, azure.

Crest: An eagle as in the Arms.

O'LALOR

Or a lion rampant guardant gules.

The blazons for arms depicted on Plate XVIII (opposite)

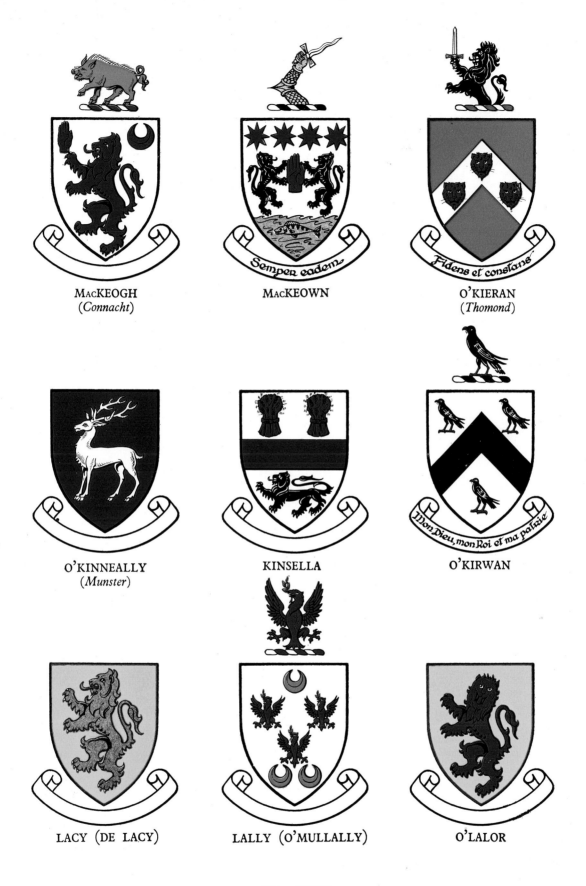

MacKEOGH
(*Connacht*)

MacKEOWN

O'KIERAN
(*Thomond*)

O'KINNEALLY
(*Munster*)

KINSELLA

O'KIRWAN

LACY (DE LACY)

LALLY (O'MULLALLY)

O'LALOR

Plate XVIII

O'LEARY

Argent a lion passant in base gules, in chief a ship of three masts sable sails set proper from the stern the flag of St. George flotant.

Crest: Out of a ducal coronet or an arm in armour embowed holding a sword proper pommel and hilt or.

O'LONERGAN

Argent on a chevron azure three estoiles or, in chief two arrows in saltire points downwards gules.

Crest: An arrow in pale point downwards distilling drops of blood all proper.

O'LOUGHLIN

Gules a man in complete armour facing the sinister shooting an arrow from a bow all proper.

Crest: An anchor entwined with a cable proper.

MacLOUGHLIN

(formerly O'Melaghlin)

Per fess, the chief two coats; 1st, Argent three dexter hands couped at the wrist gules; 2nd, Argent a lion rampant gules armed and langued azure; the base wavy azure and argent a salmon naiant proper.

MacLOUGHLIN

(Tirconnell)

Per fess azure and gules, in chief a lion rampant or between two swords erect argent pommels and hilts or, in base three crescents argent.

LYNCH

(Galway)

Azure a chevron between three trefoils slipt or.

Crest: A lynx passant azure collared or.

MacLYSAGHT

Argent three spears erect in fess gules, on a chief azure a lion passant guardant or.

Crest: Issuant from clouds a naked arm bent holding a short sword by the blade all proper.

O'MADDEN

Sable a falcon volant seizing a mallard argent.

MacMAHON

(Oriel)

Argent an ostrich sable holding in the beak a horse shoe or.

Crest: A naked arm embowed holding a sword all proper the point pierced through a fleur-de-lis sable.

The blazons for arms depicted on Plate XIX (opposite)

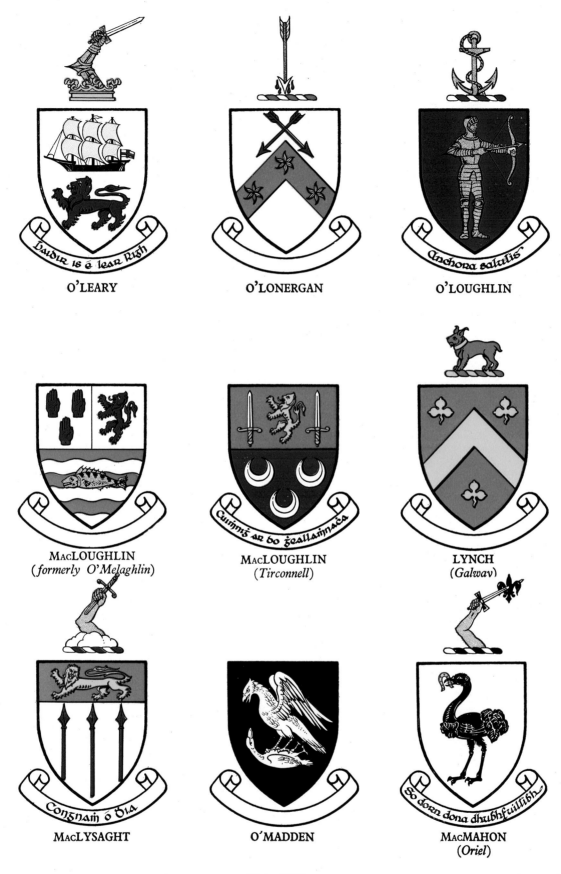

O'LEARY

O'LONERGAN

O'LOUGHLIN

MacLOUGHLIN
(*formerly O'Melaghlin*)

MacLOUGHLIN
(*Tirconnell*)

LYNCH
(*Galway*)

MacLYSAGHT

O'MADDEN

MacMAHON
(*Oriel*)

Plate XIX

MacMAHON

(*Thomond*)

Argent three lions passant reguardant in pale gules armed and langued azure.

Crest: A dexter arm in armour embowed proper garnished or holding in the hand a sword both proper pommel and hilt or.

O'MAHONY

Quarterly: 1st and 4th, Or a lion rampant azure; 2nd, Per pale argent and gules a lion rampant counterchanged; 3rd, Argent a chevron gules between three snakes tongued proper.

Crest : Out of a viscount's coronet or an arm in armour embowed holding a sword proper pommel and hilt or pierced through a fleur-de-lis azure.

O'MALLEY

Or a boar passant gules.

Crest: A ship with three masts sails set all proper.

O'MALONE

Vert a lion rampant or between three mullets argent.

Crest: A man in complete armour in the dexter hand a spear resting on the ground all proper.

MANNIX

(O'MANNIS)

Vert a griffin segreant wings elevated or, in chief three crescents argent.

Crest: A hand couped at the wrist elevated proper, holding a long cross gules.

MacMANUS

(*Fermanagh*)

Vert a griffin segreant or, in chief three crescents argent.

Crest: A hand and arm couped below the elbow erect holding a long cross proper.

MARTIN

(*Galway*)

Azure a cross calvary on three grieces argent, the dexter arm terminating in a sun in splendour or, the sinister in a decrescent argent.
Crest: An estoile or.

O'MEAGHER

Azure two lions rampant combatant or supporting a sword argent pommel and hilt of the second, in base two crescents of the third.

Crest: A falcon argent belled or.

O'MEARA

Gules three lions passant guardant in pale per pale or and argent, a border azure charged with eight escallops argent.

Crest: A pelican vulning herself proper.

The blazons for arms depicted on Plate XX (opposite)

MacMAHON
(*Thomond*)

O'MAHONY

O'MALLEY

O'MALONE

MANNIX (O'MANNIS)

MacMANUS
(*Fermanagh*)

MARTIN
(*Galway*)

O'MEAGHER

O'MEARA

Plate XX

O'MEEHAN

Gules on a chevron argent three bucks' heads erased of the field attired or, in base a demi-lion rampant argent.

Crest: A griffin's head erased wings endorsed or.

O'MOLLOY

Argent a lion rampant sable between three trefoils slipt gules.

Crest: In front of an oak tree growing out of a mount all proper a greyhound springing sable collared or.

O'MOLONY

Azure, on the dexter side a quiver of three arrows, on the sinister a bow erect all or.

O'MONAHAN

Azure a chevron between three mullets or.

Crest: A knight in complete armour resting the sinister hand on the hip and holding in the dexter a tilting spear thereon a forked pennon argent charged with an escutcheon of the Arms.

O'MOONEY

Argent a holly tree eradicated vert thereon a lizard passant or, a border compony counter compony of the first and second.

O'MORAN

Sable three stars rayed or.

Crest: A star rayed or.

O'MORE

Vert a lion rampant or, in chief three mullets of the last.

Crest: A dexter hand lying fessways couped at the wrist holding a sword in pale pierced through three gory heads all proper.

O'MORIARTY

Argent an eagle displayed sable.

Crest: An arm in armour embowed holding a sword fessways entwined with a serpent all proper.

O'MORONEY

Azure a chevron or between three boars' heads couped argent langued gules.

Crest: A boar's head couped argent, langued gules.

The blazons for arms depicted on Plate XXI (opposite)

O'MEEHAN

O'MOLLOY

O'MOLONY

O'MONAHAN

O'MOONEY

O'MORAN

O'MORE

O'MORIARTY

O'MORONEY

Plate XXI

MORRIS

(*Galway*)

Or a fess dancettée, in base a lion rampant sable.

Crest: A lion's head erased argent guttée de sang.

O'MULLAN

(*Connacht*)

Argent a dexter hand couped at the wrist in fess gules holding a dagger in pale proper between three crescents gules.

Crest: Out of a crescent gules a dagger erect proper.

O'MULVIHIL

Per fess argent and gules, in chief two lions rampant combatant azure supporting a dexter hand couped at the wrist gules and in base a salmon naiant proper, in base an Irish harp or stringed argent between two battle-axes proper.

Crest: A dexter arm couped below the elbow and erect holding two battle-axes in saltire proper.

O'MURPHY

(*Muskerry*)

Quarterly argent and gules, on a fess sable between four lions rampant counterchanged three garbs or.

MURPHY

(O'MORCHOE)

Argent an apple tree eradicated fructed proper, on a chief vert a lion passant or.

Crest: On a chapeau gules turned up ermine a lion rampant also gules holding between the paws a garb or. Motto over "Vincere vel mori".

MacMURROGH

Gules a lion rampant argent.

O'NAGHTEN

Quarterly: 1st and 4th, Gules, three falcons close proper; 2nd and 3rd, Vert three swords argent pommels and hilts or, one in pale point downwards the others in saltire points upwards.

Crest: A falcon close proper.

NAGLE

Ermine on a fess azure three lozenges or.

Crest: A nightingale or.

MacNALLY

Gules an arm in armour proper garnished or and embowed couped at the shoulder holding in the hand a battle-axe of the second between six martlets argent three and three palewise, in the centre chief point an ancient Irish crown or.

Crest: A naked arm couped at the elbow erect proper holding a dagger of the first hilt and pommel or.

The blazons for arms depicted on Plate XXII (opposite)

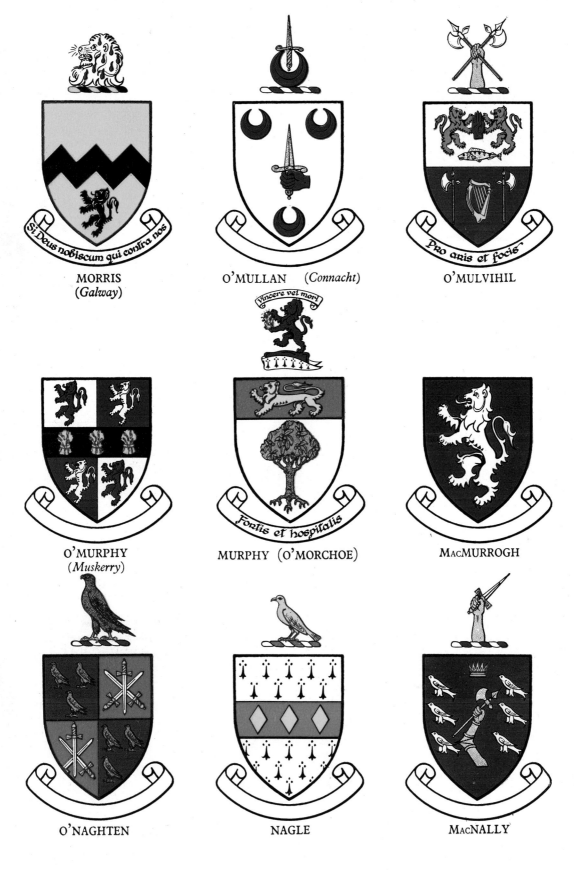

MORRIS
(*Galway*)

O'MULLAN   (*Connacht*)

O'MULVIHIL

O'MURPHY
(*Muskerry*)

MURPHY (O'MORCHOE)

MacMURROGH

O'NAGHTEN

NAGLE

MacNALLY

Plate XXII

MacNAMARA

Gules a lion rampant argent, in chief two spearheads or.

O'NEILAN

Sable two unicorns passant in pale argent horned and hoofed or.

Crest: A dexter hand erect couped at the wrist grasping a dagger all proper.

O'NEILL

Argent two lions rampant combatant gules supporting a dexter hand couped at the wrist of the last, in chief three estoiles of the second, in base waves of the sea therein naiant a salmon all proper.

O'NOLAN

Argent on a cross gules a lion passant between four martlets of the first, in each quarter a sword erect of the second.

Crest: A martlet argent.

NUGENT

Ermine two bars gules.

O'PHELAN

Argent four lozenges in bend conjoined azure between two cotises of the last, on a chief gules three fleur-de-lis of the first.

Crest: A stag's head or.

PLUNKET(T)

Sable a bend argent, in the sinister chief a tower triple-towered of the second.

Crest: A horse passant argent.

POWER

Argent a chief indented sable.

PURCELL

(of *Loughmoe*)

Or a saltire between four boars' heads couped sable.

Crest: A cubit arm erect proper habited azure cuffed argent grasping a sword proper pommel and hilt or piercing through the jaw a boar's head couped sable vulned and distilling drops of blood.

The blazons for arms depicted on Plate XXIII (opposite)

MacNAMARA

O'NEILAN

O'NEILL

O'NOLAN

NUGENT

O'PHELAN

PLUNKETT

POWER

PURCELL
(of Loughmoe)

Plate XXIII

O'QUIGLEY

Gules an orle argent, over all a bend erminois.

Crest: An estoile argent.

MacQUILLAN

Gules a wolf rampant argent, a chief or.

Crest: A demi-dragon azure.

O'QUIN
(*Annaly*)

Vert a pegasus passant wings elevated argent, a chief or.

O'QUIN
(*Thomond*)

Gules a hand couped below the wrist grasping a sword all proper between in chief two crescents argent and in base as many serpents erect and respecting each other tails nowed or.

Crest: A boar's head erased and erect argent langued gules.

O'QUINLAN

Per pale ermine and or two lions rampant combatant between in chief a mullet surmounted of a crescent and in base a dexter hand couped at the wrist and erect all gules.

O'RAFFERTY

Ermine an eagle displayed sable, over all a fesse or charged with 2 salmon naiant gules.

Crest: On a mount vert an eagle displayed or.

MacRANNALL
(REYNOLDS)

Vert a lion rampant between three escallops or.

Crest: On a mount a stag couchant proper.

REDMOND

Gules a castle with two towers argent between three woolpacks or.

Crest: A beacon fired proper.

O'REGAN

Or a chevron ermine between three dolphins azure.

The blazons for arms depicted on Plate XXIV (opposite)

O'QUIGLEY

MacQUILLAN

O'QUIN
(*Annaly*)

O'QUIN
(*Thomond*)

O'QUINLAN

O'RAFFERTY

MacRANNALL (REYNOLDS)

REDMOND

O'REGAN

Plate XXIV

O'REILLY

Vert two lions rampant combatant or supporting a dexter hand couped at the wrist erect and apaumée bloody proper.

O'RIORDAN

Quarterly: 1st and 4th, Gules out of clouds in the sinister side a dexter arm fessways proper holding a dagger in pale argent pommel and hilt or; 2nd and 3rd, Argent, a lion rampant gules against a tree in the dexter couped proper.

Crest: A fleur-de-lis gules.

ROCHE

Gules three roaches naiant in pale argent.

Crest: On a rock proper an osprey rising argent beaked and legged or holding in the claws a roach argent.

O'ROURKE

Or two lions passant in pale sable.

Crest: Out of an ancient Irish crown or an arm in armour erect grasping a sword proper pommel and hilt of the first.

RYAN
(O'MULRIAN)

Gules three griffins' heads erased argent.

Crest: A griffin segreant gules holding in the sinister claw a dagger proper.

SARSFIELD

Per pale argent and gules a fleur-de-lis counterchanged.

O'SCANLAN

(*Munster*)

Per fess indented argent and azure three lions rampant counterchanged.

MacSHANLY

Azure a lion passant or, in chief three estoiles of the last.

O'SHAUGHNESSY

Vert a tower triple towered argent supported by two lions rampant combatant or.

Crest: An arm embowed the hand grasping a spear point downwards all proper.

The blazons for arms depicted on Plate XXV (opposite)

O'REILLY

O'RIORDAN
Pro Deo et patria

ROCHE
Mon Dieu est ma roche

O'ROURKE

RYAN (O'MULRIAN)

SARSFIELD

O'SCANLAN
(*Munster*)

MacSHANLY

O'SHAUGHNESSY

Plate XXV

O'SHEA

Per bend indented azure and or two fleur-de-lis counterchanged.

O'SHEEHAN

Azure on a mount in base vert a dove argent holding in the beak an olive branch proper.

Crest: A dove as in the Arms.

MacSHEEHY

Quarterly: 1st, Azure a lion passant guardant argent; 2nd, Argent three lizards vert; 3rd, Azure three pole-axes in fess or; 4th, Argent a ship with three masts sable.

Crest: An arm in armour couped below the elbow and erect holding in the hand a sword, blade entwined with a serpent all proper.

O'SHERIDAN

Or a lion rampant between three trefoils vert.

Crest: Out of a ducal coronet or a stag's head proper.

O'SHIEL

Argent a lion rampant between two dexter hands couped at the wrist erect apaumée in chief and a mullet in base all gules.

Crest: Out of a ducal coronet or an arm erect vested gules holding a sword proper.

O'SULLIVAN

Per fess, the base per pale, in chief or a dexter hand couped at the wrist gules grasping a sword erect blade entwined with a serpent proper between two lions rampant respecting each other of the second, on the dexter base vert a stag trippant or, on the sinister base per pale argent and sable a boar passant counterchanged.

Crest: On a ducal coronet or a robin red-breast holding in the beak a sprig of laurel all proper.

O'SULLIVAN BEARE

Per pale argent and sable, a fess between in chief a boar passant and in base another counter passant all counterchanged armed hoofed and bristled or.

Crest: On a lizard vert a robin redbreast proper.

MacSWEENY

Or on a fess vert between three boars passant sable a lizard argent.

Crest: An arm in armour embowed holding a battle-axe all proper.

TAAFFE

Gules a cross argent fretty azure.

Crest: An arm in armour embowed holding in the hand a sword all proper pommel and hilt or.

The blazons for arms depicted on Plate XXVI (opposite)

O'SHEA   O'SHEEHAN   MacSHEEHY

O'SHERIDAN   O'SHIEL   O'SULLIVAN

O'SULLIVAN BEARE   MacSWEENEY   TAAFFE

Plate XXVI

MacTIERNAN

Ermine two lions passant gules.

Crest: A griffin statant gules wings erect vert.

O'TIERNEY

(*Co. Limerick*)

Argent a chevron sable, a chief gules.

Crest: An oak tree proper.

TOBIN

Azure three oak leaves argent.

O'TOOLE

Gules a lion passant argent.

Crest: A boar passant proper.

O'TREHY

(TROY)

Azure two griffins segreant combatant or.

Crest: A tiger's head erased or.

TULLY

MacATILLA

Vert a chevron between three wolves' heads erased argent.

Crest: A wolf's head couped argent.

WALL

Azure a lion rampant between three crosses crosslet or.

Crest: A naked arm embowed holding a scymitar the blade guttée de sang all proper.

WALSH

(*Iverk*)

Argent a chevron gules between three broad arrow heads points upwards sable.

Crest: A swan pierced through the back and breast with a dart all proper.

WOULFE

Per fess argent and azure, in chief on a mount vert in front of an oak tree a wolf passant both proper, in base two salmon naiant barways in pale argent.

Crest: A stork wings elevated sable.

The blazons for arms depicted on Plate XXVII (opposite)

MacTIERNAN

O'TIERNEY
(*Co. Limerick*)

TOBIN

O'TOOLE

O'TREHY (TROY)

TULLY (MacATILLA)

WALL

WALSH
(*Iverk*)

WOULFE

Plate XXVII

PART FOUR

ANGLO-IRISH SURNAMES

In treating of Irish surnames it is necessary to decide what is meant by Irish in this connexion. We have already without hesitation accepted as such the families of Norman stock which came to this country in the twelfth and thirteenth centuries. Next we have to consider those elements of the population which settled in Ireland later than the foregoing but before the sixteenth century, that is to say while the Gaelic order still continued to function almost undisturbed outside the Pale. Families in this category are much less numerous than their Norman predecessors. They did not, like them, become *hiberniores ipsis Hibernicis* but they did become assimilated in the Irish nation (if that term be permissible in a mediaeval context) through environment, intermarriage and also the inability of the country of their origin to protect them in that of their adoption. For the most part their names are associated with the towns and we do not meet them as territorial magnates except when success in commerce or favourable marriages had enabled them to acquire country estates. In this class may be included twelve of the celebrated " Tribes of Galway ", though most of the families in question were actually domiciled elsewhere in Ireland before migrating to Galway. In their case the most potent element in their assimilation was religion. The towns, particularly Galway, were constantly at enmity with the Gaelic septs outside their walls until the impact of the Reformation, followed by the continuous military aggression of England during the next 150 years, caused the townsmen to make common cause with their neighbours and former foes.

It is not, in fact, until we come to the seventeenth century that any serious difficulty confronts us in the problem under consideration. In that century Ireland was for the first time really conquered and subdued by her powerful and aggressive neighbour. Notwithstanding the notable Irish victories at Benburb and the Yellow Ford the defeat at Kinsale in 1602 seemed to seal the doom of the Irish nation ; and the Rising of 1641 and the support of the Stuart cause fifty years later only made the situation far worse, for in the seventeenth century these events led to three major plantations or wholesale transfers of land from the ancient owners to strangers from overseas—commonly called The Plantation of Ulster (up to that the most Gaelic part of Ireland), the Cromwellian Settlement and the Williamite Forfeitures. This meant that the settlers were able to look to Britain for support and protection : the centre of gravity, so to speak, for large numbers of persons living in Ireland became London, where previously men's loyalties had centred around the castle of their chief or at farthest the city of Dublin.

Thus was deliberately created what is termed the Anglo-Irish ascendancy. The families comprising this class have been slow to become an integral part of the Irish nation, if indeed they can be said to have done so even now. It is only right to observe that the " Ascendancy " included many families of Gaelic origin which, as a result of the anti-papist Penal Code, conformed to the state religion and, becoming landlords in the modern sense, threw in their lot with the new Cromwellian gentry so much despised by their ancestors.

The fact that certain individual members of the dominant caste were conspicuous as leaders in recurring revolts against all that caste stood for merely emphasizes the truth of the general statement : such men as the Sheares brothers, Lord Edward Fitzgerald, Robert Emmet, Thomas Davis, Charles Stewart Parnell and Roger Casement were regarded as traitors by their own class. It was proud to describe itself as " England's faithful garrison " ; and even to-day (when the Prime Minister of Northern Ireland, whose family has been in Co. Fermanagh for three centuries, proclaims himself an Englishman) it is probably true to say that the majority of this group on either side of the border feel a keener sense of loyalty to Queen Elizabeth II than to the Republic of Ireland, and to them " the Army " suggests Aldershot rather than the Curragh. In saying this I do not seek to disparage these people who have personally sterling qualities for which the average Irishman is not usually conspicuous. To the Anglo-Irish, indeed Ireland owes much : not only in those untypical individuals who espoused the national cause, but more so perhaps in the promotion of science and culture—for example in the activities of the Royal Dublin Society and the Royal Irish Academy and in the architecture of eighteenth century Dublin. I am considering the question as to how far they can be counted as Irish, with particular reference to the inclusion of their names in this book. It is obvious that the mere fact of birth in Ireland, though constituting a man an Irish citizen by law does not *ipso facto* make him an Irishman in the sense required of us in a work on Irish families and surnames. If birth were the sole test we would have to count Tom Clarke and James Connolly as English or Scottish, and Lord Kitchener as Irish, the former lifelong Irish republicans, signatories of the 1916 Proclamation and executed for their part in the Rising, the latter a typical Briton who happened to be born in a garrison town in Ireland.

We have considered mediaeval immigrants and those of the seventeenth century. The families which were established here in the Elizabethan period may perhaps be included with the latter because, although they were not planted in the country as part of a deliberate policy aimed at the consolidation of conquest, they did actually come either as officers in one of the invading armies or as high officials of the English Queen. The plantations attempted in Leix and Offaly under Philip and Mary may be disregarded as they had no lasting effect.

The preponderance of English names among the landowners of Ireland in the nineteenth century, which arose from the causes outlined above, is immediately apparent in the pages of such publications as de Burgh's *Landowners of Ireland* (1878) or indeed Burke's *Landed Gentry of Ireland* (1912) ; for it was not until the combined effect of the 1903 Land Act, the taxation following the First World War and the establishment of the Irish Free State produced another agrarian revolution, albeit a peaceful one, that the Ascendancy began gradually to disappear. Nevertheless, though English names predominate, there are for the reasons stated above many Gaelic-Irish surnames to be found in these lists.

In addition to those completely hibernicized and numerically strong Norman names like Burke, Fitzgerald and Roche, which are dealt with individually in Part II of this book, there are a number of other naturalized surnames. A list of the more important of these is given in Appendix E. That appendix includes only those names which may be regarded as thoroughly hibernicized. Many others are found in the early mediaeval records, but the present-day bearers of such names are for the most part descendants of much more recent immigrants from England, and so may be properly counted as Anglo-Irish.

Before passing on to that extensive category it should be mentioned that there are a few non-Gaelic surnames still extant in Ireland which were found here before the Anglo-Norman invasion. Of these the best known, (all of Norse origin), are :

Arthur : leading citizens of Limerick from the twelfth century, of whom many have been mayors and sheriffs of that city and two were bishops of the diocese. The most notable member of the family was Thomas Arthur (1593–1675), the celebrated physician and diarist. This name is quite distinct from MacArthur, which is of Scottish origin. Two Irish Arthurs were noteworthy in the eighteenth century history of France.

Coppinger : settled in Co. Cork and remained there ; several were mayors of the city. The name is seldom met with elsewhere.

Esmonde : always associated with Co. Wexford and prominent in that county's history for the past 800 years. Dr. John Esmonde was hanged as a rebel in 1798.

Hammond : no doubt families descended from comparatively recent immigrants of this name are to be found in Ireland, but Ostmen of the name were in East Leinster before the coming of the Anglo-Normans.

Harold : settled both in Dublin, where they gave their name to Harold's Cross, and in Limerick where they were prominent in civic history until the Catholic submergence. The name has now spread to Co. Cork and Co. Kerry.

Skiddy : the Skiddys formed a sept in Co. Cork and elected a chief in the Irish fashion ; from 1360 they are chiefly associated with the city of Cork and provided many mayors up to 1646 when Catholics ceased to hold that office.

Sweetman : an influential family in Co. Kilkenny, very well known in recent generations on account of the numerous Sweetmans who have been prominent in Irish political and cultural activities. Of this family was Milo Sweeteman, Archbishop of Armagh from 1362 to 1380, who was one of the most distinguished and influential mediaeval prelates.

Woulfe : *vide* p. 284 *supra*.

Having regard to the circumstances we have been considering it would seem proper to give a place in this section only to those Anglo-Irish families which have produced one or more individuals prominently associated with some important Irish activity, whether it be political, military, scientific or cultural. Inevitably such a classification must be somewhat arbitrary and no doubt names will be omitted from the resultant selection which some readers will consider should have been included. It will be observed, for example, that the family of Wellesley (formerly Colley) is not among them : several of its members, notably the great Duke of Wellington, had very distinguished careers but their renown was won in the service of England or the British Empire and they contributed nothing to the welfare of Ireland and only indirectly, if at all, to her prestige.

The following, however, will probably be generally accepted as worthy of inclusion.

ASHE. Families called Ashe settled in Counties Kildare and Meath in the fourteenth century and they are recorded in the sixteenth century as amongst the leading gentry there ; one was M.P. for Trim in 1613 and another was poll-money commissioner for Co. Meath in 1661. In recent times they are chiefly located in Kerry and Antrim. Thomas Ashe (1884–1917), the I.R.A. officer whose long hunger-strike ending in death had a far reaching effect, was born in Co. Kerry. The well-known Limerick and Kerry name Nash is etymologically of the same origin.

BALFE. The Balfes were fourteenth century settlers in Co. Meath. One of the earliest recorded instances of the name is the excommunication of William Balfe, a burgess of Athboy, for usury in 1409. By the end of the next century we find them among the leading gentry of Co. Meath, and two were M.P.s for Kells in 1585 and 1613. Michael William Balfe (1808–1870), the composer of " The Bohemian Girl " and other operas, is the most famous Irishman of the name.

BARRINGTON. First to settle in Ireland was an Elizabethan captain who obtained O'Moore lands in Leix, which he managed to retain in spite of constant feuds with the dispossessed owners. This family was among the chief gentlemen of Leix in 1598 ;

one was M.P. for Maryborough in 1613. The best known Barrington family came with Cromwell : they settled in Limerick in 1692. The principal branch resided at Glenstal, now the Benedictine Abbey and well known secondary school. Their association with Limerick is marked by Barrington's Hospital in that city. Best known of the name is Sir Jonah Barrington (1760–1834), author of *Personal Sketches* and *The Rise and Fall of the Irish Nation*. As M.P. he voted against the Union. It may be added that the Gaelic surname Ó Bearain was sometimes anglicized as Barrington.

BERESFORD. The family came to Ireland at the time of the Plantation of Uster, Tristram Beresford being manager of the London Company ; they settled at Coleraine. Their later connexion with Co. Waterford arose from an alliance with the de la Poer family. John Beresford (1739–1805), whose mother was a de la Poer, exercised almost unlimited political influence which he employed in suppression of the 1798 Insurrection and in furthering the passing of the Act of Union. He should also be remembered for the fact that many of the best architectural features of Dublin can be attributed to his efforts. In the nineteenth century the Beresfords distinguished themselves rather in the service of the British Empire than in that of Ireland. The family is now represented by the Marquessate of Waterford.

BROOKE. Descended from Basil Brooke, a high-ranking Elizabethan officer, the earliest of the name to be noted in Ireland, the Brookes acquired Rantavan, Co. Fermanagh, in 1685. Charlotte Brooke (1745–1793), almost the first in modern times to appreciate and collect poems in the Irish language, was born there, as was her father Henry Brooke (1706–1783) a poet of some note. Lord Brookeborough— Sir Basil Brooke—is Prime Minister of Northern Ireland. In other parts of the country families called Brooks (usually so spelt) settled under the Cromwellian régime.

CROKE. This name in Ireland is best known in the person of Most Rev. Thomas William Croke (1824–1902), the patriotic Archbishop of Tuam, whose early patronage of native Irish games is commemorated in Croke Park, the headquarters of the Gaelic Athletic Association. The family has been associated with Kilkenny from the fifteenth century : in the MacFirbis Annals under date 1443 it is spelt Croc. Many of the name appear in the Elizabethan Fiants.

CROKER. As landed gentry the Crokers are associated with Co. Limerick where they settled early in the seventeenth century. Since then the name is found in various parts of the country. Thomas Crofton Croker (1798–1854), author of

Researches in the South of Ireland etc., was born in Cork. From the same county came Richard Croker (1841–1922), better known as Boss Croker, prize fighter, Tammany Hall leader and famous race-horse owner. Place names in Co. Kilkenny indicate the early presence of Crokers there, Crokersland being mentioned in a deed of 1432.

DAUNT. The Daunts established themselves in Co. Cork as peaceful settlers in the sixteenth century, acquiring lands at Tracton, between Cork and Kinsale : they are listed among the leading gentry of 1598. Later they moved westwards to Kilcascan, where they still are. Of this family was William John O'Neill Daunt (1807–1894) the prominent Protestant Nationalist M.P. and author of several notable books.

DAVIS. The name Davis is found in many sixteenth century Irish records in various parts of the country though not among the landed gentry. The outstanding figure of the name was Thomas Osborne Davis (1814–1845), poet and patriot. His father was a British army surgeon, his mother an Atkins of the well known Mallow family, in which town Thomas Davis was born and lived. The name Davis, used a synonym of MacDavid in Co. Wexford, now hides the identity of that branch of the MacMurroughs.

EDGEWORTH. The Edgeworth family has been continuously resident in Co. Longford since 1583. The town Edgeworthstown, formerly called Meathus Truim, perpetuates their name. Three very famous Irish people were of this family : Richard Lovell Edgeworth (1744–1817), author, inventor, original member of the Royal Irish Academy, anti-Union M.P. and father of twenty-one children ; one of these was Maria Edgeworth (1767–1849) whose Irish novels are classics ; his nephew, the saintly and talented Abbé Henry Essex Edgeworth (1745–1807), is best remembered as the priest who attended Louis XVI on the scaffold. The Abbé's father emigrated to France from Edgeworthstown in 1751 and became a Catholic there.

EMMET. Christopher Emmet (b. 1702) lived in Co. Tipperary. The family moved to Dublin, where Robert Emmet (1778–1803) was born and was executed after his abortive but historic insurrection. His brother Thomas Addis Emmet (1764–1827) made his name as a lawyer in the U.S.A., having emigrated after the 1798 Insurrection in which he was implicated. Another brother Christopher Temple Emmet (1761–1788) was also a patriot. Their father Robert Emmet F.R.S. was state physician in Ireland.

FAY. The name Fay is not very common in Ireland. Its present day representatives are chiefly found in the city and suburbs of Dublin, the remainder being in Meath and adjacent counties. These are the Fays (called de Fae in Irish) who came to Ireland with the Anglo-Norman invaders at the end of the twelfth century and settled in Co. Westmeath. Their senior descendants are represented by the Fay family of Ballymoon, Co. Kildare. Not many Fays are of Gaelic origin—in the *Dictionary of American Biography* there are four Fays all Puritan and non-Irish. However, it must be remembered that there was a native Irish family of O'Fay in Ulster who were erenaghs of a church near Enniskillen. Their name in Irish is Ó Fiaich from *fiach*, a raven. Under the name of O'Fee they are numerous in Co. Fermanagh in the census of 1659. In the Elizabethan Fiants the name appears in north-west Ulster as O'Feye. Their descendants are now usually called Foy and sometimes Fee. Of Irish Fays much the best known are the Dublin born brothers Frank Fay (1879–1931) and Willie Fay (1872–1940) pioneers of the Irish dramatic movement in the early days of the Abbey Theatre.

FERRITER. The Ferriters have been in Kerry since 1400 if not earlier. Ballyferriter in the Dingle peninsula is named from them. They ranked as gentry in the sixteenth century : Pierce Ferriter (*c.* 1600–1653), who lost his life as a result of his participation in the Cromwellian war, was a leading Gaelic poet as well as a gentleman of standing. They were for some centuries the owners of the Blasket Islands (recently abandoned by their Irish-speaking population).

FIELD. This well-known English name has been in Ireland, chiefly in Dublin, since the thirteenth century. Field is also found as an anglicized synonym of O'Fihilly or Feely. John Field (1786–1837), the musician who is best known for his introduction of the nocturne, was born in Dublin of a family long established there.

FITZSIMONS. This name might have been treated as Hiberno-Norman, but it has been placed here rather than in Part II because it differs from the names included there, in that category (like Fitzgerald and Burke) in two main respects : first, it is by no means peculiar to Ireland being, indeed, much more usual in England, and secondly there are no basic arms common to all armigerous Irish Fitzsimons families. Nevertheless the first records of the name in Ireland are of a period very shortly after the Anglo-Norman invasion. Among the Norman families brought to Co. Down by John de Courcy in 1177 were some called Fitzsimon, while others of the name followed the Prendergasts to Mayo early in the next century and were still strong there in 1585, when a Fitzsimon possessed Castlereagh and other castles.

People are particular nowadays about the way their names are spelt, but even as late as the eighteenth century we find the same families using FitzSimon and

FitzSymon (with or without a final S), as well as FitzSymonds and even Fitz-Simmons, while occasionally the Fitz is dropped and Symons—the use or disuse of the capital S after Fitz was quite arbitrary— (or variants thereof) is used. The majority of births recorded by Matheson are entered as Fitzsimons.

The most important line of FitzSimons is that which came to Ireland from Simonshide, in Herefordshire, and settled in the Pale in 1323, since when they have been continuously leading gentry in Counties Dublin and Westmeath. There are no less than seven Dublin men in the Funeral Entries of Ulster King of Arms between 1568 and 1610, four being civic dignitaries (Mayor, Recorder etc.). By 1659 they had become not only influential in Co. Westmeath but numerous, too, for in the census of that date FitzSimons appears as a principal Irish name in the barony of Demifore. Some of these adopted the Gaelic patronymic Mac an Ridire, anglicized MacRuddery, which, in turn, was sometimes changed by translation to MacKnight. The Four Masters record the death in 1505 of Edmund Dorcha Fitzsimon " of the descendants of the Knight ", who was prior of Fore. There was a connexion between the Mayo Fitzsimonses and those of Dublin, for in the " Composition Book of Connacht " (1585) Nicholas FitzSymons is described as " gent. of Downmackniny " (barony of Clanmorris) and also alderman of Dublin. They are now represented by the family of O'Connell-FitzSimon of Glencullen, Co. Dublin.

Especially noteworthy among the distinguished bearers of the name in Ireland are Walter FitzSimons (d. 1511), Archbishop of Dublin from 1484, who also ably performed the duties of Lord Deputy and of Lord Chancellor for several years ; and Father Henry Fitzsimon, S.J. (1566–1643), whose remarkable career is described in Rev. E. Hogan's *Distinguished Irishmen of the Sixteenth Century*. In America, Irish-born Thomas FitzSimmons (1741–1811) was one of the leading men in the War of Independence.

FORBES. The Forbeses of Castle Forbes, Co. Longford (Earls of Granard) settled there in 1620. They were a very important family in Scotland. The majority of the people of the name in Ireland to-day are of Scottish stock, but in Connacht they may be of the sept of Mac Firbisigh whose name was anglicized Forbes. These were hereditary historians to the O'Dowds and had special privileges : the most distinguished of them was Donal MacFirbis (1585–1670).

GALWEY. This surname is topographical in origin but the place from which it is derived is usually stated to be Galloway in Scotland ; some Galwey families, however, claim to be descended from Burkes of Co. Galway. Up to the end of the seventeenth century the surname was usually spelt Gallaway. Though found elsewhere, e.g. in Dundalk and Armagh in 1369, the Galweys may be regarded as belonging to south-west Munster, particularly to Cork, of which city they were frequently mayors between 1430 and 1632. They were among the leading merchants not only of mediaeval Cork but of Youghal, Kinsale and to a lesser extent of Limerick also. Thirteen families of the name appear in the census of 1659, all in Co. Cork.

The leading Co. Cork family of Galwey, whose estates were confiscated after the Jacobite débâcle, like so many Irish exiles settled at Nantes in France, where they were ranked among the nobility of that country.

GRATTAN. I have placed Grattan in the Anglo-Irish section, but it is possible that further investigation may show that the name should have appeared in Part II. In all the biographies of Henry Grattan (1746–1820), perhaps the greatest statesman that Ireland has produced, nothing is revealed about his ancestors further back than his great-grandfather, one Patrick Grattan who in 1668 was Senior Fellow in Dublin University. Henry's father, James Grattan, as we know, was Recorder of Dublin and M.P. for that city from 1761 to 1766 ; a Dubliner himself, he is traditionally believed to have come of a family long established there. Woulfe hazards the guess— it is nothing more—that Grattan may be Mag Reachtain in Irish, a corruption of Mac Neachtain (i.e. the Scottish-Ulster name MacNaughton). The name MacGrattan certainly exists in north-east Ulster to-day, and in the Dublin records for 1641 I notice the use of the alias MacGrattan in the case of a clergyman called Grattan in the parish of St. John. Henry Grattan junior (1789–1859) M.P., has some claim to recognition in the literary field as the biographer of his father, the statesman. The line is continued in the well known families of Grattan-Bellew and Esmonde, his co-heiresses having married respectively a Bellew and an Esmonde.

GRAVES. The name of Graves is associated primarily with Trinity College, Dublin, and with the Protestant Church of Ireland. The principal landed family of Graves, which was until recently seated at Cloghan Castle, Co. Offaly, was earlier of the city of Limerick where John Graves was sheriff in 1719. Of the many divines and professors in their pedigree the most distinguished were Rev. James Graves (1815– 1866) co-founder of the Royal Society of Antiquaries of Ireland ; Right Rev. Charles Graves (1818–1899) Bishop of Limerick, F.R.S., mathematician and authority on ogham ; and Rev. Richard Graves (1763–1829) F.T.C.D. The best known, no doubt, was Arthur Perceval Graves (1846–1931) author of the ever popular song " Father O'Flynn ". The name appears in the 1659 census in Counties Dublin, Meath and Louth.

GRAY. Grays in Ireland are of various origins : Norman (de Grey and Le Grey), English, Scottish and to a small extent native Irish. This small minority derives its surname from the Irish Mac Giolla Riabhaigh (son of grey youth), sometimes corrupted to Mac Cúil Riabhaigh. The latter form is phonetically rendered Colreavy or Culreavy, and in certain parts of the country, chiefly in Co. Longford, this is interchangeable with Gray. The same name is rendered Gallery in Co. Clare and McAreavy etc. elsewhere. A few Grays may have acquired the name by translation of the Irish adjective *liath* (meaning grey), as such replacement of an original surname by a descriptive epithet does occur, though rarely (cf. Bane, Reagh, Lauder etc.). The majority of the Grays in Ireland to-day are Anglo-Irish and are mostly located in Ulster.

Among prominent Irishmen of the name may be mentioned Sir John Gray (1816–1875) and his son Edmund Dwyer Gray (1845–1888), proprietors of the *Freeman's Journal* and Nationalist members of Parliament. The most famous historical character is no doubt Betsy Grey (1777–1798), Ulster heroine of the 1798 insurrection.

GREGORY. The principal Gregory family in Ireland came to this country in the Cromwellian period. The first of these to be noteworthy were Robert and George Gregory who were prominent in the defence of Derry during the siege of that city in 1689. After the siege the latter settled in Co. Kerry where the family remained until 1774. The small town of Castlegregory in Kerry is not, however, named after them but from the christian name of one Gregory de Hora. This family of Gregory next migrated to Co. Galway : the Coole estate was acquired in 1768. Coole, of course, inseparably associated with the name of Lady Gregory (1852–1932) née Augusta Persse, was famous as the country house frequented by all the well-known figures of the Irish literary revival. Her father-in-law Sir Robert Gregory (b. 1790) was Under Secretary for Ireland and her husband Sir William Gregory was M.P. for Co. Galway and Trustee of the National Gallery. Before them several other members of the family were notable, particularly Robert Gregory (1727–1810), who devoted much of the wealth he acquired while chairman of the East India company to the improvement of agriculture in Co. Galway. The name was not unknown in Ireland in earlier times : it appears as early as 1362 at Swords, Co. Dublin, and 1346 in the Ormond Deeds.

GRUBB. The Grubb family of English stock were located in Counties Waterford and Tipperary in 1656. They are notable on account of Thomas Grubb (1800–1878), whose work in the field of optics was outstanding. It is possible that some families of Grubb are of Scottish origin, the name MacRob having been corrupted to Grubb.

GWYNN. The Gwynns are of Welsh origin. They were established as a clerical family in Co. Down in the seventeenth century shortly after the Cromwellian war.

They have been closely associated with Dublin University, especially since the time of the Rev. John Gwynn (1827–1917). He was the editor of " The Book of Armagh " etc. and a scholar of renown. His eldest son Stephen Gwynn (1865–1951), Nationalist M.P., was a versatile writer who published many valuable books, chiefly in the historical field. Edward J. Gwynn (1868–1941) was one of the most distinguished provosts of Trinity College, Dublin. At the present time three members of the family are University professors in Ireland.

HAMILTON. The majority of Irish Hamiltons came to this country from Scotland at the time of the Plantation of Ulster, but some families of the name were established in Ulster before that : a Hamilton appears in the contemporary list of Co. Down gentry for 1598 and another in Co. Cavan. The name is now very numerous in Ulster, particularly in Counties Antrim, Down, Tyrone and Derry. Of the many landed families the most prominent is that of the Duke of Abercorn. His ancestor the 3rd Earl of Abercorn was a Jacobite, and like his relative Count Anthony Hamilton (1645–1719), served James II in Ireland. The latter (of a Catholic branch) had a distinguished career in France as soldier and courtier ; he is best known as the author of *Memoirs de la vie du Comte de Grammont*. For the most part the Hamiltons were staunch supporters of William of Orange, two being very prominent on that side. The Hamiltons of Ireland have distinguished themselves in many spheres—literature, medicine, art and particularly the sciences. In the latter James Archibald Hamilton (1747–1815), astronomer, Rev. William Hamilton (1755–1797), naturalist, and Sir William Rowan Hamilton (1805–1855), of quaternions fame, may be specially mentioned. All these except the last were Ulstermen. Several of the Hamiltons of Co. Tyrone distinguished themselves in Sweden in the seventeenth century as soldiers and diplomats.

HARVEY. The Irish Harveys are mostly of English extraction, notably the most prominent family of the name, viz. the Harveys of Bargy, Co. Wexford. It is of interest to note, however, that a distinguished though small sept of Kilmacduagh in Co. Galway, long dispersed from their original habitat, anglicized their name Ó hAirmheadhaigh as Harvey. Occasionally, too, the O'Harrihys of Co. Fermanagh used Harvey as an alternative form of their name. The majority of Harveys in Ireland to-day are Ulster Protestants.

Though a Protestant landlord of English stock, Bagenal Harvey (1752–1798) of Co. Wexford is renowned for his part in the 1798 Rising, for which he was hanged. William Henry Harvey (1811–1866) was famous in his day as a botanist.

HENEBRY. Philip de Hynteberge was lord of the manor of Rath, Co. Dublin, in 1250. Thence the family, later called Henebry, migrated to Counties Kilkenny and Waterford. They are chiefly found in the latter county to-day, though the name is not common. Father Richard Henebry (1863–1916) was a foremost Gaelic scholar and collector of Irish music.

HYDE. The Hydes of Castle Hyde, Co. Cork acquired many extensive estates in that county in 1588. Dr. Douglas Hyde (1859–1949), first President of Ireland and probably the best known of all the leaders of the Gaelic revival, was of this family : his father, Canon Arthur Hyde, was a clergyman in Co. Roscommon. The name Hyde appears in the Ormond Deeds relating to Co. Kilkenny several times in the fourteenth and fifteenth centuries.

KENT. Though now regarded as belonging to Co. Cork, the more so as Eamonn Kent (1881–1916), one of the leaders of the 1916 Rising, was from that county, the name Kent, when first it came to Ireland soon after the Anglo-Norman invasion, was to be found only in Meath and Dublin. There Kent of Daneston and several others were among the leading gentry of the Pale in 1598, and their name is perpetuated in the modern parish of Kentstown, Co. Meath.

KICKHAM. The Kickhams are not an old family in Ireland. The name is included here because Charles James Kickham (1826–1882), author of *Knocknagow* etc., has a well earned place in the Anglo-Irish roll of honour. His father was a substantial shopkeeper at Mullinavat, of a family completely hibernicized though not many generations in the country. There was one family of the name in Dublin city in 1659.

KING. Some of the most famous Irishmen named King have been of Anglo-Irish stock, notably Archbishop William King (1650–1729), a vigorous Protestant : he was an ornament to the nation by reason of his encouragement of the Irish language in Dublin University, his collection of manuscripts, and his support of Swift, e.g. in his campaign against " Wood's halfpence ". Another Protestant, Rev. Robert King (1815–1900) was a distinguished Irish language scholar. He was from Co. Cork, as were the Kings (Earls of Kingston) who were prominent members of the Anglo-Irish ascendancy. On the other hand Rev. Paul King (d. 1665) was a noted Irish Franciscan. For King as the anglicized form of several Gaelic patronymics, see *sub* Conroy p. 90 *supra.*

LAWLESS. The best known family of Lawless is that of Cloncurry, Co. Kildare, originally of Herts., England. Nicholas Lawless, who conformed in 1770, was created Lord Cloncurry in 1789. Hon. Emily Lawless (1845–1913), Irish novelist and poet, was his great-great-grand-daughter. Some families of the name were established near Dublin soon after the Anglo-Norman invasion, branches of which migrated to Counties Galway and Mayo. They were nearly all staunch Jacobites and among the exiles after 1691 was Patrick Lawless who became Spanish Ambassador to London in 1713 and afterwards to Louis XIV of France. William Lawless (1772–1824), a professor of anatomy, was outlawed as a member of the United Irishmen organization and later became a distinguished general in Napoleon's army. The name Lillis, of Counties Cork and Limerick is the same in origin as Lawless, of which it is a local variant.

LEDWICH. This family was established in Co. Meath at least as early as 1270 ; they are included among the leading gentry of that county in 1329. Later they spread to Co. Westmeath where Ledwichtown indicates their location. By 1598 they are found also among the gentry of Co. Kilkenny. Rev. Edward Ledwich (1737–1823), the antiquary, states that they were originally a German family settled in Cheshire, England, who came to Ireland with de Burgo in 1200, when they obtained land in Co. Westmeath. The Ledwich Medical School in Dublin was named after his grandson, Thomas Ledwich (1823–1858). Francis Ledwidge (1891–1917), labourer and poet, came from the same area.

LOMBARD. Originally Lombard meant a native of Lombardy but the word was later applied to a banker or moneylender of any nation. In Ireland, where the name is on record as far back as the thirteenth century, the Lombards have been chiefly identified with Cork as merchants. Several have been mayors of that city since 1380. Lombardstown, Co. Cork, was named after them. Most Rev. Peter Lombard (c. 1560–1625), Archbishop of Armagh, was a noted author.

MITCHELL. Mitchell is an old English form of Michael. Families of the name have come to Ireland as immigrants at various times in and since the seventeenth century, but none are found among the great Anglo-Irish landed proprietors. A John Mitchell, however, was one of the poll-money commissioners for King's County (Offaly) in 1661. Mitchelstown, Co. Cork, however, does not take its name from a family called Mitchell but from the christian name Mitchel (i.e. Mitchel Condon). The name has an honoured place in Irish history in the person of John Mitchel (1815–1875), revolutionary and author, whose ancestor was a Scottish Covenanter who fled to Donegal, his father being a Presbyterian minister at Newry.

PAKENHAM. The first of this family to come to Ireland accompanied his relative, Sir Philip Sidney, in 1576. At the beginning of the next century they were established at Tullynally, Co. Westmeath, which was renamed Pakenham Hall, and have remained there since. In 1756 the head of the family was created Baron (later Earl of) Longford, a title formerly held by the Aungier family, whose heiress he had married. Several Pakenhams had brilliant careers in the British military, naval and diplomatic services; but the outstanding figure in Ireland was Father Paul Mary Pakenham, C.P. (1820–1856) who established the Passionist retreat at Mount Argus. He was formerly Hon. Charles Reginald Pakenham and his conversion was one of the most notable of the nineteenth century: to-day we have Edward Arthur Henry Pakenham, Earl of Longford, of the Gate Theatre, Dublin, he and his wife being notable playwrights, while his brother Francis Aungier Pakenham (Baron Pakenham) is author of *Peace by Ordeal*, a striking work on the Anglo-Irish Treaty of 1921.

PARNELL. The name Parnell, one of the most famous in Irish history, is very rare in Ireland to-day. Of a family long resident at Congleton, Cheshire, whence was taken the title of the peerage conferred on Sir Henry Parnell in 1841, the first of the Irish branch was Thomas Parnell, father of Rev. Thomas Parnell (1679–1717), Archdeacon of Clogher, poet and friend of Dean Swift. His brother and his nephew were both M.P.s for Queen's Co. (now Leix) and in the next generation a younger son acquired the property of Avondale, Co. Wicklow, famous as the birthplace and home of Charles Stewart Parnell (1846–1891), whose career as leader of the Nationalist Party needs no description. His sister Fanny Parnell (1854–1882) was a poetess of merit who devoted her talents to the Nationalist cause. Of his predecessors Sir John Parnell (1744–1801), 2nd Bart., was Chancellor of the Irish Exchequer and an opponent of the Union; Sir Henry Parnell (1776–1842), 4th Bart., mentioned above, was a prominent Protestant advocate of Catholic Emancipation.

PARSONS. The Parsons family has been of importance in Offaly (King's County) since the end of the sixteenth century when the brother of the celebrated Sir William Parsons settled at Birr. The name of that thriving town was changed to Parsonstown: the old name, however, was restored some fifty years ago. The head of the family is the Earl of Rosse who is resident at Birr Castle. Sir William Parsons (c. 1570–1650), Surveyor General of Ireland, was one of the most active and efficient of English officials in Ireland. His nephew, Sir Lawrence Parsons (c. 1630–1698), born at Birr, took an active part against James II. More recent members of the family have been distinguished for their work in the spheres of science and agriculture. Especially noteworthy was Sir William Parsons (1800–1867), 3rd Earl of Rosse, whose observations by means of the great telescope he installed at Birr Castle are of lasting importance. His father, Sir Lawrence Parsons, the 2nd Earl, was one of the prominent opponents of the Union in Grattan's Parliament. The name Parsons, which is very common in England, is now found in small numbers in several widely separated parts of Ireland, presumably as the result of comparatively recent commercial immigration from England.

PIERCE. There are many variants of this name. In the form Pers it is recorded in Alen's Register as of Dublin in the thirteenth century. Pearce is the form in the 1659 census (Co. Kildare), while Pierce and Peirce appear in various parts of the country at that date. A Co. Cork probate of 1677 shows the name as Pearce and for the same county Peirce and Pierce are frequent in the eighteenth century. Richard Pierce was Bishop of Waterford and Lismore from 1701 to 1735. Pearse is of course famous on account of Padraig Pearse (1879–1916), schoolmaster, orator, poet and revolutionary leader. The Pearse brothers executed in 1916 were sons of an Englishman living in Dublin and of a Gaelic Irish mother.

PRESTON. The Prestons, who were Lords of Preston in Lancashire, have been of importance since they came to Ireland about the year 1270. The first of note was made a judge in 1327 ; his son Sir Robert de Preston was Lord High Chancellor and acquired the estate of Gormanstown, Co. Dublin and Co. Meath, which has remained in the family since and from which the title Viscount Gormanston, conferred in 1478, was taken. The active participation of the Prestons on the Irish side in 1641 and again in 1690 resulted in their attainder and outlawry, but their titles were restored by the British sovereign in 1800. In addition to Nicholas Preston, 6th Viscount, leader of the Catholic gentry of the Pale, attainted by Cromwell, and his son Jenico Preston, 7th Viscount, who was colonel of Gormanston's Infantry in James II's army and was likewise attainted, another member of the family was prominent in the same cause, viz. Thomas Preston, 1st Viscount Tara (1585–1655) who returned from Spain to lead one of the armies of the Confederate Catholics : but his want of success in that capacity and his quarrels with Owen Roe O'Neill contributed to the ultimate defeat. The name is found to-day in small numbers in various parts of Ireland.

ROTHE. This name, now rather rare in Ireland and usually spelt Ruth, is on record here as early as the thirteenth century ; but no family of the name became firmly established until about 1390, when the close association of the Rothes with Kilkenny began. By the end of the sixteenth century they had become one of the leading families of that city and county. Robert Rothe (1550–1622), M.P. and Mayor and

Recorder of Kilkenny was an antiquary and historian ; his descendant Rev. Bernard Rothe, S.J. (1693–1768) had a distinguished career in France after leaving Kilkenny ; Most Rev. David Rothe (1573–1650), Bishop of Ossory, is remembered as an author of note as well as for his support of Rinnuccini at the Confederation of Kilkenny ; while another Kilkenny-born Rothe, General Michael Rothe (1661–1741), served with great distincion first in King James's Army in Ireland and later as Commander of Rothe's Regiment of Cavalry in the Irish Brigade.

RUSSELL.   It might be held that Russell should not be included in this chapter in as much as some families of the name came to Ireland at the time of the Anglo-Norman invasion and as such were prominent in early mediaeval times. Very few present day Russells, however, can claim descent from these early settlers, except perhaps those of Downpatrick, who are known to have been there for seven centuries. Later immigrants of the name have reached Ireland at various periods. Many were well established in Counties Cork, Limerick, Galway, Meath and particularly in the Swords area of Co. Dublin by the end of the sixteenth century ; more followed in the Plantation of Ulster and under Cromwell. It must not be forgotten, however, that many Russells served in King James II's Army. Perhaps the most distinguished family of Russell in Irish life was that of Ballybot, Newry, Co. Down. Unlike most Russells this family remained Catholic through the penal times : of these Charles Russell, Lord Russell of Killowen (1832–1900) the famous advocate, who defended Parnell at the " Times " Commission, his uncle Rev. Charles William Russell (1812–1880), President of Maynooth and co-editor of four volumes of the Calendar of State Papers, his sister Katherine Russell (1829–1898) of the Sisters of Mercy in America, and his brother Rev. Mathew Russell, S.J. (1834–1912), poet, are the best known. Most Rev. Patrick Russell (1629–1692), one of the greatest Catholic Archbishops of Dublin, was of the Swords family mentioned above. Thomas Russell (1767–1803) was one of the foremost Ulster Protestant United Irishmen. George William Russell (1867–1935), known as AE, poet, painter and economist, came from Lurgan, Co. Armagh. In addition to these there have been many other Russells of note in Ireland.

SHAW. Shaw is quite a common name in Ireland especially in north-east Ulster ; in Leinster it is particularly associated with Mullingar. Originally it is Scottish. The main Shaw family in Ireland is that of Bushy Park, Terenure, Dublin. The first of these was William Shaw, an officer in the army of William III : he was grandfather of Sir Robert Shaw, first baronet and anti-Union M.P. From there on the christian name Bernard appears in every generation of the pedigree, which includes George Bernard Shaw (1856–1950), the dramatist. Mid-seventeenth century records, which show that the name was not uncommon then both in Dublin city and in north-east

Ulster, indicate the presence of at least one family of Shaw in Co. Galway at that time, but the well-known family of Shawe-Taylor of Castle Taylor, Co. Galway, has no connexion with them since the name Shawe was only assumed by the Taylors in 1843 consequent upon the marriage of their heiress with an Englishman. Bernard Shaw is, of course, the outstanding Irishman of the name—in spite of 68 years residence in England he always insisted upon his Irish nationality. Other prominent Shaws were Sir Frederick Shaw (1799–1876), M.P. for Dublin University and Recorder of Dublin for forty-eight years, and William Shaw (1823–1895) of Cork, leader of the Irish Party after Isaac Butt until superseded by Parnell.

SHEARES. The name Sheares is rare in Ireland as it is in England, the country of its origin. It is famous in Irish history on account of the execution outside Newgate Prison of the brothers Henry Sheares (1753–1798) and John Sheares (1766–1798), condemned for complicity in the 1798 Insurrection. Their father Henry Sheares (1702–1768), a prominent banker, was M.P. for Clonakilty ; his father, the first of the family to settle in Ireland, was sheriff of Cork in 1716. There was an English family of Sheares in Co. Wexford (Fort Chichester) in 1659. One Sir Henry Sheares (d. 1710), though he had been imprisoned as a Jacobite, was trustee of Irish grants in 1700.

STACK. The Stacks, who originally came from England, have been in Co. Kerry since the beginning of the fourteenth century and by the sixteenth had become thoroughly Irish, being among the foremost Kerry opponents of the English in the Elizabethan wars. They were allied by marriage to several of the great families of Desmond. John Stack was Bishop of Ardfert from 1558 to 1588 and Philip Stack from 1588 to 1595. General Edward Stack (c. 1750–1833) was a notable officer in the Irish Brigade in France, and also in Pitt's Irish Brigade. Their association with Clanmaurice is perpetuated in the Stack Mountains between Tralee and Abbeyfeale and a district in the vicinity was long known as Pobble Stack or Stack's Country.

STOKES. This name is not uncommon in Leinster and Munster. It is derived from the English place name Stoke. It is found in Ireland as early as the Anglo-Norman invasion, but modern families of Stokes in Ireland do not claim to be of Hiberno-Norman stock. Those of Co. Kerry and Co. Limerick are descended from an Elizabethan officer. Their importance lies in the number of notable persons of the name in the nineteenth century. The first of these was Professor Whitley Stokes (1763–1845), a remarkable man who was a United Irishman in politics, a brilliant and self-sacrificing medical doctor and patron of Irish scholarship; his son William Stokes (1804–1878) was another doctor of European reputation and his grandson Whitley Stokes (1830–1909) was a leading Gaelic scholar; Margaret McNair Stokes (1832–1900) was a first-class archaeologist. These by no means exhaust the list of people called Stokes who have distinguished themselves in the field of science and literature.

SWIFT. The name Swift does not occur in Irish mediaeval records. Early in the seventeenth century a branch of the family of Swift, which had been of importance in Yorkshire since 1300, settled in Dublin and one member of it acquired lands in Co. Kilkenny and elsewhere. In the next century they moved to Swiftsheath in that county, where his descendants still live. Jonathan Swift (1667–1745), the famous Dean of St. Patrick's, was of a junior branch of this family. The name is found in Dublin and in Counties Kilkenny and Waterford to-day. The Swifts of Co. Mayo are not of English origin, Swift, by a mistranslation, having been adopted as the anglicized form of the Gaelic Ó Fuada, also called Foody in English.

SYNGE. The name Synge has been prominent in the history of the Protestant Church of Ireland since the seventeenth century. Beginning with two Englishmen who were respectively Bishops of Cloyne (1638) and of Cork and Ross (1663), they were followed by a succession of bishops and deans in the southern dioceses. John Millington Synge (1871–1909), one of the best known of the authors and dramatists connected with the Irish literary revival, was born in Dublin.

TONE. The Anglo-Irish records indicate that the surname Tone was not unknown in Ireland in the sixteenth century, but no person of the name of any note appears before Theobald Wolfe Tone (1763–1798). His father, Peter Tone, was a coachbuilder in Dublin, where Wolfe Tone, who was one of the great figures of Irish history, was born. His son William Theobald Wolfe Tone (1791–1828), who became a French citizen, published his father's remarkable journal. The name Tone is now very rare if not extinct in Ireland.

USSHER. The Usshers are an old Anglo-Irish family. Sir William Ussher of Donnybrook was one of the leading gentry of Co. Dublin in 1598. His father was mayor of Dublin in 1561. The Usshers were also identified with Co. Armagh and with Co. Waterford as gentry and members of Parliament. All the famous Usshers were born in or near Dublin. The most remarkable was the Most Rev. James Ussher (1581–1656), Archbishop of Dublin, whose library formed the nucleus of the famous library at Trinity College, Dublin. His brother Ambrose Ussher (1582–1629) was a noted Hebrew and Arabic scholar. Rev. Henry Ussher (1741–1790), royal astronomer, was instrumental in establishing the Dunsink Observatory. Another remarkable character, not of the same family, was Fr. James Ussher (1720–1772) a Protestant farmer who became a Catholic priest. Richard John Ussher (1841–1913) was a naturalist whose *Birds of Ireland* is a standard work.

WESTROPP. The name Westropp is not found in Ireland before 1657 when the ancestor of the Anglo-Irish Westropps settled in Co. Limerick, a branch of the family going soon afterwards to Clare. With these two counties they have since been closely associated. In the latter the family is now represented by the O'Callaghan-Westropps, an O'Callaghan of Maryfort (or Lismehane) near O'Callaghan's Mills having married the Westropp heiress in 1859. The most distinguished of the family was Thomas Johnson Westropp (1860–1922), the antiquary and historian.

WHITE. The name White is so numerous in Ireland and so many distinguished Irishmen have borne it that this book must not be without some more than passing reference to it. They came, chiefly from England, at intervals throughout the centuries and settled in every province in widely separated areas. I can only refer here to the most important of these. In Limerick the name occurs very frequently in the list of mayors and sheriffs from soon after the Anglo-Norman invasion, the earliest being in 1213. A branch of this city family became landed proprietors in Co. Clare. Father James White, who compiled a History of Limerick in 1738 (now in the Royal Irish Academy), was of this family. The story of the Whites of Waterford is very similar, though the name does not appear in the list of mayors till 1414 : in this case the landed family resided at Whyteshall, Co. Kilkenny, and near Clonmel. The famous Jesuit Father Stephen White (1575–c. 1648) was born at Clonmel ; and John Davis White (1820–1893), who did much useful historical work, was a Co. Kilkenny man. Another landed family of note was that of Leixlip, which subsequently went to Loughbrickland, Co. Down.

WILDE. The first of the family came from Durham and became a builder in Dublin ; his son Ralph Wilde went to Mayo as a land agent about the year 1750. So the Wildes were in Connacht and connected by marriage with several of the old Gaelic families a hundred years before the best known of them, Sir William Wilde (1815–1876), the oculist and antiquary, was born there. In their lifetime his wife and son were more famous than himself : Jane Francesca Wilde (1826–1896) better known as " Speranza " the political authoress, and Oscar Wilde (1856–1900) playwright and author of *Ballad of Reading Gaol.*

YEATS. The name Yeats, alias Yates and Yeates, is on record in Dublin in the seventeenth century. The ancestor of the well known Co. Sligo family was Jervis Yeats, a citizen of Dublin who died in 1712. The first in Co. Sligo was Church of Ireland rector of Drumcliff. He was grandfather of John Butler Yeats (1839–1922), the artist, who had two famous sons, William Butler Yeats (1865–1939), the poet, and Jack Butler Yeats (1870–1957) the leading artist in Ireland in the present century.

APPENDIX A

SURNAMES INDIGENOUS AND COMMON IN BRITAIN WHICH ARE USED AS THE ANGLICIZED FORMS OF GAELIC IRISH SURNAMES.

* The asterisk denotes that the older form in italics is now obsolete.

ADRIAN (*O'Dreane**)
AGNEW (*O'Gnieff**)
ALLEN (*Hallion*)

BADGER (*Brick*)
BANKS (*Brohan*)
BARNACLE (*Coyne*)
BARNES (*Berrane*)
BARRON (*Berrane*)
BATTLE (*Duncahy, MacEncaha**)
BERRY (*O'Beara**)
BIGGINS (*Biggane*)
BIRD (*MacAneeny, Heanahan, Heaney*)
BISHOP (*MacAnaspie*)
BLAKE (*Blowick*)
BLESSING (*Mulvanerty*)
BLOOMER (*Gormley*)
BONAR (*Kneafsey*)
BOWEN (*Bohane, Nevin*)
BOWES (*Bogue*)
BOYCE (*do.*)
BRADLEY (*O'Brallaghan*)
BRIDGEMAN (*O'Drehitt**)
BRODERICK, BROTHERS (*O'Broder*)
BURNS (*O'Beirne, Birrane, Byrne*)
BYRON (*do.*)

CAIRNS (*Kerin, O'Kieran*)
CALDWELL (*Colvan, Houriskey*)
CANNING (*O'Cannon, Cunneen*)
CAREY (*Keary, Kerin etc.*)
CARPENTER (*MacAteer*)
CARLTON (*O'Carolan*)
CARR (*MacIlhair, Kerin etc.*)
CARTON (*MacCartan*)
CASHMAN (*Kissane*)
CAULFIELD (*MacCall, Gaffney, MacCarron, Goonan*)
CAWLEY (*MacAuley*)
CHAFF (*Lohan*)
CLARKE (*O'Clery*)
CLIFFORD (*Cluvane*)
CLOSE (*O'Closse**)
COLE (*MacCool, Gilhool*)
COLEMAN (*O'Colman*)
COLLINS (*O'Cullane*)
COMBER (*Kerin, Kerrigan*)

COMYN (*MacComin*, O'Comin**)
CONWAY (*MacConowe*, O'Conowe*, Convey etc.*)
CORBETT (*Corbane*)
CORBY (*MacCorboy*, O'Corboy**)
CORKELL (*MacCorkill*)
COTTER (*MacCotter*)
COULTER (*O'Colter*)
COX (*MacQuilly*)
CRAVEN (*Cravane*)
CRAWLEY (*MacCraly*, Crowley*)
CREED (*Creedon*)
CROSBIE (*MacCrossan*)
CULLINGTON (*Collotan*)
CUMMINGS (see Comyn)
CUNNINGHAM (*MacCunnigan, O'Cunnigan*)

DAVENPORT (*Donarty*)
DAVEY (*Davin, MacDavitt*)
DAVIS (*do.*)
DEANE (*O'Dane*, MacDigney*)
DIVER (*O'Deere*)
DORE (*O'Dower**)
DOWNES (*Duane etc.*)
DREW (*O'Drea, MacEdrue**)
DRURY (*do.*)
DUCK (*Lohan*)
DUNCAN (*Donegan*)
DUNLOP (*Dunlevy*)
DYER (*O'Dwyer*)

EARLY (*O'Mulvochory**)
EARNER (*Seery*)
EASON (*MacKee*)
EIVERS (*Heever, MacKeever*)
EVANS (*O'Hevine**)

FANE (*Feehin*)
FANNING (*Fenning, O'Finan*)
FARLEY (*O'Farrelly*)
FARMER (*MacScollog*)
FAY (*Fee*)
FENNELL (*O'Finnell*)
FENTON (*Feeheny, Feenaghty*)
FERRIS (*Fergus*)
FIELD (*Fihilly*)
FIELDING (*do.*)
FINLAY (*Finnelly*)
FISHER (*Bradden*)
FLOOD (*MacAtilla*)

305

FORBES (*MacFirbis*)
FORD (*Foran, MacKinnawe*)
FORTUNE (*O'Fortyn**)
FOX (*Kearney, Shanahan, Shinnick etc.*)
FOY (*Fee*)
FREEMAN (*MacAteer, Seery*)

GILBEY (*MacElwee etc.*)
GILL (abbrev. of many *Gil-* names)
GODWIN (*O'Dea, Doddan*)
GOFF, GOUGH (*MacGeough*)
GOLDEN, GOULDING (*O'Gullin**)
GOW (*MacGowan*)
GRAHAM (*Grehan*)
GRAY (*MacArevy*)
GREEN (*Fahy, MacGlashan, O'Hooneen*)
GRIFFIN (*O'Griffy*)
GRIMES (*Gormley, Grehan, Quinlisk*)

HALES, HAYLES (*MacHale, Healy*)
HALFPENNY (*Halpin*)
HALVEY (*O'Halwick*)
HAND (*Claffey, Lavin*)
HANLEY (*O'Hanley*)
HARDIMAN (*Hargaden*)
HARE (*MacGarry, O'Hehir*)
HARLEY (*O'Harrily**)
HARRINGTON (*Harroughten, O'Hingerdell**)
HARTLEY (*O'Hartily**)
HARVEY (*O'Harvey**)
HASTINGS (*Hestin*)
HATTON (*MacIlhatton*)
HAUGHTON (*Haughan*)
HAWE (*Haugh*)
HAWKINS (*Haughan*)
HAYDEN (*O'Headan**)
HAYES (*O'Hea etc.*)
HEARNE (*Ahearne*)
HOLLAND (*Holohan, Hylan*)
HOLLY (*MacCullen*)
HONE (*O'Howen**)
HOOD (*O'Hood*)
HOWARD (*Heever*)
HOWE (*Hoey*)
HOWLEY (*O'Howley**)
HUGHES (see *Hayes*)
HUNT (*Fee, Feeheny*)
HUSSEY (*Hosey*)

INGOLDSBY (*Gallogly*)
IVERS (see Eivers)

JOHNSON (*MacShane*)
JUDGE (*Breheny*)

KANE (*O'Cahan*)
KETTLE (*MacKetyll**)
KEYES (*MacKee*)
KIDNEY (*Duane*)

KING (*MacAree, Conroy, MacIlroy, O'Kinga**)
KINGSTON (*MacCloughry*)
KIRBY (*Kerwick*)
KIRK (*Quirke*)
KNIGHT (*MacNaughton, MacRuddery*)
KNOWLES (*O'Newill**)

LAMBE (*O'Loan, Noone*)
LANE (*Lehane, Leyne etc.*)
LAWTON (*Loughnane*)
LEE (*Maclea, O'Leye**)
LEECH (*Logue*)
LEIGH (see Lee)
LEONARD (*MacAlinion, Lenane, Lennon etc.*)
LESTRANGE (*MacConchogrye**)
LILLY (*MacAlilly*)
LINDSAY (*MacClintock, Lynchy, O'Lynn*)
LITTLE (*Beggane*)
LITTLETON (*do.*)
LOFTUS (*Loughnane*)
LONG (*Longan, O'Longy**)
LORD (*Kiernan, Tierney*)

MANLEY (*Monnelly*)
MANNING (*Mannion*)
MARKHAM (*Markahan*)
MARLEY (*Marrilly*)
MARTIN (see p. 222 *supra*)
MASTERSON (*MacMaster*)
MATTHEWS (*MacMahon*)
MAXEY (*Mackessy*)
MAY (*O'Mea*)
MEADE (*Miagh**)
MEARS (*O'Meere**)
MELVILLE (*Mulfaal, Mulvihil*)
MERRIMAN (*MacMenamin*)
MERRY (*Mariga*)
MEYER (*O'Myer**)
MICHAEL (*MacGillemichell*, Mulvihil*)
MILES (*MacMoylie*, Mullery*)
MILEY (*O'Mealue, Mullee*)
MILFORD (*Mullover*)
MILLIN (*Mulleen*)
MITCHELL (see Michael)
MOLYNEUX (*Mulligan*)
MONDAY (*MacAloon*)
MONKS (*MacEvanny, Monahan*)
MONTAGUE (*MacTeigue*)
MORGAN (*Morahan, Murrigan*)
MORLEY (*Morrolly, Murhila*)
MORRIS (see p. 231 *supra*)
MORRISON (see p. 231 *supra*)
MORRISSEY (see p. 231 *supra*)
MORROW (*MacMorrough, Murray*)
MOSS (*Mulmona*)
MYERS (see Meyer)

APPENDIX A

NEVILLE (*O'Nee, Nevin*)
NEWELL (see Knowles)
NORTON (*O'Naghten*)

OAKES (*MacDara*)
OWEN (*O'Howen*, MacKeon*)

PALMER (*Mullover*)
PATTERSON (*Cussane, MacPadden*)
PATTON, PEYTON (*O'Petane**)
POWELL (*Gilfoyle*)

RABBITT (*MacAneany, Cunneen*)
RALEIGH (*O'Rawley**)
RAY (*Reavey*)
REDDINGTON (*Mulderrig, Redehan*)
REEVES (*O'Rive**)
REID (*Mulderrig, Mulready*)
REYNOLDS (*MacRannal*)
RICE (see p. 256 *supra*)
RING (*O'Rinne**)
ROCK (*Carrigy*)
ROE, ROWE (*MacEnroe, O'Rowe**)
ROGERS, RODGERS (*MacRory*)
ROWLAND (*Roolane*)
ROWLEY (*do.*)
RUSH (*Loughry*)
RUTLEDGE (*Mulderrig*)
RYDER (*Markahan, Markey*)

SALMON (*Bradden*)
SAVAGE (*Savin*)
SEWELL (*O'Swally**)

SEXTON (*Shasnan*)
SHALLOW, SHELLEY (*Shalvey*)
SHIELDS (*O'Shiel*)
SILKE (*O'Sheedy*—not *MacSheedy*)
SMALL (*Begg, Kielty, Quilty*)
SMALLWOODS (*MacNecollen**)
SMITH (*MacGowan, O'Gowan*)
SOMERS, SOMERVILLE, SUMMERS (*Somahan, O'Saura**)
SPELMAN (*Spillane*)
STAUNTON (see p. 51 *supra*)
STONE (*Cloherty, Muckley*)
SWIFT (*Foody*)
SWORDS (*Clavin*)

TARRANT (*Torran*)
THORNTON (*Drennan, Meenahan, Skehan, Torran*)
THYNNE (*O'Tyne**)
TORRENS, TORRANCE (see Tarrant)
TUCKER (*Togher*)

VAUGHAN (*Mohan*)
VICTORY (*MacNaboe*)

WARREN (*Murnane*)
WATERS (*Heskin, Hourisky, Toorish etc.*)
WEIR (*MacEwire*, Corry*)
WHITE (*Bannon, Galligan*)
WHITEHEAD (*Canavan*)
WOODS (*MacElhoyle, MacEnkelly*, Kielty, Quilty*)
WREN (see Ring)
WYNNE (*Geehan, Mulgeehy*)

APPENDIX B

Surnames commonly and correctly regarded as Gaelic Irish which are nevertheless found indigenous outside Ireland (though less commonly than those in Appendix A).

Begg	Donegan	Glynn	Keane
Boyle	Doyle	Guerin	
		Guinness	Lowry
Conan			Lynch
Considine	Fallon		
Cosgrave	Fearon		
Coveney	Foley*	Hart	Melody
Crowe		Healy	Moore
Crowley	Gaynor	Higgins	
Curry	Geary	Hurley	Ward

* See page 149.

APPENDIX C

GAELIC IRISH SURNAMES WHICH HAVE AN ENGLISH APPEARANCE BUT ARE NEVERTHELESS RARELY IF EVER FOUND INDIGENOUS IN BRITAIN.

ARKINS	DELAHUNT	GATELY	NESTOR
	DENROCHE	GERTY	NORMILE
	DIAMOND*	GLEESON	
	DIGGIN	GOING	PRUNTY
BLOWICK	DOOLADY	GORMLEY	
BOLGER	DOWLING*		RAFTER
BRODER	DOWNING*	HALPENNY	(or WRAFTER)
BRUEN	DROUGHT	HAMILL	RIGNEY
BUGGY	DUNWORTH	HARKIN*	RING
	DURACK	HARTNETT	RODDEN
		HASSETT	ROWAN*
		HYNES*	RUDDEN
CADDEN			
CANNY	ENNIS		SCULLION
CANTY		KERLEY*	SHARKEY
CARRY		KETT*	SHERRY
CASSERLEY	FERRIS	KNEAFSEY	SLOWEY
CHEASTY	FLATLY	KNEE	SWORDS
COAKLEY	FLATTERY	KYNE	
CONWELL	FOODY		TONER
CORKELL	FORKIN	LYNAM	
CRAMPSEY	FORTUNE*		WARNOCK*
CRIBBIN	FRAWLEY	MELDON	
CUFFE	FURY	MESCALL	ZORKIN

* Names so indicated are occasionally found indigenous in England.

APPENDIX D

GAELIC IRISH SURNAMES WHICH HAVE A FOREIGN APPEARANCE BUT ARE NEVERTHELESS RARELY IF EVER FOUND INDIGENOUS OUTSIDE IRELAND.

BRAZIL

COEN*
CONOLE

DELACOURT†
DELARGY
DE YERMOND

GAUSSEN§
GEON

GHEE
GIHON
GNA
GWEEHIN

HARGADON
HARKAN
HEDERMAN
HESSION

JERETY

KEHOE

LAVELLE†
LEVY*
LEYDEN
LOMASNEY

MANASSES
MANNIX
MARIGA
MELIA
MINOGUE
MULFAAL

NIHIL

SCHAILL
SHERA
SHOVELIN
SLOYAN

THULIS

WILHERE

* Cf. Jewish Cohen, Levi.   † Found in France.   § Found in Switzerland.

APPENDIX E

THE BEST KNOWN OF THE NORSE, NORMAN AND ENGLISH NAMES WHICH HAVE BECOME "NATURALIZED" BY LONG ASSOCIATION WITH IRELAND.

Many of them are not found in England except among families which emigrated from Ireland. A few are used occasionally as synonyms of Gaelic surnames : these are indicated by an asterisk.

ARTHUR
AYLWARD

BALFE
BARNEVILLE (or
  BARNWALL)
BARRETT
BARRON*
BARRY*
BARTON
BASTABLE
BEAMISH
BELLEW
BELLINGHAM
BELTON
BERMINGHAM
BINCHY
BLAKE*
BLANEY
BODEN
BREDIN
BRETT*
BROWNE*
BRYAN*
BURKE
  (or BOURKE)
BUTLER

CANTILLON
CARRICK*
CODD
CODY
COGAN*
COLL*
COMERFORD*
CONDON
COPPINGER
DE COURCY
CROKE
CRUISE
CUSACK
CUSSEN

DALTON
DARCY*
DEVEREUX*
DILLON
DONDON
  (or DUNDON)
DOWDALL

ENGLISH
ESMOND
EUSTACE

FAGAN*
FITZGERALD
FITZGIBBON
FITZMAURICE
FLEMING
FLOOD*
FRENCH
FURLONG

GALWEY
GERNON
GLENN
GOGAN*
GRACE

HACKETT
HAROLD
HAUGHTON
HEADON*
HENEBRY
HERBERT
HONE*
HOWLIN
HUSSEY*

IVERS*
  (or EIVERS)

JENNINGS
JORDAN
JOYCE

KEATING*

DE LACY*
LAFFAN
LANDERS
LAVALLIN
LAWLESS
LEDWICH
LILLIS
LISTON
LOMBARD
LUTTRELL

MARTIN*
MASTERSON*
MAUNSEL
MOCKLER
MOLYNEUX*

NAGLE
NANGLE
NETTERVILLE
NUGENT*

PLUNKETT
POWER
PRENDERGAST
  (or PENDER)
PRESTON
PUNCH
PURCELL

REDMOND
RICE*
ROCHE
ROCHFORT
ROSSITER
ROTHE (or RUTH)

ST. LEGER
SARSFIELD
SAURIN*
SEGRAVE
SHORTALL
SINNOTT
  (or SYNOTT)
STACK
STACPOOLE
STAFFORD
STAUNTON
STRITCH
SWEETMAN
SWIFT*

TAAFFE
TALBOT
TALLON
TEELING
TERRY*
TOBIN
TRANT
TUITE
TYRRELL

UNIACKE
USSHER

VEALE
VERDON

WADDING
WALDRON
WALL
WALSH
WELDON
WHITE*
WOGAN
WOULFE
WYSE

311

APPENDIX F

IRISH SURNAMES RARELY FOUND OUTSIDE PARTICULAR COUNTIES OR BARONIES (APART FROM IMMIGRANTS TO DUBLIN AND OTHER LARGE URBAN CENTRES).

Names dealt with in Part II and IV are not included in the following list. The great majority of the surnames in it are properly Mac or O names. These prefixes, however, have in most cases been dropped and rarely if ever resumed ; they are therefore omitted here except when generally used. Only names extant at the present day are included. The rentals referred to in Chapter I contain many names peculiar to certain districts a century ago which are now extinct, often because they have been absorbed in commoner ones.

The list is mainly of value for the counties of the Atlantic seaboard.

I regret that it is not possible to mention by name all the people who have given me information on this subject. I wish, however. especially to acknowledge the very valuable and detailed notes which I received from Mr. P. J. Kennedy on Co. Galway and from Mr. J. C. MacDonagh on Counties Donegal and Sligo ; while the observations on Westmeath surnames which Mr. Séamus Ó Conchobhair kindly sent me were most helpful. I also thank Mr. Seán Ó Súilleabháin of the Irish Folklore Commission and Mr. Hubert Butler for useful advice relating to Counties Kerry and Kilkenny.

ADRAIN : Antrim.
AGNEW : Antrim.
MACALINDEN : Armagh.
MACANDREW : Mayo.
ANGLIN (or ANGLIM) : Cork.
MACATEER : Tyrone.

BALLISTY : Westmeath.
BANNIGAN : Donegal.
BASTABLE : Cork.
BATTLE (alias DUNCAHY) : Sligo.
BERKERY : East Limerick and Co. Tipperary.
BERREEN : Sligo.
BLEHAN : East Galway.
BOLGER : Wexford.
BORAN : East Limerick and West Tipperary.
BRACKEN : Offaly.
BREHENY : Sligo and North Roscommon.
BRICK : Kerry.
BRIODY : North Longford and W. Cavan.
BRODY* : Clare.
BROSNAN : Kerry and West Limerick.
BUGLER : East Clare.

CAHALANE : Kerry and West Cork.
MACCALLION : East Donegal and West Derry.

CANTY : Cork and South Limerick.
CARRIGY : Clare.
CASHMAN : Cork.
CHEASTY : Kerry.
CLOHERTY : West Galway.
CLOHESSY : Limerick and East Clare.
CLUNE : East Clare.
CODD : Wexford.
CODYRE : S. Galway.
MACCOLE : Donegal.
COLLOPY : Limerick.
COLUMBY : Wetmeath.
CONEFRY : Leitrim.
CONHEADY : Clare.
CONNAIRE : East Galway.
CONNEELY : Galway.
CONOLE : North Clare.
CONVERY : Derry.
COOLAHAN : East Galway.
CORKERY : West Cork.
COURNANE : Kerry.
CREHAN : North East Galway.
CREMIN : Cork and East Kerry.
MACCROHAN : Kerry.
MACCRORY : East Tyrone.

*Though a rare name, Brody (MacBrody, MacBruodin) might well have been given a place in Part II on account of the distinguished persons the sept has produced. An admirable article dealing with this family by Father Cuthbert MacGrath, O.F.M. will be found in *Éigse* (Vol. IV. part 1, pp. 48–66).

APPENDIX F

MacCrossan : North Tyrone.
Cryan : Roscommon.
Culhane : Limerick.
Culkin : Galway.
Culloty : Kerry.
Cunnane : Roscommon, East Mayo.
Cunniffe : North Galway, South Mayo.
Currane : Kerry.
Currigan : Roscommon.
Cussen : Limerick and North Cork.

Daffy : Clare.
Dahill : Tipperary.
MacDaid : Donegal and adjacent areas in Tyrone and Derry.
Darragh : Antrim.
Deady : Kerry.
Deeley : South Galway.
Deeny : East Donegal and West Derry.
Deery : North Monaghan and South Tyrone.
Deloughery : Cork.
Dennehy : Cork and East Kerry.
Derrig : Mayo.
Desmond : Cork.
Dever : Mayo (cf. Diver *infra*).
MacDevitt : North Donegal.
Diamond : East Derry and West Antrim.
Dirrane : Galway (Arran Islands).
Diskin : North Galway.
Diver : Donegal.
Divilly : Galway.
Dore : Limerick.
Duignan : East Roscommon and Leitrim.
Dullea : Cork.
Dundon : Limerick.
Durack : East Clare.
Durkin : Mayo and Sligo.

Early : Leitrim.
MacEldowney : Derry.
MacElhinney : North West Donegal.
MacElligott : Kerry.
MacEllistrum : Kerry.
MacErlean : East Derry and West Antrim.

Faherty : Galway.
MacFall : West Antrim and East Derry.
Feerick : Mayo and North Galway.
Fennelly : Kilkenny.
Fennessy : Waterford.
Fergus : Mayo.
Ferry : Donegal.
MacFettridge : West Antrim and East Derry.
Flattery : Westmeath and North Offaly.
Flattley : Mayo.
Folan : Galway.

Forkin : Mayo.
Forrestal : Kilkenny.
Fortune : Wexford.
Frain : Mayo and North Roscommon.
Furey : Galway.
Furlong : Wexford.

Gahan : Wexford and North Kilkenny.
MacGahan : Louth.
MacGahey : Monaghan.
Gallery : North Clare.
Galligan : Cavan.
Gallivan : Kerry.
Gately : Roscommon and North Galway.
Gaughan : Mayo.
Gavaghan : Mayo.
MacGeady : North-West Donegal.
Geany : Cork.
MacGeough : Monaghan and North Louth.
MacGeown : Armagh.
Gerety : Westmeath.
MacGettigan : Donegal.
Giblin : Roscommon and East Mayo.
Gilhooly : Leitrim.
Gillick : Cavan.
MacGinley : Donegal.
Ginnane : Clare.
Ginty : Mayo.
MacGinty : Donegal.
MacGivern : Armagh and North Down.
MacGivney : Cavan.
MacGlinchy : Tyrone and East Donegal.
MacGloin : Donegal.
MacGlone : Tyrone.
MacGonigle : South West Donegal and West Tyrone.
Gorham : West Galway.
MacGreal : Mayo.
Grealish : Galway.
Greally : Galway and South Mayo.
Groarke : Mayo.
Grory : Donegal and West Derry.
MacGuane : Clare.
Guihan : West Kerry.
Guihen : Roscommon.
Guinan : Offaly and North Tipperary.
MacGuinn : Sligo.
Guiry : Limerick.

Hallahan : Cork.
Hallissy : West Cork and South Kerry.
Hanafin : Kerry.
Hanna : Antrim and North Down.
O'Hare : East Armagh and West Down.
Hargadon (Hardiman) : Galway.
Hassett : Clare and North Tipperary.
Heanue : West Galway.
Henehan : Mayo.

HENNELLY : Mayo.
HENRION : Westmeath.
HESSION : North and East Galway and South Mayo.
HEVER : Sligo.
HISTON : Limerick.
HOBAN : Mayo.
HOLIAN : South Galway.
HONAN : Clare.
HOOD : West Antrim and East Derry.
HORAHO (alias HARRISON) : Sligo.
HORGAN : Cork and South Kerry.
HOSTY : Mayo and North Galway.
HOUNEEN : Clare.
HOURIHANE : Cork.
HOYNE : Kilkenny.
MacHUGO : Galway.
HULTAGHAN : Fermanagh.

KEADY : South-West Galway.
KEARON : Wicklow.
KEAVENEY : North-East Galway.
MacKEEVER : Derry and West Antrim.
KEOHANE : Cork.
KERNAGHAN : Armagh.
KERWICK : Kilkenny.
KETT : West Clare.
KEVANE : Kerry.
KEVILLE : Galway.
MacKIBBIN : Down and Antrim.
KIDNEY : Cork.
KIELTY : Roscommon and East Galway.
KILBANE : Mayo.
KILCASH : Sligo.
KILCULLEN : Sligo.
KILGALLON : Mayo.
KILGANNON : Sligo.
KILKELLY : South Galway.
KILKENNY : Roscommon.
KILLACKY : North Tipperary.
KILLIAN : Westmeath and South Roscommon.
KILLILEA : Roscommon and East Galway.
KILLORAN : Sligo and North Roscommon.
KINNEEN : Galway.
MacKINNEY : Tyrone and West Antrim.
KISSANE : Kerry.
KITTERICK : Mayo.
KYLE : Derry and West Antrim.

LAHEEN : Galway.
LAHIFF (alias FLAHY) : East Clare.
LAVALLIN : Cork.
LAVAN : Mayo and North Roscommon.
LAVELLE : Mayo.
LEO : Limerick.
LESTRANGE : Westmeath.
LISTON : Limerick.

LOGUE : Derry and East Donegal.
LOHAN : Galway.
LOMBARD : Cork.
MacLOONE : Donegal.
LORDAN : Cork.
LOWNEY : Cork.
LUCEY : Cork.
LYDON : Galway and South Mayo.
LYNAM : Offaly.

MAGNER : Cork.
MacMANAMON : Mayo.
MAUGHAN : Mayo.
MEA : Mayo.
MELLON : Tyrone.
MacMENAMIN : Donegal and North Tyrone.
MERLEHAN : Westmeath.
MEYLER : Wexford.
MILLIGAN : Antrim and South Derry.
MILMO : Sligo.
MINIHANE : Cork.
MINOGUE : Clare.
MOLAMPHY : North Tipperary.
MOLPHY : Westmeath.
MacMONAGLE : Donegal.
MONAHER : Offaly.
MONGEY : Mayo.
MONNELLY : Mayo.
MORLEY : Mayo.
MORRISROE : Roscommon.
MOYNIHAN : Kerry and West Cork.
MULKEEN : Mayo.
MULKERRIN : Galway.
MULLANY : Limerick and North Cork.
MULLARKEY : Roscommon and East Mayo.
MULQUEEN(Y) : Clare.
MULROY : Mayo.
MULVENNY : Antrim.
MUNGOVAN : West Clare.
MURNANE : Limerick and North Cork.

MacNABOE : Cavan.
MacNAMEE : Derry.
NEE : Galway.
MacNELIS : Donegal.
MacNICHOLAS : Mayo.
MacNIFF : Leitrim.
NIX : West Limerick.
NOONE : Roscommon, East Galway and East Mayo.
NORMOYLE : Clare.
NYHAN (formerly NEHANE) : Cork.

ORMOND : Waterford and South Kilkenny.

PEOPLES : Donegal.
PHILBIN : Mayo.

APPENDIX F

PHYLAN (or FYLAND) : Westmeath and North Offaly.
MacPOLIN : Armagh.
O'PREY : Down.
PRIOR : South Cavan and North-East Longford.
PRUNTY : Longford.

QUALTER : North Galway.
QUEE : Antrim.
QUEENAN : Sligo.
QUILTER : North Kerry.

RAFTISS : Kilkenny.
RAGGET : Kilkenny.
RATTIGAN : Mayo.
O'RAWE : Antrim.
RELEHAN : Kerry.
RIGNEY : Offaly.
RINEY : South Kerry.
RODDEN : Donegal.
RODDY : East Mayo and North Roscommon.
ROHAN : Kerry.
RONAYNE : East Cork.
ROSSITER : Wexford.
ROSSNEY : West Kerry.
RUANE : Mayo and East Galway.

SCALLY : Westmeath and South Roscommon.
SCARRY : East Galway.
SCULLION : Antrim and East Derry.
SEERY : Westmeath.
SHRYHANE : Roscommon.
SILKE : East Galway.
SINNOTT : Wexford.

SNEE : Sligo.
SPELLISSY : Clare.
SPELMAN : Galway and South Roscommon.
SPILLANE : Cork and West Kerry.
MacSTAY : Down.
STRITCH : East Clare.
STUDDERT : Clare.
SUGRUE : Kerry.
SUMMAGHAN : Sligo–Roscommon.

TAGGART : Antrim.
TALTY : West Clare.
TANGNEY : Kerry.
TANNIAN : South Galway.
TANSEY : Sligo.
TARPEY : Mayo and North Roscommon.
TEAHAN : Kerry.
THYNNE : West Clare.
TIMLIN : Mayo.
TONRA : Sligo.
TUNNY : Sligo.

VALLELLY : Armagh.
VEALE : Waterford.
VERLING : Cork.

WALDRON : Roscommon and East Mayo.
MacWEENEY : Leitrim.
WEIR : South Antrim and North Armagh.
WHELEGHAN : Westmeath.
WOOLAHAN : Kilkenny.

YOURELL (or URELL) : Westmeath.

BIBLIOGRAPHY

I have indicated in a general way in Chapter I the principal manuscript and printed sources from which the information in the text of this book has been compiled. To give a complete list of such sources for printed material, to say nothing of manuscripts, would be impossible, since every book dealing with Irish history or literature, or indeed any aspect of Irish life, is a potential source.

The bibliography which follows is a selection of printed works suitable for consultation in a search for information relating to families not dealt with in Parts II and IV, or to supplement the necessarily brief accounts which do appear there. It must be emphasized that it is merely a general indication of printed sources and (with the exception of Section I which is fairly comprehensive) is not intended to be by any means exhaustive. In particular, no attempt has been made to list the vast number of local and parish histories which have appeared from time to time, usually in pamphlet form.

I

IRISH FAMILY HISTORIES.

(N.B.—The value and reliability of the books etc. listed in this section varies considerably—see p. 12 supra.

ABBREVIATIONS.

Ardagh = Ardagh and Clonmacnoise Antiquarian Society Journal
Breifny = Breifny Antiquarian Society Journal.
Cork = Journal of the Cork Historical and Archæological Society.
Galway = Journal of the Galway Archæological and Historical Society.
Kildare = Journal of the County Kildare Archæological Society.
Louth = Journal of the County Louth Archæological Society.
N. Munster = North Munster Antiquarian Society Journal.
Ossory = Transactions of the Ossory Archæological Society.
R.S.A.I. = Journal of the Royal Society of Antiquaries of Ireland.
Ulster = Ulster Journal of Archæology.
Waterford = Journal of the Waterford and South-East of Ireland Archæological Society.

ADAMS. A genealogical history of Adams of Cavan. By Rev. W. Adams. London, 1903.

AGNEW. The Agnews in Co. Antrim. By John M. Dickson. *Ulster*, N.S. 7, 166-'71. 1901.

ALEN. Alen of St. Wolstan's. By Henry J. B. Clements. *Kildare* I, 340-'1. 1892-'5.

ALEN. An account of the family of Alen, of St. Wolstan's, Co. Kildare. By H. L. Lyster Denny. *Kildare*, IV, 95-110. 1903-'5. V, 344-'7. 1906-'8.

ALLEN. Ladytown and the Allens. By Thomas U. Sadleir. *Kildare*, IX, 60-69. 1918-'21.

AMORY. Descendants of Hugh Amory 1605–1805. By G. E. Meredith. London, 1901.

ANCKETILL. A short history, with notes and references, of the . . . family of Ancketill or Anketell. Compiled by one of its members. Belfast, 1901.

ARCHDALE. Memoirs of the Archdales. By H. B. Archdale. Enniskillen, 1925.

ARCHER. An inquiry into the origin of the family of Archer in Kilkenny, with notices of other families of the name in Ireland. By J. H. Lawrence-Archer. *R.S.A.I.*, IX, 220-'32. 1867.

MACARTNEY. See MACAULAY.

ASH. The Ash manuscripts . . . and other family records. Belfast, 1890.

BIBLIOGRAPHY

ASTON. See CHAMBERLAIN.

MACAULAY. Gleanings in family history from the Antrim coast. The MacAulays and MacArtneys. By George Hill. *Ulster*, VIII, 196-210. 1860.

AYLMER. The Aylmer family. By Hans Hendrick Aylmer. *Kildare*, I, 295–307. 1892–'5.

AYLMER. Donadea and the Aylmer family. By the Rev. Canon Sherlock. *Kildare*, III, 169–'78. 1899–1902.

AYLMER. The Aylmers of Lyons, Co. Kildare. By Hans Hendrick Aylmer. *Kildare*, IV, 179–'83. 1903–'5.

AYLMER. The Aylmers of Ireland. By Sir F. J. Aylmer. London, 1931.

BAGENAL. Vicissitudes of an Anglo-Irish family, 1530–1800. By Sir P. H. Bagenal. London, 1925.

BAGGE. Genealogical account of the Bagge family of Co. Waterford. Dublin, 1860.

BAGOT. The Bagots of Nurney. By Charles M. Drury. *Kildare*, VII, 317–'24. 1912–'14.

BAILIE. History and genealogy of the family of Bailie of the north of Ireland. By George A. Bailie. Augusta, 1902.

BALL. Records of Anglo-Irish families of Ball. By Rev. W. B. Wright. Dublin, 1887.

BALL. Ball family records. By the Rev. W. B. Wright. York, 1908.

BARNARD. The Barnards. Londonderry, 1897.

BARRINGTON. The Barringtons: a family history. By Amy Barrington. Dublin, 1917.

BARRON. Distinguished Waterford families: Barron. By Father Stephen Barron. *Waterford*, XVII, 47–65, 128–'34, 137–'52. 1914. XVIII, 69–87, 91–104. 1915.

BARRY. Étude sur l'histoire des Bary-Barry. Par C. de Barry. Vieux-Dieu-Les Anvers, 1927.

BARRY. De l'origine des Barry d'Irlande. Par Alfred de Bary. Guebwiller, 1900.

BARRY. Barrymore. By Rev. E. Barry. *Cork*, N.S. V, 1–17, 77–92, 153–'68, 209–'24. 1899. N.S. VI, 1–11, 65–87, 129–'46, 193–209. 1900. N.S. VII, 1–16, 65–80, 129–'38, 193–204. 1901. N.S. VIII, 1–17, 129–'50. 1902.

BARRY. The last earls of Barrymore. By G. J. Robinson. London, 1894.

BARRY–PLACE. Memoirs of the Barry–Place family. A narrative of the family of Rev. John Barry, of Bandon, Wesleyan minister, and a pioneer missionary. Compiled in 1911. By J. Barry Deane. *Cork*, XXXIII, 19-21, 1928.

BARTON. The family of Barton. By the Rev. Canon Sherlock. *Kildare*, IV, 111–'13. 1903–'5.

BEAMISH. Pedigrees of the families of Beamish. By R. P. Beamish. Cork, 1892.

BELLEW. Some notes on the family of Bellew of Thomastown, Co. Louth. By the Hon. Mrs. Gerald Bellew. *Louth*, V, 193–'7. 1923.

BERMINGHAM (BIRMINGHAM). Notes on the Bermingham pedigree. By Goddard H. Orpen. *Galway*, IX, 195-205. 1915–'16.

BERMINGHAM. The Bermingham family of Athenry. By H. T. Knox. *Galway*, X, 139–'54. 1917–'18.

BERMINGHAM. Carbury and the Birminghams' country. By Rev. Matthew Devitt, S.J. *Kildare*, II, 85–110. 1896–'9.

BERMINGHAM. Manual of origin, descent, etc., of Barony of Athenry. *Dublin*, 1820.

BERNARD. A memoir of James Bernard, M.P., his son, the first earl of Bandon, and their descendants. 1875.

BERNARD. The Bernards of Kerry. By J. H. Bernard. 1922.

BESNARD. Notes of the Besnard family. By T. E. Evans. *Cork*, N.S. XXXIX, 92–99. 1934.

BEWLEY. The Bewleys of Cumberland and their Irish descendants. By Sir E. T. Bewley. Dublin, 1902.

BINGHAM. Memoirs of the Binghams. By R. E. McCalmont. London, 1913.

BLACK. The Black family. Ed. by Isaac Ward. *Ulster*, N.S. 8, 176–'88. 1902.

BLACKER. History of the family of Blacker of Carrickblacker in Ireland. By L. C. M. Blacker. Dublin, 1901.

BLACKWOOD. Helen's Tower. By the Hon. Harold Nicholson. London, 1937.

BLAKE. Blake family records. By Martin J. Blake. London, 1902–'05.

BLAYNEY. The family of Blayney. Notes relating to the Blayney family of Montgomeryshire and Ireland . . . By E. Rowley-Morris. London, 1890.

BLENNERHASSETT. The Blennerhassetts of Kerry: earlier English stock. *Kerry*, V, 34–'9. 1919.

BOLTON. Bolton families in Ireland . . . By C. K. Bolton. Boston, 1937.

BOURCHIER. The Bourchier tablet in the cathedral church of St. Canice, Kilkenny, with some account of that family. By Richard Langrishe. *R.S.A.I.*, XXXIV, 365-'79. 1904. XXXV, 21-33. 1905.

BOWEN. Ballyadams in the Queen's County, and the Bowen family. By Lord Walter Fitzgerald. *Kildare*, VII, 3-32. 1912-'14.

BOWEN. Bowen's Court. By Elizabeth Bowen. London, 1942.

BOYLE. Memoirs of the illustrious family of the Boyles . . . By Eustace Budgell. Dublin, 1755.

BOYLE. Genealogical memoranda relating to the family of Boyle of Limavady. Attempted by E. M. F. - G. Boyle. Londonderry, 1903.

BRABAZON. Genealogical history of the family of Brabazon. By H. Sharp. Paris, 1825.

BRADSHAW. The Bradshaws of Bangor and Mile-Cross, in the Co. of Down. By Francis J. Bigger. *Ulster*, N.S. 8, 4-6, 55-'7. 1902.

O'BRENNAN. The O'Brennans and the ancient territory of Hy-Duach. By the Rev. Nicholas Murphy. *Ossory*, I, 393-407. 1874-'9.

O'BRIEN. Carrigogunnell Castle and the O'Briens of Pubblebrian in the Co. of Limerick. By Thomas J. Westropp. *R.S.A.I.*, XXXVII, 374-'92. 1907. XXXVIII, 141-'59. 1908.

O'BRIEN. The O'Briens in Munster after Clontarf. By Rev. John Ryan, S.J. *North Munster*, II, 141-'52. 1941.

O'BRIEN. The sept of Mac-I-Brien Ara. By Rev. W. B. Steele. *Cork*, 2nd Ser. III, 10-21. 1897.

O'BRIEN. Historical memoir of the O'Briens. By John O'Donoghue. Dublin, 1860.

O'BRIEN. History of the O'Briens from Brian Boroimhe A.D. 1000 to A.D. 1945. By Hon. Donough O'Brien. London, 1949.

O'BRIEN. The O'Briens. By W. A. Lindsay. London, 1876.

O'BRIEN. Genealogical notes on the O'Briens of Kilcor, Co. Cork. 1887.

BROWNE. Pedigree of the Brownes of Castle MacGarrett. By Lord Oranmore and Browne. *Galway*, V, 48-59, 165-177, 227-'38. 1907-'8.

BROWNLOW. See CHAMBERLAIN.

BUCHANAN. The Buchanan book. By A. W. P. Buchanan. Montreal, 1911.

BUCHANAN. Later leaves of the Buchanan book. By A. W. P. Buchanan. Montreal, 1929.

BULLOCK. Bullock or Bullick of northern Ireland. Compiled by J. W. Beck. London, 1931.

BOURKE (BURKE).

BOURKE. The Bourkes of Clanwilliam. By James Grene Barry. *R.S.A.I.*, XIX, 192-203. 1889.

BOURKE. The de Burgos or Bourkes of Ileagh. By M. Callanan. *North Munster*, I, 67-77. 1936-'9.

BURKE. The family of Gall Burke, of Gallstown, in the Co. of Kilkenny. By John O'Donovan. *Kilkenny*, N.S., III, 97-120. 1860.

BURKE. The Rt. Hon. Edmund Burke (1729-97). A basis for a pedigree. By Basil O'Connell, K.M. *Cork*, N.S. LX, 69-74. 1955.

BURKE. Some notes on the Burkes. By M. R. *Galway*, I, 196-'7. 1900-'01.

BURKE. The De Burgo clans of Galway. By H. T. Knox. *Galway*, I, 124-131. 1900-01. III, 46-58. 1903-'4. IV, 55-62. 1905-'6.

BURKE. Portumna and the Burkes. By H. T. Knox. *Galway*, VI, 107-9. 1909-10.

BURKE. The Burkes of Marble Hill. By Thomas U. Sadleir. *Galway*, VIII, 1-11. 1913-14.

BURKE. Seanchus na mBurcach and Historia et genealogia familiae De Burgo. By Thomas O'Reilly. *Galway*, XIII, 50-60, 101-'37. 1926-'7. XIV, 30-51, 142-'66. 1928-9.

BURKE. The de Burghs of Oldtown. By Lt.-Col. Thomas J. de Burgh. *Kildare*, IV, 467-'72. 1903-5.

BUTLER. Some account of the family of Butler, but more particularly of the late Duke of Ormonde . . . London, 1716.

BUTLER. Genealogical memoranda of the Butler family. By W. Butler. Sibsagor, Assam, 1845.

BUTLER. A genealogical history of the noble . . . house of Butler in England and Ireland . . . London, 1771.

BUTLER. The testamentary records of the Butler families in Ireland (genealogical abstracts). By Rev. Wallace Clare. Peterborough, 1932.

BUTLER. The Butlers of co. Clare. By Sir Henry Blackall. *North Munster*, VI, 108-'29. 1952.

BIBLIOGRAPHY

BUTLER. Original documents relating to the Butler lordship of Achill, Burrishoole and Aughrim (1236-1640). By Professor Edmund Curtis. *Galway*, XV, 121-'28. 1931-'3.

BUTLER. The Butlers of Poulakerry and Kilcash. By P. J. Griffith. *Waterford*, XV, 24-29. 1912.

BUTLER. The descendants of James, ninth earl of Ormond. By Wm. F. Butler. *R.S.A.I.*, LIX, 29-44. 1929.

BUTLER. An Irish legend of the origins of the barons of Cahir. By W. F. Butler. *R.S.A.I.*, LV, 6-14. 1925.

BUTLER. The Butlers of Dangan and Spidogue. By George D. Burtchaell. *R.S.A.I.*, XXX, 330-'33. 1900.

BUTLER. The Butlers of Duiske Abbey. By the Rev. James Hughes. *R.S.A.I.*, X, 62-75. 1868-'9.

BYRNE. The Byrnes of Co. Louth. By Patrick Kirwan. *Louth*, II, 45-'9. 1908-'11.

O'BYRNE. Historical reminiscences of the O'Byrnes, O'Tooles, and O'Kavanaghs and other Irish chieftains. By O'Byrne. London, 1843.

O'BYRNE. The O'Byrnes and their descendants. Dublin, 1879.

O'BYRNE. History of the clan O'Byrne and other Leinster septs. By the Rev. P. L. O'Toole. Dublin, 1890.

MACCABE. The Fomorians and Lochlanns. Pedigrees of MacCabe of Ireland and MacLeod of Scotland. By John O'Donovan. *Ulster*, IX, 94-105. 1861-2.

CAIRNS. History of the family of Cairnes or Cairns. By H. C. Lawlor. London, 1906.

O'CALLAGHAN. The chieftains of Pobul-I-Callaghan, Co. Cork. By Herbert Webb Gillman. *Cork*, N.S., III, 201-'20. 1897.

CAMAC. Memoirs of the Camacs of Co. Down . . . By Frank O. Fisher. Norwich, 1897.

CAMPBELL. Campbell of Skeldon and New Grange, Co. Meath.

CAMPBELL. The genealogy of Robert Campbell . . . of Co. Tyrone. By the Rev. F. Campbell. New York, 1909.

CAREW. County Cork families—Carew pedigree. *Cork*, N.S. XXIV, facing 132, 1918.

O'CARROLL. Pedigree of the O'Carroll family. By E. O'Carroll. 1883.

CARROLL. True version of the pedigree of Carroll of Carrollton, Maryland. *R.S.A.I.*, XVI, 187-'94. 1883.

CARSON. Carson of Shanroe, Co. Monaghan. By Rev. T. W. Carson. Dublin, 1879.

CARSON. A short history of the Carson family of Monanton, Co. Monaghan. By James Carson. Belfast, 1879.

MACCARTHY. The pedigree and succession of the House of MacCarthy Mór. By W. F. Butler. *R.S.A.I.*, II, 32-48. 1921.

MACCARTHY. The Clann Carthaigh. By S. J. McCarthy. *Kerry*, I, 160-'99, 195-208, 233-'51, 320-'38, 385-402, 477-'66. 1908-'12. II, 3-24, 53-74, 105-122, 181-202. 1912-'14. III, 55-72, 123-'39, 206-'26, 271-'92. 1914-'16. IV, 207-'14. 1917.

MACCARTHY. Some McCarthys of Blarney and Ballea. By John T. Collins. *Cork*, N.S., LIX, 1-10, 82-88. 1954. LX, 1-5, 75-'9. 1955.

MACCARTHY. The MacCarthys of Drishane. By S. T. MacCarthy. *Cork*, N.S., XXIII, 114-'15. 1917.

MACCARTHY. A historical pedigree of the MacCarthys. By D. MacCarthy. Exeter, 1880.

MACCARTHY. The MacFinnin MacCarthys of Ardtully. By R. MacF. MacCarthy. *Cork*, N.S., II, 210-'14. 1896.

CAULFIELD. A short biographical notice of . . . the Caulfield family. By Bernard Connor. Dublin, 1808.

CHAMBERLAIN. The Chamberlains of Nizelrath. By T. G. F. Paterson. *Louth*, X, 324-'6. 1944.

CHAMBERLAIN. The Chamberlains of Nizelrath. Notes on the allied families of Clinton, Aston, O'Doherty and Brownlow. By T. G. F. Paterson. *Louth*, XI, 175-'85. 1947.

CHETWOOD. The Chetwoods of Woodbrook in the Queen's Co. By Walter G. Strickland. *Kildare*, IX, 205-'26. 1918-'21.

CHICESTER. The history of the family of Chichester. By Sir A. P. B. Chichester. 1871.

CHINNERY. George Chinnery, 1774-1852, with some account of his family and genealogy. By W. H. Welply. *Cork*, N.S. XXXVII, 11-21. 1932. XXXVIII, 1-15. 1933.

CLAYTON. Some account of the Clayton family of Thelwall, Co. Chester, afterwards of St. Dominick's Abbey, Doneraile and Mallow, Co. Cork. By J. P. Rylands. Liverpool, 1880.

CLAYTON. Clayton family, Co. Cork. By J. Buckley. *Cork*, N.S. V, 194-'97. 1889.

O'CLERY. The O'Cleirigh family of Tír Conaill. By Father Paul Walsh. Dublin, 1938.

O'CLERY. The muintir Cleirigh of Tirawley. By A. B. Clery, *R.S.A.I.*, LXXV, 70-75, 1945.

CLINTON. Clinton records. By T. G. F. Paterson. *Louth*, XII, 109-'16. 1950.
See also CHAMBERLAIN.

CODD. Castletown Carne and its owners. By Lieut.-Col. W. O. Cavenagh. *R.S.A.I.*, XLI, 246-'58. 1911. XLII, 34-45. 1912.

COFFEY. Genealogical and historical records of the Sept Cobhthaigh, now Coffey. By H. Coffey. Dublin, 1863.

COGHILL. See CRAMER.

COLE. The Cole family of West Carbery. By Rev. R. L. Cole. Belfast, 1943.

COLE. Genealogy of the family of Cole, Co. Devon, with branches in Ireland. By J. E. Cole, 1867.

COLLES. Records of the Colles family. By R. W. Colles. Dublin, 1892.

COLVILLE. The Colville family in Ulster. By John M. Dickson. *Ulster* N.S. V, 139-'45, 202-10. 1899.

COLVILLE. The Colville family. By R. *Ulster*, N.S. 6, 12-16. 1900.

COMYN. Notes on the Comyn pedigree. By David Comyn. Munster III, 22-37. 1913.

O'CONNELL. O'Connell family tracts, No. 1-2. Ed. by Basil M. O'Connell. Dublin, 1947-'48.

O'CONNOR (O'CONOR). The O'Conors of Connaught. By C. O'Conor Don. Dublin, 1891.

O'CONNOR. (O'Conor). Memoirs of Charles O'Conor of Belenagare, with a historical account of the family of O'Conor, by the Rev. C. O'Conor. Dublin, 1796.

O'CONNOR. Memoir of the O'Connors of Ballintubber, Co. Roscommon. By R. O'Conor. Dublin, 1859.

O'CONNOR. Lineal descent of the O'Connors of Co. Roscommon. By R. O'Connor. Dublin, 1862.

O'CONNOR. Historical and genealogical memoir of the O'Connors, kings of Connaught. By R. O'Connor. Dublin, 1861.

CONOLLY. Speaker Conolly and his connections. 1907.

CONWAY. The Conways of Kerry. By S. J. M. *Kerry*, V, 71-91. 1920.

CONYNGHAM. See LENOX-CONYNGHAM.

COOTE. Historical and genealogical records of the Coote family. Lausanne, 1900.

COPINGER. History of the Copingers or Coppingers of Co. Cork. By W. A. Copinger. Manchester, 1882.

CORRY. History of the Corry family of Castlecoole. By the Earl of Belmore. London, 1891.

COTTER. Notes on the Cotter family of Rockforest, Co. Cork. By J. C. *Cork, N.S.* XIV, 1-12. 1908.

COTTER. The Cotter family of Rockforest, Co. Cork. Ed. by G. de P. Cotter. *Cork, N.S.* XLIII, 21-31. 1938.

COWLEY. Some notice of the family of Cowley in Kilkenny. By J. G. A. Prim. *R.S.A.I.*, II, 102-'14. 1852.

CRAMER. A genealogical note on the family of Cramer or Coghill. *Cork*, N.S., XVI, 66-81. 1910.

CRAMER. Cramer pedigree. By J. F. Fuller. *Cork*, N.S., XVI, 143. 1910.

CRAWFORD. The Crawfords of Donegal and how they came there. By R. Crawford. Dublin, 1886.

MCCREADY. McCreery (McCready) genealogy. By C. T. McCready. Dublin, 1868.

CRICHTON. Genealogy of the Earls of Erne. By J. H. Steele. Edinburgh, 1910.

CROFTON. Crofton memoirs: account of John Crowton of Ballymurray, Co. Roscommon . . . his ancestors and descendants and others bearing the name. By H. T. Crofton . . . York, 1911.

CROSSLE. Descent and alliances of Croslegh, or Crossle or Crossley of Scaitliffe. By Rev. C. Croslegh. London, 1904.

O'CROWLEY. A defeated clan. By Michael Crowley. *Cork*, N.S., XXVI, 24-'8. 1920.

O'CROWLEY. O'Crowley pedigree. From the Carew Mss. and other sources. By F. C. Long. *Cork*, N.S., XXXV, 89. 1930.

O'CROWLEY. The O'Crowleys of Coill t-Sealbhaigh. By John T. Collins. *Cork*, N.S., LVI, 91-'4. 1951. LVII, 1-6, 105-'9. 1952. LVIII, 7-11. 1953.

DALY. Families of Daly of Galway with tabular pedigrees. By Martin J. Blake. *Galway*, XIII, 140. 1926-'27.

O'DALY. The O'Dalys of Muintuavara: a story of a bardic family. By Dominick Daly. Dublin, 1821.

O'DALY. History of the O'Dalys . . . By E. E. O'Daly. New York, 1937.

D'ARCY. An historical sketch of the family of D'Arcy from the Norman conquest to the year 1853. 1882.

BIBLIOGRAPHY

D'ARCY. Complete pedigree of the English and Irish branches of the D'Arcy family. London, 1901.

D'ARCY. Tabular pedigrees of the D'Arcy family. *Galway*, X, facing 58, 1917-'18.

DAUNT. Account of the family of Daunt. By John Daunt. Newcastle-on-Tyne, 1881.

O'DAVOREN. The O'Davorens of Cahermacnaughten, Burren, Co. Clare. By Dr. George U. Macnamara. *N. Munster*, II, 63-93, 149-'64, 194-201. 1912-'13.

DAWSON. The Dawsons of Ardee. By Rev. L. P. Murray. *Louth*, VIII, 22-33. 1933.

DE LACY. Notes on the family of De Lacy in Ireland. By Nicholas J. Synnott. *R.S.A.I.*, IL, 113-'31. 1919. See also LACY.

O'DEMPSEY. The O'Dempseys of Clanmaliere. By Lord Walter Fitzgerald. *Kildare*, IV, 396-431. 1903-'5.

DENHAM. Denham of Dublin. By C. H. Denham. Dublin, 1936.

DENNY. Dennys of Cork. By the Rev. H. L. L. Denny. *Cork*, N.S., XXVIII, 45-6. 1922.

DE RIDELESFORD. The De Ridelesfords. By E. St. John Brooks. *R.S.A.I.*, LXXXII, 45-61. 1952.

D'ESTERRE. Pedigree of Captain D'Esterre, who was fatally wounded by Daniel O'Connell in a duel in 1851. *Cork*, N.S., XXXIV, 47. 1929.

O'DEVELIN. The O'Develins of Tyrone: the story of an Irish sept . . . By J. C. Develin. Rutland, Vt., 1938.

DEVENISH. Records of the Devenish families. By Robert T. Devenish and Charles H. MacLaughlin. Chicago, 1948.

DE VERDON. The De Verdons of Louth. By the Rev. Denis Murphy, S.J. *R.S.A.I.*, XXV, 317-'28, 1895.

DE VERDON. By W. H. Grattan Flood. *R.S.A.I.*, XXIX, 417-'19. 1899.

DE VERDON. The De Verdons and the Draycots. By Charles MacNeill. *Louth*, V, 166-'72. 1923.

DEVEREUX. Account of the Anglo-Norman family of Devereux of Balmagir, Co. Wexford. By G. O'C. Redmond. Dublin, 1891.

DICKSON. Dickson genealogy. By C. T. M'Cready. Dublin, 1868.

DILL. The Dill Worthies. By the Rev. J. R. Dill. Belfast, 1888.

DILLON. Pedigree of Dillon, Viscounts Dillon. c. 1912.

DIXON. Dixon, of Kilkea Castle. By Henry B. Swanzy. *Kildare*, IX, 392-4. 1918-'21.

DOBBYN. Ancient and illustrious Waterford families. The Dobbyns and Waddings. By Patrick Higgins. Waterford, IV, 247-'50. 1898.

O'DOHERTY. See CHAMBERLAIN.

MACDONALD. The MacDonalds of Mayo. By G. A. Hayes-McCoy. *Galway*, XVII, 65-82. 1936-'37.

MACDONNELL. The Macdonnells of Tinnakill Castle. By Lord Walter Fitzgerald. *Kildare*, IV, 205-'15. 1903-'15.

MACDONNELL. Chiefs of the Antrim MacDonnells prior to Sorley Boy. By G. H. *Ulster*, VII, 247-'59. 1859.

MACDONNELL. Notices of the Clan Iar Vór, Clan-Donnell Scots, especially of the branch settled in Ireland. By George Hill. *Ulster*, IX, 301-'17. 1861-'2.

MACDONNELL. Historical account of the Macdonnells of Antrim. By George Hill. Belfast, 1873.

MACDONOGH. The lords of Ella: the Macdonoghs of Duhallow. By W. F. Dennehy. *Cork*, III, 157-'62. 1894.

O'DONNELL. John O'Donnell of Baltimore: his forbears and descendants . . . By E. T. Cook. London, 1934.

DRAKE. The Drake family. By Frederick W. Knight. *Cork*, N.S., XXXVIII, 20-30. 1933.

DRAYCOT. The De Verdons and the Draycots. By Charles Mac Neill. *Louth*, V, 166-'72. 1923.

DRAYCOTT. Some early documents relating to English Uriel, and the towns of Drogheda and Dundalk. I, The Draycott family. By Charles McNeill. *Louth*, V, 270-'75. 1924.

O'DRISCOLL. The O'Driscolls and other septs of Corca Laidhe. By J. M. Burke. *Cork*, N.S., XVI, 24-31. 1910.

DUNLEVY. A genealogical history of the Dunlevy family. By G. D. Kelley. Columbus, Ohio, 1901.

O'DWYER. The O'Dwyers of Kilnamanagh. By Sir M. O'Dwyer. London, 1933.
See also O'KENNEDY.

EAGAR. The Eagar family of Co. Kerry. By F. J. Eagar. Dublin, 1860.

EAGAR. Genealogical history of the Eagar family. By F. J. Eagar. Dublin, 1861.

ECHLIN. Genealogical memoirs of the Echlin family . . . By Rev. J. R. Echlin. Edinburgh, N.D.

EDGEWORTH. The Black Book of Edgeworthstown and other Edgeworth memories, 1585-1817. Ed. by H. J. Butler and H. E. Butler. London, 1917.

MacEGAN. Two Irish Brehon scripts : with notes on the MacEgan family. By Martin F. Blake. *Galway*, VI, 1-9. 1909-'10.

ELLIS. Notices of the Ellises of England, Scotland, and Ireland . . . By W. S. Ellis. London, 1857-1881.

EMMET. The Emmet family with . . . a bibliographical sketch of Professor John P. Emmet and other members. By Thomas A. Emmet. New York, 1898.

EUSTACE. Kilcullen new abbey and the FitzEustaces. By James Fenton. *Kildare*, XII, 217-'21. 1935-'45.

EVANS. The last six generations of the Evans family . . . By W. S. Evans. 1864.

EYRE. A short account of the Eyre family of Eyre Court, and Eyre of Eyreville in Co. Galway. By the Rev. A. S. Hartigan. Reading, n.d.

FALKINER. The Falkiners of Abbotstown, Co. Dublin. By George H. Frederick Nuttall. *Kildare*, VIII, 331-'63. 1915-'17.

FALKINER. A pedigree with personal sketches of the Falkiners of Mount Falcon. By F. B. Falkiner. Dublin, 1894.

FITZEUSTACE. Fitz-Eustace of Baltinglass. *Waterford*, V, 190-'95. 1899.

FITZGERALD. Geraldines, Earls of Desmond. By the Rev. C. P. Meehan. Dublin, 1852.

FITZGERALD. The story of the Slught Edmund (From 1485 to 1819.). An episode in Kerry history. By S. M. *Kerry*, III, 186-205. 1915.

FITZGERALD. The Fitzgeralds of Lackagh. By Lord Walter Fitzgerald. *Kildare* I, 245-'64. 1892-'5.

FITZGERALD. The Fitzgeralds a n d t h e MacKenzies. By W. Fitz G. *Kildare*, II, 269. 1896-'9.

FITZGERALD. The Fitzgeralds of Ballyshannon (Co. Kildare), and their successors thereat. By Lord Walter Fitzgerald. *Kildare*, III, 425-'52. 1899-1902.

FITZGERALD. The history of Morett Castle, and the Fitzgeralds. By Lord Walter Fitzgerald. *Kildare*, IV, 285-'96. 1903-5.

FITZGERALD. The Geraldines of Desmond. From Michael O'Clery's Book of pedigrees. Ed. by Canon Hayman. *R.S.A.I.*, XV, 215-'35, 411-'40. 1880-'81. XVII, 66-92. 1885.

FITZGERALD. The Fitzgeralds of Rostellane, in the Co. Cork. By R. G. Fitzgerald-Uniacke. *R.S.A.I.*, XXV, 163-'70. 1895.

FITZGERALD. The Geraldines of the Co. Kilkenny. By George Dames Burtchaell. *R.S.A.I.*, XXII, 358-'76. 1892. XXIII, 179-'86, 408-'20. 1893. XXXII, 128-'31. 1902.

FITZGERALD. The Fitzgeralds of Glenane, Co. Cork. By R. G. Fitzgerald-Uniacke. *R.S.A.I.*, XLII, 164-'9. 1912.

FITZGERALD. The Fitzgeralds, barons of Offaly. By Goddard H. Orpen. *R.S.A.I.*, XLIV, 99-113. 1914.

FITZGERALD. The Desmonds' castle at Newcastle Oconyll, Co. Limerick. By Thomas J. Westropp. *R.S.A.I.*, XXXIX, 42-58, 350-'68. 1909.

FITZGERALD. The descendants of the last Earls of Desmond. By John O'Donovan. *Ulster*, VI, 91-'7, 1858.

FITZGERALD. The Fitzgeralds of Farnane, Co. Waterford. By G. O'C. Redmond. *Waterford*, XIV, 27-39, 72-81. 1911. XV, 168-'76. 1912.

FITZGERALD. Unpublished Geraldine documents. Ed. by the Rev. Samuel Hayman. *R.S.A.I.*, X, 356-416. 1869. XI, 591-616. 1871. XIV, 14-52, 157-'66, 246-'64, 300-'35. 1876-'77.

FITZGERALD. The Fitzgerald family—unpublished Geraldine documents. Ed. by the Rev. S. Hayman. Dublin, 1870.

FITZGERALD. Descents of the Earls of Kildare, and their wives. By the Marquis of Kildare. Dublin, 1869.

FITZGERALD. Sketch of the history and descent of the Geraldines of Queen's Co. Mountmellick, 1913.

FITZGERALD. The Earls of Kildare and their ancestors from 1057-1773. By the Marquess of Kildare. Dublin, 1858, 1862.

FITZGERALD. Memoirs of an Irish family, Fitzgerald of Decies . . . By Mrs. M. MacKenzie. Dublin, 1905.

FITZGERALD. Initium, incrementum et exitus familiae Geraldinorum Desmoniae . . . By Dominic O'Daly. 1655.

FITZMAURICE. The Fitzmaurices, Lords of Kerry. By M. J. Bourke. *Cork*, N.S. XXVI, 10-18. 1920.

FitzRery. The Fitz Rerys, Welsh lords of Cloghran, Co. Dublin. By E. Curtis. *Louth,* V, 13-17. 1921.

O'Flaherty. The flight of the O'Flahertys, lords of Moy Soela, to Iar Connaught. By the Very Rev. J. Fahy, P.P. *R.S.A.I.,* XXVII, 19-27. 1897.

Flatesbury. The family of Flatesbury, of Ballynasculloge and Johnstown, Co. Kildare. By Sir Arthur Vicars. *Kildare,* IV, 87-94. 1903-'5.

Fleetwood. The Fleetwoods of the Co. Cork. By Sir Edmund T. Bewley. *R.S.A.I.,* XXXVIII, 103-'25. 1908.

Fleetwood. An Irish branch of the Fleetwood family. By Sir E. T. Bewley. Exeter, 1908.

Fleming. Historical and genealogical memoir of the family of Fleming of Slane. By Sir W. Betham. 1829.

O'Flynn. The O'Flynns of Ardagh. By J. M. Burke. *Cork,* N.S., XI, 99-101. 1905.

Follin. Follin family. By G. Edmonston. Washington, 1911.

Folliott. The Folliotts of Londonderry and Chester. By Sir E. T. Bewley. 1902. N.P.

Forbes. Memoirs of the earls of Granard. By the Hon. John Forbes. London, 1868.

Fox. Some notes on the Fox family of Kilcoursey in King's Co. By M. E. Stone. Chicago, 1890.

Frazer. Notes and papers connected with Persifor Frazer in Glasslough, Ireland . . . By P. Frazer, 1906.

French. The families of French of Dures, Cloghballymore, and Drumharsna, with tabular pedigree. By Martin J. Blake. *Galway,* X, 125-38. 1917-18.

French. The origin of the families of French of Connaught, with tabular pedigree of John French of Grand-Terre in 1763. By Martin J. Blake. *Galway,* XI, 142-'49. 1920-'21.

French. Some account of the family of French of Belturbet. By the Rev. H. B. Swanzy. *Ulster,* N.S., VIII, 155-'60. 1902.

French. The families of French and their descendants. By the Rev. H. B. Swanzy. Dublin, 1908.

French. Memoir of the French family (De la Freyne, De Freyne, Frenshe, ffrench). By John D'Alton. Dublin, 1847.

Fuller. Some . . . descents of the Kerry branch of the Fuller family . . . By J. F. Fuller. Dublin, 1880.

Fuller. Pedigree of the family of Fuller of Cork, Kerry and Halstead. By J. F. Fuller. 1909.

Fulton. Memoirs of the Fultons of Lisburn. By Sir T. Hope. 1903.

Galwey (Galway). The Galweys of Lota. By C. J. Bennett. Dublin, 1909.

Galwey. The genealogy of Galwey of Lota . . . *Cork,* N.S., XXX, 59-74. 1925.

Garde. The Garde family. By R. Bickersteth. *Cork,* N.S., V, 200-'02. 1899.

Gayer. Memoirs of the Gayer family in Ireland. By A. E. Gayer. Westminster, 1870.

Gerrard. Gerrards and Geraldines. By Capt. Henry Gerrard. *Cork,* N.S., XXXIV, 30-35, 71-75. 1929.

MacGillycuddy. The Macgillycuddy family. *Kerry,* III, 176-'85. 1915.

Gillman. Searches into the history of the Gillman or Gilman family . . . in . . . Ireland . . . By A. W. Gillman, London, 1895.

Gorges. The story of a family through eleven centuries. By Raymond Gorges. Boston, 1944.

McGovern. An Irish sept. By the Rev. J. B. and J. H. McGovern. Manchester, 1886.

McGovern. Genealogy and historical notes of the MacGauran or McGovern Clan. By J. H. McGovern. Liverpool, 1890.

O'Gowan. A memoir of the name of O'Gowan, or Smith. By an O'Gowan. Tyrone, 1837.

Grace. A survey of Tullaroan, etc., being a genealogical history of the family of Grace. Dublin, 1819.

Grace. The origin of the Grace family of Courtstown, Co. of Kilkenny, and of their title to the Tullaroan estate. By Richard Langrishe. *R.S.A.I.,* XXX, 319-'24. 1900. XXXII, 64-67. 1902.

Grace. Memoirs of the family of Grace. By S. Grace. London, 1823.

Green. Green family of Youghal, Co. Cork . . . By H. B. Swanzy and T. Green. Dublin, 1902.

Greene. Pedigree of the family of Greene. By Lt.-Col. J. Greene. Dublin, 1899.

Gregory. The house of Gregory. By V. R. T. Gregory. Dublin, 1943.

Guinness. See Magennis.

HAMILTON. Monea Castle, Co. Fermanagh, and the Hamiltons. By the Rt. Hon. the Earl of Belmore. *Ulster*, N.S., I, 195-208, 256-'77. 1895.

HAMILTON. Pedigree of the Hamilton family of Fermanagh, Co. Tyrone. By J. F. Fuller. London, 1889.

HAMILTON. Hamilton mss. Ed. by T. K. Lowry. Belfast, 1848.

HAMILTON. Hamilton memoirs. By E. Hamilton. Dundalk, 1920.

O'HANLON. Redmond Count O'Hanlon's descendants. *Louth*, II, 61. 1908-11.

O'HART. The last princes of Tara, or a brief sketch of the O'Hart ancient royal family. By J. O'Hart. Dublin, 1873.

HART. Family history of Hart of Donegal. By H. T. Hart. 1907.

HARTPOLE. Notes on the district of Ivory, Coolbanagher Castle, and the Hartpoles. By Lord Walter Fitzgerald. *Kildare*, IV, 297-311. 1903-'05.

HARVEY. The Harvey families of Inishowen, Co. Donegal . . . By G. H. Harvey. Folkestone, 1927.

HASSARD. Some account of the Hassard family. By the Rev. H. B. Swanzy. Dublin, 1903.

HEACOCK. Richard Heacock pedigree. *Cork*, N.S., XI, 47. 1905.

HEALY. The Healys of Donoughmore. By John T. Collins. *Cork*, N.S., XLVIII, 124-'32. 1943.

HEFFERNAN. The Heffernans and their times. By Patrick Heffernan. London, 1940.

HENCHY. The O'Connor Henchys of Stonebrook. By V. Hussey-Walsh. *Kildare*, II, 407-'12. 1896-'9.

HENRY. The Henry family in Kildare. By the Rev. Canon Sherlock. *Kildare*, III, 386-'8. 1899-1902.

HEWETSON. The Hewetsons of the Co. of Kildare. By John Hewetson. *R.S.A.I.*, XXXIX, 146-'63. 1909.

HEWETSON . . . of the Co. Kilkenny. By John Hewetson, *R.S.A.I.*, XXXIX, 369-'92. 1909.

HEWETSON . . . of Ballyshannon, Donegal. By John Hewetson, *R.S.A.I.*, XL, 238-'43. 1910.

HEWETSON. Memoirs of the house of Hewetson or Hewson in Ireland. By the Rev. H. B. Swanzy. Dublin, 1903.

HEWSON. Hewsons of Finuge, Kerry, of royal descent. By John Hewson. 1907.

HILL. The house of Downshire from 1600 to 1868. By H. McCall. 1880.

HOARE. Account of the early history and genealogy, with pedigrees from 1330 unbroken to the present time, of the families of Hore and Hoare with all their branches. By Captain Edward Hoare of Cork. London, 1883.

HORT. The Horts of Hortland. By Sir Arthur F. Hort. *Kildare*, VII, 207-'16. 1912-'14.

HOVENDEN. Lineage of the family of Hovenden (Irish branch). By a member of the family. London, 1892.

O'HURLEY (O'HURLY). The family of O'Hurley. By the Rev. P. Hurley. Cork, **1906.**

O'HURLEY. Some account of the family of O'Hurly. *Cork*, N.S., XI, 105-'23, 177-'83. 1905. *Cork*, N.S., XII, 26-33, 76-88. 1906.

JACOB. History of the families of Jacob of Bridgewater, Tiverton and S o u t h e r n Ireland. By H. W. Jacob. Taunton, 1929.

JACOB. Historical and genealogical narration of the families of Jacob. By A. H. Jacob of Dublin and J. H. Glascott. Dublin, 1875.

JEPHSON. The English settlement in Ireland under the Jephson family. By H. F. Berry. *Cork*, N.S., XII, 1-26. 1906.

O'KANE. Some account of the sept of the O'Cathains of Ciannachta Glinne-Geinhin. Now the O'Kane's of the Co. of Londonderry. By J. Scott Parker. *Ulster*, III, 1-8, 265-'72. 1855. IV, 139-'48. 1856.

KAVANAGH. The fall of the Clan Kavanagh. By the Rev. James Hughes. *R.S.A.I.*, XII, 282-305. 1873.
See also O'BYRNE.

KEATING. Records of the Keating family. By Thomas Mathews.

MCKEE. A history of the descendants of David McKee, with a general sketch of the early McKees. By James McKee. Philadelphia, 1872.

KELLS. The Kells and Philpotts in Mallow, 1749. By H. J. Berry. *Cork*, N.S., XV, 95-98. 1909.

O'KELLY. The O'Kellys of Gallagh, counts of the Holy Roman Empire. By Richard J. Kelly. *Galway*, III, 180-'5. 1903-'04.

O'KELLY. Notes on the family of O'Kelly. By Richard J. Kelly. *Galway*, IV, 92-'6. 1905-'06.

BIBLIOGRAPHY

O'KELLY. The pedigree of Maria Anna O'Kelly, countess of Marcolini. *Galway,* IV, 108-'10. 1905-'6.

O'KELLY. Notes on the O'Kelly family. By E. Festus Kelly. *Galway,* XVI, 140-'43. 1934-'5.

KEMMIS. A short account of the family of Kemmis in Ireland. By Lewis G. N. Kemmis. *Kildare,* XII, 144-'69. 1935-'45.

KENNEDY. A family of Kennedy of Clogher and Londonderry c. 1600-1938. By Major F. M. E. Kennedy. Taunton, 1938.

O'KENNEDY. Records of four Tipperary septs : the O'Kennedys, O'Dwyers, O'Mulryans, O'Meaghers. By M. Callanan. Galway, 1938.

KENNEY. Pedigree of the Kenney family of Kilclogher, Co. Galway. By J. C. F. Kenney. Dublin, 1868.

McKINLEY. The McKinleys of Conagher, Co. Antrim, and their descendants. With notes about the president of the United States. By Thomas Camac. *Ulster,* N.S., III, 167-'70. 1897.

LACY. The roll of the house of Lacy. By E. de Lacy—Bellingarri. Baltimore, 1928.

LALLY. A sept of O'Maolale (or Lally) of Hy-Maine. By Miss J. Martyn. *Galway,* IV, 198-209. 1905-'6.
See also O'MULLALLY.

LANGTON. Memorials of the family of Langton of Kilkenny. By J. G. A. Prim. Dublin, 1864.

LANGTON. Memorials of the family of Langton of Kilkenny. By John G. A. Prim. *R.S.A.I.,* VIII, 59-108. 1864.

MacLAUGHLIN. The MacLaughlins or Clan Owen. By T. P. Brown. Boston, 1879.

LA TOUCHE. The La Touche family of Harristown, Co. Kildare. By Miss M. F. Young. *Kildare,* VII, 33-40. 1912-'14.

LA TOUCHE. Genealogy of the "De La Touche" family seated in . . . France, prior to and continued after a branch of it had settled in Ireland, 1690-95. By Sir A. B. Stransham. London, 1882.

LATTIN. The Lattin and Mansfield families, in the Co. Kildare. By the Rev. Canon Sherlock. *Kildare,* III, 186-'90. 1899-1902.

LATTIN. Notices of the family of Lattin. By John M. Thunder. *R.S.A.I.,* XVIII, 183-'88. 1887.

LAVALLIN. History of the Lavallins. By George Berkeley. *Cork,* N.S., XXX, 10-15, 75-83. 1925. XXXI, 36-43, 53-59. 1926.

LAWE. Lawe of Leixlip. By Rev. H. L. L. Denny. *Kildare,* VI, 730-'39. 1909-'11.

LE FANU. Memoir of the Le Fanu family. By T. P. Le Fanu. Manchester, 1945.

LEFROY. Notes and documents relating to Lefroy of Carrickglass, Co. Longford . . . By a cadet (Sir J. H. Lefroy). 1868.

LENOX-CONYNGHAM. An old Ulster house and the people who lived in it. By M. Lenox-Conyngham. Dundalk, 1946.

LE POER TRENCH. Memoir of the Le Poer Trench family written by Richard, 2nd Earl of Clancarthy, about 1805. Dublin, 1874.

LESLIE. The Leslies of Tarbert, Co. Kerry, and their forebears. By P. L. Pielou. Dublin, 1935.

LESLIE. Of Glaslough in the kingdom of Oriel, and of noted men that have dwelt there. By Seymour Leslie. Glaslough, 1913.

LEVINGE. Historical notes on the Levinge family, baronets of Ireland. By J. C. Lyons. Ladestown, 1853.

LEVINGE. Jottings for the early history of the Levinge family. By Sir R. Levinge. Dublin, 1873.

LIMRICK. The family of Limrick of Schull, Co. Cork. By the Rev. H. L. L. Denny. *Cork,* N.S., XIII, 120-'27. 1907.

LINDSAY. The Lindsay memoirs. A record of the Lisnacrieve and Belfast branch of the Lindsay family during the last two hundred years. By J. C. Lindsay and J. A. Lindsay. Belfast, 1884.

LLOYD. Genealogical notes on Lloyd family in Co. Waterford. By A. R. Lloyd.

LOWTHER. Lowthers in Ireland in the 17th century. By Sir E. T. Bewley. 1902.

LUTTREL. The Luttrels of Luttrelstown. By M. J. Bourke. *Cork,* N.S., XXVII, 65-69. 1921.

LYNCH. Genealogical memoranda relating to the family of Lynch. London, 1883.

LYNCH. Lynch record, containing biographical sketches of men of the name Lynch, 16th to 20th century . . . By E. C. Lynch. New York, 1925.

LYNCH. Account of the Lynch family and of the memorable events of the town of Galway. By John Lynch. *Galway,* VIII, 76-93. 1913-'14.

LYNCH. Pedigree of Lynch of Lavally, county Galway. By Martin J. Blake. *Galway,* . . . X, 66-'9. 1917-'18.

MacLysaght. Short study of a transplanted family in the seventeenth century. By E. MacLysaght. Dublin, 1935.

O'Madden. Records of the O'Maddens of Hy Many. By T. M. Madden. Dublin, 1894.

O'Madden. The O'Maddens of Silanchia, or Siol Anmachadha, and their descendants, from the Milesian invasion of Ireland to the present time. By Thomas More Madden. *Galway*, I, 184-'95. 1900-'01. II, 21-33. 1902.

Madden (Madan). The Madan family and Maddens in Ireland and England. By F. Madan. London, 1933.

Magennis. The Magennises of Clanconnell. By the Rev. E. D. Atkinson. *Ulster*, N.S., I, 30-32. 1895.

Magennis. Magennis of Iveagh. By Henry S. Guinness. *R.S.A.I.*, LXII, 96-102. 1932.

Magennis. Notes on the family of Magenis, formerly lords of Iveagh, Newry and Mourne. By E. F. Danne. Salt Lake City, 1878.

Magennis. Pedigree of the Magennis (Guinness) family of N. Ireland and of Dublin. By Richard Linn. Christchurch, N.Z., 1897.

O'Mahony. A history of the O'Mahony septs of Kinelmeky and Ivagha. By Rev. Canon O'Mahony. *Cork*, N.S., XII, 183-'95. XIII, 27-36, 73-80, 105-'15, 182-'92. XIV, 12-21, 74-81, 127-'41, 189-'99. XV, 7-18, 63-75, 118-'26, 184-'96. XVI, 9-24, 97-113. 1906-'10.

O'Mahony (Mahony). The Mahonys of Kerry. *Kerry*, IV, 171-'90, 223-'55. 1917-'18.

O'Malley. Genealogy of the O'Malleys of the Owals. Philadelphia, 1913.

O'Malley. Note on the O'Malley lordship at the close of the XVIth century. By Sir Owen O'Malley. *Galway*, XXIV, 27-57. 1950-'51.

Mansfield. The Lattin and Mansfield families, in the Co. Kildare. By the Rev. Canon Sherlock. *Kildare*, III, 186-'90. 1899-1902.

MacManus. Genealogical memoranda relating to the Sotheron family and the sept MacManus. By C. Sotheron. 1871-'73.

Marisco. The family of Marisco. By E. St. J. Brooks. *R.S.A.I.*, LXI, 22-38, 89-112. 1931.

Marshal. The Marshal pedigree. By Hamilton Hall. *R.S.A.I.*, XLIII, 1-29. 1913.

Massy. Genealogical account of the Massy family. Dublin, 1890.

Mathew. Genealogy of the earls of Llandaff of Thomastown, Co. Tipperary. 1904.

Maunsell. History of the Maunsell or Mansel family. By R. G. Maunsell. Cork, 1903.

Maxwell. Farnham descents. By Henry Maxwell, Lord Farnham. Cavan, 1860.

Meade. The Meades of Inishannon. By J. A. Meade. Victoria, B.C., 1956.

Meade. The Meades of Meaghstown Castle and Tissaxon [By J. A. Meade, n.d.].

O'Meagher. Historical n o t i c e s of the O'Meaghers of Ikerrin. By J. C. O'Meagher. London, 1887.

O'Meagher. See also O'Kennedy.

Mercer. The Mercer chronicle : an epitome of family history. By E. S. Mercer. 1866.

Merry. The Waterford Merrys. *Waterford*, XVI, 30-35. 1913.

Molyneux. An account of the family and descendants of Thomas Molyneux. By Capel Molyneux. Evesham, 1820.

Molyneux. Pedigree of Molyneux of Castle Dillon, Co. Armagh. By Sir T. Phillips. Evesham, 1819.

Montgomery. The Montgomery manuscripts (1603-1706). Compiled . . . by W. Montgomery . . . Belfast, 1869.

Montgomery. A genealogical history of the family of Montgomery, of Mount Alexander . . . By Mrs. E. O'Reilly, 1842.

Montgomery. A family history of Montgomery of Ballyleck, Co. Monaghan. By By G. S. M. Belfast, 1887.

Moore. The family of Moore. By the Countess of Drogheda. Dublin, 1906.

Moore. The genealogy of John W. Moore. Dublin, 1900.

Moore. The Moores of Moore Hall. By Joseph Hone. London, 1939.

Moore. Sir Thomas More: his descendants in the male line: the Moores of Moorehall, Co. Mayo. By Martin J. Blake. *R.S.A.I.*, XXXVI, 224-'30. 1906.

Moran. The Morans and the Mulveys of South Leitrim. By V. Rev. Joseph McGivney. *Ardagh*, I, iii, 14-19. 1932.

O'More. Notes on an old pedigree of the O'More family of Leix. By Sir Edmund T. Bewley. *R.S.A.I.*, XXXV, 53-'9. 1905.

O'More. Historical notes on the O'Mores and their territory of Leix, to the end of the sixteenth century. By Lord Walter Fitzgerald. *Kildare*, VI, 1-88. 1909-'11.

O'MORE. The O'More family of Balyna in the Co. Kildare, by James More of Balyna, circa 1774. *Kildare*, IX, 277-'91, 318-'30. 1918-'21.

MORRIS. Morris of Ballybeggan and Castle Morris, Co. Kerry. By the Marquis of Ruvigny and Raineval. 1904.

MORRIS. Memoirs of my family : together with some researches into the early history of the Morris families of Tipperary, Galway and Mayo. By E. M. Chapman. Frome, 1928.

O'MULCONRY. The O'Maolconaire family. Ed. by Edmund Curtis. *Galway*, XIX, 118-'46. 1940-'41.

O'MULCONRY. The O'Maolconaire family. A note. By E. de Lacy Staunton. *Galway*, XX, 82-'8. 1942-'3.

O'MULLALLY. History of O'Mullally and Lally Clans . . . By D. P. O'Mullally. 1941.

O'MULLANE. The O'Mullanes and Whitechurch. By Sir Henry Blackall. *Cork*, N.S., LVIII, 20-21. 1953.

O'MULLANE. The O'Mullanes. By John T. Collins. *Cork*, N.S., LVIII, 97. 1953.

MULOCK. The family of Mulock. By Sir E. Bewley. Dublin, 1905.

O'MULRYAN. See O'KENNEDY.

MULVEY. See MORAN.

MACNAGHTEN. Gleanings in family history from the Antrim Coast. The MacNaghtens and MacNeills. By Geo. Hill. *Ulster*, VIII, 127-'44. 1860.

MACNAMARA. The story of an Irish sept. By N. MacNamara. London, 1896.

MACNAMARA. Histoire d'un sept irlandais : Les Macnamara. Par Eugène Forgues. Paris, 1901.

MACNAMARA. The pedigrees of MacConmara of . . . Co. Clare. By R. W. Twigge. 1908.

NANGLE. Ballysax and the Nangle family. By Omurethi. *Kildare*, VI, 96-100. 1909-'11.

NASH. The genealogy of the Nash family of Farrihy . . . 1910.

MACNEILL. See MACNAGHTEN.

O'NEILL. The O'Neills of Ulster : their history and genealogy. By Thomas Mathews. Dublin, 1907.

NESBITT. History of the family of Nisbet or Nesbitt in Scotland and Ireland . . . By A. Nesbitt. Torquay, 1898.

NUGENT. Historical sketch of the Nugent family. By J. C. Lyons. Ladestown, 1853.

NUTTALL. The Nuttalls of Co. Kildare. By R. W. Smith, Jr. *Kildare*, VIII, 180-'84. 1915-'17.

OLIVER. The Olivers of Cloghanodfoy and their descendants. By Major-Gen. J. R. Oliver. London, 1904.

ONSELEY. The name and family of Onseley. By Richard J. Kelly. *R.S.A.I.*, XL, 132-'46. 1910.

ORPEN. The Orpen family : being an account of the life and writings of Richard Orpen of Killowen, Co. Kerry, together with some researches into the early history of his forebears . . . By G. Orpen. Frome, 1930.

PALLISER. See CODD.

PALMER. Genealogical and historical account of the Palmer family of Kenmare, Co. Kerry. By the Rev. A. H. Palmer. 1872.

PALMER. Account of the Palmer family of Rahan, Co. Kildare. By T. Prince. New York, 1903.

PARSONS. Notes on families and individuals of the name of Parsons. London, 1903.

PATTERSON. Some family notes. By W. H. Patterson. Belfast, 1911.

PENN. Admiral Penn, William Penn, and their descendants in the Co. Cork. By J. C. *Cork*, N.S., XIV, 105-'14, 177-'89. 1908.

PENTHENY. Memoir of the ancient family of Pentheny or De Pentheny, of Co. Meath. Dublin, 1821.

PHAIRE. Colonel Robert Phaire, "Regicide". His ancestry, history, and descendants. By W. H. Welply. *Cork*, N.S., XXIX, 76-80. 1924. XXX, 20-26. 1925. XXXI, 31-36. 1926. XXXII, 24-32. 1927.

PILKINGTON. Harland's history of the Pilkingtons, from the Saxon times . . . to the present time. 2nd ed. Dublin, 1886.

PIPHOE. See TRAVERS.

POE. Origin and early history of the family of Poë, or Poe, with full pedigrees of the Irish branch of the family . . . By Sir E. T. Bewley. Dublin, 1906.

POLLOCK. The family of Pollock. By the Rev. A. S. Hartigan. Folkestone, n.d.

PONSONBY. Bishopscourt and its owners. By the late Captain Gerald Ponsonby. *Kildare*, VIII, 3-29. 1915-'17.

POWER. The Powers of Clashmore, Co. Waterford. By Matthew Butler. *Cork*, N.S., XLVII, 121-'22. 1942.

POWER. An historical account of the Pohers, Poers and Powers. By G. O'C. Redmond. Dublin, 1897.

POWER. Notes and pedigrees relating to the family of Poher, Poer or Power. By Edmund, 17th Lord Power. Clonmel, n.d.

PRATT. Pratt family records : an account of the Pratts of Youghal and Castlemartyr, Co. Cork. Millom, 1931.

PUNCH. Punch family of city and county of Cork. *Cork*, N.S., XXXIII, 106. 1928.

PURCELL. Family papers belonging to the Purcells of Loughmoe, Co. Tipperary. By Rev. St. John D. Seymour. *N. Munster*, III, 124-'9, 191-203. 1914.

MACQUILLIN. The Clan of the MacQuillins of Antrim. By M. Webb. *Ulster*, VIII, 251-'68. 1860.

MACQUILLIN. The MacQuillins of the Route. By George Hill. *Ulster*, IX, 57-70. 1861-'62.

REDMOND. Military and political memoirs of the Redmond family. By J. Raymond Redmond. *Cork*, N.S., XXVII, 22-35, 73-78. 1921. XXVIII, 1-11, 81-89. 1922. XXIX, 19-28, 87-93. 1924. XXX, 34-40, 96-99. 1925.

O'REILLY. The O'Reillys of Templemills, Celbridge . . . with a note on the history of the clann Ui Raghallaigh in general. By E. O'H. Dundrum, Co. Dublin, 1941.

O'REILLY. The descendants of Col. Myles O'Reilly in Co. Leitrim (1650-1830) from tradition. By Thomas O'Reilly. *Breifny*, II, i, 15-19. 1923.

RENTOUL. A record of the family and lineage of Alexander Rentoul. By E. Rentoul. Belfast, 1890.

REYNOLDS. Notes on the MacRannals of Leitrim and their country : being introductory to a diary of James Reynolds, Lough Scur, Co. Leitrim, for the years 1658-1660. By the Rev. Joseph Meehan, C.C. *R.S.A.I.*, XXXV, 139-'51, 1905.

RICHARDSON. Six generations of Friends in Ireland. By J. M. R. London, 1890.

ROBERTS. A Roberts family quondam Quakers of Queen's Co. By E. J. Adeir Impey. London, 1939.

ROBERTS. The Roberts family of Waterford. By William T. Bayly. *Waterford*, II, 98-103. 1896.

ROBERTS. Some account of the Roberts family of Kilmoney. By Bessie Garvey. *Cork*, N.S., XXXIV, 107-110. 1929.

ROCHE. The Roches, lords of Fermoy. By Eithne Donnelly. *Cork*, N.S., XXXVIII, 86-91. 1933. XXXIX, 38-40, 57-68. 1934. XL, 37-42, 63-73. 1935. XLI, 20-28, 78-84. 1936. XLII, 40-52. 1937.

ROCHFORD. A Cork branch of the Rochford family. By James Buckley. *Cork*, N.S., XXI, 112-'20. 1915.

RONAYNE. Some Desmond incidents and notes on the Ronayne famliy. By E. C. R. *Cork*, N.S., XXIII, 104-'7. 1917.

RONAYNE. Notes on the family of Ronayne, or Ronan, of Counties Cork and Waterford. By F. W. Knight. *Cork*, N.S., XXII, 56-63, 109-'14, 178-'85. 1916. XXIII, 93-104, 142-'52. 1917.

MACRORY. The Past-MacRorys of Duneane, Castle-Dawson, Limavady and Belfast. By R. A. MacRory. Belfast.

ROSBOROUGH. Later history of the family of Rosborough, of Mullinagoan, Co. Fermanagh. By H. B. Swanzy. 1897.

ROTHE. The family of Rothe of Kilkenny. By George Dames Burtchaell. *R.S.A.I.*, XVII, 501-'37, 620-'54. 1886.

RUDKIN. The Rudkins of the Co. Carlow. By Sir E. T. Bewley. Exeter, 1905.

RUMLEY. The Rumley family of Cork. By "Huguenot". *Cork*, N.S., VII, 127. 1901.

RYLAND. Pedigree of Ryland of Dungarvan and Waterford. *R.S.A.I.*, XV, 562-'5. 1881.

ST. LAWRENCE. Notes on the St. Lawrences, lords of Howth, from the end of the twelfth to the middle of the sixteenth century. By Lord Walter Fitzgerald. *R.S.A.I.*, XXXVII, 349-'59. 1907.

SANDYS. Some notes for a history of the Sandys family of Great Britain and Ireland. By C. Vivian and Col. T. M. Sandys. 1907.

SARSFIELD. Dr. Caulfield's records of the Sarsfield family of the County Cork. By J. C. *Cork*, N.S., XXI, 82-91, 131-'6. 1915.

SARSFIELD. The Sarsfields of Co. Clare. By R. W. Twigge. *N. Munster*, III, 92-107, 170-'90, 32-'43. 1914-15.

SARSFIELD. Patrick Sarsfield, Earl of Lucan, with an account of his family and their connection with Lucan and Tully. By Lord Walter Fitzgerald. *Kildare*, IV, 114-'47. 1903-'05.

SAUNDERS. The family of Saunders of Saunders' Grove, Co. Wicklow. By T. U. Sadleir. *Kildare*, IX, 125-'33. 1918-'21.

SAUNDERSON. Saunderson of Castle Saunderson. By H. Saunderson. Frome, 1936.

SAVAGE. Ancient and noble family of Savages of Ards . . . By G. F. Armstrong. London, 1880.

BIBLIOGRAPHY

SAVAGE. A genealogical history of the Savage family in Ulster . . . Ed. by G.F.S.-A. London, 1906.

SEAVER. History of the Seaver family. By George Seaver. Dundalk, 1950.

SEGRAVE. The Segrave family, 1066 to 1935. By C. W. Segrave . . . London, 1936.

O'SHAUGHNESSY. O'Shaughnessy of Gort (1543-1783) : tabular pedigree. By M. J. Blake. *Galway*, VII, 53. 1911-'12.

SHAW. Some notes on the Shaw family of Monkstown Castle. By James B. Fox. *Cork*, N.S., XXXVII, 93-'5. 1932.

SHAW. Concluding notes on the Shaw family of Monkstown castle. By J. B. Fox. *Cork*, N.S., XL, 53-'4. 1935.

SHERLOCK. Distinguished Waterford families. I. Sherlock. *Waterford*, IX, 120-'28, 171-'5. 1906. X, 42-44, 171-'83. 1907.

SHERLOCK. Notes on the family of Sherlock: from state papers and official documents. By the Rev. J. F. M. ffrench. *Kildare*, II, 33-47. 1896-'9.

SHERLOCK. The family of Sherlock, No. II. Notes by Rev. Canon ffrench. *Kildare*, VI, 155-'9. 1909-'11.

SHERLOCK. Extract from the pedigree of Sherlock of Mitchelstown, Co. Cork. By W. Devereux. *Cork*, N.S., XII, 51. 1906.

SHIRLEY. Stemmata Shirleiana, or annals of the Shirley family. By E. P. Shirley. London, 1873.

SINCLAIR. The Sinclair genealogy. By C. T. McCready. 1868.

SINCLAIR. Genealogy of the Sinclairs of Ulster. By Sir John Sinclair. 1810.

SINNETT, SINNOTT, SYNNOTT. Sinnett genealogy . . . records of Sinnetts, Sinnotts, etc. in Ireland and America. By Rev. C. N. Sinnett. Concord, N.H., 1910.

SIRR. A genealogical history of the family of Sirr of Dublin. London, 1903.

SITLINGTON. The Sitlington family, of Dunagorr, Co. Antrim. By Edmund Getty. *Ulster*, N.S., XV, 161-'72. 1909.

SKERRETT. Some records of the Skerrett family. By Philip Crossle. *Galway*, XV, 33-72. 1931-'3.

SLACKE. Records of the Slacke family in Ireland. By Helen A. Crofton. 1900-'02.

SMITH. The chronicles of a Puritan family in Ireland. [Smith (formerly) of Glasshouse]. By G. N. Nuttall-Smith. London, 1923.
    See also O'GOWAN.

SMYTH. Généalogie de l'ancienne et noble famille de Smyth de Ballyntray, Comté de Waterford en Irlande.

SOMERVILLE. The Somervilles and their connexions in Cork. Ed. by P. S. O'Hegarty. *Cork*, N.S., XLVII, 30-33. 1942.

SOMERVILLE. Records of the Somerville Family of Castlehaven and Drishane, from 1174 to 1904. Compiled by E. Œ. Somerville and Boyle Townshend Somerville. Cork, 1940.

SPEDDING. The Spedding family, with short accounts of a few other families allied by marriage. By Captain J. C. D. Spedding. Dublin, 1909.

SPENSER. Pedigree of the poet Spenser's family. *Cork*, N.S., XI, facing 196. 1905.

SPENSER. Spenser's pedigree. By W. Devereux. *Cork*, N.S., XV, 101-'02. 1909.

SPENSER. Memorials of Edmund Spenser, the poet, and his descendants in the county of Cork . . . By J. C. *Cork*, N.S., XIV, 39-43. 1908.

SPENSER. The family and descendants of Edmund Spenser. By W. H. Welply. *Cork*, N.S., XXVIII, 22-34, 49-61. 1922.

STEWART. The Stewarts of Ballintoy: with notices of other families of the district in the seventeenth century. By the Rev. George Hill. *Ulster*, N.S., VI, 17-23, 78-89, 143-'61, 218-'23. 1900. VII, 9-17, 1901.

STONEY. Some old annals of the Stoney family. By Maj. Stoney. London, 1879.

STOUT. The old Youghal family of Stout. By Henry F. Berry. *Cork*, N.S., XXIII, 19-29. 1917.

STUART. Genealogical and historical sketch of the Stuarts of Castle Stuart in Ireland. By the Hon. and Rev. Andrew G. Stuart. Edinburgh, 1954.

SULLIVAN. Materials for a history of the family of Sullivan . . . of Ardee, Ireland. By T. C. Amory. Cambridge, Mass., 1893.

SULLIVAN. A family chronicle derived from the notes and letters selected by Lady Grey . . . London, 1908.

O'SULLIVAN. Bantry, Berehaven, and the O'Sullivan sept. By T. D. Sullivan. Dublin, 1908.

SWEETMAN. Notes on the Sweetman family. By the Rev. Canon Sherlock. *Kildare*, III, 389-'90. 1899-1902.

TAAFFE. Memoirs of the family of Taafe. Compiled by Count E. F. J. Taaffe. Vienna, 1856.

TALBOT. Genealogical memoir of the . . . family of Talbot of Malahide, Co. Dublin. 1829.

TERRY. Terry pedigree. By J. F. Fuller. *Cork*, N.S., IX, 274-'76. 1903.

TIERNEY. The Tierneys and the Egmont estates. By M. J. Bourke. *Cork*, N.S., XXVII, 10-14. 1921.

TOBIN. The genealogy of Walter Tobin and his family. Presented by Mr. Thomas Shelly. *Ossory*, II, 92-'5. 1880-'83.

TONE. The family of Tone. By T. U. Sadleir. *Kildare*, XII, 326-'29. 1935-'45.

O'TOOLE. The O'Tooles, anciently lords of Powerscourt . . . By John O'Toole. Dublin, N.D.

O'TOOLE. Les O'Toole : notice sur le clan ou la tribu des O'Toole . . . La Réole, 1864.

O'TOOLE. History of the Clan O'Toole and other Leinster septs. By the Rev. P. L. O'Toole. Dublin, 1890.
See also O'BYRNE.

TOWNSHEND. An officer of the Long Parliament and his descendants, being an account of the life and times of Colonel Richard Townshend of Castletown (Castle Townshend), and a chronicle of his family. By R. and D. Townshend. London, 1892.

TRANT. Trant family. By J. F. Fuller. *Kerry*, V, 18-26. 1919.

TRANT. The Trant family. By S. M. *Kerry*, II, 237-'62. 1914. III, 20-38, 1914.

TRAVERS. Hollywood, Co. Wicklow : with an account of its owners to the commencement of the seventeenth century. By Lord Walter Fitzgerald. *Kildare*, VIII, 185-'96. 1915-'17.

TRENCH. Memoir of the Trench family. By T. R. F. Cooke-Trench. 1897.

TUTHILL. Pedigree of Tuthill of . . . Kilmore and Faha, Co. Limerick. By Lt.-Col. P. B. Tuthill.

TYNTE. Some notes on the Tynte family. By H. T. Fleming. *Cork*, N.S., IX, 156-'57. 1903.

TYRRELL. Genealogical history of the Tyrrells of Castleknock in Co. Dublin, Fertullagh in Co. Westmeath and now of Grange Castle, Co. Meath. By J. H. Tyrrell. London(?), 1904.

TYRRELL. The Tyrels of Castleknock. By E. St. John Brooks. *R.S.A.I.*, LXXVI, 151-'54. 1946.

UNIACKE. The Uniackes of Youghal. By R. G. Fitzgerald-Uniacke. *Cork*, III, 113-'16, 146-'52, 183-'91, 210-'21, 232-'41, 245-'55. 1894.

USSHER. The Ussher memoirs, or genealogical memoirs of the Ussher families in Ireland. By the Rev. W. B. Wright. London, 1899.

VANCE. An account historical and genealogical of the family of Vance in Ireland. By W. Balbirnie. Cork, 1860.

VILLIERS. Pedigree of the family of Villiers . . . of Kilpeacon, Co. Limerick. By Lt.-Col. P. B. Tuthill. London, 1907.

WADDING. See DOBBYN.

WALSH. Notes on the Norman-Welsh family of Walsh in Ireland, France and Austria. *R.S.A.I.*, LXXV, 32-44. 1945.

WALSH. Nota et synopsis genealogiae comitum de Walsh aut Wallis. *Ossory*, II, 95-'8. 1880-'3.

WALTER. See WATERS.

WANDESFORDE. The story of the family of Wandesforde of Kirklington and Castlecomer. By H. B. M'Call. London, 1904.

WARBURTON. Memoir of the Warburton family of Garryhinch, King's Co. Dublin, 1848.

WARREN. History of the Warren family. By Rev. Thomas Warren. 1902.

WARREN. Some notes on the family of Warren of Warrenstown, Co. Louth. By the Hon. Mrs. Richard Bellew. *Louth*, IV, 26-34. 1916.

WATERS. The Waters or Walter family of Cork. By E. W. Waters. Cork, 1939.

WATERS. The Waters family of Cork. By Eaton W. Waters. *Cork*, N.S., XXXI, 71-8. 1926. XXXII, 17-23, 104-113. 1927. XXXIII, 35-41. 1928. XXXIV, 36-42, 97-105. 1929. XXXV, 36-43, 102-113. 1930. XXXVI, 26-38, 76-86. 1931. XXXVII, 35-41. 1932.

WAUCHOPE. The Ulster branch of the family of Wauchope . . . By G. M. Wauchope. London, 1929.

WEST. The Wests of Ballydugan, Co. Down; the Rock, Co. Wicklow; and Ashwood, Co. Wexford. By Edward Parkinson and Captain E. E. West. *Ulster*, N.S., XII, 135-'41, 159-'65. 1906.

WHITE. The Whites of Dufferin and their connections. By Major R. G. Berry. *Ulster*, N.S., XII, 117-'25, 169-'74. 1906. XIII, 89-95, 125-'32. 1907.

WHITE. The history of the family of White of Limerick, Knockentry . . . By J. D. White. Cashel, 1887.

WILKINSON. Fragments of family history. By S. P. Flory. London, 1896.

BIBLIOGRAPHY

WILLIAMS. The Groves, and L a p p a n ; Monaghan county, Ireland. An account of a pilgrimage thither, in search of the genealogy of the Williams family. By J. F. Williams. Saint Paul, 1889.

WINGFIELD. Muniments of the family of Wingfield. By Viscount Powerscourt. London, 1894.

WINTHORP. Some account of the early generations of the Winthorp family in Ireland. Cambridge, Mass., 1883.

WOGAN. Mémoire historique et généalogique sur la famille de Wogan . . . Par le comte Alph. O Kelly de Galway. Paris, 1896.

WOLFE. The Wolfe family of Co. Kildare. By George Wolfe. *Kildare*, III, 361-'67. 1899-1902.

WOLFE. Wolfes of Forenaghts, Blackhall, Baronrath, Co. Kildare and Tipperary. By Lt.-Col. R. T. Wolfe. Guildford, 1893.

WRAY. The Wrays of Donegal, Londonderry and Antrim. By C. V. Trench. Oxford, 1945.

WYSE. Ancient and illustrious Waterford families. The Wyses of the Manor of St. John's, Waterford. By P. Higgins. *Waterford*, V, 199-206. 1899.

YARNER. A collection concerning the family of Yarner of Wicklow. By J. C. H. 1870.

YOUNG. Three hundred years in Inishowen being more particularly an account of the family of Young of Culdaff . . . By A. J. Young. Belfast, 1929.

YOUNG. The extinct family of Young of Newtown-O'More, Co. Kildare. By W. FitzG. *Kildare*, III, 338. 1899-1902.

II.

GENERAL

COLLECTIVE WORKS ON FAMILY HISTORY AND SURNAMES.

BARDSLEY, C. W. Dictionary of English and Welsh surnames with special American instances. London, 1901.

BURKE, J. B. A genealogical and heraldic list of the landed gentry of Ireland. London, 1912.

BURKE, J. B. General armoury of England, Scotland, Ireland and Wales. London, 1878.

CLARE, REV. W., ed. A guide to copies and abstracts of Irish wills. March, 1930.

CLARE, REV. W. A simple guide to Irish genealogy. London, 1937.

COKAYNE, G. E. The complete peerage of England Scotland Ireland . . . New ed. London, 1910.

CRONNELLY, R. F. Irish family history. Dublin, 1864-65.

DALTON, JOHN. Illustrations, historical and genealogical of King James's Irish Army List. Dublin, 1855. 2nd ed., 1860.

HARRISON, HENRY. Surnames of the United Kingdom. London, 1912.

O'CALLAGHAN, J. C. History of the Irish Brigades in the service of France. Dublin, 1854.

O'HART, JOHN. Irish pedigrees. 4th ed. Dublin, 1887-88.

ROBSON, T. The British herald ; or, cabinet of armorial bearings of the nobility and gentry of Great Britain and Ireland . . . Sunderland, 1830.

WOULFE, REV. P. Sloinnte Gaedheal is Gall. Dublin, 1923.

IRISH FAMILIES

BIOGRAPHICAL DICTIONARIES ETC.

AGNEW, D. C. Protestant exiles from France in the reign of Louis XIV ; or, the Huguenot refugees and their descendants in Great Britain and Ireland. 2nd ed. with index-volume. London, 1871–74.

ALUMNI DUBLINENSES. A register of the students of Dublin University. Ed. by G. D. Burtchaell and T. U. Sadleir. Dublin, 1924.

BRADY, W. MAZIERE. Clerical and Parochial Records of Cork, Cloyne and Ross. Dublin, 1863–64.

BROWN, REV. S. J. M., S.J. Ireland in fiction. 2nd. ed. Dublin, 1919.

CRONE, J. S. Concise dictionary of Irish biography. Dublin, 1928.

DICTIONARY OF AMERICAN BIOGRAPHY. New York, 1928–44.

DICTIONARY OF AUSTRALIAN BIOGRAPHY. By Percival Serle. Sydney, 1949.

DICTIONARY OF CANADIAN BIOGRAPHY. By W. S. Wallace. Toronto, 1926.

DICTIONARY OF NATIONAL BIOGRAPHY. London, 1908–49.

HAYES, RICHARD. Biographical dictionary of Irishmen in France. Dublin, 1949.

LESLIE, J. B. and H. B. SWANZY. Biographical Succession Lists—Dioceses of Armagh, Ardfert, Clogher, Derry, Down, Ferns, Ossory and Raphoe.

[*N.B.*—similar compilations for many other dioceses were made by Rev. J. B. Leslie and these are in the Manuscripts Department of the National Library of Ireland and the Church of Ireland, Representative Body Library.]

NEW CENTURY CYCLOPAEDIA OF NAMES. New York, 1954.

O'DONOGHUE, D. J. The geographical distribution of Irish ability. Dublin, 1906.

O'DONOGHUE, D. J. The poets of Ireland : a biographical and bibliographical dictionary. Dublin, 1912.

O'HANLON, REV. J. Irish-American history of the United States. Dublin, 1903.

O'REILLY, EDWARD. Irish writers down to 1750 with a descriptive catalogue of their works. Dublin, 1820.

RENNISON, WM. H. Succession List of Bishops and Clergy of the Dioceses of Waterford and Lismore. [Waterford, 1922].

RONAN, REV. MYLES V. The Irish martyrs of the penal laws. London, 1935.

WEBB, ALFRED. A compendium of Irish biography. Dublin, 1878.

STATISTICAL LISTS AND DIRECTORIES.

CENSUS OF IRELAND. A census of Ireland, circa 1659. Ed. by Séamus Pender. Dublin, 1939.

DE BURGH, U. H. H. The landowners of Ireland. Dublin, 1878.

DESCRIPTION OF IRELAND 1598. Ed. by Rev. E. J. Hogan, S.J. Dublin, 1878.

DIRECTORIES. Directories of Dublin, the earliest of which is Wilson's Directory for 1751, and Directories of Ireland of which the earliest is Slater's Directory for 1846. Thom's Directory began in 1844 and it now embraces the whole of Ireland. (annual).

FIANTS OF EDWARD VI, PHILIP & MARY and ELIZABETH I with indexes. In Reports of the Deputy Keeper of Public Records in Ireland, 6–21. 1874–'89.

GRIFFITH, RICHARD. Valuation of Ireland. Dublin, 1848–'66.

HIERARCHIA CATHOLICA . . . Ed. by C. Eubet, R. Ritzler & P. Sefrin. Münster & Padua, 1901–'52.

INQUISITIONS. Inquisitionum in officio Rotulorum Cancellariae Hiberniae asservatarum, repertorium, 1603–49. For Leinster and Ulster. 1826–'29.

LIBER MUNERUM PUBLICORUM HIBERNIAE. Compiled by Rowley Lascelles, London, 1824-30.

MATHESON, R. E. Special report on surnames in Ireland. Dublin, 1909.

MATHESON, R. E. Varieties and synonymes of surnames and christian names. Dublin, 1901.

MEMORIALS OF THE DEAD IN IRELAND. Dublin, 1892–1937.

PATENT ROLLS. Calendar of the Patent and. Close Rolls of Chancery in Ireland. Ed. by J. Morrin. Dublin, 1861–'62.

PUBLIC RECORD OFFICE. The reports of the Deputy Keeper of Public Records in Ireland. Dublin. 1869—.

REGISTRY OF DEEDS, DUBLIN. Abstracts of Wills 1708–'85. Ed. by P. B. Eustace. Dublin, 1954–'56.

VICARS, SIR ARTHUR, ed. Index of the Prerogative Wills of Ireland 1536–1810. Dublin, 1897.

BIBLIOGRAPHY

HISTORICAL WORKS (PRE-1700).

ANNÁLA RÍOGHACHTA ÉIREANN. Annals of the kingdom of Ireland by the Four Masters . . . to 1616. Ed. by John O'Donovan. Dublin, 1851.

ANNALS. Miscellaneous Irish annals (A.D. 1114–1437). Ed. by Séamus Ó h-Innse. Dublin, 1947.

ANNALES HIBERNIAE, A.D. 1074-1504. Jacobi Grace, Kilkenniensis, Annales Hiberniae. Dublin, 1842.

ANNALS OF CLONMACNOISE . . . to A.D. 1408. Ed. by Rev. D. Murphy. Dublin, 1896.

ANNALS OF CONNACHT, A.D. 1224–1544. Dublin, 1944.

ANNALS OF INISFALLEN, A.D. 433-1320. Ed. by Seán Mac Airt. Dublin, 1951.

ANNALS OF IRELAND, THE, UP TO A.D. 1600. Ed. by John Clyn and Thady Dowling. Dublin, 1849.

ANNALS OF IRELAND, A.D. 571–913. Copied by Dubhaltach Mac Firbisigh. Ed. by John O'Donovan. Dublin, 1860.

ANNALS OF LOUGH CÉ, 1014-1590. Ed. by W. M. Hennessy. Dublin, 1939.

ANNALS OF ULSTER, 431–1541. Ed. by W. M. Hennessy and B. MacCarthy. Dublin, 1887–1901.

BOOK OF FENAGH, THE. Ed. by W. M. Hennessy. Dublin, 1875.

BOOKS OF SURVEY AND DISTRIBUTION : being abstracts of various Surveys and Instruments of Title 1636–1703. Prepared for publication by R. C. Simington. Volume I : Roscommon, Dublin, 1949. Volume II : Mayo, Dublin, 1956.

CALENDAR OF THE STATE PAPERS RELATING TO IRELAND, 1509–1670. London, 1860–1908.

CAREW MANUSCRIPTS, CALENDAR OF, 1515–1624. Ed. by J. S. Brewer and W. Bullen. London, 1867–'73.

CIVIL SURVEY, THE, A.D. 1654–1656. Prepared for publication by R. C. Simington. Dublin, 1931.

COMMENTARIUS RINUCCINIANUS DE SEDIS APOSTOLICAE LEGATIONE AD FOEDERATOS HIBERNIAE CATHOLICOS PER ANNOS 1645–1649. Ed. by Rev. Fr. Stanislaus Kavanagh, O.F.M. Cap. Dublin, 1932-'49.

COMPOSSICION BOOKE OF CONOUGHT, THE. 1585. Transcribed by A. M. Freeman. Dublin, 1936.

KEATING, GEOFFREY. The history of Ireland : Foras Feasa ar Éirinn. London, 1902-'14.

LEABHAR MUIMHNEACH, AN. Ed. by Tadhg Ó Donnchadha. Dublin, 1940.

LEABHAR NA GCEART, or The Book of Rights. Ed. by John O'Donovan. Dublin, 1847.

LYNCH, JOHN. Cambrensis Eversus. Ed. by the Rev. Matthew Kelly. Dublin, 1848–'52.

LYNCH, JOHN. De praesulibus Hiberniae potissimis Catholicae religionis in Hibernia serendae propagandae, et conservandae authoribus. Ed. by the Rev. J. F. O'Doherty. Dublin, 1944.

MAC FIRBISIGH, DUBHALTACH. Chronicon Scotorum . . . to A.D. 1135. Ed. by W. M. Hennessy. London, 1866.

Ó DÁLAIGH, AENGUS. The tribes of Ireland together with an historical account of the family of O'Daly. Ed. by John O'Donovan. Dublin, 1852.

Ó DUBHAGÁIN, JOHN. The topographical poems of John Ó Dubhagáin and Giolla na Naomh Ó Huidhrin. Ed. by John O'Donovan. Dublin, 1862.

O'FLAHERTY, RODERICK. A chorographical description of West or H-iar Connaught. Ed. by James Hardiman. Dublin, 1846.

O'KELLY, CHARLES. The Jacobite war in Ireland, 1688–1691. Ed. by George Plunkett and the Rev. Edmund Hogan, S.J. Dublin, 1894.

O'KELLY, CHARLES. Macariae excidium, or the destruction of Cyprus ; being a secret history of the War of the Revolution in Ireland. Ed. by J. C. O'Callaghan. Dublin, 1850.

ORMOND DEEDS. Calendar of Ormond Deeds 1172–1603 A.D. Ed. by E. Curtis. Dublin, 1932–'43.

STAFFORD, THOMAS. Pacata Hibernia ; or, a history of the wars in Ireland during the reign of Queen Elizabeth. Ed. by Standish O'Grady. London, 1896.

IRISH FAMILIES

HISTORICAL WORKS (MODERN).

BUTLER, W. F. T. Confiscation in Irish history. Dublin, 1917.

BUTLER, W. F. T. Gleanings from Irish history. London, 1925.

BURKE, REV. W. P. The Irish priests in the Penal Times (1660–1760). Waterford, 1914.

CORKERY, DANIEL. The hidden Ireland. Dublin, 1925.

CURTIS, EDMUND. A history of mediaeval Ireland. London, 1950.

DE BLÁCAM, AODH. Gaelic literature surveyed. 2nd ed. Dublin, 1933.

FITZGERALD, BRIAN. The Anglo-Irish. London, 1952.

GLEESON, D. F. The last lords of Ormond. London, 1938.

GREEN, A. S. The making of Ireland and its undoing, 1200–1600. London, 1908.

HANDLEY, J. E. The Irish in modern Scotland. Cork, 1947.

HARDIMAN, JAMES, ed. Irish minstrelsy, or bardic remains of Ireland. London, 1831.

HICKSON, MARY. Ireland in the seventeenth century or the Irish massacres of 1641–2. London, 1884.

HILL, GEORGE. An Historical Account of the Plantation in Ulster. Belfast, 1877.

HYDE, DOUGLAS. A literary history of Ireland from earliest times to the present day. London, 1899.

KIERNAN, T. J. The Irish exiles in Australia. Dublin, 1954.

MAC NEILL, EOIN. Celtic Ireland. London, 1921.

MAC NEILL, EOIN. Phases of Irish history. Dublin, 1919.

MEEHAN, REV. C. P. The Confederation of Kilkenny. Dublin, 1846.

MURRAY, THOMAS. The story of the Irish in Argentina. New York, 1919.

O'KELLY, J. J. Ireland's spiritual empire. Dublin, 1952.

ORPEN, G. H. Ireland under the Normans. Oxford, 1911–'20.

PRENDERGAST, J. P. The Cromwellian settlement of Ireland. Dublin, 1922.

SIMMS, J. G. The Williamite confiscation in Ireland. London, 1956.

WALSH, REV. PAUL. Irish men of learning. Ed. by Colm O'Lochlainn. Dublin, 1947.

WITTKE, CARL. The Irish in America. Baton Rouge, 1956.

PERIODICALS CONTAINING MUCH MATERIAL FOR FAMILY HISTORY.

ANALECTA HIBERNICA. Dublin, 1930——.

ARCHIVIUM HIBERNICUM. Maynooth, 1912——.

DUBLIN HISTORICAL RECORD. Dublin, 1938——.

GENEALOGIST. London, 1877–1922.

GENEALOGISTS' MAGAZINE. London, 1925——.

IRISH ECCLESIASTICAL RECORD. Dublin, 1864——.

IRISH GENEALOGIST. London, 1937—.

IRISH HISTORICAL STUDIES. Dublin, 1938—.

IRISH REVIEW. Dublin, 1911–'14.

IRISH SWORD. Dublin, 1949——.

JOURNAL OF THE AMERICAN-IRISH HISTORICAL SOCIETY. Boston, 1898——.

JOURNAL OF THE CORK HISTORICAL AND ARCHAEOLOGICAL SOCIETY. Cork, 1892——.

JOURNAL OF THE GALWAY ARCHAEOLOGICAL AND HISTORICAL SOCIETY. Galway, 1900——.

JOURNAL OF THE CO. KILDARE ARCHAEOLOGICAL SOCIETY. Dublin, 1892——.

JOURNAL OF THE CO. LOUTH ARCHAEOLOGICAL SOCIETY. Dundalk, 1904——.

JOURNAL OF THE NORTH MUNSTER ARCHAEOLOGICAL SOCIETY. Limerick, 1909–'15.

JOURNAL OF THE ROYAL SOCIETY OF ANTIQUARIES, IRELAND. Dublin, 1849——

JOURNAL OF THE WATERFORD AND SOUTH-EAST OF IRELAND ARCHAEOLOGICAL SOCIETY. Waterford, 1894–1920.

NORTH MUNSTER ANTIQUARIAN JOURNAL. Limerick, 1936——.

NOTES AND QUERIES. London, 1849.

ROYAL IRISH ACADEMY PROCEEDINGS. Dublin, 1836——.

ROYAL IRISH ACADEMY TRANSACTIONS. Dublin, 1785——.

STUDIES. Dublin, 1912——.

ULSTER JOURNAL OF ARCHAEOLOGY. Belfast, 1853——.

BIBLIOGRAPHY

COUNTY DIOCESAN AND LOCAL HISTORIES.

ATKINSON, E. D. Dromore an Ulster Diocese. Dundalk, 1925.

BALL, FRANCIS ELRINGTON. History of the County of Dublin. Dublin, 1902–20.

BEGLEY, JOHN. The Diocese of Limerick. Dublin, 1906–38.

BENNETT, GEORGE. History of Bandon. Cork, 1869.

BURKE, WILLIAM P. History of Clonmel. Waterford, 1907.

CARRIGAN, WILLIAM. History and Antiquities of the Diocese of Ossory. Dublin, 1905.

COMERFORD, M. Collections relating to the Dioceses of Kildare and Leighlin. Dublin, 1883.

COOKE, T. L. Early History of the Town of Birr. Dublin, 1875.

COTTER. James. Tipperary. New York, 1929.

CRAIG, MAURICE. Dublin, 1660–1860. Dublin & London, 1952.

CUSACK, MARY FRANCES. A history of the city and county of Cork. Dublin, 1875.

DALTON, JOHN. History of the archdiocese of Tuam. Dublin, 1928

DALTON, JOHN. The history of Drogheda with its environs. Dublin, 1863.

DALTON, JOHN & J. R. O'FLANAGAN. The history of Dundalk and its Environs. Dundalk, 1864.

DOWNEY, EDWARD. The story of Waterford. Waterford, 1914.

DWYER, PHILIP. The diocese of Killaloe from the Reformation to the close of the 18th century. Dublin, 1878.

FAHY, J. History and antiquities of the diocese of Kilmacduagh. Dublin, 1893.

FARRELL, JAMES P. History of the county Longford. Dublin, 1891.

FITZGERALD, P. & J. J. McGREGOR. History, topography and antiquities of the county and city of Limerick. Dublin, 1826.

FLYNN, PAUL. The book of the Galtees and the Golden Vein. Dublin, 1926.

FROST, JAMES. History and topography of the county of Clare. Dublin, 1893.

GILBERT, JOHN T. History of the city of Dublin. Dublin, 1861.

HARDIMAN, JAMES. History of the town and county of the town of Galway. Dublin, 1820.

HARKIN, MICHAEL. Inishowen: its history, traditions, and antiquities. Cardonagh, 1935.

HARRIS, WALTER. The ancient and present state of the county Down. Dublin, 1744.

HARRIS, WALTER. The history and antiquaries of the city of Dublin, from the earliest accounts . . . Dublin, 1766.

HEALY, JOHN. History of the diocese of Meath. Dublin, 1908.

HOGAN, JOHN. Kilkenny, the ancient city of Ossory. Kilkenny, 1884.

HOLLAND, REV. W. History of west Cork and the diocese of Ross. Skibbereen, 1949.

HORE, PHILLIP. History of the town and county of Wexford. Dublin, 1900–11.

KING, JEREMIAH. County Kerry past and present. Dublin, 1931.

KNOX, ALEXANDER. History of the county of Down. Dublin, 1875.

KNOX, H. T. Notes on the early history of the diocese of Tuam, Killala and Achonry. Dublin, 1904.

KNOX, H. T. History of the county of Mayo to the close of the 16th century. Dublin, 1908.

LENIHAN, MAURICE. Limerick; its history and antiquities. Dublin, 1866.

MAGUIRE, E. A history of the diocese of Raphoe. Dublin, 1920.

MacNAMEE, JAMES J. History of the diocese of Ardagh. Dublin, 1954.

M'SKIMIN, SAMUEL. History and antiquities of Carrickfergus. Belfast, 1909.

O'CONNELL, PHILIP. The diocese of Kilmore, its history and antiquities. Dublin, 1937.

O'HANLON, JOHN. History of the Queen's County. Dublin, 1907–14.

O'LAVERTY, JAMES. Historical account of the dioceses of Down and Connor. Dublin, 1878–89.

O'RORKE, T. The history of Sligo: town and county. Dublin, n.d. [1889].

O'SULLIVAN, M. D. Old Galway. The history of a Norman colony in Ireland. Cambridge, 1942.

OWEN, D. J. History of Belfast. Belfast, 1921.

PARKINSON, EDWARD. The city of Downe from its earliest days. Belfast, 1927.

POWER, REV. PATRICK. History of county Waterford. Waterford, 1933.

POWER, REV. PATRICK. Waterford and Lismore. Dublin and Cork, 1937.

RUSHE, D. C. History of Monaghan 1660–1860. Dundalk, 1921.

RYAN, JOHN. History and antiquities of the county of Carlow. Dublin, 1833.

RYLAND, R. H. The history, topography and antiquities of the county and city of Waterford. London, 1824.

335

SEYMOUR, ST. JOHN D. The diocese of Emly. Dublin, 1913.

SHIRLEY, EVELYN PHILLIP. History of the county of Monaghan. London, 1879.

SMITH, CHARLES. Ancient and present state of the county and city of Cork. New edition. Cork, 1893-94.

SMITH, CHARLES. Ancient and present state of the county of Kerry. Dublin, 1756.

SMITH, CHARLES. The antient and present state of the county and city of Waterford. Dublin, 1746.

STEVENSON, J. Two centuries of life in Down : 1600–1800. Belfast, 1921.

STUART, JAMES. Historical memoirs of the city of Armagh. Dublin, 1900.

TRIMBLE, W. C. History of Enniskillen with some manors of Fermanagh. Enniskillen, 1919–1921.

WARBURTON, JOHN ; JAMES WHITELAW and ROBERT WALSH. History of the City of Dublin. Dublin, 1818.

WEBSTER, C. A. The diocese of Cork. Cork, 1920.

WHITE, J. GROVE. Historical and topographical notes etc. on Buttevant, Castleroache, Doneraile, Mallow . . . Cork, 1905–25.

WOOD-MARTIN, W. G. History of Sligo, county and town. Dublin, 1882-'92.

INDEX

When page numbers are given in heavy type this indicates that the name referred to is the subject of an article in Part II or Part IV of the book.

Abbreviations used for counties in references to the map:

Ant*rim*	Down	Leix	Ros*common*
Arm*agh*	Dub*lin*	Lim*erick*	Sligo
Car*low*	Fer*managh*	Long*ford*	Tip*perary*
Cav*an*	Gal*way*	Lou*th*	Tyr*one*
Cla*re*	Ker*ry*	Mayo	Wa*terford*
Cork	Kild*are*	Mea*th*	West*meath*
Der*ry*	Kilk*enny*	Mon*aghan*	Wex*ford*
Don*egal*	Lei*trim*	Off*aly*	Wick*low*

Surnames are indexed in alphabetical order—the prefixes Mac, O and De being disregarded; e.g. for Mac/Adam see under Adam.

Surnames are indexed in alphabetical order—the prefixes Mac, O and De being disregarded;
e.g. for O/Beirne see under Beirne.

Surnames are indexed in alphabetical order—the prefixes Mac, O and De being disregarded; e.g. for Mac/Bride see under Bride.

Surnames are indexed in alphabetical order—the prefixes Mac, O and De being disregarded; e.g. for Mac/Carthy see under Carthy.

Surnames are indexed in alphabetical order—the prefixes Mac, O and De being disregarded;
e.g. for O/Clery see under Clery.

Surnames are indexed in alphabetical order—the prefixes Mac, O and De being disregarded; e.g. for O/Connell see under Connell.

*Surnames are indexed in alphabetical order—the prefixes Mac, O and De being disregarded;
e.g. for de/Courcey see under Courcey.*

Surnames are indexed in alphabetical order—the prefixes Mac, O and De being disregarded;
e.g. for O/Daly see under Daly.

Surnames are indexed in alphabetical order—the prefixes Mac, O and De being disregarded; e.g. for Mac/Dermot see under Dermot.

*Surnames are indexed in alphabetical order—the prefixes Mac, O and De being disregarded;
e.g. for O/Duffy see under Duffy.*

Surnames are indexed in alphabetical order—the prefixes Mac, O and De being disregarded;
e.g. for O/Farrell see under Farrell.

O'Ferral: **139**.
  Ferris: 305, 309.
  Ferriter: **291**. Map: Ker.
  Ferry: 313.
MacFettridge: 313.
O'Feye: 291.
Mac an Fhailghigh: 239.
Mac Fhearadhaigh: 91.
Mag Fhearadhaigh: 155.
Mac Fhiachra: 73.
Mac Fhiarais: 177.
Mac Fhinn: 141.
Mac Fhiodhbhuidhe: 136.
Mag Fhionnáin: 154.
Mac Fhlannchaidh: 79.
Mag Fhógartaigh: 149.
  Ó Fiachnach: 35.
  O'Fiaich: 291.
  Ó Fiannaidhe: 140.
  Ó Fidhne: 140.
  Field: 292.
  Fielding: 305.
O'Fihilly: 25, 292, 305. Map: Cork.
O'Finaghty: Map: Ros.
O'Finan: 305. Map: Mayo.
  Finegan: see O'Finnegan.
  Finglas: 19.
  Finlay: 305.
MacFinn: 141.
O'Finn: **140**. Map: Mon., Sli.
O'Finnegan: **141**. Plate XI.
O'Finnell: 305.
  Finnelly: 305.
  Ó Fionnagáin: 141.
MacFirbis: 292, 306. Map: Mayo, Sli.
  Ó Firghil: 152.
  Fisher: 305.
  Fitch: 33, 145.
  Fitz: 145.
  FitzEustace: 322.
  Fitzgerald: 15, 17, 29, 31, 32, 33, 41,
    51, 52, 55, 68, **142**, 144, 195, 202,
    230, 270, 281, 286, 311, 322. Map:
    Cork-Ker., Kild., Lim. Plate XI.
  Fitzgibbon (see MacGibbon): 7, 142,
    144, 311. Map: Lim. Plate XI.
  Fitzhenry: 135.
  Fitzjames: 20.
  Fitzmaurice: 17, **231**, 248, 268, 311,
    322. Map: Ker.
  Fitzpatrick: 17, 32, 33, **145**. Plate XI.
  FitzRery: 323.

Fitzsimon(s), Fitzsymon(s): 17, 33,
  291, Map: Westm.
  Fitzwalter: 68.
O'Flaherty: 136, **145**, 146, 189, 208,
  323. Map: Gal. Plate XI.
  Flahy: 314.
Ó Flaithbheartaigh: 146
O'Flanagan: 15, 56, **146**. Map: Fer.,
  Off., Ros. Plate XI.
Ó Flannabhra: 147.
Ó Flannagáin: 146.
O'Flannelly: Map: Mayo.
O'Flannery: **147**. Map: Lim., Mayo.
  Flatesbury: 323.
  Flatly: 309, 313.
O'Flattery: 309, 313. Map: Off.
  Fleetwood: 323.
  Fleming: **147**, 311, 323. Map: Mea.
    Plate XI.
Ó Floinn: 148.
  Flood: **278**, 305, 311.
O'Flynn: **148**, 149, 323. Map: Cork,
  Mayo, Ros. Plate XI.
Ó Fógartaigh: 149.
O'Fogarty: **149**. Map: Tip. Plate XII.
Ó Foghladha: 150.
  Folan: 313.
O'Foley: 31, **149**, 308.
  Follin: 323.
  Folliott: 323.
  Foody: 302, 307, 309.
  Foran: **150**, 306.
  Forbes: **292**, 306, 323.
  Ford(e): 10, **150**, 306. Map: Gal.,
    Leit.
  Forker: 24.
  Forkin: 309, 313.
  Forrestal: 313.
O'Fortin: Map: Wex.
  Fortune: 306, 309, 313. Map: Wex.
O'Fortyn: 305.
  Fowler: 150.
  Fowloo: 150.
  Fox: **151**, 192, 306, 323. Map: Off.
    Plate XII.
  Foy: 291, 306.
  Frain: 313.
  Frawley: 309.
  Frazer: 323.
O'Freel: 152.
  Freeman: 10, 306.
  French: 49, **152**, 311, 323. Map: Ros.
    Plate XII.
de Freyne(s): 152.

*Surnames are indexed in alphabetical order—the prefixes Mac, O and De being disregarded;
e.g. for O/Flynn see under Flynn.*

Surnames are indexed in alphabetical order—the prefixes Mac, O and De being disregarded; e.g. for Mac/Gibbon see under Gibbon.

Surnames are indexed in alphabetical order—the prefixes Mac, O and De being disregarded;
e.g. for Mac/Gilligan see under Gilligan.

Surnames are indexed in alphabetical order—the prefixes Mac, O and De being disregarded; e.g. for O/Hagan see under Hagan.

Surnames are indexed in alphabetical order—the prefixes Mac, O and De being disregarded; e.g. for O/Hegarty see under Hegarty.

Surnames are indexed in alphabetical order—the prefixes Mac, O and De being disregarded; e.g. for O/Hurley see under Hurley.

Surnames are indexed in alphabetical order—the prefixes Mac, O and De being disregarded; e.g. for O/Kelly see under Kelly.

*Surnames are indexed in alphabetical order—the prefixes Mac, O and De being disregarded;
e.g. for De/Lacy see under Lacy.*

Surnames are indexed in alphabetical order—the prefixes Mac, O and De being disregarded;
e.g. for O/Lennon see under Lennon.

Surnames are indexed in alphabetical order—the prefixes Mac, O and De being disregarded;
e.g. for O/Mahony see under Mahony.

Surnames are indexed in alphabetical order—the prefixes Mac, O and De being disregarded;
e.g. for O/Merry see under Merry.

Surnames are indexed in alphabetical order—the prefixes Mac, O and De being disregarded;
e.g. for O/Mulcahy see under Mulcahy.

Surnames are indexed in alphabetical order—the prefixes Mac, O and De being disregarded; e.g. for Mac/Nulty see under Nulty.

Surnames are indexed in alphabetical order—the prefixes Mac, O and De being disregarded;
e.g. for O/Regan see under Regan.

Surnames are indexed in alphabetical order—the prefixes Mac, O and De being disregarded; e.g. for O/Rourke see under Rourke.

Surnames are indexed in alphabetical order—the prefixes Mac, O and De being disregarded;
e.g. for O/Sheehan see under Sheehan.

*Surnames are indexed in alphabetical order—the prefixes Mac, O and De being disregarded;
e.g. for O/Sullivan see under Sullivan.*

Surnames are indexed in alphabetical order—the prefixes Mac, O and De being disregarded;
e.g. for Mac/Tully see under Tully.

CORRIGENDA

Page 9, par. 3, line 2: Delete comma after " plates ".

Page 18, par. 2, lines 18 and 19: For " Ballyviniter " read " Ballyvaddock "; for "Viniter" (*recte* Miniter) read " Maddock ".

Page 30, footnote: For " 20, 19 " read " 20, 21 ".

Page 128, line 8: For " Mác Dunadhagh " read " Mac Dúnadhaigh ".

Page 312: For "Columby: Wetmeath" read "Columby: Westmeath".

Map, Co. Roscommon: Delete " McDonnell ".